New Products Management

Tenth Edition

Merle Crawford
University of Michigan—Emeritus

Anthony Di Benedetto
Temple University

McGraw-Hill
Irwin

NEW PRODUCTS MANAGEMENT, TENTH EDITION

Published by McGraw-Hill, a business unit of The McGraw-Hill Companies, Inc., 1221 Avenue of the Americas, New York, NY 10020. Copyright © 2011 by The McGraw-Hill Companies, Inc. All rights reserved. Previous editions © 2008, 2006, and 2003. No part of this publication may be reproduced or distributed in any form or by any means, or stored in a database or retrieval system, without the prior written consent of The McGraw-Hill Companies, Inc., including, but not limited to, in any network or other electronic storage or transmission, or broadcast for distance learning.

Some ancillaries, including electronic and print components, may not be available to customers outside the United States.

This book is printed on acid-free paper.

1 2 3 4 5 6 7 8 9 0 DOC/DOC 1 0 9 8 7 6 5 4 3 2 1

ISBN   978-0-07-340480-6
MHID   0-07-340480-2

Vice President & Editor-in-Chief: *Brent Gordon*
Vice President EDP/Central Publishing Services: *Kimberly Meriwether David*
Publisher: *Paul Ducham*
Sponsoring Editor: *Laura Hurst Spell*
Editorial Coordinator: *Jonathan Thornton*
Marketing Manager: *Jaime Halteman*
Project Manager: *Melissa M. Leick*
Design Coordinator: *Margarite Reynolds*
Cover Designer: *Studio Montage, St. Louis, Missouri*
Cover Image: *Comstock Images/Getty Images*
            Photographer's Choice/Getty Images
            Digital Vision/Getty Images
            Royalty-Free/CORBIS
            © Brand X Pictures/PunchStock
            Digital Vision/PunchStock
Buyer: *Nicole Baumgartner*
Media Project Manager: *Balaji Sundararaman*
Compositor: *MPS Limited, a Macmillan Company*
Typeface: *10/12 Palatino*
Printer: *R. R. Donnelley*

All credits appearing on page or at the end of the book are considered to be an extension of the copyright page.

Library of Congress Cataloging-in-Publication Data

Crawford, C. Merle (Charles Merle), 1924-
   New products management / Merle Crawford, Anthony Di Benedetto. — 10th ed.
       p. cm.
   ISBN 978-0-07-340480-6
1. New products—Management. I. Di Benedetto, C. Anthony.   II. Title.
   HF5415.153.C72   2010
   658.5'75—dc22

                                                            2010037323

www.mhhe.com

Preface

New products have always been of interest to both academics and practitioners, and organized, college-level instruction on the subject of new products management traces to the 1950s. By the 1990s, a new products management discipline had evolved. Today, the Product Development & Management Association has flowered to over 3,500 members all around the world, over 300 colleges have courses on the subject of new products, and the field's journal, the *Journal of Product Innovation Management,* is now successfully into its 27th year of publication. The job title of new products manager or director is becoming much more common and is offering much earlier entry than 15 or 20 years ago; we also see the emergence of higher level positions for careers to build to. The Association now offers a practitioner certification (New Product Development Professional, or NPDP), it has a strong international operation, and it has been able to do what those in many fields have not, that is, merge the thinking and activity of professors and practitioners.

How This Book Views the Field of New Products Management

Such exploding growth means that we still take a variety of approaches to the teaching of the new products subject—marketing, technical, creative, design, and so on. This book provides the management approach, with the perspective of marketing. In every organization (industry, retailing, government, churches, etc.) there is a person or group of persons who, knowingly or unknowingly, are charged with getting new goods and services (both are products) onto the market. Increasingly, those people are new products managers, or project managers, or team leaders. They lead a multifunctional group of people, with the perspective of a general manager, operating as a company within a company. They must deal with the total task—strategy, organization, concept generation, evaluation, technical development, marketing, and so on. They are not finished with their work until the new product has achieved the goals assigned to the team—this usually means some form of sales or profit, and certainly means the task is not finished when the new product is put onto the shipping dock.

We try to avoid a functional myopia, and it is rare today to hear that, "Marketing tells everyone what to do" or "R&D runs our new products activity." When a functional specialist is assigned leadership of a new products team, that person must learn the general manager viewpoint, but one usually has to succeed as a functional member of new products teams before getting a shot at being a team leader. Marketing people, working as team members or as team leaders, need the types of information in this book.

Some Basic Beliefs That Guided the Writing

People who have used the first nine editions of this book know its unique viewpoints on the subject. But for newcomers, and of course all students are newcomers, here are some of them.

1. Product innovation is one single operation in an organization. It has parts (strategy, teams, plans, etc.), but they are all just parts. Any operation that runs as separate pieces misses the strength of the whole.

2. The field is still new enough that it lacks a systematic language. This makes it very difficult for students, who are accustomed to studying subjects where a term means one thing, and only that one thing. We use all product terms consistently throughout the book, and we urge students to use them. Naturally, new terms come and go; some survive and some don't.

   Because of the terminology problem in a rapidly growing field, every term that might require definition has been made bold the first time it is used, and the index directs the reader to that section. We agree with the past users who recommended this approach when they argued that a definition of a term should be presented in the context of its actual use in the text, not separately in a glossary. (A glossary is available at the Product Development & Management Association website, **www.pdma.org**.)

3. Ideas learned without application are only temporary residents in your mind. To become yours, a concept must be applied, in little ways or in big ones. Thus, the book is peppered with applications, short cases, and other opportunities for using the concepts studied. Projects are encouraged in the Instructor's Manual. There are many examples from the business world, and up-to-date references on all important topics.

4. As much as we would like them and have diligently tried to find them, we believe there is no standard set of procedures for product innovators, nor particular sets for makers of consumer packaged goods, or of consumer durables, industrial goods, services, and so on. Like a marketing plan, there is a best plan for any particular situation. A manager must look at a situation and then compile a set of tools and other operations appropriate to that situation. All large firms use scores of different approaches, not one.

5. Next, there is the halo effect, which is a problem in the field of new products. The halo effect shows in the statement, "It must be a good thing for us to do—3M does it, or GE does it, or Hewlett-Packard does it." Those are excellent companies, but one reason they're good is that they spend lots of time and money studying, learning from others. They have huge training programs in product innovation and bring in every expert who appears on the scene with what looks like a good new products management idea. They assume everything they do is wrong and can be improved. You should too. This book does. Citations of their actions are given as examples, not recommendations. These well-known firms have many divisions and hundreds of

new products under development at any one time. Managers there can't know what others are doing, nor do they care, in the prescriptive sense. Each group aims to optimize its situation, so they look around, see what others in comparable situations are doing (inside and outside their firm), and pick and choose to fit the situation. To the extent there are generalizations (e.g., there should be some form of strategy), these will stand out as you work your way through the course. But what strategy, and exactly how should one determine it—that is situational.

6. An example of this lies in rejection of the belief that new products strategy should rest on the base of either technology or market. This choice has been argued for many years. But most firms seek to optimize on both, a dual-drive strategy. Of course, true to the previous point, firms will build on one or the other if the situation seems to fit—for example, DuPont's platform program to find applications for the superstrength fabric, Kevlar, or auto components firms that rely on process development engineering to better meet the needs of original equipment manufacturers. And yet, DuPont works to advance that technology, and the components firms are evolving their own research and development operations!

7. We believe that students should be challenged to think about concepts they have been introduced to. This book contains lists of things from time to time, but such lists are just a resource for thinking. The above belief about the best approach being situational is based on the need to analyze, consider, discuss, apply. The great variety in approaches used by business-people is not a testimony to ignorance, but to thinking. On a majority of the issues facing us today, intelligent people can have different views. Decisions are the same—they are not necessarily right or wrong at the time they are made. Instead, the manager who makes a decision then has to work hard to make that decision turn out right. The quality of the work is more important than the quality of the decision. An example of this phenomenon is the sadness we feel when a manager says, "We're looking for the really great idea." Managers of product innovation make ideas great—they don't come that way.

8. Last, we have tried to implement the view that two things are being developed—the product and the marketing plan. There are two development processes going on in tandem. Marketing strategy begins at the very start and runs alongside the technical work and beyond it.

Online Resources

The instructor will find plenty of online support for this text at the companion website, **www.mhhe.com/crawford10e**. Available on the website are an online Instructor's Manual, a set of PowerPoint slides, a test bank, and exercises and cases that can be used to accompany the text material. Some of these materials are also available to the students where appropriate.

Changes in the Tenth Edition

Past adopters of *New Products Management* will notice major changes in this edition. While there are some changes in virtually every chapter, some of the most substantial changes are as follows:

1. The first three chapters have undergone a major reorganization. Three key concepts from early chapters (new products process, product innovation charter, and product portfolio) are now introduced in Part I as the three *strategic elements of product development*. This unites all the key strategies involved in new product development and serves as a foundation for all aspects of product development presented in later chapters. Chapter 1 is no longer a "menu" and has been retitled "The Strategic Elements of Product Development." The material from Chapter 2, which introduced the basic new products process, has been moved to Chapter 1, and that introduction is now presented here as the first of the three strategic elements. The new products process is introduced in Chapter 1 as it is indeed the framework on which the rest of the text is built. The new products process is expanded on in Chapter 2. The product innovation charter and product portfolio are detailed in Chapter 3.

2. Chapter 1 includes updated data on product success and failure from the new CPAS study and expanded coverage of globalization in new product development. This newly revised introductory chapter also goes much deeper into key topics such as fuzzy gates, overlapping phases, and the third-generation new products process.

3. Chapter 2 picks up the discussion of the new products process with a much fuller discussion of important issues such as new service development, amply illustrated with new examples such as JetBlue and FedEx. Importantly, the chapter now begins with a new extended example, the "P&G Cosmetics Saga," that illustrates all three strategic elements mentioned earlier as well as the importance of new product teams. A very important addition to Chapter 2 is the increased discussion of the topic of breakthrough vs. incremental new products. We add coverage of discovery-driven planning and expand the discussion of the challenges of breakthrough innovation.

4. Chapter 4 has a new, more descriptive name ("Creativity and the Product Concept"), and it now features an expanded presentation of open innovation, one of the fastest-growing topics in product innovation, containing plenty of examples of all types of open innovation.

5. Chapter 5 is renamed simply "Finding and Solving Customers' Problems." A major improvement in this revised chapter is a new, lengthy section on online communities, illustrated with numerous successful examples. This was a critical update, felt to really bring this chapter into the 21st century as more firms adopt this as a routine way to find and solve customer problems. Other discussions, such as problem analysis and brainstorming, have been updated.

6. The discussion of A-T-A-R models in Chapter 8 has been improved in presentation and generally cleaned up; also, all commodity volume (ACV) is included as an alternate measure of availability.

7. Chapter 9 adds a new section on concept testing using BASES. This discussion adds an understanding of practical concept testing that is very commonly used by large consumer product manufacturers.

8. In Chapter 11, we add real options pricing as a method for product managers to make early decisions on product concepts, showing how a decision can be delayed on taking a concept to the next phase.

9. In both the design chapter (Chapter 13) and the public policy chapter (Chapter 20), there is greater attention placed on designing for the environment.

10. Chapter 14 is greatly reworked. The discussion of projectization, matrix structures, and similar organizational concerns has been greatly shortened, and discussion of other concerns more relevant to the modern product team is increased. These concerns include virtual teams and global product development teams, and these sections have been expanded to reflect the newest thinking.

11. In Chapter 16, there is an expanded discussion of the Rogers diffusion process with many new illustrative examples, and we add a discussion of the newer Moore diffusion model (the *crossing-the-chasm* model), because of its importance in describing the diffusion of high-tech products. There is also much new material on branding. We give examples of firms such as P&G and Clorox and discuss why they do or do not use umbrella branding strategies. We also do an extended example of ConAgra and what motivated their recent move to a corporate brand identity complete with new logo. Given the increased importance of global brand management, we also add a lengthy section on global brand decisions and provide some examples of unexpected brand strategies by firms like Unilever.

12. Finally, the reader will notice several new cases, such as the Honda Element, Aquafresh White Trays, Hulu, and Clorox Green Works; new examples worked in throughout; some general cleanup of text and tables; and other minor improvements.

We still use the analytical models to integrate the stages of the new products process. As in previous editions, perceptual mapping is introduced early in the new products process, during concept generation, but its output may guide selection of attributes in a conjoint analysis task and may later be used in benefit segmentation and product positioning. Conjoint analysis results may be used in concept generation or evaluation and may provide a set of desired customer attributes for house-of-quality development. The sequence of three Dell Computer end-of-chapter cases illustrates how the analytical models bind the new products process together. As in previous editions, many other concepts—the product innovation charter, A-T-A-R models, evaluation techniques, the multifunctional nature of new products management—are also used to integrate topics horizontally throughout the text.

As always, effort has been aimed at making the book increasingly relevant to its users. We consider a text revision to be a "new product," and thus an opportunity for us to become even more customer-oriented. Academic colleagues have made many thoughtful suggestions based on their experiences with previous editions and have provided much of the driving force behind the changes you see in this edition.

We gratefully acknowledge Geoff Lantos of Stonehill College, who once again provided extensive comments and suggestions that were extremely helpful in this revision. We also thank the anonymous reviewers who provided valuable comments on the previous edition and alerted us to many opportunities for improvement.

We are very excited about the changes to this new edition and sincerely hope they fit your needs. A new Instructor's Manual, reflecting the changes in this edition, is available through your McGraw-Hill/Irwin representative.

To the Practitioner

Because this book takes a managerial focus and is updated extensively, it is useful to the practicing new products manager. It has been used in many executive education programs. Great pains have been taken to present the "best practices" of industry and offer footnote references to business literature.

The Applications

From the first edition, the ends of chapters do not have a list of questions. Rather, we have culled mainly from many conversations with students the questions and comments they received from business managers on their fly-backs. These comments are built into a conversation with the president of a conglomerate corporation. Explanation of how to use them is given at the end of Chapter 1.

Acknowledgments

The authors wish to thank their students for all of their insights, comments, and suggestions provided over the years, and their families for their support and encouragement.

C.M.C.

A.D.B.

Contents in Brief

Contents

New Products Management

FIGURE I.1
Opportunity Identification and Selection

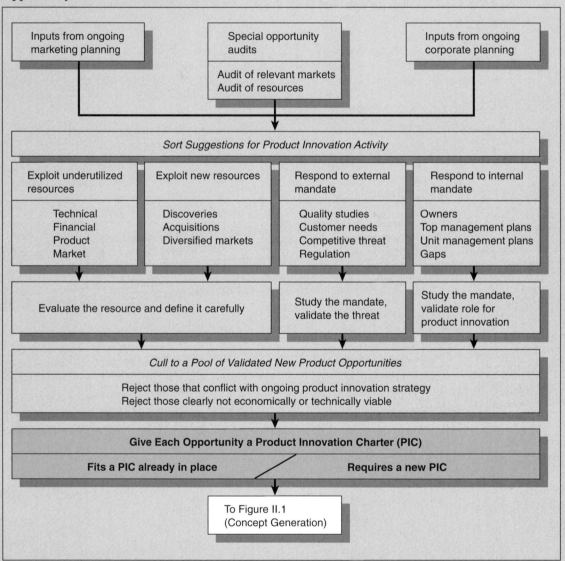

PART ONE

Overview and Opportunity Identification/Selection

This book is divided into parts. They are (1) Overview and Opportunity Identification and Selection, (2) Concept Generation, (3) Concept/Project Evaluation, (4) Development, and (5) Launch. They follow the general flow of the new products process, which we will present in Chapter 1, Figure 1.4. We will see later, however, that the phases are not sequential, compartmentalized steps. They are almost fluid and overlap each other.

At the beginning of each part is a short Part Introduction (noted with a Roman numeral) and a figure (see Figure I.1). The introduction describes briefly what aspects of the new products process will be covered in the upcoming chapters. The figure provides detailed information about what goes on at that phase in the new products process, and shows what phases come immediately before and after. Figure I.1, for example, details the opportunity identification and selection process, ending with the product innovation charter, a key topic of Chapter 3. Hence, the five part figures (Figures I.1, II.1, III.1, IV.1, and V.1) actually make up one long, detailed new products process, the essence of which is presented briefly in Figure 1.4.

Before getting to opportunity identification and selection, we begin Part I with two introductory chapters. The first introduces the three *strategic elements of product development:* the new products process, the product innovation charter, and the product portfolio. It presents the first of these, the new products process, in relatively simplified form, as a kind of introduction to the rest of the book. Chapter 1 also attempts to answer the questions most often asked about such a course and helps to define some of the concepts we will be returning to throughout the text (such as, what exactly is a new product, how many new products really do succeed, and how do firms achieve globalization in product development). Chapter 2 goes much deeper into the new products process. Chapter 2 also introduces the key concepts of radical innovation, new service development, and speed to market, and how each of these may have an impact on the new products process as presented in the chapter.

Chapter 3 completes the introductory part of the book, as it presents the second and third strategic elements. First, opportunity identification and selection are presented, which deal with the strategic planning lying at the very base of new products work and guide a new products team, just as corporate or SBU strategy guides the unit as a whole. Figure I.1 provides a flow model that describes the process of opportunity identification. Chapter 3 then discusses the product innovation charter (PIC). This can be thought of as a statement of strategy that will guide the new product development team: the arena in which they will operate, their goals and objectives, and other considerations. The last part of Chapter 3 discusses the product portfolio. Innovative ideas that can be converted into high-potential new product opportunities can come from many sources; but however the new product idea is arrived at, its fit with the firm's product innovation strategies need to be assessed. This is a portfolio issue: When assessing any potential new product, the firm needs to consider its technical viability (can we make it?) and its market viability (will customers buy it?). Most firms will have many other criteria, both financial and strategic, that they consider at this important step.

As seen in Figure I.1, once the PIC has been determined, the next step is to generate product concepts: This will be taken up in Part II of this book.

CHAPTER ONE

The Strategic Elements of Product Development

Setting

Mention new products and people think about technology—iPods, iPhones, YouTube, virtual realities, fiber optics, and the like. But most new products are far simpler—low-carb colas, new movies, new musical groups, fast foods, and new flavors of frozen yogurt. New products run the gamut from the cutting edge of technology to the latest version of the ballpoint pen. New products can be tangible goods or services. New products can be destined for the consumer market, the business-to-business market, or both.

You have chosen to study how new products are developed and managed, so it would be nice to say they come from an orderly process, managed by experienced persons well versed in product innovation. Some do, but some don't. Years ago, Art Fry became famous for an idea that became Post-it notes, when his hymnal page-marking slips kept falling out. He had a rough time persuading others at 3M that the idea was worth marketing, even though it soon became the second largest volume supply item in the office supply industry! Or consider James Dyson, an industrial designer by training who was dissatisfied with the performance of commercially available vacuum cleaners and set out to create a better one. After five years and about 5,000 prototypes, he created the Dual Cyclone bagless vacuum cleaner. Over the next eight years, he was unable to interest vacuum cleaner manufacturers or venture capitalists in the new product, frequently hearing that since he was a designer, he couldn't possibly know anything about manufacturing or marketing! In 1985 and on the verge of bankruptcy, Dyson found an interested Japanese investor, and by 1993 he had set up Dyson Appliances in the United Kingdom (his home country). Since that time, Dyson Appliances has sold over $2 billion worth of vacuums worldwide.[1]

So you may be confused by the uncertainty you meet in this book. If so, welcome to the land of creative exploration. In this field, we strive for new things, not knowing just what they will be, what they will cost, who will want them, how we will distribute and sell them, and how some regulator in a government office

[1]Anonymous, "Dyson Fills a Vacuum," @*Issue*, 8(1), 2003.

somewhere will react to them. We do know a lot about how new products *should* be developed, but the ideal conditions discussed in a textbook are rarely matched in practice. Managers face the world as it is, not as they would like it to be—downsizing, regulatory actions, competitive moves, the impact of new Internet technologies, and even personal problems such as illnesses.

Some people call this activity **product innovation management,** some call it **product planning,** and some (from a very biased perspective) call it *research & development* (R&D) or *marketing*. In this book, it is called the most descriptive term we have: **new products management,** but our viewpoint is that of the marketing manager—that is, we are primarily concerned about the specific role for marketing in the overall task.

The Importance of New Products

New products are *big business.* Over a hundred billion dollars are spent yearly on the technical phase alone. Untold thousands of new products are marketed every year, perhaps millions if we call each new Web site a new product. One Web site may be marketing hundreds or thousands of products. Hundreds of thousands of people make their living producing and marketing new products. Many managers realize that *radical innovation* is critical to future growth and even the survival of the firm. Here, we are defining radical innovation as innovation that displaces or obsoletes current products and/or creates totally new product categories.[2] The Industrial Research Institute identified "accelerating innovation" and "business growth through innovation" as the top challenges faced by technology leaders, and well-known business writer Gary Hamel has described the creation of radical innovation as "the most important business issue of our time."[3]

The reason firms invest this much in new products is that they *hold the answer to most firms' biggest problems.* Competitors do the most damage when (1) there is so little product differentiation that price-cutting takes everyone's margins away or (2) when they have a desirable new item that we don't. The fact is: *A successful new product does more good for a firm than anything else that can happen.* The very reason for a firm's existence is the value its operations provide to others, and for which they pay. And in a competitive world this means that what we offer—be it a physical good or a service—must be better than what someone else offers, at least part of the time. This is true in all organizations, including hospitals, churches, colleges, and even political parties. Look at the winners in those arenas and ask yourself which ones are popular and growing.

[2]M. Rice, R. Liefer, and G. O'Connor, "Assessing Transition Readiness for Radical Innovations," *Research-Technology Management,* 45(6), 2002, pp. 50–56; and Gina O'Connor, Joanne Hyland, and Mark P. Rice, "Bringing Radical and Other Innovations Successfully to Market: Bridging the Transition from R&D to Operations," in *The PDMA Toolbook 2 for New Product Development*, P. Belliveau, A. Griffin, and S. M. Somermeyer (eds.), (Hoboken, NJ: Wiley, 2004), pp. 33–70.
[3]Industrial Research Institute 2001/2002 Annual Reports, Washington, DC, Industrial Research Institute; and Gary Hamel, "Innovation Now! (It's the Only Way to Win Today)," *Fast Company*, December 2002, pp. 114–124.

Another reason for studying about new products is that *the new products process is exceedingly difficult*. Hundreds of individuals are involved in the creation of a single product, but all are from separate departments (sales, engineering, manufacturing, and so on) where they may have their own agendas. When a product flops miserably, it often generates huge publicity, much to the chagrin of the producers: think of New Coke, Premier smokeless cigarettes, the movies *Gigli* and *Catwoman*, or countless others. Perhaps, as a result, we think failure rates are higher than they really are. New products do fail, of course, but at around a 40 percent rate, not the 90 percent rate you often hear, and this percentage holds for both goods and services. The best product-developing firms can improve their odds further: They require only about four ideas to generate one winning product, as compared to over nine ideas for other firms. This is probably because the best firms are better at screening out bad ideas earlier.[4] And after many years of research, we know many of the most important reasons why products fail. The firm doesn't understand the customer, or underfunds the required research and development, or doesn't do the required homework before beginning development (sometimes called the *ready—fire—aim approach*), or doesn't pay enough attention to quality, or lacks senior management support, or chases a moving target (we will see moving-target issues such as unstable specifications and scope creep in Chapter 3).[5]

The goal at most firms is not necessarily to reduce failure rates to zero. Having too low a failure rate might mean that the firm is playing it too safe with close-to-home innovations, while missing out on the (risky) breakthroughs. "Too low," a failure rate here also probably depends on the industry and on how inherently risky product development is. The goal here is to minimize the dollar losses on the failures (don't bankrupt the company!) and to learn from them. Regardless of the actual failure rate you encounter, the amount at stake and the risk of failure are high in new product development.

Success rates have remained remarkably consistent over the years. The most recent best-practices study, the Comparative Performance Assessment Study (CPAS), was conducted in 2003 by the Product Development & Management Association (PDMA).[6] In this study, for every 100 ideas, a little under 70 make it through the initial screen; fewer than 50 pass concept evaluation and testing and

[4]Griffin, op. cit., and Marjorie Adams, *Competitive Performance Assessment (CPAS) Study Results*, PDMA Foundation, 2004. Success rate holds steady at around 59 percent of products marketed. In Cooper's research reported in *Winning at New Products*, about one-third of products failed. There is evidence that the 40 percent figure holds in the Netherlands and the United Kingdom as well; see Erik Jan Hultink, Susan Hart, Henry S. J. Robben, and Abbie Griffin, "Launching New Products in Consumer and Industrial Markets: A Multi-Country Empirical International Comparison," Proceedings of the Product Development & Management Association International Research Conference, Monterey, CA, 1997, pp. 93–126.

[5]Robert Cooper, *Winning at New Products: Accelerating the Process from Idea to Launch*, 3rd ed. (New York: Perseus Books, 2001).

[6]2003 CPAS results on www.pdma.org; Doug Boike and Marjorie Adams, "PDMA Foundation CPAS Study Reveals New Trends—While the 'Best-Rest' Gap in NPD Widens," *Visions*, 28(3), July 2004, pp. 26–29; Gloria Barczak, Abbie Griffin, and Kenneth B. Kahn, "Perspective: Trends and Drivers of Success in NPD Practices: Results of the 2003 PDMA Best Practices Study," *Journal of Product Innovation Management*, 26(1), January 2009, pp. 3–23.

are moved to the development phase; a little more than 30 make it through development; about 30 make it through testing; about 25 of them are commercialized; and about 15 are considered to be successes (about 60 percent of those that were commercialized). Interestingly, the percent success rate does not vary too much from one category to the next. The percent success rate ranges from 51 percent (frequently purchased consumer goods) to 65 percent (health care). If one splits the CPAS sample into two groups, the "Best" and the "Rest," a slightly different pattern emerges: The Best firms attain a success rate of 75.5 percent, while the Rest's success rate is much lower at 53.8 percent. The Best, therefore, have greater success with new product development![7]

Business firms expect, and get, a *high percentage of their sales and profits from new products*. A 1997 study of business managers by the PDMA showed that, on average, about a third of company sales come from products introduced within the past five years.[8] A later best-practices study by Robert Cooper showed that the top-performing firms did even better, gaining over 49 percent of current sales from new products. This same study also showed how profitable new products can be: Among the successful new products studied, half achieved at least a 33 percent return on investment, half had payback periods of two years or fewer, and half achieved at least 35 percent market shares![9]

Actually, the percent of sales and profits derived from new products (products less than three years on the market) has slightly declined since the first PDMA Best Practices study. In 1990, about 33 percent of both sales and profits were derived from new products; these had declined to about 28 percent by the 2003 CPAS study. This trend might have been due to a poorer business climate and a tendency toward more risk-averse business strategies. Nevertheless, the "Best" firms did not lose their focus on new products over this time. In the 2003 study, the "Best" firms reported obtaining about 48 to 49 percent of their sales and profits from new products as compared to only 21 percent for the "Rest." The results suggest that the firms that maintained their commitment to new products tended to do well, even in a poor business climate!

Globalization and New Product Development

Like all aspects of modern business, product development has become more challenging due to increased **globalization.** To a greater extent than ever before, firms are seeing new product development as a global process in order to take advantage of worldwide opportunities and increase their efficiency and effectiveness of innovation. According to a 2007 study by consultants Booz & Company, the top global firms in terms of R&D spending deployed about 55 percent of their R&D

[7]The "Best" are defined in the CPAS study as those firms that are in the top third in their industry and above the mean in both program success and sales and profit success from new product development.
[8]Abbie Griffin, *Drivers of NPD Success: The 1997 PDMA Report* (Chicago: Product Development & Management Association, 1997).
[9]Robert G. Cooper, *Winning at New Products: Accelerating the Process from Idea to Launch,* 3rd ed. (New York: Perseus Publishing, 2001).

spending in foreign countries. Among the 80 top U.S. R&D firms, $80.1 billion out of $146 billion was spent overseas, and similar percentages were found for top European and Japanese R&D firms.[10] The Booz & Company study also showed that the firms with higher percentages of R&D spending deployed elsewhere did better than average on many important performance measures, such as return on investment and total shareholder return.

This study found that firms have multiple reasons for increasing their global R&D efforts. In many foreign countries, R&D engineers are lower paid than in the United States, Western Europe, or Japan—but the salary gap is narrowing, especially for the most skilled engineers and scientists. Now, many firms look overseas not just to access a cheaper labor force, but to access the talent residing in these markets and the ideas generated by these skilled personnel. Huge markets such as India and China are obvious sources of talented engineers, and there is some evidence of specialization: India boasts strengths in automotive engineering, China in electronics. Another reason for increased R&D is the increasing globalization of the innovating firms themselves. For example, as automakers seek to penetrate new markets such as China or India, it makes sense to conduct more of their design work in or near these markets than back in the home office located in Michigan or Bavaria.

Many multinational firms seek to leverage their product development skills across their subsidiaries and gain competitive advantage by setting up *global new product teams*.[11] A large firm may have R&D skills in its German subsidiary, its manufacturing in Asia, and its suppliers somewhere else again. A firm's global presence, however, is no guarantee that it will automatically know how to efficiently manage its global operations. Effectively coordinating and marshaling the efforts across multiple countries to develop and to launch successful new products is a major challenge. There are many decisions to make that impact global product development effectiveness: how much autonomy should the subsidiaries have, how should they be rewarded, what work conditions should be imposed such that teamwork within and between subsidiaries is encouraged, and so forth. There is also the possibility of outsourcing some of the required new product capabilities, for example, through strategic alliances with global partners. Similarly, the global network of suppliers and distributors needs to be managed and coordinated so as to improve global product development as well as global launch. Selecting the best organizational structure for the global product team is more difficult than if only one culture is involved, as differences among team individuals as well as linguistic barriers and national culture differences must be taken into account. At

[10]For a summary of the Booz & Company findings, see Barry Jaruzelski and Kevin Dehoff, "'Beyond Borders: The Global Innovation 1000' Study Reveals a Global Shift in R&D Spending," *Visions*, 33(3), October 2009, pp. 27–30.

[11]Good references are: Roger J. Calantone and David A. Griffith, "From the Special Issue Editors: Challenges and Opportunities in the Field of Global Product Launch," *Journal of Product Innovation Management*, 24(5), September 2007, pp. 414–418; and Ram Mudambi, Susan Mudambi, and Pietro Navarra, "Global Innovation in MNCs: The Effects of Subsidiary Self-Determination and Teamwork," *Journal of Product Innovation Management*, 24(5), September 2007, pp. 442–455.

the time of launch, even more decisions arise: Should a product be positioned the same way throughout the world, or should positioning, branding, or packaging decisions be localized? Many firms react to these challenges with well-defined, formal processes, while others leave the new products process relatively unstructured and adaptable to product or environmental considerations.

The best research available on this topic finds that firms with a *global innovation culture* have the most effective global new product programs.[12] Having a global innovation culture means that a firm is open to global markets, mindful of differences in customer needs and preferences, and respectful of different national cultural and business environments. Firms with such a corporate culture are able to recognize the specialized skills, resources, and ideas they possess in different subsidiaries around the world. In fact, at these firms, all operations and strategies (not just new product development) are defined in terms of the realities of the international market. A firm with a global innovation culture is better at integrating its global knowledge, can better manage the R&D tasks associated with the new products process, and has an advantage in implementing global launches.[13] All of these factors contribute to improved global new product performance. Throughout this book, you will see examples of firms that practice innovation on a global basis, which includes managing virtual and highly diverse global product development teams—no easy task! Figure 1.1 provides several samples of firms that take the global aspect of product development very seriously.

FIGURE 1.1   **Product Development as a Global Process**

Procter & Gamble: According to the P&G Web site, P&G products are developed as global R&D projects. P&G has 22 research centers in 13 countries from which they can draw expertise. As a good example of a global product, consider the Swiffer mop. P&G made use of its research centers in the United States and France to conduct market research and testing in support of this new product.

Apple: In the development of the iPod, Apple worked with about ten different firms and independent contractors throughout the world, and did product design and customer requirement definition in both the United States and Japan.

Ikea: The Swedish furniture retailer knows that its target market (middle-class strivers) crosses international and intercontinental lines, so it operates globally in a streamlined fashion. It identifies an unmet customer need (say a certain style of table at a given price point), commissions in-house and outsourced designers to compete for the best design, then its manufacturing partners worldwide compete for the rights to manufacture it. Excellent global logistics complete the value delivery to customers.

Bungie Studios: This boutique software company, now owned by Microsoft, developed the MS Halo gaming software series in the United States, but product-tested it in Europe and Asia. Like Ikea customers in the prior example, gamers are much alike the world over.

Source: Loida Rosario, "Borderless Innovation™: The Impact of Globalization on NPD Planning in Three Industries," *Visions,* June 2006.

[12]Elko J. Kleinschmidt, Ulrike de Brentani, and Sören Salomo, "Performance of Global New Product Development Programs: A Resource-Based View," *Journal of Product Innovation Management,* 24(5), September 2007, pp. 419–441.

[13]Roger J. Calantone, S. T. Cavusgil, J. B. Schmidt, and G.-C. Shin, "Internationalization and the Dynamics of Product Adaptation: An Empirical Investigation," *Journal of Product Innovation Management,* 22(2), March 2004, pp. 185–198.

Global new product teams are a way of life now for many firms, and we will see more about the challenges facing such teams in Chapter 14. There, we will focus on the issues facing the global new product development team, and how firms overcome these hurdles to take advantage of product knowledge residing in many corners of the world. We touch on some of the issues regarding global positioning and branding decisions in Chapter 16.

How Product Development Is Different

It is likely that this course is located in your university's business school, within the marketing department. Or it might be part of your engineering training, or part of a specialized program in technology innovation management. In any case, this is a good time to note an underlying principle of product development: It's all about teamwork. The *new products team* ideally is cross-functional, comprising personnel from marketing, R&D, engineering, manufacturing, production, design, and other functional areas as well. Unlike other courses you may be taking, we spend much time in this text on *how you interact with people from other fields of study*: discussing how team members work together, how they can improve communication, what they need to achieve when working together, and so on. So, whatever your background, and whatever course of study you are pursuing, remember that in product development you will spend a lot of your time coordinating and working closely with people from other functional areas. Above all else, product development is a joint effort.

All members of a new products team make an important contribution to product development, so we must be aware of, and try to avoid, narrow functional viewpoints. Marketers have to learn to work with scientists, engineers, lawyers, production managers, and so on. We may come from marketing, and we will often return there when the project is finished, but, for now, we are all *new products people,* working with all functions, being biased to no one. A marketing type may not appreciate the thoroughness of a research scientist. And that scientist may not appreciate the marketer's enthusiasm, which sometimes leads to what the scientist thinks are rash and unwarranted conclusions. Now is a good time to begin thinking like a general manager.

This course of study calls for a *strong creative contribution*. Not only do we create new product concepts; in many firms, that's easy. The tough creativity is *how best to develop and market them*—devising a concept-testing method that works, screening a totally new idea the firm has never faced, figuring out how to integrate engineers into a trade show booth effectively, how to position a product that creates its own new category, how to produce it on present equipment, how to name it in a way that communicates yet doesn't confuse, and so on. No answers are found in the back of this book. We never will know whether any one decision was right, just whether the total package of decisions worked out.

Being creative means we *travel on unmarked roads*. Most of our decisions are made on grossly inadequate facts. Not that we don't know what facts we need or how to get good estimates of them—we usually do. But there's never enough time or money. Worst of all, *what seems to be a fact in January may not be a fact come June, when we actually introduce the new item.* As a result, we often do things that make others nervous. For example, we use **heuristics**—rules of thumb that firms have found work for them: "On items such as this, about 30 percent of the people who hear of a new brand, try it," or "When the product engineer from R&D disagrees with the process engineer from manufacturing, it's better to go with manufacturing." Heuristics sometimes leave us holding an empty bag; but without them, projects just won't move forward fast enough. Another technique is to use *simple intuition* or hunch, or gut feel. This explains why most managers want new products people to have spent time in ongoing operations before moving on to new products work.

This suggests another key difference between this course and many of your others. We are *dealing with people under intense pressure*, making tough decisions under impossible conditions. Consider a classic example: a group of about 15 people sent by IBM from Armonk to Boca Raton during the dawn of the personal computer era, 1980. They were given one year to create and market a new product, which eventually became known as the IBM PC. Literally billions of dollars were at stake—the difference between becoming a major player in a new market or missing the boat completely. Virtually every day, someone on that team had to make a decision that could close the show. When studying how strategy guides teams throughout a project, or how firms telescope their market testing into simultaneous regional rollouts, remember that pressure.

You may also be taking a course that deals with innovation in manufacturing (often called *operations* in service firms), and you may wonder how *process* innovation differs from *product* innovation. The term *process innovation* usually applies to functions, especially the manufacturing or distribution process, and every new product benefits from this type of innovation. The term *product innovation* applies to the total operation by which a new product is created and marketed, and it includes innovation in all of the functional processes.

The last difference worth noting here is in *application*. Sometimes the new product process is accidental, or **serendipitous** (see Figure 1.2). But remember the old adage that chance favors the prepared mind. At least two dozen scientists had observed mold killing off their bacteria colonies before Alexander Fleming pursued the phenomenon into the discovery of penicillin. More recently, Pfizer researchers noticed that several of the men in a test study of a new angina medication reported that it was ineffective at treating their angina, but it did have an unexpected alternative effect on the body. Soon, Pfizer was marketing Viagra, one of their top products in recent years.[14] So, we must practice. You cannot learn how to develop a new product concept by reading about attribute analysis or gap analysis. You must *do* them. The same goes for product use testing, positioning, contingency planning, and many more. There are

[14]Jenny Darroch and Morgan P. Miles, "Sources of Innovation," in V. K. Narayanan and Gina C. O'Connor (eds.), *Encyclopedia of Technology & Innovation Management* (Chichester, UK: John Wiley, 2010), Chapter 14.

FIGURE 1.2   Not All New Products Are Planned

A Raytheon engineer working on experimental radar noticed that a chocolate bar in his shirt pocket melted. He then "cooked" some popcorn. The firm developed the first commercial microwave oven.

A chemist at G. D. Searle licked his finger to turn a page of a book and got a sweet taste. Remembering that he had spilled some experimental fluid, he checked it out and produced aspartame (NutraSweet).

A 3M researcher dropped a beaker of industrial compound and later noticed that where her sneakers had been splashed, they stayed clean. ScotchGard fabric protector resulted.

A DuPont chemist was bothered by an experimental refrigerant that didn't dissolve in conventional solvents or react to extreme temperatures. So the firm took the time to identify what later became Teflon.

Another scientist couldn't get plastic to mix evenly when cast into automobile parts. Disgusted, he threw a steel wool scouring pad into one batch as he quit for the night. Later, he noticed that the steel fibers conducted the heat out of the liquid quickly, letting it cool more evenly and stay mixed better. Bendix made many things from the new material, including brake linings.

Others? Gore-Tex, dynamite, puffed wheat, Dextro-Maltose, LSD, penicillin, Dramamine, X rays, pulsars, and many more. In each case, a prepared mind.

Sources: DuPont and Bendix cases, *The Innovators* (New York: Dow Jones, 1968); Raytheon, Searle, and 3M cases, Kenneth Labrich, "The Innovators," *Fortune*, June 6, 1988, p. 56.

opportunities at the end of every chapter to think about the chapter's material in a market setting.

What Is a New Product, and What Leads to Success?

The term **new product** can mean different things to different people. Figure 1.3 shows that new products can include **new-to-the-world** (sometimes called **really-new**) products, as well as minor repositionings and cost reductions. The list in Figure 1.3 may include things you would exclude. For example, can we have a new item just by repositioning an old one (telling customers it is something else)? Arm & Hammer did, several times, by coming up with a new refrigerator deodorant, a new carpet freshener, a new drain deodorant, and more, all in the same package of baking soda, even with the same brand name. These may be considered just new uses, but the firm's process of discovery and development is the same. And a new use (particularly in industrial firms) may occur in a completely separate division. DuPont, for example, uses basic fibers in many different ways, from technical to consumer. Financial firms use their common databases for different markets. Similarly, brand names have long been used as platforms for launching line extensions. The Dove soap name, for example, has been extended to almost two dozen box soaps and almost as many liquid body washes.[15]

[15]Deborah L. Vence, "Just a Variation on a Theme," *Marketing News,* February 2007, pp.18–20.

FIGURE 1.3 **What Is a New Product?**

New products can be categorized in terms of how new they really are to the world, or to the firm. One common set of categories is as follows:

1. **New-to-the-world products, or really-new products.** These products are inventions that create a whole new market. Examples: Polaroid camera, Sony Walkman, the Palm Pilot, Hewlett-Packard's laser printer, Rollerblade brand inline skates, P&G's Febreze and Dryel. This category accounts for about 10% of new products.

2. **New-to-the-firm products, or new product lines.** Products that take a firm into a category new to it. The products are not new to the world, but are new to the firm. Examples: P&G's first shampoo or coffee, Hallmark gift items, AT&T's Universal credit card, Canon's laser printer. About 20% of new products.

3. **Additions to existing product lines.** These are "Flanker" brands, or line extensions, designed to flesh out the product line as offered to the firm's current markets. Examples: P&G's Tide Liquid detergent, Bud Light, Apple's iMac, Hewlett-Packard's LaserJet 7P (an inexpensive laser printer designed for home computers). About 26% of new products.

4. **Improvements and revisions to existing products.** Current products made better. Examples: P&G's Ivory Soap and Tide powder laundry detergent have been revised numerous times throughout their history; countless other examples. About 26% of new products.

5. **Repositionings.** Products that are retargeted for a new use or application. Example: Arm & Hammer baking soda repositioned as a drain deodorant, refrigerator deodorant, etc.; aspirin repositioned as a safeguard against heart attacks. Also includes products retargeted to new users or new target markets; Marlboro cigarettes were repositioned from a woman's cigarette to a man's cigarette years ago. About 7% of new products.

6. **Cost reductions.** New products that simply replace existing products in the line, providing the customer similar performance but at a lower cost. May be more of a "new product" in terms of design or production than marketing. About 11% of new products.

Sources: The categorization scheme was originally presented in Booz, Allen & Hamilton Inc., *New Product Management for the 1980s* (New York: Booz, Allen & Hamilton Inc, 1982) and is now standard in new product development. The percentages are from Abbie Griffin (1997), *Drivers of NPD Success: The 1997 PDMA Report* (Chicago: Product Development & Management Association); some of the examples are from Robert G. Cooper, *Winning at New Products: Accelerating the Process from Idea to Launch*, 3rd ed. (Cambridge, MA: Perseus Publications, 2001).

All the categories in Figure 1.3 are considered new products, but it is plain to see that the risks and uncertainties differ, and the categories need to be managed differently. Generally, if a product is new to the world or new to the firm (the first two categories), the risks and uncertainties faced by the firm are higher, as are the associated costs of development and launch. It cost Gillette far more, for example, to launch the first three-blade shaving system (the Mach3) than to do upgrades to the earlier Sensor system (Sensor for Women and SensorExcel). A greater commitment of human and financial resources is often required to bring the most innovative new products to market successfully.

Note also that not all the new product categories in Figure 1.3 are necessarily innovations. Line extensions, like the Dove soap bars mentioned above, or new flavors of Oreo cookies, may have resulted from the company's desire to increase display space and shelf space. As Bob Golden of Technomic (a food industry consultancy) notes, "Many of these companies [that launch line extensions] are cannibalizing existing brands in order to stimulate the [product] category." Line extension shouldn't be confused with "true" innovation—and management must recognize that true innovation that provides enhanced value to customers is where their long-term competitive advantage may lie.[16]

New-to-the-world products revolutionize existing product categories or define wholly new ones. They are the most likely to require consumer learning and/or incorporate a very new technology. Desktop computers with word processing software defined a new product category that virtually obsoleted electric and manual typewriters, and consumer learning was required by those who type for a living. Hewlett-Packard LaserJet printers did much the same thing in the printer category. The launch of CDs required major differences at the retail level in terms of store layout and distribution of related components (such as CD players). Other familiar examples, such as hybrid cars, the iPod, and even the Swatch watch, illustrate the use of new technologies in new-to-the-world products. Manufacturers had to overcome perceived risks, perceived incompatibility with prior experience, or other barriers to customer adoption (more on this subject in Chapter 16).

Of course, launching new-to-the-world products means risk—and the encouragement to take on the risk must permeate the whole firm and must start at the highest levels of management. At highly innovative firms like Intel and Gillette (the latter now a division of Procter & Gamble), top management may even abandon the use of quarterly earnings estimates in order to keep the business units focused on innovation and other long-term strategic goals.[17]

The **new product line** category in Figure 1.3 raises the issue of the imitation product, a strictly "me-too." If a firm introduces a brand of light beer that is new to them but is identical to those already on the market, is it a new product? Yes, it is new to the firm, and it requires the new products process. Canon was not the first laser printer manufacturer, Coca-Cola was not the first orange-juice bottler, and P&G was not the first competitor in the coffee business. These were new products to these firms, however, managerially speaking, and they are managed as such by the companies.

The evidence suggests that maintaining a focus on new-to-the-world products and new product lines is easier said than done. In 1990, about 20 percent of new products were new-to-the-world, and about 39 percent were new product lines—compare these to the much lower percentages in Figure 1.3.[18] New products expert Robert Cooper attributes this finding to an increased preoccupation with minor product improvements and "tweaking" as opposed to true product innovation. Nonetheless, over this time, the best-performing businesses did not give in to this temptation—innovative products represented about 17 percent of their portfolios in 2004, about the same as in 1990.[19]

---

[16]Deborah L. Vence, op. cit.; the Bob Golden quote is from Karen Heller, "It's in the Snack Aisle, But Is It Food?" *Philadelphia Inquirier,* March 14, 2007, pp. E1, E4.
[17]Thomas D. Kuczmarski, "What Is Innovation? And Why Aren't Companies Doing More of It?" *Journal of Consumer Marketing,* 20(6), 2003, pp. 536–541.
[18]Robert G. Cooper, S. J. Edgett, and E. J. Kleinschmidt, "Benchmarking Best NPD Practices–II: Strategy, Resource Allocation and Portfolio Management," *Research-Technology Management,* 47(3), May–June 2004, pp. 50–59.
[19]Robert G. Cooper, "Your NPD Portfolio May Be Harmful to Your Business Health," *Visions,* April 2005; and Cooper *et al.,* op. cit.

Figure 1.3 shows that many new products can be considered additions to existing product lines or improvements and revisions to existing products. Many of these line extensions round out or add to existing product lines extremely well: Tide Liquid detergent, Bud Light, the Apple iMac. Nevertheless, studies suggest that the most innovative new product categories account for many more product successes. In one study, the two most innovative categories accounted for about 30 percent of new product launches, but about 60 percent of the most successful products. (Percentages, of course, will vary by industry: High-tech industries will produce proportionately more highly innovative new products.) In fact, an inverted-U shape between innovativeness and success was found: The most innovative new product categories and the least innovative categories (the repositionings and cost reductions) outperformed the middle categories in terms of meeting financial criteria, returns on investment, and resulting market shares![20] These results suggest that many firms need to reconsider the importance and potential contribution of innovative new products when making project selection decisions. In Chapter 3 we shall look at building a strategic portfolio of products that strives for balance among the innovation categories.

We have already seen that, even among the best firms, there are some product failures, and this entire book is devoted to developing new successful products, so there can be no easy answer to the question "What leads to new product success?" Nevertheless, several studies over the years on this question have yielded a consistent answer: The number one reason for success is a *unique superior product*. Additionally, common causes of failure include "no need for the product" and "there was a need but the new product did not meet that need." In other words, it was not unique and superior.[21] It did not offer the user sufficient **value added** relative to the costs of purchasing and use. Value added is a key concept to keep in mind as you travel the new product highway.

Does This Field of Activity Have a Unique Vocabulary?

Yes, it does, for two reasons. One, it is an *expanding field*, taking on new tasks and performing them in new ways. Second, it is a *melting pot field*, bringing in the language of scientists, lawyers, advertisers, accountants, marketing planners, corporate strategists, organizational behaviorists, and many more. Because many of these people talk about the same event but use different phrases to describe it, communication problems abound. The solution is to forge a common acceptance

[20]Elko J. Kleinschmidt and Robert G. Cooper, "The Impact of Product Innovativeness on Performance," *Journal of Product Innovation Management*, 5(4), December 1991, pp. 240–251; see also Abbie Griffin, *Drivers of NPD Success: The 1997 PDMA Report* (Chicago: Product Development & Management Association, 1997).

[21]Discussions of product success and failure can be found in R. G. Cooper, "New Products: What Separates the Winners from the Losers?" in M. D. Rosenau, A. Griffin, G. Castellion, and N. Anscheutz (eds.), *The PDMA Handbook of New Product Development* (New York: John Wiley, 1996), pp. 3–18; and R.G. Cooper, "The Impact of Product Innovativeness on Performance," *Journal of Product Innovation Management*, 16(2), April 1999, pp. 115–133.

of terms and to urge acceptance of one term for each new concept or activity as it arises.

But your study of new products management will be complicated by the unresolved problems. For example, there is continuing confusion over the terms **invention** and **innovation.** To managers invention refers to the dimension of uniqueness—the form, formulation, function of something. It is usually patentable. Innovation refers to the overall process whereby an invention is transformed into a commercial product that can be sold profitably. The invention may take but a few moments. We have far more inventions than we do innovations. Similarly, the average person might think that a product idea, a product concept, a product prototype, and maybe even a product are all about the same thing. As you will see in the pages of this book, we have specific, distinct definitions for each of these terms, and they are not interchangeable. For perhaps the most complete glossary of new product terms, check the online glossary published by the Product Development & Management Association (**www.pdma.org;** follow the link to the glossary).

The problem becomes much worse from a global perspective. Take, for example, the term **design.** In North American new product work, design means essentially industrial design or engineering (premanufacturing) design; in Europe, however, design means the entire technical creation function from initial specs to the shipping dock. To some design people, the term means the entire product innovation function.

The new products field has no definitional authority, as the accounting and legal professions have. The American Marketing Association publishes a glossary of definitions, and many of the new product terms came from one of the authors of the book you are reading. But we still have a long way to go.

Does the Field of New Products Offer Careers?

It does, though not many are entry positions for people right out of college. Generally, top managers want new products people to know the industry involved (for the customer understanding mentioned earlier) and the firm's various operations (that multidimensional, orchestration task also mentioned). So, most new products managers get assigned to new products work from a position in a functional department. For example, a scientist finds working with marketing and manufacturing people interesting, a market researcher specializes in benefit segmentation, or a salesperson earns a reputation for good new product concepts. Each of these people is a candidate for full-time work on new products.

The specific jobs in this field are three. First is **functional representative** on a team, sometimes full time, more often part time. An example is a marketing researcher or a production planner. These people may be representatives on several teams or just one. The second job is **project manager** or **team leader.** This role is leader of a team of people representing the functions that will be required. The third position is **new products *process* manager,** responsible for helping project managers develop and use good new product processes.

Some of the career tips we hear are:

1. Be multifunctional, not functionally parochial. Have experience in more than one function (marketing, manufacturing, and so on).
2. Be a risk taker, willing to do whatever is necessary to bring a product to market, including facing the wrath of co-workers.
3. Think like a general manager. Scientists and sales managers can lead new products teams, but they must cease being scientists and sales managers.
4. Be a combination of optimist and realist, aggressor and team player, leader and follower.
5. Develop your creative skills, both for new product concepts and for new ways of doing things.
6. Be comfortable in chaos and confusion. Learn to work with depressives, euphorics, and those with no emotion at all.

Fortunately, such managers do exist—and in increasing numbers. We hope you become one of them.

The Strategic Elements of Product Development

We cover a lot of product development material in this book, from opportunity identification right through to launch and postlaunch. Underlying all of this are three **strategic elements,** which will be a major focus in this book. These strategic elements provide a framework to guide management through product development and help them focus on what is most important. Top product development consultants, like Robert Cooper of the Product Development Institute, recommend a framework of this type to firms of all sizes to help guide product development.[22] A key point here is that *all three of the strategic elements must be in place*, and each is coordinated with, and supports, all the others. The three elements are a **new products process,** a **product innovation charter,** and a well-managed **product portfolio.**

The *new products process* is the procedure that takes the new product idea through concept evaluation, product development, launch, and postlaunch. This procedure is usually depicted as a phased process with evaluative steps between the phases, but as you will see in upcoming chapters, there is much more here than meets the eye. The *product innovation charter* can be thought of as a strategy for new products. It ensures that the new product team develops products that are in line with firm objectives and strategies and that address marketplace opportunities. *Product portfolio management* helps the firm assess which new products would be the best additions to the existing product line, given both financial and strategic objectives. In this chapter, we introduce the first strategic element, the new products process, as it serves as a framework for everything that follows in this book, and explore it more deeply in Chapter 2. In Chapter 3, we discuss the last two strategic elements, the product innovation charter and product portfolio management.

[22]Roger J. Calantone, S. T. Cavusgil, J. B. Schmidt, and G.-C. Shin, "Internationalization and the Dynamics of Product Adaptation: An Empirical Investigation," *Journal of Product Innovation Management*, 22(2), March 2004, pp. 185–198.

The Basic New Products Process

Figure 1.4 shows a simple new products process described in terms of phases and tasks. Research has shown that about 65 to 75 percent of firms use some kind of adaptable, phased new products process, and about 47 percent use clearly defined evaluation criteria after each phase. At least 40 percent of firms assign a process manager whose job it is to manage the phased new products process.[23] The phased new products process is certainly well established among firms involved in new product development.

The idea behind the new products process is that the phases represent *activities* that are conducted by the new product team; between the phases are *evaluation tasks*, or decision points.[24] It is at these points that the hard Go/No Go decisions

FIGURE 1.4
The Basic New Products Process

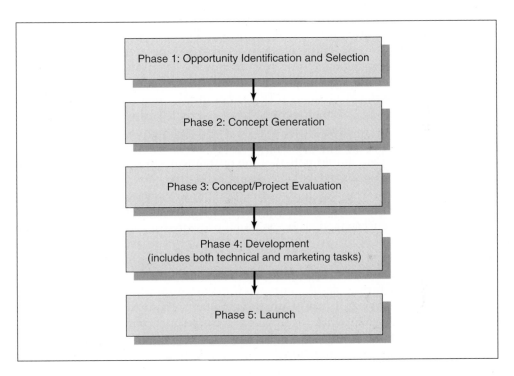

[23]Abbie Griffin, "PDMA Research on New Product Development Practices: Updating Trends and Benchmarking Best Practices," *Journal of Product Innovation Management,* 14(6), 1997, pp. 429–458; Robert G. Cooper, Scott G. Edgett, and Elko J. Kleinschmidt, *Improving New Product Development Performance and Practices: Benchmarking Study* (Houston, TX: American Productivity and Quality Center, 2002); Marjorie Adams, *Competitive Performance Assessment (CPAS) Study Results,* PDMA Foundation, 2004; and Kenneth B. Kahn, Gloria Barczak, and Roberta Moss, "Perspective: Establishing a NPD Best Practices Framework," *Journal of Product Innovation Management,* 23(2), March 2006, pp. 106–116.
[24]Robert G. Cooper, *Winning at New Products: Accelerating the Process from Idea to Launch,* 3rd ed. (Cambridge, MA: Perseus Publishing, 2001).

need to be asked (that is, whether the project looks promising enough to go on to the next phase). Throughout this book, we will be looking at the kinds of tests (from concept tests, to product use tests, to market tests) that are used to gather information for project evaluation.

The goal of a new products process is to manage down the amount of risk and uncertainty as one passes from idea generation to launch. There are periodic evaluations all the way through the process. A firm may have access to hundreds of ideas; weaker ones are immediately eliminated, and the better ones are refined into concepts. Later in the process, only the best concepts are approved and moved forward to the development phase. The product is continuously refined during the development phase and could close up still be halted before the launch phase if preliminary product use test results are not positive. By the time the product is launched, it has a much higher likelihood of succeeding (recall the roughly 60 percent success rate across many product categories cited earlier). Managing down the amount of uncertainty is important, because each additional phase means greater financial investment (possibly much greater), not to mention greater commitment of human resources. Firms using a new products process have reported improvements in product teamwork, less rework, greater success rates with new products, earlier identification of failures, improved launch, and up to 30 percent shorter cycle times.[25] This is not to say, however, that all firms implement the process well. Other studies show that many firms that claim to have a new products process either designed it or implemented it poorly; thus, there is much room for improvement.[26]

One should note that the neat, linear sequencing of phases shown in Figure 1.4 is just not typical. The reality is that the activities are not sequential, but overlapping. It is not implied that one phase must be completed before work can begin on the next one, like a pass-the-baton relay race. In fact, this kind of overlapping is encouraged. There is much pressure for firms to **accelerate time to market** for new products, and a certain amount of phase overlapping is an important tool in speeding new products to market. To do this right, of course, requires that the product team members from different functional areas (marketing, R&D, manufacturing, design, engineering) communicate very effectively.[27] Product development is truly **multifunctional,** where all functions (and, increasingly, the customer as well!) work together on a **cross-functional team** to accomplish the required tasks. The whole of Chapter 14 investigates the organization and management of these cross-functional teams in depth. But even though we discuss teams later in the text, keep in mind that the team must become involved as early as possible

[25]Robert G. Cooper, "New Products: What Separates the Winners from the Losers," in M. D. Rosenau, A. Griffin, G. Castellion, and N. Anscheutz (eds.), *The PDMA Handbook of New Product Development* (New York: John Wiley, 1996), pp. 3–18.
[26]Robert G. Cooper, Scott J. Edgett, and Elko J. Kleinschmidt, *Best Practices in Product Innovation: What Distinguishes the Top Performers,* Product Development Institute, 2003; Robert G. Cooper, "Perspective: The Stage-Gate® Idea-to-Launch Process—Update, What's New, and NexGen Systems," *Journal of Product Innovation Management,* 25(3), May 2008, pp. 213–232.
[27]Preston G. Smith and D. G. Reinertsen, *Developing Products in Half the Time* (New York: Van Nostrand Reinhold, 1991).

in the new products process. It is the responsibility of the team leader to bring together the right individuals with the right skill sets, and to encourage communication within the team, between the team and top management, and between the team and communities of customers. The effective team leader knows how to deal with power conflicts as well as technical complexity.[28]

Another way that firms have been able to avoid delays and speed up time to market is to streamline the evaluation tasks. At Johnson & Johnson, the preparation for an evaluation task might have included preparing a 30- to 90-page review document. This was cut to a standardized presentation, with a one-page summary and a handful of slides—enough to inform senior management about the risks and commitments being decided upon. It was reported that weeks of preparation time were saved with the new format.[29]

Furthermore, we should clear up something about the evaluation tasks that occur after every phase in the new products process. Figure 1.4 implies that each phase is always followed by a Go/No Go decision. While this is often the case, it might be an oversimplification. If some key information is still missing or unavailable, a third option is possible, which we can call an "On decision." This means that the project will move forward (a conditional "Go," if you will), but the missing information must be gathered and the project could still be halted at a later phase. An evaluation task that includes conditional Go decisions is sometimes called a **fuzzy gate.** For example, a new packaged food product might do reasonably well at a concept test, but management might feel they don't really have a read on the market until some product use testing (letting the customer actually taste the product) is conducted. An On decision would mean that the product is approved to move to development, but the product use test must yield positive results, otherwise the project would be halted at that point. Fuzzy gates, therefore, speed up the process because time is not wasted in obtaining complete information before the decision is made. They are relatively common; in the CPAS study, about 50 percent of projects move forward with some conditional decisions along the way. Nevertheless, the firm must indeed make a firm decision once the necessary information is obtained; in other words, fuzzy gates still have teeth. A related problem occurs when teams actually make a full "Go" decision, but fail to commit any resources to the project. This is known as a *hollow-gate* problem and results in too many projects underway and, inevitably, cost overruns and launch delays. Similarly, a poor project may never be critically evaluated because it is the CEO's pet project, or because a hidden personal or political agenda is influencing decision making. Gates without teeth, hollow gates, special treatment for executives, or hidden agendas can all hinder effectiveness of the new products process, but all are identifiable and avoidable.[30]

---

[28]Hans J. Thamhain, "Managing Product Development Project Teams," in Kenneth B. Kahn, George Castellion, and Abbie Griffin (eds.), *The PDMA Handbook of New Product Development* (New York: John Wiley & Sons, 2005), pp. 127–143.
[29]Robert G. Cooper, "What Leading Companies Are Doing to Reinvent Their NPD Processes," *Visions,* 32(3), September 2008, pp. 6–10.
[30]For more on all of these problem areas, see Cooper (2008), op. cit.

Another consideration is that the new products process might look very different for new-to-the-world, **breakthrough products** (more on these in Chapter 2) as compared to more **incremental new products.** A firm like P&G might use a simplified process for a low-risk project (such as a new detergent) in which some phases and evaluation tasks are combined or may even be omitted. The CPAS study showed that only about 40 percent of radical projects have phases that overlap or are skipped, while for incremental new products, about 59 percent have overlapping phases or skip some phases entirely. For a new-to-the-world product, such as Febreze or Dryel, P&G faces greater risks and higher expenses, and the complete new products process in all its detail will probably be followed. Thus, it is helpful to think of the process in Figure 1.4 as a guideline or framework, but to recognize that the new products process is really quite flexible. In fact, these characteristics (overlapping phases, fuzzy gates, and flexibility) are features of what is called the **third-generation new products process,** which is the way most firms interpret the process depicted in Figure 1.4.[31]

There is something else significant in Figure 1.4. Don't be misled by the titles of the phases. They do not refer to functions or departments. Technical people *lead* the technical portion of the development, but others participate, some very actively, including market research, sales, design, and so on. Launch sounds like a marketing activity, but much of the marketing is done back during earlier phases. We discuss what we call the "marketing ramp-up" in detail in Chapter 16. Also, during launch, the manufacturing people are busy setting up production capability. Legal people are clearing brand names, lab people are running tests on early product output, and so on. As seen before, the new products process is a job for a well-organized, efficient cross-functional team.

Additionally, different firms group the new product activities differently. There is certainly no agreement on the exact number of steps. That is not a cause for concern. Rather than thinking of the process as some number of discrete phases, look for the bigger picture of a large, evolving, general-purpose process, which we break up into phases partly for our benefit in presenting the story about new product activities. Different firms simply break up the same underlying process differently.

Lexmark International, manufacturer of printers and related products and associated supplies, is a prime example of a firm with a successful phased new products process. Lexmark's process requires cross-functional teams from the earliest phases and cross-functional decisions at the evaluation points. For example, preceding the launch phase, the Worldwide Marketing group conducts the Announcement Readiness Review, which is tied to the Manufacturing group's Manufacturing Readiness Review. Lexmark assigns one owner to each phase, and the evaluation task has only one owner; its new products process is tied to milestones, not the calendar, which allows some processes to be longer than others depending on complexity. Since establishing its latest new products process, Lexmark has

---

[31]See Robert G. Cooper, "Perspective: Third-Generation New Product Processes," *Journal of Product Innovation Management,* 11(1), 1994, pp. 3–14; also Cooper (2008), op. cit.; also Robert G. Cooper, "Effective Gating," *Marketing Management,* 18(2), 2009, pp. 12–17.

reported increased ability to launch new products within time and budget targets, and senior management state that its business and technical processes are in better alignment.[32]

We will go much deeper into the new products process in Chapter 2.

The Other Strategic Elements

The process depicted in Figure 1.4 is part of a firm's new product strategy, but it leaves some questions unanswered. First, what is the firm's underlying strategy for new products? What market and/or technology opportunities is it seeking to exploit? What is the strategic arena within which the firm will compete? How innovative does management want to be? Lacking a new product strategy, the firm will approach new product development in an unfocused manner. Without a clear boundary defining what new market or technology opportunities to pursue, *any* idea would seem to be all right, which leads to too many underfunded products. We call this new product strategy a product innovation charter, or PIC. The PIC is developed by senior management and provides guidance to all functional areas involved in innovation. It defines a scope of activity for new product development, helping the product team identify what opportunities lie within the boundaries and where they should focus their efforts. That way, perhaps fewer projects may be pursued, but they will generally be of higher value to the firm. And the advantages of establishing a PIC are clear-cut: In Robert Cooper's research, firms with a strong product definition had about an 85 percent chance of success and averaged a 37 percent market share, while those with a weak product definition showed a 26 percent chance of success and a market share of about 23 percent.[33]

Additionally, many new product concepts may seem to be technically feasible and marketable. Before committing scarce financial and human resources, top management must also consider whether the new product, if developed, would fit the firm's overall business strategy: whether it adds strategically to the products already being offered, or whether it throws the firm's product line off balance. This is an issue of product portfolio management. While almost every firm will consider financial criteria such as expected sales revenues or profits when approving a new product development project, the best performing firms balance financial criteria with strategic considerations, such that the firm's long-term objectives will be met and there will be a dependable flow of new products into the future.[34]

The product innovation charter, product portfolio management, and related issues are covered more deeply in Chapter 3.

---

[32]Ed Crowley, "Building a Gated Product Development Process at Lexmark International," *Visions,* 29(4), October 2005, pp. 22–23.

[33]Robert Cooper, *Winning at New Products: Accelerating the Process from Idea to Launch,* 2nd ed. (Reading, MA: Addison-Wesley, 1993).

[34]Gary E. Blau, Joseph F. Pekny, Vishal A. Varma, and Paul R. Bunch, "Managing a Portfolio of Interdependent New Product Candidates in the Pharmaceutical Industry," *Journal of Product Innovation Management,* 21(4), July 2004, pp. 227–245.

Product Development in Action

To see the ongoing efforts of the best product developers in the business, check the Web site for the Product Development & Management Association (www.pdma.org). Among other things, the PDMA sponsors an Outstanding Corporate Innovator award. This award is not for a single great new product, but rather for a sustained program of new product success over at least five years. And award winners must tell attendees at the association's annual conference how they did it. As we noted before, innovation can be taught—and managers from the best innovating firms serve as the teachers in these conference sessions. In most of these cases, one could take their systems right from this book. Winners have included Corning, Royal DSM, Merck, Hewlett-Packard, Dow Chemical, Maytag, Bausch & Lomb, Harley-Davidson, and many others (the full list is on the PDMA Web site).

The PDMA Web site also provides links to their academic journal, the *Journal of Product Innovation Management*, and their practitioner-oriented newsletter, *Visions*, as well as to the glossary mentioned earlier. As you take this course, you may want to check these publications for the most recent and timely articles on many aspects of new product development and innovation, and for the current hot topics among new product development professionals.

Summary

This chapter has introduced you to the general field of new products management. You read how the activity is (or should be) found in all organizations, not just business. You read how this course of study relates to others, what a new product actually is, and that services and business products are covered, not just cake mixes, cell phones, and cars. You learned about where the field stands today, the hallmarks of our activity, our problems with vocabulary, and possible careers. Chapter 2 will take us directly into the new product process.

Applications

At the end of each chapter are a few questions that arose (or could have) one time or another in a job interview. The candidate was a student who took a course in new products management, and the interviewer was a high-ranking person in the firm (here portrayed as the president). The questions came up naturally during discussion, and they are tough. Often, the executive didn't intend them to be answered so much as talked about. Occasionally, the executive just made a comment and then paused for the applicant's reaction. Each question or comment relates to something in the chapter.

Imagine you are the person being interviewed. You do not have the option of ducking the question or saying "I really don't know." If, in fact, you really don't know, then glance back over the reading to see what you missed. It's also a good idea to exchange answers with another student taking the course, given that most of the applications involve opinions or interpretations, not recitation of facts.

1. "When you were talking a while ago about taking risks, I wondered just whose money you were talking about. A fellow I know out in California insists that all new product team members invest their own money (with his) in their projects. Fifty thousand dollars is not unusual. In that system I'll bet you would be seeking to *avoid* risks, not trying to *find* them."

2. "Funny thing, though, it sure does frustrate me when I hear a division general manager's strategy is to imitate other firms. Now, I know some firms might reasonably use imitation, but none of my divisions should. Should they?"

3. "I would like to be sure as many of our people as possible support innovation, but I know some people in the firm just can't react positively to proposed innovation, no matter how much we need it. Tell me, how do you think I should go about spotting the worst offenders, and what should I do with them when I find out who they are?"

CHAPTER TWO

The New Products Process

Setting

Chapter 1 provided a view of the *overall new products process*—that combination of steps/activities/decisions/goals and so on that, if performed well, will churn out the new products the organization needs. This process appeared in Figure 1.4, which serves as a framework for the rest of this book. As noted in the introduction to Part I, the five figures that introduce each part of this book (Figures I.1, II.1, and so on) are indeed simply the five boxes of Figure 1.4, expanded to show more detail on what happens at each phase in the process. In this chapter, we go more deeply into the phases of the new products process model of Figure 1.4, illustrating what tasks are required at each phase and who is responsible for what. We then explore several issues important to product managers: how the new products process can be sped up (without sacrificing product quality or running up the budget), how the process would have to be adapted for the development of new services, how to develop breakthrough innovations, and how the skills and resources of external partners can be leveraged to improve the process.

We begin by relating a short new product story to illustrate some of the key activities in the new products process in action. This will lead into a deeper discussion of the new products process and its managerial aspects. In particular, the story clearly shows how the new products process is interwoven with the other strategic elements introduced in Chapter 1, that is, the product innovation charter and the new product portfolio. It also introduces the idea of the cross-functional team and the importance of effective team management in implementing the new products process.

The Procter & Gamble Cosmetics Saga[1]

In 1989, leading U.S. consumer goods manufacturer Procter & Gamble established itself in the cosmetics business by acquiring two leading cosmetics brands, Cover Girl and Clarion. By 1991, they also owned Max Factor. P&G established a new

[1]The P&G saga is drawn from Robert G. Cooper and Michael S. Mills, "Succeeding at New Product Development the P&G Way: A Key Element Is Using the 'Innovation Diamond,'" *Visions*, 29(4), October 2005, pp. 9–13.

Cosmetics strategic business unit (SBU) and tried developing and launching new products using the procedures it had mastered in the detergent, food, and other packaged-goods lines. By the mid-1990s, however, P&G senior management was considering its options for its Cosmetics SBU. Some new products had done poorly, Clarion was sold, and some managers were even wondering whether P&G should leave the cosmetics business for good.

P&G, one of the leading product developers worldwide, certainly knew the long-term importance of new products to the firm's bottom line. P&G's CEO, A. G. Lafley, said that "innovation is a prerequisite for sustained growth. No other path to profitable growth can be sustained over time. Without continual innovation, markets stagnate, products become commodities, and margins shrink." Senior management felt that this was not the time to get out of cosmetics; rather, the challenge was to turn new product development around within the ailing SBU. With this strong commitment to new products at the highest levels within the firm, the Cosmetics SBU's challenge was clear: fix the new products process, so that new products can become a sustaining, vital part of their business into the long term.

Cosmetics SBU management understood its new product weaknesses. At the time, there was little evidence of a clear product development strategy in the Cosmetics SBU. Product initiatives were all over the place, too many different product categories were being pursued, and too many customer segments were being targeted. In short, the SBU lacked a product development focus.

Within a few years, P&G's Cosmetics SBU had engineered a complete turnaround by following and implementing the three strategic elements we introduced in Chapter 1. It's not so simple, of course; senior management had to recognize new products as the lifeblood of their SBU and a key component of their success. They had to adequately fund new products and assign the right people to the tasks. However, the cosmetics SBU turnaround is almost a textbook case of the value of the strategic elements. It also clearly shows that one or two of the strategic elements alone won't be enough. All three were put into action, and each complemented and supported the others. Let's examine each in turn.

The Product Innovation Charter (PIC)

The starting point for the turnaround was a clear product innovation charter (PIC), which starts with an honest situation assessment and opportunity identification. At the time, the Cosmetics SBU was trying to develop products for the entire body and having difficulty carving out a competitive position. The situation assessment showed that there was an underserved consumer market, who wanted quality products for facial use only (facial cleanser, eye or lip products, and so on). Also, a problem was identified in the supply chain, which had become uncoordinated. Production and shipments were not tied to fluctuations in market demand, with the result that products spent too long in the supply network. Some new products were almost obsolete (not really competitive any more) by the time they were launched! Management realized that the supply chain needed to be under better control, such that market demand forecasts drove production and shipping schedules. If they succeeded in improving the supply chain, fewer launches would be delayed, and new products would be more competitive at the time of launch.

While you will learn more about the PIC in Chapter 3, the important thing to know is that it is a systematic way for managers to develop a new product strategy that considers the goals for their product innovation efforts and how these efforts fit overall business strategy. It involves identifying a strategic focus (which markets and which technologies will be targeted). In this case the market was defined in terms of products for the face. Essentially, this became a statement of the strategic arena or battlefield the Cosmetics SBU was going to compete in. Any new product opportunities that did not clearly help Cosmetics achieve its objectives in this arena would no longer be pursued.

The New Products Process

A second strategic element is the new products process, which is the path the new product takes from idea to the time of launch and beyond. P&G's Cosmetics SBU did not have an effective new products process in place, with the result that product development often proceeded without clear inputs from customers early in the process. Cosmetics implemented a new products process quite similar to the five-phase process introduced in Chapter 1, which ensured that project teams were established early in the process, that consumer research was done early, and that consumer insights were actually used in the development of new product concepts. (A term you will see in upcoming chapters is the *voice of the customer* or VOC: Think back to this example and consider how the VOC was used to drive product development in the Cosmetics SBU.) Note here that having a new products process, and actually implementing it correctly, are two different things. Cosmetics made its new products process work by having tough evaluation steps between the phases. At each phase, the project team had a set of current best practices against which to evaluate the product, as well as clear end-points or expectations. In addition, the evaluations were two-step, consisting of both a team recommendation and a decision by top management. In the past, the evaluations were not so carefully done, with the result that too many poor ideas would be allowed to pass.

The New Product Portfolio

In addition to a well-functioning new products process, there needs also to be an assurance that the firm is developing the right products with respect to its product portfolio. P&G's Cosmetics SBU established a plan for managing its product portfolio and systematically adding new products to the portfolio. Given the nature of the products they were making, it was important for new launches to create buzz and excitement in the marketplace—for that reason, excellent launch timing was important. Cosmetics added new products to the existing portfolio strategically, in terms of both product selection and launch timing. For example, a new eye makeup would not be launched onto the market if there were already too many similar products in the portfolio, or if a similar product had just been launched. SBU management spoke of establishing an "initiative rhythm" for its products: New products would come through the development pipeline such that they would be ready for market launch at the best moment. We will see much more about portfolio management in Chapter 14.

Supporting the Strategic Elements: Effective Team Management

Finally, new product team management within the Cosmetics SBU was excellent. First and foremost, senior SBU management was committed to turning new product development around and to properly implementing the new products process. Certainly, senior P&G management such as CEO A. G. Lafley was behind them as well, judging from his quote above. Cosmetics management ensured that a positive innovative culture was in place within their SBU, one in which employees worked effectively in empowered, cross-functional teams. One important step, established in Cosmetics as well as in other SBUs, was to create initiative success managers (ISMs), who reported to senior SBU management. These ISMs led strategy development sessions, managed new product evaluation meetings, took part in resource planning, trained employees, and (importantly) shared what they learned with ISMs working in other business units, so that their expertise could spread quickly throughout the firm. A solid set of metrics was also established, so that the performance of each development team could be honestly assessed every six or twelve months on key indicators established by SBU management. As with all other SBUs within P&G, great emphasis was placed on identifying the best team leaders, who could come from any of the functional areas (marketing, engineering, R&D, or elsewhere) and were rewarded based on how they performed relative to the established indicators. We will see much more about cross-functional teams and related organizational issues in Chapter 14.

What Happened in That Saga?

We just read several years worth of product development activity in a few minutes. The story began with an ongoing operation that was facing a difficult situation. The saga illustrates how the managers involved applied the strategic elements effectively. We also saw how important it was to get support for the process from top management—in this case, from the CEO himself.

This situation is typical in that the new products process *does not usually begin with a new product idea*. It is folklore that someone, somewhere, wakes up in the middle of the night with a great insight. It can happen, but successful new product programs are not built on such slender hopes. As the saga shows, the process usually begins with what amounts to strategy. With top management's support and good execution of all the strategic elements, P&G was able to turn the weak Cosmetics SBU around.

Note too that development does not take place behind the closed doors of a research lab. The cross-functional team includes personnel from many departments, not just the product engineers or R&D people. Also, marketing doesn't start when the product is finished. It becomes involved very early in the process—in this saga, marketing provided key information for the development of the PIC.

Last, the process is not over when the new product is launched. It ends when the new product is *successful*, usually after some in-flight corrections. P&G monitors the sales, profits, and market shares of its new products and takes corrective actions if interim goals are not reached.

The next section looks more deeply at the phases of the new products process, first introduced in Chapter 1.

The Phases in the New Products Process

Figure 2.1 shows a more detailed version of the **new products process.** Let's examine each of the phases individually to understand the basics.

FIGURE 2.1

The Phases of the New Products Process

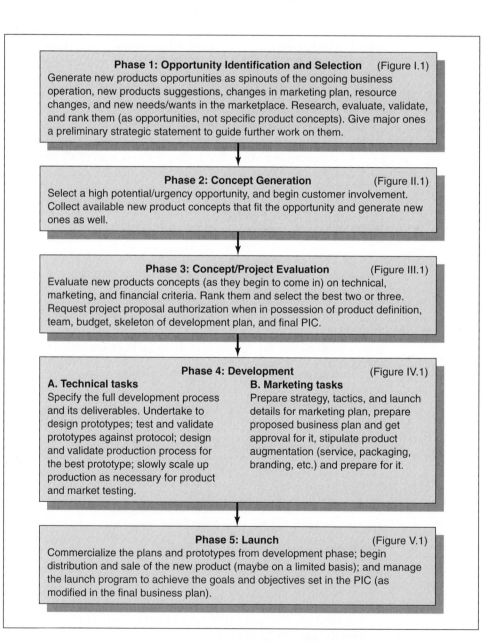

Phase 1: Opportunity Identification and Selection   (Figure I.1)
Generate new products opportunities as spinouts of the ongoing business operation, new products suggestions, changes in marketing plan, resource changes, and new needs/wants in the marketplace. Research, evaluate, validate, and rank them (as opportunities, not specific product concepts). Give major ones a preliminary strategic statement to guide further work on them.

Phase 2: Concept Generation   (Figure II.1)
Select a high potential/urgency opportunity, and begin customer involvement. Collect available new product concepts that fit the opportunity and generate new ones as well.

Phase 3: Concept/Project Evaluation   (Figure III.1)
Evaluate new products concepts (as they begin to come in) on technical, marketing, and financial criteria. Rank them and select the best two or three. Request project proposal authorization when in possession of product definition, team, budget, skeleton of development plan, and final PIC.

Phase 4: Development   (Figure IV.1)

A. Technical tasks
Specify the full development process and its deliverables. Undertake to design prototypes; test and validate prototypes against protocol; design and validate production process for the best prototype; slowly scale up production as necessary for product and market testing.

B. Marketing tasks
Prepare strategy, tactics, and launch details for marketing plan, prepare proposed business plan and get approval for it, stipulate product augmentation (service, packaging, branding, etc.) and prepare for it.

Phase 5: Launch   (Figure V.1)
Commercialize the plans and prototypes from development phase; begin distribution and sale of the new product (maybe on a limited basis); and manage the launch program to achieve the goals and objectives set in the PIC (as modified in the final business plan).

Phase 1: Opportunity Identification and Selection

The first phase is strategic in nature and is the most difficult to describe or define. The best approach probably is to tell you what businesses actually do, and then show how this yields strategic guidance to the firm.

At least three main streams of activity feed strategic planning for new products. They are (with an example for each) as follows.

- **Ongoing marketing planning.** Example: The annual marketing plan for a CD-ROM line calls for a line extension to meet encroachment of a new competitor selling primarily on price.
- **Ongoing corporate planning.** Example: Top management adopts a strategy that says either own a market (meaning get either a first- or second-place share) or get out of it. This will require new product activity in all desirable markets where the firm holds a minor position.
- **Special opportunity analysis.** One or more persons (in the firm or a consulting firm) are assigned to take an inventory of the firm's resources (people, facilities, reputations, whatever). Example: A firm in the auto parts business called for an audit of its manufacturing operation. It turned out that manufacturing process engineering had been overlooked or just not appreciated—that skill could serve as the base for a new products program.

From these activities, the opportunities identified sort naturally into four categories, again with examples:

- **An underutilized resource.** Example: A bottling operation, a strong franchise with dealers, or that manufacturing process engineering department.
- **A new resource.** Example: DuPont's discovery of Surlyn, a material with hundreds of potential uses.
- **An external mandate.** Example: The market may be stagnant, the competition may be threatening, or customer needs may be evolving. Challenges like this will cause the firm to search for new opportunities, as did the Tasty Baking Company in the case at the end of this chapter.
- **An internal mandate.** Example: Long-range planning often establishes a five-year-out dollar sales target, and new products people often must fill part of the gap between current sales and that target. That assignment is called the **product innovation** (and/or *acquisition*) **gap.** Other common internal mandates are simply upper management desires.

The process of creatively recognizing such opportunities is called **opportunity identification.** The opportunities are carefully and thoroughly described, then analyzed to confirm that a sales potential does, indeed, exist. Recall that one of the first things P&G Cosmetics did was recognize that the new products process for cosmetics could be fixed, and that new products in this category could be a viable business direction.

Of course, no firm wants to exploit *all* opportunities; some are better than others. Some may not fit with company skills, some are too risky, some require more money than the firm has. So, most firms have **ongoing strategies** covering product innovation. For example, Waterford had a strategy that no new product would jeopardize the firm's great image. Cincinnati Milicron's strategy demanded that any new product be highly innovative, not a me-too. Gillette and Sony usually choose leading-edge innovation strategies.

Once an opportunity is approved, managers turn to various techniques to guide new product people in exploiting it. This we will call the **product innovation charter (PIC),** and it will be explained in Chapter 3.

Phase 2: Concept Generation

In some cases, merely identifying an opportunity pretty well spells out what is wanted (for example, an opportunity to add a small size of deodorant for travelers). Most times, however, it's not so clear, so an immense set of ideation tools has evolved. Creating new product ideas, usually called **product concepts** by new products people, is not the simple, fun-and-games thing it might appear.

The most fruitful ideation involves identifying problems people or businesses have and suggesting solutions to them. For example, if the opportunity focused on "people moving their families over long distances," the first ideation step is to study those people and find what problems they have. This problem-finding-and-solving activity has become quite sophisticated; it is no longer the caricature of a group sitting around a table, pouring out ideas.

While the systematic problem-based ideation is going on, unsolicited ideas are pouring in on phone, mail, and e-mail from customers, potential or former customers, employees (especially sales, technical, and operations), and every other source imaginable. These ideas are reviewed briefly by whomever receives them to see if they are even relevant to the firm and its strategies. They are then put into the pool with the ideas that came from problem-solving activities.

Concept generation is covered in Part II, Chapters 4 through 7.

Phase 3: Concept/Project Evaluation

Before development work can begin on new ideas, they need to be evaluated, screened, sorted out. This activity, sometimes called **screening** or **pretechnical evaluation,** varies tremendously. But most firms more or less follow a sequence from quick looks to complete discounted cash flows and a net present value. The quick look is necessary because the flow of new product concepts is huge—into the thousands in many firms.

But what happens next is the first formal type of evaluation. Depending on the idea, this may be end-user screening or technical screening, or both. The work may be extensive and difficult, or it may take no more than a few telephone calls. In the P&G Cosmetics example, some of the proposed new products may have originated among the technical people; this would have to be followed by a **concept test** to see what potential consumers thought about it. Ultimately, these views all come together in what is often called the **full screen.** It uses a scoring model of some type and results in a decision to either undertake development or quit.

If the decision is to go ahead, the evaluation turns into **project evaluation,** where we no longer evaluate the idea but rather the plan we propose for capitalizing on that idea. This involves preparing a statement of what is wanted from the new product. Firms using **Quality Function Deployment** (a method of project management and control) see this as the first list of customer needs. A more common generic term is **product description** or **product definition.** In this book it will be called **product protocol.** Protocol means agreement, and it is important that there be agreement between the various groups *before* extensive technical work gets under way. The protocol should, to the extent possible, be *benefits* the new item is to yield, not the features the new item is to have.

The lack of good hard information complicates all pretechnical evaluation. In fact, the first three phases (strategic planning, concept generation, and, especially, concept/project evaluation) comprise what is popularly called the **fuzzy front end** (of the new product process). By the end of the project, most fuzz will have been removed, but for now, we move with more daring than the data allow.[2] The various pretechnical evaluation actions are covered in Part III, Chapters 8 through 12.

Phase 4: Development

This is the phase during which the item acquires finite form—a tangible good or a specific sequence of resources and activities that will perform an intangible service. It is also the phase during which the **marketing plan** is sketched and gradually fleshed out. Business practice varies all over the map, but we often find the following pieces.

Resource Preparation

Often overlooked by new products managers is a step called **resource preparation.** For product improvements and some line extensions, this is fine, because a firm is already up and going in a mode that fits products that are close to home. The culture is right, market data are more reliable, and ongoing managers are ready to do the work. But a particular innovation charter may leave familiar territory, forcing problems of fit. If a firm wants new-to-the-world products (more about them later in this chapter), then the team may need special training, new reward systems, revisions in the firm's usual project review system, and special permissions. Without adequate preparation of the ball field, a firm doesn't get much home advantage.

The Major Body of Effort

Next comes what all of the previous steps have been leading up to—the actual development of, not one thing, but three—the item or service itself, the marketing plan for it, and a business (or financial) plan that final approval will require. The product (or better, the concept) stream involves industrial design and bench work (goods) or systems design (services), **prototypes,** product specifications, and so on. It culminates in a product that the developers hope is finished—produced, tested, and costed out.

---

[2]The fuzzy front end has been the subject of much research the past few years. A good resource is Peter A. Koen, Greg A. Ajamian, Scott Boyce, Allen Clamen, Eden Fisher, Stavros Fountoulakis, Albert Johnson, Pushpinder Puri, and Rebecca Seibert, "Fuzzy Front End: Effective Methods, Tools, and Techniques," in P. Belliveau, A. Griffin, and S. M. Somermeyer, *The PDMA Toolbook for New Product Development* (New York: John Wiley, 2002), Ch. 1.

While the technical developers are at work, marketing planners are busy making periodic market scans (to keep up with changes out there) and making marketing decisions as early as they can be made—first strategic and then tactical. Marketing decisions are completely interlaced with technical ones and involve package design, brand name selection, and tentative marketing budgets. A technical disappointment down the line may junk the early package design, name, or whatever. But we have to pay that price; we can't wait for each step to be conclusive before going to the next one.

Along the way, concept evaluation continues; we evaluated the concept well enough to permit development work (discussed earlier), but we have to keep evaluating technical and marketing planning *results*. We evaluate prototypes primarily, checking to be sure that the technology being developed meets the needs and desires of the customers in a way that creates value for them, while at the same time being profitable commercially.[3] By the time this phase winds down, we want to be assured that the new product actually does solve those problems we began with.

Comprehensive Business Analysis

If the product is real and customers like it, some firms make a comprehensive **business analysis** before moving into launch. The financial analysis is still not firm, but it is good enough to assure management that this project will be worthwhile. The financials will gradually be tightened during the launch phase, and where the actual Go/No Go point is reached varies with the nature of the industry. Approval for a new food product can be held until just before signing TV advertising contracts, but a new chemical that requires a new manufacturing facility has to Go much earlier, and the pharmaceutical industry really makes the Go decision when it undertakes the 10-year, $50 million R&D research effort. The development phase is covered in Part IV, Chapters 13 through 15.

Phase 5: Launch

Traditionally, the term **launch,** or *commercialization,* has described that time or that decision when the firm decides to market a product (the Go in Go/No Go). We associate this decision with building factories or authorizing agencies to proceed with multimillion-dollar advertising campaigns.

It's more subtle than that now. The launch decision has a healthy component of attitude. A firm can always pull out, even during a test market, so some people say most projects actually don't have a Go/No Go decision. Regardless, the last few weeks or months just before and after announcing the new product is really a launch *phase*. New products teams are enjoying life in the fast lane (or, unfortunately, life in a pressure cooker). Manufacturing is now doing a gradual scale-up of output. The marketing planners, who got a good glimpse of their ultimate target market as early as the opportunity, are

---

[3]Edward U. Bond, III and Mark B. Houston, "Barriers to Matching New Technologies and Market Opportunities in Established Firms," *Journal of Product Innovation Management,* 20(2), March 2003, pp. 120–135.

now deep into the hundreds of tactical details required for launch. The critical step—if a company takes it—is the **market test,** the first time the marketing program and the product dance together. This step is pure dress rehearsal, and managers hope any problems discovered are fixable between dress rehearsal and opening night. If they aren't, the opening has to be delayed. Given the time pressures involved, managers have come up with many new ways to do reliable market tests quickly, to complement the familiar **test market,** which can be inordinately time-consuming and costly. We will review many market test techniques in Chapter 18.

Sooner or later (it is hoped), these preparation activities lead to a public announcement of the new product—advertising, sales calls, and so forth. The announcement is often called *launch,* meaning that launch takes place one day, or even at one hour. Dramatically, yes, but practically most firms today are gradually moving the new item into commerce over a period of at least several weeks—there are suppliers to bring on line, sales forces to be trained, distributors to be stocked and trained, and a large set of market support people to be educated (columnists, scientists, government people, and thousands more). These things cannot happen one day, nor can the secret be kept—details yes, but the emergence of a new item, no.

One thing that is often overlooked at this point is the activity of planning for **launch management.** Everyone knows that when space shuttles leave the launch pad in Florida, a plan of tracking has been carefully prepared. "Houston Control" runs it, seeking to spot every glitch that comes up during launch and hoping it was anticipated so that a solution is on board, ready to use. New products managers often do the same thing, sometimes formally but often *very* informally.

The launch phase is covered in Part V, Chapters 16 through 20.

Evaluation Tasks Throughout the New Products Process

Figure 2.2 illustrates the evaluation tasks encountered in the new products process. As shown, different kinds of questions need to be asked after different phases. For example, once concepts are generated, each is subject to an initial review: Is it any good, and is it worth refining? At the concept evaluation phase, careful screening is required, as concepts that pass this phase move on to development and begin incurring significant costs. In development, relevant questions are "Are we done yet?" and "If not, should we continue to try?" These questions are best answered through progress reports. Finally, at launch, the main questions concern whether the product should be launched, and later, how well it has done relative to expectation. We pick up discussion of Figure 2.2 later, in Chapter 8, when we go much more in depth into which evaluation techniques are the most useful at each point in the new products process.

You may have noticed by now that the new products process essentially turns an opportunity (the real start) into a profit flow (the real finish). It begins with something that is not a product (the opportunity) and ends up with another thing that is not a product (the profit). The product comes from a situation and turns into an end.

FIGURE 2.2
The
Evaluation
Tasks in the
New Products
Process

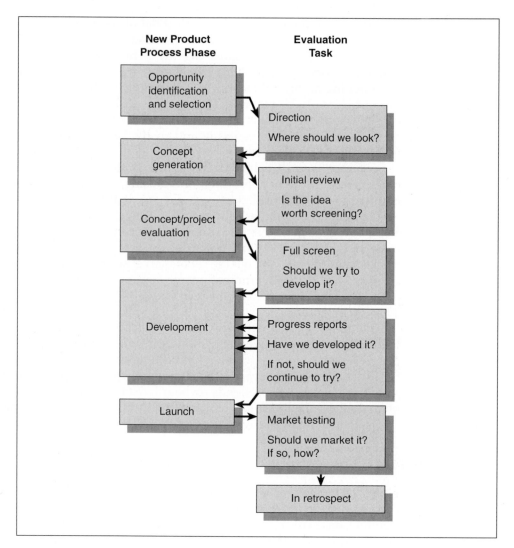

What we have, then, is an **evolving product,** or better, an evolving concept that, at the end, if it is successful, becomes a new product. Even a new product announcement just tells the world about a concept, hopefully a winner, but actually just in temporary form. Forces are standing by to see what revisions need to be made, even now, if it is off track.

This evolution is linked to the phases of the new products process (see Figure 2.3). Here are the phases in that process, using a new skim milk product as an example:

Phase 1: Opportunity Identification

- *Opportunity concept*—a company skill or resource, or a customer problem. (Assume that skim milk drinkers tell us they don't like the watered look of their favorite beverage.)

FIGURE 2.3
The Evolution
from Concept
to New
Product

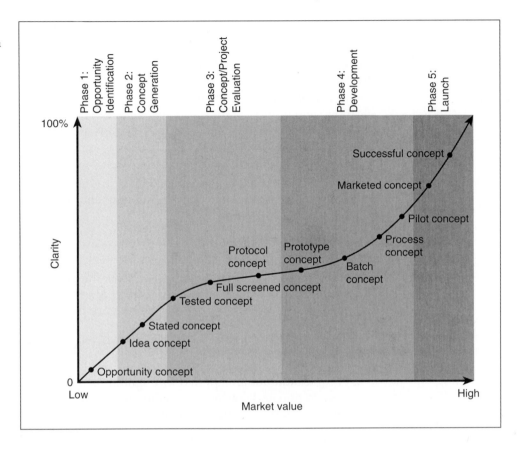

Phase 2: Concept Generation

- *Idea concept*—the first appearance of an idea. ("Maybe we could change the color ...")
- *Stated concept*—a form or a technology, plus a clear statement of benefit. (See Chapter 4.) (Our firm's patented method of breaking down protein globules might make the liquid more cloudy; emphasis on the *might*, at this time.)

Phase 3: Concept/Project Evaluation

- *Tested concept*—it has passed an end-user concept test; need is confirmed. (Consumers say they would very much like to have such a milk product, and the method of getting it sounds fine.)
- *Fully screened concept*—it passes the test of fit with the company's situation.
- *Protocol concept*—a product definition that includes the intended market user, the problem perceived, the benefits that a less watery skim milk would have to have, plus any mandatory features. (Our new product must taste as good or better than current skim milk, and it must yield exactly the same nutritional values.)

Phase 4: Development

- *Prototype concept*—a tentative physical product or system procedure, including features and benefits. (A small supply of a full-bodied skim milk, ready to consume, though not yet produced in quantity.)
- *Batch concept*— first full test-of-fit with manufacturing; it can be made. Specifications are written stating exactly what the product is to be, including features, characteristics, and standards. (Skim milk ingredients: Vitamin A source, fat, fiber, and so on.)
- *Process concept*—the full manufacturing process is complete.
- *Pilot concept*—a supply of the new product, produced in quantity from a pilot production line, enough for field testing with end users.

Phase 5: Launch

- *Marketed concept*—output of the scale-up process from pilot—milk product that is actually marketed, either for a market test or for full-scale launch.
- *Successful concept (i.e., new product)*—it meets the goals set for it at the start of the project. (New, Full Body Skim has achieved 24 percent of the market, is very profitable, and already competitors are negotiating licenses on our technology.)

The idea that a new product suddenly emerges from R&D—like a chicken from an egg—is simply incorrect. In fact, throughout this book we will be examining how analytical techniques are applied throughout the new product process, from early idea generation and concept evaluation, through screening, and on to positioning, market testing, and launch management.

Speeding the Product to Market

One of today's most discussed management goals in product development is **accelerated product development (APD),** or speeding the product to market. Accelerating time to market offers many benefits to the firm. The product will be on the market for a longer period of time before becoming obsolete, it can attract customers early and possibly block competitors with similar products that hit the market at a later time, or it can help to build or support a firm's reputation. A firm that implements the strategic elements outlined in Chapter 1—the product innovation charter, the new products process, and portfolio management—has advantages in reducing cycle time. New products consultant Robert Cooper identifies five sure methods to accelerating time to market, some of which have been mentioned previously:

- A clear product innovation charter—doing the opportunity identification homework and having a clean product definition—leads to better product design specifications and less time lost due to "recycling" (returning to earlier phases in the process to fix errors).
- A third-generation new products process that permits overlapping phases or *parallel processing* results in more getting accomplished in a shorter span

of time; streamlined evaluation tasks means that less time is wasted in evaluation.

- A portfolio management approach minimizes the chance that the firm's human and financial resources are spread too thinly over too many projects; better project selection focuses the firm's scarce resources and uses them more efficiently.
- A focus on quality at every phase complements the PIC; by following the adage "do it right the first time," the firm will avoid unnecessary recycling.
- An empowered *cross-functional team,* including individuals from marketing, R&D, manufacturing, and other functional areas, that works on the project from the earliest phases, supports parallel processing and eliminates "over-the-wall" product development (for example, marketing or production do not even begin their participation until the product is out of technical product development).[4]

Notice that the first three methods are the three strategic elements, while the last two (focus on quality and multifunctional product teams) are methods that help the firm to implement the strategic elements.

There is plenty of evidence that these techniques contribute greatly to increasing speed to market. Software development is often marked by intensive "crunch time" periods due to approaching deadlines, and many firms in this industry rely on small, cohesive cross-functional teams to meet time goals while at the same time not sacrificing quality.[5] Parallel processing is typical in the car industry: A car's drive train may be 70 or 80 percent designed (but not 100 percent) before body design work is initiated. Then, an early prototype (but not the final car) may be built and ready for controlled test-driving. Some observers have noted that the use of parallel processing by the Japanese automakers was a big factor in their emergence on the world market.[6] Figure 2.4 shows many techniques that have been advocated for shortening cycle times.

Note that the *cycle time metric,* that is, the way management measures speed to market (or, frequently, *time to market*), is often "getting the idea to the shipping dock faster." This assumes that there has already been technical accomplishment—the R of R&D has been concluded successfully. But from the point of view of technical development, speed to market success means not just time to the shipping dock, but also *postshipping technical speed:* For example, are corporate services (such as legal and environmental) in place? Also, if one uses the metric of

---

[4]Robert G. Cooper, *Winning at New Products: Accelerating the Process from Idea to Launch,* 2nd ed. (Reading, MA: Addison-Wesley, 1993), p. 210.
[5]B. J. Zirger and Janet L. Hartley, "The Effect of Acceleration Techniques on Product Development Time," *IEEE Transactions on Engineering Management,* May 1996, pp. 143–152, look at cross-functional teams in electronics firms; and Alfredo M. Choperena, "Fast Cycle Time: Driver of Innovation and Quality," *Research-Technology Management,* May–June 1996, pp. 36–40, examines the development of an immunoassay diagnostic system. Both found evidence that teams drive speed to market without sacrificing quality.
[6]K. B. Clark and T. Fujimoto, *Product Development Performance: Strategy, Organization, and Management in the World Auto Industry* (Boston, MA: Harvard Business School Press, 1991).

FIGURE 2.4   **Techniques for Attaining Speed in a New Product Project**

Organization Phase

1. Use dedicated cross-functional teams.
2. Use small groups and other techniques to minimize bureaucracy.
3. Empower a team, motivate it through incentives and rewards, and protect it.
4. Destroy turf and territory.
5. Make sure the supporting departments are ready when called on.
6. Develop effective team leadership.
7. Encourage organizational learning; transfer knowledge from one project to the next.

Intensify Resource Commitments

1. Integrate vendors; reduce numbers as necessary.
2. Integrate other technology resources.
3. Integrate resellers; reduce numbers as necessary.
4. Get users involved early; capture the Voice of the Customer.
5. Use simultaneous or concurrent engineering.
6. Get suppliers involved through alliances, ventures, etc; develop long-term relations with them.

Design for Speed

1. Computer-aided design and other forms of rapid prototyping.
2. Design-aided manufacturing, reduce number of parts, consider the manufacturing process.
3. Use common components across families.
4. Make the product easy to test.
5. Design in the qualities that lead to fast trial, including relative advantage.
6. Use effective design practices; minimize costly design changes late in the new products process.

Prepare for Rapid Manufacturing

1. Simplify documentation.
2. Use standardized process plans.
3. Use computer-aided manufacturing.
4. Go to just-in-time delivery of materials and components (flexible manufacturing).
5. Integrate product use testing, and start it early.

Prepare for Rapid Marketing

1. Use rollouts in place of test markets.
2. Seed the firm's reputation ahead of marketing.
3. Spend what it takes to get immediate market awareness.
4. Make trial purchasing as easy as possible.
5. Get customer service capability in place ahead of need, and test it.

Sources: Compiled from many sources, but some particularly useful articles on the subject are: Edward F. McDonough III and Gloria Barczak, "Speeding Up New Product Development: The Effects of Leadership Style and Source of Technology," *Journal of Product Innovation Management*, 8(3), September 1991, pp. 203–211; Murray R. Millson, S. P. Raj, and David Wilemon, "A Survey of Major Approaches for Accelerating New Product Development," *Journal of Product Innovation Management*, 9(2), March 1992, pp. 53–69; Ed J. Nijssen, Arthur R. L. Arbouw, and Harry F. Commandeur, "Accelerating NPD: A Preliminary Empirical Test of a Hierarchy of Implementation," *Journal of Product Innovation Management*, 12(2), March 1995, pp. 99–109; Ashok K. Gupta and William E. Souder, "Key Drivers of Reduced Cycle Time," *Research-Technology Management*, 41(4), July-August 1998, pp. 38–43; J. Daniel Sherman, William E. Souder, and Svenn A. Jenssen, "Differential Effects of the Primary Forms of Cross-Functional Integration on Product Development Cycle Time," *Journal of Product Innovation Management*, 17(4), July 2000, pp. 257–267; Morgan Swink, "Product Development – Faster, On-Time," *Research-Technology Management*, 45(4), July-August 2002, pp. 50–58.

"time to success" rather than "time to the shipping dock," marketing has a much bigger role to play in accelerating cycle time. Marketing can strive to accelerate *premarket speed* (i.e., pretesting the marketing plan more quickly, or getting up to speed on field coverage through alliance formation), and also *postannouncement* speed (i.e., speeding up coupon redemption, or getting the sales reps into the field more quickly).

We are now also hearing about the value of being **first to mindshare** rather than being first to market. The firm with mindshare in a given product category is the one that the target market associates with the product category and that is seen as the standard for competitors to match (such as Intel microprocessors or Hewlett-Packard laser printers). Firms that strive for mindshare think not about the speed of an individual product's development and launch, but rather about creating a dominant position in the mind of the customer.[7]

Finally, the role of *top management* in speeding products to market cannot be ignored. It is not enough for top management simply to say "Cycle times are to be cut by 50 percent, effective now!" Employees will no doubt interpret such blanket statements as a thinly disguised command to work twice as hard. Real resources need to be committed to a cycle time reduction program. An expert in cycle time reduction, Preston Smith, reports that many firms expect the process to be quick and easy. Executives sometimes ask for a one- or two-day training program in cycle-time reduction, believing that to be adequate training. The idea is not to skip critical steps in the new products process—the goal is to figure out how to get through the process faster without sacrificing quality. In the early 1990s, Chrysler spent over $1 billion on a development center designed to allow colocation of its project teams, while at the same time investing heavily in new CAD systems, team training, and supplier development.[8]

Senior management will also know the value of strategic alliances to obtain technical and marketing resources and assistance. Alliances can be upstream to vendors, downstream to resellers and customers, and even sideways to competitors. Apple, for example, turned to Sony for assistance in speeding up the development of the PowerBook notebook.[9]

Risks and Guidelines in Speeding to Market

There are plenty of advantages to speeding to market, not the least of which is that the product that is launched early is on the market for a longer period of time before becoming obsolete. A launch delay of, say, six months means six months less to earn profits and may give a competitor a chance to be first to market and establish a positive reputation.

---

[7]Denis Lambert and Stanley F. Slater, "First, Fast, and On-Time: The Path to Success. Or Is It?" *Journal of Product Innovation Management,* 16(5), September 1999, pp. 427–438.
[8]Preston G. Smith, "From Experience: Reaping Benefit from Speed to Market," *Journal of Product Innovation Management,* 16(3), May 1999, pp. 222–230.
[9]For the Apple example, see Douglas W. LaBahn, Abdul Ali, and Robert Krapfel, "New Product Development Cycle Time: The Influence of Project and Process Functions in Small Manufacturing Companies," *Journal of Business Research,* June 1996, pp. 179–188.

Nevertheless, there are lots of costs involved in speed, costs that are not evident and which can sometimes be disastrous. A firm facing increased competitive intensity, rapid technological change, and fast-changing market demographics may be tempted to concentrate on only easy, incremental product projects, or to cut critical steps in the new products process in order to get cycle time down. Cutting corners in technical product development may result in quality sacrifices, resulting in annoyed customers and distributors. By rushing the early steps, the firm may decide late in the process that the product quality is inadequate, which delays the launch, further infuriates dealers, and encourages customers to drift to the competition. Alternatively, rushing through the marketing ramp-up may result in inadequate attention to key marketing tasks in readying the product for launch. In these cases, the firm wins the speed-to-market battle but may lose the war.

The temptation to go too fast must be resisted, so that the firm does not mishandle a new-to-the-world opportunity, miss out on key customer information, or develop a technologically inferior product.[10] A better way to cope when facing a high-turbulence environment is to keep product development as flexible as possible: Do not freeze the product concept until the last possible moment, but allow later phases in the new products process to run concurrently with concept development.[11]

Another related concern is that accelerating time to market might result in bringing the product out too soon, while it still has bugs. In some situations, where there are high opportunity costs and relatively low development risks (such as with a new personal computer), it would be better to speed up cycle time. When Boeing develops and launches a new aircraft, however, there are relatively low opportunity costs (less direct competitors) but much higher development risks. In this case, getting the product "100 percent right" is the more appropriate goal.[12] Another risk of focusing exclusively on speed to market is that management might be tempted to concentrate on quick, close-to-home innovations at the expense of really new products, thus putting new product development efforts out of strategic balance.[13]

---

[10]Christer Karlsson and Pär Åhlström, "Technological Level and Product Development Cycle Time," *Journal of Product Innovation Management,*16(4), July 1999, pp. 352–362; R. G. Cooper and S. J. Edgett, "The Dark Side of Time and Time Metrics in Product Innovation," *Visions,* April–May 2002, pp. 14–16; see also C. Merle Crawford, "The Hidden Cost of Accelerated Product Development," *Journal of Product Innovation Management,* 9(3), September 1992, pp. 188–199; and Abdul Ali, Robert Krapfel, Jr., and Douglas LaBahn, "Product Innovativeness and Entry Strategy: Impact on Cycle Time and Break-Even Time," *Journal of Product Innovation Management,* 12(1), January 1995, pp. 54–69.

[11]Marco Iansiti, "Shooting the Rapids: Managing Product Development in Turbulent Environments," *California Management Review,* Fall 1995, pp. 37–58. Roger J. Calantone, Jeffrey B. Schmidt, and C. Anthony Di Benedetto, "New Product Activities and Performance: The Moderating Role of Environmental Hostility," *Journal of Product Innovation Management,* 14(3), May 1997, pp. 179–189, looked specifically at high-hostility environments.

[12]E. G. Krubasik, "Customize Your Product Development," *Harvard Business Review,* 66, November–December 1988, pp. 46–52.

[13]C. Merle Crawford, op. cit.

FIGURE 2.5   Other Considerations in Cycle Time Acceleration

Do the job right the first time. A small amount of time in the early phases can save many times that later, in rework alone.

Seek lots of platinum BBs rather than one silver bullet. This means look at every step, every action, every meeting; small savings add up.

Train everyone involved. People who don't know their jobs, who are assigned work without proper skill-building, won't know how to speed things up.

Communicate. Huge amounts of delay can be traced to someone, somewhere, waiting for a piece of information. E-mail and the Internet have made collaboration much easier and quicker, speeding up communication.

Be flexibile. Look for machines that can do many jobs, people who can switch from one job to another, stand-by vendors, and more. Attitudes too: a new product may require finding a more open-minded designer.

Make fast decisions. Managers know that people sometimes get blamed more for things they *do* than for things they *don't do*. Retraining them to make decisions as soon as they reasonably can, *and* managing them in such a way that we don't destroy that willingness, is a key step to a fast program.

Cut things wisely. There is a common bureaucratic practice of meeting a budget cut of 10% by cutting all of its components 10%. A better method is to take perhaps a 50% cut in noncritical steps, and 0% in the key ones. It's all risky, but why not take the risk on things that are more forgiving?

Some other considerations in cycle time acceleration may be summarized as in Figure 2.5.

P&G successfully cut development time on a pharmaceutical product by over 80 percent, while improving quality by over 60 percent, using many of the techniques described above. New product personnel carefully documented all work activities involved in product development and set aggressive goals for time reduction—"This activity should take 50 percent of the time it currently takes" (more modest goals could be easily achieved through only minor improvements). Stretch goals were set: To achieve a 75 percent reduction, one could set a goal of 50 percent reduction in the first year and a further 50 percent reduction in the second year. They also practiced several of the techniques described in this chapter and the previous one: team motivation through clear goal setting, empowerment, and reward mechanisms; and senior management commitment.[14]

In Chapter 16 we will see other metrics that can be used to complement speed-to-market, such as the *cash-to-cash metric*. Using this tool, the firm will measure not just how quickly the product is launched, but also how long it takes to break even. Using metrics such as this help the firm manage the *whole* launch phase, not just the moment of launch.

[14]R. W. Boggs, Linda M. Bayuk, and David A. McCamey, "Speeding Development Cycles," *Research-Technology Management,* September–October 1999, pp. 33–38.

What about New Services?

Before we leave the new products process, let's take a look at a group of products that might not seem to have a technical component to their development—**services.** Services and goods are often arrayed on a scale of (1) pure service, (2) primarily service and partly a good, (3) primarily a good and partly service, and (4) pure good. Examples, in order, are counseling, insurance policy, automobile, and candy bar. Only in the first category does the product provider have nothing tangible on which to do R&D, and there are very few of them. Even on pure or primarily service products, there are tangible support items such as ads, warranties, policies, and instructions, which need design and production. For an example of a good/service blend, consider a cell phone. The phone itself is tangible, yet it provides services: certainly communication, and possibly also entertainment (music, games) and other services as well.

The creation of service products tends to mirror the systems used on goods. The strategic elements all fit (the product innovation charter, the new products process, and the balanced portfolio). Perhaps the concepts must be applied creatively, but still the parallels are there. Indeed, a study of successful new services found that these tended to come from companies that used a systematic, comprehensive new service development process with clearly defined phases and regular evaluations and reviews. In fact, the new services process is very similar to the new products process we have presented in this chapter![15]

The new products process needs a little refinement to be most useful in service development, mostly due to fundamental differences between services and manufactured goods.[16] Services are individualized to the individual customer. Whereas goods are mass-produced, services are provided through interaction between service provider and customer, and the most successful service providers are those that can deliver a "customized" experience to each customer. Services, unlike goods, are also intangible, which means that a key component of the service is indeed the experience of receiving the service. For this reason, the human interaction between service provider and customer is of utmost importance; service providers must strive to meet customer expectation and leave a positive impression. Services are also instantly and continuously being evaluated by customers at every interaction with the service provider. The service provider therefore needs to obtain feedback from the customer and act on it quickly so as to continuously improve performance. Finally, services are often evaluated by customers as the sum of their parts. A family looking back on a trip to a theme park considers the friendliness of the ticket agent on the phone, the ease of parking, the number and

[15]Scott Edgett, "The Traits of Successful New Service Development," *Journal of Services Marketing,* 8(3), 1994, pp. 40–49. For a discussion of whether a formal new products process works in service development, see Ian Alam and Chad Perry, "A Customer-Oriented New Service Development Process," *Journal of Services Marketing,* 16(6), 2002, pp. 515–532.
[16]The next paragraphs, and the JetBlue example, are drawn from Thomas D. Kuczmarski and Zachary T. Johnston, "New Service Development," in Kenneth B. Kahn, George Castellion, and Abbie Griffin (eds.), *The PDMA Handbook of New Product Development* (New York: John Wiley & Sons, 2005), pp. 92–107.

entertainment value of rides and other activities, the cleanliness of the park, and the quality of interaction with park personnel when forming an overall opinion of the experience. Poor performance on any of these leads to a lower evaluation of the whole trip. These fundamental differences between services and products pose challenges to the service provider, but the same basic new products process can still be used.

Consider how JetBlue has managed to be a successful airline in an extremely difficult and competitive market through excellent service development. Rather than focusing on cost-cutting, as many of its competitors have done, JetBlue has strived to provide a customized experience, offering travelers free television, friendlier flight crews, comfortable seats, and a simple but useful Web site. JetBlue also is a leader in adding safety measures, such as "paperless cockpit" flight technology and security cameras in the passenger cabin. These safety measures, important to today's air travelers, help to differentiate JetBlue from competitors. Also, JetBlue obtains opinions (good and bad) from customers throughout the service experience: when the customer is on the company Web page, at the ticket counter, or on the actual flight, JetBlue strives to obtain customer satisfaction information so they can target any areas for improvement and increase the customer's overall level of satisfaction with the firm. The guiding objective at JetBlue, according to its founding CEO, David Neeleman, was to bring "humanity back to air travel." This is clearly a service provider that understands the importance of customer interaction!

Given the importance of customer interaction in service success, it is no surprise that getting customer participation early is critical to successful new service development. Service delivery personnel—the staff that actually deals with customers, obtains their feedback, and handles their complaints—are in the best position to identify unmet customer needs and are therefore critical players at the concept generation phase. Involving them this early in the new products process increases their motivation and excitement about the new service, which results in more enthusiastic service delivery and more satisfied customers. As the service progresses through development, the best prototype concepts can be taken to customers and tested in product use tests much like those outlined above. Unfortunately, prototype testing is not always well done by service providers. Since services are by definition unpatentable and often easy for competitors to replicate, it is important to ensure that the service has been "tweaked" as much as possible before launch to make sure customers are very satisfied with the offering. A prototype test would be an ideal opportunity to do this kind of tweaking.

Finally, the launch phase for services can be particularly challenging. For one thing, services need constant monitoring to ensure they are efficiently meeting customer needs and expectations; this is why the best service providers (think restaurants, hotels, and hospitals) are constantly getting customer feedback. Also, the successful launch of a new service depends greatly on the service delivery personnel training. Coca-Cola employees, for example, rarely interact with the final consumer; by contrast, services of all types are delivered by company personnel (the bank teller, the hotel clerk, the hairdresser, the financial advisor). Excellent training of the service delivery personnel is a key component of any service firm's customer retention program. A training program will include instruction on the strategic importance to the firm of excellent service delivery as well as lessons on crisis management and troubleshooting, in addition to basic service delivery training.

FedEx is a prime example of a service provider that excels in new service development.[17] FedEx places the customer experience at the center of its new products process. Customers are involved early in the new products process as co-innovators; this helps FedEx identify their needs early. FedEx has set up market councils comprising executives, sales and marketing personnel, and even corporate lawyers to call on key customers and learn from them. They complement these activities with ethnographic studies (such as the observational techniques to be discussed in Chapter 5) to get at the heart of emerging customer needs. A classic example of this was FedEx's realization that the customer's experience would be enhanced if they provided greater access and more digital services. The solution was the 2004 acquisition of Kinko's (now FedEx Office), which immediately increased the number of shipping points, and at the same time widened service offerings to include photocopying, faxing, binding, and printing. As customer needs evolved (in particular those of small business customers), FedEx was able to grow with them and keep pace.

A key factor in FedEx's new products success was the establishment of the Portfolio Management Team (PMT), a group of senior executives that lead business units and functional areas. The PMT is charged with developing strategic direction, conducting the evaluation tasks in the new products process, and maintaining a balanced portfolio of projects. FedEx has found that the principles stated in Chapter 1 are effective: Following a phased new products process, risk is managed down through time, such that it is effectively reduced by the time costly development and launch phases are reached, and there is a high degree of confidence that a newly launched service will be successful and provide expected returns on investment. For its excellent service development program, FedEx won the 2007 PDMA Outstanding Corporate Innovator award.

What about New-to-the-World Products?

As seen in Chapter 1, the term *new products* can refer to new-to-the world products, close-to-home extensions of existing products, or just about anything in between. The phased process seen in Figure 2.1 may not work as well with new-to-the-world products due to the high levels of technical and market uncertainty and associated risks. Research confirms these risks: Firms that launch pioneering new-to-the-world products into the market incur a significantly lower long-term survival rate than those that enter the market later. That is, the long-term advantage of going first is greater for firms that launch incrementally new products than for those that launch really new ones! Still, the lower survival rate for a

---

[17]The FedEx example is drawn from Donald Comer, "How FedEx Uses Insight and Invention to Innovate," *Visions*, 31(4), December 2007, pp. 12–14.

new-to-the-world product is offset by higher profits, since the market for such a product is often larger and also often offers bigger profit margins.[18]

Part of the reason for the higher failure rate for new-to-the-world products is that they are difficult to manage. Almost by definition, new-to-the-world products, like the first cell phone or the first personal computers, require discontinuities (sometimes several of them) in order to succeed. Consider the introduction of the personal computer. Contributing to its rapid adoption were discontinuities in technology (computer companies, including some new startups, had to design essentially a totally new computer), in the market (individual homeowners and small businesses now were buying computers, and not just big firms), organizational (personal computers were sold in electronics shops and department stores, not through a professional sales force), and social (millions of people realized how much they needed a computer).[19] Much new research is aimed at understanding the management processes that are most appropriate for high-uncertainty, high-ambiguity environments,[20] yet we still have a long way to go.

Many managers recognize how profitable a well-managed new-to-the-world product can be: Corning's optical fiber, General Electric's CT scanner, Apple's iPhone, and many other examples come to mind.[21] They also realize that one successful breakthrough product is usually not enough to guarantee success. The best innovating firms, like Apple, seem to be able to launch one successful breakthrough product after another, seemingly at will. These firms seem to have a system for *breakthrough innovation* that provides them with a competitive capability, and other managers have caught on to the idea that they too need a system to increase their breakthrough capabilities as well.

We are still learning about how such a system works, and it may vary from one firm to another. But a good starting point is the recognition that the process for managing breakthrough innovation will differ from managing ongoing product development processes. Once a breakthrough innovation is identified, it must be nurtured. Many business opportunities may present themselves, and some may look very promising, but all have uncertain outcomes. Experimentation in the marketplace can assess the opportunities and may even identify new ones. The goal is to consider the innovation, together with the identified business opportunities, and to develop from this a new business model that provides the market with breakthrough value and, ultimately, is profitable for the firm. This can be an expensive proposition, and certainly management must not plan on instant decision making, but the due diligence is required due to the uncertainties involved. This

---

[18]Sungwook Min, Manohar U. Kalwani, and William T. Robinson, "Market Pioneer and Early Follower Survival Risks: A Contingency Analysis of Really New Versus Incrementally New Product-Markets," *Journal of Marketing,* 70(1), 2006, pp. 15–33.

[19]Rosanna Garcia, "Types of Innovation," in V. K. Narayanan and Gina C. O'Connor (eds.), *Encyclopedia of Technology & Innovation Management* (Chichester, UK: John Wiley, 2010), Chapter 13.

[20]A good reference is Gina C. O'Connor, Richard Liefer, Albert S. Paulson, and Lois S. Peters, *Grabbing Lightning: Building a Capability for Breakthrough Innovation* (San Francisco, CA: Jossey-Bass, 2008).

[21]Much of this section derives from O'Connor *et al.*, op. cit.

process sounds a little like a business laboratory, and indeed this is sometimes called the *incubation* stage.[22] As leading researcher Gina O'Connor says, "Companies do not realize that breakthrough technologies do not yield breakthrough businesses without enormous investment far beyond the technology itself, requiring lots of experimentation on many fronts."

To do incubation correctly, failure must be tolerated, but at the same time learning from the failure so that the firm continues to move toward the launch of a successful breakthrough innovation. According to Marissa Meyer, vice president for search products and user experience at Google Notes, Google's failure rate of innovative products is over 60 percent, but this is the cost of doing cutting-edge technology.[23] It should be noted that incubation is not the same as business development (finding new customers, managing acquisitions, etc.). Business development is often done over a one- to two-year time horizon and may be completely done by marketing or management personnel. Due to its focus on business model development for a radical innovation (in an uncertain environment), the time horizon for incubation can be three to five years, and typically technical development, as well as customer and market interaction, is involved.

Breakthrough innovation requires a planning approach that acknowledges the unknowns and uncertainties involved. This approach, called *discovery-driven planning*,[24] requires that managers make assumptions about the future in order to build their forecasts and targets, recognizing that these assumptions may be quite wrong. As more information becomes available, the targets are rethought, the forecasts adjusted, and the plan evolves. This is different from the approach more typically seen in less-uncertain markets, where past results can be used to build predictable forecasts of the future. A guiding principle in discovery-driven planning is the reverse income statement, which starts from the bottom (required profits) and works backward to required levels of revenues and allowable costs. Management would also need to keep track of assumptions, and set up periodic checkpoints to test assumptions and to update market and technology information as it becomes available. Coupled with discovery-driven planning, the firm should also be pursuing a real-options orientation to investment.[25] The firm can make low-cost test investments to gather information on the technology and its marketplace potential. The test investment can be thought of as buying an option to continue the development of the breakthrough innovation. If the small investment suggests there is great upside potential, the project is continued to the next phase; otherwise it is terminated.

To accomplish all of this may require organizational shakeups. At Corning, a new senior position, vice president for Strategic Growth and New Business Development, was created, who reports to the chief technology officer and who is located in the R&D division. This individual's main role is to assist in opportunity

[22]O'Connor *et al.*, Chapter 4; the quote is from p. 82.

[23]P. Sellers, "The Net's Next Phase," *Fortune*, November 13, 2006, pp. 71–72.

[24]Rita Gunter McGrath, and Ian C. MacMillan, "Discovery-Driven Planning," *Harvard Business Review*, July–August 1995, pp. 44–54.

[25]Ian C. MacMillan, Alexander B. van Putten, Rita Gunther McGrath, and James D. Thompson, "Using Real Options Discipline for Highly Uncertain Technology Investments," *Research-Technology Management*, January–February 2006, pp. 29–37.

identification, and in particular, those that required breakthrough innovation. In addition, breakthrough innovation project teams are assisted by a newly created business development team, which helps identify potential applications and business partners, build the customer base, and plan a technology development path.[26]

While the challenges involved in the development of new-to-the-world products are different, the first phase must still be opportunity identification and the development of a strategic statement. Later phases may be quite different, depending on how new-to-the-world (or to-the-company) the product is, but these must always roll out from some strategic starting point. There should be a clear connection between the radical innovation and the firm's strategic vision as articulated by senior management.[27] Without top management encouragement, business units involved in product development will often focus on improving operational efficiency and will therefore be reluctant to accept radically new product projects because of the new product personnel involvement in corporate strategic planning when the environment is very changeable and turbulent.[28] In order to move promising radical innovation projects forward, senior management at some firms establishes a *transition management* team charged with moving an R&D innovation project to business operating status. The transition team receives appropriate funding as well as support and oversight from senior management.[29] Figure 2.6 illustrates the transition management process at Eastman Kodak.

FIGURE 2.6   **The Transition Management Process at Eastman Kodak**

In 2001, Eastman Kodak successfully implemented a Transition Management process to be able to move R&D projects more effectively to its business units and ultimately improve its innovation rate. In order to get the required commitment, Eastman Kodak held several transition management workshops, and System Concepts Center (SCC) team members were involved directly in the tasks of transition management. Senior managers in R&D and at the business units were called on to champion the new innovation program, and senior SCC members got involved in business unit strategy development. By 2003, an unprecedented number of projects were being successfully transfered to Eastman Kodak's business units, and were meeting Eastman Kodak's initial requirements for commercialization (the equivalent of Phase I in this text's new products process) on the first pass. Though Eastman Kodak designed this process to facilitate transfer of radical innovation projects, it discovered it was also successfully speeding fast-track incremental innovation opportunities into development.

Source: Gina O'Connor, Joanne Hyland, and Mark P. Rice, "Bringing Radical and Other Major Innovations Successfully to Market: Bridging the Transition from R&D to Operations," in P. Belliveau, A. Griffin and S. M. Somermeyer (eds.), *The PDMA Toolbook 2 for New Product Development* (Wiley, 2004).

[26]O'Connor *et al.*, pp. 7–8.

[27]A good general reference on radical new products is Gary S. Lynn and Richard R. Reilly, *Blockbusters: The Five Keys to Developing Great New Products* (New York: HarperCollins, 2002). An influential article on this topic is Erwin Danneels, "Disruptive Technology Reconsidered: A Critique and Research Agenda," *Journal of Product Innovation Management*, 21(4), July 2004, pp. 246–258.

[28]Roger Calantone, Rosanna Garcia, and Cornelia Dröge, "The Effects of Environmental Turbulence on New Product Development Strategy Planning," *Journal of Product Innovation Management*, 20(2), March 2003, pp. 90–103.

[29]Gina O'Connor, Joanne Hyland, and Mark P. Rice, "Bringing Radical and Other Major Innovations Successfully to Market: Bridging the Transition from R&D to Operations," in P. Belliveau, A. Griffin, and S. M. Somermeyer (eds.), *The PDMA Toolbook 2 for New Product Development* (New York: John Wiley, 2004).

Leading firms in radical product development tend to use a more informal process, supported by a budget, for idea selection for radical new product projects. Alliance partners make a larger contribution, so more effort and time is spent on identifying the best partners in order to obtain resources and negotiate the terms of the relationship.[30]

The fundamental market-related question for a new-to-the-world product is whether the market will ultimately value the offering.[31] It is usually very difficult for potential customers to provide useful information about likely acceptance (or perceived value) of a new-to-the-world product, since they have nothing to which they can compare it; they may not even be able to visualize its potential. (For example, the microwave oven took a long while to catch on despite obvious consumer benefits.) As Alexis Girard from the Future Image Report noted, "Ninety-nine percent of the time with technological breakthroughs, people hadn't been asking for it."[32] Hence, gauging market opportunity is challenging, and conventional market research may not be as much help as one would like. Consider the personal digital assistant (PDA). While most people might be able to draw a crude sketch of their dream car or dream kayak, it is hard to imagine someone drawing their dream PDA before having ever seen one! Complicating the matter is the fact that new-to-the-world products often require major commitments in firm resources and technology, and years or decades of R&D. Yet, in the case of the PDA, product development proceeded, and quite successfully.

Nevertheless, this does not mean that one goes about new-to-the-world product development without consideration of possible customer need, especially given the high financial stakes and resource commitments involved. To be able to make the difficult link between breakthrough technology and market need, firms need to be adept at market visioning. While this process is not well understood yet, some have likened it to focusing on "what could be"—identifying how things will be in the future and then figuring out a way to get there. For example, senior management at Black & Decker simply called for the next big idea and allocated an appropriately sized budget: The Snake Light emerged.[33] In such a case, the process is more exploratory, becoming more customer-oriented as the product becomes further formulated and developed. While the technology may be breakthrough, the firm cannot simply guess at its customer applications.

[30]Marjorie Adams, *Competitive Performance Assessment (CPAS) Study Results,* PDMA Foundation, 2004; also Christopher M. McDermott and Gina Colarelli O'Connor, "Managing Radical Innovation: An Overview of Emergent Strategy Issues," *Journal of Product Innovation Management,* 19(6), November 2002, pp. 424–438; and Mark P. Rice, Donna Kelley, Lois Peters, and Gina Colarelli O'Connor, "Radical Innovation: Triggering Initiation of Opportunity Recognition and Evaluation," *R&D Management,* 31(4), October 2001, pp. 409–420.

[31]Gina Colarelli O'Connor, "Market Learning and Radical Innovation: A Cross-Case Comparison of Eight Radical Innovation Projects," *Journal of Product Innovation Management,* 15(2), March 1998, pp. 151–166.

[32]Laurie J. Flynn, "LightSurf Piggybacks a Tiny Camera on a Cell Phone," *The New York Times on the Web,* July 9, 2001.

[33]Gina Colarelli O'Connor and Robert W. Veryzer, "The Nature of Market Visioning for Technology-Based Radical Innovation," *Journal of Product Innovation Management,* 18(4), July 2001, pp. 231–246.

Obviously, with a new-to-the-world product, it is especially important that the **voice of the customer (VOC)** be brought in as early as possible. In fact, customers can be brought in as early as concept generation to provide input to both marketing personnel and the R&D department. A critical issue here is identifying the right customers to bring in: For example, a medical-equipment manufacturer developing a next-generation diagnostic machine might want to partner with the leading research hospitals to determine what performance features need to be built in. Researchers at these hospitals, having found available products to be unsatisfactory, may already have internally developed simple working prototypes of their own. What better guidance could the equipment manufacturer obtain? Identifying and working with these customers is central to **lead user analysis,** which we will explore more fully in Chapter 5.

Early customer involvement for new-to-the-world products is sometimes accomplished by using **focused prototypes:** early, limited-performance versions that customers can try out and comment on. Early in 1994, Iomega's first internally developed prototypes of the Zip Drive (a plug-in laptop drive that allowed the user to access large-storage floppy disks called zip-disks) were plain-looking gray boxes with a flip-up lid (much like many CD players); early focus groups disliked the top-loading feature and wanted something "personal, portable, and powerful." Several days later, R&D hit upon the front-loading design (much like a floppy-disk drive); ultimately, over 50 prototypes were built to test out many different ideas before one was selected. The Zip Drive ultimately marketed by Iomega featured the now-familiar front-loading mechanism and was indeed personal (attractive blue plastic cover), portable (small enough to fit in a briefcase), and powerful (capable of storing 100 megabytes of data).[34] Figure 2.7 recounts how an electric bicycle was developed using a succession of focused prototypes.

The new products process employed in these examples is sometimes called **probe-and-learn:** Through interaction with customers, designers are inspired to probe, experiment, and improvise, and as a result, may come up with a successful new-to-the-world product. Another term sometimes used to describe this iterative process is **lickety-stick:** The developing team develops prototypes from dozens of different new product ideas ("lickety"), eventually settling on a prototype that customers like ("stick").[35] As Mike Santori of National Instruments said, the goal at this early stage is not to determine how to cut costs, but to see what functionality customers are looking for. Rolling out several prototypes quickly and efficiently "gives you flexibility to try out different ideas and audiences."[36] Thus, the new products process for radical new products may be less linear and more flexible than is implied in Figure 2.1: Several versions of focused prototypes might be built and tested before concept generation takes place!

The story of General Electric's computed tomographic (CT) scanner illustrates the development of a new-to-the-world product with a large assist from the voice

[34]For the Iomega story, see Gary S. Lynn and Richard R. Reilly, *Blockbusters,* op. cit.
[35]"Lickety-stick" was coined by Gary S. Lynn and Richard R. Reilly in *Blockbusters,* op. cit.
[36]Quoted in Heidi Bertels, "The 7th Annual Front End of Innovation Conference Adopts a New Format and Content," *Visions,* 33(3), October 2009, pp. 34–37.

FIGURE 2.7   **Prototype Development of an Electric Bicycle**

The initial opportunity seemed relatively clear: Fitness-conscious Americans would like an electric-powered bicycle that would be superior to Japanese-made competitive products about to hit the U.S. market. In 1996, Charger Electric Bicycles, LLC, embarked on a project to develop a "fast and fun" electric bicycle that would be the "Mercedes-Benz of electric bikes." The designers put together pieces of all sorts: various electric parts, old bicycle frames, and so on. A major design contributor, Peter Zwaan, built several nonfunctional models of the bike as well as of its component parts (such as the drive train and power pack), using wood, foam carvings, and plastic models. With these nonworking prototypes, the designers could make assessments of appearance, performance, weight, and cost tradeoffs.

A crude working prototype was finished within eight weeks—suitable for the team to "play around with." Several prototype improvements later, an improved (though still crude) bicycle was ready to be tried out by potential users. Inputs from this early prototype test were gathered and built into later prototypes, presented at the Interbike trade show. The final round of technical and cosmetic tradeoffs were made by taking the best parts and accessories from the various prototypes. The bike went into production a short 18 months from the start of the product project and has gone on to win several design awards.

The process employed for this bicycle did not have any traditional stages or gates, but rather was driven by continuous prototyping—sometimes called a "probe and learn" procedure. The designers were inspired to probe, experiment and improvise and, as a result, came up with a few brilliant ideas.

Source: Ronald Mascitelli, "From Experience: Harnessing Tacit Knowledge to Achieve Breakthrough Innovation," *Journal of Product Innovation Management* 17, no. 3, May 2000, pp. 187–188.

of the customer. The original instrument was developed as a head scanner; later versions included a breast scanner and a full-body scanner. In each case, the physicians said the product did not work appropriately. On the fourth try, GE developed the 8800 full-body scanner, which was a huge success when launched, eventually gaining a 68 percent market share. GE did not simply create a solution looking for a problem—that implies having no strategy. GE did have a strategy: Develop a breakthrough scanner technology for medical diagnostic applications, and learn from early trials specifically what applications would be the most valuable to their physician customers.[37]

Closing Thoughts about the New Products Process

As we discussed in Chapter 1, many firms use a new product process much like the one shown in this chapter, though of course the details will vary. We have, however, not yet achieved full adoption of the best methods (see Figure 2.8). Some of the best techniques are widely used by the most successful new product firms, but many still are used only by a minority. It is clear from the recent PDMA Comparative Performance Assessment study, however, that the best firms in new product development do indeed have some kind of new products process, resulting in

[37]Gary S. Lynn, Mario Mazzuca, Joseph G. Morone, and Albert S. Paulson, "Learning Is the Critical Success Factor in Developing Truly New Products," *Research-Technology Management*, May–June 1998, pp. 45–51.

FIGURE 2.8   Rates of Use of Selected New Products Process Steps

Step	PDMA Members*	Canada[†]	Australia, England, and Belgium[‡]	PDMA Members Plus Others**
1. Detailed market study	Not reported	25%	57%	NR
2. Concept searching	90%	NR	NR	57%
3. Concept screening	76	92	96	55
4. Concept testing	80	NR	NR	NR
5. Business analysis	89	63	76	59
6. Product development (technical)	99	89	93	64
7. Customer field (use) testing	NR	66	78	NR
8. Market testing	NR	23	34	61
9. Use testing or market testing	87	NR	NR	NR
10. Trial production setup	NR	49	70	NR
11. Separate marketing plan	NR	68	NR	NR

*Product Development & Management Association, in Albert L. Page, "Assessing New Product Development Practices and Performance: Establishing Crucial Norms," *Journal of Product Innovation Management,* September 1993, pp. 273–290.
**In Abbie Griffin, "PDMA Research on New Product Development Practices: Updating Trends and Benchmarking Best Practices," *Journal of Product Innovation Management,* November 1997, pp. 429–459.
[†]Robert G. Cooper and Elko J. Kleinschmidt, "An Investigation into the New Product Process: Steps, Deficiencies, Impact," *Journal of Product Innovation Management,* June 1986, pp. 71–85.
[‡]Larry Dwyer and Robert Mellor, "New Product Process Activities and Project Outcomes," *R&D Management,* January 1991, pp. 31–41.

a higher success rate of products as they move through development, test, and commercialization.[38]

Some exciting developments are being noted in the auto industry. Almost half of the automotive engineers in a recent survey said their companies used a traditional new products process, while about a third used a modified process, which allows them to improve efficiency without sacrificing product novelty.[39] Using a modified process has allowed as much as a 50 percent reduction in time to market while maintaining new product quality and novelty.

The role of senior management cannot be overlooked, especially in the case of radical new products. Speaking at a PDMA meeting, Al Lopez, former vice president of R&D at ExxonMobil, mentioned his company's many radical new products, including high-strength steel for pipelines, low-sulfur fuel processes, improved catalysts, and so on. Senior management supports productive R&D in several key ways: by recognizing and building the firm's core technical competencies and capabilities, by encouraging knowledge flow (both internal and external) throughout the firm, by developing effective, streamlined work processes,

[38]Marjorie Adams, *CPAS Study Results,* op. cit.; see also Abbie Griffin, "PDMA Research on New Product Development Practices: Updating Trends and Benchmarking Best Practices," *Journal of Product Innovation Management,*14(6), November 1997, pp. 429–458.
[39]John E. Ettlie and Jorg M. Eisenbach, "Modified Stage-Gate® Regimes in New Product Development," *Journal of Product Innovation Management,* 24(1), January 2007, pp. 20–33.

by clearly linking basic and applied research, and by assuring an exciting work environment in which learning and achievement are rewarded.[40]

Finally one can ask whether firms can be ambidextrous—that is, be excellent in both new-to-the-world and incremental innovations. Barriers to ambidexterity no doubt exist: Fears of brand dilution, channel conflict, or even a "we've always done it this way" culture. There is also the issue of resource allocation: Investing in developing competencies that lead to radical new products may mean divesting those resources away from bettering one's existing competencies. These are serious concerns of managers at highly innovative firms; to avoid problems of this sort, often a highly projectized venture is spun out as a separate organizational unit to pursue the radical innovation;[41] more on this topic in Chapter 14.

Summary

In this chapter, we studied essentially one thing: the system of phases and activities used in the process of developing and marketing new products. We looked at a simplistic version of this process in a hypothetical situation in P&G's cosmetics division. We then went through the basic process phase by phase. Be careful: don't think this, or any, new product process is etched in stone. It is a guide and an integrator, not a straitjacket.

We now turn to Chapter 3, in which we will discuss two more strategic elements: the product innovation charter and managing the portfolio of new products. Chapter 3 introduces the first of the five major phases in the process—Opportunity identification and Selection. This will include the various forms of strategy to guide the evaluation of available opportunities. That will prepare us to begin the study of concept generation.

Applications

1. "I've got to make a speech down in Dallas next month. It's part of a conference SMU is having on the general topic of opportunity identification (OI). They want me to explain why OI is sometimes more important than brainstorming and other techniques of concept generation. Seems to me it isn't. What do you think?"

2. "I work for a financial services firm. We do new product development all the time, and a lot of it is of the incremental variety. You know, bundle credit card access to a savings account, bundle the savings account to a money market account, add an IRA investment option, things of that sort. Explain how the new products process is relevant in my industry, and to my company. Seems like it's more tailored to physical goods. Isn't it a little misleading?"

[40]For more information, see Peter Koen, "Tools and Techniques for Managing the Front End of Innovation: Highlights from the May 2003 Cambridge Conference," *Visions,* October 2003.
[41]Erwin Danneels, "From the Guest Editor: Dialogue on the Effects of Disruptive Technology on Firms and Industries," *Journal of Product Innovation Management,* 23(1), January 2006, pp. 2–4.

3. "We are increasingly committed to really new products—we see them as the future of our company. Can you explain to me again what the new products process looks like for them? I'm not really convinced that the process you outlined is applicable to them. Seems like it will generate more incrementally new products rather than bold new ideas."

Case: Tastykake Sensables[42]

For generations, Tastykakes have been one of the most popular snack foods in and around the Philadelphia area. The local Tasty Baking Co., founded about 90 years ago, turns out about five million snack cakes, pies, cookies, and doughnuts each day. Sales, however, had been stagnant in recent years. The top sales year was 2001, when Tasty Baking hit $166 million in sales, netting $6 million profit. About this time, new CEO Charles Pizzi announced to shareholders that in 2004, an innovative line extension would be launched. While this would not be the only company action designed to boost performance, the new line would certainly be an important step.

In the snack business, the previous decade had seen a major trend toward healthier products. Nabisco SnackWell's lowfat cakes and cookies were a prominent example from the early 1990s. Even Tastykake had some low-fat products out at this time. By the late 1990s, a newer diet-conscious trend, low-carb products, was emerging, due to the popularity of the low-carbohydrate Atkins Diet. By 2003, dozens of food companies had launched about 600 low-carb products onto the store shelves, and the healthy, low-carb product trend showed no signs of abating. It seemed logical to all concerned that Tasty Baking's new line would be a low-carb version of Tastykakes. As noted by chief marketing officer Vince Melchiorre, "It was a wave, and we wanted to ride it." If successful, the low-carb Tastykake could be the first of several new lines, targeted at a variety of health concerns.

Karen Schutz had about 20 years of marketing experience at Campbell Soup before becoming a marketing manager at Tastykake. In January 2004, she was given the task of making the low-carb Tastykake a reality. The deadline was short: The product was to be out by fall. From her Campbell days, Schutz was aware of the challenge. A new consumer packaged good of this type might require a year to 18 months for product formulation, assessing shelf life, market testing, and advertising planning. As an added constraint, the new line would have to be produced using existing equipment and personnel.

By mid-January, John Sawicki, Tasty Baking's manager of research, obtained the first trial batches of low-carb cookies and doughnuts from an ingredient supplier and arranged for a private tasting by Tasty Baking managers, including Schutz, at company headquarters. Schutz and her colleagues liked the taste (she feared her doughnut would taste like "hamster food") and agreed that this supplier's mixes

[42]This case was based on Marian Uhlman, "A Trimmer Tastykake," *The Philadelphia Inquirer*, May 16, 2004, pp. E1, E8; and Marian Uhlman, "Low-Cal Strategy to Fatten Profit," *The Philadelphia Inquirer*, August 10, 2004, pp. E1, E12.

were a good starting point. At this time a code name was selected for the still-secret low-carb project: Greta (for "Greta Carbo").

Sawicki and his team began development of a low-carb chocolate cookie bar on January 27, 2004. A sugar alcohol called maltitol would be the sugar substitute, and some flour in the mix would be replaced by modified cornstarch. Meanwhile, Melchiorre asked Schutz if it would be possible to make Greta sugar-free. He explained, "I needed to address the issue of people who had grown up on Tastykakes who can't eat it any more. It was good for business, and good for them." Schutz knew this would be difficult, as sugar is in milk, berries, and other ingredients. She e-mailed Sawicki to see if this were feasible. Sawicki's response: "Possibly. It probably depends on the product. Should we be targeting this?"

Things were soon going to get exciting for Schutz and Sawicki. In February, senior management rescheduled Greta's launch to late June—three months earlier than expected! But early research results were promising from a low-carb viewpoint. Early batches of low-carb chocolate cookie bars contained only seven net carbs (the statistic used by low-carb dieters), comparable to Atkins low-carb cookies. Sawicki brought these, as well as chocolate cookies and blueberry muffins, to a taste test attended by Schutz and her co-workers. They liked the taste, but other details like product shape and toppings still had to be decided on. Schutz reminded the team that "people eat with their eyes," emphasizing that the products had to look good.

She also noted that the low-carb cookies, muffins, and doughnuts were planned for preview at the upcoming March 10 board meeting. Considering that the doughnut mix wasn't ready, the blueberries sank in the muffins, and the cookie bars needed icing, this would be difficult. Somehow, Sawicki pulled it all together for the meeting, even arranging the snacks on serving trays, and the board thanked Schutz and the Greta team for having come so far so fast.

Later that day, Schutz was speaking to a supplier, who happened to mention that he could not eat products with maltitol, because it gave him side effects in the lower intestine. As it turned out, some people are more sensitive to maltitol. She spoke to Melchiorre the next morning. He needed no convincing that maltitol levels had to be decreased: He had the same discomfort. In addition, two days after the board meeting, the FDA announced they were going to monitor the usage of terms like "carb free" or "reduced carb" on product labeling; violating companies would face sanctions.

Schutz and Sawicki thought fast to solve these problems. A new cookie with polydextrose and glycerin (a sugar alcohol with fewer side effects than maltitol) was in preparation. Portion sizes were also reduced. To avoid the FDA low-carb regulatory web, Schutz decided to position Greta as a sugar-free product, with low-carb being a secondary attribute. The product was also about to get a name: "Sensables" evoked diet moderation and could potentially be reused on other snacks with different health benefits.

By May 12, Sensables were introduced to Tasty Baking's district sales managers. The team was unable to work out problems with the blueberry muffins (too much sugar in the blueberries) and replaced them with orange and chocolate-chip finger cakes. The rest of the lineup was plain and chocolate doughnuts, and the chocolate and chocolate-chip cookie bars. Schutz and her team had tried out the reformulated line, with no intestinal side effects. In her presentation, Schutz stressed the Sensables message: no sugar, low-carb, and portion control, and announced that the product would hit the shelves on July 15. At the end of her presentation, something happened that is rare for a district sales manager meeting: She received a standing ovation. Jim Roche, a Pennsylvania district sales manager, said, "This is a winner."[43]

After Sensables were introduced to the sales force, consumer taste testing was undertaken. According to Schutz, a few of the products were modestly "tweaked": the chocolate chip finger cakes and cookie bars received more chips, and more orange flavor was added to orange finger cakes. The chocolate doughnut was dropped, as customers didn't like its taste or its appearance. The consumer testing delayed the launch by a few weeks. Once the final adjustments were made to the product line, Sensables were launched in and around Philadelphia on August 10, 2004. The launch received coverage in Philadelphia area newspapers and on news radio.

Question: How does the Sensables process compare with the new products process in this chapter? Would you question anything Tastykake did? Do you think the Sensables line will succeed? Why or why not?

Case: The Levacor Heart Pump[44]

Since 1982, when the first artificial heart (the Jarvik-7) was implanted in the chest of Barney Clark, a major quest of the medical device companies has been to improve the well-being of heart failure patients. The goal for the patient is independent existence. Dr. Clark needed to be attached to a large external machine that powered his mechanical heart, which managed to prolong his life 112 days. Today, of course, the goal is to make the devices as thin as possible, such that they can be implanted in the body and allow the patient essentially to go about a normal existence. In view of the ultra-thin iPods, RAZR phones, and other similar products already available to consumers, medical device engineers are eager to use similar technologies to develop slim devices to support the functioning of the heart.

According to the American Heart Association, about 80 million adults in the United States have cardiovascular disease of one type or another, and about 5 million suffer from heart failure. When looking at the demand for medical devices to aid the heart, the aging baby-boomer market cannot be ignored. This active age group "wants to live, and demands, a full, rich life.... now we have medical consumers, a market that didn't exist twenty years ago," notes designer Allan Cameron. This target audience would certainly be receptive to a device that would allow long-term freedom and independence, even if major heart disease strikes. In fact, the heart pump industry is profitable and growing. In 2005, the leading

[43]Not everyone was convinced. A local food critic tried the snacks and wasn't impressed, offering the opinion that devotees of real Tastykakes would not find the Sensables line to be an acceptable substitute.
[44]This case was based on information in Reena Jana, "A Smaller, Sleeker Heart Pump," businessweek.com, January 16, 2007.

heart-pump maker, Thoratec, had annual sales of $201 million on its HeartMate XVE. Analysts see the market as going nowhere but up, especially after Medicare announced that it will be expanding the number of hospitals permitted to do heart-pump implants.

Recent efforts have been to develop implantable heart pumps that assist the patient's own heart, rather than mechanical devices that actually replace the heart. One of the most promising of these is the Levacor, which by late 2006 was in development at WorldHeart, based in Oakland, California. By this time, the Levacor had been in feasibility trials in Europe only for a few months; clinical trials in the United States (and ultimate FDA approval) were still far into the future. The most distinctive feature of the Levacor is that it uses magnetically levitated rotary technology to power the pump.

The Levacor story begins in the early 1990s at a company called Medquest (since acquired by WorldHeart). Pratap Khanwilkar and his team at Medquest were studying the heart pumps of the time and identified several problems associated with their use. Their size limited their usefulness: A pump that fit into the body of a large man might not be supported by a small adult, teenager, or child. There was also the problem of longevity. The heart pumps needed to be replaced every so often, exposing the patient to the risks and stresses of repeat surgery; this would be a concern especially in the case of a very young patient who might be relying on the pump for decades. The term used in the medical community for an implant that will never need to be replaced is "destination therapy." Another concern is the actual functioning of the pump: It must be gentle enough not to rupture blood cells, cause as little vibration as possible, and not require much power to operate.

The Medquest team settled on magnetic levitation technology as a possible solution. Magnetic levitation involves suspending a rotor using a balance of magnetic fields so that it moves without touching other parts: It literally levitates. Since nothing contacts the rotor, there is no friction or heat buildup, and also no erosion due to wear-and-tear, leading to longer life. The technology had been used for some time in large-scale projects such as power turbines, but had never been tried on such a small commercial application and certainly never in a heart device. Together with an engineering firm, LaunchPoint Technologies, Medquest developed a small, proprietary magnetic levitation system that could serve to pump blood from the heart throughout the rest of the body. The "suspension in air" of the rotor had a distinct advantage in a heart pump application, since there was less to obstruct blood flow, life-threatening clots would be unlikely to form. The development team designed a three-dimensional version of the pump using computer-aided design (CAD) software, which also was used to make a real-size, clear plastic prototype using rapid-prototyping technology. Using a blood substitute, the team was able to watch liquid flow through the prototype.

By early 2006, a working prototype made of a titanium alloy was available, about the size of a hockey puck and one-fourth the size of WorldHeart's previous model (that did not use the magnetic levitation technology). The device provides full mobility: The pump itself is implanted in the patient's abdomen, and the external device is a small battery pack and controller that the patient straps on. The first patient, a 67-year-old Greek man, was well enough 50 days after the implant to climb stairs on his own and was released from hospital to live a normal life at home not long thereafter. By this time, WorldHeart and LaunchPoint were also working on an even smaller device designed for babies.

As of early 2007, it was still unclear whether the magnetic levitation heart pumps would be the long-term industry standard; however, Mr. Khanwilkar (by now serving as WorldHeart's vice president for rotary systems and business development) was optimistic.

Based on the description in this case, discuss the new products process apparently underway at WorldHeart, in comparison to that outlined in this chapter. How is it similar or different? The launch phase is, of course, still well into the future at the time the case occurs. What are the problem areas the company might face at the time of launch? At the time of the case, what are the uncertainties that still exist? What could the company do now to manage these uncertainties?

CHAPTER THREE

Opportunity Identification and Selection: Strategic Planning for New Products

Setting

Chapter 1 introduced us to the strategic elements of new product development, and to the first of these elements, the new products process. Chapter 2 expanded on this process, showing us the phases beginning with opportunity generation and ending with the launch of a new product. Chapter 3 details the first phase of the process, opportunity analysis and strategic planning. It is in this context that we present the two remaining strategic elements: the product innovation charter (PIC) and product portfolio management, since these two strategic elements are such essential parts of this first phase.

We will explore in detail the process shown in Figure I.1 in the Introduction to Part I. The first part of this chapter discusses the importance of product strategic planning, focusing on the role of product platforms and also on the process of opportunity identification. This leads up to the second part of the chapter, the development of the PIC. This is essentially the product team's new product strategy, and it can be thought of as a foundation for new products management that serves as a loose harness for the integration of all people and resources used in generating new products. We look at what a team needs in its strategy statement and then at where its inputs originate—that is, in corporate strategy, in platform strategy, and in influences from many other sources. We explore the components of the PIC—its drivers, its goals and objectives, and its rules of the road. The final part of the chapter presents new product portfolio strategy: the strategic importance of having a portfolio strategy, what the components of a good portfolio are, and how some of the top firms develop their portfolios.

A Product Strategy for a "Company within a Company"

The group of people who lead the development of a new product act as *a company within a company*. They may be loosely tied together in a committee, or they may be fully dedicated (full-time) managers sent off somewhere in a *skunkworks* to address a difficult assignment. Regardless of the precise form, the group represents all of the necessary functions. They are led by a group leader, a team manager, or a project manager. They, as a group, essentially do everything the company as a whole would do: develop and allocate a budget, do financial analysis and projections, assign and implement tasks and responsibilities, and so on.

For these people, a new products strategy does several things. It charts the group's direction—where it must go, and where it must *not* go. It also tells the group its goals and objectives and provides some rules of the road. As new product researcher Peter Koen recently said, managers of the best firms at product innovation ask, "What sandbox should I be playing in?" before thinking of specific products—much as successful venture capitalists ask first what market areas they should be looking for new businesses in.[1] We first explore the inputs to this new products strategy—which we will later define as the **product innovation charter (PIC)**—then we detail the PIC's components and explore ways in which it can be built.

New Product Strategy Inputs and Identifying Opportunities

Corporate leaders make many strategy statements. Figure 3.1 shows a list of such statements, and you can see how important they would be to a new products team. Top-level statements like these guide a whole firm and are parts of what are sometimes called **mission statements.** Explicit consideration of the role of new products in the organization is strongly related to success. In Robert Cooper's research, 59 percent of managers from top-performing firms report their new products are a key part of their stated business goals, while only 3 percent of the lowest-performing firms do so.[2]

Product Platform Planning

A **product platform** is defined as a set of systems and interfaces that form a common structure. It is from this common structure that a family, or stream, of products can be developed efficiently. In simple terms, a product platform can be thought of as a basis for all individual product projects within a family of products.[3]

[1]Peter Koen, "Tools and Techniques for Managing the Front End of Innovation: Highlights from the May 2003 Cambridge Conference," *Visions*, October 2003.
[2]Robert G. Cooper, *Product Leadership: Pathways to Profitable Innovation*, 2nd ed. (New York: Basic Books, 2005).
[3]The formal definition is from Moreno Muffatto and Marco Roveda, "Developing Product Platforms: Analysis of the Development Process," *Technovation*, 20, 2000, pp. 617–630; for more information see also Johannes Halman, Adrian Hofer, and Wim van Vuuren, "Platform-Driven Development of Product Families: Linking Theory with Practice," *Journal of Product Innovation Management*, 20, 2003, pp. 149–162. For a good discussion of the top-down platform procedure, see Timothy Simpson, "Product Plaform Design and Customization: Status and Promise," *AI EDAM*, 18(1), pp. 3–20.

FIGURE 3.1   Corporate Strengths

These are examples of actual corporate strengths that managements have asked be used to differentiate the firm's new products. Many others are discussed in this chapter. These terms can be used to complete the following sentence: *New products in this firm will:*

Technologies

Herman Miller: Utilize our fine furniture designers
Braun: Utilize innovative design in every product
Otis Elevator: Build in new levels of service as key benefit
Coca Cola: Gain value by being bottled in our bottling system
White Consolidated: Be made on our assembly lines

Markets

Gerber: Be for babies and only babies
Nike: Be for all sports and not just shoes
IBM: Be for all people in computers, not just techie types
Budd: Be specially created to meet the needs of Ford engineers

Guidelines

Rubbermaid: Proliferate our lines
Lexus: Offer genuine value
Polaroid: Be almost impossible to create
Cooper: Never be first to market
Ford Tractor: Not upset the regulators
Bausch & Lomb: Use only internal R&D
Ganz: Be offered to the market hard-to-get (Webkinz)
Kodak: Have high value to us and to the customer
Toro: Solve outdoor environmental problems
Sealed Air: Offer more protection with less material
Argo: Copy Deere, at lower price

In many industries, corporate strategy affects product platforms as well as individual product projects. Product platform strategy will affect all projects related to the common platform. So a new products team has some strategies from corporate, some from platforms and other parts of the firm, and some developed by the team itself. A PIC (defined, in these cases at the product project level) will contain corporate mandates as well as product platform-level mandates.

Though long used in the auto industry, the term *platform* gained widespread usage shortly after Chrysler's success with the LH car platform, from which the Concorde and Intrepid models came. Note that a platform can be a technology, a design, a subsystem—anything that can be shared by one or more product families. Due to rapid market turbulence and the number of product varieties demanded by customers, many firms find that it is not efficient to develop a single product. It can cost as much as $3 billion to develop a new car platform, for example, so carmakers look for ways by which they can spread these costs over several models.

It makes sense for carmakers, and other manufacturers, to think in terms of product families that share similarities in design, development, or production process. Among many others, consider the following examples:

- Sony developed four platforms for the Walkman between 1980 and 1990, and from these launched about 160 Walkman product variations.
- From Toyota's U.S. Camry platform, at least five different made-in-America cars were developed.
- Honda's World Car platform is used to make Accords for the North American, European, and Japanese markets, each slightly different in size according to market preferences. Honda also makes minivans, SUVs, and Acura luxury cars from the same platform.

- Boeing makes passenger, cargo, short-haul, and long-haul aircraft from the same design, with many shared components.
- From a common set of ingredients, P&G developed Liquid Ariel, Liquid Tide, and Liquid Cheer for the European, U.S., and Japanese markets, respectively.
- Intel develops a microprocessor generation (platform), then concentrates on developing derivative products such as MMX or speed doubler technology.[4]

Many firms report promising results. Black & Decker redesigned its power tool groups into product families, allowing for more sharing of components. For example, where once 120 different motors were used in consumer power tools, a single universal motor is now used. The emphasis on platforms reduced product costs by 50 percent and helped Black & Decker achieve the highest market share in the category. And IBM used a standard set of subcomponents for all ThinkPad products, cutting both number of parts needed and base manufacturing costs in half.[5]

The examples illustrate a couple of different ways platforms evolve. In the Black & Decker example, the procedure was *bottom-up*: The firm found a way to consolidate components within an existing family of products to gain scale economies. But the Sony and Honda examples show a *top-down* platform procedure: The platform was designed at the outset to become the basis for a family of products, possibly for years into the future. Managers may need to be convinced to commit to top-down platform development rather than development of a single product, as it will certainly be more expensive and time-consuming. But the benefits are the cost and time efficiencies that will be obtained with future products built from the same platform, and ultimately, greater future competitive advantage. (Actually, once Black & Decker successfully converted to platform-based design, it then was able to generate even more products by "reusing" its platforms: It transformed its product design into a kind of top-down procedure.[6])

Platforms are a possibility in service industries as well as for manufactured goods. From a single platform for managed health care services, one provider offered several derivative insurance products: self insurance, group insurance, and extra coverage insurance.[7]

---

[4]Definition is from William L. Moore, Jordan J. Louviere, and Rohit Verma, "Using Conjoint Analysis to Help Design Product Platforms," *Journal of Product Innovation Management,* 16(1), January 1999, pp. 27–39. Examples are from Moore *et al.*; Tamar Krichevsky, "Leveraging and Managing Platforms," *Visions,* 24(1), January 2000, pp. 12–13; and Marc H. Meyer and Arthur DeTore, "Perspective: Creating a Platform-Based Approach for Developing New Services," *Journal of Product Innovation Management,* 18(3), May 2001, pp. 188–204.

[5]Identified industries, and examples, are from Niklas Sundgren, "Introducing Interface Management in New Product Family Development," *Journal of Product Innovation Management,* 16(1), January 1999, pp. 40–51; Krichevsky, op. cit.; and Meyer and DeTore, op. cit.

[6]Marc Meyer and Alvin Lehnerd, *The Power of Product Platforms* (New York: Free Press, 1997).

[7]James Walter, "Managing Services Platforms: The Managed Comp Experience," presentation at the 1999 Product Development & Management Association International Conference, Marco Island, FL.

There is a tradeoff involved here: Customers (or segments) want distinct products, while common products produce the greatest cost efficiencies.[8] To find the best balance, the manufacturer needs to decide on the level of commonality to be attained (that is, which designs or processes to standardize, and which to adapt). Suppose a product team is designing the dashboard for a new line of cars. The desired attributes in a dashboard no doubt depend on type of car being designed. A sports coupe buyer would probably like a roadsterlike dashboard, while a family sedan buyer would prefer a more functional look. Once the key attributes have been identified, the team considers the components of the dashboard: HVAC, electrical, steering system, radio, insulation, and so on, and decides where commonalities could be found. Possibly the electrical and radio designs could be shared, as could some HVAC parts (only the ends of the air conditioning ducts might need to be adapted). To achieve the desired differences between the two types of cars, the steering systems may need to be completely different, as would the insulation system: One might want to design the insulation for the sporty car such that it lets in more road noise![9]

Planning for product platforms clearly is difficult work. Excellent cross-functional communication and serious top management involvement and support are needed to ensure everyone agrees on the platform's architecture and how it is to be adapted to market segment needs.[10] It is also clear that firms can have very different philosophies on platform planning. Within the car industry, Volkswagen might have a single platform underlying its lowest-priced Skoda Oktavia model and its Audi TT sports car; Ford might use a common platform across its Jaguar or Lincoln models but would not share it with cheaper cars. And BMW continues to develop each model individually, believing that sharing a common platform would hurt its cars' appeal![11] Ford established a common platform from which small Fords, Mazdas, and Volvos are produced. Through its strategic alliance with Suzuki, GM gains access to small-car platforms as well as low-cost manufacturing skill; Suzuki obtains access to GM's low-cost global sourcing of car parts and its skill at alternative energy systems.[12]

Brand platforms can also be strategically important and are widely used. Brands may be billion-dollar assets, so many brand platforms are personally driven by CEOs. Brands can serve as the launching pad for scores of products, all having in common the brand and any strategies applying to that brand. Kodak built a new platform when it marketed the FunSaver, from which came what some call *derivatives:* Weekender, a flash format; FunSaver II; Portrait; Weekender II; and other

[8]As the U.S. carmakers found out in the 1980s, it may have been more cost efficient for compacts and luxury sedans to share parts and design features, but customers complained that the cars looked too much alike.
[9]David Robertson and Karl Ulrich, "Planning for Product Platforms," *Sloan Management Review*, 39(4), Summer 1998, pp. 19–32.
[10]Mohan V. Tatikonda, "An Empirical Study of Platform and Derivative Product Development Projects," *Journal of Product Innovation Management*, 16(1), January 1999, pp. 3–26.
[11]Thomas Osegowitsch, "The Art and Science of Synergy: The Case of the Auto Industry," *Business Horizons*, March–April 2001, pp. 17–23.
[12]Larry J. Howell and Jamie C. Hsu, "Globalization within the Auto Industry," *Research-Technology Management*, 45(4), July–August 2002, pp. 43–49.

versions, all perhaps planned from the beginning. Note, however, that any team using a platform brand must conform to the strategy of that brand; in the case of Waterford glass, all products had to have top quality, no exceptions.[13]

The *value* of an established brand is called its **brand equity.** Market research can measure the value of any brand for any particular market (for example, the Duracell brand, if put onto a line of heavyweight industrial batteries). The measurements actually tell the amount of free promotion and integrity the brand equity brings to a new item that uses it. Estimating this value accurately can be challenging; furthermore, a poor product concept won't succeed just because of a good brand name, and may indeed damage that brand's equity. We will return to the issue of managing brand equity in Chapter 16.

Another common platform is the **category platform,** either product type or customer. Most marketing effort today is conducted at category group levels—one overall plan for cake mixes, for do-it-yourself tools, or for finance courses in a college. For example, DuPont has special finishes platforms for doing business with the automobile industry, the marine industry, and the furniture industry, among others. Any strategic change in one of those areas influences all new products developed under that umbrella. Oddly, though Intel has its chips (e.g., Pentium) as corporate strategic platforms (remember "Intel inside"?); they are not *new product* platforms because each is a product, not a group of products. Customers such as Gateway will have the latest Intel chip as a platform for a line of products using it.

In sum, any new products team that sets out to develop its own product innovation charter for management's approval had better look around for all the baggage that comes from corporate and platform strategies. Most of them would hope they could be so lucky as the teams at Calvin Klein Cosmetics, where the CEO has a rule that there will be "no rules"—he thinks it permitted the first (and very successful) unisex scents.

Opportunity Identification

Many firms have persons working full time looking for new opportunities. They essentially audit the firm and any environment relevant to it. Throughout the firm people in the course of doing their jobs discover new opportunities—a salesperson learns that a customer is moving into a new market, a scientist finds unexpected activity in a compound, a finance VP notes a fall in the prime rate, a director urges that we look more carefully at what the Environmental Protection Agency is doing. A new regulation, for example, may restrict the use of petroleum-based synthetics, and a CEO may want all divisions to seek new products that actively capitalize on the regulatory change.

As shown in Figure I.1, new opportunities can come from many different sources: underutilized or new resources, mandates originating external to the firm (e.g., new regulatory restrictions), or internal mandates (e.g., from new corporate

---

[13]Guidance on using brand platforms for product innovation can be found in Dennis A. Pitts and Lea Prevel Katsanis, "Understanding Brand Equity for Successful Brand Extension," *Journal of Consumer Marketing*, 12(4), 1995, pp. 51–64. For a discussion of benefits and issues in platform planning, see David Robertson and Karl Ulrich, "Planning for Product Platforms," *Sloan Management Review*, Summer 1998, pp. 19–32.

FIGURE 3.2   Identifying the "Greenfield Markets"

1. Find another location or venue. Once McDonald's had taken up the best locations for traditional fast-food restaurants, it continued its U.S. expansion by placing stores inside Wal-Marts, in sports arenas, and elsewhere. Starbucks coffee complemented coffee-shop sales by selling its coffee beans and ice creams in supermarkets.

2. Leverage your firm's strengths in a new activity center. Nike has recently moved into golf and hockey, and Honeywell is looking into casino opportunities.

3. Identify a fast-growing need, and adapt your products to that need. Hewlett-Packard followed the need for "total information solutions" that led it to develop computing and communications products for the World Cup and other sporting events.

4. Find a "new to you" industry: P&G in pharmaceuticals, GE in broadcasting (NBC), Disney in cruises, Rubbermaid in gardening products—either through alliance, acquisition, or internal development.

Recommendations for scouting for such opportunities:

1. Look for emerging trends: increased globalization of freight flow meant more global opportunities for FedEx.

2. Find fringe markets that are becoming mainstream: gourmet coffee, extreme sports, home carbon monoxide testing are recent examples that spelled opportunities for many firms.

3. Find bottlenecks in the flow of trade, and seek to eliminate them. Need for better hospital patient record retrieval led 3M to develop its Health Information Systems business.

4. Look for "ripple effects" on business opportunities. The trend toward "immediacy" has led to products such as electronic banking and 24-hour food stores. Health concerns have opened up opportunities in fitness products, vitamins, seminars, etc.

Source: Allen J. Magrath, "Envisioning Greenfield Markets." *Across the Board*, May 1998, pp. 26–30. Reprinted with permission.

leadership). Figure 3.2 suggests several ways in which firms can identify opportunities for growth in new markets as their existing ones become less desirable.

Many futurists advocate studying the emerging trends in society and deriving product opportunities from them. A team of experts from the consulting firm Social Technologies identified six important and provocative modern trends including:

Just-in-time life: People like making spur-of-the-moment decisions based on real-time information.

Sensing consumers: People can sense their environment better now than ever before; what might be "too much information" for some might be essential information for others.

The transparent self: There is more information about consumers available to product managers now than ever before.

In search of "enoughness": Consumers are increasingly adopting simpler lifestyles marked by fewer material possessions and an increasing concern about quality of life.

Virtual made real: As more people become accustomed to virtual spaces, the boundary between these and the real world will become increasingly blurred.

FIGURE 3.3   **Product Opportunities as Derived from Six Societal Trends**

Trend	Related Product Opportunities
Trend 1: Just-in-Time Life	PhillyCarShare or Zipcar: carsharing systems with hourly rentals. Twitter or related services that allow instantaneous updates about friends. Real-time people tracking services such as Loopt.
Trend 2: Sensing Consumers	Home-testing kits for cholesterol, allergens, and so on. Technology that allows parents to track their children around the clock. Consumers taking part in environmental sensing networks.
Trend 3: The Transparent Self	GyPSii displays friends' whereabouts. Services that generate personal data such as bank accounts. 23andme, a home DNA test (*Time* Invention of the Year in 2009).
Trend 4: In Search of "Enoughness"	Products servicing environmental concerns. "Slow food" and "slow life" related products. Products supporting leisure time activities.
Trend 5: Virtual Made Real	Products and services related to virtual economies. Websites offering avatars for socialization and play in virtual cities. Virtual nightclubs and similar activities.
Trend 6: Co-Creation	iPhone apps number in the tens of thousands and are still growing. Lego has an online factory for visitors to make their own Lego toys. NikeID for custom shoes, and other similar product "configurators."

Source: Andy Hines, Josh Calder, and Don Abraham, "Six Catalysts Shaping the Future of Product Development," *Visions*, 33(3), October 2009, pp. 20–23.

Co-creation: Due to increases in e-commerce and online communities, it is easier for customers to communicate with each other, cooperate, and share information.[14]

Each one of these trends suggests possible opportunities for new product development, as shown in Figure 3.3. As an example, Tremont Electric developed the nPower PEG, a "Personal Energy Generator" that allows the user to charge a phone or other electronic device just by plugging it in and putting it in his or her pocket—the device charges from the kinetic energy generated from walking or running. Product developers at Tremont may have been thinking about the "just-in-time life" trend. If one is traveling or camping, or just forgot to plug in the phone the night before, this product can help the person use the phone again quickly and without waiting to find a plug. It also adds a cost-saving benefit as well as an eco-friendly charging option.[15]

Truly, there is no end to these opportunities, every one of which may reveal additional opportunities for new products. Unfortunately, each opportunity takes time and money to investigate, so we don't exploit nearly as many as we would like.

[14]Andy Hines, Josh Calder, and Don Abraham, "Six Catalysts Shaping the Future of Product Development," *Visions*, 33(3), October 2009, pp. 20–23.
[15]Tremont Electric's Web site for the charger is www.greennpower.com.

Noncorporate Strategic Planning

Although the major thrust of strategic planning comes from the top down (i.e., corporate and platform strategy development), much of it also comes from the heads of the functions (**silos** or chimneys) in the firm—marketing, technical, manufacturing, and finance, and from the planning of suppliers, customers, and others. Such groups frequently have the power to affect new product work. For example, paper manufacturing is done on huge, expensive machines; such firms often have strategies with a statement: "All new items, if paper-related, must be manufacturable on our current lines." Financial conditions may warrant restrictions such as "no new products that require more than $3,000,000 capital investments." Suppliers of materials (e.g., chemicals or metals) often require (usually smaller) firms to buy and use what they make. But the greatest functional inputs may come from technical, especially in technology- or supply-push conditions, or from marketing, where ongoing planning uses a range of techniques designed to give sharper market focus and new positionings. For example, look at Figure 3.4. It shows a variation on the traditional **product-market matrix.** The cells show variations in *innovativeness risk* as a firm brings in new product types or technologies (operating mode change, across the top) or markets products that require changes in how people buy or use them (use mode down the left side). A simple flavor change

FIGURE 3.4
Degree of Innovativeness as a Matter of Strategic Risk

Risk		Change in operations or marketing mode		
		None	Some	Great
Change in use/ user mode	None	Low	Low	Medium
	Some	Low	Medium	High
	Great	Medium	High	Dangerous

Application: This matrix has gone by several names: Product/Market, Technology/Application, and Market-Newness/Firm-Newness. In all cases, the issue is the risk of innovativeness. Risk on the user side is just as much a concern to us as risk within the firm. Every new product can be positioned on this chart somewhere, and that position is important if it is accepted as a project. Selecting one section to be preferred over the others is a matter of strategy.

(product improvement) would probably involve little or no risk, but substituting a computer line for face-to-face dealings in the field of medicine (**diversification for a computer services firm**) would involve dangerous risk to the producer of the service (great change in both technology and use mode).

Miscellaneous Sources

In contrast to the corporate-platform downward pressure approach and the horizontal functional pressure approach, some inputs can start at the lower level of activity and influence upward, as when a new product is so successful it drives corporate strategy to change. For example, an ethical pharmaceutical firm once unintentionally marketed a very successful new proprietary food product, with the result that a new division was created (to isolate the consumer advertising activity from the rest of the firm) and new strategies created to optimize its opportunity. Sometimes, a slow and gradual restructuring of business practice can influence new product strategies almost without anyone realizing it. For example, managers of service products frequently add a tangible component (FedEx and UPS offer branded packaging materials and even require that their drivers look neat), while managers of tangible products may add or emphasize a service component (such as a car-warranty program).

The Product Innovation Charter

All of the above inputs (corporate mission, platform planning, strategic fit, and so on) are potentially used in the development of a company's new product strategy. Because of the importance of this step in driving all that comes later in product development, we advocate a special name for this strategy: the **product innovation charter (PIC).** Typically, the PIC is a document prepared by senior management designed to provide guidance to the business units on the role of innovation.[16] The term PIC reminds us that the strategy is for *products*, not processes and other activities, it is for *innovation*, and it is indeed a *charter* (a document that gives the conditions under which an organization will operate). The PIC can be thought of as a kind of mission statement, but applied at a more micro level within the firm and adapted to new product activities.[17] It allows delegation, permits financing, and calls for personnel assignments, all within an agreed-upon scope of activity. For new product teams plowing off into unknown waters, such a charter is invaluable.[18]

[16]Erika B. Seamon, "Achieving Growth Through an Innovative Culture," in P. Belliveau, A. Griffin, and S. M. Somermeyer, *PDMA Toolbook 2 for New Product Development* (New York: John Wiley, 2004), Ch. 1.

[17]Christopher K. Bart, "Product Innovation Charters: Mission Statements for New Products," *R&D Management,* 32(1), 2002, pp. 23–34.

[18]See Robert G. Cooper and Elko J. Kleinschmidt, "Winning Businesses in Product Development: The Critical Success Factors," *Research-Technology Management,* July–August 1996, pp. 18–29. An example at Kodak is given in Diana Laitner, "Deep Needs and the Fuzzy Front End," *Visions,* July 1997, pp. 6–9.

FIGURE 3.5
The Product
Innovation
Charter

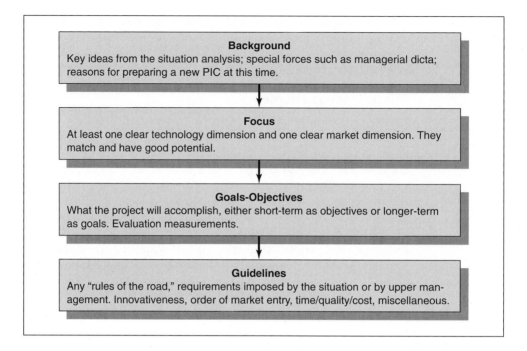

Most firms have a PIC, though it may not go by that name. In fact, some firms claim they have no strategy and then go on to describe methods of project management that are clearly strategic![19] In an empirical study of PDMA member managers, about three-fourths of the firms investigated had a formal new product policy of some type (that is, at least a partial PIC), while 29 percent reported having a formal, written PIC.[20] A more recent study of senior executives found that innovation rates are substantially higher in cases where the PIC has detailed and specific content, and where there is general satisfaction with the new products process within the firm. The more specific the corporate mission is presented in the PIC, and the more clearly senior management's strategic directions are spelled out, the better the performance of new products developed by the firm.[21] The value of PICs is clearly shown in the CPAS study introduced in Chapter 1. In that study, 86 percent of the "Best" firms had a PIC, as opposed to only 69 percent for the "Rest."[22]

The components of a PIC are provided in Figure 3.5. In the PDMA study, well over 80 percent of the firms had formalized at least some of these components. To ensure that the PIC is effective, it should be put in place early by senior management, and the latter should stay involved and not delegate its implementation.[23]

[19]Albert L. Page, "Product Strategy for Product Development," *Visions,* July 1997, pp. 15–16.
[20]Bart, op. cit.
[21]Chris Bart and Ashish Pujari, "The Performance Impact of Content and Process in Product Innovation Charters," *Journal of Product Innovation Management,* 24(1), January 2007, pp. 3–19.
[22]Gloria Barczak, Abbie Griffin, and Kenneth B. Kahn, "Perspective: Trends and Drivers of Success in NPD Practices: Results of the 2003 PDMA Best Practices Study," *Journal of Product Innovation Management,* 26(1), January 2009, pp. 3–23.
[23]Seamon, op. cit.

FIGURE 3.6   **An Illustrative PIC for the Apple iPad**[i]

Focus: Apple's technology strengths include Apple's operating system, hardware, applications, and services. It also has product design and development strengths by which it can provide products that are intuitive, simple, and fun to use. On the marketing side, the customer wants the newest products on the "cutting edge" that provide seamless integration, high performance, and ease of use.

Goals: Revolutionary new products should also be platforms for a line of products into the future. This is a necessity due to the high costs of product development for Apple's "really new" products. New products should also become the "standard bearer" establishing a leadership position in its market.

Special Guidelines: Apple aims to be the best, not necessarily the first, in new product categories.

One can see how this PIC would lead to the development of the iPad. Much of the required technology had been previously developed for the Mac, iPod, or iPhone. The product itself would be Apple's first tablet computer, which was a revolutionary new product that was seen by many to be the "next big thing" in computers. Some skeptics were less impressed, noting that it lacked a "killer app," but the iPad is designed to be the first of a line of tablet computers with increasing numbers of capabilities and applications. At the time of launch, no one tablet computer had really established a dominant position yet in that industry. Apple's goal appears to be to have the iPad become the standard bearer of tablet computers much as iPhones have become almost synonymous with music players.

[i]This PIC is speculative only and meant to be an illustration, yet it is realistic and derived from published news reports about the time of the iPad launch. These include: Apple's 2009 annual report; Scott Steinberg, "Apple iPad Impressions: The Skeptic's Take," **digitaltrends.com**, January 27, 2010; Reena Jana, "Apple iPad Product Development Approach," blog appearing on the Harvard Business Review site, **hbr.org**, January 27, 2010.

An illustrative example of what the PIC might have looked like for the Apple iPad is shown in Figure 3.6.

We will expand the discussion of the PIC soon, but let's first examine the various inputs that help managers make strategic decisions.

Strategy statements take almost as many forms as there are firms preparing them, but they tend to build around the structure given in Figure 3.5. They can be for an *entire firm* (if very small or very narrowly conceived), or for a *standing platform* of activity within a larger firm (for example, Black & Decker brand of tools), or for a *specific project* (for example, Hewlett-Packard's newest laser printer). A PIC generally speaks to an opportunity (the focus), not to the specific product or products the group is yet to create. Oscar Mayer embarked on the development of the "big wiener" only to find later they needed Big & Juicy in six different flavors for U.S. regions. Of course, when products are very complex (a new car platform, an air express service for the Asian market, or a nation's new health plan), one product is all the team can handle.

The PIC should be in writing, but for various reasons it often is not, and it should be given to all participants, but again it often is not. This is unfortunate, because a secret, mind-only strategy will not do much for a team of 30 people.

Why Have a PIC?

Think back to Peter Koen's "sandbox" comment mentioned earlier. We have already seen how many different places we can find opportunities for new product development. Without a strategy, it is easy to lose focus and to spend time and resources chasing the wrong opportunities. The PIC provides the direction, or directions, the team should concentrate on in new product development—in other words, it defines what sandbox the team is in, or wants to be in, and also where it does not want to be. Without putting down the boards that define the size and shape of the sandbox (metaphorically speaking), then *any* opportunity would seem to be a good one!

Consider a team developing a small, portable computer printer. One member is thinking of using a new battery-based technology, while another team member is concentrating on potential customers who happen to work in environments where wall plugs are available! Marketing research people plan to pretest the product extensively, while manufacturing engineers assume time is critical and are designing finished production capability from the beginning! A vendor picked to supply the tractor mechanism has to check with the team leader almost every day because the team has not decided exactly what functions the printer will serve or the target user! And the team is being guided by requests from the sales department, which is currently calling on smaller firms although, in fact, the biggest potential is thought to be in large firms and governments! This team has not developed strategy.

Team guidance, just like corporate or strategic business units (SBUs) guidance, comes partly in the form of strategy. Its purpose is *to focus and integrate team effort and to permit delegation.* Bausch & Lomb almost lost its market position when its managers concentrated for too long on improving old products and thus almost missed new products like extended-wear contact lenses. Being forced to review their strategy, they found many more opportunities and went on to capitalize on them (e.g., disposable contact lenses).

Lacking a focused and integrated effort, new products teams are likely to face the related problems of *scope creep* and *unstable product specifications*.[24] Both of these problems occur if the "sandbox" is not defined, or only poorly or vaguely defined. Scope creep refers to the constant changing of a project's definition: Is the project meant to be a product designed for a specific customer, a large number of users, or a platform for a whole new line of products? *Unstable product specifications* refer to the product requirements or desired performance level changing as the product goes through the development phase. In either case, the product team is chasing an elusive target (Robert Cooper would call this the "moving goalpost"), with inevitable wastes of both time and resources. A clear-cut PIC, designed to overarch the entire new products process, helps to minimize these costly and time-consuming problems. There is even value to be gained in the very process of working together and formulating a PIC. A good process fosters high levels of commitment from the participants, consensus on goals and objectives, and agreement on the ways the goals will be achieved. Indeed, in a recent empirical study, the most innovative firms in the sample were those that had a clear PIC and also

---

[24]For more on scope creep and unstable specifications, see Robert G. Cooper, "What Separates the Winners from the Losers and What Drives Success," in Kenneth B. Kahn, George Castellion, and Abbie Griffin, *The PDMA Handbook of New Product Development,* 2nd ed. (Hoboken, NJ: John Wiley & Sons, 2005).

had a satisfactory process for PIC development.[25] This finding complements an earlier study, in which 70 percent of the highest-performing firms had a specific PIC, while only 51 percent of low-performing firms did.[26]

The Sections of the PIC

The PIC is a plan for the firm's initiatives in new product development. It provides clarification of goals and a common language for all personnel involved in new products. The roles of all participants throughout the new products process are clearly specified. An effective PIC communicates to the product team members exactly how their efforts fit into the big corporate picture.[27]

Background Section of the PIC

This section of the PIC answers the question: "Why did we develop this strategy, anyway?" To the extent necessary, it recaps the analysis behind it.

The Arena (Area of Focus) Section of the PIC

In today's competitive marketplaces, it takes focus to unlock the necessary power of innovation. Just as a laser can take a harmless light and convert it into a deadly ray, so can a commitment to, say, the delivered-pizza business or to the Web site construction process convert limited resources into a strong competitive thrust. As one developer said, "We like to play on fields that tilt in our direction."

In recent years we have heard a great deal about **core competencies**. They are an excellent place to start the search for charter arena definitions. Marketers narrow their focus by targeting and segmentation. Technical people, all too often fenced in by time, limited facilities, and money, don't relish yet another focus mechanism. But the idea of a new products arena, or area of focus, is growing. Focus is generally achieved by use of four types of strengths or leverage capabilities: *technology* (such as Kimberly-Clark's paper processing technology), *product experience* (Stroh's chose to focus on the beer business), *customer franchise* (Stanley Tools' hold on the woodworker), and *end-use experience* (Chase Manhattan's international division). **Licensing** or **acquisition** to acquire technologies or market strengths are also fair game for inclusion in strategies. The original *Star Wars* creator, George Lucas, opened bids from toy makers for licenses when planning *Episode 1*. Some of them approached $1 billion.[28]

[25]Chris Bart and Ashish Pujari, "The Performance Impact of Content and Process in Product Innovation Charters," *Journal of Product Innovation Management,* 24(1), January 2007, pp. 3–19.
[26]Abbie Griffin, "PDMA Research on New Product Development Practices: Updating Trends and Benchmarking Best Practices," *Journal of Product Innovation Management,* 14(6), November 1997, pp. 429–458.
[27]Roger J. Calantone, S. K. Vickery, and Cornelia Droge, "A Business Performance and Strategic New Product Development Activities: An Empirical Investigation," *Journal of Product Innovation Management,* 12(3), May 1995, pp. 214–223.
[28]Lisa Bannon and Joseph Pereira, "Toy Makers Offer the Moon for New 'Star Wars' Licenses," *The Wall Street Journal,* August 19, 1997, p. B1.

Relying solely on a technology is risky, as no one knows whether the technology-based product is something customers want (Polaroid's Polavision instant movies, for example, or the Iridium satellite-based telephone). Likewise, letting customers' stated wants drive product innovation is unlikely to work well, except in a market with enormous unmet needs and very slow-reacting competitors. One recent report told how two PC makers differed on drivers. One, Fujitsu, bet on technology and lost, while NEC bet on customer needs and won.[29] Gambles like this are too expensive today. So consumer giants Frito-Lay and P&G have major laboratory research facilities, and technology-driven Hewlett-Packard has announced that it wants a strong market commitment behind every new product program. These firms have realized that the best option is a balanced, or **dual-drive,** strategy. Let's explore technology and market drivers separately, then see their value when taken in combination.

Technology Drivers

The most common technological strengths are in the *laboratories*. Corning used to say it would develop those products—and only those products—that exploited the firm's fabulous glass technology. Today's global competition makes it tougher for Corning (and others) to hold a superior position in a technology defined so broadly.

Many times, a firm finds it has a valuable *non*-laboratory technology. Avon has an efficient small-order-handling technology. Other operations technologies include soft drink distributed bottling systems and White Consolidated's efficient appliance production lines. Big business consulting firms have built new services around capabilities of analysis and interpretation of financial information. For a firm with superior technical skills, applying the dual-drive idea means turning technical specifications into product features that satisfy market needs. Consider a firm that manufactures semiconductors and has developed the capability to produce smaller-size, highly efficient, higher-resistance semiconductors (the technical specifications). These specifications by themselves may mean little to customers or end users, but they do provide capabilities and features, such as longer battery life, lower temperature operation, or lower manufacturing or maintenance costs, that might provide useful benefits to customers. The firm will need to think first of what products might be developed from the basic technology, such as a chip for use in cell phones, laptops, PDAs, or electric motors. Then, what particular market segments would be interested in such products? Here, the firm will need to match these products, offering these features and benefits, to unmet market needs. Cell phone, laptop, or PDA users who require longer and more dependable battery life, possibly, or electric motor users who need lighter-weight, lower-cost units that run at lower temperatures. This procedure of converting technical specifications to product features and benefits, to market needs, has sometimes been called the **T-P-M linkage.**[30]

[29]David T. Methé, Ryoko Toyama, and Junichiro Miyabe, "Product Development Strategy and Organizational Learning," *Journal of Product Innovation Management,* 14(5), September 1997, pp. 323–336.
[30]Stephen K. Markham and Angus I. Kingon, "Turning Technical Advantage into Product Advantage," in P. Belliveau, A. Griffin, and S. M. Somermeyer, *The PDMA Toolbook 2 for New Product Development* (New York: John Wiley, 2004).

Even harder to see are the technologies in marketing. For example, some packaged goods firms view their product management departments as technologies. Other examples include physical distribution systems, customer technical service, or creative advertising departments.

Market Drivers

The other half of the dual-drive strategy also comes from two market sources: *customer group* and *end-use*. The best new product ideas are based on customer problems, and these problems serve as the heart of the concept generation process described in Chapter 4.

The Hoover Company once had a strategy of developing new vacuums for people who already had one—the two-vacuum home concept. (Today they may be working on the five-vacuum home!) Other firms have relied on demographic dimensions for focus, for example, Toro's young couples, and Olivetti's banks and law offices. As examples of more abstract dimensions, Hallmark famously concentrates on "people who care enough to send the very best." Welch Allyn, maker of high-tech medical devices that are used in doctors' offices and hospitals, once said, not jokingly, if you have a cavity we want to see it, and if you don't have a cavity but need one we will make it. The latter part of that strategic focus brought about their device for doing noninvasive gall bladder removal.

Firms producing services find customer-focus comfortable, since many of their operations involve the customer as an actual **coproducer** of the service. The logic of this arrangement has led many service firms, in all industries, to involve the customer as an integrated partner in the new product development process.

Occasionally, a firm can concentrate on one single customer; for example, an auto-parts firm may build new items for Ford or for General Motors. A variation on the single-customer focus is **mass customization**—where we offer all customers a product of their individual choice. Marriott's Courtyard, for example, has made this successful in the motel business. We will see more of mass customization in Chapter 16.

The second way of focusing on the market side is on a particular *end-use*, such as sports or skiing. *User* (previous paragraph) and *end-use* (here) may sound alike, but they are not. For example, focusing on skiers or skiing would both provide new equipment, but skiing would also lead to new lodges, new slopes, new travel packages, and services for lodge owners (who may not even be skiers). Industrial firms make great use of end-use. You may say, but how do we know when to use which? The answer lies in the opportunity analysis that took place earlier—you studied markets, people in them, and activities they engage in. You selected a given opportunity because you thought its needs fit the firm's capabilities.

A variation on market drivers is the *distributor*—when a producer develops new products to meet the needs of, or capitalize on the franchise of, resellers. Hallmark's line of small gift items, for example, was originally developed to help their card shop franchisees make more money.

Combinations: Dual-Drive

Now, putting one technical driver together with a market driver yields a clear and precise arena focus. University Microfilms International (UMI) has been using the *technology of microfilming* and the *market activity of education* as their original mainstay, but later added *photocopiers* for schools and microfilm readers for *law offices.* Penn Racquet Sports switched species of markets, putting their *tennis ball technology* to work making a line of ball toys for *dogs.*[31] Toro had years of success with a series of dual-drives, one of which is *global-satellite technology* and *golf course superintendents.*[32]

The Signode Corporation set up a series of seven new product venture operations and asked each group to select one company technology and one market opportunity that matched that company strength. The first team chose *plastics extrusion* (from Signode's primary business of strapping materials) and *food manufacturing.* This team's first new products were plastic trays for packaged foods headed into microwave ovens.

Gap has been extremely successful with a dual-drive of European styles and American women. Both drives are a bit general, but to date they have produced the nation's most successful apparel retailer.

Goals and Objectives Section of the PIC

Anyone working on product innovation ought to know the purpose, because work can change in so many ways if the purpose changes. The PIC uses the standard definition that **goals** are longer-range, general directions of movement, whereas **objectives** are short-term, specific measures of accomplishment. Thus, a PIC may aim for market dominance (as a goal) and 25 percent market share the first year (as an objective).

Both goals and objectives are of three types: (1) *profit,* stated in one or more of the many ways profit can be stated; (2) *growth,* usually controlled, though occasionally a charter is used defensively to help the firm hold or retard a declining trend; and (3) *market status,* usually increased market share. Many top managements insist that new product teams entering new markets plan to dominate them. But the American Regitel Corporation, marketers of point-of-sale machines, aimed to be number three in its markets, even though the parent firm wanted to be number one as a general policy. There has been lots of criticism of market share as a new product goal, but it is still a popular objective. Wendy's, Burger King, Dunkin' Donuts, and Starbucks all rolled out breakfast menus in 2007 in order to capture a larger share of the enormous breakfast market that has been dominated by McDonald's.[33]

---

[31]Dennis Berman, "Now, Tennis Balls Are Chasing the Dogs," *BusinessWeek,* July 13, 1998, p. 138.
[32]Richard Gibson, "Toro Charges into Greener Fields with New Products," *The Wall Street Journal,* June 22, 1997, p. B4. This article gives lots of details on a very sophisticated use of the dual-drive system of defining an arena.
[33]For more on goals and objectives used by business, see Abbie Griffin and Albert L. Page, "PDMA Success Measurement Project: Recommended Measures for Product Development Success and Failure," *Journal of Product Innovation Management,* 13(6), November 1996, pp. 169–195. For developments in the fast-food industry, see Bruce Horovitz, "Fast-Food Rivals Suit Up for Breakfast War," *USA Today,* February 20, 2007.

Special Guidelines Section of the PIC

Up to this point, we have filled out three sections of the PIC form. We know the team's arena or focus and we know what they are supposed to accomplish there. But research shows that almost every new product strategy has a fourth section— some guidelines or rules of the road. They may be managerially imposed, or consensus thinking of team members. They are certainly strategic. We have no research study that shows what such guidelines *should* be, but we do have lots of research showing what firms put into this section, right or wrong.

Degree of Innovativeness

How **innovative** does a management want a particular group to be? The options range from first-to-market (whether a synthetic fiber or a Frisbee) to strict imitation.

First-to-market is a risky strategy. It goes by several other names, including *pioneering*. There are three ways to get it, the first of which is by *state-of-the-art breakthrough*. Pharmaceutical firms use that route most of the time. Other products that came from such programs include bubble memory, the pacemaker, compact discs, and television. But most first-to-market products do not extend the state of the art; instead they tweak technology in a new way. This second way, sometimes called **leveraged creativity,** constitutes the most common first-to-market category. For example, DuPont researchers find the special properties (such as durability or oil and grease resistance) of synthetic materials such as Surlyn and Kevlar, then think up creative applications to arrive at new products. Surlyn's grease resistance led to its application in the meat packing industry. The third way to be first is **applications engineering,** where the technology may not be changed at all, but the use is totally new. Loctite has done this dozens of times, for example, by using glue to replace metal fasteners in electronics and automotive products.

Far more common than pioneering is the strategy of developing an **adaptive product.** Being adaptive means taking one's own or a competitive product and improving it in some way. The improvement may be technical (a CD drive for the PC) or nontechnical (the 17-inch PC screen). It may be useful, or trivial. Adaptation is especially popular where the firm needs cash, fast.

Some adapters seek almost any change that can be used in advertising. Others follow what is called *second but best*; the improvement is to be major, and the follower intends to take over the market, if possible. Maytag followed this strategy for many years. Harris Corporation, on the other hand, entered markets where others had pioneered and used its great technical know-how to create a niche with a slightly improved product. The firm's chairman said Harris tried to be strong in technology and to enter a product in a timely manner.

Adaptation, alone, is risky. The pioneer often obtains a permanent advantage; if other things are equal, the first product in a new market gains an average market share of around 30 percent. But the second firm can take over the market and win the category if its adaptation is clearly superior. Often, the firm that enters first-to-market will follow the successful entry with less innovative adaptive extensions or even straight imitations, opening up an opportunity window for competitors. The third level of innovativeness is **imitation,** or **emulation.** Firms such as Cooper Tire & Rubber, Matsushita, and White Consolidated (appliances) deliberately wait to see winners emerge from among the pioneers and early adopters. Imitation has its risks, too: A firm cannot wait too long to enter the market, by which time the earliest firms to enter have well-established, loyal customer bases and ties to the supply networks and distribution channels. Furthermore, an incumbent firm may take an innovator to court over alleged patent, trademark, or copyright infringement; trademark protection is returned to in Chapter 16.[34]

Timing

This category of guidelines variation has four options: first, quick second, slower, and late. The decision to be *first* is pioneering, just discussed. A *quick second* tries to capture a good second-share position, perhaps making no significant improvement, or just enough to promote. The strategy is very demanding, because such a firm has to make the decision to enter the market *before the innovator is successful or has even come to market*. This turns the quick second into a forecaster—how successful will the innovator be? Waiting risks letting the second spot go to aggressive competitors. Striving for a *slower* entry is safer in the sense that a firm knows the outcome of the pioneer's efforts and has time to make a more meaningful adaptation. But the good market opportunities may be taken by quick seconds. The last timing alternative, *late* entry, is usually a price entry keyed to manufacturing skills.

Miscellaneous Guidelines

Innumerable specialized guidelines can be found in product innovation charters. Some are surprising. Hewlett-Packard was trying to decide what to do with its new digital photography for use in printers and scanners. But it took hard selling for the technical people to persuade HP's printer division it should try to compete with Kodak. An unwritten guideline had banned it for many years.[35]

Some firms recognize weaknesses. For example, a large mining machinery firm told its product innovators to come up with products that *did not* require strong marketing; the firm didn't have it and didn't want to invest in getting it. A pharmaceutical firm said, "It must be patentable." A small computer firm said all new products must be parts of systems, while an even smaller computer firm said, "Nothing that must be part of a system!" A food firm said, "Don't put anything in a can that Frito-Lay can put in a bag." Another miscellaneous guideline is **product integrity,** meaning that all aspects of the product are internally consistent. An example: Honda was very successful using the new four-wheel steering system because it put the innovation into a two-door coupe with a sporty image, whereas Mazda failed when putting it on a five-door hatchback that was positioned for safety and durability.

[34]For a discussion of pioneering benefits and risks, see M. B. Lieberman and D. B. Montgomery, "First-Mover (Dis)advantages: Retrospective and Link with the Resource-Based View," *Strategic Management Journal,* 19(12), 1998, pp. 1111–1125. Information on several later entrants who overtook pioneers can be found in Steven P. Schnaars, *Managing Imitation Strategies* (New York: Free Press, 1994).
[35]Eric Nee, "What Have You Invented for Me Lately?" *Forbes,* July 28, 1997, pp. 76–82.

How to Prepare a Product Innovation Charter

The process for developing a PIC lies in its contents. *First*, we are always looking for opportunities, inside the firm or outside it. Each strategy can be traced to a strength of the company involved. No one firm can be strong in everything. *Second*, we have to evaluate, rate, and rank them. *Third*, we simply begin filling out the PIC form—focus, goals, and guidelines. Usually there is no shortage of suggestions for all the sections—not unlike any marketing situation analysis.

Consider first the opportunity identification step. Potentially fruitful options in technologies or marketplaces may seem hard to find, but we are surrounded by them. Figure 3.7 shows a partial list. Every one has been the basis for a team's new product assignment, at least once.

The second step, evaluating and ranking the opportunities, is extremely difficult. In fact, one of the most valuable creative skills in product innovation is the ability to look at a building, an operation, a person, or a department and visualize how it could be used in a new way. This skill can be developed, and should be practiced. Not only is there no ready quantitative tool for measuring, say, the strength of the pharmaceutical chemistry department of a small drug manufacturer, there is also politics, because people are involved. And, unfortunately, it is a lot easier to see the potential in some technology or market *after the fact*. Take Amazon.com, for example. Thousands of people have said how obvious was their idea of selling books on the Internet, but where were they when Amazon.com stock was selling for $10 a share?

FIGURE 3.7
Market and
Technology
Opportunities

Market Opportunities	Technology Opportunities
User (category)	Product type
User (for our product)	Specific product
Customer (buyer)	Primary packaging
Influencer	Secondary packaging
Potential user	Design process
Nonuser	Production process
Demographic set	Distribution process
Psychographic set	Packaging process
Geographic set	Patent
Retailer	Science
Wholesaler	Material
Agent	Individual
Use	Management system
Application	Information system
Activity	Analytical skill
Franchise	Expert system
Location	Project control
Competitor	Quality attainment
Regulator	Project design

To get through these disputes and arrive at a mutually agreeable PIC, a firm needs to do an honest assessment of itself, its goals, its strengths, its customers, and so on. Figure 3.8 illustrates the procedure followed by a real firm, Creative

FIGURE 3.8   **PIC Development for Creative Problem Solving Group—Buffalo***

Who are we, and what do we do?
- We provide professional services and resources that help people
  - Ignite creative potential
  - Lead creative change
  - Achieve creative results

Who are our customers?
- Human resource professionals
- Business unit and line leaders
- Senior managers
- Researchers (potential)
- Professors (potential)
- New product professionals

What are their demographics?
- Western Europe and North America
- Aiming for global industrialized nations
- Professionals in organizations (profit, not for profit, government)

What are their behavioral traits?
- Work with their minds
- Interested in research
- Personally committed
- Bright
- Possess integrity and honesty
- Willing to collaborate and partner

What technology/core competency do we leverage?
- Understanding of creative problem solving, leadership, etc.
- Understanding of curriculum design
- Understanding of assessment techniques
- Human interface and high-touch

What are our growth expectations?
- 40 percent per year

What is our marketing plan?
- Target a new level of distribution

What do we want to accomplish?
- Fill gaps in existing line
- Maintain or improve marketplace image
- Take existing products to new markets
- Enhance brand name

How much risk are we willing to take?
- Strive for integration and synthesis with current operations

How should we time our entry to the market?
- ASAP

Any other factors important to consider?
- Pay attention to patents

Based on the above question and answer session, the following PIC was developed:

Creative Problem Solving Group—Buffalo provides professional services and resources that help people ignite creative potential, lead creative change, and achieve creative results. These services and resources are used in training courses, learning programs, and creativity and change-related consultancy. Our customers are adult professionals in organizations with interest in affecting change and enhancing creativity. These customers are primarily located in Western Europe, North America, and increasingly in industrialized nations around the globe. Existing and potential customers and associates will be the primary distribution channels.

We aspire to grow at least 40% each year by expanding our own efforts and increasing our offering to associates. New products will fill gaps in our existing line as well as improving our image and brand identity.

Leveraging our brand and reputation, we will take existing and new products to new markets. Integration and synthesis is our key approach and we will release products to new markets as they are validated. New products will be protected as much as possible by copyright, patent, trade secrets, and trademarks.

*The authors wish to thank Len Kistner for providing this detailed example of PIC development.

Problem Solving Group—Buffalo, in developing its PIC. The figure shows a set of assessment questions, together with some of the answers provided by firm's managers in a PIC workshop. The PIC that was ultimately developed is shown at the end of the figure.

At the end of this chapter are two cases involving Kellogg and Honda. In each case, the assignment is to write out *what the PIC might have been*. Doing that will demonstrate some of the difficulties we have been talking about, because you will have to replicate their knowledge and process.

Product Portfolio Analysis: The New Product's Strategic Fit

Now that a new products manager has written a PIC, *is that it*? Not at all. Upper management must approve it. Importantly, the newly chartered product must fit as part of the firm's overall business strategy. It should provide an appropriate balance to other products already being offered before any scarce financial resources are allocated to it. Many firms use a product-portfolio approach in which management allocates R&D and other scarce resources across several categories defined by strategic dimensions.[36] This approach bears some similarity to the familiar Boston Consulting Group portfolio model, but allows great flexibility in the choice of dimensions, which can include:

- Strategic goals, such as defending current base of products versus extending the base.
- Project types, such as fundamental research, process improvements, or maintenance projects.
- Short-term versus long-term projects.
- High-risk versus low-risk projects.
- Market familiarity (existing markets, extensions of current ones, or totally new ones).
- Technology familiarity (existing platforms, extensions of current ones, or totally new ones).
- Ease of development.
- Geographical markets (North America, Europe, Asia).

Current spending within each of the categories is assessed and compared to desired spending (which may be expressed as a dollar amount or as a percent), and adjustments are made. Thus, a firm would not allocate funds to yet another close-to-home, low-value product project when it would be strategically more advisable to take on a riskier, higher-potential-return project.

---

[36]For discussions of the portfolio approach, see Robert G. Cooper, Scott J. Edgett, and Elko J. Kleinschmidt, *Portfolio Management for New Products* (Hamilton, Ontario: McMaster University, 1997), pp. 59–69; and Robert G. Cooper, Scott J. Edgett, and Elko J. Kleinschmidt, "Portfolio Management: Fundamental to New Product Success," in P. Belliveau, A. Griffin, and S. Somermeyer (eds.), *The PDMA Toolbook for New Product Development* (New York: John Wiley, 2002), pp. 331–364.

FIGURE 3.9
Strategic
Portfolio
Model for
One SBU
in Exxon
Chemical

	Low Market Newness	High Market Newness
Low Product Newness	Improvements to Existing Products (35%)	Additions to Existing Product Lines (20%)
Medium Product Newness	Cost Reductions (20%)	New Product Lines (15%)
High Product Newness	Repositioning (6%)	New-to-the-World Products (4%)

Source: Adapted from Robert G. Cooper, Scott J. Edgett, and Elko J. Kleinschmidt, *Portfolio Management for New Products*, McMaster University, Hamilton, Ontario, Canada, 1997, p. 63. Reprinted with permission.

Managing a strategic product portfolio in order to maintain a dependable, continuous flow of products is a reality in most industries. Consider pharmaceuticals, agrochemicals, or other highly regulated industries. Product managers face incredibly difficult challenges: low likelihoods of success, high development and regulatory costs, limited financial and human resources, even the sheer difficulty of coming up with a good new product idea! Add to this the need to time product launches with marketplace demand, and it's easy to see why managers in such industries resort to complex decision models to help them manage their product portfolios.[37]

One SBU within Exxon Chemical uses a strategic portfolio approach for funding allocation, using two dimensions: product newness and market newness (see Figure 3.9). If current allocations to, say, improvements to existing products total much more than the desired 35 percent, another product project of this type would be less likely to be funded. The SBU would rather invest in a project of higher product and/or market newness. Both Eastman Chemical and Dow Corning are among the firms that use similar dimensions of technology and market newness to define their strategic categories.[38] As another example, Allied Signal has three strategic categories: platform projects, new products, and minor projects, and maintains a portfolio within each category.[39] Procter & Gamble uses a phased new products process much like that seen in Chapter 2 in conjunction with a portfolio that includes all its new product initiatives to ensure the right balance and mix of products. This portfolio method permitted P&G to build a pipeline of new

[37]Gary E. Blau, Joseph F. Pekny, Vishal A. Varma, and Paul R. Bunch, "Managing a Portfolio of Interdependent New Product Candidates in the Pharmaceutical Industry," *Journal of Product Innovation Management,* 21(4), July 2004, pp. 227–245.
[38]The examples are from the Cooper *et al.* book, pp. 62–63.
[39]Robert G. Cooper, Scott J. Edgett, and Elko J. Kleinschmidt, "New Products, New Solutions: Making Portfolio Management More Effective," *Research-Technology Management,* March–April 2000, pp. 18–33.

FIGURE 3.10
A Sample
Portfolio
Diagram

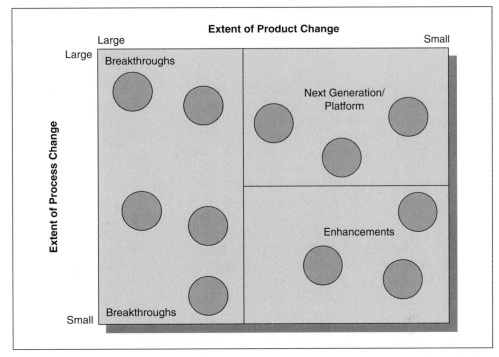

Source: Adapted from a real portfolio diagram used by a division of Hewlett-Packard, as reported in Randall L. Englund and Robert J. Graham, "From Experience: Linking Projects to Strategy," *Journal of Product Innovation Management* 16, no. 1, January 1999, pp. 52–64.

products for each of its product lines (face, lips, eyes, etc.) to be released or upgraded at the most appropriate times. Among their recent winning products are Prilosec OTC and Crest White Strips Premium Tooth Whiteners.[40]

Senior management can also check strategic balance using a portfolio diagram. While a wide variety of dimensions can be used to construct the diagram, the example in Figure 3.10 (similar to one used by a division of Hewlett-Packard) uses *extent of product change* and *extent of process change*. Incremental change on both dimensions leads to enhancement products; major change on the product dimension leads to breakthrough (or really new) products. Next-generation products and new product platforms are also represented in the diagram. Too many products in any one region of the diagram represent an imbalance that would have to be rectified.[41]

Another example is given in Figure 3.11, which is a portfolio evaluation model proposed by the Strategic Decision Group (SDG).[42] This method uses expected commercial value (or ECV, measured as the net present value of the future

[40]Robert G. Cooper and Michael S. Mills, "Succeeding at New Product Development the P&G Way: A Key Element Is Using the Innovation Diamond," *Visions,* October 2005, pp. 9–13.
[41]Randall L. Englund and Robert J. Graham, "From Experience: Linking Projects to Strategy," *Journal of Product Innovation Management,* 16(1), January 1999, pp. 52–64.
[42]See Robert G. Cooper, *Winning at New Products: Accelerating the Process from Idea to Launch,* 2nd ed. (Reading, MA: Addison-Wesley, 1993), pp. 184–185.

FIGURE 3.11
Strategic
Decision
Group
Portfolio
Evaluation
Model

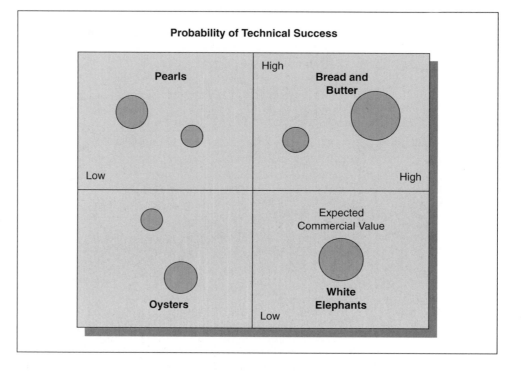

earnings stream) and probability of technical success to build the grid that appears in Figure 3.11. As shown in the grid, four categories emerge. *Oysters* and *Pearls* are projects with high ECV. Pearls are projected to have high technical success as well and are therefore highly desirable. Oysters are currently assessed to have a lower likelihood of technical success but potentially are highly profitable; with additional investment, the firm can "cultivate" some of these into Pearls. On the other side of the grid are the projects with lower ECV. The *Bread and Butter* projects are low risk but low ECV, and typically include incrementally new projects such as extensions and product modifications. *White Elephants* have low ECV and low probability of success and should be avoided. This portfolio model stresses balance between the three desirable categories. As with other portfolio models, the Strategic Decision Group model alerts the firm if it is investing too heavily in incremental Bread and Butter projects, or if it has taken on too many risky Oyster projects.

Persistence in applying portfolio techniques is rewarded: Many firms report that their portfolio efforts are weakly implemented, resulting in an unhealthy preference for incremental projects and inefficient resource allocation.[43]

[43]Robert G. Cooper, Scott J. Edgett, and Elko J. Kleinschmidt, *Improving New Product Development Performance and Practices, Benchmarking Study* (Houston, TX: American Productivity and Quality Center, 2002).

Summary

Chapter 3 has dealt with the most important and difficult step in the entire new products process: developing a sound strategy to guide the company within the company—the subset of people and resources charged with getting new products. Strategy turns such a group into a miniature firm, a microcosm of the whole. We looked at what such strategic guidance might be—a format here called a product innovation charter. We then studied the opportunities and mandates that yield the charters and how the charters can vary. The chapter ended by looking at some important issues that often arise when discussing new product strategy.

We can now begin the study of concept generation—the subject of four chapters in Part II.

Applications

1. "I'm afraid I don't follow your reasoning very well when it comes to this matter of innovativeness—being a pioneer, an adapter, quick second, and so on. Seems you've always got to come up with something new, or it simply won't sell. I believe we agreed on that earlier when we discussed the concept that winners market unique, superior products. Further, if you've got something new, why in the world would you ever want to be less than first to market with it? You'll lose your uniqueness that way. Sounds like you've taken a simple practice and made it complex."

2. "Somewhere along the line, R&D gets the short end of the stick. Now, I know about the arguments for strategy, but I really do feel that R&D deserves a better shake than to simply be told to do this or that. Some of our top people are in R&D—our electronics division has a couple of the world's best fax technicians. If I were doing it, I think I would have R&D prepare the first draft of a PIC, at least their areas of a PIC, and then have other areas like manufacturing add to it. When all of the interior departments have their sights properly set, I would ask marketing to reconcile the PIC with the marketplace. Otherwise, we'd have the tail wagging the dog when it comes to the new products function."

3. "I saw the other day where filmmakers (large ones as well as small ones) are finding profits in low-budget films. It seems they aim for narrow, but very reachable market segments (e.g., young kids), and they use standard film-making technologies but use only what they call emerging actors and directors (meaning cheap now). They try hard to capture the interests of their core target group, and they mean it when they say low-budget. I also read where several of them are trying to move out rapidly from the core when they have a winner: little kids, bigger kids, and so on. They think this approach yields the best return on investment even though it causes them to miss out on the occasional blockbuster winner. Some of these low-budget specials included *American Pie, There's Something About Mary, Rush Hour,* and *The Wedding Singer.* That last one focused on boys and men, but they added a love story line with Drew Barrymore that brought women in too. Now, can you fit all that into what might be the PIC of these films? What are the negatives of this approach?"[44]

[44]This application is taken from Bruce Orwall, "Hollywood's Champs: Cheap Little Flicks," *The Wall Street Journal,* November 11, 1998, p. B1.

Case: New Product Strategy at Kellogg[45]

The Kellogg Company of Battle Creek, Michigan, has been producing cereals since 1906. With reported annual sales in the $9 billion range, it is a leading manufacturer of cereals and other convenience foods (cookies, crackers, toaster pastries, frozen waffles, etc.). Aside from the familiar Kellogg's cereals, company brands include Keebler (acquired by Kellogg in 2001), Kashi (acquired in 2000), Pop-Tarts, Eggo, Famous Amos, and Morningstar Farms. Kellogg advertising has long featured cartoon spokespersons such as Tony the Tiger, Toucan Sam, and Snap, Crackle, and Pop, the Rice Krispies elves. Kellogg manufactures in 19 countries and has a presence on store shelves in over 150 countries. Many Kellogg's brands are particularly popular in Europe, where peanut- and chocolate-flavored corn flakes coexist on store shelves with the original recipe.

Kellogg, long the number-one cereal maker, was bypassed by General Mills in 1999. Many factors seemed to contribute to Kellogg's loss in cereal market share (from over 40 percent to about 31 percent): few successful new product introductions, high prices, and slashed advertising budgets. Meanwhile, its many competitors were thinking up new ways to compete: General Mills successfully launched line extensions such as Honey Nut Cheerios; Post focused on the adult market; and Quaker slashed prices by switching to bag packaging.

Kellogg CEO Carlos Gutierrez, who took over in 1999 (and who later became U.S. Secretary of Commerce), planned to respond to the competitive challenges by getting Kellogg to rethink its corporate strategy. Under his leadership, Kellogg has turned to a greater emphasis on snack products while not ignoring its core cereal products. It is building its traditional cereal business through heavy advertising and promotions (such as a Special K sweepstakes offering a chance to meet model Cindy Crawford). At the same time, however, it is leveraging its well-known cereal and snack products to increase its presence in the snack food business. New snack products are being spun off familiar cereal brand names (Snack 'Ums are large-size Froot Loops that come in small cans), and new flavors of familiar snacks are constantly being tried out (such as butterscotch Rice Krispies Treats and S'Mores Nutri-Grain Bars). The 2001 acquisition of Keebler also quickly increased Kellogg's snack portfolio. Gutierrezpredicted that cereal would soon make up less than half of Kellogg's business, as the company increasingly pursues the convenience foods market with products such as Nutri-Grain Bars. As Gutierrez said, "People snack—that's the way the world is moving."

By year-end 1999, Kellogg's snack food lines were already showing substantial sales and profit increases. New product development efforts at Kellogg have

[45]This case is based on Keith Naughton, "Crunch Time at Kellogg," *Newsweek,* February 14, 2000, pp. 52–53; Stephanie Thompson, "Kellogg Has Megabrand Ambitions for Special K," *Advertising Age,* November 6, 2006; Anonymous "Adwatch: Kellogg's Special K—Drop a Jeans Size," *Marketing,* February 1, 2006, p. 21; Anonymous, "Special K Seals David Lloyd Tie," *Marketing,* July 5, 2006, p. 6; Lawrence C. Strauss, "Barron's Insight: Kellogg Seems Underrated," *Wall Street Journal,* January 8, 2006, p. 2; and on information available at www.kellogg.com. Many thanks to Geoff Lantos who provided additional material to update this case.

focused on new snack items, many being line extensions of familiar Kellogg snacks. Among the items tested were kimchi- and seaweed-flavored Rice Krispies Treats (both aimed at overseas markets, neither ultimately launched). Another was Krave, a refueling snack bar intended as a midday snack. Krave was to be supported with a $2–3 million advertising budget; on the packaging, the "K" in Krave was written as the familiar red-script Kellogg's K. Snack 'Ums (see above) made the cut. At the same time, major cereal brands such as Special K are being supported with significant advertising and sales promotion budgets: At one time, Beanie Babies were stuffed inside Kellogg cereal boxes.

By 2002, Kellogg had regained the leadership position, largely due to its successful new products and shrewd marketing investments. In 2003, more new cookies were launched: E. L. Fudge in Butterfingers and S'Mores varieties. In keeping with the line extension strategy, new cereals included Special K Red Berries and Special K Vanilla Almond, as well as Maple Brown Sugar Frosted Mini Wheats, Smart Start, and Tony's Cinnamon Crunchers. In 2004, low-sugar Frosted Flakes and Froot Loops were launched, as well as Fruit Twistables (a snack). Kellogg has also got into licensing in a big way recently with SpongeBob SquarePants items such as Pop-Tarts, Eggo waffles, and Cheez-Its. By 2006, Kellogg was focusing on Special K as a "mega brand" under which it launched several new snack products (Snack Bites, K_2O Protein Water, and Protein Bars) as well as fruit- and yogurt-flavored Special K cereals. These launches have been tied to aggressive promotions aimed at the calorie-counting crowd. During 2006 it sponsored a "Drop a Jeans Size" ad campaign, ran a joint promotion with David Lloyd health clubs in Britain, supported a special "get-fit" Web site, and offered Special K Personal Trainer watches. Noting the obsession with healthy eating in North America and elsewhere, Kellogg also tied its promotion of All-Bran to better digestion.

Question: Given what you know about the cereal industry and the information provided above, choose one of the products or product lines marketed by Kellogg (it can be an older brand or a new release) and try to write out its PIC for 1999, around the time of Gutierrez's assumption of the CEO position. Follow the format of Figure 3.5. Be sure to flesh out all components of the PIC, and include in the background section of your PIC what higher level strategic plans may have been in place. Comment also on how Kellogg's PIC seems to have evolved from 1999 to 2006. As a further challenge, try to think of future products and/or product lines that would be consistent with your PIC and might be appealing directions for new product development at Kellogg.

Case: The Honda Element[46]

Honda, like most automakers, is an expert in the use of product platforms. This case takes you through all new products process phases, highlighting how Honda applied its expertise in product platforms to develop a cost-efficient new light truck, the Element, that was highly appealing to the targeted market segment.

[46]This case was derived from Marc H. Meyer, "Perspective: How Honda Innovates," *Journal of Product Innovation Management,* 25(3), May 2008, pp. 261–271.

The development of the Element began in 1998 with an idea for a new kind of light truck. At the time, Honda was already producing several lines of light trucks and SUVs, including the CR-V, Pilot SUV, and Odyssey minivan. At that time, a new cross-functional team was charged with developing a new light truck to add to this line, targeting a different customer segment and usage situation. In particular, the target was Generation Y males (aged 19–29) about to buy their first car. Gen Y was a potentially lucrative market: It was a sizeable segment, almost as large as the "baby boom" (individuals born between 1946 and 1964). Also, 52 percent of first-time car buyers were in this demographic. In the original business model, Element sales were forecasted to reach about 50,000 units in the first year. This number was based on comparison against CR-V sales, which reached about 100,000 per year in North America.

Senior salespeople at Honda recognized that several of their cars and light trucks were popular with young women or with families, but nothing appealed to young men. Honda also knew that several competitors had SUVs in the $20,000 price range that appealed to this segment. Getting loyalty at an early age has always been a strategy of automakers, as they expect that customers will trade up to more expensive or luxurious cars in the line as they become more affluent. For example, an Element buyer might trade up to an Accord, then an Odyssey, through time. Honda was clearly using demographics as a segmentation base and identifying a segment with very high growth potential.

The original charge of the product team was to develop a compelling new design that target users would respond to, while keeping the retail price affordable. Therefore, the first task was to try to understand the core values and beliefs of this unfamiliar segment. Ethnographic "fly-on-the-wall" research was conducted at the X-Games, featuring competitions in extreme events such as hot-dog skiing, snowboarding, and dirt-course motorcycle racing. Researchers with camcorders watched X-Games participants and spectators before, during, and after competitions. Later analysis of the videos provided a clear picture of the young males in the target market: They exhibit strong cohort identification, support social and environmental causes, are well educated, and tend to be less career driven than older segments. These observations provided clues to Honda designers on what features would need to be built in to appeal to this target. For example, typical users of this age group would need a vehicle that provided flexibility: it should be able to easily carry sporting equipment, dorm room furniture, or plenty of friends, and could even serve as sleeping quarters for weekend trips.

Product planners recognized that the light trucks currently in the line each had a clear positioning statement. The CR-V was for single, active individuals or small families; the Pilot was for larger families; and the Odyssey appealed to more settled families. The Element could fill a gap in the positioning map: the light truck for the single individual with an unconventional lifestyle.

Designers realized they would have to build flexibility into the Element's design. It would need a unique appearance and would also have to provide a fun driving experience. In all, four design themes were identified for the Element: adaptability/modularity, authenticity, functionality, and attitude/expression. These were added to the three design themes that drive development of all Honda cars: performance, safety, and value, to get the seven design themes that guided designers and engineers working on the Element.

Several different activities were then conducted simultaneously. Designers sketched several new versions of a bold new exterior appearance. Meanwhile, engineers worked on building in adaptability, focusing on fold-away seats that provided plenty of cargo or sleeping space when folded. Side doors were attached in such as way as to permit easier entry and exit, and the tailgate was also redesigned in a "clamshell" shape to improve access. A removable moon roof would allow the user to carry a tall piece of furniture vertically, with the top part sticking out. Armed with sketches of their progress so far, team members (both engineers and marketers) visited several universities and met with male students at frat houses. After obtaining feedback, they made adjustments and were able to achieve many "quick-turn" improvements.

To get top management support for the Element, the product team invited Honda executives to San Onofre Surf Beach in California, together with several Gen Y university students, for a weekend camping trip. The group discussed Gen Y lifestyle as well as car issues. The team felt that top management would support the project if they "lived the life" of the target user. It worked. The top executives were convinced of the value of the Element to the Honda car line, and the project got approval. A launch date of late 2003 was chosen.

Once the project was approved, stylists updated their sketches, quarter-size clay models were built, and eventually full-size prototypes were created and submitted to top executives for approval. At the same time, a user group of 30 men in the target age group, all living near Honda's Design Center in Torrance, California, was selected. They also reviewed sketches and prototypes, and gradually a design that this group found really interesting was finalized.

Here is where Honda's platform experience was put to use. New car product development is usually broken down into subsystems. In the case of the Element, four subsystems were used: exterior, interior, suspension, and power train. For each, a design strategy was created, and work progressed with periodic review by top management. The exterior subsystem consists of frame, bumpers, windshield, sunroof, tailgate, and so forth. Many of these components were specifically designed for the Element target segment, such as the unique side doors and the clamshell tailgate. The exterior panels were also designed with extra durability. In short, the Element's exterior was different enough from other Honda autos that it had to be designed uniquely, from the ground up. Similarly, the interior was a unique design. The driving principle behind the Element's interior design was the flexibility in cargo storage. The seats could be easily reconfigured into many different positions, or removed entirely. It was also expected that sand or mud would likely find its way into the storage area, so easy cleaning would be required. The flooring was urethane-coated, and electronics were located above the floor or put into waterproof barriers. Even waterproof seat fabric was used.

There was little need to develop a totally unique suspension for the Element, however. The ride needed to be maneuverable, sporty, and fun, and the current CR-V suspension would not have delivered the desired benefits. Honda engineers solved the problem by combining the basic CR-V chassis with the power steering gearbox used in the CR-V, MDX, and Pilot, making the Element wider and lower to the ground, and adding wider tires. Finally, for the power train, they used the existing 2.4 liter VTEC (variable valve timing and emissions control) engine, specifically adapted for the Element to deliver 160 horsepower at 5,500 RPM—plenty of power for the target customer. This engine also provided 26 miles per gallon (highway rating) and met all California emission standards. Since the power train accounts for about 20 to 30 percent of each car's cost of goods, Honda has historically invested in excellent power trains; product teams such as the Element team are actually not authorized to design new power trains but indeed must work with Honda's central Power Train Group. This same engine was used in the 2002 CR-V and Acura RSX, as well as the 2003 Accord. Together with the Element, four different products were supported by the same engine, and any advances made by the Power Train Group benefit all of these products.

In summer 2003, initial manufacturing runs began and early versions of the Element were delivered to dealerships. Marketing worked on finalizing the brand name; "Element" was the favorite of the user panel and also in research studies with prospective buyers. Communications had to be carefully chosen, given Gen Y's notorious aversion to traditional advertising. Honda selected a more grass-roots approach, creating buzz in auto enthusiast groups, at auto shows, and at colleges. Honda sponsored surf events and tailgate parties at universities, highly unusual for an automaker. More traditional television advertising used a lifestyle theme, showing groups of young Gen Y friends going to the beach or to a party.

The product team's hard work paid off. The Element was named *Automobile Magazine*'s small SUV of the year for 2003, and sales have been good—2004 sales reached 75,000 cars, substantially above the forecast. The biggest surprise was that the Element proved popular across all age groups: 40 percent of Element buyers were in their mid- to late-30s, and baby boomers also bought the Element in large numbers. Still, the buyers were mostly (not totally) male, and lived more active lifestyles than typical Civic buyers. Older buyers seemed to like the fact that it was clearly a young person's car.

Comment on the factors leading to the success of the Element. Include Honda's platform strategy as well as any other aspects of the new products process that you feel are relevant. In your answer, try also to work out what the product innovation charter (PIC) might have been for the Element. What tangible benefits resulted from bringing in the voice of the customer? What could be learned from this case for firms in industries other than automobile manufacture?

PART TWO

Concept Generation

In Chapters 1 and 2, we saw the overall new products process and learned that the first phase is all about strategic planning—the rationale being that one should seek new products that are best for the particular firm.

Ideation goes on constantly. Many employees of every organization come up with new product possibilities, and in no way will the act of creativity ever be constrained into a diagram. That's part of the fun of it! But there are common patterns, and we manage those.

Look at Figure II.1. Starting at the top, we see Prepare for Ideation, the topic of Chapter 4. People inside, and outside, the firm don't hold up ideating until we "prepare," of course, but managed creativity is much more successful if we assign much of the task to people with strong creative capabilities. Then, early on, we want to focus on problems and needs. So, by one means or another, we try to identify and clarify one or more specific problems that creativity can be focused on. Identifying problems and finding creative ways to solve them are the subject of Chapter 5. Most of what follows in Part II does just that, but there still is a lot of freelance ideation going on.

Activity takes place in five areas, shown in the figure. On the left, most firms have a technology operation (R&D, engineering, whatever) in which completely new technologies (e.g., Kevlar, OCR) are being sought. Technical people are also on hand to help solve problems identified earlier. On the right side, end users (indeed, all stakeholders in the marketplace) also do freelance ideation, and some of them actually design their own products, produce prototypes, and put them to work. For example, a dentist or an X-ray technician may well conjure up some device this way. They, too, stand ready to help us solve problems we identify.

In the meantime, in the middle of the diagram, the in-house team or group of people working on this project do their own problem solving. And they engage in other activities (Chapters 6 and 7) that produce "surprise" products. These, of course, are not problem-driven, so they must find out if someone has a problem that fits the "solution." While all of this is going on, people everywhere are telling us about their ideas—employees throughout the organization, their families, complete strangers . . . everybody, it seems. They come in on the left and right sides of the figure, lower down. The consequence is a pool of ideas— we will call them concepts—and filling this pool is the subject of Chapters 4–7. We will take up the issue of evaluating and refining these concepts in Part III of the book.

One caveat: Ideation is a huge topic, and there are hundreds of methods. The best are here, and a set of others often used is in Appendix B. What works on a pizza would not work on a fiber-optic sensor. And nothing in the world of creativity lends itself very well to research, so what most firms do is what satisfies them.

CHAPTER FOUR

Creativity and the Product Concept

Setting

This chapter takes us through several topics. First, to managers comes the task of preparing the firm for ideation—the first step in Figure II.1.[1] This means getting the right people, putting them in the correct environment, and generally getting them ready for the ideation process. Second, a creative person needs to know what is being searched for—that is, what is a concept and how is it typically found and identified? Third, you will explore a specific system of active (not reactive) concept generation, including approaches that seem to work. One part of that system—using employees and nonemployees in a search for ready-made ideas—will be discussed in this chapter, and the others will follow in Chapters 5, 6, and 7.

Preparation

Many people think of product innovation beginning with a new product idea. But Chapter 3 showed that it is far better to select a playing field and some rules (have a strategy) before starting the game.

The Product Innovation Charter

Think about these items from a hypothetical charter (Chapter 3) in a firm making bathtubs:

- Our new product concepts should be useful to older people and others with physical handicaps.
- New products coming from these concepts must make use of the firm's strong design capabilities, as well as copper metal.

Assuming the PIC work was well done, any person trying to come up with new bathtub ideas for this firm had better know the game plan, or many ideas created will simply be wrong. In a case like this, having a strategy helps.

---

[1]Anonymous, "Inspiring Innovation," *Harvard Business Review*, August 2002, pp. 39–49.

Finding the Right People

Creativity has been described by Craig Wynett, a senior manager at P&G, as "the everyday task of making nonobvious connections." Firms like P&G that are known for their innovative product programs are also known for being staffed with highly creative people—those that get original ideas with a high degree of usefulness. One such highly creative person was Harry Coover, the discoverer of superglue (cyanoacrylate adhesives). He was working on plastics from which to cast precision gunsights. He noticed that the plastic he was working with stuck to everything, and thereby ruined a refractometer he was using to study it with. He also was the first to get the idea that superglues could be used by doctors as an adhesive for human tissues.[2] Harry Coover's example demonstrates that originality and usefulness are both important characteristics of creative ideas.

Most people think reproductively—solve problems in ways that have worked for us in the past. Creative geniuses think productively, rethinking how to visualize the problem. Nobel Prize–winning physicist Richard Feynman called it "inventing new ways to think." For example, what is half of 13? Most of us would say 6½. But by redefining the problem we can identify other solutions.

- One half of "thirteen" is "thir."
- One half of "1-3" is "1."
- Cutting XIII horizontally through the middle gives VIII.

Can you think of others? The key here is to keep looking, even after you have found a solution![3] Several thinking strategies seem common to creative geniuses in all walks of life (see Figure 4.1).

A common stereotype is that creative persons are eccentric. While this may not always be the case, creative individuals do announce themselves by leaving a lifetime trail of creative accomplishments. They are creative as children and never become uncreative. This is the bottom line for us, since people being considered for new product team assignments can be evaluated on their past. People without a lifetime trail usually blame unfamiliar environments, overpowering bosses, limited opportunities, and the like.

Creativity can be measured using the standard MBTI® (Myers-Briggs Type Indicator) Creativity Index. This index is based on the MBTI personality measurement instrument, used to assess individuals on four personality scales (intuitive-sensory, perceiving-judging, extraverted-introverted, and thinking-feeling). The MBTI Creativity Index uses an individual's personality scores to assess his or her creativity: Creative types tend to be more intuitive, perceiving, extraverted, and thinking than other individuals.[4] More recent studies of new product development personnel found that those with high MBTI Creativity Index scores did more new

[2]Harry W. Coover, "Discovery of Superglue Shows Power of Pursuing the Unexplained," *Research-Technology Management,* September–October 2000, pp. 36–39.
[3]Michael Michalko, "Thinking Like a Genius," *The Futurist,* May 1998, pp. 21–25. For dozens of problems of this type, try thinks.com/brainteasers. Good luck finding creative solutions!
[4]Avril Thorne and Harrison Gough, *Portraits of Type: An MBTI Research Compendium* (Palo Alto, CA: Consulting Psychologists Press, 1991).

FIGURE 4.1 Genius Thinking Strategies

1. Geniuses find many different ways to look at a problem. Einstein, for example, and da Vinci, were well known for looking at their problems from many different perspectives.

2. Geniuses make their thoughts visible. Da Vinci's famous sketches, and Galileo's diagrams of the planets, allowed them to display information visibly rather than relying strictly on mathematical analysis.

3. Geniuses produce. Thomas Edison had a quota of one invention every 10 days. Mozart was among the most prolific composers over his short life.

4. Geniuses make novel combinations. Einstein found the relationship between energy, mass, and the speed of light (the equation $E = mc^2$).

5. Geniuses force relationships. They can make connections where others cannot. Kekule dreamed of a snake biting its tail, immediately suggesting to him that the shape of the molecule he was studying (benzene) was circular.

6. Geniuses think in opposites. This will often suggest a new point of view. Physicist Neils Bohr conceived of light as being both a wave and a particle.

7. Geniuses think metaphorically. Bell thought of a membrane moving steel, and its similarity to the construction of the ear; this led to the development of the telephone earpiece.

8. Geniuses prepare themselves for chance. Fleming was not the first to see mold forming on a culture, but was the first to investigate the mold, which eventually led to the discovery of penicillin.

Source: From Michael Michalko, "Thinking Like a Genius," *The Futurist*, May 1998, pp. 21–25. Originally published in *The Futurist*. Used with permission for the World Future Society, 7910 Woodmont Avenue, Suite 450, Bethesda, Maryland 20814 USA. Telephone: 01-656-8274; www.wfs.org.

product projects and identified new product opportunities that were much more profitable than those identified by other personnel![5] This suggests that choosing the right persons and getting them involved in the new products process in the earliest phases may be just as important as the process itself!

Management's Role in Creativity

Certainly, management has a role in getting the best out of its "ideas people." Some firms, like General Electric, seem to truly embrace new ideas, treating them like corporate initiatives, organizing learning sessions, and importantly, sticking with them—rather than moving on to the "next big thing." This stress on business innovation allows GE to gain advantage over competitors who focus solely on financial results.[6] Recent work on idea generation in large organizations suggests that top managers should keep control over innovative projects, while at the same time allowing the employees to do as much of the work as possible. In short, top

[5]Greg Stevens, James Burley, and Richard Divine, "Creativity + Business Discipline = Higher Profits Faster from New Product Development," *Journal of Product Innovation Management*, 16(5), September 1999, pp. 455–468; and Greg Stevens and James Burley, "Piloting the Rocket of Radical Innovation," *Research-Technology Management*, 46(3), March–April 2003, pp. 16–25.

[6]Thomas H. Davenport and Laurence Prusak with H. James Wilson, *What's the Big Idea? Creating and Capitalizing on the Best Management Thinking* (Cambridge, MA: Harvard Business School Press, 2003).

FIGURE 4.2 Obstacles to idea generation*

Group think: We think we are being creative, when in reality we are only coming up with ideas that our group will find acceptable. Remember that we are not trying to find the "conventional wisdom," but truly original ideas.

Targeting error: We keep going back to the same simple demographic targets (for example, the under-35 or under-50 markets. Great new product opportunities may be missed as a result.

Poor customer knowledge: Despite the money spent on market research by the top firms, the reality is that little is understood about prospective customers. Lavish research spending doesn't guarantee that it was done well.

Complexity: Creative types within organizations, as well as senior management, often think that the more complex the idea, the better it is (or the smarter and more promotable they seem). Complexity, however, is a major barrier to new product adoption (see discussion in Chapter 8).

Lack of empathy: These same managers are also well-educated, high-income individuals accustomed to an upscale lifestyle. They may simply not understand the "typical" customer they are trying to sell to.

Too many cooks: A small new product team works fine, but large companies especially are prone to internal competition for power and influence. This is not a healthy climate for a new product in the earliest phases of development.

*Source: Jerry W. Thomas, "In Tough Times, "Hyper-Creatives" Provide an Advantage," *Visions*, 33(3), October 2009, 24–26.

management must stay involved; and participants who had a hand in the design of the innovation will be more likely to adopt it.[7]

Creative people can benefit from training. Training programs range from introductory classes in traditional brainstorming to elaborate sessions that include games and horseplay. Obvious, but often overlooked, is training in the company's products, its markets, competition, technologies used, and so forth.

Newly born ideas are extremely fragile, quite the opposite of the strong and almost unstoppable concepts that are 80 percent of the way through the process. By then, many ideas have picked up one or more powerful owners. So, if we give these people a hard time, show no appreciation for their ideas, offer no particular encouragement, they simply let the ideas slide by, vowing to "not waste my 'genius babies' on those idiots." Figure 4.2 shows the kind of roadblocks that exist within firms and keep them from generating creative new ideas: not knowing the customer, not being empathetic to customers' needs, preferring ideas that everyone agrees with rather than the truly creative ones, and so on.

John Cleese, formerly of Monty Python, is now a training consultant. He jokes, "No more mistakes and you're through!" This sparks a sense of excitement in creative people, and there's nothing like excitement to get the innovative juices going. Michael Dell, CEO of Dell Computers, says that it is important to keep his employees unafraid of failure, as he believes that innovation involves learning from failure.[8]

Managements therefore have two packages of activity, one designed to encourage the creative function, and the other to remove roadblocks that thwart it.

[7]Davenport *et al.*, 2003, p. 171.
[8]"Inspiring Innovation," op. cit.

Activities to Encourage Creativity

Today's managers recognize that innovators are apt to be different and need special treatment. "Accommodative" is the word. Innovators can't be allowed to violate rules at will, but it's good to recognize individuality, be tolerant of some aberrations, and be supportive under stress. Also, management should allow innovators freedom to associate with others in similar positions. This freedom extends to all functional areas and to outside the firm as well—no locked cells. Management should also permit innovators to help select projects for development, though this is often difficult. Job assignments should be challenging. Creative people don't lack confidence and, in fact, often consider their present assignments a waste of time. This means *they* will determine whether an assignment is worthy—no one can tell them.

Some firms deliberately create competitive teams and have them race to a deadline. Bell & Howell's management once faked the news of an impending competitive breakthrough to urge a scientific group to speed up. Another technique is free time. It runs as high as 20 percent in some firms. The 3M Company is a major follower of this technique (with Post-it notes being one beneficiary). Flextime is a similar tool, but for creative types it means letting employees take work home or stay in their workplaces and work all night if they want.

Surprisingly perhaps, transferring creative personnel also helps. Creative people have a need for novelty and want to change situations occasionally.

Then, of course, we see a wide range of unique techniques developed by individual firms, especially those known for their creative achievements. Texas Instruments, for example, had a program called IDEA (identify, develop, expose, and action). Sixty IDEA representatives throughout TI could dole out funds (without higher approval) for projects proposed by personnel who did not have enough influence to get funds through normal channels. Speak & Spell and Magic Wand were two notable results of such funds. 3M also awards genesis grants of up to $30,000 to fund innovative new projects that don't fit the business structure. Polaroid's SX-70 system began this way too: The project was actually "special experiment number 70," developed outside the normal structure at Polaroid. Sony and Toshiba will give teams a six-month project budget to take a new product concept all the way through development and out to market, on a small scale. This investment not only gives the team development resources, but also allows the firm to establish a technology standard and identify the early adopters in the market.[9]

The 3M Company has a long history of innovation, so it is not surprising that a chairman once said: "We do expect mistakes as a normal part of running a business, but we expect our mistakes to have originality."[10] One very creative product design firm, IDEO of Palo Alto, California, takes several specific steps to create a culture of creativity and innovation. They seek out individuals who love product design, set up offices in cities like Chicago, San Francisco, Boston, and Tokyo that attract creative types, and permit employees to swap positions and locations

[9]Karen Anne Zien and Sheldon A. Buckler, "From Experience: Dreams to Market: Crafting a Culture of Innovation," *Journal of Product Innovation Management*, 14(4), 1997, pp. 274–287.
[10]L. W. Lehr, "The Role of Top Management," *Research Management*, November 1979, pp. 23–25.

frequently. To generate ideas, IDEO designers take objects apart and may visit places like airplane junkyards or the Barbie Hall of Fame. They collect assorted parts and pieces of items in Tech Boxes and index all pieces on the company intranet. Tech Box curators conduct weekly conference calls.[11]

Creative firms often use a computerized database, or "idea bank," to store and document ideas from earlier, unused new product projects for reuse later. These ideas can come from market research or test market results, project audits, design plans, engineering notes, and elsewhere. To help transfer information, managers that worked on the earlier project can be assigned to the project where the idea might be reused.[12] Guinness Breweries, for one, periodically reviews its idea bank, viewing it as an important component of the concept generation phase of its new products process. Oce, a computer peripheral manufacturer, calls this database their "refrigerator of ideas."[13] In general, creative operations should be in areas conducive to exchange of ideas; office arrangements should make people comfortable; and distractions should be held to a minimum. The offices of the Internet start-up factory Idealab!, and also IDEO, are laid out such that employees can hear each other's problems and interact with each other as much as possible.[14]

These firms actively encourage creativity among their employees and get the desired results. Design Continuum, for example, had to design a new pulsed lavage (a product that cleans wounds with saline solution); battery-powered squirt guns were the inspiration. This firm also created a new kitchen faucet design after considering valves used in toys, cars, and medical products. Earlier, Design Continuum had been responsible for the Reebok Pump shoe, having applied ideas from inflatable splints, intravenous bags, and diagnostic valves.[15]

Another highly creative firm, Qualcomm, uses an *innovation engine* technique to generate ideas. Senior managers carefully select employees who have proven to be highly creative and innovative, and form several groups of twelve. Each individual receives a homework assignment, which is to prepare six ideas they think Qualcomm should be working on. The groups are sent to offsite brainstorming sessions, where they discuss and extend the ideas brought in by each individual, the goal being to identify new, big ideas (not incremental new products). Each member receives an allocation of "Qualcomm Bucks," which they can invest in what they think is the best new idea. This procedure might generate about twelve good new ideas, which are then narrowed down in successive rounds to about four. Qualcomm can turn these four "Big Bang" ideas into products within about

[11]Andrew Hargadon and Robert L. Sutton, "Building an Innovation Factory," *Harvard Business Review*, May–June 2000, pp. 157–166.
[12]Sarah J. Marsh and Gregory N. Stock, "Building Dynamic Capabilities in New Product Development through Intertemporal Integration," *Journal of Product Innovation Management*, 20(2), March 2003, pp. 136–148.
[13]Robert G. Cooper, Scott J. Edgett, and Elko J. Kleinschmidt, "Optimizing the Stage-Gate System: What Best-Practices Companies Do—I," *Research-Technology Management*, September–October 2002, pp. 21–27; and Tekla S. Perry, "Designing a Culture for Creativity," *Research-Technology Management*, March–April 1995, pp. 14–17, and Zien and Buckler, op. cit.
[14]Hargadon and Sutton, op. cit.
[15]Hargadon and Sutton, op. cit.

three months. One of the more prominent Big Bang ideas: Flo TV, a service by which owners of iPhones and similar devices can watch TV, for a modest monthly fee, without experiencing the poor video quality and slow download times usually encountered with this kind of service.[16]

Special Rewards

There is no question about the value of recognizing creative achievement. But creative people are usually unimpressed by *group* rewards. They believe group contributions are never equal, especially if the group is company employees, for many of whom creatives have great disdain. This is unfair; large portions of successful creativity are now set in groups, and we know more now about how to make group judgments work. But creatives do like personal accolades—preferably immediately. The famous Thomas Watson of IBM commonly carried spare cash in his pockets so he could reward persons with good ideas when he heard them. Campbell Soup has Presidential Awards for Excellence. Many firms have annual dinners to recognize employees who obtained patents during the year. At IDEO, there are no organization charts or job titles: Parties and trophies, rather than job promotions, are the rewards for a job well done. In one of the most dramatic reward systems, Toyota and Honda have their champions follow the new product out the door and take over its ongoing management.[17]

The Removal of Roadblocks

As seen in Figure 4.2, some organizations set up roadblocks, perhaps unintentionally, that stop new product concept creativity. Managers will say that the concept "simply won't work," or "it's against policy," or "we don't do things that way." These statements are often well intentioned, and they may be accurate statements of status quo. But they are extremely discouraging to fragile ideas, and only conscious effort by managers can help scare them away.

Some organizations use a technique called **itemized response.** All client trainees must practice it personally. When an idea comes up, listeners must first cite all its advantages. Then they can address the negatives, but only in a positive mode. The recommended language for bringing up a negative is "OK. Now—let's see what would be the best way to overcome such-and-such a problem." Note that this constructive comment assumes the problem can be overcome, and the listener offers to help. To encourage creativity, some firms deliberately encourage conflict by putting certain employees together on the same team—for example, a blue-sky creative person and a practical type. This technique is sometimes called *creative abrasion.*[18]

The bottom line here is that managers need to be aware of the barriers to group creativity. New product teams are, by definition, cross-functional, which means

[16]The Flo TV example is documented from several news articles on the Qualcomm Web site, qualcomm.com.
[17]These ideas, and many more, are discussed in Tekla Perry, "Designing a Culture for Creativity," op. cit.
[18]James Krohe, Jr., "Managing Creativity," *Across the Board*, September 1996, pp. 16–22.

FIGURE 4.3 **Barriers to Firm Creativity**

1. *Cross-functional diversity.* A diverse team means a wide variety of perspectives and more creative stimulation, but also can lead to difficulties in problem solving and information overload.

2. *Allegiance to functional areas.* The team members need to have a sense of belonging and to feel they have a stake in the team's success. Without this, they will be loyal to their functional area, not to the team.

3. *Social cohesion.* Perhaps a little unexpectedly, if the interpersonal ties between team members are too strong, candid debate might be replaced by friendly agreement, resulting in less innovative ideas.

4. *The role of top management.* If senior management stresses continuous improvement, the team might stick with familiar product development strategies and make only incremental changes. Top management should encourage the team to be adventurous and try newer ideas.

Source: Reprinted by permission of *Harvard Business Review*. Exhibit from "How to Kill a Team's Creativity," by Rajesh Sethi, Daniel C. Smith, and C. Whan Park, August 2002. Copyright © 2002 by the Harvard Business School Publishing Corporation; All rights reserved.

a greater variety of perspectives but also potential difficulties in reaching a solution acceptable to all. Further, if the team members share strong interpersonal ties, the creative abrasion might be lacking: Team members may simply reach friendly agreements. Figure 4.3 describes these and other barriers to overcome in stimulating group creativity.

The Product Concept

Given creative and exciting people, just what is it we want them to produce? What is this thing called concept? How does it differ from a new product? When does it come about?

Let's start with the end point, the successful marketing of a new product, and back up. A new product only really comes into being when it is *successful*—that is, when it meets the goals/objectives assigned to the project in the PIC.

When launched, it is still in tentative form, because changes are quite apt to be necessary to make it successful. Therefore we say it is still a concept, an idea that is not fulfilled.

Back before technical work was finished, the product was even more of a concept. To understand this and see how it relates to the ideation process, we have to look at the three inputs required by the creation process.

- **Form:** This is the physical thing created, or in the case of a service, it is the sequence of steps by which the service will be created. Thus with a new steel alloy, form is the actual bar or rod of material. On a new mobile phone service it includes the hardware, software, people, procedures, and so on, by which calls are made and received.

- **Technology:** This is the source by which the form was attained. Thus for the steel alloy it included, among others, the steel and other chemicals used for the alloy, the science of metallurgy, product forming machines, cutting machines, and more. Technology is defined in product innovation as the power to do work, as you will recall from Chapter 3. In most cases there is one clear technology that is at the base of the innovation, the one that served as the technical dimension of the focus-arena. Sometimes there are two.

- **Need/Benefit:** The product has value only as it provides some benefit to the customer that the customer sees a need or desire for.

We put these together this way: *Technology permits us to develop a form that provides the benefit.* If any of those three is missing, there cannot be product innovation, unless one buys a product ready-made and resells it without change. Even then, there would be some change in the service dimension—where it is sold, how it is serviced, and so on. Even clone makers add value, if nothing more than price; we even hear computer buffs say something like: "XYZ makes better clones than PDQ does!"

Oddly, the innovation process can start with any one of the three dimensions and can vary in what happens second (see Figure 4.4). Here are the primary ways (which we will illustrate with the Designer Decaf example later in this chapter):

Customer has a NEED, which a firm finds out about. It calls on its TECHNOLOGY to produce a FORM that is then sold to the customer. A firm has a TECHNOLOGY that it matches with a given market group, and then finds out a NEED that group has, which is then met by a particular FORM of product.

A firm envisions a FORM of a product, which is then created by use of a TECHNOLOGY and then given to customers to see if it has any BENEFIT.

Any of the three can start the process, and in each case either of the other two can come second. Now, you may say, so what is the difference? The difference is too often that between success and failure. Putting benefit last is very risky, since it comprises a solution trying to find a problem. DuPont, for example, spent several years finding applications where Kevlar could yield a profitable benefit.

Apple's experience with the Newton Message Pad personal digital assistant shows the risk firms take when they put benefits last. Technology developed by Apple's R&D department allowed a user to enter handwritten inputs, eliminating the keyboard. From this technology, a form was conceived: a pen-based, digitized notepad designed to capture and process ideas and data. Apple didn't check with customers, however, to see if this form actually satisfied customer needs or addressed customer problems. Customers were apparently satisfied with the tried-and-true ways of capturing ideas and data: pen and paper, sticky notes, calendars, and electronic address books. The fact that it retailed at about $800, and that handwriting recognition did not work flawlessly, did not help Newton's case either. The Newton never sold well.[19]

Therefore we often put benefit first. Incidentally, even technology-driven scientists actually put benefit first in most cases because they have some idea of need that is leading them in their efforts. For example, a pharmaceutical chemist seeking a new compound for lowering blood pressure knows how widespread that problem is. Given the benefit, preferences vary. Some people like to visualize what type of finished product could meet the need, and then design that form. Others like to give technical people the basic benefit(s) and let them use their available technologies

[19]Abbie Griffin, "Obtaining Customer Needs for Product Development," in *The PDMA Handbook of New Product Development*, M. Rosenau, A. Griffin, G. Castellion, and N. Anscheutz, eds. (New York: John Wiley, 1996), pp. 153–166.

FIGURE 4.4
The New Product Concept

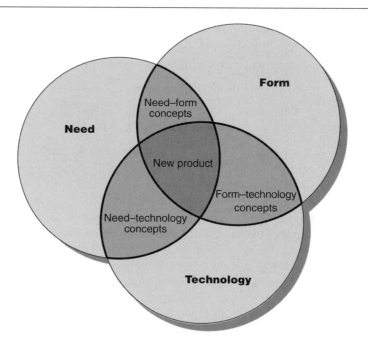

Concept: "A far better way of meeting the learning needs of computer users is to utilize modem-based online systems to let them see training videos on the leading software packages." (This has a well-known need/benefit and stipulates the several technologies that will be used; but exactly how this service will function is still to be worked out.)

Another way of stating this concept would be: "XYZ Corporation has a national telecommunications network in place, and also owns a chain of video rental stores. Surely there is some way we can use these capabilities to help meet the training needs of home-based computer users." Again, this offers the market need and the technologies; it still lacks method/process, which is the service product's equivalent of form. (Note how close a new product concept can come to sounding like the focus/arena of a product innovation charter.)

Here are two statements that may sound like new product concepts, but clearly aren't. In each case, to be worked-out concepts, another piece of the puzzle must be added.

"Let's create a new way of solving the in-home training/educational needs of personal computer users." (Need, but no form and no technology. Just a wish, like a cure for cancer.)

"I think we ought to develop a line of instructional videos." (No specific market need/benefit, and no form—just a technology.)

without restraint on form. This book follows the latter. Granting that in practice, all versions exist, and no one would throw out a good idea just because it came up in the wrong way, the fact remains that we are speaking about management. If one wants to design the best way to go about product innovation, then, in general, the best way is to have first the benefit, then the technology, and then the finished form.

Think about toilet brushes for a moment. Old-fashioned brushes do the job, but one could imagine someone (a thoughtful customer, perhaps, or a research chemist at a detergent company) having the idea that a new, improved brush that somehow makes toilet cleaning easier would be a big seller. Note that we said "idea" here and not "concept" as all we have so far is a need: a new brush that offers convenience. What does that mean? Longer handle? Disposable bristles? Probably not. How about a brush that contains detergent, which is refillable and easy for the customer to attach to the brush? Now we have something resembling a simple product concept, as we have a need (convenient brush) based on use of a technology (detergent suitable for toilet scrubbing). Apparently at least three companies hit upon that concept at about the same time a few years back. But these companies developed and launched products whose forms are very different. Reckitt Benckiser produced the Lysol Ready Brush: An aerosol can of cleanser is mounted into the brush. The can is replaced when empty; the brush is not disposable. SC Johnson's entry is the Scrubbing Bubbles Fresh Brush: Here, a disposable pad containing Scrubbing Bubbles cleaner is attached to the end of the brush. The Clorox Toilet Wand is much like the Fresh Brush, but with a round, disposable sponge instead of a pad. Think of this as a kind of translation process: In each case, the idea was developed into a concept, but the concept was translated three different ways, resulting in three different products (that offer pretty much the same benefit to customers). Which of these will do the best in the marketplace? Probably the one that offers the greatest benefit to customers? (Which do you think that would be?)

Chapter 5 will deal with how we go to customers and find out what their problems are. In Chapter 10 we will talk about a form of product description (called a protocol) that is written out prior to undertaking technical development; the description is primarily benefits. Features (form) are put into it only if they seem absolutely essential (e.g., required by law).

Let's put this all into a simple case, and maybe the issues will become clearer.

The Designer Decaf Example

Many years ago, coffee was, well, coffee. One went to one's favorite restaurant, diner, or food truck in the morning or at lunch and ordered an inexpensive "regular." Typically, coffee sold in North America contained a blend of cheaper coffee beans, and that was that. With the emergence of Starbucks and competitors, the North American coffee-drinking culture changed abruptly. Fancy coffee bars, based on the Italian coffee bar model, sprang up everywhere, and Italian-style espresso soared in popularity. Espresso-based concoctions like cappuccinos and lattes, often selling for three to four times the price of restaurant coffee, became big sellers overnight. Let's imagine we worked at a major coffee roasting company at about this time. Imagine also three different people walked into the new product office one week, at different times, each with an idea for a new product. Each was unaware the others were coming in.

One person said, "Our most recent customer satisfaction report disclosed that customers would like a decaffeinated espresso coffee that tastes identical to regular espresso and can deliver a full-flavored cappuccino. No current decafs offer this *benefit*." The second person was a product manager who said, "I was thinking last week about our coffees and our competitors, and noticed they were all about the same color and thickness. I wonder if we could mass-produce a darker espresso that actually pours out thicker, something like Turkish coffee" (*form*).

The third person was a scientist who had just returned from a technical forum and said, "I heard discussion of a new chemical extraction process that can isolate and separate chemicals from foods cheaply and effectively; maybe it could be applied to taking caffeine out of coffee" (*technology*).

Each of these people had a germ of an idea, but as a concept each suggestion wasn't really very useful. The first person had something on a par with a cancer cure—benefit, but no way to supply it. The product manager had no idea whether consumers would like darker, thicker espresso or how it might be made. The scientist didn't know whether the technology would work on coffee or even whether consumers wanted a change.

A new product concept would result if the first person met with either the second or the third. If the second, they would ask the lab for a technology that would produce the sought form and benefit. If the third, they would undertake lab work to find the exact form of the new technology (for example, should all or only some of the caffeine be extracted; if darker or thicker in appearance, how dark or thick). What might best sum up the point that a concept is evolving from its creation until it metamorphoses into a new product is the saying of one manager: "Don't waste your time trying to find a *great* new product idea; it's our job to take a rather ordinary idea and *make it* into a successful new product."

The Concept Statement

Ideas, concepts, new products, and so on are all words in common use. But, as in all disciplines, we have to clarify them for understanding. Medical books draw a sharp distinction between common cold, sinusitis, upper respiratory infection, and so on, even though as patients, we don't care.

Figure 4.4 showed that any two of the three (form, benefit, technology) can come together to make a concept, a potential product. All three together produce a new product that may or may not be successful. Often, there is little difference. For example, inventors frequently call on companies with a prototype in hand. This is a concept that is virtually finished—it has form, based on a technology, and you can be sure the inventor knows a benefit it provides. Of course, firms know from experience that the inventor usually overstates the benefit; the technology will have drawbacks that make it impractical to use in a plant; and the form is very tentative based primarily on tools and space in a crude workshop.

At the other extreme the very first thought about a new product may be so incomplete that nothing can be done with it as is. For example, the scientist returning from the technical forum had only capability—nothing that had value to anyone in the coffee roasting company.

Once a concept appears, with two of the three dimensions (technology, form, benefit), we have to screen it before undertaking development. That part of the process comes in Chapter 9, and it requires what we call a **product concept statement.** Technical people and intended customers must tell us the concept is worthy of development. Their review of the concept statement allows this, *if* the concept tells them what they need to know to make that judgment. A concept statement will usually do this if it has two of the three basic essentials (technology, form, benefit).

If you were asked, "How would you like zero calorie ice cream?" you could not really answer. You probably already find yourself thinking, what will it taste like, what is it made of, what's the catch? To do concept testing, we need a concept statement that meets these information needs. It would be a waste of time to ask taxi company owners whether they would like a cab with a 10-cents-per-mile operating cost. They might say sure, but that answer would change quickly if told we planned to use Caterpillar tractor technology.

Sometimes the technology will tell us something useful about the concept: a flashlight that burns 10 times as bright because it uses arc-welding technology. Or a light based on fiber-optics technology that comes wound on a wooden spool of the size used for thread. Or a flashlight that uses a pyramidal reflector rather than a conical one. Each of these statements offers more or less information and permits you to get better or worse reactions.

A concept, then, is *a verbal and/or prototype expression that tells what is going to be changed and how the customer stands to gain (and lose)*. Early on, the information is quite incomplete, but when marketed the concept is (hopefully) complete. Anything that doesn't communicate gain and loss to the intended buyer is still just an idea that needs work.

An interesting demonstration of the three-facet concept source came when Eddy Goldfarb, a famous toy inventor, was asked how he did it. He replied, "Notice what things your child plays with, and try to spot what's lacking." He also said he likes to look for new processes and materials and "for holes—you know, a lack of a certain item on the market." These statements cite benefit, technology, and form, in that order.[20]

The importance of these three dimensions varies by industry. In most industries, one of the three often needs no attention because of general knowledge within the industry. Pharmaceutical new products people do not have to check out the desirability of stopping body fluid buildup, or of eliminating cancer. Furthermore, pharmaceutical expertise is available to manufacture virtually any new drug, so technology is the only unknown and thus the focus of attention. On the other hand, the leading food companies presume the kitchens and factory can put together anything the customer wants, so benefit (ascertained through taste tests, for example) becomes the prime variable. In the automobile industry, car manufacturers so dominate the new products process that components suppliers are told what benefit is wanted and then work with either technology or form for its innovation.

In these three different industry situations, discussion with new products people quickly indicates the critical avenue of innovation for *their* firm or industry. And the distinctions are not moot—they provide the direction for the idea stimulation process. Still, it takes all three. If a project aborts, it may be the fault of the department with the easy task. For example, a television manufacturer's marketing research may show that consumers want a television set that will increase in volume as room noise picks up and decrease in volume as room noise subsides. This research engenders the idea for the new product, so the process would be demand-induced. But, in reality, the technical side of the business has the toughest task.

The reverse of this can happen as well. Not long ago, a small Michigan firm attempted to find markets for a new development in reticulated vitreous carbon. The situation was clearly one where technology provided the breakthrough; but,

[20]Fran Carpentier, "Can You Invent a Toy?" *Parade*, December 1981, pp. 14–15.

again ironically, the pressure was on marketing to find applications to yield adequate volume for a profit. It couldn't, and the firm folded.

Two Basic Approaches

Now, given some agreement on language, we can go back to the original question: How should we go about generating new product concepts? The diagram given in the figure at the start of Part II showed five routes—technology, end user, team, other insiders, and other outsiders. Two of these involve receiving product ideas created by others, and three of them involve a managed process run by the team. This distinction is the one that makes a managerial difference, and it is the one we will use in this book. Like getting a new garment; we can buy one ready-made or make it ourselves. Here we will discuss the ready-made source, and in Chapters 5 through 7 doing it ourselves.

Of course, most firms use both ready-made and tailored. But in each industry it is common knowledge as to which has a better batting average. For example, food manufacturers usually will not even read new product suggestions sent in by consumers. They have more than enough concepts of their own; consumer suggestions are very repetitive or old ideas; and even just glancing at hundreds of thousands of ideas every year would be almost impossible.

Yet, in some other industries (e.g., toys and tools) inventors thrive. There are even inventors' fairs, where inventors are invited to display their creations. Haystack Toys Inc. periodically holds a Great American Toy Hunt, inviting toy inventors from all over the United States to present their prototype products. Each inventor gets 15 minutes to present his or her product before Haystack judges. About 100 make the final judging round, and of these, Haystack will select at most 10 to develop and market. Dan Lauer, cofounder of Haystack, believes that the biggest toy companies overlook the best and most innovative toy ideas, preferring to extend well-entrenched brands (like Barbie) or to get movie licensing rights. In fact, most big toymakers will routinely turn down walk-in-the-door ideas regardless of their potential value. Says Lauer of his experiences trying to sell one of his toy ideas (novel, fun tub toys) to the big companies, "I had to start a company to make what I want."[21]

Some manufacturers have employee and customer idea contests. Even in the food industry, one firm (Pillsbury) has found it profitable to run an annual Bake-Off Contest to capture thousands of new recipes for their possible use. Nordic-Track had outstanding success relying almost entirely on ideas from inventors; they have no internal R&D. Alan Klingerman, head of AkPharma Inc., seems to have a knack for thinking up products that give people relief, having developed both Lactaid (lactose-reduced milk) and Beano antiflatulence pills, the success of which he attributes partly to the humorous-sounding name. Both Lactaid and Beano were eventually sold to big drug companies. Each also resulted in at least one spinoff product: CatSip (lactose-reduced milk for cats) and CurTail (a kind of Beano for dogs). Klingerman claims to always have other products in development and keeps file drawers full of what he calls "ideas and stuff."[22]

[21]Samuel Fromartz, "Creation Theory," *Inc.*, March 2000, pp. 86–103.
[22]Robert Zausner, "An Inside Job," *Philadelphia Inquirer Magazine*, February 25, 2001, pp. 16–25.

One thing we know for sure, concept generation should be an *active*, not *reactive* process. This is no time to be thinking like the Maytag repairman, waiting for something to happen.

Important Sources of Ready-Made New Product Ideas

Experience in the field of product innovation has it that 40 to 50 percent of new product ideas are ready-made, coming at least partially from employees, suppliers, end users and other stakeholders, and published information. (See Figure 4.5.) More recent additions to the list are consulting engineering firms and smaller firms with expertise in idea exploration. Among the latter are small biotech companies that have the expertise to do early-stage pharmaceutical research, but lack the

FIGURE 4.5
Sources of Ready-Made New Product Concepts

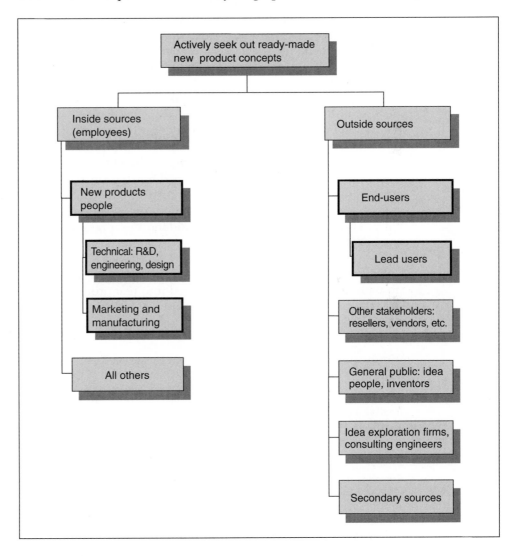

resources and skills to carry out extensive development, testing, or commercialization. Large pharmaceutical firms turn to these biotech companies as a rich source of new product ideas. The product design firm IDEO discussed earlier often plays this "reconnaissance" role for larger firms in other industries seeking market or technological opportunities.[23]

Many organizations have evolved ways (seminars, visits to customers' plants, and so on) to more systematically involve user groups because these groups have been so productive. ARCO actually ran full-page *Wall Street Journal* ads that reproduced good suggestions sent in by the public and encouraged more.

Appendix A lists and discusses the most common sources of ideas already created. They are many, diverse, and of varying quality. However, one of those sources deserves special attention—the end user (customer or consumer). People who use a product often have ideas for improving it, but unfortunately, their ideas are sometimes rather obvious. Black & Decker reportedly received over a thousand suggestions for a new product that would be a DustBuster–type bug catcher.

Sometimes, the ideas can be unexpected and insightful. Reportedly, when designing the Fiat 500 for relaunch in 2005, Fiat invited potential customers to suggest design ideas via the Web site fiat500.com. Many of these suggestions (colors, rally stripes, decals, wheel covers, and the like) found their way onto the Web site's car configurator (the design-your-own link on the Fiat 500 Web site), which boasts 500,000 different possible combinations. Similarly, Dell's Idea Storm initiative encouraged customers to submit ideas for new products and improvements to existing products online. Over 10,000 ideas were obtained from sources around the world.[24] The term that is sometimes used for this kind of open idea solicitation is **crowdsourcing**.[25] It was reported that Apple made use of crowdsourcing in generating ideas for the iPad. Apple monitored reviews and blogs and also obtained voice of the customer data to understand the most pressing needs of potential users, not just of the iPad tablet itself but also of related devices such as the iPhone.[26]

Even if new, most consumer users' concepts are for product improvements rather than new-to-the-world products. Also, the typical user is less likely to come up with ideas that are easily developed into real products: Product development professionals (or more experienced users) will have a more realistic view of what is and is not feasible.[27] The role of the end user also depends on the industry. For

---

[23]For a discussion of consulting engineering firms, see Ian Alam, "Commercial Innovations from Consulting Engineering Firms: An Empirical Exploration of a Novel Source of New Product Ideas," *Journal of Product Innovation Management*, 20(4), July 2003, pp. 300–313; other examples are from Christopher Meyer and Rudy Ruggles, "Search Parties," *Harvard Business Review*, August 2002, pp. 14–15.

[24]See ideastorm.com.

[25]A source on crowdsourcing is Gary P. Pisano and Roberto Verganti, "Which Kind of Collaboration Is Right for You?" *Harvard Business Review*, 86(12), pp. 78–86.

[26]Reena Jana, "Apple iPad Product Development Approach," The Conversation blog, *Harvard Business Review*, January 27, 2010.

[27]Per Kristensson, Anders Gustafsson, and Trevor Archer, "Harnessing the Creative Potential among Users," *Journal of Product Innovation Management*, 21(1), January 2004, pp. 4–14. For an excellent resource on the importance of establishing a dialogue with customers, see C. K. Prahalad and Venkat Ramaswamy, *The Future of Competition: Co-Creating Unique Value with Customers* (Cambridge, MA: Harvard Business School, 2004).

example, manufacturers of scientific instruments and plant process equipment report the *majority* of their successful new products came originally from customers. In other industries, such as engineering polymers and chemical additives for plastics, customers provide little or no help.

Lead Users

Many firms seek to elicit new product ideas from their **lead users,** that is, the customers associated with a significant current trend (for example, fiber optics in telecommunications).[28] The lead user firms (or individuals) are at the front edge of the trend, have the best understanding of the problems faced, and expect to gain significantly from solutions to those problems. Although usually fairly easy to identify, they may also be outlanders, or not established members of that trade. And, if they are really leaders, they may think they have already solved their problems. But in an *evolving* trend, their solutions may not hold up; product developers can work with them to anticipate their next problem.

Lead users are especially helpful in giving new product ideas because their work is of the problem-find-solve type, a method stressed in the next chapter. For example, suppose your firm makes snowboards for use by extreme athletes in competitions such as the X-Games. While there are always improvements in equipment for established sports such as football or golf, there are many, many more uncertainties in designing products such as high-performance snowboards. The top athletes are even today still creating new moves and pushing the boundaries of the sport. So what should your next generation of snowboard be like? Shorter? Longer? Lighter? Heavier? Wider? More aerodynamic? More flexible? How would you know, and whom should you ask? It is those very same top athletes who would know—they are your lead users. They probably care little about the appearance of the board, as they are most concerned about improving high-level performance. By partnering with these athletes, your firm would be able to develop radical new snowboards that address these rapidly emerging needs. What is more, these same athletes are also quicker to adopt new products than ordinary users, and are therefore also influential in speeding adoption of your new product in the marketplace.[29]

One issue in lead user analysis is identifying lead users. While this will certainly depend on the product in question, it is possible that the lead users may display key characteristics. In a study of product development in kite surfing, Nikolaus Franke and his coauthors found two characteristics that could identify lead users: high expected benefits and being "ahead of the trend." These characteristics identified people who were more likely to come up with commercially attractive innovations.[30]

[28]The best summaries regarding lead user analysis are Eric von Hippel, *The Sources of Innovation* (New York: Oxford University Press, 1988); and Lee Meadows, "Lead User Research and Trend Mapping," in P. Belliveau, A. Griffin, and S. M. Somermeyer, eds., *The PDMA Toolbook for New Product Development* (New York: John Wiley, 2002), pp. 243–265.

[29]Martin Schreier and Reinhard Prügl, "Extending Lead-User Theory: Antecedents and Consequences of Consumers' Lead Userness," *Journal of Product Innovation Management*, 25(4), 2008, pp. 331–346.

[30]Nikolaus Franke, Eric von Hippel, and Martin Schreier, "Finding Commercially Attractive User Innovations: A Test of Lead-User Theory," *Journal of Product Innovation Management*, 23(4), July 2006, pp. 301–315.

Regardless of whether the firm turns to typical end users or lead users, one important principle is to ask customers for *outcomes*—that is, what it is they would like the product, or service, to *do for them*. Too often, product developers ask customers what product improvements they *want*. Note the difference: Customers said they wanted low-fat fast food, low-salt canned soup, and nicotine-free cigarettes, but didn't buy them! One product expert, Anthony Ulwick, suggested that product developers be "informed" by customers. As an illustration, he notes that Kawasaki, seeking to improve its original Jet Skis, asked current Jet Ski customers what they wanted. Most suggested adding padding, or some other features that would make it more comfortable for the standing rider. No one suggested adding a seat, which of course provides the desired outcome (increased comfort). By the time Kawasaki added seats to its Jet Skis, other competitors had already done so, reducing the one-time leader to a "me-too" competitor. Ironic, since Kawasaki could have looked to the motorcycles it produced and got the seat idea![31] For another example, see Figure 4.6.

After a disappointing product launch with Vista, an operating system often described as not user-friendly, Microsoft's goal with the Windows 7 operating system was to "make your PC simpler." Software engineers, working with typical users as well as partner firms, sought to make the new operating system simpler and better than previous ones, offering quick access to programs, greater compatibility, better remote streaming, and several other advantages. During development, Windows 7 was extensively beta-tested with potential users (a subject we will explore in Chapter 15). Many new ideas obtained from typical users were incorporated into the finished product. To emphasize they were listening to their customers, Windows 7 advertising featured typical computer users saying "I'm a PC and Windows 7 was my idea."[32]

One way to determine whether a particular industry can benefit from working directly with users to gather concepts is to ask whether customers are tinkerers. For example, dentists are; so are medical technicians and farmers. In some of these

FIGURE 4.6   **How Cordis Corporation Turned Customer Input on Desired Outcomes into Innovation**

Cordis Corporation was a Florida-based medical device maker looking to improve angioplasty balloons. They carried out a series of interviews with cardiologists, nurses, hospital administrators, and other health professionals to determine what outcomes they wanted in an improved angioplasty product, before, during, and after surgery. The customers interviewed agreed that a major outcome to focus on was "minimizing the recurrence of blockages." The stated outcomes led to the development of the angioplasty stent, which became at the time the fastest-growing medical device in history, generating about $1 billion in revenues in its first year. Other outcomes generated suggested possible market segments: Some physicians highly valued "precision placement of the device," while others wanted "speed in completing the procedure."

Source: Anthony W. Ulwick, "Turn Customer Input into Innovation," *Harvard Business Review,* January–February 2002, pp. 91–98.

[31]Anthony W. Ulwick, "Turn Customer Input into Innovation," *Harvard Business Review*, January–February 2002, pp. 91–98.
[32]Source: Microsoft News Center, www.microsoft.com, Oct. 9, 2009; Windows 7 page on en.wikipedia.org; and other public sources.

industries, the participants not only have good ideas, but have prototypes as well, and may even have undertaken a form of manufacturing by making prototypes for their friends. In fact, some research suggests that it is especially important to turn to end users with a wide diversity of perspectives and experience in order to identify highly innovative product ideas.[33]

Reportedly, Chrysler got the idea for building 32-ounce cup holders into their Ram pickup trucks by observing that many pickup drivers had installed their own large-size cup holders themselves. Sometimes, observing the customer identifies the problem, leaving it to the firm to find a solution. A Chrysler engineer noticed that his wife struggled putting a child's car seat into their minivan. He came up with the idea of integrating car seats into the van's seating system; Chrysler added this feature, which turned out to be extremely popular. Being a customer of your competitors' products as well as your own can also provide insights on customer problems and needs. A company that makes checkout scanner systems has its employees work as checkout clerks a few days a year to get a sense of the product in use and the kind of problems that can crop up. GM requires its employees to rent GM cars when on business—thus passing up an opportunity to compare its cars with the competition in a real use situation.[34]

Many firms now get end-user input for new product ideas by involving end users effectively, from the earliest phases of the new products process, on their new product teams (see Chapter 14). This brings their needs and problems directly onto the table. But there will always be firms where they don't wait to be asked—they go right ahead and prototype their ideas. A new example of this today is the information technology field, especially computers and telecommunications, where end users have become quite sophisticated.

Some manufacturing firms are turning to *toolkits for user innovation*, a method that formally turns the innovation task over, to some extent, to the users themselves.[35] A toolkit is a user-friendly set of design tools that customers can use, together with their understanding of their own needs, to customize a product that would be best suited to them. The toolkit allows for the customer-designed product then to be directly transferred to manufacturing or production. There are many firms that have turned to toolkits of this type, as they find them to be a way to speed up the time required to respond to customer needs, or to minimize the number of iterations required to fully satisfy the customer. These toolkits are also particularly useful when many customers require customized products and/or have been making do with standardized products, especially if the firm's manufacturing processes are set up to do small batches of custom products. Web-based toolkits for customized products are available for many consumer products such as running shoes or personal computers. The newest research in Web-based toolkits finds that novice users

[33]Joseph M. Bonner and Orville C. Walker, Jr., "Selecting Influential Business-to-Business Customers in New Product Development: Relational Embeddedness and Knowledge Heterogeneity Considerations," *Journal of Product Innovation Management*, 21(3), May 2004, pp. 155–169.

[34]The examples from this paragraph are from A. Griffin, "Obtaining Customer Needs for Product Development," op. cit.

[35]Eric von Hippel, "Toolkits for User Innovation," in P. Belliveau, A. Griffin, and S. M. Somermeyer, *The PDMA Toolbook 2 for New Product Development* (New York: John Wiley, 2004).

can benefit from the assistance of other customers. In an experiment involving ski design, skiers were able to design better skis (more preferred, higher purchase intention, and greater willingness to pay) if they were able to examine other skiers' opinions on interim designs and improve on them. We may see more peer-assisted user toolkits in the future.[36] Clearly, a firm could also integrate techniques to be discussed in Chapter 13, such as CAD/CAM or rapid prototyping, into a toolkit.

Figure 4.7 shows how a couple of companies have incorporated user toolkits into their product development processes. Note how both examples show how the manufacturer actually has outsourced product innovation, at least partially, to its customers. A study of customers who actually used toolkits to create new products showed that they were willing to pay substantially more for them.[37] In

FIGURE 4.7 Two Examples of Toolkits for User Innovation*

International Flavors and Fragrances (IFF)

This company makes specialty flavors added into processed foods. Typically, a customer would place a requirement, such as a "meaty flavor to add to a soy product," and IFF starts working. A sample might be shipped back to the customer within a week. The trouble is that the customer firm may not be entirely happy, but finds it difficult to define exactly what it wants (e.g., "make it 'gutsier'"). Several iterations might need to occur between IFF and the customer before the latter is satisfied. This is especially problematic to IFF since customers typically expect they will get it right the first time.

   To respond to this problem, IFF created an Internet-based user toolkit that provides a huge database of flavor profiles as well as design rules used in combining or modifying these. The actual chemical formulations are not provided in the toolkit, of course, in order to protect IFF's intellectual property. The customer firm now can design its own flavor and send it directly to a machine that will make up a sample within a few minutes. The customer can easily make adjustments, using the easy-to-understand customer interface appearing on the computer screen, until the desired flavor is obtained.

3M Telecom Enclosure Division

This 3M division makes enclosures for telecom firms like Verizon, used in mounting external equipment. In the past, a telecom customer firm would give 3M the equipment about to be installed in a customized enclosure, and 3M would design the appropriate enclosure using a CAD program. The customer checks the design, and may at that point rethink the required equipment or some other part of the specification. As in the above example, numerous iterations might occur.

   3M's solution is to provide the customer with a simple-to-use version of its own CAD program. (As above, intellectual property rights are protected by providing customers with only the customer-interface parts of the program.) The customer inputs the required equipment and other specifications, and allows the program to do its work. It can make whatever adjustments are necessary until satisfied, then sends the complete design back to 3M that can then put it right into production.

*Examples are taken from Eric von Hippel, "Toolkits for User Innovation," in P. Belliveau, A. Griffin, and S.M. Somermeyer, *The PDMA Toolbook 2 for New Product Development,* John Wiley & Sons, Inc., 2004. Reprinted with permission of John Wiley & Sons, Inc.

[36]Nikolaus Franke, Peter Keinz, and Martin Schreier, "Complementing Mass Customization Toolkits with User Communities: How Peer Input Improves Customer Self-Design," *Journal of Product Innovation Management*, 25(6), 2008, pp. 546–559.

[37]Nikolaus Franke and Frank Piller, "Value Creation by Toolkits for User Innovation and Design: The Case of the Watch Market," *Journal of Product Innovation Management,* 21(6), November 2004, pp. 401–415.

another study, increased costs of customer support associated with user toolkit use were shown to be partially offset by encouraging interaction and support among the users, with the result that the learning from the toolkit is enhanced.[38] Taken together, these studies suggest that using even simple toolkits to get customer design input can create much value for the firm.

Open Innovation[39]

One of the most exciting new developments in new product development is the adoption by many firms of an *open innovation* policy. Open innovation has been defined as "the process a company employs to externally search for . . . research, innovation, new technologies, and products."[40] The first advocate of open innovation was Henry Chesbrough, who viewed it as a new paradigm for innovation in which the firm makes a strategic commitment to use the knowledge in the external environment to improve innovation performance. Open innovation has, in fact, been described as the dominant model of innovation for the twenty-first century.[41]

For years, firms have sought to externally acquire technologies that they lack, but on an as-needed basis. Outsourcing is common, for example, in the pharmaceutical industry, where top firms such as Eli Lilly and GlaxoSmithKline outsource a substantial amount of their new product research due to the enormous costs involved in new drug product discovery, development, regulatory approval, and launch.[42] Under an open innovation policy, firms start with the understanding that much, if not most, of the knowledge they could use resides outside the firm (that is, "not all the smart people work for us"). They systematically and intentionally set out to acquire knowledge from external resources to complement their own internal resources and accelerate innovation. Accessing this innovative pool is critical, even more so as global competition heats up. The result, ultimately, is improved joint value for all partners. And open innovation does not stop with inflows of knowledge. Inevitably, a firm will have invested in innovations that they ultimately don't use: They may no longer fit their business model, for example. With an open innovation policy, a firm could spin off this innovation (sell outright to a willing buyer), offer it under license, form a joint venture with a partner, or otherwise profit from it.[43]

[38]Lars Bo Jeppesen, "User Toolkits for Innovation: Consumers Support Each Other," *Journal of Product Innovation Management*, 22(4), July 2005, pp. 347–362.
[39]Much of this section was derived from Henry Chesbrough, *Open Innovation: The New Imperative for Creating and Profiting from Technology* (Boston, MA: Harvard Business School Press, 2003); Henry Chesbrough, "Why Companies Should Have Open Business Models," *Sloan Management Review*, 48(2), Winter 2007; and Henry Chesbrough and Melissa M. Appleyard, "Open Innovation and Strategy," *California Management Review*, 50(1), Fall 2007.
[40]R. M. (Skip) Davis, "How to Make Open Innovation Work in Your Company," *Visions*, January 2006, pp. 10–13
[41]Larry Huston and Nabil Sakkab, "Connect and Develop: Inside Procter & Gamble's New Model for Innovation," *Harvard Business Review*, March 2006, pp. 58–66.
[42]Roger J. Calantone and Michael A. Stanko, "Drivers of Outsourced Innovation: An Exploratory Study," *Journal of Product Innovation Management*, 24(3), pp. 230–241.
[43]Michael Docherty, "Primer on 'Open Innovation,' Principles, and Practice," *Visions*, April 2006, pp. 13–17

Open innovation does not mean that the firm outsources its R&D. Rather, the firm's goal is to reach out beyond its familiar research partners and to access R&D carried out globally, so that it will complement the knowhow it develops internally. By partnering with an outside firm, the innovating firm leverages and supports its *own* R&D and product development staff. In a sense, intellectual property (IP) in open innovation is like building blocks that allow the firm to build and execute its business model. A firm can acquire IP from a partner if it supports its business model; and it can profit from an unused IP building block if another firm has a use for it. Aside from these obvious leverage advantages, the firm benefits in other ways: It has a much larger pool of innovative ideas from which to draw; it speeds up its new products process by linking with partners that have required technology; and it obtains access to its partner's IP with lower risk.

A key to making open innovation work is to select the best partner or partners. Some researchers have suggested that the innovating firm evaluate prospective partners in terms of their technological, strategic, and relational characteristics. A high level of trust between the partners is also critical to success.[44]

Open innovation is seen as a valuable counterpoint to more traditional closed innovation models. The closed innovation model allows for inputs to come from internal sources (marketing or strategic planning inputs) as well as external ones (such as customer inputs or market information). Under open innovation, firms at the fuzzy front end of product innovation are now no longer looking externally only for inputs such as unmet needs or unsolved problems. Now, inventors, startup companies, or various sources or technology (such as independent, government, or industry labs) are all actively sought out as possible joint venture partners, or as the basis for leveraging internal product development skills. An established firm with commercialized products can also benefit from open innovation by accessing technologies that allow it to more easily move up by emerging product generation.

While open innovation may have originated in high-tech industries, it is increasingly used in lower technology environments. In fact, two of the foremost proponents of open innovation are Procter & Gamble and Kimberly-Clark.[45] In 2000, P&G was going through a rough period: Innovative successes were scarce and stock prices were low. The incoming CEO at that time, A. G. Lafley, felt that the problem was P&G's closed innovation model. He instituted a now-famous open innovation policy known as Connect and Develop, in which no fewer than 50 percent of new initiatives had to include at least one external partner. The results soon emerged: P&G worked with a French partner involved in wound-care R&D to jointly develop Olay Regenerist, an antiwrinkle cream. Pringles Stix originated with an innovation by a Japanese partner firm. P&G licenses the Mr. Clean

[44]Zeynep Emden, Roger J. Calantone, and Cornelia Dröge, "Collaborating for New Product Development: Selecting the Partner with Maximum Potential to Create Value," *Journal of Product Innovation Management*, 22(4), July 2006, pp. 330–341.

[45]The P&G example is drawn from www.pgconnectdevelop.com, and the Kimberly-Clark example from Patrick Clusman and Amy Achter, "How Kimberly-Clark Uses Open Innovation to Enhance NPD Success: Interview with Cheryl Perkins," *Visions*, 30(4), September 2006, pp. 10–11.

FIGURE 4.8 Open Innovation at P&G

The philosophy behind Procter & Gamble's Connect and Develop program is that no one firm, even one with the resources of P&G, holds any more than a fraction of the innovative capacity that could be useful or relevant. Looking outside one's industry for technology is a key component of open innovation. It is less risky for P&G to transfer a technology from a different industry than to develop a new technology from scratch. The environment is constantly sourced for ideas that show some connection to P&G's business lines, then products are developed using this idea. P&G's Magic Eraser cleaning pad, designed to remove dirt and marks from just about any surface, was first noted by P&G in use in Japan; the original idea was sourced from a chemicals company based in Germany. The Mr. Clean scrubbing sponge uses a technology that was originally used as insulation in the auto industry.

Source: Deborah L. Vence, "Just a Variation on a Theme," *Marketing News*, February 1, 2007, pp. 18–20.

trademark to partner firms that make cleaning gloves, mops, and car-cleaning kits. P&G has even founded joint ventures with direct competitors: It provides technology that is used in Clorox's Glad Force Flex bags. Connect and Develop has resulted in over 1,000 active agreements between P&G and external partners. Kimberly-Clark counts universities, entrepreneurial startups, health care companies, and packaged goods manufacturers among its open innovation partners. When forming a relationship with a new partner, Kimberly-Clark begins by carefully considering the partner's strategic fit, vision, mission, and culture to make sure they are choosing the best partner for that situation. Kimberly-Clark also manages a venture capital fund so that it has the option of taking an equity stake in its partner. Among the ideas generated though open innovation at Kimberly-Clark: a free sample of UV sensors, produced by SunHealth Solutions, placed on packages of Huggies Little Swimmers® Swimpants so that parents can monitor the child's exposure to ultraviolet B radiation. Figure 4.8 provides details on two recent P&G innovations.

Another application of open innovation is seen in the pharmaceutical industry. Merck, for example, instituted its Merck Gene Index, in which Merck funded university research on genetic markers. These markers would prove valuable in later pharmaceutical development. Merck published these markers in the Gene Index, accessible to any interested researchers. Why would Merck put the results of its heavily funded research initiative in the public domain? The reason was strategic: Though Merck lost exclusivity to the markers, they also blocked small biotech startups from patenting the markers themselves. Had a small firm patented a marker, it would have kept Merck from being able to develop it further into new, marketable drugs. By creating an open source of inputs (the markers), Merck hoped to capture value downstream in the compounds derived from the markers.

Danish toymaker LEGO implemented an open innovation system to generate ideas from customers. Company management had identified a new robotics building-blocks system as a high-potential new product. Relying on the high brand equity and reputation for reliability and quality associated with its name, LEGO was able to identify and attract knowledgeable lead users and offer them the opportunity to play the role of co-creators of the new robotics offering for little more than the cost of supplying them with early versions of the product. LEGO used inexpensive but effective ways to keep in touch with their lead user community: a closed Web forum, Web sites, and blogs, in which participants could share and improve ideas and even purchase them. The company also invited the participants to tour the actual production facilities, which raised their excitement level and stimulated very positive word-of-mouth. The result: a solid, highly engaged online community that helped LEGO make its robotics system its most successful product ever.[46]

One interesting approach to open innovation is taken by the Dutch electronics company Philips, which created a specialized facility in Singapore known as the InnoHub.[47] This facility provides several realistic environments simulating an apartment, a fashion store, and a hospital ward, as well as office and workshop areas. In these environments, end users, product developers, and other partners work together to develop new ideas for breakthrough innovations. As an example, a mirror display in the fashion store triggered a couple of ideas: shoppers viewing videoclips of products at home via the Internet, then ordering online; or sending images of themselves wearing different outfits to their friends via multimedia messaging. In its first four years, over 4,000 people involved in innovation visited the InnoHub; visitors interact spontaneously to the concepts they see and often generate even more ideas.

Finally, another form of open innovation is the completely online system. One of these is InnoCreative, which describes itself on its Web site as a Web community that exists to match scientists to the research challenges of global firms.[48]

One of the complicated issues a firm must manage in an open innovation policy is intellectual property protection. Without careful partner selection, the firm opens itself up to the possibility that intellectual property could be accidentally disclosed by a partner, or worse, deliberately used illegally or given to competitors. Leading product consultants suggest that it is up to the firm to do its due diligence on prospective partners early and to make sure that all of the legalities are handled correctly, including letters of intent, memoranda of understanding, and detailed contracts.[49] Some general advantages and risks of open innovation are found in Figure 4.9.

Firms such as P&G and Kimberly-Clark that have committed to open innovation have adjusted their new products process accordingly. In short, the new products process must be able to incorporate externally developed ideas, intellectual property, technology, and/or commercialized products. To accomplish this,

[46]Jennifer Dominiquini, "Dispelling the Myths About Product Innovation," at www.prophet .com (undated).

[47]Elke den Ouden, Darren Ee, and Nicky Goh, "The Philips InnoHub—Generating Breakthrough Innovation in an Open Innovation Setting," *Visions*, Vol. 32, No. 1, March 2008, pp. 20–21.

[48]See www.innocentive.com; see also description in Mariann Jelinek, "Open Innovation," in V. K. Narayanan and Gina C. O'Connor (eds.), *Encyclopedia of Technology & Innovation Management* (Chichester, UK: John Wiley, 2010), Chapter 18.

[49]Robert Cooper, "What Leading Companies Are Doing to Reinvent Their NPD Processes," *Visions*, Vol. 32, No. 3, September 2008, pp. 6–10.

FIGURE 4.9   **Advantages and Risks of Open Innovation***

- Importing new ideas multiplies innovation building blocks—ideas and expertise, resulting in more total sales generated from new products.
- Exporting ideas raises cash (IBM gets about $2 billion per year in patent royalties), and improves employee retention, since creative types know that good ideas will be exported and not buried.
- Exporting signals true worth of an innovation. Eli Lilly offers pharmaceutical licenses, but if outsiders don't bite it suggests the value of the new drug is perceived to be low.
- Exporting clarifies core business: Boeing sticks with design and systems integration, and often finds partners for manufacturing.
- Risk: deal is not structured in a way that captures the financial value of your innovation – ask Xerox!
- Proprietary secrets can be lost to a partner, even inadvertently.

Theft of technology, or poaching of top researchers, is a concern.

*Source: Darrell Rigby and Chris Zook (2002), "Open-Market Innovation," *Harvard Business Review*, 80(10), 2002, 80–89; and Mariann Jelinek, "Open Innovation," in V. K. Narayanan and Gina C. O'Connor (eds.), *Encyclopedia of Technology & Innovation Management*, Chichester, UK: John Wiley, 2010, Chapter 18.

changes in the new products process can be made at any or all of the phases. In the concept generation and evaluation phases, these firms actively seek inventors, new startups, entrepreneurial firms, and other possible open innovation partners and assess the potential value of joint product development. During the development phase, firms may be looking for technical assistance from scientists and other individuals outside the firm, or may seek to acquire externally developed innovations or intellectual property that can push the project along. As would be expected, this is also an opportune time for the firm to find a licensee for intellectual property not currently being used. Finally, at the time of launch or commercialization, firms may look to sell or license newly commercialized products if this provides good value, or may acquire products already launched elsewhere to obtain immediate growth potential.[50]

Summary

Chapter 4 has introduced concept generation for new products. First we noted that management has the task of preparing an organization for concept generation. This includes applying the strategic guidance of a product innovation charter, finding and training creative people, and then creating an environment for them to work in where they can be motivated to produce.

Next came a look at the concept itself, what it is, what it isn't, and how it comes into existence. The concept is built around ideas of technology, form, and benefit and is tested by whether it can communicate to an intended buyer what the proposed product is all about and whether it appears useful.

[50]Robert G. Cooper, "Perspective: The Stage-Gate ® Idea-to-Launch Process—Update, What's New, and NexGen Systems," *Journal of Product Innovation Management*, 25(3), May 2008, pp. 213–232.

After noting that there are two broad categories of approaches to getting good new concepts, we explored the one that involves looking for ready-made concepts. Many firms use this approach heavily, and all should make at least some use of it. There are legal problems here, of course, and the chapter concluded by outlining the steps to follow in handling ideas that come from end users, lead users, employees outside the new products loop, and so on.

This prepares us to look at the most difficult, but by far the best method for creating new product concepts: problem-based ideation. This is the subject of Chapter 5.

Applications

1. "Lots of our people try to get good new product ideas from outsiders, but they are careful to keep it legal. I wonder, though, about something I ran into on a trip to Australia last fall. I met what our company people there called a professional espionage agent. He employs a network of flight attendants to gather tidbits of information overheard in the first-class compartments of international flights. And sells this information for over a million dollars a year! I wonder what suggestions I should put in a memo for employees to minimize the chances that our key new product information will be stolen by competitors."

2. "In-house inventors are tough to deal with. Right now we have this PhD in physics, a really great person, bright as they come, and terribly creative. She has had no less than 11 ideas go to market since she joined the firm four years ago. But she feels we don't reward her properly, even though she is on a good salary, shares an annual bonus with all the other persons in research, and even got a special bonus of $5,000 last year. Frankly, I think she will leave us if I don't find some way to let her have an equity position in some of her ideas. What do you think of her argument, and how might I arrange something if I wanted to?"

3. "In these days of intensive ideation, it sure surprised me to read that a man named Reuben Ware, a retired furniture upholstery restorer in Savannah, Georgia, had to reactivate a successful business he had shut down—producing and selling a special formulation of carpet shampoo. Seems that he had invented a formulation that removed almost anything (blood, lipstick, doggie stains, whatever) from your carpets, your laundry, or even your windshield. Sold it for a while, then dropped it. People clamored for it, so Rich's department store bankrolled him for more product. He says he chose the product's name, Aunt Grace's, because he was paying the trademark attorney by the hour, so he accepted the first name that got through. When people ask him about his not being a chemist, he answers, 'Was Edison an electrician?'" Seriously, how in the world, in these days of expensive R&D laboratories, could someone out there come up with a formulation that seems to be better than anything industry can make? And after first marketing his formulation in 1965, how was he able to keep his lead?"

Case: P&G CarpetFlick[51]

In 1999, Procter & Gamble launched the Swiffer, a floor sweeper with a disposable cloth that fits over a rectangular head. The cloth actually trapped dust and thus was a big improvement over regular sweepers and brooms. But one thing the Swiffer could not do was clean a carpeted floor. Since about three-quarters of the floors in U.S. homes are carpeted, this posed a unique challenge and an opportunity for P&G. In late 2003, the company decided to do something about it and set a target launch date of mid-2005.

P&G had a long-standing relationship with IDEO, the Palo Alto, California, design consulting firm. Over the years, IDEO had worked on several "one-off" projects with P&G, such as on the redesign of a toothpaste tube. Recently, the two firms moved closer together with the intention of collaborating on innovative products. By 2003, the collaboration was already showing a promising track record: Pringles Prints (potato chips with trivia questions written on them) and Mr. Clean Magic Reach (a bathroom-cleaning wand with a removable scouring pad). While successful in their own right, these products didn't really break into any new markets. P&G was turning to IDEO for help in the design of a new Swiffer product for use on carpets, which would be the most ambitious joint project so far, but one that potentially opens up a whole new market for P&G.

The P&G chemist assigned to the project was Bob Godfroid, and his first day at IDEO headquarters was an interesting one, to say the least. IDEO had started by visiting homeowners, asking them questions about existing sweepers and taking pictures. They discovered that there was a real need for an effective sweeper that didn't make a lot of noise and could pick up just about anything. Then, in November 2003, IDEO went into "deep dive" mode. About 15 IDEO designers went to the local hardware store and bought all sorts of random items that might be even remotely handy in crpet cleaning. Then they placed several carpets all over their facility and got them as filthy as possible. When Bob walked into the session, he noticed one designer sucking up dirt with a suction gun, while several others were busy trying to pick up dirt by rolling balls of Play-Doh around on it. He observed that the room "looked like a bomb went off.... I don't know if we're going to come out of here with anything other than a bunch of pictures of a trashed room."

On the morning of the second day, Bob took a squeegee blade and scraped a dirty carpet with it. To his surprise, dirt and paper confetti particles popped up in the air, as if they were Tiddly-Winks. He angled the blade differently, and the pieces popped up higher. Someone else thought of suspending a balloon overhead, which trapped the pieces of paper with static electricity. Soon enough, Bob and IDEO's Mike Strasser had built a prototype—a plain box, really, with a slit in the bottom to mimic the action of the squeegee blade—which they immediately named the Shagilator. By the end of the two-day period, IDEO had several crude

---

[51]Information for this case was obtained from Sarah Lacy, "How P&G Conquered Carpet," *BusinessWeek Online*, businessweek.com, September 23, 2005; Beth Belton (ed.), "Lafley on P&G's Gadget 'Evolution,'" *BusinessWeek Online*, businessweek.com, January 28, 2005; and other public sources.

but working prototypes, which used either suction, glue, or scraping to get the dirt up, and the Shagilator was judged to be the best. Bob returned to P&G's Ohio head offices and demonstrated the Shagilator to Gilbert Cloyd, P&G's chief technology officer, by spilling crushed Froot Loops on the carpet and successfully sweeping them up. Impressed, Cloyd wrote out a check for several hundred thousand dollars in seed money to keep the project rolling.

IDEO's "deep dive" model resembled a kind of lickety-stick approach (see discussion in Chapter 3), except it was company designers and engineers, not customers, who were trying out and evaluating the crude prototypes. IDEO employees were trying out all kinds of variations on the box-and-slit idea. Thinking P&G all the way, one even made a Shagilator out of a Pringle's can, crushed and spilled the Pringles, and made the can "eat" them back up! By early 2004, a more refined version of the Shagilator had been designed. IDEO tried another novel touch, a disposable strip that ejected out of the box, but decided against it for manufacturing cost reasons.

By late September 2004, the design was fixed, and the prototype was being beta tested in 350 homes. The beta test households noticed one drawback—the sweeper couldn't pick up hair or lint. P&G was planning an August 2005 launch, but were reluctant to go without addressing the hair and lint problem. IDEO staffers took another "deep dive," buying lint rollers, Brillo pads, glue, and anything else they could find. The P&G lab engineers did the same. The P&G engineers thought adhesive paper was the way to go, but it kept sticking to the carpet. Finally, one of them tried gluing a chopstick down the center of the adhesive paper (to keep the latter from touching the carpet). This solution worked: The paper was high enough not to stick to the carpet, but was low enough to trap hair and lint.

A few additional tweaks were made. The sweeper's color was changed from "Swiffer green" to a new bright orange, to emphasize that this product was to clean a whole new kind of surface. A more appropriate name, CarpetFlick, was chosen. It was shipped, first to Europe, then on to other parts of the world, by the end of July 2005, exactly on time.

What was IDEO's contribution in the development of the CarpetFlick? What was unusual about it, and in what unusual ways did P&G gain from this contribution? How else might P&G have generated a concept or concepts that would address this market opportunity? Suppose you are called in as a creativity consultant to assist in further development of this product. How could new product concepts that would further satisfy P&G's wishes be generated?

Case: Aquafresh White Trays[52]

This case details how GlaxoSmithKline (GSK) entered into an open innovation relationship with a small manufacturing company, Oratech LLC, to get into the teeth whitening market with Aquafresh White Trays. In one sense, the partnership seems to be a perfect match, a textbook example of open innovation in action. GSK

[52]This case is drawn from Scot Andersen, Kevin Foley, and Lee Shorter, "A Story of What Happens When Opposites Attract—Hint: It's Something to Smile About," *Visions*, 31(4), December 2007, pp. 16–17.

noted the rapid growth in teeth whitening products and was experienced in product marketing, sales, and distribution. Also aware of the potential in this category, Oratech had already developed the product, owned the patents, and could handle manufacturing. But the road was not as smooth as expected.

The first successful teeth whitening product was P&G's Crest Whitestrips, launched in 2001, followed by several competitors. While the market showed great interest in these products, there were frequent customer complaints. Most notably, customers found the first few products difficult to use, foul-tasting, and messy. This suggested to GSK a market opportunity based on improved customer value. By offering better teeth whitening properties, and at the same time delivering a product that was tastier and easier to use, GSK could capture a share of this market. GSK was already in the oral care business with its Aquafresh toothpaste line; GSK management felt that only a product that offered superior customer value would be worthy of carrying the Aquafresh name. They also recognized that the most efficient way to enter this market was with a partner that had the required technology knowhow.

Oratech, a small private-label manufacturer, was already making a teeth whitening tray and selling it to dentists and other professionals. They too recognized the growth potential in the consumer market, but needed a partner who owned the requisite marketing skills and brand equity. Oratech identified a small number of potential partners and soon chose GSK due to their marketing and R&D capabilities, in addition to competency in working with regulatory agencies.

Some problems arose in the early going, due to differences in corporate culture. Oratech was initially surprised by the complexity of development and regulatory standards, which were second nature to a huge global corporation like GSK. Perhaps more unexpectedly, the new products processes employed by the two firms were somewhat different as well, with Oratech's version of the process being a little simpler and somewhat more streamlined, typical of a smaller manufacturing firm.

The partnership went well, taking only about eighteen months to get the new product ready for launch. GSK ran into some development challenges, which required that they make some decisions typical of late-phase product development: Do we sacrifice quality, or slow down time-to-market? Despite this slight setback, there was really never any doubt at GSK: The commitment to bring the best-quality product to the consumer, under the Aquafresh name, was the number-one priority. Oratech managers were quite impressed with how seriously this commitment was taken by GSK, who brought in consultants to try to fix the development problems and not slow down development time too much. Scot Andersen, VP of marketing and sales at Oratech, said that the "level of sophistication with which GSK treats its own brands resulted in an improvement in our own processes."

Aquafresh White Trays were launched in early 2007, beating all sales forecasts and going on to be a top player in the teeth whitener category. Executives from both companies agreed that a key factor leading to this success was open communication throughout the new products process. As it turned out, if one partner ran into a manufacturing problem, the other was able to find a solution. A good example of this was the manufacturing process for the trays themselves. GSK preferred individual molding of the trays, but knew that this would run up production time and cost; the alternative was to vacuum-form and cut them, which led to imperfections at the edges. With its technical and manufacturing expertise, Oratech figured out a way to trim the edges, resulting in a desirable finished product. In turn, Oratech was very surprised to see how accessible GSK employees (and even senior management) were throughout the new products process; they were not expecting such a close relationship given GSK's size.

What accounts for the market success of the Aquafresh product? Keep in mind: As large and knowledgeable as GSK is, both P&G and Colgate already had similar products on the market, and both could easily defend themselves against the competitive launch of Aquafresh. More generally, what can be learned from GSK's perspective, and also from Oratech's perspective, about making open innovation work?

Finding and Solving Customers' Problems

Setting

Chapter 5 will be devoted to the most productive concept-generating system that we know—the problem-based approach of finding and solving customers' problems. It seems obvious and easy: Ask customers what their problems are and have a scientist put together the solution! But it's not always so simple.

Just getting customers involved is often difficult. Learning their toughest problems is more difficult, partly because they often don't know their problems very well. Many departments of a firm may be involved, not just the technical ones. You might want to glance back at Figure II.1 in the introduction to Part II, which briefly depicts the problem-based approach to generating concepts, and see how problem-based ideation fits in with other methods for gathering new product concepts.

But ask product managers, and you'll find that they are passionate about identifying customer problems and figuring out how to best solve them—for them, this is fun and exciting work! Think about toy companies. The most innovative ones recognize that one cannot just ask young children what problems they experience with existing toys. But watch them playing in a room with a variety of toys and observe what appears to be missing to them and what they do about it (for example, using the box a toy car came in as a garage), and you may be on to something!

The Overall System of Internal Concept Generation

Every ideation situation is different and varies by the urgency, the skills of the firm and its customers, the product, the resources available, and so on. But one general approach, that of problem-based ideation, works best and can be modified to fit virtually every situation. The steps are diagrammed in Figure 5.1.

The flow essentially is from the study of the situation, to use of various techniques of problem identification, to screening of the resulting problems, and to development of *concept statements* that will then go into the evaluation phase. The whole system is based on close involvement with parties who have information to help us, primarily stakeholders, which include end users, of course, but also advisors, financiers, consultants, maybe architects, physicians, or other professional groups,

FIGURE 5.1
Problem-
Based
Concept
Generation

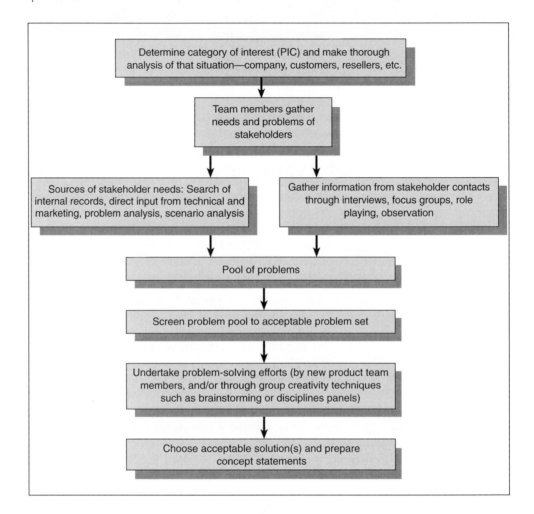

Determine category of interest (PIC) and make thorough analysis of that situation—company, customers, resellers, etc.

Team members gather needs and problems of stakeholders

Sources of stakeholder needs: Search of internal records, direct input from technical and marketing, problem analysis, scenario analysis

Gather information from stakeholder contacts through interviews, focus groups, role playing, observation

Pool of problems

Screen problem pool to acceptable problem set

Undertake problem-solving efforts (by new product team members, and/or through group creativity techniques such as brainstorming or disciplines panels)

Choose acceptable solution(s) and prepare concept statements

possibly resellers—even current nonusers certainly have information that may be useful to us!

Recall from Chapter 2 that the leading cause of new product failure is the absence of a perceived need by the intended end user. If our development process begins with a problem/need the end user has and agrees is important, then we have answered the toughest question. Fortunately, organizations today are getting close to their stakeholders. But stakeholder integration is especially tough on high-security *new product* matters. So we figure out how to do it, just as customer satisfaction managers have.

Gathering the Problems

Figure 5.1 showed four sources for needs and problems of stakeholders: internal records, direct inputs from technical and marketing departments, problem analysis, and scenario analysis. Let's explore each of these.

Internal Records

The most common source of needs and problems comes from an organization's routine contacts with customers and others in the marketplace. Daily or weekly sales call reports, findings from customer or technical service departments, and tips from resellers are examples. Sales files are peppered with customer (and reseller) suggestions and criticisms. Warranty files will show where problems are. In addition to these routine contacts, a firm may conduct formal marketing research to gather information on customer satisfaction. Studies of this type are useful, as are the files of the groups working on total quality management.

Industrial and household consumers sometimes misunderstand products and erroneously project into their use of products what they are *seeking*. A complaint file thus becomes a psychological projective technique. One approach to handling user complaints is the toll-free complaints number or complaints Web site. It helps defuse criticism and can lead to new products. Engineers or other employees may be collocated (sent to work at customer sites) to observe customer problems first-hand.

Information gained through routine market contacts can be profitably combined with other methods, such as the problem-solving technique or customer surveys. A consumer study commissioned by the SC Johnson Company in 2006 found that about one-third of homeowners cleaned the shower only once a month or less, and that a common reason was that they thought this job was difficult and took a long time to do. Over half of the respondents said that they waited until there was visible scum or dirt on the shower before they attempted to clean it! A couple of years later, another survey commissioned by the Soap and Detergent Association found that having a "sparkling shower" was one of the most satisfying cleanup jobs in the house. Since most people in the same survey said they would not employ a housekeeper or cleaning service, this job would have to be done by the homeowner him- or herself. Putting the results of the internal consumer study and the industry association study together, management identified a potentially huge unmet need: a shower cleaner that made the job easy. The result was the Scrubbing Bubbles Automatic Shower Cleaner: attached to the shower head; it sprays cleaning solution throughout the tub/shower area effortlessly by push-button. The product was a natural extension of SC Johnson's popular Scrubbing Bubbles bathroom cleaners and sprays and became quite popular.[1]

Direct Inputs from Technical and Marketing Departments

Understanding about end users and other stakeholders also lies in the minds of marketing and technical people.[2] Most of them have spent time with customers and end users, sometimes many years of it. Team representatives from these two functions should canvass their colleagues, seeking out every piece of evidence on

---

[1]From an SC Johnson press release dated March 16, 2006.
[2]A good reference on using firm employees as sources of new product ideas is Christine Gorski and Eric J. Heinekamp, "Capturing Employee Ideas for New Products," in P. Belliveau, A. Griffin, and S. Sommermeyer (eds.), *The PDMA Toolbook for New Product Development* (New York: John Wiley, 2002), pp. 219–241.

problems. They have to take the initiative on this because most of these people are busy; it's strictly "you call me."

It's good to remember that technical people may be found anywhere in the business, not just in R&D or engineering—especially in manufacturing, technical service, and regulatory affairs. Salespeople may not be considered in marketing, and thus are sometimes overlooked.

The only real problems with using in-house people to report on customer problems are (1) each suggestion is usually someone's *perception* of what the customer problem is, and (2) there is usually a solution given with each suggestion. In fact, sometimes we have to ask what new product customers are asking for and then ask why; the why is what we want to know at this time.

These problems, including the time and difficulty of actually gathering memories, lead us to depend more on *active* searching for stakeholder problems. That is, making direct contact with all relevant stakeholders, asking *them* what their problems and needs are. And, although all of the above market contacts and searches around the firm help us compile useful problems, the methods of direct user contact are what we usually mean when we say problem analysis.

Problem Analysis

It seems that every history of an industry, a business firm, or a famous businessperson cites some key time when a new good or service capitalized on a problem that others didn't sense or appreciate. But problem analysis is much more than a simple *compilation* of user problems. Although the term problem *inventory* is sometimes used to describe this category of techniques, taking the inventory is only the beginning—analysis is the key.

As an advertising agency executive once said: If you ask people what they want in a new house and also ask them what are their problems with their current house, you will get distinctly different subject matter on each list. If you then observe their subsequent behavior, it becomes clear their problem list is a far better predictor than the want list. Users verbalize their wants in terms of current products, whereas problems are not product specific. Thus, if you ask what a person needs or wants from a shampoo, the answers will be clean hair, manageable hair, and so on—replies reflecting recent promotions of product benefits. But if you ask, "What problems do you have with your hair?" the answers may range into areas (for example, style or color) unrelated to shampoo. See Figure 5.2 for an example of what we are looking for in problem analysis, as applied to cell phones.

Several recent award-winning product designs have resulted from the application of problem analysis. In one case, homeowners reported several problems with smoke and carbon monoxide detectors: ugly designs, too hard to shut off (without climbing up on a chair), nuisance alarms, poor instructions on what to do in case of an emergency. Coleman developed its line of Safe Keep Monitors to be aesthetically pleasing in appearance and added a broom button for easy reach. The carbon monoxide monitor comes with a door that opens to reveal instructions when activated (thus eliminating the need to hunt for a manual during an emergency). When developing the Aptiva S computer line, IBM sent researchers out to get pictures of home PCs. They found that space is at a premium for home

FIGURE 5.2
Problem
Analysis
Applied to the
Cell Phone

Here are 24 cell phone problems that came up in a consumer study. See if you can generalize to a smaller number of problems. Then select the one big problem that sounds most productive for cell phone new products people.

Keeping the phone clean.
Breaks when I drop it.
Battery doesn't stay charged long enough.
Finding it in the dark.
Battery dies when I am in the middle of a conversation.
Who "out there" can hear me?
Dropped calls (line goes dead for no reason).
Difficulty in looking up numbers.
Other party's voice fades in and out.
Hard to hold, if arthritic.
I've heard about health risks—are they true?
Can't cradle it between ear and shoulder.
Antenna breaks off.
Flip cover breaks off.
My arm and ear get tired.
Ringing is usually too loud, but sometimes I can't hear it.
It is a very disruptive instrument.
I can't see facial or body language.
Getting flustered making emergency calls.
People who call the wrong number in the middle of the night.
The call doesn't go through.
Fear of what the ringing might be for.
Avoiding "If you want sales, push 1," etc.
Knowing when is the best time to call people.

computer users, as home desks tend to be smaller than office desks. The research also suggested that IBM was not a favored brand for home PCs. The Aptiva S was given a sleek design in which only the CD-ROM, diskette drive, and power switch are located in a console sitting on the desk—the rest of the computer is hidden under the desk. Speakers are built into the monitor to avoid taking up more space, and the keyboard can be stored on the console under the monitor when not in use. By being designed to solve real customer problems, both the Safe Keep line and the Aptiva S line have done well in terms of sales.[3] In a business-to-business application, Cemex (a large Mexican cement company) conducted customer research and discovered a previously hidden problem: Customers were unhappy with late supply arrivals at the project site. Cemex seized the opportunity and repositioned itself as the on-time supplier—a virtual "Domino's Pizza" of the cement industry![4]

[3]Examples are from Bruce Nussbaum and contributing writers, "Winners: The Best Product Designs of the Year," *BusinessWeek*, June 2, 1997, pp. 94–111.
[4]Erika B. Seamon, "Achieving Growth through an Innovative Culture," in P. Belliveau, A. Griffin, and S. M. Somermeyer (eds.), *The PDMA Toolbook 2 for New Product Development* (New York: John Wiley, 2004).

Problem analysis was, at least informally, used by James Dyson in the development of the Dual Cyclone bagless vacuum cleaner (which you saw at the beginning of Chapter 1). Existing vacuum cleaners were unsatisfactory in terms of performance, maneuverability, and ease of disposing of dirt, and Dyson set out to create a better vacuum. In later years, Dyson produced a powerful hand dryer, the Airblade, sold to the business market, and by 2009 adapted the technology behind the Airblade to create a better fan. Like vacuums, regular household fans have remained quite unchanged in design for decades. Dyson's innovation was guided by a quick but thorough problem analysis that identified several points of improvement. As Dyson said, conventional fans have "spinning blades [that] chop up airflow, causing annoying buffeting. They're hard to clean, and children always want to poke their fingers through the grille."[5] One could add a few more problems: Fans can tip over and are not very energy efficient. The Air Multiplier, as it was called, was purported to address many of the problems. It was bladeless, increasing safety and ease of cleaning, as well as creating a smooth stream of air. The Airblade technology provided for effective and efficient cooling, and its low center of gravity prevented dangerous tipping. It featured functional and "cool" design elements associated with the other Dyson products. The product was successfully developed and launched in late 2009, at a price point significantly above conventional fans (about $300), but within reach of customers who appreciate good design and substantially improved performance.

Note that in this and the earlier examples, it is up to senior management to encourage new product teams to look beyond their normal boundaries when they explore customer problems.

Problem Analysis Procedure

There are several variations in problem analysis. But one commonly used procedure is **reverse brainstorming.** In this procedure, participants generate a list of key problems with the product currently in use, then group and prioritize these such that product development can focus on addressing the most important problems.[6] The general approach is the following:

Step One Determine the appropriate *product or activity category* for exploration. This has already been done if the product innovation charter has a use, user, or product category dimension in the focus statement.

Step Two Identify a group of *heavy product users* or activity participants within that category. Heavy users are apt to have a better understanding of the problems, and they represent the bulk of the sales potential in most markets. A variation is to study *non*users to see if a solvable problem is keeping them out of the market.

---

[5]Rebecca Smithers, "Latest for the Dyson Touch: The Fan Without Blades," *The Guardian,* October 13, 2009.
[6]Robert G. Cooper, Scott J. Edgett, and Elko J. Kleinschmidt, "Optimizing the Stage-Gate Process: What Best-Practice Companies Do—I," *Research-Technology Management,* September–October 2002, pp. 21–27.

FIGURE 5.3
The Bother-
someness
Technique
of Scoring
Problems

The following is an abbreviated list of pet owners' problems found by manufacturers of pet products.

	A Problem Occurs Frequently	B Problem Is Bothersome	C A × B
Need constant feeding	98%	21%	.21
Get fleas	78%	53%	.41
Shed hairs	70%	46%	.32
Make noise	66%	25%	.17
Have unwanted babies	44%	48%	.21

Source: From Burton H. Marcus and Edward M. Tauber, *Market Analysis and Decision Making*, Little, Brown, 1979, p. 225. Reprinted with permission.

Step Three   Gather from these heavy users or participants a set of *problems* associated with the category. Study the entire system of product use or activity. This is the inventory phase mentioned earlier, but far more is involved than just asking respondents to list their problems. A good method of doing this is asking respondents to rate (1) the benefits they *want* from a set of products and (2) the benefits they are *getting*. The differences indicate problems. Complaints are common and often taken as requests for new products. But they are apt to be just the result of *omniscient proximity*, meaning that users face a minor problem frequently, so it is the first one mentioned. Some firms have had success *observing* consumers or business firms actually using products in a given category; for example, observing skiers as they shoot down a hill or office workers handling a mailing operation.

Step Four   *Sort and rank* the problems according to their severity or importance. Various methods can be used for this, but a common one is shown in Figure 5.3. It uses (1) the extent of the problem, and (2) the frequency of its occurrence. This *bothersomeness index* is then adjusted by users' awareness of currently available solutions to the problem. This step identifies problems that are important to the user and for which the user sees no current solutions.

Methodologies to Use

The generalized structure of problem analysis still contains the question of how to gather the list of customer problems. Many methods have been used, but the task is dificult. The customer or user often does not perceive problems well enough to verbalize them. And, if the problems are known, the user may not *agree* to verbalize them (for many reasons, including being embarrassed). Much of the sophistication in newer technologies was developed specifically to deal with these problems and will be discussed in Chapter 6.

Experts   We have already mentioned going to the experts—using them as surrogates for end users based on their experience in the category under study. Such experts can be found in the sales force, among retail and wholesale distribution personnel, and in professionals who support an industry—architects, doctors, accountants, and the staffs of government bureaus and trade associations. Zoo experts first publicized the problem of elephant keepers being killed when trying to cut the big animals' toenails. Today an Elephant Hugger grabs an elephant, rolls it over on its side and holds it there, while the keeper cuts away. Later, the inventor turned his attention to a giraffe-restraining device.[7] In another example, Nokia of Finland has an R&D team of 8,000 scientists and managers who collect environmental information on wireless communications and identify the main challenges. This has helped Nokia sustain growth in this market through the introduction of innovative, successful new products.[8]

Published Sources   Also as mentioned earlier, published sources are frequently useful—industry studies, the firm's own past studies on allied subjects, government reports, investigations by social critics, scientific studies in universities, and many others.

Stakeholder Contacts   The third, and most productive, is to seek out the voice of the customer (VOC)—that is, we will ask household or business/industry customers directly, via interviewing, focus groups, direct observation, or role playing.

- **Interviewing** The most common method by far is direct, one-on-one interviewing. Sometimes this is a full-scale, very formal, and scientific survey. Other times the discussion is with lead users, an idea-generating method discussed in Chapter 4; lead users often are the first to sense a problem, and some go on to respond to it themselves. Still other times, it may be no more than conversations with some key customer friends at a trade show, because a problem statement may come from only one person and yet be very significant for us. Phone interviews have been shown to be a quick and effective way to get useful new product ideas and help to ensure that the targeted respondent (for example, a professional or a senior manager at a customer firm) actually responds, rather than a last-minute fill-in.[9] Because many end users don't think that much about the products they use and often just accept them as parts of living, even very informal discussions with individuals at a trade show or over the telephone can reopen thinking, bringing to mind things forgotten.
- **Focus Groups** The **focus group** is designed to yield the exploratory and depth-probing type of discussion required, and it *can be* easy and inexpensive to set up and use. If done wrong, it only *appears* that way. Granted, in this case we are not seeking facts or conclusions, just genuine problems, and the focus group method works well by stimulating people to speak out about things

---

[7]Laura E. Keeton, "Marketers Debate the Best Way to Trim an Elephant's Toenails," *The Wall Street Journal*, February 25, 1995, p. B1.

[8]Muammer Ozer, "A Survey of New Product Evaluation Models," *Journal of Product Innovation Management,* 16(1), January 1999, pp. 77–94.

[9]For more on telephone interviews and qualitative interviewing in general, see George Castellion, "Telephoning Your Way to Compelling Value Propositions," in P. Belliveau, A. Griffin, and S. Somermeyer (eds.), *The PDMA Toolbook for New Product Development* (New York: John Wiley, 2002), pp. 63–86.

they are reluctant to mention when in one-on-one interview situations. It's much easier to talk about one's problems when others in the group have already admitted they have problems, too.

But, even in a single focus group, the costs are deceptive. Such sessions can cost from $3,000 to $10,000 in normal usage. Even at $3,000, a two-hour meeting of 10 people will yield about 10 minutes talk per participant. Since the cost is $300 per participant, that's talk at the rate of $30 per minute, or $1,800 an hour! It had better be very good indeed.

Although the focus group technique is common, the outcome is not always, or even usually, successful. The focus group is a **qualitative research** technique. Unlike the traditional survey, it depends on in-depth discussions rather than the power of numbers. A problem analysis focus group should be asked:

What is the real problem here—that is, what if the product category did not exist?
What are the current attitudes and behaviors of the focus group members toward the product category?
What product attributes and benefits do the members of the focus group want?
What are their dissatisfactions, problems, and unfilled needs?
What changes occurring in their lifestyles are relevant to the product category?[10]

In a typical example, Nissan conducted focus groups of American children between the ages of 8 and 15 to get ideas for storage, cup holders, and other features as part of the design of its full-size minivan.[11]

Other suggestions for helping guarantee the usefulness of focus group findings are to invite scientists and top executives to the sessions and to avoid what some people call *prayer groups:* Managers sit behind the mirror and pray for the comments wanted rather than really listening to what users are saying. Be sure the focus groups are large enough for the interactions and synergy that make them successful, and don't expect focus group members to like your products! Focus group moderators know not to begin the session cold, but instead to let people get comfortable and introduce themselves—a rule of thumb is to treat participants as one would treat strangers at a party. The best moderators genuinely like people and generate openness and trust by asking ice-breaker questions and by contributing personal experiences and practices.[12]

- **Observation** Observation methods are rooted in sociological studies, and involve watching customers (or noncustomers) using products in their own environments. Video cameras or photos are sometimes used to record

[10]"When Using Qualitative Research to Generate New Product Ideas, Ask These Five Questions," *Marketing News*, May 14, 1982, p. 15.
[11]Norihiko Shirouzu, "Tailoring World's Cars to U.S. Tastes," *The Wall Street Journal*, January 15, 2001, pp. B1, B6.
[12]Joseph Rydholm, "Respondent Collages Help Agency Develop Ads for New Pontiac," *Quick's Marketing Research Review*, March 1995, p. 7; and Tim Huberty, "Sharing Inside Information," *Quick's Marketing Research Review*, March 1995, p. 10.

observational data. The new product team observes the data carefully for actions, body language, and so on and tries to identify customer needs and wants, and new product ideas that might satisfy these needs.[13]

In developing a revolutionary new hand-held instrument for the chemical industry, Fluke Corporation visited chemical industry trade shows and customer plants, talking informally with end users (the instrument engineers). Internally this technique was known as *fly on the wall* or *day in the life* research.[14] Nokia has sent teams of employees to developing nations like Uganda for up to twelve days at a time to understand phone usage better. They learned that phone sharing is more common in these nations and sought to make their mobile phones more amenable to sharing.[15]

When redesigning its popular Explorer sport-utility vehicle, Ford sent a team of designers out to parking lots in order to watch how people used their cars. The researchers' duties were not unlike those of zoologists watching animals in their natural habitat—in fact, the work was colloquially known internally as "gorilla research." Among other ideas, the research suggested ways the Explorer could be made easier to get into.[16] Similarly, Honda engineers and executives visited the homes of U.S. families that owned Ford SUVs and noted, to their surprise, how many parents put their children and their neighbors' children in the first two rows and the dogs in the third row. Had the research been conducted only in Japan, the researchers would have entirely missed the American love affair with dogs and might consequently have made the passenger compartment too small.[17]

Role Playing   Though role playing has long been used in psychology to enhance creativity, there is little evidence of its successful use in generating ideas for new products. Presumably, it would be valuable in instances where product users are unable to visualize or verbalize their reactions. It should also be valuable where consumers are emotionally unable or unwilling to express their views—for example, in areas of personal hygiene.

Unfortunately, though users are the best place to begin the ideation, and problem analysis is widely used in one form or another, most firms still do not have

---

[13]Dorothy Leonard and Jeffrey F. Rayport, "Spark Innovation through Emphatic Design," *Harvard Business Review,* 75(6), November–December 1997, pp. 102–113. For a look at how the design firm IDEO uses observation, brainstorming, and rapid prototyping to identify and refine product concepts, see Bruce Nussbaum, "The Power of Design," *BusinessWeek,* May 17, 2004, pp. 86–94, or check the IDEO Web site, www.ideo.com. (We explore prototyping issues in Chapter 13 of this book.)

[14]Robert G. Cooper, "From Experience: The Invisible Success Factors in Product Innovation," *Journal of Product Innovation Management,* 16(2), March 1999, pp. 115–133; see also Cooper, Edgett, and Kleinschmidt, op. cit.

[15]Anonymous, "Nokia's Design Research for Everyone," www.businessweek.com, March 14, 2007.

[16]Al Haas, "Spying Helps to Improve Explorer," *Philadelphia Inquirer,* December 24, 2000, p. G1.

[17]Norihiko Shirouzu, op. cit.

organized systems to exploit this source. Considering that Levi Strauss got the idea for steel-riveted jeans from a Nevada user in 1873, one must wonder why not.

An alternative way to generate concepts is based on **product function analysis.** A product can be expressed in two words, a verb and an object (for example, toothpaste "cleans teeth"). Thinking of new combinations of verbs and objects can suggest new product functions. In this method, hundreds of these two-word mini-concepts can be generated and shown via computer to respondents, who rate them in terms of likely interest. The highest scoring concepts are identified and in-depth interviews are conducted to explore feelings and ideas further. In an application in the food processing industry, several novel mini-concepts emerged (have fun with food, touch food), while several others fared poorly (sponge food, vaporize food). To develop these concepts further, one would need to examine why these mini-concepts were liked.[18]

Problem Analysis in Action

One unmet need that had existed for years was the noisy candy wrapper in the theater. Gene Shalit, of NBC's *Today Show,* complained one morning about crackling candy bar wrappers. An expressway-commuting executive from Hercules Inc. overheard his comment and asked the laboratory for a silent candy wrapper. Polypropylene provided the answer, though not without tricky effort on heating, waterproofing, and airproofing.

Toyota, Mitsubishi, and other carmakers redesigned their sport-utility vehicles to appeal more to the U.S. marketplace demand. Often, these changes come about after disappointing sales with early SUV versions. The Toyota T100 pickup had disappointing sales in the United States; consumer research suggested that the reason was that it was viewed as too small. The full-size Tundra comes complete with a V8 engine and a passenger compartment reportedly large enough for "a passenger wearing a ten-gallon cowboy hat."[19]

Noting that children are heavy ketchup consumers, the H. J. Heinz Company conducted research with children to identify ways to improve ketchup. Some strides were made in package redesign: softer, curvier squeeze bottles that emit a thinner stream of ketchup (so that kids could draw with it). The real breakthrough came, however, when someone thought to ask kids for their own suggestions—and they immediately said, "try different colors." Apparently no adults had thought of changing its color (ketchup has been red since Heinz began mass-producing it in 1876). It probably surprised no one that the kids' favorite color was a disgusting (to adults) shade of green. By adjusting color, Heinz came up with a significantly new product idea: EZ Squirt Ketchup in red and "Blastin' Green," greeted with enthusiasm by loyal, young ketchup users in the fall of 2000. Heinz followed this

[18]Jeffrey F. Durgee, Gina Colarelli O'Connor, and Robert W. Veryzer, "Using Mini-Concepts to Identify Opportunities for Really New Product Functions," *Journal of Consumer Marketing,* 15(6), 1998, pp. 525–541.

[19]Norihiko Shirouzu, "Tailoring World's Cars to U.S. Tastes," *The Wall Street Journal,* January 15, 2001, pp. B1, B6.

initial success by launching purple ketchup.[20] (Initially skeptical parents were won over by the fact that all the EZ Squirt colors had plenty of added Vitamin C, something regular ketchup lacks.)

Finally, ongoing problem analysis is critical to identification of newly emerging problems and continued improvement. Consider Domino's Pizza. Decades ago, Domino's founders identified a real unmet need in the market: quick, reliable pizza delivery service. Late-night customers, in fact, were satisfied with an average-quality pizza, as long as it was delivered fast and hot. Generations of customers knew Domino's promise: "thirty minutes or it's free." But by 2009, competition in the pizza business had heated up; major delivery competitors such as Papa John's had achieved immense success and even the traditional-restaurant Pizza Hut chain was getting into the delivery business. Fast and hot was no longer enough. Domino's focus groups found that customers had lots to say about the taste, most of it negative. Company president Dan Boyle decided to respond to the threat by assigning a product team to develop a new, better-tasting pizza. Marketing employees used focus groups and other research methods to capture the voice of the customer; the food engineers developed a totally new recipe to meet the specifications. Over a dozen different sauces and crusts were tried, as well as dozens of types of cheese. Despite the risks of such a dramatic strategy (what if it were New Coke all over again and customers demanded the old product back?), the new pizza was just what the market ordered.[21]

Scenario Analysis

So far, we have talked about going to technical and marketing people within the firm for ideas on customer problems, about searching the many files and record-keeping places where customer concerns can be found, and about problem analysis. The fourth general source of stakeholder needs shown in Figure 5.1—**scenario analysis**—comes into play because the ideal problem for us to find is one that customers or end users don't know they have at this time. As hockey star Wayne Gretzky said, "I don't skate to where the puck is. I skate to where it's going to be." Similarly, we have to stay one step ahead of the customers by anticipating their problems.[22]

A future problem is a good problem because most problems we find in interviews and focus groups have already been told to competitors and anyone else who will listen. Providers of the goods and services have been working on them for many years, for example, flimsy music stands and steam on bathroom mirrors. We have time to solve a *future* problem and have that solution ready to market when the time comes.

[20]Peter Mucha, "Ketchup: The Color of Money," *Philadelphia Inquirer,* October 26, 2000, pp. C1, C3.

[21]Anonymous, "New Domino's Pizza Recipe Doubles Quarterly Profits," nydailynews.com, March 2, 2010; Domino's Pizza 2009 Financial Results.

[22]Mark Henry Sebell, "Staying Ahead of Customers," *U.S. Banker,* October 1997, p. 88.

Unfortunately, end users usually don't know what their future problems will be. And they often don't really care, at least not right now. So they are not much help in interviews. This is where scenario analysis becomes valuable. Here's how it works.

If we were to describe apartment life 20 years from now, we would probably see lots of windows and sunlight coming in. If a furniture manufacturer were doing this scenario analysis, an analyst could immediately see problems, such as: Those apartment dwellers will need (1) new types of upholstery that are more resistant to the sun, and (2) new types of chairs that will let them continue such activities as conversing and eating but also let them gain exposure to all that sunlight.

The scenario analysis procedure is evident: First, paint a scenario; second, study it for problems and needs; third, evaluate those problems and begin trying to solve the most important ones. The ideal scenario is a "stylized narrative"—that is, it should be like a story: painting a clear picture of the future state, containing a "plot" or sequence of believable events. Painting a scenario does not yield a new product concept directly; it is only a source of problems, which still must be solved. In fact, it is often valuable for concept generation if several future states are described. Creative people can then choose to focus on the most likely scenario, or possibly attempt a *multiple coverage strategy* in which a separate strategy is pursued for each of several possible scenarios. A carmaker might develop several different alternative engine technologies (gas/electric hybrid, hydrogen cell, etc.) in parallel if it is unclear which of these will be dominant in the future.[23]

Scenarios take several different forms. First, we distinguish between (1) *extending* the present to see what it will look like in the future, and (2) *leaping* into the future to pick a period that is then described. Both use current trends to some extent, of course, but the leap method is not constrained by these trends. For example (hypothetically) an extend study might be: Currently, homeowners are converting from individual housing to condominium housing at an annual rate of 0.9 percent. If this keeps up for 20 years, there will be 7 million condominium units in use, which will present a need for 250,000 visitors' motel units in major condominium areas to house visitors who cannot stay in the smaller units with their hosts. The thinking of the utopian school is sometimes used. By contrast, a leap study might be: Describe life in the year 2030 in a major urban area of Germany contrasted with life in a similar setting in France.

Leap studies can be *static* or *dynamic*. In dynamic leap studies, the focus is on what changes must be made between now and then if the leap scenario is to come about—the interim time period is the meaningful focus. In static leaps, there is no concern about how we get there. Figure 5.4 shows a dynamic leap period in which the auto dealer service problem no longer exists. The time between now and then is broken down to yield the technical breakthroughs needed soon to

---

[23]For more on using scenarios, see Steven Schnaars and Paschalina (Lilia) Ziamou, "The Essentials of Scenario Writing," *Business Horizons*, July–August 2001, pp. 25–31.

FIGURE 5.4
The Relevance
Tree Form of
Dynamic Leap
Scenario

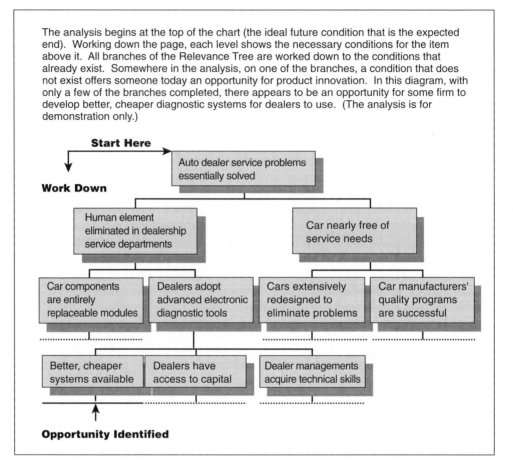

reach that ideal condition. As another illustration, one professional forecaster made several rather bold predictions regarding technologies and our lifestyles in the future (see Figure 5.5). Any of these could be viewed as a leap scenario into some time in the not-too-distant future: These scenarios (if not too farfetched) might suggest opportunities for several new products. (Which do they suggest to you?)

Another variant is a study of **wild cards**—high-impact, low-probability events (see Figure 5.6 for a set of wild cards identified recently by the Arlington Institute). In a wild card study, one assesses the likelihoods of occurrence of the identified events and investigates the threats or new product opportunities they suggest. While any one of them might be rather unlikely, it does not mean that one should not develop a contingency plan, especially if it may set off a chain of events that can have an impact on innovation. For example, a natural disaster may result in an epidemic, triggering border closings and quarantines and threatening the airline industry. A key here is to try to recognize the early

FIGURE 5.5 One Professional Forecaster's View of the Future

Graham Molitor is a professional forecaster who relies on a variety of sources to develop his forecasts: census documents, government statistics, trade journals and similar publications, weekly newsmagazines, and his own 40 years of experience. Here are a few of the trends and forecasts he envisions for the 21st century:

1. Investment in communication will allow more people to work at home; by 2020, telecommuting and videoconferencing will have largely replaced in-person business meetings.

2. Internet use will continue to increase rapidly, and Americans will spend more on computers than on televisions. Handheld videophones will be a commercial hit by 2025.

3. Medical technology breakthroughs will continue to happen: Improved cloning technology will extend human life, and computerized health monitors will be of wearable size.

4. Ethical and social issues related to health and lifestyle will continue to be prevalent: These will include euthanasia, cloning, genetic manipulation, and biological engineering.

5. The traditional "nuclear family" will continue to become a thing of the past; by 2020 the average household size will be down to 2.35 persons.

6. By 2050, over a quarter of the U.S. population will be over 65. Large-type and recorded books, and cars that can be operated by people with reduced dexterity, will become popular.

7. By 2100, Americans of European descent will be in the minority (that is, less than 50 percent of the population). Continued diversity and multiculturalism will be stimulated by increased immigration.

8. In the far future (2200 to 2500), biotechnology and related life-science industries will have replaced tourism as a key employer in the U.S.

9. Greater globalization of manufacturing industries, more outsourcing of capital-intensive functions, and more electronic commerce, will mark business and industry.

10. Supplies of petroleum will shrink and prices will rise; by 2050, electricity demand will multiply by a factor of four.

What new products do each of these forecasts suggest? Do any of them suggest any changes in the new product development process? Do any of them seem too far-fetched to believe?

Source: Graham T. T. Molitor, "Trends and Forecasts for the New Millennium," *The Futurist,* July–August 1998, pp. 53–59. Reprinted with permission.

warning signs of the wild cards, as often they will exist (possibly outside one's own discipline).[24]

Scenario analyses lead to great learning and insights, but are hard to do well. Several guidelines have been suggested for conducting a good scenario analysis:

1. *Know the now.* The participants must have a good understanding of the current situation and its dynamics, otherwise the future they envision will not be realistic or useful for idea generation.

2. *Keep it simple.* Participants will likely have difficulty understanding really complex scenarios.

[24]John L. Petersen, "The 'Wild Cards' in Our Future: Preparing for the Improbable," *The Futurist,* July–August 1997, pp. 43–47.

FIGURE 5.6
Wild Card
Events
and Their
Consequences

Human Cloning: Raises ethical issues, as well as the possibility of extending human life thanks to organ and tissue cloning.

No-Carbon Policy: Global warming may cause governments to put high taxes on fossil fuels, shifting demand to alternative sources of energy. This changes the allocation of R&D investment toward alternative energy, possibly causes new "energy-rich" nations to emerge, and ultimately may lead to a cleaner environment for everyone.

Altruism Outbreak: This is the "random acts of kindness" movement—solve social problems rather than leaving it up to the government. Schools and other institutions will revive due to community actions, and perhaps inner cities would be revitalized.

Cold Fusion: If a developing country perfects free energy, it becomes prosperous overnight. It gains further advantages by becoming an energy exporter.

Other wild cards identified in the study: Civil war in the U.S., revolt in the inner cities, computer hackers blackmail the Federal Reserve. Secession of a Western state, collapse of the U.N. . . . not a bright picture! Luckily, none of these might happen, though their possible occurrence should not be ignored.

Source: John I. Petersen, "The 'Wild Cards' in Our Future: Preparing for the Improbable," *The Futurist*, July–August 1997, pp. 43–47. Reprinted with permission.

3. *Be careful with selecting group members.* A group of about six, with contrasting or complementary viewpoints and prior experiences, works best.

4. *Do an 8- to 10-year projection.* Too far out, and the participants are guessing. Not far enough out, and the respondents will just extend whatever is going on now.

5. *Periodically summarize progress.* This keeps the group on track and avoids contradictions.

6. *Combine the factors causing changes.* Scenarios should not be determined by just one factor.

7. *Check fit* or consistency at the end.

8. Once you have done the scenario analysis, *plan to use it several times.* These can be expensive.

9. *Reuse the group.* The more scenario analyses they do, the more they enjoy the task, and the better they get at it.[25]

Solving the Problems

Once an important user problem has been identified, we can begin solving it. Most problem solving is probably done by members of the new products group that has been leading the concept generation work so far. They do it instinctively, from the moment they hear of a problem. There is no way we can quantify or describe the

[25]These points are from David Mercer, "Scenarios Made Easy," *Long Range Planning*, August 1995, pp. 81–86; and Audrey Schreifer, "Getting the Most out of Scenarios," *Planning Review*, September–October 1995, pp. 33–35. See also Schnaars and Ziamou, op. cit.

methods they use, most of it being intuitive. It is probably best for the group to attempt to solve one problem at a time, however—taking on too much in the real world can be confusing and may foster communication difficulties.

Many problems are sent into the technical areas for more systematic attempt at solution. Here science and intuition rule, side by side. Some firms have it as strategy that problem solutions must come from R&D or engineering, with the solution itself being found in the application of some specific technology. A bus line wants travel problems solved by buses, and a bank probably wants problems solved by borrowing money. Besides technical people, the creative talents of marketing people are often used as well.

Note that the problem has to be carefully specified in order to find a good, creative solution. P&G product developers reportedly spent months trying to solve the problem, "How can we make a green striped soap that will draw sales from Irish Spring?" It was only when they focused their attention on a new problem, "How can we make a soap that connotes freshness in its appearance, shape, and color better than Irish Spring?" that Coast (a soap with blue and white swirl patterns and a more oval shape) was developed and was ultimately successful.[26]

Group Creativity

New products people use individual problem-solving effort, but many think that **group creativity** is more effective. Some scientists protest loudly that this is not true, that the synergism of groups is way overplayed. Generally, individuals can handle really *new* ideas and find *radical* solutions to problems better than groups can. Some feel that one reason small firms are more innovative than large firms is that they do not often use group creativity.

Back in 1938, advertising executive Alex Osborn wrote a book about a technique he called **brainstorming.** All of the group ideation techniques developed since that time are spin-offs of his process and embody one idea: One person presents a thought, another person reacts to it, another person reacts to the reaction, and so on. This presenting/reacting sequence gives group creativity its meaning, and the various techniques developed simply alter how ideas are presented or how reactions take place.

Brainstorming

Because brainstorming techniques have been around so long, they are widely abused and misused. It is good to be able to recognize bad brainstorming , because bad brainstorming just does not work. Thomas Kelley of the design firm IDEO laid out several rules for making brainstorming sessions more effective. These include: *mind the rules* (go for a large quantity of ideas, defer judgment, no snickering allowed); *number the ideas* (can you hit 100 ideas per hour?); *jump and build* (when the group hits a plateau, the facilitator suggests a new direction); and *get physical* (as in the Carpet Flick case, by using odds and ends to build models and prototypes).[27]

[26]Peter Wilson, "Simplex Creative Problem Solving," *Creativity and Innovation Management*, 6(3), September 1997, pp. 161–167.
[27]Tom Kelley, *The Ten Faces of Innovation* (New York: Currency Books, 2005).

The biggest change in the practice of problem solving over the past 20 years is to use brainstorming combined with other tools of creativity. We still try to avoid the *bazooka effect* (state an idea only to have someone shoot it down), but also to avoid the scores of easel sheets with hundreds of ideas scribbled on them. Instead, we aim for group deliberations that are exploratory, evaluative in a constructive way, hours long (versus the 20-minute brainstorming session), and built toward a few specific solutions that appear operational. IDEO uses brainstorming in combination with "lickety-stick" prototype development (see Chapter 2) to speed up innovation.[28]

There have been many attempts to stick with the basic idea of brainstorming, but to tweak it in some way to overcome the problems. In *brainsketching*, participants draw their ideas rather than expressing them in words. Some evidence shows that brainsketching helps participants draw more connections with earlier ideas when coming up with new ideas.[29] Another emerging technique is called *speedstorming*. It is described as a round-robin format, similar to speed-dating, in which participants pair off (at random, or with some pattern in mind such as that the two participants must be from different functional areas) and discuss a topic for a three- to five-minute round. The goal of each round is to come up with ideas that can be pursued by the new product team. After each round, partners switch around and another round begins. At the end of the session, numerous new ideas have been generated, and participants have identified which partners they seem to collaborate with the best. For this reason, the proponents of speedstorming claim that it is particularly good at overcoming the communication difficulties typical of cross-functional teams.[30]

Some other common techniques are described in Appendix B.

Electronic Brainstorming and Computer-Assisted Creativity Techniques

Despite its popularity, brainstorming has several drawbacks. Only one person can talk at a time, and social loafing may occur (average work intensity may be lower in a group setting). Further, some individuals may still fear being criticized for having unpopular ideas. **Electronic brainstorming,** a form of brainstorming assisted by **group support systems** (or **GSS**) **software,** is said to overcome these limitations of traditional brainstorming, as it allows participants to all answer at once, and also to answer anonymously.

A GSS-assisted brainstorming session may take place in a room set up with a network of computer terminals. Participants sit at the terminals and respond to questions provided by the moderator, who runs the GSS software. The GSS software gathers the participants' responses and projects them onto a large screen at the front of the room or on the participants' monitors. Seeing the responses stimulates even more ideas and encourages follow-up discussion. The GSS also

[28]Bruce Nussbaum, op. cit.
[29]Remko Van Der Legt, "Brainsketching and How It Differs from Brainstorming," *Creativity and Innovation Management,* 11(1), 2002, pp. 43–54.
[30]Caneel K. Joyce, Kyle E. Jennings, Jonathan Hey, Jeffrey C. Grossman, and Thomas Kalil, "Getting Down to Business: Using Speedstorming to Initiate Creative Cross-Disciplinary Collaboration," *Creativity and Innovation Management,* 19(1), 2010, pp. 57–67.

automatically takes electronic notes of all the proceedings, so nothing is lost or erroneously transcribed![31]

One is not restricted to a single location, either. GSSs can facilitate activity at many sites simultaneously (through computer linkups or videoconferencing) and handle group sizes into the hundreds.

GSSs are becoming much more popular in facilitating meetings, and there is increasing evidence that electronic brainstorming outperforms traditional brainstorming in terms of productivity and output of unique ideas.[32]

An increasing number of firms are using computer programs such as Mindlink, Mindfisher, and NamePro to assist their creative efforts in idea generation and management, and also to help out in other creative tasks such as brand name generation and selection. While they come in many forms, many of these work by drawing from large databases of words, phrases, or even pictures, encouraging the user to *think laterally* (gather unrelated thoughts, then try to associate them with the problem at hand). Most are straightforward and stimulating to use.[33] Also, many are adaptable to use in a GSS setting.

Online Communities[34]

Online communities (or *virtual communities*) have revolutionized customer information gathering. An online community can be defined as any group that interacts using a communications medium such as online social networking. Numerous firms, including P&G, Kraft, Dell, and Hewlett-Packard, use online communities as a key part of their voice of the customer efforts and, indeed, throughout their new products process. Familiar online communities such as Facebook, MySpace, or LinkedIn are open to everyone and widely popular. But there are alternatives, some of which are much less well known. Some online communities such as tivocommunity.com are set up by lead users with an interest in a particular product or service; some such as Johnson & Johnson's babycenter.com are launched by firms. In addition, service providers like MarketTools or Vision Critical obtain rich customer insights by setting up *private online communities* of 500 or fewer carefully selected members. Firms can also access *proprietary online panels (POPs)*, which may contain hundreds of thousands of individuals who are statistically representative of a target market. These panels can be used to supplement online communities

[31]An assessment of GSSs is found in Robert O. Briggs and Gert-Jan De Vreede, "Meetings of the Future: Enhancing Group Collaboration with Group Support Systems," *Creativity and Innovation Management*, 6(3), June 1997, pp. 106–116.

[32]Keng L. Siau, "Group Creativity and Technology," *Journal of Creative Behavior*, Third Quarter 1995, pp. 201–217.

[33]Tony Proctor, "New Developments in Computer Assisted Creative Problem Solving," *Creativity and Innovation Management*, 6(2), June 1997, pp. 94–98; and Mark Turrell, "Technology Spotlight: Unfuzzing the Front-End with Web-Based Idea Management," *Visions*, 27(1), January 2003, pp. 18–21. For a critique of several of these computer programs, see Arvind Rangaswamy and Gary L. Lilien, "Software Tools for New Product Development," *Journal of Marketing Research* 34, February 1997, pp. 177–184.

[34]Much of this section derives from Claire-Juliette Beale, "How Online Communities Are Changing the NPD Landscape—An Introduction to the Value of This New Tool," *Visions*, 32(4), December 2008, pp. 14–18.

in a number of ways. For example, POPs can validate promising ideas or insights generated from a private online community.

Firms may have a range of objectives when initiating an online community. As a VOC technique, online communities provide a listening function: They allow firms to obtain new ideas from customers and get feedback on new concepts. Working with a service provider like MarketTools, firms can monitor public communities and blogs to spot new customer trends and emerging opportunities. Online communities are also a way to establish rapport with customers, enable customer support, and build emotional bonds between customers and the firm.

Del Monte Foods (makers of many pet food brands such as Kibbles 'n Bits, Milk-Bone, Meow Mix, and 9 Lives) used online communities extensively to get a better understanding of changes in its consumer market, identifying opportunities early and quickly developing products. In 2006 they joined forces with Market-Tools and brand monitoring agency Umbria to start the I Love My Dog initiative. By analyzing data from millions of blogs, user forums, and message boards, Del Monte was able to identify the things that pet owners cared about, and wrote about, the most. In fact, a new customer segment of dog lovers (named the "Dogs Are People, Too" segment) was identified. Next, an online community was created to encourage innovative solutions from consumers within this segment. A community of 500 consumers was contacted and asked to enter a by-invitation-only, password-protected site that encouraged interaction and mutual understanding among participants. The community generated and refined ideas for a new breakfast product, which was immediately put into development by Del Monte. During the development process, Del Monte contacted community members, either individually or in group format, about a dozen times. By summer 2007, the new product, Sausage Breakfast Bites, was launched. The process from idea to launch took only six months, half the normal time for a product in this category. Since then, Del Monte has continued to explore ways to exploit online communities. In 2008, the firm partnered again with MarketTools, this time to tap into the latter's Moms Insight Network and quickly identify cat owners. The newly created cat owner community, named Meow Mixer, is used by Del Monte to generate ideas, develop concepts, sample new products, and obtain packaging and marketing suggestions.

Like anything else, online communities take work, and the firm seeking to institute an online community must be aware of the drawbacks.[35] Building and managing an online community requires hiring moderators and facilitators, and can take time—a good-sized community may take more than a year to mature. Also, the longer the community is in operation, the more difficult it becomes to organize the content and make it easy for participants to find their way around. There are also legal issues, such as member privacy, confidentiality of statements, and content ownership, that would need to be considered. Usually, participants would be expected to sign a service agreement so that the sponsoring firm could avoid legal problems down the road. Despite the drawbacks, it is likely that online communities will be a major source of customer input for years to come.

---

[35]Claire-Juliette Beale, "Creating Your Own Online Community—How to Avoid the Pitfalls," *Visions*, 33(1), March 2009, pp. 15–19.

Disciplines Panel

Several of today's leading new products consulting firms believe creativity groups should actually work on a problem, not just talk about it, particularly in situations calling for significant innovation. Their approach is to assemble experts from all relevant disciplines and have them discuss the problem as a **disciplines panel.** A panel on new methods of packaging fresh vegetables might include representatives from home economics, physics, nutrition, medicine, ecology, canning technology, marketing, plastics, chemistry, biology, industrial engineering, agriculture, botany, and agronomy. The panel may also include outside experts.

One panel working in the shampoo industry was focusing on a consumer need: to put on hair conditioner that actually sought out split ends and went to work there. An R&D person on the panel noted that the then-current products all did that! This surprising comment led to a new product that made the claim others had overlooked, and which turned out to be very successful.

Concept Generation Techniques in Action

This chapter provided several **creativity-stimulating techniques** that can be used to generate concepts; Appendix B provides many more. Throughout the chapter, we have provided examples of firms that have successfully applied these techniques. Here are a few additional recent examples that illustrate the successful use of some other, perhaps less common, techniques.

1. *Using Props.* Life Savers Company wanted to develop new flavors. They hired a consultant who filled a room with samples of fruits, varieties of perfumes, and lists of dozens of ice cream flavors. Life Savers' Fruit Juicers line came out of the session. P&G's Duncan Hines Pantastic party cakes came from an idea stimulation session where greeting cards were among the props used.

2. *Role Playing.* Bausch and Lomb's Polymer Technologies Division came up with the idea of cushioning material bonded to the lens surface by getting pairs of executives to play the roles of eyeball and contact lens. The actors had to think of ways the lens could stop hurting the eyeball while role playing.

3. *Imitating Nature.* Goats eat waste and emit it in the form of small pellets. This idea inspired Whirlpool in its development of the Trash Smasher compactor.[36]

Summary

Chapter 5 began our study of the many specific techniques developed by concept creators to aid them in their work. The most common approach is based on the paradigm of "find problem, solve problem," requiring participation by many people in the firm, plus stakeholders and others outside the firm. Then, we looked at the many techniques developed to spot problems. These included (1) inputs

[36]Bryan Mattimore, "Eureka: How to Invent a New Product," *The Futurist,* March–April 1995, pp. 34–38.

from technical and marketing departments; (2) search of internal records from sales calls, product complaints, customer satisfaction studies, and more; (3) problem analysis as a way of involving end users and other stakeholders; and (4) scenario analysis as a way of learning about future problems. Once problems are discovered, efforts at solution can begin; most efforts are individual thinking and analysis, whether in the office or in the lab. One major group of techniques uses the label of group creativity; it includes a great variety of approaches, but most are variations of brainstorming.

Next we will turn to some methods called analytical attributes, created over the years to aid marketing managers in seeking improvements while they are waiting for the approach of problem-find-solve to bear fruit. This is the approach where we start with form, then see if there is a need, and if so, then develop the necessary technology.

Applications

1. "I recently met the president of a Florida university who had previously researched the new products operation in Silicon Valley firms. He wasn't impressed. Said that sales reps told over and over about getting suggestions and tips from their customers and sending them in on call reports, but nothing ever happened. Apparently, upper-level sales and marketing executives only rarely have much customer contact, yet don't capitalize on the contacts of salespeople. You have any ideas on how I might go about being sure this condition doesn't exist in our various divisions?"

2. "I believe in problem analysis—that's at the heart of things. But I sure don't like those focus groups. I sat in on a couple last year, and all the people did was chat. And the chatting never seemed to lead to anything. After the second one was over, I quizzed the moderator, and she agreed that there had been a lot of rambling. She kept talking about the gems of knowledge we found—common threads, I believe she said. Now, honestly, isn't that pure bunk? However, she did say she thought focus groups would be especially useful in Eastern Europe, where businesses have so many needs, and we have to be sure to cull down to the most critical ones. I wonder, suppose our Swiss trucking division could use focus groups to help them develop new services for Eastern European businesses?"

3. "You know a lot about personal digital assistants, I imagine. Can you take me through a problem analysis using the PDA market as an example? We are getting into the PDA business in our electronics division, with the idea of having a direct competitor to Palm, and I'm curious to see what problems you come up with that we haven't solved yet."

Case: Campbell's IQ Meals[37]

In 1990, Campbell Soup was the undisputed leader among U.S. soup manufacturers, with a market share of over 75 percent. Soup consumption, however, was leveling off, and top management was looking for opportunities for growth in related markets. Competitors such as ConAgra (Healthy Choice brand) and H. J. Heinz (Weight Watchers brand) were making sizeable sales and profit gains in their frozen foods lines, stressing their dietary benefits, and this seemed like a good place for Campbell to begin generating new product ideas.

At the time, the U.S. public was becoming more interested in the relationship between diet and disease prevention. It seemed that, every day, health benefits were turning up in one food or another, causing fads such as oat bran to sweep the country. Campbell's R&D department soon turned to investigating the diet-disease relationship, focusing on foods that could be used to prevent illnesses such as diabetes or cardiovascular disease (including high blood pressure). Given that 58 million Americans have some form of cardiovascular disease and another 16 million have diabetes, this focus seemed very reasonable. Soon enough, the rough idea had been generated: a line of foods with medical benefits. The rough idea now needed to be further developed.

The challenge was to develop a food line that not only played a role in the prevention of these diseases, but also would be accepted and adopted by the U.S. population. Dr. R. David C. Macnair, Campbell's chief technical officer, built an advisory board consisting of leading nutrition, heart disease, and diabetes specialists, who would scientifically analyze the new products. Campbell's CEO at the time, David W. Johnson, was 100 percent behind the food-with-medical-benefits idea, saying that it had "explosive potential." Soon, he was attending the advisory board meetings as well. Mr. Johnson said, "Wouldn't you be dumbfounded by the opportunity to take a quantum leap and develop a product that could help improve the health and nutrition of the world?"

With the backing of the Campbell CEO, the project was underway, with a clear goal: to make the concept of healthy, vitamin-and-mineral-rich meals a reality. The Campbell food technologists found this a challenging task—one of the early prototype fiber-enriched rolls "could have been marketed as a hockey puck," according to Macnair. By fall 1994, however, about 24 meals that passed early taste tests were ready for clinical trials to determine health benefits. Over 500 subjects ate the meals for 10 weeks, and most reported improvements in cholesterol, blood pressure, and blood sugar levels. None experienced side effects, and many reported they liked the taste. Meanwhile, Mr. Johnson created Campbell's Center for Nutrition and Wellness, based in the Camden, New Jersey, head office and employing 30 nutrition scientists and dietitians.

Next came the market test. Campbell marketing staff selected the name "Intelligent Quisine" (or IQ Meals), and a blue box or can for packaging. The plan was

---

[37]This case is largely based on Vanessa O'Connell, "Food for Thought: How Campbell Saw a Breakthrough Menu Turn into Leftovers," *The Wall Street Journal*, October 6, 1998, pp. A1, A12.

for UPS drivers to deliver 21 meals (mostly frozen, a few in cans) each week to test subjects' doors. By January 1997, the product was being test marketed in Ohio, backed up with a print ad campaign and a 10-minute infomercial designed to stimulate toll-free calls to Campbell's information line. Campbell also hired part-time pharmaceutical sales reps to pitch IQ Meals to doctors, and contacted leading hospitals such as the Cleveland Clinic to distribute IQ Meals and promotional material. Things were looking up!

The first sign of trouble was at the phone bank. Callers found out that the one-week sample pack cost $80, and the recommended plan (10 weeks) cost $700, and promptly hung up. Fixed-income households found the price especially steep. At the American Heart Association's Columbus office, Campbell sponsored a lunch to promote IQ Meals' benefits, but failed to impress many of the dietitians present. Further, Wall Street analysts had their doubts as well: One of them wrote a report titled, "UPS T.V. Dinners Drive Top Line?"

Soon, Campbell executives were doubting the IQ Meals as well. Consultants were called in to assess the project's viability, and Dale Morrison, head of international and specialty foods, cut IQ's budget drastically. By May 1997, sales in the Ohio market test were dismal, and another problem was arising. Those that had stuck with the program since January were showing health benefits, but now many of them were reporting that they were getting tired of the same nine meals over and over again.

The fate of IQ Meals was sealed in a corporate shakeup at Campbell in July 1997. Mr. Johnson, its biggest supporter, gave up his CEO position (and became Campbell's chairman). Mr. Morrison rose to president and CEO, with a plan to expand international sales and to focus on key brands. Swanson, Vlasic, and other Campbell brands were spun off—and the marketing and promotion for IQ was terminated (though clinical trials were continued). The Center for Nutrition and Wellness researchers were reassigned. By fall 1997, Campbell announced plans to sell IQ Meals.

Question: IQ Meals seemed to be a classic case history. The idea that was generated seemed foolproof with respect to the marketplace opportunity and the associated demographic trends. Campbell would appear to be the perfect company to pull it off, given its core competencies and its willingness to expand into growth areas. The line even did well in both clinical trials and early consumer tests. But, somehow, something got lost in the translation. And clearly, this is not an isolated incident. What went wrong? And what might Campbell product developers or executives have done differently? Or was this one just doomed from the start?

Case: Earning Organizational Respect

In this case, you and your classmates play the role of the marketing department in a firm involved in new product development. Your firm is struggling with instituting team-based product development, and over the last several months several of the marketing staff have been placed on product teams with personnel from engineering, design, and manufacturing. The experience so far has not been positive for you and your marketing colleagues. You feel that marketing is routinely left out of key team decisions and that top management seems more sympathetic to the engineers when conflicts arise within the team. You suspect that part of the reason is that most top management personnel in your firm come from an engineering background and just understand the perspectives and the decision-making style of the engineers better. You also feel that marketing has a lot to contribute to product development. There is an excellent marketing research department that can provide quick feedback on customer behavior using state-of-the-art equipment, and the sales force is second to none in the industry and routinely gathers key market information and intelligence. There are several very good creative people on staff responsible for generating high-potential ideas, which your firm has developed into many successful new product launches.

One of your creative colleagues in product development suggests using a problem-based ideation approach, commonly used to generate new product ideas, to try to find a way to get top management to respect the marketing department more. Ideally, you would like them to recognize your skills, training, and experience and to appreciate and use the unique information you can bring to the new product process. You succinctly state your problem as follows:

"How can we communicate the value and potential contributions of the marketing department effectively to top management, so that they will respect us more?"

Using the ideation techniques given in Appendix B (or any others you prefer), develop creative solutions to this problem. First, generate at least half a dozen ideas individually. Keep a basic rule in mind: There are no bad ideas—the more, the merrier. Then, with your instructor working as a group facilitator, boil these down to the four or five best ideas and, as a group, discuss and refine these. Your goal is to arrive collectively at one or more clear, well-thought-out programs that you could realistically begin implementing soon. One other rule: Use your imagination! This is an exercise where you can really stretch. Though you can try any of the techniques given in Appendix B, some you might find particularly useful are the following:

Scenario Analysis: Identify a set of trends (fashions, hot places to live/work, celebrities, exciting new products, etc.). Think about what might be suggested by or associated with any of these.

Creative Stimuli: Look at the set of stimulus words provided in Appendix B and select a few of these at random. Ask yourself how each of your words suggests something that helps you solve your problem. Be creative.

Forced Relationships: Forget about your problem altogether for a little while. Select a magazine. Turn randomly to a page and look at the picture on that page. (If none, leaf through the magazine until you get to one.) What does the picture suggest to you? Jot down at least half a dozen thoughts. Now, return to your problem and use the thoughts you came up with to help you think creatively about possible solutions. For a variation, use a dictionary, encyclopedia, or the Yellow Pages instead and find a random word on a random page.

Use of the Ridiculous: Think of the most ridiculous idea you can. Then ask yourself if it suggests to you a not-so-ridiculous new idea.

CHAPTER SIX

Analytical Attribute Approaches: Introduction and Perceptual Mapping

Setting

In Chapter 5, we studied an approach to concept generation that involves identifying users' problems and finding solutions to them. The problem-based approach is the best because product concepts found by the problem/solution route are most likely to have value for the user.

This chapter introduces a different set of techniques that are commonly used in the problem-solving phage (see Figure II.1 at the beginning of Part II). Everyone involved with the creation and sale of goods and services can make use of these techniques, including some who don't even know they are doing formal concept generation. What these techniques do is create views of a product different from the usual ones—they can seem almost magic, but are quite deliberate. They can appear to be strictly fortuitous, or lucky, when they work, and they have indeed worked—many times, as with adding a third stocking to a package, quick-drying inks, and cell phones that search the Internet. But actually, they are quite deliberate and purposeful, allowing discovery—serendipitous findings that come to people who know what they are looking for. We refer to these techniques as analytical attribute techniques, and they are our concern in Chapters 6 and 7.

Understanding Why Customers Buy a Product

Products Are Groups of Attributes

What is a **product attribute?** Figure 6.1 shows the set of them. A product is really nothing but attributes, and any product (good or service) can be described

FIGURE 6.1
A Typology
of Attributes

A. Product attributes (for our purposes) are of three types:

Features	Functions	Benefits

Features can be many things:

Dimensions	Esthetic characteristics	Components
Source ingredients	Manufacturing process	Materials
Services	Performance	Price
Structures	Trademarks	And many more

Benefits can be many things:

Uses	Sensory enjoyments	Economic gains
Savings (time, effort)	Nonmaterial well-being	And many more

Benefits are either direct (e.g., clean teeth) or indirect (e.g., romance following from clean teeth).

Functions are how products work (e.g., a pen that *sprays* ink onto the paper). They are unlimited in variety, but are not used nearly as often as benefits and features.

B. Analytical attribute approaches use different attributes:

Dimensional analysis uses features
Checklists use all attributes
Trade-off analysis also uses determinant attributes
Several methods in Appendix B use functions and benefits

by citing its attributes.[1] Attributes are of three types: **features** (what the product consists of), **functions** (what the product does and how it works), and **benefits** (how the product provides satisfaction to the user). Benefits can be broken down in an almost endless variety—uses, users, used with, used where, and so on. Concept generation is a creative task, so great liberty has been taken with definitions in its activity. The classification system used in this book is an attempt, and no more than that, to arrange them for study. It is important here to recognize that it makes sense for us to define attributes broadly. A pair of shoes can be thought of as a group of attributes; a person may buy a given pair because she likes the appearance of the leather (*feature*), because they are excellent walking shoes (*function*), or because they are very comfortable (*benefit*). (And if you disagree with the classification of these attributes as features, functions, or benefits, that's OK too!)

A spoon is a small shallow bowl (*feature*) with a handle (another *feature*) on it. The bowl enables the spoon to *function* as a holder and carrier of liquids. The *benefits* include economy and neatness of consuming liquid materials. Of course, the spoon has many other features (including shape, material, reflection, and pattern), not to mention other functions (it can pry, poke, project, and so on, as school cafeteria managers know all too well) and benefits (such as pride of ownership, status, or table orderliness).

---

[1]For a useful perspective on how to conduct research on identifying what attributes are most valued by customers, see Charles Miller and David C. Swaddling, "Focusing NPD Research on Customer-Perceived Value," in P. Belliveau, A. Griffin, and S. Somermeyer (eds.), *The PDMA Toolbook for New Product Development* (New York: John Wiley, 2002), pp. 87–114.

Theoretically, the three basic types of attributes occur in sequence. A feature permits a certain function, which in turn leads to a benefit. A shampoo may contain certain proteins (feature) that coat the hair during shampooing (function), which leads to more shine on the hair (benefit).

Analyzing Product Attributes for Concept Generation and Evaluation

Analytical attribute techniques allow us to create new product concepts by changing one or more of its current attributes, or by adding attributes, and to assess the desirability of these concepts if they were to be developed into products. That is, these techniques can be used in concept generation (which will be approached in this chapter), but also in concept evaluation and even further along in the new products process, as you will see in succeeding chapters. If we were to change current product attributes in all the ways they could be changed, or to think of many additional attributes that could be built into the product, we would eventually discover every change that could ever come about in that product. Other techniques capitalize on relating one attribute with another attribute (or to something else in the environment), forcing these relationships whether normal and logical or strange and unanticipated. They all can work, as you will see. And they have been used in all product categories from polymer processing technologies at Kodak to the newest car lines at Ford or Toyota to eyeglasses and cereal.

Analytical attribute techniques are felt to be more useful in Western culture than in Eastern. Western (particularly European and North American) thought goes heavily toward rearranging things, while Eastern (Asian) thought tends to start work anew.[2] Commodity-type products are a major focus because slight rearrangements can differentiate one item from its competitors, thus allowing it to carry a higher price.

There are a variety of quantitative and qualitative **attribute analysis** techniques available. In this chapter, we explore one common quantitative technique: **perceptual gap analysis.** After an introduction to determinant gap maps, we will show how perceptual mapping techniques such as factor analysis and multidimensional scaling (MDS) can be used to generate perceptual gap maps. These techniques are frequently used in concept generation, and indeed, throughout new product development, during launch, and even beyond. We shall be returning to them from time to time as we proceed through the new products process. Chapter 7 examines a second common quantitative technique, conjoint analysis, and several qualitative techniques such as dimensional analysis, checklists, relationships analysis, and analogy. Many more techniques are also given in Appendix B.

Gap Analysis

Gap analysis is a statistical technique with immense power under certain circumstances. Its *maps of the market* are used to determine how various products are

[2]Jacquelyn Wonder and Jeffrey Blake, "Creativity East and West: Intuition versus Logic," *Journal of Creative Behavior*, Third Quarter 1992, pp. 172–185.

perceived by how they are positioned on the market map. On a geographical map, New York City is much closer to Pittsburgh than it is to Los Angeles. But on a *nearness-to-the-sea* map, New York City would be right next to Los Angeles. On any map, the items plotted tend to cluster here and there, with open space between them. These open spaces are gaps, and a map that shows gaps is, not surprisingly, called a **gap map.**

Several levels of sophistication will be cited, because many firms prefer to use the technique in a simple form, while others have achieved their greatest success with the more complex versions. Gap maps are made in three ways: (1) *Managerial expertise and judgment* is used to plot products on a map and make a **determinant gap map;** (2) a manager uses customer *attribute ratings* to get data from users for an **AR perceptual gap map;** and (3) a manager uses *overall similarities* to get data from users for an **OS perceptual gap map.**

Determinant Gap Maps

Figure 6.2 shows a map of snacks prepared by members of a new products team seeking to enter the snack market. The map consisted of two dimensions (they personally thought crunchiness and nutritional value were important in snacks). Scales ran from low to high on both factors. Each brand then in the market was scored by the managers on each of the two factors.

While the scoring may seem arbitrary and subject to managerial error, determinant gap maps are often a good place to start. Remember, concept generation takes place *after* strategy (the PIC) has targeted a market or user group on which to

FIGURE 6.2
Gap Map for Snack Products

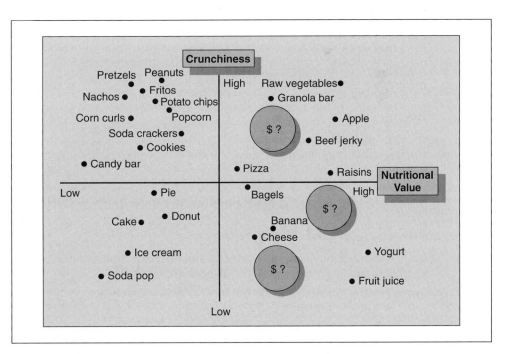

focus. Either the firm had experience in this market (a strength) or the market was researched. Each brand was then entered on the diagram (Figure 6.2) according to its scores. The result was a map of the brands, each in relationship to all others, on these two factors. Many maps could have been prepared, each with a different pair of attributes. They can also be three-dimensional. But the managers providing inputs to the determinant gap map are not new to this industry; they would have valuable and useful beliefs and judgments that may be very helpful in guiding concept generation. (Of course, they can still be wrong. Do you disagree with any of the assigned positions in Figure 6.2? Look closely!)

Attributes used in gap analysis should normally be *differentiating* and *important*. Consumers differentiate snacks on their crunchiness and on their nutritional value. And these attributes are important in buying snacks. Snacks also have different shape esthetics, but these are not often used to differentiate one from another. Even if they were, most people would probably not think them important.

Attributes that both differentiate and are important are called **determinant attributes,** because they help determine what snacks are bought. In an industrial study of vinyl siding, some of the determinant attributes identified were appearance/status, maintenance/weathering, application/economy, and dent resistance.[3]

The reason it is important to use determinant attributes in making the maps is that our purpose in this method is to find a spot on the map where a gap offers potential as a new item, one that people might find different and interesting.

For example, on the snacks map in Figure 6.2 the circles marked "$?" are gaps, and thus offer new product possibilities. Note that the large number of snacks makes our gaps few and small—for example, the gap of semi-high crunchy and semi-high nutritional is close to the granola bar, the apple, beef jerky, and soda crackers.

Determinant gap maps are speedy and cost-efficient, but have the weakness of being driven by only managerial judgment. Customer perceptions may indeed be quite different. Plus, brand perceptions might be more difficult for managers to judge correctly. In Figure 6.2, we might all agree that potato chips have lower nutritional value than granola bars, but how do customers perceive different brands of granola bars? Do they really think Nature Valley bars are the most nutritious, best tasting, or lowest in calories? And how important are each of these attributes to customers when they form preferences? Techniques that gather customer perceptions use them to develop gap maps that can provide important (and perhaps surprising) insights to the manager. We now explore two commonly used types of perceptual gap maps.

Perceptual Gap Maps Based on Attribute Ratings (AR)

Unlike the determinant gap map method, attribute ratings (AR) perceptual gap mapping asks market participants (buyers and users of the product) to tell what attributes they believe products have. For example, product users may think candy bars are high in nutrition—doubtful, but if this were so, then any map putting candy bars low in nutrition is incorrect for seeing perceptual gaps. Determinant

[3]Steven A. Sinclair and Edward C. Stalling, "Perceptual Mapping: A Tool for Industrial Marketing: A Case Study," *Journal of Business and Industrial Marketing*, Winter/Spring 1990, pp. 55–66.

FIGURE 6.3
A Data Cube

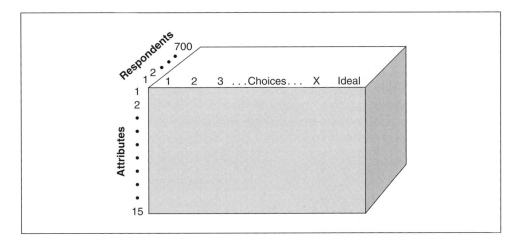

maps are based on reality as viewed by the new products manager (or, perhaps, by the firm's R&D personnel). Perceptual maps, as the name implies, are based on marketplace perceptions of reality, which may or may not be accurate. They can complement each other, and both have a place in our work.

In AR perceptual gap mapping, we begin with a set of attributes (again, these can be features, benefits, or functions) that describe the product category being considered. We gather customers' perceptions of the available choices (brands, manufacturers, etc.) on each of these attributes. Typically, this is done using 1-to-5 or 1-to-7 scales (commonly called "Likert-type" scales), where the endpoints are "strongly disagree" and "strongly agree" with each attribute statement provided. We also ask customers which attributes are important in their purchases of products in this category. This procedure results in a formidable **data cube** (Figure 6.3), which while perhaps impressive in size, is not very helpful to managers. In Figure 6.3, the perceptions of the available choices on each attribute would appear under Brands 1 through X, while the importances of the attributes would be given in the Ideal column.

The challenge is then to reduce the data cube into something more manageable—namely, a perceptual map. **Factor analysis,** a statistical technique available in computer packages, is typically used to reduce the large number of attributes to a small number of underlying dimensions (also called factors), which can then serve as the axes of the perceptual map. Other techniques beyond the scope of this book, such as multiple discriminant analysis, can also be used. **Cluster analysis** (to be presented in a later chapter) can then be used to group individual respondents together into benefit segments based on their preferences.

Suppose, for example, that you are a product manager at a firm that makes women's swimsuits. Based on your industry experience and your knowledge of the market, you have developed a set of attributes that customers use in evaluating and comparing swimsuits. You have commissioned a research study in which female respondents were asked to identify all the brands of swimsuits they are familiar with and to rate them on each of the attributes on 1-to-5 Likert-type scales (see Figure 6.4). They are also asked to state how important each of these attributes is when deciding which brand of swimsuit to buy, again using 1-to-5 Likert type

FIGURE 6.4
Attribute
Perceptions
Questionnaire

Rate each brand you are familiar with on each of the following:

	Disagree	Agree
1. Attractive design	1..2..3..4..5	
2. Stylish	1..2..3..4..5	
3. Comfortable to wear	1..2..3..4..5	
4. Fashionable	1..2..3..4..5	
5. I feel good when I wear it	1..2..3..4..5	
6. Is ideal for swimming	1..2..3..4..5	
7. Looks like a designer label	1..2..3..4..5	
8. Easy to swim in	1..2..3..4..5	
9. In style	1..2..3..4..5	
10. Great appearance	1..2..3..4..5	
11. Comfortable to swim in	1..2..3..4..5	
12. This is a desirable label	1..2..3..4..5	
13. Gives me the look I like	1..2..3..4..5	
14. I like the colors it comes in	1..2..3..4..5	
15. Is functional for swimming	1..2..3..4..5	

scales. The average ratings of each brand on each attribute are presented in the snake plot of Figure 6.5.

The **snake plot** (the name refers to the snakelike shape of the lines that join the points) reveals some useful information. For example, respondents tend to think

FIGURE 6.5
Snake Plot of
Brand Ratings

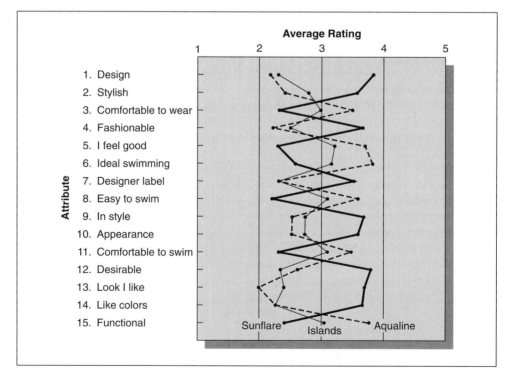

that Aqualine is more comfortable to wear and easier to swim in than Sunflare (attributes 3 and 8), while Sunflare has a more attractive design and is more stylish than Aqualine (attributes 1 and 2). But there is just too much in Figure 6.5 for it to be of much help in identifying a lucrative perceptual gap, and we still seem to be far away from a simple pictorial representation as seen in Figure 6.2.

Closer inspection of Figure 6.5 suggests that there may be underlying patterns in the data. We notice, for example, that choices that are rated high on "attractive design" tend also to be perceived as "fashionable," "designer label," and so on. We might say that these attributes seem to *hang together*. Similarly, other attributes ("comfortable to wear," "easy to swim in," and "comfortable to swim in") also seem to hang together. There may be a small number of such underlying dimensions or factors that explain most of the variation in perceptions presented in Figure 6.5. If we could identify these factors, then we would no longer need all the attributes: We could present most of what we know about customer perceptions using just the factors. We apply a factor analysis computer program to the customer perception data to identify these factors.

The first challenge we face is to determine how many underlying factors to retain in the model, as this is seldom clearcut. One rule of thumb is to plot incremental percent variance explained as shown in Figure 6.6. As this figure shows,

FIGURE 6.6
Scree Plot and Eigenvalue Test

Factor	Eigenvalue	Percent Variance Explained
1	6.04	40.3
2	3.34	22.3
3	0.88	5.9
4	0.74	4.9
5	0.62	4.2
6	0.54	3.6
7	0.52	3.5
8	0.44	3.0
9	0.40	2.7

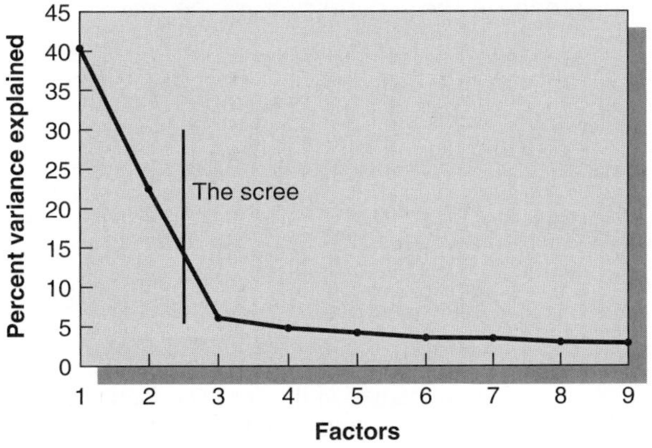

FIGURE 6.7
Factor
Loading
Matrix for
Swimsuit
Data

Attribute	Factor 1 "Fashion"	Factor 2 "Comfort"
1. Attractive design	**.796**	.061
2. Stylish	**.791**	.029
3. Comfortable to wear	.108	**.782**
4. Fashionable	**.803**	.077
5. I feel good when I wear it	.039	**.729**
6. Is ideal for swimming	.102	**.833**
7. Looks like a designer label	**.754**	.059
8. Easy to swim in	.093	**.793**
9. In style	**.762**	.123
10. Great appearance	**.758**	.208
11. Comfortable to swim in	.043	**.756**
12. This is a desirable label	**.807**	.082
13. Gives me the look I like	**.810**	.055
14. I like the colors it comes in	**.800**	.061
15. Is functional for swimming	.106	**.798**

Factors 1 and 2 both explain a lot of variance, but going from two to three factors does not add very much to the model. This provides some evidence that the first two factors should be retained. This procedure is called the *scree test*. (A scree is a pile of rocks at the foot of a mountain. Figure 6.6 resembles the side of a mountain, and the cutoff is made at the scree.) The factor analysis procedure also provides a useful statistic (called the *eigenvalue*) for each factor, which is mathematically related to the amount of variance explained. A second rule of thumb is to keep only those factors whose eigenvalues are greater than 1. Figure 6.6 shows that the first two eigenvalues pass this hurdle (they are 6.04 and 3.34, respectively). Thus, both the scree test and the eigenvalue rule suggest that the two-factor solution is satisfactory.

The factor analysis program then calculates a factor loading (or factor pattern) matrix, showing the correlation of the original set of attributes to their underlying factors. Figure 6.7 shows the rotated factor loading matrix obtained for the swimsuit data.[4] Attribute 1 ("attractive design") clearly loads on the first factor much more than on the second factor (the loadings are 0.796 and 0.061, respectively; in Figure 6.7, the large loadings are underlined and boldfaced for clarity). As the table shows, Attributes 2, 4, 7, and five others also load on the first factor in addition to Attribute 1. Similarly, a different set of attributes (3, 5, 6, and so on) load on the second factor.

So what should we call the two factors? Again, there is no right answer; this is part of the analyst's art. But, glancing at the attributes that loaded onto Factor 1 ("attractive design," "stylish," "fashionable," "looks like a designer label," "in style," and so on), we see a common thread. We might call this factor "fashion." The second factor

[4]The factor loading matrix of Figure 6.7 has been varimax rotated. This procedure rotates the axes to aid in interpretation of the resulting factors by forcing the column entries to be close to 0 or 1. For details, see Gilbert A. Churchill, Jr. and Dawn Iacobucci, *Marketing Research: Methodological Foundations*, 8th ed. (Fort Worth, TX: Dryden, 2002).

FIGURE 6.8
Factor-Score
Coefficient
Matrix

Attribute	Factor 1 "Fashion"	Factor 2 "Comfort"
1. Attractive design	0.145	−0.022
2. Stylish	0.146	−0.030
3. Comfortable to wear	−0.018	0.213
4. Fashionable	0.146	−0.017
5. I feel good when I wear it	−0.028	0.201
6. Is ideal for swimming	−0.021	0.227
7. Looks like a designer label	0.138	−0.020
8. Easy to swim in	0.131	0.216
9. In style	−0.021	−0.003
10. Great appearance	0.146	0.021
11. Comfortable to swim in	−0.029	0.208
12. This is a desirable label	0.146	−0.016
13. Gives me the look I like	0.148	−0.024
14. I like the colors it comes in	0.146	−0.022
15. Is functional for swimming	−0.019	0.217

Sample calculation of factor scores: From the snake plot, the mean ratings of Aqualine on attributes 1 through 15 are 2.15, 2.40, 3.48, . . . , 3.77. Multiply each of these mean ratings by the corresponding coefficient in the factor-score coefficient matrix to get Aqualine's factor scores. For example, on Factor 1, Aqualine's score $(2.15 \times 0.145) + (2.40 \times 0.146) + (3.48 \times -0.018) + \ldots + (3.77 \times -0.019) = 2.48$. Similarly, its score on Factor 2 can be calculated as 4.36. All other brands' factor scores are calculated the same way.

might be called "comfort" as its attributes all seem to have to do with comfort or ease of wear. Figure 6.7 shows the factor names at the top of each column. Incidentally, the fact that these two factors are easily interpretable is further proof that the two-factor solution is good. Several apparently unrelated attributes can sometimes get forced together onto a single factor: This may be a sign that too few factors were chosen.

The program also calculates the matrix of factor-score coefficients (see Figure 6.8). These are regression weights that relate the attribute scales to the factor scores. Thus, since we know how each choice is rated on each individual attribute (this information is in the snake plot), we can use the factor-score coefficient matrix to estimate how they would have been rated relative to the underlying factors. These estimates, called *factor scores*, can be used to draw the perceptual map, which appears in Figure 6.9.

The perceptual map shows that Aqualine is perceived as the most comfortable brand (score on Factor 2 is 4.36), but is low in fashion (score on Factor 1 is 2.48). Sunflare is the most fashionable swimsuit but is also perceived to be the most uncomfortable; Splash is rated quite low on both factors; and the other two choices occupy intermediate positions in perceptual space. Recall that this is information on how *customers* perceive the products; it may be quite unlike what management had previously believed.

So we have gone from the messy snake plot of Figure 6.5 to the perceptual map of Figure 6.9. Granted, the perceptual map does not have *all* the information contained in the snake plot. But we have retained the two most important factors (in terms of variance explained) underlying customer perceptions. Thus we have a simple visual representation that is easily used and understood by managers, and that contains *most* of the information we started with.

FIGURE 6.9
AR Perceptual
Map of
Swimsuit
Brands

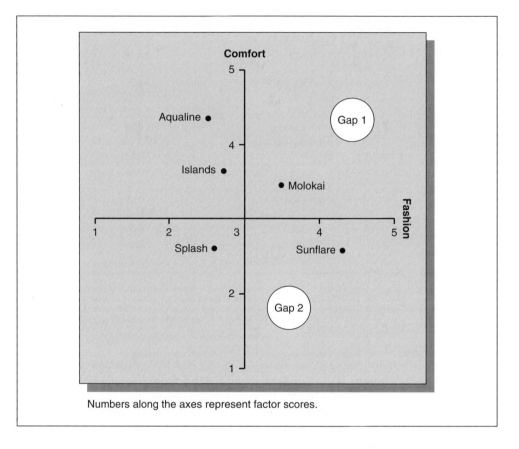

Numbers along the axes represent factor scores.

The perceptual map we just built resembles the snack map of Figure 6.2, and the search for gaps can proceed as before. Since the perceptual map was built using actual customer perceptions, any gaps found are more likely to interest the potential users.[5] For example, the perceptual map suggests that customers perceive some swimsuits to be comfortable and others to be fashionable, but none offers both high comfort and high fashion (Gap 1 in Figure 6.9). Congratulations—you've just uncovered a gap!

Perceptual Gap Maps Based on Overall Similarities (OS)

AR perceptual maps early on suffered a criticism that led to a variation preferred by some product innovators. The problem was that users sometimes make purchase decisions using attributes they cannot identify. These phantom attributes don't show up on the lists, are not included as map dimensions, and by their absence distort the analysis. Also, some users have difficulty scoring attributes, even when they are aware of them, because they are simply unable to, or are unwilling to do so. In a focus group setting, some participants may not want to reveal

[5]For more information on the use of factor analysis in new products, see Uwe Hentschel, "On the Search for New Products," *European Journal of Marketing* 5, 1976, pp. 203–217.

something they feel is socially undesirable, for example. AR methods essentially view products as bundles of attributes. For AR to be effective, then, the attribute set needs to be complete. (If we had forgotten to include comfort-related attributes in the above analysis, our results would have been very different, and very misleading!) Also, customers should, by and large, make their purchase decisions according to these attributes. In a product category like cologne, for example, the customer's decision may be driven more by brand image, aesthetics, or other attributes that are notoriously difficult for them to verbalize.

DuPont offered an early example of the phantom problem. The company sold filler material for pillows and wanted to find the best type and form of filler to enhance its sales to pillow manufacturers. But DuPont market analysts found that consumers could not clearly describe the attributes of pillows and could not communicate the attributes they wanted in pillows. So the firm created many different types of pillows and then gave them to consumers three at a time, along with the question, "Which two are most similar, or which one is least like the other two?" DuPont's research was much more complex than this question implies; but, in essence, the firm was now able to use a computer algorithm to convert the similarities data into a map showing closeness of products, *without knowing a priori which attributes created that closeness.*

OS techniques do not require customers to rate choices on individual attributes. Rather, these techniques run on perceptions of overall similarities between pairs of brands. If there are five choices (as in the swimsuit example), there are 10 possible pairs. There are a couple of ways the data can be collected. Respondents could rank the pairs from most similar to most dissimilar, or rate pairs on, say, a 1-to-9 Likert-type scale where 1 is "very similar" and 9 is "very dissimilar." If we had gathered similarities data on swimsuits using Likert-type similarity scales, we might have ended up with average similarity ratings as shown in Figure 6.10. This figure shows that customers tend to see Sunflare and Molokai as relatively similar (recall that lower ratings mean greater similarity), and Aqualine and Sunflare as very dissimilar.

The next step is to convert the customer data (similarity ratings or rankings, depending on what data were gathered) into a perceptual map. In a very simple example, if you think Coke and Pepsi are very similar, and both are very different from Dr Pepper, you could easily draw a map of your perceptions on a single line: Put Coke and Pepsi on the left and put Dr Pepper on the right. In the same way, we could eyeball the ratings in Figure 6.10, though the task would admittedly be difficult. Alternatively, we could use a computer program such as **multidimensional scaling (MDS)** to develop a perceptual map from the similarities data.

FIGURE 6.10
Dissimilarity Matrix

	Aqualine	Islands	Sunflare	Molokai	Splash
Aqualine	X	3	9	5	7
Islands		X	8	3	4
Sunflare			X	5	7
Molokai				X	6
Splash					X

FIGURE 6.11
OS Perceptual
Map of
Swimsuit
Brands

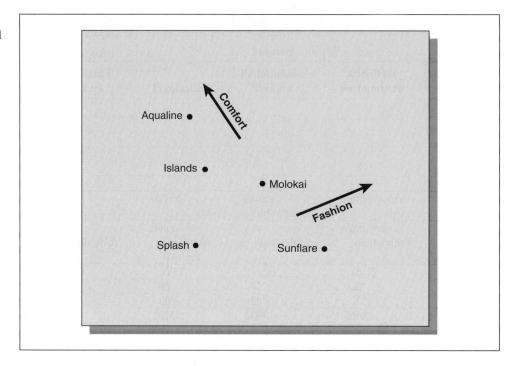

MDS attempts to plot the choices on a map such that the similarities are best preserved (i.e., swimsuits that should be together, are together). Figure 6.11 shows the perceptual map obtained from the similarity ratings.

The MDS-based perceptual map seems very similar to Figure 6.9, which was derived from factor analysis. In fact, the relative positions of the swimsuits are not that different. There is one important difference, however: The axes are not defined! MDS provides the relative positions only; follow-up analysis must be done to define the axes (there may be more than two) and determine what the relative positions mean. A manager knowledgeable about the industry might be able to infer the meanings by examining the points. For example, since Aqualine is known to be the most comfortable brand, and Splash and Sunflare are generally viewed as less comfortable, the north-south direction might represent comfort (north being more comfortable). In the same way, the more fashionable swimsuits seem to be toward the right, suggesting that the east-west direction represents fashion.

Alternatively, computer programs can be used to assist in naming the axes if measures on specific attributes had been obtained from the respondents. One of the most common of these is PROFIT (for PROperty FITting), which fits vectors to the map that best correspond to the swimsuits' positions. If, for example, customers were asked to rate each brand on comfort and fashion, PROFIT might have fit vectors corresponding to these attributes as shown in Figure 6.11. The most fashionable swimsuits tend to be in the direction of the fashion vector.

FIGURE 6.12
Comparing
AR to OS
Perceptual
Mapping

AR Methods	OS Methods
Input Required	
Ratings on specific attributes	Overall similarity ratings
Attributes must be prespecified	Respondent uses own judgment of similarity
Analytic Procedures Commonly Used	
Factor analysis	Multidimensional scaling (MDS)
Graphical Output	
Shows product or brand positions on axes	Shows product positions relative to each other
Axes interpretable as underlying dimensions (factors)	Axes obtained through follow-up analysis or must be interpreted by the researcher
Where Used	
Situations where attributes are easily articulated or visualized	Situations where it may be difficult for the respondent to articulate or visualize attributes

Source: Adapted from Robert Dolan, *Managing new Product Development Process*, 1st Edition, Copyright © 1993. Reprinted by permission of Pearson Education, Inc., Upper Saddle River, New Jersey.

Figure 6.12 compares the advantages and disadvantages of AR and OS perceptual mapping methods. Both methods are readily available as parts of easy-to-use commercial software packages and can generate detailed results at quite a low cost.

Comments on Gap Analysis

All gap mapping is controversial, but perceptual maps especially so. The input data come entirely from responses to questions about how the choices differ. Nuances and shadings are necessarily ignored, as are interrelationships and synergies. Creations requiring a conceptual leap are missed. In the early 1800s, for example, gap analysis might have led to breeding faster horses or to wagons with larger wheels, but it probably would not have suggested the automobile.

The most troublesome aspect is that gap analysis discovers gaps, not demand. Gaps often exist for good reasons (e.g., fish-aroma air freshener or aspirin-flavored ice cream). New products people still have to go to the marketplace to see if the gaps they discovered represent things people want.

Returning to Gap 1 in Figure 6.9, we do not know yet whether the market wants a very comfortable, very fashionable swimsuit. Inspection of Figure 6.9 also suggests there is a gap at medium fashion, low comfort (Gap 2). Maybe this is a better bet for a new concept. To answer this question, we need to turn to the importance data, which, as you will recall, we collected at the same time as we gathered the perceptual data. We will continue this example in Chapter 9 when we analyze customer preferences and identify benefit segments.

And, as in all ideation of new products, people must avoid being bound by what is now impossible. For example, for years gap maps on analgesics showed a big hole where strength was paired with gentleness. The strong/gentle part of the map was always empty, and everyone knew why—an over-the-counter analgesic that was potent yet didn't irritate the stomach could not be made. Of course, Extra-Strength Tylenol and later products such as Aleve were eventually developed that filled this gap, offering both strength and gentleness. As another example, most popular brands of soap were positioned as either deodorants (like Dial) or moisturizers (like Dove), and a perceptual gap (a brand that offered both attributes) existed. In 1991, Lever 2000 soap very successfully filled that gap, having been launched as a combination deodorant/moisturizing bar and supported by a first-year advertising campaign of $25 million—raised to $40 million in the second year![6]

Summary

In this chapter, we have examined the use of gap maps in identifying potential product concepts. As we have noted, this technique will come in handy in later phases of the new products process, when we begin working with customer preferences and positioning (and repositioning) our products. We have looked in depth at both attribute-based and overall similarity–based perceptual mapping, each technique having its own advantages and disadvantages.

Other attribute-based approaches are also available to us at the concept generation stage. Chapter 7 will introduce us to conjoint (trade-off) analysis and several other less-quantitative approaches, which can also be useful in generating potentially lucrative product concepts.

Applications

1. "One method you say you studied is of great interest to me, for reasons I'll not go into. It's gap analysis, especially the idea of maps. Several of our best divisions produce and sell services. Is the gap map method applicable to services? Could you please take, say, the college education market and draw up a product map for it? I understand it can be done by a manager at a desk, although, of course, it wouldn't be nearly as accurate as if we had all the technical data, and so on. But could you try?"

2. "OK, you've identified a gap in the swimsuit market in your little example. Some customers like fashionable swimsuits, some like comfortable ones. We already know that. So isn't it obvious you should design a swimsuit that's both fashionable and comfortable? What insights did you get from the gap analysis that you couldn't have figured out on your own?"

3. "A few years ago, most peanut butters were sold on the basis of their perceived quality (well-known brands vs. store brands), and crunchiness. There wasn't a

[6]See Robert M. McMath and Thom Forbes, *What Were They Thinking?* (New York: Times Business Books, 1998), pp. 184–185.

lot of difference among the competitors. Then Skippy hits the market, claiming to be healthier than other brands because it uses less salt. They didn't even position themselves on the traditional attributes in their market. How does your gap map account for that?"

Case: Dell Computers (A)[7]

Dell Computers was founded by Michael Dell in 1984 and has its head offices in Round Rock, Texas. Recent annual sales revenues have been well over $40 billion, and Dell employs almost 48,000 people worldwide. Michael Dell's original vision was to sell computer systems directly to customers. By eliminating the retailer, Dell was able to better understand emerging wants and needs and to provide the best computing solutions to satisfy those needs, while at the same time reducing time and costs. Effectively, every system is built to order in response to a customer need. Dell is also able to roll out advanced technology more rapidly than competitors that rely on traditional, indirect distribution channels. In fact, Dell claims that it turns its inventory over once every three days!

Dell was one of the pioneers in selling computers over the Internet. Its Web site, www.dell.com, was launched as early as 1994, with e-commerce capability added in 1996. By 1997, Dell reached sales of $1 million in daily online sales, being the first firm to do so. Currently, Dell's Web site receives over a billion page requests per quarter across 84 country sites. It also allows business and institutional customers to use its Premier Dell.com Web pages to conduct online transactions.

The market for personal computers has been growing rapidly for several years with little end in sight. As of the end of the year 2000, approximately 120 million PCs were sold worldwide. Projections for the next five years of industry sales are as shown below:

Year	2001	2002	2003	2004	2005
Market size (in millions)	136	152	168	184	200

The PC industry has four major competitors: Lenovo (the former producer for IBM), Dell, Compaq, and Hewlett-Packard (HP). All four make and sell competitive midrange performance PCs, with the typical configuration for home or small business use costing approximately $1,000. Dell's variable costs per unit total about $800, and it is believed that competitors face a similar variable cost structure. Dell's Executive would be priced competitively, at about the same price level of $1,000.

A recent study of the home/small-business PC market found that most customers considered two important nonprice attributes when selecting a PC: flexibility and

[7]This case was written by Prof. C. Anthony Di Benedetto and is based on public information, including www.dell.com. The "Executive" is a disguised product name. Market size and market share information is realistic for the leading competitors. Note that there are more than four key players in the computer industry but that some simplifying assumptions were made for the sake of presentation. Positioning information and company/industry financial information is not based on fact but is meant to illustrate concepts of product positioning, advertising decision making, and financial analyses.

performance. Flexibility refers in this situation to a PC's ability to run several different kinds of software, to be easily connected to printers and other peripherals, suitability for business as well as educational or game use, and so forth. Performance, by contrast, referred to speed of Internet connection and internal calculations, support of the highest-end software programs, and reliability and accuracy of calculations (the study was done soon after the infamous Pentium "bug" was found, which caused a very small percentage of numerical calculations to be slightly wrong). Using familiar customer survey methods, the consultants conducting the study found the perceived positions of each of the four major brands on the two key nonprice attributes. The results of the study are summarized below. (The positions are on scales of −2 to +2.)

Brand Positions	Attribute 1 (Performance)	Attribute 2 (Flexibility)
Dell	1	−1
Lenovo (IBM)	2	−1.5
HP	1	3
Compaq	0.5	0.5

Construct the positioning map for this industry using the information presented in the case. Discuss the relative positions of the Executive and its major competitors on the two key attributes. Do you think Dell is well positioned with respect to its competitors? Which competitor(s) should Dell be the most concerned about? Why? What additional information might you want to have about the competitors and/or about the marketplace at this point? How might a seemingly "weaker" later competitor (i.e., outpositioned by Dell on both key attributes) make a dent in Dell's market share, given that by the time they enter, the Executive will have been on the market for at least several months?

CHAPTER SEVEN

Analytical Attribute Approaches: Trade-Off Analysis and Qualitative Techniques

Setting

The previous chapter presented market research techniques that are very frequently used to analyze customer perceptions and tradeoffs and to generate promising product concepts. We begin this chapter with another useful and common quantitative technique: trade-off (or conjoint) analysis. These techniques will be encountered in subsequent phases of the new products process and, in a way, serve to provide continuity and guidance to the process (i.e., customer perceptual and preference data generated here can be used as inputs into protocol specification).

We will then encounter several analytical attribute approaches that are more qualitative in nature. While less numbers-oriented, they are very helpful in getting customers and managers to think in creative ways to generate new product concepts. These and the quantitative approaches complement each other well in concept generation and development. For example, dimensional or relationships analysis could be used to help identify determinant attributes for subsequent use in an AR gap analysis; or any of the qualitative approaches could aid in interpreting a perceptual map produced by AR or OS methods.

Trade-Off Analysis

Trade-off analysis (often called **conjoint analysis**) is a technique that is more commonly used in concept evaluation, so we will meet it again in Chapter 9; but it can be used in generating high-potential concepts for future evaluation, and so it is introduced here. You will likely encounter both terms, though they are not interchangeable. Trade-off analysis refers to the analysis of the process by which customers compare and evaluate brands based on their attributes or features. Conjoint analysis is the name of one of the most common analytical tools used to assess tradeoffs (much like factor analysis is a tool that is used to develop perceptual maps). Trade-off analysis is thus the broader term. In this text, we will use "conjoint analysis" when we are specifically referring to that technique for assessing tradeoffs.

Recall that after finding the determinant attributes (important attributes on which the available products differ), gap analysis plots them on maps. In using conjoint analysis, we assume we can represent a product as a set or bundle of attributes. Conjoint analysis puts all of the determinant attributes together in new sets and identifies which sets of attributes would be most liked or preferred by customers. In fact, AR gap analysis output can be used to select the attributes used in conjoint analysis.

Using Trade-Off Analysis to Generate Concepts

Let's say coffee has three determinant attributes: flavor, strength, and intensity of aroma. As Figure 7.1 shows, there are several different levels available for each of these attributes. If somehow we could get customer preferences (or **utilities**) for each attribute separately, we could combine the best level of each attribute into an overall favorite product. As shown in Figure 7.1, customers prefer medium strength, no (added) flavor, and regular aroma. Unless this particular combination was already on the market, we would have our new product concept. Other high-potential concepts are also suggested in the figure: For example, a strong hazelnut coffee might not be a bad idea.

Trade-off analysis was used by the Sunbeam Corporation when it wanted to expand its kitchen mixing appliances sales in various countries around the world. The company identified three types of attributes—silhouette, features, and benefits. The determinant attributes for each appliance were identified, and the range for each selected. For instance, silhouettes had about 10 combinations—low versus high, strong versus stylized, and so on.

FIGURE 7.1   Factor Utility Scores—Coffee Example

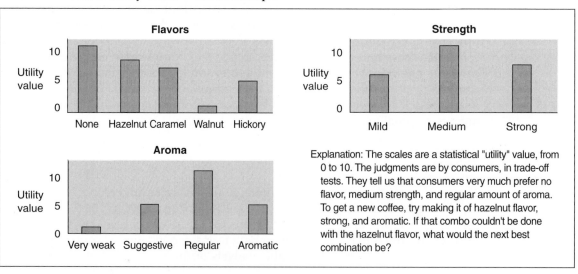

Explanation: The scales are a statistical "utility" value, from 0 to 10. The judgments are by consumers, in trade-off tests. They tell us that consumers very much prefer no flavor, medium strength, and regular amount of aroma. To get a new coffee, try making it of hazelnut flavor, strong, and aromatic. If that combo couldn't be done with the hazelnut flavor, what would the next best combination be?

Cards representing new products that combined specific silhouettes, features, and benefits were prepared. Consumers in the various countries were asked to sort the cards by preference from top to bottom. If a person wanted a low, strong silhouette, a large number of variable speeds, a very quiet motor, and the ability to use on semiliquids, one card may have had the right silhouette, speed, and noise, but couldn't be used on liquids. Another could be used on liquids and had the right silhouette and noise but had only three speeds. To choose one, the consumer would have to trade off speed variety against use on liquids. With hundreds of consumers doing this, a good picture for each attribute can be obtained and the optimization process begun.

Though our first couple of examples have centered on consumer goods, don't think that trade-off techniques can't be used elsewhere. In fact, because business buyers tend to make a more rational analysis of product features, trade-off analysis has become quite valuable in industrial product innovation. Applications include snowmobiles, health care systems, aircraft, lift trucks, and computer software, as well as business services of all kinds.[1] Conjoint analysis was also used by Marriott Corp. when designing and developing the Courtyard chain to build in the most desired needs and wants of both business and leisure customers.[2]

A Conjoint Analysis Application

We begin by illustrating *a full-profile conjoint analysis,* that is, one for which we obtain information on all possible levels of all the product's attributes. We will see alternatives to this method later.

Suppose you are managing a line of prepared salsas for a food company. You are looking to add to your product line and need to generate some new concepts that can be evaluated and brought to product development. Based on your understanding of the market and recent consumer research, you have found that three attributes are uppermost in customers' minds when they choose a brand of salsa: (1) spiciness (mild, medium-hot, or extra-hot), (2) color (green or red), and (3) thickness (regular, thick, or extra-thick). There are $3 \times 2 \times 3 = 18$ different types of salsa that can be made by combining the levels of these attributes in all possible ways (a mild, green, thick salsa is one way).

We begin by designing 18 cards, each with a picture and/or verbal description of one of the combinations.[3] Each respondent customer is then asked to rank the

---

[1] For details on usage of the trade-off technique, see Dick R. Wittink and Philippe Cattin, "Commercial Use of Conjoint Analysis: An Update," *Journal of Marketing,* July 1989, pp. 91–96; and Dick R. Wittink, Marco Vriens, and Wim Burhenne, "Commercial Use of Conjoint Analysis in Europe: Results and Critical Reflections," *International Journal of Research in Marketing,* January 1994, pp. 41–52.

[2] Gary L. Lilien, Arvind Rangaswamy, and Timothy Matanovich, "The Age of Marketing Engineering," *Marketing Management,* Spring 1998, pp. 48–50.

[3] Some research suggests that verbal representations were good for facilitating judgment, while pictorial representations are good for improving respondents' understanding of design attributes. See Marco Vriens, Gerard H. Loosschilder, Edward Rosbergen, and Dick R. Wittink, "Verbal versus Realistic Pictorial Representations in Conjoint Analysis with Design Attributes," *Journal of Product Innovation Management,* 15(5), September 1998, pp. 455–467.

FIGURE 7.2
Preference
Rankings
of One
Respondent

Thickness	Spiciness	Color	Actual Ranking*	Ranking as Estimated by Model
Regular	Mild	Red	4	4
Regular	Mild	Green	3	3
Regular	Medium-Hot	Red	10	10
Regular	Medium-Hot	Green	6	8
Regular	Extra-Hot	Red	15	16
Regular	Extra-Hot	Green	16	15
Thick	Mild	Red	2	2
Thick	Mild	Green	1	1
Thick	Medium-Hot	Red	8	6
Thick	Medium-Hot	Green	5	5
Thick	Extra-Hot	Red	13	13
Thick	Extra-Hot	Green	11	11
Extra-Thick	Mild	Red	7	7
Extra-Thick	Mild	Green	9	9
Extra-Thick	Medium-Hot	Red	14	14
Extra-Thick	Medium-Hot	Green	12	12

*1 = Most preferred, 18 = Least preferred.

cards from 1 to 18, where 1 is "like most" and 18 is "like least."[4] As this task may be challenging, we can suggest that the respondent make three piles of cards ("like," "neutral" and "don't like"). The six or so cards within each pile can more easily be sorted, then the piles can be combined and final adjustments to rank order can be made. The rankings provided by one respondent are given in Figure 7.2. (Figure 7.2 also shows rankings as estimated by the model, which can be ignored for now.)

Suppose a given customer likes extra-hot salsa. There are several cards in the stack (six, to be exact) that depict extra-hot salsa, in combination with other attributes. He or she would tend to rank these cards favorably (that is, give them a low rank number—the lower the rank number, the more the concept is liked). If he or she *really* likes extra-hot, we might expect almost all of the extra-hot cards to be assigned low rank numbers—that is, a pattern would be evident in the rank orderings. If the customer couldn't care less about whether the salsa was green or red, we would expect the rank numbers assigned to red salsa to be not that different from those assigned to green—no patterns would emerge.

Conjoint analysis uses monotone analysis of variance (**MONANOVA**), a data analysis technique, to find these patterns within the rank order data. That is to say, we identify the customer's underlying value system: which attributes are important, and which levels of the important attributes are favored. To do this, we use the rank orderings to estimate the utilities (sometimes called *part-worths*) of each level of each attribute for each customer. The graphical conjoint analysis output for the data of Figure 7.2 is given in Figure 7.3(a).

[4]In addition to ranking, other types of responses can also be gathered. For example, respondents can be presented with pairs of cards and asked to state which they prefer. The different techniques lead to similar results. See Gilbert A. Churchill, Jr., *Marketing Research: Methodological Foundations,* 6th ed. (Fort Worth, TX: Dryden, 1995).

FIGURE 7.3 Conjoint Analysis Output—Salsa Data

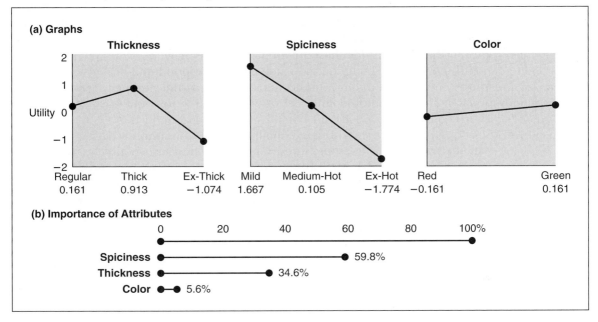

The graphs in Figure 7.3(a) provide a visual representation of the relative importances of the attributes. The largest range in utilities is found for spiciness—the utilities assigned to mild and extra-hot are 1.667 and 1.774, for a range of 3.441—thus, spiciness is this individual's most important attribute influencing likes and dislikes in salsa (using the same logic, color is the least important). The graphical output also indicates which levels of each attribute are preferred. As shown, mild salsa is favored over medium-hot or extra-hot, other things being equal. This particular customer also prefers medium-thick salsa to both regular and extra-thick, and likes green salsa very slightly more than red salsa.

Figure 7.3(b) expresses the relative importances of the three attributes as percentages.[5] As can be seen, the relative importance of spiciness to this individual is almost 60 percent. Thickness is also relatively important (about 34.5 percent), while this respondent seemed to be almost indifferent to color. One should keep in mind that these results are very dependent on the levels actually selected for the conjoint task. The customer might not have been indifferent to color if the options were red, green, and shocking pink.

---

[5]These are estimated by looking at the ranges of utilities of the three attributes (that is, the gap between the highest and lowest utilities). As seen, the range for spiciness is 3.441. The ranges for thickness and color can be calculated as 1.987 and 0.322. Summing the three ranges yields a total of 5.750, and each range is divided by this amount to get its relative importance. For spiciness, 3.441/5.750 = 59.84 percent.

How well does our model predict this customer's choice patterns? We can check predictive accuracy by adding the utilities comprising each of the 18 choices to get estimates of overall preference. For example, the estimate we would obtain for the extra-thick, mild, red salsa would be $-1.074 + 1.667 - 0.161 = +0.432$. We can then rank order these preferences as predicted by the model and compare these to the rankings actually made by the respondent. As shown in the last column of Figure 7.2, the estimates predict the actual preference order almost perfectly for this customer and identify the most-favored and least-favored combinations easily.

In a typical application, trade-off analysis allows the manager to identify which attributes are the most important overall and also which levels of these attributes are the most popular. Assume that a large sample of individuals performed the trade-off task, and that the rankings shown in Figure 7.2 were average rankings over the sample rather than one individual's responses. In this case, we might concentrate on developing a medium-thick, green, mild salsa. (Note that these are the levels of each attribute with the highest utilities in Figure 7.3(a).)

Clearly, there may be segments within the market. It may be that about half the market likes mild salsa and about half likes extra-hot. If we only examined the average, we might conclude that medium-hot is best, though in reality nobody may like it! Thus, the next analytical step is to identify benefit segments based on the utilities. This will be discussed later in Chapter 9.

The ranking task was relatively easy in this simple case, as there were only 18 cards to rank order. What if you had to consider many more attributes and/or levels? For example, in addition to the three attributes given above, you might need to consider type of container (glass jar vs. plastic bucket), size of container (10 ounce vs. 16 ounce), type of ingredients (organic vs. not organic), and three different potential brand names. That's $3 \times 2 \times 3 \times 2 \times 2 \times 2 \times 3 = 432$ different cards—equivalent to eight decks of playing cards stacked together, including jokers! No respondent, however well intentioned, will have the patience for this task.

Fortunately, the full set of cards need not be rank ordered. By using a fractional factorial design, we can still estimate the relative preferences of all possible products using only a small subset of the cards.[6] With a reduced set of cards, most respondents won't be able to find the exact combination they want. So they must choose the combination that most closely meets their desires by trading off attributes wanted more against those wanted less. We all do this when our favorite brand of something is not in the store and we have to find a close substitute.

---

[6]See discussion in David R. Rink, "An Improved Preference Data Collection Method: Balanced Incomplete Block Designs," *Journal of the Academy of Marketing Science* 15, Spring 1987, pp. 54–61; also Joel H. Steckel, Wayne S. DeSarbo, and Vijay Mahajan, "On the Creation of Acceptable Conjoint Analysis Experimental Designs," *Decision Sciences* 22, Spring 1991, pp. 435–442.

A set of practical guidelines for the use of conjoint analysis would include the following:

1. One should be able to specify the product as a bundle of attributes. As seen in our discussion of factor analysis in Chapter 6, this is not always easily done, especially in the case of image products such as perfumes, where attributes may be more difficult for the respondent to articulate.
2. We need to know what the determinant attributes are before we do the conjoint analysis. As mentioned above, AR gap mapping or one of the qualitative techniques can be helpful in this regard.
3. Respondents should be familiar enough with the product category and the attributes to be able to provide meaningful data on preference or purchase likelihood. Thus, conjoint may be less useful in the case of completely new to-the-world products.
4. The firm should be able to act on the results—in other words, actually develop a product that delivers the combinations of attributes preferred in the conjoint analysis.[7]

Finally, we should reiterate that trade-off (conjoint) analysis is most commonly used in concept evaluation, and we will pick up the discussion of this technique in Chapter 9.

Alternatives to Full-Profile Conjoint Analysis

Sometimes the decision problem just has too many attributes, and it cannot be easily solved using full-profile conjoint analysis. Another weakness of the full-profile approach is that it does not measure interactions among attributes. As an example of an interaction effect, a customer may like mild salsa, and may like medium-thick salsa, but may *really* like mild, medium-thick salsa—even more than you might have imagined from the conjoint analysis! There are adaptations of the full-profile conjoint analysis that can make up for these shortcomings.[8]

Adaptive conjoint analysis, developed by Sawtooth Software, shows only a few attributes at a time to the respondent and adapts to the respondent as the conjoint exercise goes on. In the adaptive technique, the respondent is first asked which attributes are most important and which levels are most liked or disliked, then pairs of options are shown to the respondent that focus only on the most important attributes and levels that are most liked or disliked. In a car design application, if the respondent says that the number of car doors and country of manufacture are highly important, one question might ask if he or she prefers a four-door car made in the USA or a two-door car made in Japan. After a series of questions, the respondent is presented with "calibration concepts"—combinations of several

[7]Adapted from Robert J. Dolan, *Managing the New Product Development Process: Cases and Notes* (Reading, MA: Addison-Wesley, 1993), p. 125.
[8]The techniques and examples are adapted from the Sawtooth Software Web site, www.sawtoothsoftware.com. Sawtooth Software is one of the leading providers of conjoint analysis software.

attributes to which he or she states likelihood of purchase, given as a number between 0 and 100. (Example: On a scale of 100 where 100 is "definitely buy," how likely would you be to buy a red, two-door, rear-wheel-drive USA-made car that costs $16,000?)

Another alternative sometimes used is *choice-based conjoint analysis*, in which the respondent is shown several alternative product choices and is asked which he or she would prefer (if none, then "none of the above" is a possible response). As an example, the respondent may be asked if he or she would prefer:

- A red, two-door, rear-wheel-drive USA-made car that costs $16,000.
- A blue, four-door, front-wheel-drive Japanese-made car that costs $18,000.
- A green, two-door, all-wheel-drive German-made car that costs $20,000.
- None of the above.

Both of these procedures minimize the number of attributes and levels any one respondent has to be exposed to. Note that there are also other simple trade-off techniques available for concept development, similar to the conjoint analyses described above in terms of required data but not requiring any specialized software.[9]

Recent Modifications in Conjoint Analysis

Other techniques are sometimes used to handle large numbers of determinant attributes and levels. In a property insurance example, analysts had to restructure a traditional form of conjoint measurement called **SIMALTO** by adding *cost* and *savings* to each of the attribute trade-off utilities. They then gave consumers budgets to spend on their choices, and thus captured a lot of variables in a *willingness to pay*. They kept the power of the original set of trade-off attributes without having to use the data-losing method of conjoint calculations.[10]

Recent work has examined some of the practical difficulties and concerns encountered in concept testing. Since concept testing is done so early in the new product process, often before a prototype is available for customer trial, can the respondent conceptualize the product and its uses well enough? If not, does the method still produce valid results? A study of a simple product line extension (a baking-soda toothpaste) suggested that conjoint results obtained when customers were only exposed to the product concept were very similar to those obtained if customers were actually allowed to try the product.[11] Thus, conjoint results are a valid early indicator of ultimate product success, at least for product line extensions. Of course, conjoint analysis and perceptual mapping, as well as product trial, will be rich sources of customer information later in the new products process.

[9]For a good, fully worked-out example, see Nelson Whipple, Thomas Adler, and Stephan McCurdy, "Applying Tradeoff Analysis to Get the Most from Customer Needs," in A. Griffin and S. M. Somermeyer, *The PDMA Toolbook 3 for New Product Development* (New York: John Wiley, 2007), Chapter 3.

[10]Peter D. Morton and Crispian Tarrant, "A New Dimension to Financial Product Innovation Research," *Marketing and Research Today*, August 1994, pp. 173–179.

[11]John R. Dickinson and Carolyn P. Wilby, "Concept Testing With and Without Product Trial," *Journal of Product Innovation Management*, 14(2), March 1997, pp. 117–125.

In the case of major innovations (such as a new computer or telecommunications technology), customers without a high level of expertise in the product category may be unable to assess the innovation's benefits, and concept test results may not validly predict how well the actual product will be received. Some have advocated using only customers with at least moderate levels of expertise, even for minor innovations.[12]

Virtual Prototypes in Concept Testing

Virtual prototypes can be used in concept testing as well. These are either static pictures of the prototypes, or video clips that simulate the product in action, which can be presented to respondents via the Internet. These virtual prototypes are, of course, far less costly to produce and test than actual physical prototypes, allowing the firm to test a wide range of concepts quickly and cheaply.[13]

Improvements in **virtual reality** computer and video technology are providing marketers with many exciting new ways to test concepts with customers. One new measurement method, called **information acceleration (IA)**, has recently been developed and was first applied by General Motors in testing new electric car concepts.[14] The unique feature of IA is that respondents are brought into a virtual buying environment that simulates the information typically available in a realistic purchase situation. Through the use of a video monitor and laser videodisk player, the respondent can see ads, read car magazines, and hear statements from salespeople and word-of-mouth comments from customers. Using surrogate travel technology, customers can virtually walk around a dealer showroom and look at computer-generated car prototypes.

While expensive (an application might cost $100,000 to $300,000), IA is a potentially valuable complement to existing concept testing methods. Simple concept pictures or descriptions may not provide enough information to customers to enable them to make a realistic purchase decision, especially in the case of a very complex product like a new electric automobile. IA also allows testing of many virtual variations of the same basic concept, so that preferences can be observed. As video technology improves, IA will become less expensive and further extensions to it will be made (for example, the respondent may be able to virtually drive the car).[15]

---

[12]Jan P. L. Schoormans, Roland J. Ortt, and Cees J. P. M. de Bont, "Enhancing Concept Test Validity by Using Expert Consumers," *Journal of Product Innovation Management,* 12(2), March 1995, pp. 153–162.

[13]Ely Dahan and V. Srinivasan, "The Predictive Power of Internet-Based Product Concept Testing Using Visual Depiction and Animation," *Journal of Product Innovation Management,* 17(2), March 2000, pp. 99–109.

[14]For detailed information on information acceleration, see Glen L. Urban, Bruce D. Weinberg, and John R. Hauser, "Premarket Forecasting of Really New Products," *Journal of Marketing,* January 1996, pp. 47–60. See also Phillip J. Rosenberger III and Leslie de Chernatony, "Virtual Reality Techniques in NPD Research," *Journal of the Market Research Society,* October 1995, pp. 345–355.

[15]Reportedly, Caterpillar lets its customers virtually test drive tractors under different driving conditions using a similar virtual reality technique. See Brian Silverman, "Get 'Em While They're Hot," *Sales and Marketing Management,* February 1997, pp. 47–52.

Qualitative Techniques

We have seen several quantitative techniques that can be used to incorporate customer input into concept generation. As seen at the beginning of this chapter, however, these techniques have natural complements: namely, a collection of qualitative techniques, which we will now explore.

It is tempting to be dazzled by the fancy outputs generated by MDS or factor analysis, especially if one is not that familiar with them. Managers, however, should resist this temptation and not take the results at face value. The qualitative techniques presented below are useful ways to challenge the assumptions (for example, about what attributes are really determinant) that underlie the sophisticated approaches and can very frequently bring the manager perspectives that may go overlooked otherwise. Although our discussion of these is briefer, they are by no means less important or useful in concept generation.

Dimensional Analysis

Dimensional analysis uses any and all features, not just measurements of dimensions (such as spatial—length, width, and so on). The task involves listing *all* of the physical features of a product type. Product concept creativity is triggered by the mere listing of every such feature, because we instinctively think about how that feature could be changed. Rarely is anything worthwhile found in dimensional analysis until the list is long. It takes a lot of work to push beyond the ordinary and to visualize dimensions that others don't see.

Some of the most interesting features are those that a product doesn't *seem* to have. For example, a spoon may be described in terms of its aroma, sound, resilience, bendability, and so on. Granted, the aroma may be hard to detect, the sound (at the moment) may be zero, and the resilience may be only when pushed by a vise. But each feature offers something to change. How about spoons that play musical notes as children move them to the mouth? How about spoon handles that can be squeezed to play notes? How about spoons that smell like roses?

Listing hundreds of features is not uncommon. Figure 7.4 shows a shorter list, but perhaps it suggests what must be done. Successful users claim that just citing a unique dimension sparks ideation, and that the technique has to be used to be believed.

Checklists

From early forms of dimensional analysis evolved one of today's most widely used idea-generating techniques—the **checklist.** The most widely publicized checklist was given by the originator of brainstorming:

Can it be adapted?	Can something be substituted?
Can it be modified?	Can it be magnified?
Can it be reversed?	Can it be minified?
Can it be combined with anything?	Can it be rearranged in some way?

These eight questions are powerful; they do lead to useful ideation.

FIGURE 7.4
Dimensional
Attributes of a
Flashlight

Using dimensional analysis, here are 80 dimensions. There were almost 200 in the analyst's original list. A change in any one of them may make a new flashlight.

Overall unit:
Weight
Rust resistance
Balance
Gripability
Shock resistance
Shear force
Heat tolerance
Insulation material
Automatic flasher
Manual flasher
Distance visible
Length
Hangability
Stain resistance
Cold tolerance
Flexibility
Insulation color
Translucence
Focus of beam
Closure type
Lining material
Buoyancy
Flammability
Malleability
Compressibility
Reflectiveness
Surface area/color
Closure security
Material of case

Color
Number body seams
Water resistance
Diameter
Washability
Weight of metal
Explosiveness
Smell of unit
Number of tags
Snagability
Sealant material

Lens:
Material
Opacity
Color
Strength
Texture

Springs:
Number
Material
Length
Strength
Style

Switches:
Number
Pressure
Noise
Type
Location

Bulb:
Number
Shape
Size
Gas type
Thread strength
Length of stem
Filament shape
Thread size
Filament material
Shatter point
Thread depth
Amperage

Batteries:
Number
Size
Terminal type
Direction
Rechargeability

Reflector:
Depth
Diameter
Shape
Durability
Surface
Color
Temperature limit

Business and industrial goods analysts use such features as source of energy, materials, ease of operation, subassemblies, and substitutable components. (See Figure 7.5 for an abbreviated list of such industrial checklist questions.)

Checklists produce a multitude of potential new product concepts, most of them worthless. Much time and effort can be spent culling the list. Another more recent technique for generating new concepts systematically manipulates the existing product's attributes in certain specified ways. One attribute could, for example, be made dependent on another: A child's bath mat changes color if the water is too hot. An attribute might be removed, leading to an essentially different product: Removing the internal floppy drives on a PC results in an ultra-thin model. And so on. Four strategies for creatively generating new concepts in this way are presented in Figure 7.6.

FIGURE 7.5
Checklist
of Idea
Stimulators
for Industrial
Products

Can we change the physical, thermal, electrical, chemical, and mechanical properties of this material?

Are there new electrical, electronic, optical, hydraulic, mechanical, or magnetic ways of doing this?

Find new analogs for parallel problems.

Is this function really necessary?

Can we construct a new model of this?

Can we change the form of power to make it work better?

Can standard components be substituted?

What if the order of the process was changed?

How might it be made more compact?

What if it was heat-treated, hardened, alloyed, cured, frozen, plated?

Who else could use this operation or its output?

Has every step been computerized as much as possible?

FIGURE 7.6   **Templates for Creativity**

Goldenberg and Mazursky present several "Creativity Templates" that can be used to manipulate the existing knowledge base encoded in product attributes to discover innovative new products. Procedure: Begin by identifying the determinate attributes, then manipulate these according to the four creativity templates. The templates are:

1. *Attribute Dependency Template:* Find a functional dependency between two independent variable attributes. The interaction may suggest a creative new product. Example: the color of the ink on a coffee cup is dependent on the contents, and a warning message can be revealed if the beverage is too hot.
2. *Replacement Template:* Remove one of the components of the product and replace it with one from another environment. The function the removed component performed is done by another component. Example: the antenna on a Walkman is replaced by the headphone cord.
3. *Displacement Template:* Remove an intrinsic component and its function, in such a way as to functionally change the product. This may create a new product for a new market. For example: removing floppy and CD drives on laptop PCs resulted in the ultra-thin PCs.
4. *Component Control Template:* Identify and create a new connection between a component internal to the product and one that is external to the product. Examples: Toothpastes with added whiteners, or suntan lotions with added skin moisturizers.

Source: From Jacob Goldenberg and David Mazursky, *Creativity in Product Innovation,* Cambridge University Press, 2002.

Relationships Analysis

Several of the concept-generating methods we have been looking at *compare* things: Perceptual maps compare attributes, and group creativity is stimulated by reasoning from a known to an unknown, for example. But the comparisons are incidental to a larger issue in those methods. We will now look at two analytical attribute techniques that go right to the point—forcing things together for examination. These two techniques are the **two-dimensional matrix** and the **morphological matrix**. Both are examples of types of **relationships analysis**, so named because they require the respondent to find relationships among dimensions to generate new product concepts.

About the Dimensions Used in Relationships Analysis

Recall that Figure 6.1 said attributes are *features* (such as length), *functions* (such as coating hair with protein), and *benefits* (such as economy and health). But other aspects of products are not always included as attributes in definitions—for example, different places of use, occupations of users, or other items the product is used with. Relationships analysis techniques use them too. We seek any and all dimensions that help, and there is no fixed set of these. It is hoped that the examples shown in this chapter will suggest the view you should take in creating the matrixes.

Two-Dimensional Matrix

The simplest format for studying relationships is seen in Figure 7.7, which shows two attribute sets for insurance. Only partial lists of two dimensions (event insured against and person/animal insured) are used, but just these two provide 50 cells to consider. Notice that only by forcing relationships could we *expect* to come up with a special policy that protects new parents if they happen to misplace their new child, or that protects newlyweds from the costs of overcelebrating their honeymoon. In the case of the insurance example, to analyze the results we would just start with 1, think about it, then to 2, and so on.

In contrast to most of the methods studied to this point, relationships analysis goes directly to a new product idea (e.g., aerosol ice cream). The number of two-dimensional matrixes that can be prepared is almost unlimited. Keep looking at different ones until satisfied with the list of new possibilities found or convinced that the technique "just isn't for me."

A slightly different kind of relationships analysis employs as its dimensions the product's *utility lever* (how the product affects the customer's life) and *buyer's experience cycle* (at what point does the product affect the customer). Altering one

FIGURE 7.7 **Two-Dimensional Matrix Used for New Insurance Products**

Event Insured Against	Person/Animal Insured									
	New-borns	Geniuses	Troubled Kids	Rich Uncles	Dogs/ Cats	Tropical Birds	Salt-water Fish	New Job-holders	Newly-weds	New Parents
Injury from fire	1	2	3	4	5	6	7	8	9	10
Getting lost	11	12	13	14	15	16	17	18	19	20
Normal death	21	22	23	24	25	26	27	28	29	30
Being insulted	31	32	33	34	35	36	37	38	39	40
Being kidnapped	41	42	43	44	45	46	47	48	49	50

Examples of new product concepts: An insurance policy that protects new parents if their child gets lost (20), or that protects newlyweds from the risks of being kidnapped while on their honeymoon (49), or that protects geniuses from the damage of being insulted (32). Relationships analysis methods mostly produce nonsense, but like the others, the two-dimensional matrix often produces a surprise that, upon careful thought, makes sense.

FIGURE 7.8 **Another Form of Dimensional Analysis**

W. C. Kim and R. Mauborgne note that firms can come up with winning new product ideas by considering two key dimensions:

- *Utility lever:* How the product will affect the customer's life (such as simplicity, fun/image, environmental friendliness, reduced risk, convenience, and productivity).
- *Buyer's experience cycle:* The stage when/where the product will affect the customer (purchase, delivery, use, supplements, maintenance, disposal).

They provide examples of firms that altered one or both of these dimensions, resulting in great new product ideas:

- Typical fast-food restaurants offer cheaper coffee, focusing on offering convenience or productivity to the customer at the purchase stage. Starbucks also aims at the purchase stage, but adds the utility lever of fun/image with its trendy coffee bars and exclusive blends.
- Computer makers offer the utility of productivity at the use stage. Dell's innovation was to offer the productivity utility at the delivery stage as well by shipping direct.
- The Philips Alto disposable fluorescent light bulb offered a unique combination of enviornmental friendliness utility at the disposal stage.

Note: In addition to the novel combination of utility and experience cycle stage, the firm must also set a strategic price to improve the likelihood of success.

Source: Reprinted by permission of *Harvard Business Review*. Exhibit from "Knowing a Winning Business Idea When You See One," by W. C. Kim and R. Kauborgne, September–October 2000. Copyright © 2000 by the Harvard Business School Publishing Corporation; All rights reserved.

or both of those dimensions can result in successful new product ideas. Figure 7.8 shows how several companies have come up with product ideas that ultimately were very successful by "stretching" on one or both dimensions.

Morphological or Multidimensional Matrix

The next method, morphological matrix, simultaneously combines more than two dimensions. The matrix can include many dimensions, and the technique originated many years ago when a scientist was trying to further development on what became the jet engine.[16]

An example, shown in Figure 7.9, concerns the development of a new coffee maker. Five dimensions were identified, and for illustrative purposes, three alternatives for each dimension are shown. (In a real example, many more alternatives are generally found.)

The new product manager's task is to link combinations of those items. One common technique is to have a computer print out all possible combinations, which are then scanned for interesting sets.

Other analysts just use a simple mechanical method of reading the rows across. The top row says: How about a new coffee pot, with an element right in the pot for

[16]The scientist used 11 parameters (dimensions), each of which had between two and four alternatives; that set yielded 36,864 combinations (possible engines). Incidentally, that matrix also yielded two combinations that became the German V-1 and V-2 rockets in World War II. See Fritz Zwicky, *Discovery, Invention, Research: Through the Morphological Approach* (New York: Macmillan, 1969).

FIGURE 7.9
A Morpholog-
ical Matrix for
a New Coffee
Maker

	Dimension			
Heating	**Adding Coffee**	**Filtering Coffee**	**Keeping Coffee Warm**	**Pouring Coffee**
1. Heating element in pot	1. By spoon	1. Filter paper	1. Thermal (insulating) technology	1. Valve under pot
2. Open flame under pot	2. With built-in measuring cap	2. Porous ceramic filter	2. Warming unit in pot	2. Pump in lid of pot
3. Microwave unit	3. Automatic feed	3. Centrifuge method	3. External heat source	3. Espresso-like jets

Source: Adapted from Stefan Kohn and Rene Niethammer, "Why Patent Data Can Be a Good Source of Comparative 'Technology Intelligence' in New Product Development," *Visions*, January 2004.

heating the water, to which one adds ground coffee by spoon into a paper filter, which then keeps the coffee warm via a thermal insulator? A valve under the pot is turned on to pour the coffee. Didn't like that one? There are many other combinations! After going through the rows, the analyst systematically exchanges one item in each row with one item in another, and so on. All analytical attribute techniques produce noise from which good ideas must be picked; but what at first appears to be noise may simply be a great new idea no one would have thought of easily without the matrix.

In any event, the structure shown in Figure 7.9 should be followed. Creation of the columns was discussed at the beginning of this section of the chapter. The number of items in each column is either (1) the entire set, as in the survey above, or (2) a selection representing the full array. For example, a study of play wagons might have a column headed number of wheels, and the rows would be two, three, four, five, and six; but the height column might just have rows of 6 inches, 8 inches, and 12 inches (low, medium, and high).

Analogy

We can often get a better idea of something by looking at it through something else—an **analogy.** Analogy is so powerful and popular that it is used heavily as part of the problem-solving step in problem-based methods (Chapter 5). Just think of how many analogies are involved in common PC terminology: cut-and-paste, recycle bin, browsing, surfing, briefcase, folder, and so many other terms are familiar to us in noncomputer contexts, and the use of these terms in computer settings is intuitively obvious to PC users.

A good example of analogy was the study of airplane feeding systems by a manufacturer of kitchen furniture and other devices. Preparing, serving, and consuming meals in a plane is clearly analogous to doing so in the home, and the firm created several good ideas for new processes (and furniture) in the home kitchen. Amusement park designers watched cattle being herded and came up with the idea of queues for those waiting to go on popular rides!

An analogy for bicycles might be driving a car—both incorporate steering, moving, slowing, curving, and so on. But the auto carries more passengers, has four wheels for stability, variable power, built-in communications, on-board service diagnosis and remedial action, and the like. Each difference suggests another new type of bicycle; some of these types are already available. The bicycle could also be compared to the airplane, to skating, to the submarine, to swimming, and at the extreme (for illustration) to a mouse in a maze.

The secret, of course, is finding a usable analogous situation, which is often difficult. The analogy should meet four criteria:

1. The analogy should be vivid and have a definite life of its own.
2. It should be full of concrete images.
3. It should be a happening—a process of change or activity.
4. It should be a well-known activity and easy to visualize and describe.

Airplane feeding systems and driving a car qualify easily. And, perhaps to their surprise, an analogy of the machine gun ammunition belt helped seed company developers think of a roll of biodegradable tape studded with carefully placed seeds to be laid along a furrow.

Analogy is used in several of the specialized techniques in Appendix B.

Summary

In this and the preceding chapter, we have presented a review of several analytical attribute techniques. Qualitative techniques included the very simple yet challenging dimensional analysis and more advanced methods such as the morphological matrix. Quantitative approaches included gap analysis and trade-off analysis. These can be used in complementary fashion: As seen above, the qualitative methods can be used prior to the more numbers-oriented models (to specify or double-check the attributes included in the analysis) or after the fact (to help interpret results).

The essence of attribute analysis, in every case, is to force us to look at products differently—to bring out new perspectives. We normally have fixed ways of perceiving products, based on our sometimes long-term use of them, so forcing us out of those ruts is difficult. Anyone reading this in preparation for a specific ideation activity is encouraged to scan the list of over 40 other techniques in Appendix B.

We are now finished with concept generation and hopefully have several good concepts ready for serious review and evaluation before undertaking costly technical development. We meet evaluation in Part III, Chapters 8–12, entitled Concept/Project Evaluation. We will also find that several of the analytical techniques we encountered in these chapters will be of assistance in assessing customer preferences, specifying product design characteristics, and even beyond in the new product development process.

Applications

1. "I guess I really like checklists best—they're easy for me to understand and use. I've never seen this one by Small that you mentioned—wow, four pages of ways. Is all that really necessary? Couldn't just as good a job be done with, say, one page? And incidentally, I must confess I'm slightly confused by the terminology. Tell me, what is the difference again between the checklists I like and what you call dimensional analysis?"

2. "As you can probably tell by now, I am an engineer by training and have always enjoyed playing around with one form of attribute analysis. We call it attribute extension, where we forecast the future changes in any important attribute of a product. You know, like the amount of random access memory in a PC. I recently asked our cable TV division to take five dimensions of a cable TV service and extend each out as far as they can see it going and tell me what ideas they get from it. I mentioned number of channels and types of payment as examples. Could you do something like this for me now . . . that is, take five dimensions of cable TV service and extend them? It would help me get ready for their presentation Thursday."

3. "Several of our divisions work in the women's clothing markets. As you know, they are all specialized these days, this segment or that segment. It's getting hard to come up with a new segment, one that has some size and would be responsive. So, when you were talking about morphological matrix, which I liked, I thought about women's attire. One way to innovate would be to come up with new settings, or occasions, situations where we could devise a whole outfit. Sort of like wedding, or racetrack, or picnic, though we know of them and have clothing for them, of course. Sort of a *package* of apparel and accessories. But there must be many we don't think of now. Would that morphological matrix method work on that?"

Case: Rubbermaid Inc.[17]

Rubbermaid has consistently received awards as a well-managed company. It made the *Fortune* magazine list for three consecutive years in the early 90s. It posts growth rates of 15 percent, even in tough times, with important contributions from new products. About 200 new items are introduced each year. Some are line extensions and others enter, or even create, entirely new markets.

The firm's success is based partly on creating and producing high-quality, functional plastic products for the housewares, the office, the industrial, and the farm markets in addition to specialty products such as toys, educational and recreational products, and furniture. In recent years items have ranged from a spatula to a cooler used on a golf course and from a child's 15-pound minicar to lawn furniture. Category brands include Little Tikes, Gott, Blue-Ice, Sunshine, and others.

[17]This case was prepared from many public information sources.

The firm makes almost a half-million different items, boasts a 90 percent success rate on new products, and obtains at least 30 percent of its sales each year from products less than five years old.

The firm's new product strategy is to meet the needs of the consumer. The new product rate is high, and diversification is desired. It is market-driven, not technology-driven, although in recent years the firm has identified such technologies as recycling new plastic parts from old tires for which it is seeking market opportunities. This practice of seeking opportunities for specific technologies will increase as a fall-out of the firm's current use of simultaneous product development.

For idea generation, Rubbermaid depends on finding customer problems that can be built into the strategic planning process. Problems are sought in several ways, the principal one of which is focus groups. It also uses comments and complaints from customers, an example of which came when then-CEO Stanley C. Gault heard a Manhattan doorman complaining as he swept dirt into a Rubbermaid dustpan. Inquiry determined that the doorman wanted a thinner lip on the pan, so less dirt would remain on the walk. He got it.

Each complaint is documented by marketing people, and executives are encouraged to read the complaints. One complaint by customers in small households, who found the traditional rack-and-mat too bulky to store, led to a compact, one-piece dish drainer. The Little Tikes toy division actually molds a toll-free number into each toy to encourage complaints and comments. They have to watch the legal ramifications, of course, and may require idea submitters to sign a waiver giving up their rights to their ideas. The firm generally finds its problems by using problem analysis in focus groups and solves them internally. They occasionally use scenario analysis to spot a problem. But scenario analysis is much less useful than problem analysis because the lead times are so short; their new product cycles make them concentrate mainly on already existing problems. The organization is kept conducive to newly created ideas by promoting cross-functional association among workers. Problem-find-solve is encouraged at all levels.

Some other new items have been:

Bouncer drinkware was created for people who fear using glassware around their swimming pools.

A lazy susan condiment tray and other patio furniture products came from studies of lifestyle changes.

People working at home told of problems that led to a line of home office accessories, including an "auto-office," a portable device that straps onto a car seat and holds pens and other office articles.

The firm also runs a day care program, where researchers observe children having problems with toys and test their new toys.

Generally speaking, Rubbermaid does not make much use of attribute listing and other fortuitous scan methods of ideation, including the various mapping approaches. It does find that product life-cycle models can be useful, and it closely tracks competitive new product introductions.

Rubbermaid is, however, always looking for new ways by which it can come up with good new product concepts. They know from experience, for example, that there will be new ways by which problem-find-solve techniques can be used. And perhaps the fortuitous scan methods can be of greater use than now perceived.

FIGURE III.1

Concept/Project Evaluation

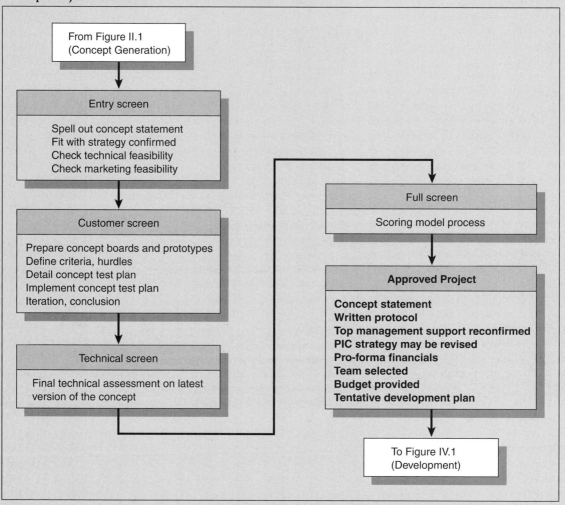

PART THREE

Concept/Project Evaluation

Part II completed our study of the various methods of generating new product concepts. The next task is to undertake evaluation of these concepts. Evaluation takes place at many different times and in different ways, by different people, for different reasons. Therefore, a *system* of evaluations is needed, an idea that will be explained in Chapter 8.

Then, beginning in Chapter 9, we will look at the different phases in that system. (See Figure III.1.) Concept testing is the first major tool and will be discussed there. Chapter 10 covers the activity generally called a *full screen*, a step where the concept is judged by how well it fits the company and its marketing strengths. Once the project has cleared the high hurdles set at the full screen, it is approved for development and ready to move into the next phase of the process. Chapters 11 and 12 focus on specific topics appearing in the last box in Figure III.1: a financial analysis, a check to make sure the project (still) fits with the product innovation charter, and the development of a protocol. At that point, development can begin, teams are assigned (if they do not exist yet), and we move to Part IV of the book.

The evaluation tools discussed in Part III are those that precede development. Once prototypes or service configurations begin to appear, evaluation begins again, first in the form of product use testing and later in market testing, and more. These are covered in later chapters. All of these efforts at evaluation are themselves major topics, so our discussions must be selective. Unfortunately, industry uses many of the tools in different ways, so they tend to blend together at the edges. When, for example, does a prototype concept test become a product use test?

Likewise, industry often combines two or even three of the tools. For example, in some industries it is very easy to prepare prototypes, so some of these firms like to do an early customer survey that is partly market analysis, partly concept test, and partly prototype test, particularly when the idea first emerged in prototype form. Finally, standardized and fully accepted terminology often doesn't exist. Therefore, we have had to do some standardizing of terms, and some of our decisions won't be acceptable to all people.

CHAPTER EIGHT

The Concept Evaluation System

Before looking into the various specific techniques used to evaluate new product concepts, we need something to give us an overview. Throughout the new product development process, we are doing evaluations, and there are evaluation techniques appropriate to each of the phases in the basic new product process. Furthermore, none of these techniques is used all the time or in all cases. Chapter 8 offers this overview, presenting models such as the cumulative expenditures curve and the A-T-A-R model as ways that can help us decide which evaluation techniques to use. We will even cover potholes and surrogates, among other ideas. In Chapters 9 and 10, we will look more closely at concept evaluation and full screen techniques that are specifically appropriate to Phase III (concept/project evaluation), while Chapters 11 and 12 round out the discussion with a look at sales forecasting, financial and strategic analysis, and product protocol specification.

You will recall from Chapter 2 that new products fail because (1) there was no basic need for the item, as seen by intended users; (2) the new product did not meet its need, considering all disadvantages; and (3) the new product idea was not properly communicated (marketed) to the intended user. In sum, they didn't need it, it didn't work, they didn't get the message. Keep these factors in mind as you see how an evaluation system is constructed.

What's Going On in the New Products Process?

New products actually build up the way rivers do. Great rivers are systems with tributaries that have tributaries. Goods that appear complex are just collections of metal shapes, packaging material, fluids, prices, and so on. A good analogy is the production of automobiles, with a main assembly line supported by scores of subsidiary assembly lines scattered around the world, each of which makes a part that goes into another part that ultimately goes onto a car in that final assembly line.

If you can imagine the quality control people in auto parts plants evaluating each part before releasing it to the next step, you have the idea of a new product **evaluation system.** The new product appears first as an idea, a concept in words or pictures, and we evaluate that first. As workers turn the concept into a formed piece of metal, or software, or a new factory site preparation service, that good or service is then evaluated. When a market planner puts together a marketing plan, its parts are evaluated separately (just as minor car parts are) and then evaluated again in total, after it is added to the product.

The fact that we evaluate the product and its marketing plan as separate and divisible pieces is what lets us telescope the development process into shorter periods of time. There was an era when we went through a new product's development step by step, nothing ahead of its time. But today we may be working on a package before we actually have finished the product, we may be filming part of a commercial before the trademark has been approved and finalized, or we may be preparing the trailer to promote an upcoming movie long before the final edits are completed.[1]

This sometimes causes some backtracking, but the cost of that is less than the costs of a delayed introduction. It does require, however, that we have thought through carefully the item's overall development needs and decided which of those needs are crucial, and which are not crucial. Any evaluation system *must* cover the crucial ones.

The Evaluation System for the Basic New Products Process

Although the overall purpose of evaluation is to guide us to profitable new products, each individual evaluation step task has a specific purpose, keyed primarily to what happens next. Recall Figure 2.2, which showed that different evaluation tasks were appropriate to specific phases in the new products process. Figure 8.1 presents the same information, but adds the most common evaluation techniques used throughout the process. Before going any farther, this is a good place to note that conducting the evaluation tasks really does improve new product performance. The 2003 CPAS study (first introduced in Chapter 1) included an analysis of the most commonly used evaluation techniques: In all cases, the "Best" firms were significantly more likely to use these techniques than the "Rest," and they ended up with better sales and profit results from their new products.[2]

In the process of Figure 8.1, ideas become concepts; concepts get refined, evaluated, and approved; development projects are initiated; and products are launched. Throughout this process, different questions need to be asked, and different evaluation techniques provide the required answers. For example, the very first evaluation *precedes* the product concept—in fact, it takes place in Phase I, when an opportunity or threat is identified and assessed. Someone decided the firm had a strong technology, or an excellent market opportunity, or a serious competitive threat—whatever. As discussed in Chapter 3 on strategy, a judgment was made that if the firm tried to develop a new product in a given area, it would

---

[1]There is a (perhaps apocryphal) story about an Alberto Culver shampoo. Television commercials were finished and at the networks ready for showing before the chemist could find an appropriate formulation!

[2]Gloria Barczak, Abbie Griffin, and Kenneth B. Kahn, "Perspective: Trends and Drivers of Success in NPD Practices: Results of the 2003 PDMA Best Practices Study," *Journal of Product Innovation Management*, 26(1), January 2009, pp. 3–23.

probably succeed. This early evaluation step (direction) is shown at the top of Figure 8.1. Where should we look, what should we try to exploit, what should we fight against? The tool is opportunity identification and evaluation, also discussed in Chapter 3. This tool keeps us out of developments where we stand a poor chance of winning; in other words, it makes sure we play the game on our home field. This direction is provided in the product innovation charter.

Now continue down Figure 8.1 to see how the evaluation tasks change as we progress through the basic new product process. In Phase II (concept generation), ideas begin to appear, and the purpose of evaluation changes: Now the goal is to avoid the big loser or the sure loser. We want to cull them out and spend no added

FIGURE 8.1
The Evaluation System, Including Common Techniques

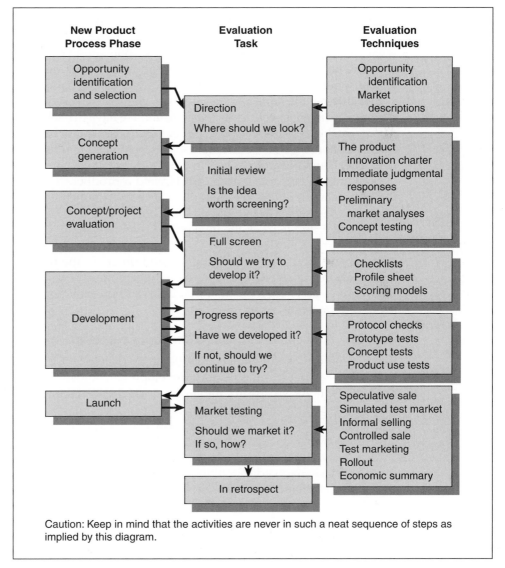

New Product Process Phase	Evaluation Task	Evaluation Techniques
Opportunity identification and selection	Direction — Where should we look?	Opportunity identification Market descriptions
Concept generation	Initial review — Is the idea worth screening?	The product innovation charter Immediate judgmental responses Preliminary market analyses Concept testing
Concept/project evaluation	Full screen — Should we try to develop it?	Checklists Profile sheet Scoring models
Development	Progress reports — Have we developed it? If not, should we continue to try?	Protocol checks Prototype tests Concept tests Product use tests
Launch	Market testing — Should we market it? If so, how?	Speculative sale Simulated test market Informal selling Controlled sale Test marketing Rollout Economic summary
	In retrospect	

Caution: Keep in mind that the activities are never in such a neat sequence of steps as implied by this diagram.

time and money on them. We're sometimes wrong, of course, but usually we're right, and this step is essential if we are to focus limited resources on the worth-while concepts.

The initial review segment of activities also tries to spot the potential big win-ners. Most good concepts are just that—good. A few are great, and we want to recognize them as soon as possible. These get added effort, usually in the form of a very complete concept testing and development program.

That activity leads us to Phase III (concept/project evaluation) and the decision on whether to send the concept into full-scale development. This decision, if the amounts to be spent make it an important decision, will benefit from a very thor-ough scoring model application. Should we try to develop it?

The decision to enter Phase IV (development) introduces the part of the process where the parallel or simultaneous technical and marketing activities are done (as seen in Figure 2.1). All through this phase we are continually asking, Have we got what we want? Is this part ready? Is that system subset cleared for use? Does the software not only work, but produce what the customer needs? A protocol check tells us whether we are ready to develop a product for serious field testing.

Development is naturally iterative: One new discovery leads to another; direc-tions are changed; specific attempts fail, and we have to back up. At Hollingsworth & Vose, an industrial specialty paper company, gaskets are tested five times in this stage—in-house lab test, customer lab test, customer engine test, car manufacturer engine test, and fleet test.

Sooner or later the technical efforts yield a product that evaluators say meets the customers' request. We then enter Phase V (launch), and attention turns to launching the item. The evaluation issue now is whether the firm has proven itself able to make, and market, the item on a commercial scale. This is usually resolved by some form of market testing.

Later on, of course, the developers (and others in the firm too, unfortunately) will be asking, in retrospect, should we have done all this? The purpose is not to find a guilty party for a product that bombed but, rather, to study the evaluation process to prevent a repetition.[3]

Product Line Considerations in Concept Evaluation

Keep in mind that any one product being evaluated is not alone. Most organiza-tions have several products under development, sometimes scores or even hun-dreds of them. As we saw in Chapter 3, managers often think in terms of a portfolio of products and evaluate new product projects in terms of how well they would fit with corporate strategy. We will see how product projects are selected relative to strategic concerns (such as strategic portfolios) in more detail in Chapter 11.

Especially at the early phases, or fuzzy front end, of the new product process, there are risks involved in making project selection decisions. Depending on the evaluation mechanism chosen, the firm may let through too many bad ideas or

---

[3]For a thorough discussion of new product evaluation techniques and their use at different phases in the new products process, see Muammer Ozer, "A Survey of New Product Evalua-tion Models," *Journal of Product Innovation Management,* 16(1), January 1999, pp. 77–94.

reject good ideas. There is no one right way to optimize project evaluation, but some experience can help set the best rules for a given firm or industry. For example, a firm that needs new product help fast may skip early checkpoints and narrow down to just one or two alternative formats during development. They will tend to put in one major check late in the process to make sure the marketing plan communicates and the distribution system is in place. In an industry like pharmaceuticals, a firm might bring two or more ideas through to development: With more potential products, there is a greater chance that one will be a winner, and the payoff for winning is large enough to offset the extra costs incurred in developing more products. Having hurdles that are too high may reduce failure rate, but contribute to major, costly delays in new product launch. If a firm makes products with very short cycle times (such as computer games), it has to control the number of products it has in the process queue at any given time so that products receive development funds in a timely manner.[4]

The Cumulative Expenditures Curve

As we have seen, the new product evaluation system flows with the development of the product. What evaluation occurs at any one point (how serious, how costly) depends greatly on what happens next. Figure 8.2 shows a key input to the design of any evaluation system: In the middle of that figure, a gradually upward-sloping

FIGURE 8.2
**Cumulative
Expenditures—
All-Industry
Average
Compared to
Occasional
Patterns**

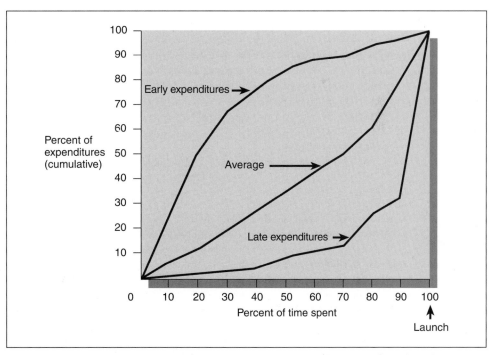

Percent of
expenditures
(cumulative)

Early expenditures →

Average →

Late expenditures →

Percent of time spent

Launch

[4]For more on this topic, see Donald G. Reinertsen, "Taking the Fuzziness Out of the Fuzzy Front End," *Research-Technology Management,* November–December 1999, pp. 25–31.

curve represents the accumulation of costs or expenditures on a typical new product project from its beginning to its full launch.

This generalized curve, taken from various studies over the years, is just an average. It need not reflect any one firm, but it is typical of many durable consumer goods, nontechnical business-to-business products, and many services. Shown with the average curve are two others. The early expenditures curve is representative of product development in technical fields, such as pharmaceuticals, optics, and computers. R&D is the big part of the cost package, and marketing costs are relatively small. The lower curve in the figure shows the opposite type of firm, say, a consumer packaged goods company. Here the technical expenditures may be small, but a huge TV advertising program is needed at introduction.

These are generalizations, and individual exceptions do occur, such as when P&G spends years developing a fat substitute called Olestra or Upjohn markets a line of generic drugs. The point is, whoever develops a concept evaluation system needs to know what situation it is for. No evaluation decision is independent of considerations on what will be done next, how much will be spent, or what points of no return are passing. An old Chinese proverb says, "Spend your energy sharpening the edge of the knife, not polishing the blade."

The Risk/Payoff Matrix

Figure 8.3 applies these ideas in a **risk/payoff matrix**. At any single evaluation point in the new product process, the new products manager faces the four situations shown. Given that the product concept being evaluated has two broad ultimate outcomes (success or failure) and that there are two decision options at the time (move on or kill the project), there are four cells in the matrix.

The AA cell and the BB cell are fine; we drop a concept that would ultimately fail, or we continue on a concept that would ultimately succeed. The managerial problem arises in the other two cells. AB is a "drop error": A winner is discarded. But BA is a "go error": A loser is continued to the next evaluation point.

Which error does the manager most want to avoid? The answer depends on the dollars. First, throwing out a winner is very costly, because the ultimate profits from a winning product are bound to be much greater than all of the development costs combined, let alone those in just the next step. So error AB is much worse than BA.

FIGURE 8.3
Matrix of Risk/
Payoff at Each
Evaluation

Decision is to: →	A Stop the project now	B Continue to next evaluation
If the product were marketed		
A. It would fail	AA (no error)	BA (go error)
B. It would succeed	AB (drop error)	BB (no error)

Comment: Cells AA and BB are "correct" decisions. Cells BA and AB are errors, but they have different cost and probability dimensions.

The exception, of course, is the opportunity cost. What other project is standing by waiting for funding? When good candidates wait in the wings, the losses of dropping a winner are much less because the money diverted will likely go to another winner. The point is, a manager must think of these matters when deciding what evaluation to do. If the net costs of the next step in any situation are low, then a decision will probably be made to go ahead, perhaps with very little information. For example, P&G supported both Febreze (an odor eliminator) and Dryel (which lets you wash dry-clean-only clothes at home) with extensive market testing, including lengthy test marketing, as they were seen as risky, new-to-the-world (and also new-to-P&G) products. P&G supports a detergent line extension with much less extensive testing (relying on some of the alternative methods we will see in Chapter 18), as that would be considered a much less risky launch. After all, who knows more about detergents than P&G?

A good example of the risk matrix in action occurred when Pillsbury announced that it had, in one year, failed with three major new consumer product launches, but succeeded with Totino's Crisp Crust Frozen Pizza. Sales of the frozen pizza were over $60 million the first year, while none of the losers cost the company as much as $1 million. There were some morale problems in this case because no developers like to have a new product fail. And the R&D people were very much aware that the losers were internal developments whereas the frozen pizza came mainly from an acquisition. But no one can fault the overall financial outcome from this package of four decisions.

In general, the new products team should consider four generic risk strategies:

Avoidance: Eliminate the risky product project altogether, though an opportunity cost is incurred (what if they had pushed through with the project and it succeeded?).

Mitigation: Reduce the risk to an acceptable, threshold level, perhaps through redesigning the product to include more backup systems or increasing product reliability.

Transfer: Move the responsibility to another organization, in the form of a joint venture or subcontractor, for example. The other party would be better equipped to handle the risk.

Acceptance: Develop a contingency plan now (active acceptance) or deal with the risks as they come up (passive acceptance).[5]

The Decay Curve

The risk matrix decisions lead to the idea of a **decay curve,** as shown in Figure 8.4. That figure depicts the percentage of any firm's new product concepts that survive through the development period, from the 100 percent starting out before concept testing to the 2 percent (estimated from various studies) going to market. The discarded 98 percent drop off at various times during the process, and when they drop off is primarily determined by the analysis of the risk matrix.

---

[5]Gregory D. Githens, "How to Assess and Manage Risk in NPD Programs: A Team-Based Risk Approach," in P. Belliveau, A. Griffin, and S. Somermeyer (eds.), *The PDMA Toolbook for New Product Development* (New York: John Wiley, 2002), pp. 187–214.

FIGURE 8.4
**Mortality of
New Product
Ideas—the
Decay Curve**

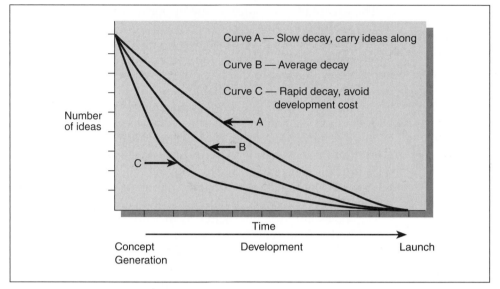

Source: Hypothetical representation based on empirical data in various sources, including *New Products Management for the 1980s* (Chicago: Booz Allen & Hamilton, 1982), p. 14.

Decay curve C is roughly the shape of one decay curve from a leading company in the paper industry that wanted to kill off all possible losers early and spend time developing only those proposals worthy of marketing. This was their strategy, and their evaluation system implemented it faithfully. Decay curve A represents one for a service firm that had very low development costs and wanted to drop a project only when there was solid evidence against it. The paper company spent time making careful financial analyses even before technical work began; the service firm started up a project and just let it keep going until the contrary evidence built up.

Thus, the decay curve is partly a plan and partly a result. The two should be synchronized. Its value as a managerial concept lies in helping the manager see the need for thinking through the stream of development costs and the risk/payoff matrix (above) for each new product concept as it starts its journey through development. When it is working, you will hear statements such as, "On that chip, let's make sure the customer will want it if we can make it; no sense in spending all that money only to find there's no buyer for it." And, in the building next door, "Don't worry about Ed's doubts at this time; we can reposition the fertilizer spreader at the last minute if we have to, even change several of the key attributes if we want. Let's just get going, now!"

Planning the Evaluation System

The previous considerations help set the tone for management decisions on an appropriate evaluation system for any particular new product concept. There are four other relevant, but less demanding concepts that help us decide whether to concept test, how long to run a field use test, whether to roll out or go national immediately, and how thorough a financial analysis to demand.

Everything Is Tentative

It's easy to imagine that building a new product is like building a house—first the foundation, then the frame, then the first floor, and so on. Unfortunately, product aspects are rarely locked in that way. Occasionally they are, as when a technical process dominates development, or when a semifinished product is acquired from someone else, or when legal or industry requirements exist.

We usually assume everything is tentative, even up through marketing. Form can usually be changed, and so can costs, packaging, positioning, and service contracts; so can the marketing date and the reactions of government regulators. So can customer attitudes, as companies with long development times have discovered.

This means two long-held beliefs in new product work are actually untrue. One is that everything should be keyed to a single Go/No Go decision. Granted, one decision can be critical—at times, for example, when a firm must invest millions of dollars in one large facility or when a firm acquires a license that commits it to major financial outlays. But many firms are finding ways to avoid such commitments by transferring risk: by having another supplier produce the product for a while before a facilities commitment, or by negotiating a tentative license, or by asking probable customers to join a consortium to ensure the volume needed to build the facility.

The other fallacy is that financial analysis should be done as early as possible to avoid wasting money on poor projects. This philosophy leads firms to make complex financial analyses shortly after early concept testing, although the numbers are inadequate. The paper products firm whose decay rate was presented in Figure 8.4 (curve C) rejected hundreds of ideas before realizing that early financial analysis was killing off ideas that would have looked great after further development. The financial analysis is best built up piece by piece, just like the product itself. We will see later how this works.

Still another tentative matter is the marketing date. Marketing actually begins very early in the development process (for example, when purchasing agents are asked in a concept test whether they think their firm would be interested in a new item). Rollouts (discussed in Chapter 18) are now so common it is hard to tell when all-out marketing begins. No one pulls a switch and marketing instantly begins. We more often sneak up on it, which clearly affects the evaluation system. What results in some cases is a sort of *rolling evaluation*. The project is being assessed continuously, figures are penciled in, premature closure is avoided, and participants avoid mindsets of good and bad. This is, in a way, dealing with risk via acceptance or mitigation. We know product development projects are risky, so we evaluate, move to the next phase if warranted, and continuously upgrade the quality of information available to us throughout the process to minimize the chances of failure (mitigation) and to expect contingencies and deal with them as they come up (acceptance).

Potholes

One critical skill of product developers is the ability to anticipate major difficulties, the potholes of product innovation. In automobile travel, potholes are always a problem, but they only become costly when we fail to see them coming in time to slow down or steer around them. The same thinking applies to new products: We should carefully scan for the really damaging problems (the deep holes) and keep them in mind when we decide what evaluating we will do. If the pothole is deep enough, the development team may have to seriously consider the risk avoidance option: Drop the project!

For example, when Campbell Soup Company undertakes the development of a new canned soup, odds are in its favor. But experience has shown two points in the process when it may fail, and if it does, the product won't sell. The first is manufacturing cost—not quality, as that's one of the company's key strengths. But there is always a question about whether the chosen ingredients can be put together to meet market-driven cost targets. The second is whether consumers think it tastes good. So the company's evaluation system is set never to overlook these two points.

A flour miller once said his biggest pothole was a quick entry by a price-cutter because that industry had virtually no patent protection or other barriers to competitive entry. He planned on it in every case and didn't go ahead without an answer. A software developer said his biggest pothole was customer unwillingness to take the time to learn to use complex new products. He had several worthwhile products in the graveyard to prove it. Among the potholes faced by pharmaceutical manufacturers is the uncertainty regarding FDA approval: For that reason a firm may go to the expense of taking two similar products through the approval process in the hopes that at least one of them makes it.

In fact, if a manager thinks through the matter of potholes carefully (scans the road ahead), there are more benefits than just to the evaluation system.

The People Dimension

Product developers also have to remember they are dealing with people, and people cause problems. For example, although R&D workers are quite enthusiastic early in the life of a new product, the idea may have little support outside of R&D; it is fragile and easy to kill. Late in the development cycle, more people have bought in on the concept and are supportive because they have played a role in getting it to where it is. Consequently, the now-strong proposal is tough to stop.

This means that an evaluation system should contain early testing that is supportive. In fact, concept *testing* is sometimes called concept *development* to reinforce the idea of helping the item, not just killing it off. Later in the cycle, hurdles should usually be tough and demanding, not easily waved aside. One firm designated its market research director as a manager of screens. His task was to impose absolute screens, such as, "A new food product, in home placement testing, must achieve a 70 percent preference against the respective category leaders." If less than 70 percent of the testers preferred the new item, it was stopped, period. This sounds severe and arbitrary, but it shows how difficult it sometimes is to kill off marginal products late in development. Another people problem relates to personal risk. All new product work has a strong element of risk—risk to jobs, promotions, bonuses, and so on. Consequently, some people shy away from new product assignments. We're always under the gun from someone—an ambitious boss, a dedicated regulator, an aggressive competitor, a power-hungry distributor, an early critic who was overruled within the company, and more. A good evaluation system, built on a thorough understanding of the road the new item will follow as it winds its way through development, protects developers from these pressures. The system should be supportive of people and offer the reassurance (if warranted) that players need.

Surrogates

The timing of factual information does not often match our need for it. For example, we want to know customer reactions early on, even before we develop the product, if possible. But we can't really know their reactions until we make some of the product and give it to them to try out. So, we look for **surrogate questions** to give us pieces of information that can substitute for what we want to learn but can't. Here are four questions to which we badly need answers and four other questions that can be answered earlier (thus giving *clues* to the real answer):

Real Question	Surrogate (Substitute) Question
Will they prefer it?	Did they keep the prototype product we gave them?
Will cost be competitive?	Does it match our manufacturing skills?
Will competition leap in?	What did they do last time?
Will it sell?	Did it do well in field testing?

Note that each response has little value except to help answer a critical question that cannot be answered directly.

Surrogates often change at different times in the evaluation process. For example, let's go back to one of the questions just above: Will cost be competitive? At different times during the project, the surrogate used might be:

Time 1: Does it match our skills?

Time 2: Are the skills obtainable?

Time 3: What troubles are we having in making a prototype?

Time 4: How does the prototype look?

Time 5: Does the manufacturing process look efficient?

Time 6: How did the early production costs turn out?

Time 7: Do we now see any ways we can cut the cost?

Time 8: What is the cost?

Time 9: What is the competitive cost?

Only when we know our final cost and the competition's cost can we answer the original question. But the surrogates helped tell us whether we were headed for trouble.

The last tool that we use for designing an evaluation system for each new project as it comes along is based on how we forecast sales and profit on a new item. The calculation is much like a pro forma income statement, an *array* of figures allowing us to see what the profits will look like based on where we are at any one time in the development.

The basic formula, shown in Figure 8.5, is based on what is known in the marketing field as the **A-T-A-R concept** (awareness-trial-availability-repeat).

FIGURE 8.5

The A-T-A-R
Model

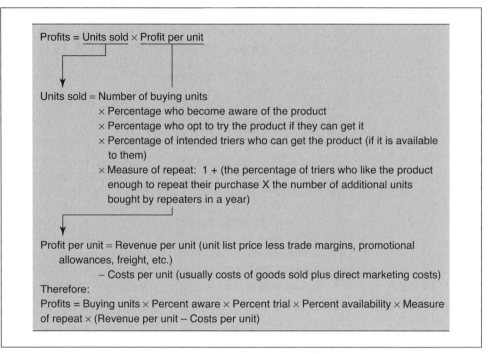

Profits = Units sold × Profit per unit

Units sold = Number of buying units
      × Percentage who become aware of the product
      × Percentage who opt to try the product if they can get it
      × Percentage of intended triers who can get the product (if it is available
        to them)
      × Measure of repeat: 1 + (the percentage of triers who like the product
        enough to repeat their purchase X the number of additional units
        bought by repeaters in a year)

Profit per unit = Revenue per unit (unit list price less trade margins, promotional
      allowances, freight, etc.)
        − Costs per unit (usually costs of goods sold plus direct marketing costs)
Therefore:
Profits = Buying units × Percent aware × Percent trial × Percent availability × Measure
of repeat × (Revenue per unit − Costs per unit)

The A-T-A-R Model

This is taken from what is called **diffusion of innovation,** explained this way:
For a person or a firm to become a regular buyer/user of an innovation, there
must first be awareness that it exists, then there must be a decision to try that
innovation, then the person must find the item available to them, and finally
there must be the type of happiness with it that leads to adoption, or repeat
usage.[6]

    We want to use the formula to calculate all the way to profit, so we expand it to
include target market size (potential adopters), units purchased by each adopter,
and the economics of the operation. But at the heart of the calculation is A-T-A-R.
We use one form of this model here in predicting first-year profitability; in Chapter 11 we revisit A-T-A-R as a market-share forecasting tool, and we see it again
later in Chapter 18 in the context of simulated test markets.

    Let's take a simple example to explain how it works. Assume we are develop-
ing a new cellular picturephone-camera: This is a regular-size cell phone with a
small video display that sends video images of the speakers as well as their voices;
the cell phone also has a camera and can take digital photos and send them via
phone lines. We presume that the product is analogous to existing cell phones

[6]The basic A-T-A-R sequence has been broken down further into many microsteps. One example
of this extension is John H. Antil, "New Product or Service Adoption: When Does It Happen?"
Journal of Consumer Marketing, Spring 1988, pp. 5–16. Some people use this model in abbreviated form, stopping at unit sales. They calculate market share and make conclusions on that.

with video display (that is, the new product will be comparable in many ways to these cell phones: similar price, similar target market, similar benefit provided). A rough estimate, then, of the potential for the new product is the size of the market for the analogous existing product (more about the use of analogous products in forecasting in Chapter 11). To apply the A-T-A-R model, we need the following (hypothetical) data:

- Number of owners of video cell phones (who are our potential buying units for the new product): 10 million.
- Percentage of owners of video cell phones we think we can make aware of our new cellular picturephone-camera the first year on the market: 40 percent.
- Percentage of aware owners who will decide to try the new phone during the first year and set out to find it: 20 percent.
- Percentage of customary consumer electronics retailers whom we can convince to stock the new phone during the market introduction period: 70 percent. (To keep things simple, assume that potential buyers probably will not seek beyond one store if they cannot find it there.)
- Percentage of the actual triers who will like the product enough to repeat-purchase within the first year: 20 percent.
- Number of additional units bought by these repeat buyers, on average: 1 (that is, they buy a total of two phones, possibly one for home use and one for office use).
- Dollar revenue at the factory, per device, after trade margins and promotion discounts: $100.
- Unit cost, at the intended volume: $50.

The profit contribution forecast, based on the A-T-A-R model as depicted in Figure 8.5, would be:

$$\text{Profit contribution} = \text{Potential} \times AW \times T \times AV \times R \times \text{margin}$$
$$= 10 \text{ million} \times 0.40 \times 0.20 \times 0.70 \times 1.20 \times (\$100 - \$50)$$
$$= \$33,600,000,$$

where AW = awareness and AV = availability,

and R is calculated as shown in Figure 8.5 as

$$1 + (\text{percentage of repeaters} \times \text{number of additional units}) = 1 + (0.20 \times 1)$$
$$= 1.20.$$

What we did was prepare a mathematical formula and run it through one set of data. Since the development was about finished when the calculation was made, the forecast was fairly solid. But the formula could have been used at the very beginning as well. Only a few figures (e.g., number of potential adopters) are known at the start, but estimates can be plugged into the other spots and the whole thing set up for use down the line.

As with the other parts of this chapter, the A-T-A-R model gives us guidance on evaluation system design. You can immediately see the importance of awareness, trial, and so on. That means tests will have to be run where customers are checked out for their interest in trying, their reactions after trying (how likely would they be to try again?), and whatever else contributes to the formula.

There is nothing magic in the formula; it simply states the critical factors and shows their relationship to one another and to the sales and profit forecasts.

Two things are important about this model's sales and profit forecasts for the new cell phone:

1. *Each factor is subject to estimation,* and in every development phase we are trying to sharpen our ability to make the estimates. For example, we may be trying to check the introductory promotion's awareness-building capability or just how much price discounting we must do to motivate a first purchase of the device. We may be worried about how we're going to get enough distribution to make the product available when the intended market seeks it.

2. *An inadequate profit forecast can be improved only by changing one of the factors.* For example, if the forecast of $33,600,000 profit contribution is insufficient, we look at each factor in the model and see which ones might be changed and at what cost. Perhaps we could increase the retail margin by 5 percent and get another 10 percent of retailers to stock it. On the other hand, perhaps an increase in advertising would produce more awareness.

Qualitative changes (such as a new advertising theme) can be made in addition to the quantitative. The proposed changes are then run through the formula again, which yields another set of results, some more changes, and so on. Sometimes the issue raised is so fundamental that it is more efficient to cycle back to an earlier phase in the development. The fact that the model is set up in spreadsheet format makes for easy simulations and what-if tests.

A-T-A-R is a term that came from consumer products marketing. Industry has traditionally used slightly different language, so a natural question is, "Does the model apply to all types of new products, including industrial ones, and services too?" The answer is absolutely, though each term may be defined slightly differently in different settings.

See Figure 8.6 for the definitions of terms that vary. A **consumer buying unit** may be a person or a home. For office furniture, it will perhaps be a facility manager; for industrial products, it will generally be a purchasing or engineering person (part of a team); and for a consumer bank loan, it will once again be a person or a family. Product developers know what these definitions should be; the target users were selected partly because we know them well.

Without a precise definition there can be no worthwhile measurement. In each case, something about the term tells you how to define it. For **awareness,** we want to know if the buying unit has been sufficiently informed to stimulate further investigation and consideration of trial. If it has only heard the product's name, it probably won't. For **trial** of our new product, we might imagine an in-store situation where the prospective customer tries out the cell phone and sees if the product is satisfactory. For other kinds of new products (such as a new electronic security device to be installed on a car), you may wonder how a

FIGURE 8.6
Definitions
Used in the
A-T-A-R
Model

Buying unit means purchase point; may be each person, household, or department who participates in the decision.

Aware means someone in the buying unit hears about the existence of a new product with some characteristic that differentiates it; subject to variation between industries and even between developers.

Available means the percentage chance that if a buyer wants to try the product, the effort to find it will be successful; often "percent of stores that stock it." Direct sellers have 100 percent availability.

Trial is variously defined; may be use of a sample in an industrial setting where such use has a cost associated with it; in most situations, means an actual purchase and at least some consumption.

Repeat is also varied; on packaged goods, means to buy at least one (or two or three) more times; on durables, may mean be happy and/or make at least one recommendation to others.

potential buyer could try the product, that is, try it in risky situations, waiting for a thief to challenge it. The answer is that we get as close to the perfect answer as we can, and that sometimes calls for ingenuity. Otis Elevator Company, for example, is not selling cake mixes—they simply take prospective buyers to a site where the elevator under consideration is already installed. The trial is not perfect, but it is close enough for real customer learning. Sometimes firms use **vicarious trial** where a person or firm who *did* try something shares results with someone who can't try it. But trial there should be, and Chrysler once wanted a new item tried so badly that they paid people $50 if they would take a demonstration ride (and later show proof of purchase of a new car within a month or so). It can be done.

In a trial, we want two things to happen:

1. The buying unit went to some expense to get the trial supply—if there was no cost, then we can't be sure there was evaluation of the product message and interest created. Anyone can taste some sausage in a supermarket, but that doesn't mean the taste was a true trial.
2. The buying unit used the new item enough to have a basis for deciding whether it is any good.

For **availability,** we want to know whether the buyer can easily get the new product if a decision is made to try it. This factor is more standard, and for consumer products it is usually the percent of those outlets where our target buyers shop where the firm has stocking of the new item. If the firm sells direct, there is always availability (unless the factory has extended back-orders). Another measure commonly used is *all commodity volume,* or ACV, which is the percentage of the market that has access to the product in local distribution channels. Business-to-business often uses distributors of some type, usually under some franchise or semifranchise agreement, again pretty much assuring availability. But many small firms cannot be sure of availability and spend much of their marketing money on trying to get it.

Repeat is easy for consumer packaged goods (usually, a repeat purchase), but it really means the trial was successful—the buying unit was pleased. For one-time purchases (industrial or consumer), we have to decide what statistic will tell us that. Some people use the direct one: "Were you satisfied?" Sometimes, an indirect one—such as "Have you had occasion to recommend the product to others?"—is better. In the case of the cellular picturephone-camera, buying a second unit would be a good measurement. In any case, a firm should arrive at some acceptable definition and stick with it, thus building up experience to measure against.

Where Do We Get the Figures for the A-T-A-R Model?

The evaluation techniques shown in Figure 8.1 (primarily concept testing, product use testing, and market testing) will provide the data needed for the A-T-A-R model. You are not yet acquainted with the various tests, but they will be tied into the A-T-A-R model as they come up. Though various evaluation events can help on several of the key factors, we are usually most interested in the one event that makes the biggest contribution—noted as *Best* in the figure. And we should know which these are prior to starting the evaluation. That way, we spend our limited funds first on the best steps and then on others if funds are available. Also, if we have to skip a step (for example, the concept test), we immediately know we are leaving open the question of whether users are likely to try the item when it becomes available. If we are going to do product use testing, then it should be set up in a way that lets us go through a concept test in the process of getting people to sign up for the use testing. It's later than we wanted, but better now than not at all.

Further Uses of the A-T-A-R Model

In this chapter, we outlined the use of A-T-A-R relatively early in concept evaluation, as a rough forecasting tool (i.e., what is the potential profit contribution of this product, is it satisfactory, and how could it be improved?). The A-T-A-R model is useful at this early point, as it provides an early sales and profit forecast based on estimates specific to the new product (i.e., the A, T, A, and R)—it calls for numbers that usually can be researched, and it uses them in a managerial way. We will use A-T-A-R at later phases in the new products process and therefore will return to it occasionally in this book. In Chapter 11, we will use it as the basis of a somewhat more detailed sales forecasting model. A-T-A-R is implicit throughout the discussion of market launch planning (Chapters 16 and 17): What else could be more important for the marketing effort to do than achieve awareness, trial, availability, and repeat use?[7] Finally, in Chapter 19, we visit it again, this time as a tool to assess the launch, identify where the problem areas are, and steer it back on course.

---

[7]One of our top sales forecasting experts addressed the new product situation, particularly the issues surrounding the many techniques. Robert J. Thomas, "Issues in New Product Forecasting," *Journal of Product Innovation Management,* 10(3), September 1994, pp. 347–353.

Summary

This chapter looked at the factors that aid in designing an evaluation system for the basic new products process, designed to provide pieces of information that guide the project in its journey to the market. First came the cumulative expenditures curve, the risk/payoff matrix, and the decay curve. Then we looked at several descriptors of most situations, the primary one being that almost everything about a process situation is tentative. The product itself is still evolving, at least until it sells successfully; the actual date of marketing is increasingly unclear as firms adopt limited marketing approaches; evaluation actually begins with the innovation charter well before ideation; and a product is an assemblage of many parts, each requiring its own evaluation.

Lastly, we introduced the A-T-A-R model, which tells us some of the critical steps, how our information about them can be used to forecast sales and profits, and how to design an evaluation system accordingly.

What are the specific tools, what can each do, and what are their weaknesses? The ones we use in Phase III of the basic process, prior to entering the development phase, are covered in the next two chapters. Others come later.

Applications

1. "During a recent management meeting, two of my division managers (both in the United Kingdom, incidentally) got into quite a tussle over the programs they use to evaluate new product ideas. One of them said he felt evaluation was very important; he wanted to do it quite completely, and he certainly didn't want anyone working to further the development of an item unless the prospects for it looked highly promising. The other manager objected to this, saying she wanted products to move rapidly down the pike, saving the serious evaluation for the time when she had the data to make it meaningful. Both persons seemed to have a point, so I just let it ride. What do you think I should have said?"

2. "I don't know what business school professors would say, but it often seems to me that we might be just as well off if we didn't do any evaluation on new products. Just produce the ones we're convinced will sell the best and really support those. Let's face it—we never have reliable data anyway, and everyone is always changing minds or opinions. Never knew so many people could say I told you so."

3. "Let me tell you another funny thing about evaluation. It seems as though the folks involved in it never use the facts or data that they should and instead use some sort of surrogate data. I don't see why you have to beat around the bush. Why not just gather the real facts in the first place and not use those substitutes?"

Case: Chipotle Mexican Grill[8]

In 1993, Steve Ells opened a burrito-and-taco restaurant in a Denver storefront, not far from the University of Denver campus and popular with students. He named it Chipotle Mexican Grill, after the dried pepper common in Mexican cooking. A trained chef and graduate of the Culinary Institute of America, Steve's idea was for Chipotle to be a cash cow to help him finance a "real," upscale restaurant. Chipotle, however, began branching out: first to several locations in and around Denver, then eventually nationwide. In 1998, McDonald's bought a 91 percent stake in Chipotle; this was followed by a 2006 initial public offering in which McDonald's retained 69 percent of the stock and 88 percent of voting rights. By the end of 2005, there were about 500 Chipotle outlets generating approximately $600 million in sales annually. Currently, about 15,000 people are employed by Chipotle. Steve Ells still serves as the chairman and CEO.

What accounts for the success? For starters: a simple menu, skilled cooking techniques, fresh preparation, served quickly, and a "cool" setting. The menu is described as "fast casual" and is at first glance rather limited: only tacos and burritos. (As the only real change in over a decade, salads were very recently added.) Steve notes, however, that there is a wide variety of flavors to choose from, and by focusing on a couple of things, Chipotle has been able to ensure that they do them very well. He argues that too big a variety leads to too much pre-preparation or processed ingredients, and notes that since its earliest days, Chipotle items are always made-to-order. He admires and tries to emulate In-N-Out Burger, a fifty-year-old chain that sells only fries, hamburgers, and milkshakes, but offers high quality for which people are willing to pay a premium. He also admires Steve Jobs of Apple, and feels that one can learn a lot from Jobs's "passion for not accepting mediocre stuff."

There are some other factors at work here as well. The pork used by Chipotle comes from pigs raised naturally, without hormones, on family farms. In 2005, Chipotle switched its dairy purchasing policy: Since then, all sour cream comes from cows that are not given the hormone rBGH. The restaurants use fresh avocados, tomatoes, and peppers, prepared from scratch. And Chipotle believes in the "open kitchen" format: People can see for themselves that the food is fresh.

Steve's term for Chipotle's vision is "food with integrity." He notes that he loves seeing high school students going into a Chipotle, spending a couple of dollars more for a meal than they might elsewhere, and maybe getting a bottle of water instead of a soda. Chipotle's has never advertised as a place for kids or teenagers to eat. In fact, it does very little advertising. Steve feels that advertising the "food with integrity" vision won't work; to use his term, it would "be too preachy." Rather, he lets the food quality, value, and convenience do the talking. The open kitchen also helps promote Chipotle's freshness and quality. He estimates that no more

[8]Information from this case was obtained from Anonymous, "Chipotle: Fast Food with 'Integrity,'" *BusinessWeek.com*, February 16, 2007; Anonymous, "Chipotle's Chef Has His Payday," *BusinessWeek.com*, January 27, 2006; Marc Gunther, "Can Fast Food Be 'Good' Food?," *cnnmoney.com*, September 13, 2006.

than 5 percent of his customers know about "food with integrity." The rest come in because they like the taste or the value, or just because "the place looks cool."

But Steve believes that "food with integrity" can mean much more. He points to the popularity of organic food stores such as Whole Foods. People respond positively to organic, sustainably grown vegetables, humanely raised meats, and fewer preservatives. At Chipotle, he has considered switching over to all-organic produce, but does not want to price a dining experience at Chipotle out of the average fast-food customer's range. According to one estimate, going organic overnight would make the retail price of a burrito jump to $15. Nevertheless, switching to natural pork increased the price of carnitas from $4.50 to $5.50, but sales also went up.

Totally organic is perhaps a long-term goal, and there are certainly interim steps. About 30 percent of its beans are organic, though other vegetables are generally not. About 60 to 70 percent of the chicken and about 40 percent of the beef is sourced naturally, as well as all of the pork. The sour cream is still not organic, though it is hormone-free. The other thing to keep in mind is that as Chipotle grows, it gets more power in the supply channel. As a tiny chain, it was unable to get natural chicken thighs from high-end supplier Bell and Evans, but at its current size, it can do so today.

Though today's Chipotle would seem to be among the leaders in providing healthy fast food to the public, Steve feels that he is still lagging behind. His goal is for all Chipotle restaurants to offer only organic, pesticide-free ingredients, lacking preservatives and artificial flavors and colors, and all natural, humanely raised meat. He would be even more delighted if every restaurant were to follow the same vision. Let's call this the "all-organic concept" for short, recognizing that organic is only a part of the whole vision here.

If you were advising Steve Ells, what could he have done to evaluate the all-organic concept? Is the concept viable at all? How would he be able to estimate the price elasticity (that is, how high does price have to get before he begins losing significant numbers of customers)? Given the fierce competition in this industry, is his concept pleasant but unrealistic? Or does the organic position provide Chipotle with sustainable competitive advantage?

Case: Concept Development Corporation[9]

Late in 1999, three bridge-playing friends in a southern college town decided to start their own firm. One, Bob Stark, worked for General Motors as a planning manager in a local assembly operation. The second, Betsy Morningside, was a speech and theater professor at the college. The third, Myron Hite, was a CPA who worked for one of the Big Eight accounting firms.

All three were exceptionally creative and especially enjoyed their bridge sessions because they had a chance to brag about their new creations and to hear the creations of the others. It was all for fun until one evening it struck them that it was time to stop the fun and start making some money from their many ideas. So they

[9]This is a real situation, slightly camouflaged.

quit their jobs, pooled their savings, rented a small, three-room office, hired a couple of people, coined the name Concept Development Corporation, and started serious work.

A professor from the college was asked to "make a contribution to local entrepreneurship" by setting up a system to evaluate their ideas. They fully realized they were better at thinking up things than evaluating them. They also were aware of their deficiencies: little staff, little money, little experience in making things like the ones they created, and little time before their meager savings disappeared completely.

They began with two product areas. One was toys, broadly defined as things children played with, especially educational activities. The other area was writing services, something they had not intended to work on but which arose as temporary spin-offs from the abilities of one of the two people they hired. These services primarily involved designing and writing instruction sheets for area firms (training manuals, copy for package inserts, instruction signs—anywhere words were used to instruct people in doing things). The individual had some background in instructions and was experienced in writing and layout work. So they decided to develop new items along that line as well.

Their strategy was to develop unique toys that required little up-front expenditures (for example, dies and packaging equipment). All three were too creative to settle for imitation. Most toys would have some game or competitive aspect, be educational, and involve paper, color, numbers, and the like. They figured "most of the stuff would be for children under 12." And, of course, they needed products that would catch on fast and sell well.

The writing services would be partly reactive in that they would do whatever clients asked them to do. But, being creative, they also planned to create innovative services—new ways of meeting industry and business needs. For example, they wanted to offer a special test/training service, whereby after developing a training manual or instruction sheet they would have some employees for whom the piece was developed come to a special room where they would read the material, apply it in some fashion, be tested on it, and so on. What they delivered to the client would be proven to work. They had many such ideas.

The professor went back to the college and decided to let a new products class assist in the assignment. The students were asked to think about the new firm's situation, the general evaluation system in Figure 8.1, and the various purposes and special circumstances discussed in Chapter 8 and then come up with one general guideline statement of evaluation policy for the toy ideas and another for the new services. They hadn't yet studied specific techniques (such as concept testing), but they could clearly indicate which of the phases in Figure 8.1 were the most critical, where the toughest decisions would be, and so on. The professor was especially interested in the differences between goods and services. He wanted the students to state, as specifically as possible, what they felt were the major differences between the evaluation of tangible goods (like toys) and services, why these differences existed, and what the consequences were with respect to evaluation techniques and methods.

CHAPTER NINE

Concept Testing

Setting

This chapter is the first of two spelling out the various tools for evaluating new products (goods and services) *prior* to undertaking technical development. Chapter 9 will cover the product innovation charter and market analysis activities, which occur before the idea appears, and the initial reaction and the concept testing, which occur immediately after the idea appears. We will be investigating the different kinds of evaluation steps leading up to, but not including, the full screen as shown in Figure III.1. Chapter 10 will examine the full screen in detail. All the evaluation steps shown in this chapter and Chapter 10 should be viewed as investments—the additional information provided far outweighs their cost, and cutting corners in getting important early information from customers can prove costly in the long run.

Recall that, at the end of Chapter 6, we had left unresolved the issue of whether customers would actually buy products corresponding to the gaps we had identified. We need to be able to relate customer needs and preferences to these gaps to ensure that we don't develop the "wrong" product. In this chapter, we will show how we can use perceptual mapping and conjoint analysis to analyze market needs and preferences, to segment the market according to benefits sought, and to test how well our concept will be accepted by the market.

The Importance of Up-Front Evaluations

In recent years there has been much more activity at this phase of the process, prior to development. There still is not nearly enough, but the practice is spreading, as product managers are under continual pressure to boost quality and reduce time to market while not incurring cost overruns. There's another reason: This is when finalizing the positioning statement, a cornerstone of our entire marketing strategy, becomes a focus of attention.

The biggest cause of new product failure is that the intended buyer did not see a need for the item—no purpose, no value, not worth the price. It is in concept testing, a key part of this chapter, where we get our first confirmation that this will be a *quality* product. We save *time* by gathering information and making decisions that help assure the product will move through development fast, and with a minimum of looping back to correct some problem. Spending time here saves time overall, and there is good evidence of this.[1] We lower cost in several ways, one coming when we avoid the rising cumulative expenditures curve you just met in Chapter 8—with the cost curve ever rising, the best time to get off a loser is at the bottom of the curve. Another cost cutter is the elimination of the many losers naturally picked up in an aggressive concept generation program. It's difficult to cut at this point, but we have to, so we want to do it in the correct way. Last, on cost, information gathered here helps us make cost forecasts—just how close are we going to be to competition on the proposed item and how draconian must our efficiencies be.

Quality, time, and cost—there is no better reason for taking action at this point. But highly relevant is that this is also the phase where we set the basic marketing strategy on firm ground. We confirm the target market (the user whose needs we are trying to find and solve) and settle on a product positioning statement (just how the new item will be better than others already out there). The positioning statement guides all the rest of the marketing activities.

In this chapter, we look at what happens at this point in the process, what firms need to be doing, and in particular how one sets about doing what seems to be the very best approach—concept testing.

The Product Innovation Charter

The earliest evaluation that a firm makes is *of itself and its situation*. That evaluation yields *a priori* conclusions about new product proposals. The firm reaches these conclusions while making basic strategic decisions, as discussed in Chapter 3 on the product innovation charter. These decisions decide what types of new products fit best. We saw earlier that Kellogg's sought snack foods that capitalized on existing food technologies and familiar brand names and trademarks.

The PIC itself will eliminate many new product ideas. In advance and without knowing the concepts, the firm decides to reject ideas that violate PIC guidelines. Following the PIC should result in excluding the following kinds of ideas:

- Ideas that require technologies the firm does not have.
- Ideas to be sold to customers about whom the firm has no close knowledge.
- Ideas that offer the wrong degree of innovativeness (too much or too little!).
- Ideas wrong on other dimensions: not low cost, too close to certain competitors, and so on.

The charter given to new products management thus eliminates more product ideas than all the other evaluations combined. By coming at the beginning of the

---

[1]Several studies show this, one being Albert L. Page and John S. Stovall, "Importance of the Early Stages in the New Product Process," *Bridging the Gap from Concept to Commercialization* (Indianapolis, IN: Product Development & Management Association, 1994). Others are Robert G. Cooper and Elko J. Kleinschmidt, "Determinants of Timeliness in Product Development," *Journal of Product Innovation Management,* 11(5), November 1994, pp. 381–395; and Mitzi M. Montoya-Weiss and Roger Calantone, "Determinants of New Product Performance: A Review and Meta-Analysis," *Journal of Product Innovation Management,* 11(5), November 1994, pp. 397–417.

new products system, it precludes the unfortunate practice of having unwanted proposals eat up valuable development funds before they are detected.

Market Analysis

The second evaluation that precedes appearance of the concept is an in-depth study of the market area that the product innovation charter has selected for focus. The study takes place immediately after the PIC is approved, and the depth of the study depends on how well the firm already knows the market selected. Ongoing ideation in support of present product lines takes place within a standing type of PIC, and no special study is necessary (assuming current product managers do their jobs correctly).

Initial Reaction

Concept generation follows the market analysis just discussed. Concepts begin flowing in, usually very fast, and opinions on them are formed instantly. But most firms have evolved some special technique to handle this deluge more systematically, which we will call **initial reaction.**

At Oster, each idea that came from the marketing or administration departments went to the sales vice president first, and each idea from the technical departments or production went to the engineering vice president first. If one of these vice presidents approved the idea, it was sent to the other. If both approved, the idea went to a committee and the system became more formal. The two people making the initial reaction primarily used their experience of many years in the small-appliance industry.

Quick and inexpensive initial reactions must resist the "bazooka effect" (where suggestions are quickly blasted out), so several provisos apply:

1. *The idea source does not usually participate in the initial reaction.* A person who has an idea may want to explain it and argue for it, but this person should probably not have a vote in the decision to advance the idea or drop it.
2. *Two or more persons are involved in any rejection decision,* based on the "fragility of new ideas" concept discussed in Chapter 8. The rejection percentage is much higher here than at any other stage, but involving two or more persons dilutes the biases of a single person.
3. *The initial reaction, though quick, is based on more than a pure intuitive sense.* The evaluators are trained and experienced; records are kept and reviewed; and objective aids are sought.

One of several techniques used in this initial reaction is the product innovation charter. Knowing such things as whether a firm wants to be first or last, high risk or low risk, internally or externally developing, and in shoes or handbags leads to quick and decisive action.

Most firms also make use of heuristics (rules of thumb) for this rough screening. For example, managers look at the scale required (is it in our league?), the competitor we would have to face, the state of the art the idea would require, and the fit with our manufacturing and marketing operations. One suggested way for firms to do a rough early screen is to evaluate it on three factors:

- *Market worth:* What is the attractiveness of the new product to the targeted customer population?
- *Firm worth:* Is the new product project viewed positively by management? Does this new product project enhance the firm's competencies?
- *Competitive insulation:* Can the product's advantage be maintained against competitive retaliation?[2]

Some managers prefer to use a small-scale informal survey at this initial reaction point, particularly when some aspect of the proposal extends beyond the evaluator's experience. But such a survey should be held to the level of telephone checks with professional colleagues.

Concept Testing and Development

Years ago, when Alan Ladd Jr. reigned as top judge of new movie scripts at Twentieth Century Fox Film Corporation, he revealed that his product proposal evaluation system ended about as soon as it began. He would just read a script and decide whether to make the movie. He and his small staff knew their markets well, had a guiding product innovation charter, and combined their knowledge and the charter with personal judgment to reach decisions. They did not use concept testing, full screening, or product use testing. Ladd said, "It's based on my intuition and experience. There's no way to put it on a chart or graph or formulate it."[3] Perhaps. Some agree with Mr. Ladd, but most do not. Most major firms make frequent use of **concept testing.** It is a mandatory part of the process for makers of consumer packaged goods. And use is growing in industrial firms, which actually invented it. Business-to-business firms have always spent much time talking with users about their needs and problems, what suggestions they have, what they think about various ideas, and so on. They just never called it **concept testing.**

But first, let's deal with some concerns about this activity—there are times when it doesn't help. When the prime benefit is a *personal sense,* such as the aroma of a perfume or the taste of a new food, concept testing usually fails. The concept cannot be communicated short of actually having some product there to demonstrate. A type of kids' gum popular in the early 90s (sour gums called Cry Baby and Warhead) tasted so bad that even product use testing showed children hated it. But, when the gum became available, kids became masochistic to the tune of almost $100 million a year.

[2]Rita Gunther McGrath, "Advantage from Adversity: Learning from Disappointment in Internal Corporate Ventures," *Journal of Business Venturing,* 10(2), March 1995, pp. 121–142.
[3]Earl C. Gottschalk, "How Fox's Movie Boss Decides That a Script Is a Powerful Winner," *The Wall Street Journal,* May 17, 1979, p. 1. Many years later, he was still doing the fast reaction and had some major successes—e.g., *Star Wars, Nine to Five,* and *Thelma & Louise.* But he had also worked at several different studios and had marketed some misses—*The Right Stuff, Quigley Down Under,* and *Not Without My Daughter.* Ronald Grover, "Can Alan Ladd Jr. Make Leo the Lion Roar?" *BusinessWeek,* August 12, 1991, pp. 65–66.

Second, concepts embodying new *art and entertainment* are tough to test. Whistler could not have concept-tested his idea for a painting of his mother. The inventor of the Ferris wheel could not have surveyed people to ask what they thought of it. The thrill simply had to be experienced personally. The WB Network (now part of the CW Network) stopped using test audiences to decide which pilot shows should be bought and added to the prime-time lineup since over 80 percent of shows fail whether they did well in audience testing or not. Long-running shows including *Seinfeld, Gilligan's Island,* and *All in the Family* did poorly in tests, while others that aced the audience tests such as *Gabriel's Fire* and *I'll Fly Away* never caught on. Network executives decided it was best to go with "gut instincts."[4]

Third, when the concept embodies some *new technology* that users cannot visualize, it is also a weak tool. Kodak realized this when it tried to concept test its new disc camera. So did Alberto-Culver when it first tested the concept of hair mousse. Women accustomed to sprays could not imagine putting "stuff like that" on their hair. Only after the company developed the product and set up training classes in salons did women agree to try the mousse. Another example was when physicians rejected the concept of a heart pump—they could not know the full attributes (and thus the risks) of such a product before work was completed.

Fourth, there are times when firms mismanage concept testing and then blame the tool for misleading them. Coca-Cola asked their customers to taste-test a New Coke and got favorable replies. But they then took that taste testing to mean customers would buy the product when it got a new name. This is actually the same problem as the heart pump—customers were asked to predict their behavior without knowing all the facts. They can't, but will if asked, and will deceive developers who aren't careful. Another mismanagement was when several fast-food chains asked customers if they wanted diet burgers. Not only was it an unknown taste situation (see above), but people are notoriously inclined to predict "worthy" behavior and then do something else.

Fifth, consumers sometimes simply do not know what problems they have. We discussed this in the chapter on problem-based ideation. Steelcase, for example, found they could not use concept testing on special furniture for use by teams. The team members had no feeling for what they didn't have, so Steelcase observed them in action and came up with a winner: furniture that lets them do some of their work collaboratively and some privately. The microwave oven was another similar example—we didn't know what to do with it even after it hit the market, and we certainly could not have responded helpfully to researchers asking us what we thought about the concept.[5]

Oddly, in spite of evidence to the contrary, some new products people have doubts about concept testing on business and industrial products and on services. Regarding the former, if one sticks to situations where the customer has the ability to make judgments, those judgments are worth gathering; but major technological breakthroughs don't qualify for that, and we just have to take the risk. On services,

---

[4]Brooks Barnes, "Trusting Gut Instincts, WB Network Stops Testing TV Pilots," *The Wall Street Journal,* May 3, 2004, pp. B1, B7.
[5]Some of these examples are discussed in Justin Martin, "Ignore Your Customer," *Fortune,* May 1, 1995, pp. 121–128.

there is no question as to whether people can tell us what they see useful if they can see it (but watch for the intangibles above). They can. But because there is usually little technical development, there is less *need* to do concept testing. If it is simple to go from concept to full service description (a form of prototype), then the services firm can proceed to what is called **prototype concept testing.** Such testing is, of course, much more reliable with a physical prototype to talk around.

Concept testing is useful in most cases, and right now the burden of argument lies with the person who wants to skip it. Unfortunately, we will for a long time hear about such firms as CalFare Corporation, which, without concept testing, developed shopping carts with a "special fifth wheel" that locked into place if the cart was taken from the premises (and run over a rough surface). The cart would then only go in circles. But most stores said no thanks. They feared negative publicity, and customers being scared away. A competitor said it often happened that the cart went awry and started circling around the dairy departments. The developers were caught off guard by the very negative reactions they got.[6]

What Is a New Product Concept?

Webster's says a concept is an idea or an abstract notion. Businesspeople use the term *concept* for the product promise, the customer proposition, and the real reason why people should buy. We have, of course, previously seen it in Chapter 4, describing it as a stated relationship between product features (form or technology) and consumer benefits (needs satisfied). That is, the product concept is a claim of proposed satisfactions.

This promise is open to four interpretations:

1. The *producer's* perception of the *features* of the new product;
2. The *consumer's* perception of the *features* of the new product;
3. The *producer's* estimate of the *benefits* delivered by that set of features;
4. The *consumer's* estimate of the *benefits* delivered by that set of features.

These are only forecasts, or guesses, at this time—not reality, even with a prototype in hand. They rest on expectations.

Thus a complete new **product concept** is a statement about anticipated product features (form or technology) that will yield selected benefits or problem solutions relative to other products already available. An example is "A new electric razor whose screen is so thin it can cut closer than any other electric razor on the market."

Sometimes a part of the concept can be assumed; for example, saying "a copier that has twice the speed of current models" assumes the benefits of speed can go without saying.

The Purposes of Concept Testing

Recall that concept testing is part of the **prescreening** process, preparing a management team to do the full screening of the idea by providing input into the

---

[6]David Jefferson, "Building a Better Mousetrap Doesn't Ensure Success," *The Wall Street Journal,* November 18, 1991, p. B2.

full screen just before beginning serious technical work. We look at information to help the screeners use scoring models and write out product protocols in Chapter 10.

Therefore, the *first* purpose of a concept test is to identify the very poor concept so it can be eliminated. If music lovers, for example, cannot conceive of a compact disc that will last forever and thus reject it out of hand, the concept is probably a poor one.

If the concept passes the first hurdle, a *second* purpose is to estimate (even crudely) the sales or trial rate that the product would enjoy—a sense of market share or a general range of revenue dollars. Some people believe this buying prediction is worthless. Others claim a clear, positive correlation between intention and purchase. One longtime practicing market researcher claimed to have confidential data showing correlations of 0.60 and well above.[7]

The buying intention question appears in almost every concept test. The most common format for purchase intentions is the classic five-point question: How likely would you buy a product like this, if we made it?

1. Definitely would buy.
2. Probably would buy.
3. Might or might not buy.
4. Probably would not buy.
5. Definitely would not buy.

The number or percentage of people who definitely would buy or probably would buy are usually combined and used as an indicator of group reaction. This is called the **top-two-boxes** score, as it is the total number of times one of the top two boxes on the questionnaire (definitely or probably) were checked. Incidentally, Nabisco says "try" (not "buy"), because buyers really are still quite tentative at this point.

Whether this many people actually purchase the item is not important. Researchers have usually calibrated their figures, so they know, for example, that if the top two boxes total 60 percent, the real figure will be, say, 25 percent. They do this from past experience, discounting what people tend to say in interview situations. Direct marketers can do the best calibration because they will later be selling the tested item to market groups they surveyed; they can tell exactly how actual behavior matches stated intentions. The data banks of the BASES Group, the largest supplier of concept tests, literally let a client company calibrate all of its concept test questions by product type. For a price, BASES translates a client's raw intentions data into probable intentions.[8]

Incidentally, sometimes experience calibrates the probable intention *higher* than the respondents say now. On complex products, people often use caution at

[7]Personal communication with Anthony Bushman, now professor of marketing, San Francisco State University.
[8]Other concept testing suppliers listed recently in a publication from the Leo Burnett Advertising Agency were Conway/Milliken, Custom Research, Elrick & Lavidge, FRC Research, Information Resources, Longman-Moran Analytics, Market Decisions, Moskowitz Jacobs, NFO Research, Total Research, and The Vanderveer Group. Most of these have international operations.

concept testing time but end up buying the product when they have a chance to see the final item and hear all about it. (Recall the heart pump.)

Obviously, the concept's sales potential will be closely related to how well it satisfies customer needs or offers desired benefits to the customer. Later sections of the chapter show more advanced analytical procedures that identify customer segments based on benefits sought. Knowing the benefit segments that exist in the marketplace, the firm can identify concepts that would be particularly desirable to specific segments or niches.

The *third* purpose of concept testing is to help develop the idea, not just test it. Concepts rarely emerge from a test the way they went in. Moreover, a concept statement is not enough to guide R&D. Scientists need to know what attributes (especially benefits) will permit the new product to fulfill the concept statement. Because the attributes frequently oppose or conflict with each other, many trade-offs must be made. When better to make them than when talking with people for whom the product is being developed? Near the end of this chapter, we will see how conjoint (trade-off) analysis, a technique we discussed in Chapter 7, is frequently used for this task.

Considerations in Concept Testing Research

Prepare the Concept Statement

A concept statement states a difference and how that difference benefits the customer or end user: "This new refrigerator is built with modular parts; consequently, the consumer can arrange the parts to best fit a given kitchen location and then rearrange them to fit another location." If you think this sounds somewhat like a positioning statement, you are correct. And if the interviews are with a logical target group of potential buyers, the principal parts of a marketing strategy are in place—target market and product positioning. This is consistent with the basic new products process, where we say that the product and its marketing plan are developed simultaneously.

Format

Practitioners urge that any concept statement should make the new item's difference absolutely clear, claim determinant attributes (those that make a difference in buying decisions), offer a chord of familiarity by relating in some way to things familiar to the customer, and be completely credible and realistic. And short, as short as possible, although there have been concept statements of 3–5 pages that worked very well in complex technical situations.[9]

This information is usually presented to potential buyers in one of several formats: a narrative (verbal) format, a drawing or diagram, a model or prototype, or in virtual reality. Early in concept testing, it apparently does not make too much

---

[9]Regarding clarity, Anheuser-Busch said consumers had difficulty understanding Bud Dry, even when it was marketed. Perhaps the reason lies in what an executive said it was: "A cold-filtered draft beer—not pasteurized—with no aftertaste, basically a full-alcohol, light beer, a cleaner beer." (So, is other beer not clean?)

FIGURE 9.1 Mail Concept Test Format—Plain Verbal Description of the Product and Its Major Benefits

A major soft-drink manufacturer would like to get your reaction to an idea for a new diet soft drink. Please read the description below before answering the questions.

New Diet Soft Drink

Here is a tasty, sparkling beverage that quenches thirst, refreshes, and makes the mouth tingle with a delightful flavor blend of orange, mint, and lime.

It helps adults (and kids too) control weight by reducing the craving for sweets and between-meal snacks. And, best of all, it contains absolutely no calories.

Comes in 12-ounce cans or bottles and costs 60¢ each.

1. How different, if at all, do you think this diet soft drink would be from other available products now on the market that might be compared with it?

- ❏ Very different
- ❏ Somewhat different
- ❏ Slightly different
- ❏ Not at all different

2. Assuming you tried the product described above and like it, about how often do you think you would buy it?

	Check one
More than once a week	❏
About once a week	❏
About twice a month	❏
About once a month	❏
Less often	❏
Would never buy it	❏

Source: NFO Research, Inc., Toledo, Ohio, now part of TNS, a worldwide market information company. See www.tns-global.com.

difference which of these formats is used, as all yield about the same answers from the respondents.[10] All the concept testing techniques we discuss here are commonly used for business-to-business product development, though in those cases it is especially important to provide sketches, models, and/or other renditions of the concept such that meaningful, objective reactions can be obtained.[11]

Figure 9.1 shows an example of the narrative format. Some people prefer a very brief presentation, giving only the minimum of attributes and letting the respondent offer additional ones. Others prefer a full description, approaching what a diagram or prototype would provide.

Drawings, diagrams, and sketches comprise a second way to present concepts to respondents. Figure 9.2 demonstrates the use of a drawing. Drawings and the like

[10]Gavin Lees and Malcolm Wright, "The Effect of Concept Formulation on Concept Test Scores," *Journal of Product Innovation Management,* 21(6), November 2004, pp. 389–400.
[11]Ronald L. Paul, "Evaluating Ideas and Concepts for New Business-to-Business Products," in M. Rosenau, A. Griffin, G. Castellion, and N. Anscheutz (eds.), *The PDMA Handbook of New Product Development* (New York: John Wiley, 1996), pp. 207–216.

FIGURE 9.2
Mail Concept
Test—Sketch

Aerosol Hand Cleanser

A large-size can of hand cleanser concentrate that completely eliminates those lingering unpleasant odors that come from handling fish, onions, garlic, furniture polish, etc. Not a covering odor! Just press the button and spray directly on the hands, rub for a few seconds, and rinse off under the faucet. 24-ounce aerosol can will last for months and can be easily stored. Costs $2.25.

1. How interested would you be in buying the product described above if it were available at your supermarket?

	Check one	Responses in sample (%)
I would definitely buy	☐	5%
I would probably buy	☐	36%
I might or might not buy	☐	33%
I would probably not buy	☐	16%
I would definitely not buy	☐	10%
		100% Total

Note: These hypothetical response percentages are for illustrative purposes only.
Source: NFO Research Inc., Toledo, Ohio, now part of TNS, a worldwide market information company. See www.tns-global.com.

usually must be supplemented by a narrative statement of the concept. Figure 9.2 also shows what the results might look like. As shown, 5 percent of respondents said they would definitely buy the product and 36 percent said they would probably buy it, so the top-two-boxes score is 5 + 36 = 41 percent. Note that while Figures 9.1 and 9.2 present classic concept tests administered by mail, these concept statements can obviously be converted to online testing with minimal difficulty.

Prototypes, or models, are a third, more expensive form of concept statement because many decisions have to be made about the new product to get it into a prototype. Whoever builds an early prototype makes lots of decisions about the item that probably should be kept open at this early date. Prototypes are useful only in special situations, as, for example, with simple-to-prepare food products or, at the other extreme, with concepts so complex that the buyer cannot react without more knowledge than a simple narrative would give. A firm in Canada was trying to get reactions to the concept of a traveling medical examining unit that would be driven to various corporation offices where examinations would be given. The answer was to build a small model of the unit, showing layout, equipment, and so on.[12]

[12]Robert G. Cooper, *Winning at New Products*, 3rd ed. (Cambridge, MA: Perseus Publishing, 2001), p. 162.

The fourth type of concept format, virtual reality, captures the advantages of the prototype without most of the disadvantages. Steelcase, the office supply firm, has a software system that allows them to virtually build three-dimensional images of office concepts. The interviewee can actually walk around rooms, seeing things from any angle.[13] The real question is "What does it take to communicate to the buyer what we have in mind?" From that point on, it is a question of the cost of better displays versus the need for that information in making forecasts of buying intentions. For office furniture, most buyers want lots of details, but for turnip-flavored yogurt, one sentence would probably work.[14]

Commercialized Concept Statements

A special variation, regardless of format, concerns whether to make the statement as a **commercialized concept statement,** which is to present it in promotional style. Compare these two concept statements:

> Light Peanut Butter, a low-calorie version of natural peanut butter that can provide a tasty addition to most diets.

> A marvelous new way to chase the blahs from your diet has been discovered by General Mills scientists—a low-calorie version of ever-popular peanut butter. As tasty as ever and produced by a natural process, our new Light Peanut Butter will fit most weight-control diets in use today.

These statements show little *substantial* difference, yet they will draw different reactions. Commercialized formats produce more realistic evaluations (that is, greater acceptance), but they risk the bias of good or poor advertising copy writing. Proponents say noncommercialized statements won't provoke typical market reactions in this commercial world. Critics answer, why evaluate the advertising when all we want at this time is reaction to the concept?

Neither form is *better* than the other, and many managers simply go for a compromise—a gentle sell that puts advantages in language stakeholders are used to. Some practitioners say that it is most important to keep the idea simple and to be clear and realistic—don't oversell the concept. Also, if you are testing several concepts, remember to use the same format for all of them so they can be directly compared![15]

Offering of Competitive Information

Customers of all types know much less about their current products and other options than we would like. A new concept may well offer a benefit that the customer

[13]Information from William Miller, director of research and business development, at a Product Development & Management Association conference in Southfield, Michigan, January 1995.
[14]Actually, Green Giant Vegetable Yogurt in four "flavors" (cucumber, beet, tomato, and garden salad) scored well on concept tests (87% top two boxes). But the firm couldn't deliver what the concept seemed to promise to consumers (should it be crunchy?). This one failed in the marketplace.
[15]Ned F. Anscheutz, "Evaluating Ideas and Concepts for New Consumer Products," in M. Rosenau, A. Griffin, G. Castellion, and N. Anscheutz (eds.), *The PDMA Handbook of New Product Development* (New York: John Wiley, 1996), pp. 195–206.

doesn't realize is new. One solution is to provide a full data sheet about each competitive product. Many new product managers, however, don't like to overload the concept statement; it diffuses the message and confuses the customer.

Price

Another issue turns on whether to put a price in the concept statement. The examples in Figures 9.1 and 9.2 both mention price. Some people object, saying reaction to the concept is wanted, not to its price. Yet price is part of the product (actually, a product attribute in the customer's eyes), and buyers can't be expected to tell purchase intentions without knowing price. An exception occurs for those complex concepts (for example, the medical examinations van, above) requiring many decisions before the cost is known.

Define the Respondent Group

We would like to interview any and all persons who will play a role in deciding whether the product will be bought and how it might be improved. When the New Zealand Wool Testing Authority came up with a new wool testing service, it had to test the concept with three levels in its channel—brokers who sell the raw wool, scourers who scour the wool and prepare it for shipment, and exporters who sell the wool to manufacturers.[16] A cement company, which created a new concept in cement for use in construction, had to seek advice from brick makers, siding makers, architects, builders, designers, and regulators, among others, in addition to the people who would be buying the buildings. Some industrial products may involve 5–10 different people at each buying point, and durable consumer goods usually involve more than one person. Yet that peanut butter mentioned above could probably be tested with just one person in a family setting—the homemaker who does the buying—or could it?

The solution is to think in terms of **stakeholders**—any person or organization who has a stake in the proposed product. Our new product wastebaskets are filled with products that made sense to the end users but could not get to them— for example, when professional sanitary engineers refuse to endorse a new system of water treatment.

Reaching this full set of influencers sounds simple, but it is complex and expensive. Some people try to seek a small number of lead users (see Chapter 4), or influencers, or large users. This approach saves some money and gets more expert advice but often fails to reflect key differences (and misunderstandings) in the marketplace. It would seem to be a technique for situations where there is a right understanding or perception or preference. Of course, we should always watch out for critics, people who have a reason for opposing the concept. A developer came up with a device that read electrocardiograms and needed the reactions of cardiologists, but the obvious conflict of interest made the interviewing tricky.

---

[16]Arch G. Woodside, R. Hedley Sanderson, and Roderick J. Brodie, "Testing Acceptance of a New Industrial Service," *Industrial Marketing Management* 17(1), February 1988, pp. 65–71.

Some new products people, aware that they will first have to interest the innovators and early adopters in a market, concentrate their concept testing solely on them. If this group is interested, it's a good bet others will be also.

Select the Response Situation

There are two issues in the response situation: (1) the mode of reaching the respondent, and (2) if personal, whether to approach individually or in a group.

Most concept testing takes place through personal contact—direct interviewing. Survey samples typically run about from 100 to 400 people, though industrial samples are usually much smaller. Personal contact allows the interviewer to answer questions and to probe areas where the respondent is expressing a new idea or is not clear. Examples earlier in this chapter show that mail contact is frequently used instead of personal contact, and firms have also used the phone and the Internet as other, less expensive means to conduct these tests.

Some research suppliers offer a service of interviewing in which the client can submit product concepts on a shared-cost basis. In the Omnibus program at Moskowitz Jacobs, a fully equipped central testing facility conducts periodic waves of interviewing, which yield 100 interviews at a cost per concept of around $3,000. Other research firms use pseudo stores in vacant locations at shopping malls.

The second issue concerns individual versus group. Both are widely used. Groups (that is, focus groups) are excellent when we want respondents to hear and react to the comments of others and to talk about how the product would be used.

Newer methodologies allow for almost instantaneous evaluation of a great number of product concepts. One such technique, the **real-time response survey**, combines the best features of focus groups and surveys and has proved useful in screening new consumer product concepts. Briefly, about 100 participants observe price, positioning, and attribute information about the concept, perhaps via a simulated ad. A moderator guides the respondents through a computer exercise, in which they use a keypad to input their purchase intentions, responses to proposed prices, and similar data using 11-point scales. The responses are sent to a central computer where they can be read directly, in real time, by the moderator and client. Based on these early results, the moderator can develop original open-ended questions and ask them while the respondents are still present. Responses to the open-ended questions might suggest whole new concepts or attribute combinations, which can then be further evaluated by the respondents. Response rates are virtually guaranteed; hundreds of questions can easily be asked in a three-hour session using the keypads; and dozens of concepts can be evaluated in a single session (thus reducing the number of sessions needed).[17] Another similar technique now used in concept evaluation is to employ group support systems (GSS) software (see Chapter 5) in a focus group setting and to have the participants react to different versions of products. For the aerosol hand cleanser of Figure 9.2 as an

[17]Lynne R. Kahle, Douglas B. Hall, and Michael J. Kosinski, "The Real-Time Response Survey in New Product Research: It's About Time," *Journal of Consumer Marketing*, 14(3), 1997, pp. 234–248.

example, different spray applicators, package sizes, effectiveness levels, and price points could be tried. The group's responses can be averaged and immediately displayed at the front of the room, and good concepts can be selected and even improved upon.

Prepare the Interviewing Sequence

Simple interviewing situations state the new product concept and ask about believability, buying intentions, and any other information wanted. The whole interview may take only two or three minutes per product concept if the item is a new packaged good and all we really want is a buying intention answer.

Usually we want more than that. In such cases, we first *explore the respondent's current practice* in the area concerned, asking how people currently try to solve their problems, what competing products they use, and what they think about those products. How willing would they be to change? What specific benefits do they want? What are they spending? Is the product being used as part of a system?

This background information helps us understand and interpret *comments about the new concept*, which are asked for next. The immediate and critical question is, "Does the respondent understand the concept?" Given understanding, we then seek other reactions:

Uniqueness of the concept.	Does it solve a problem?
Believability of the concept.	How much they like the concept.
Importance of the problem.	How likely would they buy?
Their interest in the concept.	Their reaction to the price.
Is it realistic, practical, useful?	Problems they see in use.

We are especially interested in what changes they would make in the concept, exactly what it would be used for and why, what products or processes would be replaced, and who else would be involved in using the item.

You can see that services present a problem here. A service offers an image, or a feeling, or a hard-to-measure convenience. This makes it difficult for the respondent to give useful information along the lines just listed.

In all this interviewing, remember we are not taking a poll but, rather, *exploring what people are doing and thinking*. Only a few questions will be in standard form for tabulation. Each new concept addresses a very specific problem (or at least it should), and we need to know what people think about that problem in the context of the new concept. It doesn't pay to get too formal in the questioning, unless conducting many concept tests where there is a database for comparison.

Variations

There are variations to all these procedures. The above procedure assumed one-on-one contact with potential buyers. The real-time response surveys employing GSS, discussed earlier, can provide information on buying intentions efficiently as groups of customers respond to the product concepts presented to them. In another example, Avon markets 50 new products every 60 days, with a three-month development cycle. Every two weeks they meet with some of their test bank of 150 sales reps. Many ideas are shown to them for their quick reaction, by computer-driven projectors. Their appeal rating correlates very well with sales, in some cases more accurately than field consumer concept testing predicted. A garment must be cut to fit a body, and bodies vary greatly.

Note also that there are research firms that offer concept evaluation as part of their package of product development services. One example is the Inno Suite Concept Screener, a product of TNS (www.tns-global.com).

Analyzing Research Results

A great number of firms rely on a simple top-two-boxes score (or top-two-boxes plus 30 percent, based on industry experience) in doing concept testing. Occasionally, more information is needed. We cannot assume all customers will have the same needs or look for the same benefits when making a purchase. In fact, through **benefit segmentation,** a firm may identify unsatisfied market segments and concentrate its efforts on developing concepts ideally suited to the needs of these segments. We now turn our attention to ways in which we can identify benefit segments in our desired market and develop products that will be most preferred by key benefit segments.[18]

Identifying Benefit Segments

Let's return to the swimsuit example of Chapter 6. Recall that, when we were collecting respondents' perceptions of the existing swimsuit brands, we also asked them to rate how important each attribute was in determining their preference among brands. These **importance ratings** can be used to model existing brand preferences and predict likely preferences for new concepts.

Suppose there were only two attributes to consider: comfort and fashion. It might be very simple to identify benefit segments on an *importance map* as in Figure 9.3. Each customer is indicated by a dot in this figure, according to the importance she attaches to each of the two attributes. In this simple case, three obvious benefit segments emerge of approximately equal size: customers that think comfort alone is important, those that think fashion alone is important, and those that think both are important.

Rarely are the benefit segments so easily visualized, however. In this case, like most others, there were many more than two attributes that are important to customers in forming their preferences. We need to turn to one of the many computer programs that can do **cluster analysis,** which puts observations (in this case, individuals) together into relatively homogeneous groups on an importance map.

---

[18]Note that, in our typology, benefits are one type of attribute (the others being features and functions). The terms "benefit segmentation" and "benefit segments" are commonly used for the procedure described in this section and should not imply that only benefit-type attributes can be considered.

FIGURE 9.3
Importance
Map Showing
Benefit
Segments

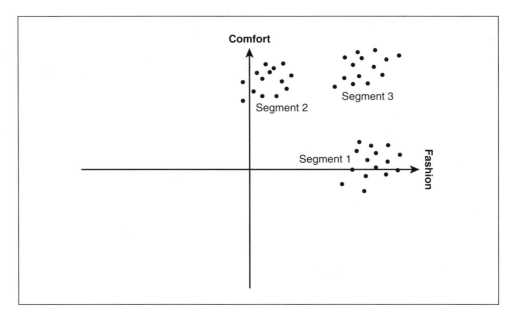

Like factor analysis, cluster analysis is also a data reduction method. In Chapter 6 we learned that factor analysis reduces the data cube by grouping many attributes together into a small number of underlying factors; cluster analysis groups together many individuals into a small number of benefit segments.

Different criteria and rules of thumb can be used to select the best number of clusters (benefit segments) that exist in the market since there is no one correct answer. Generally, practical judgment or experience play an important role. For example, in this case we may feel it is unlikely that more than five or six benefit segments exist. When cluster analysis was run on the swimsuit importance data, a satisfactory solution with three benefit segments was obtained. Conceptually, it is not too different from Figure 9.3, even though we considered many more attributes: The three clusters we obtained more or less correspond to those depicted in that figure.

Joint Space Maps

We can now overlay the benefit segments onto our perceptual map (previously built in Chapter 6). The result is called a **joint space map,** and it allows us to assess the preferences of each benefit segment for different product concepts. Joint space maps can be developed using ideal brand ratings or preference regression.

Ideal Brands

The most direct way is to get customers to rate their **ideal brand** on each attribute. Using the factor score coefficient matrix (which we obtained in Chapter 6 from the perceptions of existing brands), we convert the ideal brand ratings to factor scores and plot the ideal brand positions directly on the perceptual map. Clusters of individuals may be detected visually from this map—each cluster represents a segment

FIGURE 9.4
Joint Space
Map Showing
Ideal Points

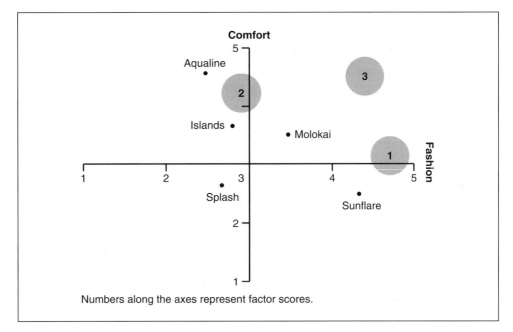

Numbers along the axes represent factor scores.

with its own ideal brand positioned at the center of the cluster. Figure 9.4 shows what a joint space might look like if three segments existed as shown in Figure 9.3.

The preferences of each segment can be obtained from Figure 9.4. We expect the brand that is located closest to a segment's ideal brand will be preferred by that segment. Market share estimation models often assume that the market shares obtained by the various brands are inversely proportional to the square of the distance of that brand from the ideal point: This technique makes brands very close to the ideal highly preferable.

In Figure 9.4, Segment 1 is likely to prefer Sunflare, while Segment 2 seems to be satisfied with either Aqualine or Islands. The brand nearest to Segment 3s ideal point is Molokai, but none of the brands is really that close. Thus, a new brand high in both fashion and comfort has a chance to draw substantial market share from competitors.

Figure 9.5 provides a fully worked-out benefit segmentation of the car-driving market. At the left are four benefits identified through factor analysis: need to haul people and belongings, good performance, practical, and safe. The figure shows that five segments were identified:

1. *Experience Seekers:* While performance and safety are important, they really care about hauling lots of stuff.
2. *Pragmatic:* They care mostly about practical transportation.
3. *Performance Seekers:* They seek out high performance cars only.
4. *Affordable Performance:* They care about performance but also about practicality.
5. *Safety Conscious:* Only the safety benefit comes out important.

FIGURE 9.5 **Benefit Segment Profiles**

Benefits	Experience Seekers	Pragmatic	Performance Seekers	Affordable Performance	Safety Conscious
			Segment		
Need to haul people and belongings	**				
Good performance	*		**	*	
Practical		**		*	
Safe	*				**
Preferred Vehicle	SUV	Hybrid	Luxury Performance	Performance	Sedan
Preferred Way to Seek Car Information	Visit dealerships	Read *Consumer Reports*	Visit dealerships	Web and dealerships	Web
Male/Female	50/50	35/65	75/25	65/35	35/65
Median Age	40	49	42	33	40
Children	80%	60%	30%	20%	50%
Median Income	$70K	$60K	$85K	$35K	$60K

Note: **This cluster's factor score is *very* high for this benefit.
*This cluster's factor score is *relatively* high for this benefit.
Source: Adapted from Brian Ottum, "Segmenting Your Market So You Can Successfully Position Your New Product," in A. Griffin and S. M. Somermeyer, *The PDMA Toolbook 3 for New Product Development,* John Wiley & Sons, Inc., 2007, Ch. 7. Reprinted with permission of John Wiley & Sons, Inc.

What the figure then shows is how all of this information is put to use by management. Additional rows in the figure suggest the kinds of cars each of these segments might prefer, show how each segment tends to get information about car purchases, and provide key segment demographics. Information like this is very useful to managers in developing ideal new products for targeted segments, and also for making positioning decisions (to be taken up later in Chapter 16).[19]

Preference Regression

Preference regression is another method that can be used to identify the optimum combination of attributes desired by the market. This method relies on a different kind of numerical input—often, rankings of brands are obtained (paired comparisons can also be used). In preference regression, we do a regression analysis to relate the factor scores of each brand to the rankings of brands. The relative sizes of the regression coefficients we obtain give us an indication of the relative importance of each factor. Preference regression can also be done on attribute ratings instead of factor scores.

Instead of the importance ratings we discussed above, assume that customers were asked to provide rank orderings of the five existing brands, where 1 = most

[19]The car example is adapted from Brian Ottum, "Segmenting Your Market So You Can Successfully Position Your New Product," in A. Griffin and S. M. Somermeyer, *The PDMA Toolbook 3 for New Product Development* (New York: John Wiley, 2007), Ch. 7.

favored, and 5 = least favored. First, we reverse scale the rank orderings such that higher numbers represent more favored brands. Then, we can solve the regression equation:

$$\text{(reversed) preference rank} = b_0 + (b_1 \times \text{attractiveness score}) + (b_2 \times \text{comfort score}) + e$$

If we ignore benefit segments and put all the respondents together, we find the values of b_1 and b_2 are 0.28 and 0.21. Thus, the relative importance of fashion to customers is 0.28/(0.28 + 0.21), or 57 percent, and the relative importance of comfort is 43 percent. Hence, while fashion comes out as the more important factor, we cannot ignore the fact that customers also place a lot of importance on comfort when we are assessing product concepts. We can also plot the regression line on the perceptual map as shown in Figure 9.6.[20] This line is referred to as the **ideal vector,** as it visually represents the optimum proportion of attributes desired by this market. A product concept lying near the regression line, at Point X on the map, is in a desirable position for this market.

We can also cluster analyze the rank orderings to get benefit segments. In this case, two benefit segments were found to exist in this market, represented by the two lighter lines in Figure 9.6. One of these appears to consider only fashion (the relative importance of this factor is 94 percent), while the other considers a blend

FIGURE 9.6
Joint Space Map Showing Ideal Vectors

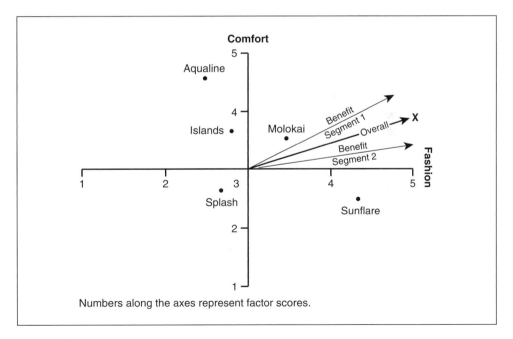

Numbers along the axes represent factor scores.

[20]Though we actually do estimate b_0 in the regression equation, we ignore it when drawing Figure 9.6, as we are most interested in the relative importance of the revealed weights b_1 and b_2. The b_0 term simply defines the scale. Thus, in Figure 9.6, the regression line is shown passing through the origin.

of fashion and comfort (the relative importances are 30 and 70 percent, respectively). Product concepts aimed at one or the other of these segments may do better than the concept represented by Point X, which in fact may not directly appeal to either segment.

Conjoint Analysis in Concept Testing

We were first introduced to conjoint analysis in the context of concept generation. In actuality, conjoint analytic techniques are extremely useful in concept testing as well and are frequently used at this point.

In the conjoint analysis of Chapter 7, you had assumed the role of product manager for a line of salsas. We selected three key attributes of salsa and two or three levels for each attribute, and used conjoint analysis to identify high-potential gaps: combinations of attributes that (a) customers like and (b) are not on the market yet.

Without going through the quantitative analysis again, it should be clear how conjoint analysis can be used at concept testing. The model identified the levels of the key attributes that are preferred by customers and rank ordered the possible combinations from most to least preferred. Each of these combinations could be thought of as a concept, and the top-ranking concept or concepts are the ones that hold the highest potential and should be considered for further development. Of course, the model also identified the real losers!

As was mentioned earlier, many attributes and levels can feasibly be tested in conjoint analysis using a reduced set of cards. The most preferred concept(s) will still come out ranked on top, even if they were not included in the original set of cards. Overall, conjoint analysis is extremely useful in concept testing because of its ability to uncover relationships between attributes (features, functions, benefits) and customer preferences, as illustrated in the salsa example.

We had used a set of product description cards as the stimuli in our original example, since we were at the very earliest phases of the new products process. Note, however, that conjoint analysis can easily use concept statements in other forms as stimuli. At concept testing, we may have concept statements in any of the forms discussed earlier in this chapter (verbal narratives, drawings, sketches, models or prototypes, even virtual-reality representations). The analysis would proceed in the same way regardless of the stimuli used.

To illustrate: Conjoint analysis was used to evaluate how well drivers in New York and New Jersey would respond to the EZPass electronic toll collection system.[21] With the EZPass system, drivers attach an electronic "tag" to their windshield. The tag is read using high-speed radio waves as the car passes through the toll lane and the toll amount is deducted from the driver's prepaid account. The tag can be read while the car is moving; thus EZPass eliminates the need for the driver to stop completely to pay the toll and ultimately should result in fewer

---

[21]Terry G. Vavra, Paul E. Green, and Abba M. Krieger, "Evaluating EZPass: Using Conjoint Analysis to Assess Consumer Response to a New Tollway Technology," *Marketing Research,* Summer 1999, pp. 5–16.

traffic tie-ups at toll plazas. The transportation authorities had already decided to adopt EZPass, but needed assistance on how it should be designed in order to meet driver needs.

Seven key attributes were identified by the transportation authorities:

- The number of EZPass accounts a user would need to open.
- How to apply and pay for an account.
- The number of EZPass lanes available at each toll plaza.
- Transferability of the EZPass tag to another vehicle.
- Acquisition cost and/or service charge (if any) for the tag itself.
- The toll price with EZPass.
- Other uses for EZPass, such as airport parking or gasoline purchase.

Because EZPass was a new product concept for most drivers at the time of the study (1992), the concept description took the form of an 11-minute videotape demonstration of the system "in action" and its effectiveness in relieving toll plaza congestion. Respondents were mailed a copy of the videotape together with a questionnaire and eight scenario cards (each showing a different combination of the above attributes). The conjoint analysis revealed that the most important attribute by far was the number of lanes available and how they would be controlled, while price of the toll, application procedure, and acquisition cost were also relatively important. The analysis also revealed which levels of each attribute were preferred. For example, the four options provided for acquisition cost were rated in order as follows:

1. $10 deposit, plus $15 yearly service charge (most preferred).
2. $2 per month service charge.
3. $10 charge plus $1.50 per month service charge.
4. $40 credit card charge if tag not returned, plus $20 annual fee.

The results from the conjoint analysis were used to design the implementation plan for the EZPass system. The system was adopted rapidly by drivers in New York and New Jersey. By 1999, rush hour use of EZPass had reached 60 percent, about 2 million drivers in the two states that were enrolled in the program, and about 3.1 million tags had been distributed.

Benefit segments can also be identified in conjoint analysis. Recall that conjoint identifies each customer's value system, that is, the relative importances of the attributes to each customer and the preferred levels of each attribute. We took a shortcut in Chapter 7 by assuming that all customers had about the same value system, so we identified the medium-hot green salsa as the best combination.

As we have seen earlier in this chapter, however, there may be underlying benefit segments. We noted in Chapter 7 that aggregating all customers may disguise the fact that half of the market might like extra-hot salsa, and half the market might like mild. We can apply cluster analysis techniques to the importances and preferences generated by conjoint analysis to identify benefit segments of customers who have similar value systems. For example, in the industrial service example of Chapter 7, price came out as the most important variable (with a relative importance of about 27 percent) when all the respondents were aggregated. Follow-up cluster analysis revealed as many as five benefit segments, which varied widely with respect to the importance ascribed to price. In one segment, more concerned with performance quality, price's relative importance was under 9 percent, while in a second, price-driven segment, the comparable figure was about 35 percent![22]

The benefits sought by potential subscribers to TrafficPulse System, by Mobility Technologies Inc., were assessed using a variation of conjoint analysis. This system allows subscribers to get information on traffic conditions, travel times, and preferred routes. The analysis found five benefit segments, differing in their levels of interest in a personalized system, a voice/wireless system, and an Internet-only system.[23]

Market Research to Support Concept Testing

There are a few well-known research firms that support the concept testing phase. One of the best known is BASES, part of the A. C. Nielsen company. BASES helps firms evaluate and optimize new product concepts and also predict sales, operates worldwide, and studies over 10,000 new product ideas per year. BASES provides three levels of concept testing studies.[24] Pre-BASES is a concept test that provides rough sales predictions. BASES I is a more advanced concept test that incorporates media selection decisions, levels of consumer and trade promotion, and extent of distribution to estimate awareness and availability, and can attain a forecasting accuracy range of 25 percent. BASES II combines the concept test with a customer taste test and post-taste customer responses, and achieves an accuracy range of 20 percent.

Nestlé Refrigerated Foods relied on BASES for support during concept development of their Contadina refrigerated pasta and pizza products. To concept-test a line of refrigerated pastas and sauces, a BASES I methodology was used. Preliminary study assessed the appeal of the refrigerated pasta concept and current levels of customer satisfaction. Then the concept was tested among 300 adult female respondents. Each stated a purchase intention and also assessed what they liked, disliked, and found unique about the product. A summary of the results is found in Figure 9.7.

The refrigerated pasta earned a 75 percent top-two-boxes score (24 percent stating "definitely would buy" and 51 percent stating "probably would buy"). An advantage of using BASES is that it can compare these figures to similar products in its database as a rough benchmark. In this case, the median top-two-boxes score for similar products was 61 percent, so these results are encouraging so far for the pasta. The respondents were then split into two groups: favorable (the 75 percent with positive purchase intentions) and unfavorable (everyone else). Both groups liked the same things about the new product: It's natural, it offers variety, it's

---

[22]Y. Wind, J. Grashof, and J. Goldhar, "Market-Based Guidelines for Design of Industrial Products," *Journal of Marketing*, July 1978, pp. 27–37.

[23]Abba Krieger, Paul Green, Leonard Lodish, Jim D'Arcangelo, Chris Rothey, and Paul Thirty, "Consumer Evaluations of 'Really New' Services: The TrafficPulse System," *Journal of Services Marketing*, 17(1), 2003, pp. 6–36.

[24]This section is adapted from the Nestlé Refrigerated Foods: Contadina Pasta and Pizza (A) case, by V. Kasturi Rangan and Marie Bell, Case no. 9-595-035 (Cambridge, MA: Harvard Business School Press, 1995).

FIGURE 9.7
Summary of
Concept Test
Results—
Refrigerated
Pasta

	Total (%)	Favorable (%)	Unfavorable (%)
Likes			
General variety	28	28	28
Filled variety	16	16	16
Natural/not artificial	28	30	23
Quick/fast/saves time	20	22	16
Easy to prepare/already prepared	17	20	11
Good/reasonable price	8	9	4
Fresh/made fresh & dated	26	27	21
Dislikes			
Too expensive	8	3	23
Not like green/spinach color	6	5	11
Not like spinach taste	3	2	5
Concept Uniqueness			
Extremely new and different	15	17	8
Very new and different	38	41	32
Somewhat new and different	35	32	41

Explanation:
These are the results of the concept test for the refrigerated pasta product. The figure reports the percent of respondents agreeing with each statement, broken down by (1) overall percent, (2) percent of respondents who are favorable toward the product concept, and (3) percent of respondents who are unfavorable toward the product concept. For example, 20% of those who liked the concept thought it was easy to prepare, while only 11% of those who disliked the concept thought it was easy to prepare (the overall average was 17%). The statements are organized into likes, dislikes, and statements of uniqueness.

Source: V. Kasturi Rangan and Marie Bell, "Nestlé Refrigerated Foods: Contadina Pasta and Pizza (A)," Case no. 9-595-035, Cambridge, MA: Harvard Business School Press, 1995.

fresh, it saves time, and it's easy to prepare. Of those who were unfavorable to the product, they most often mentioned price.

Although not shown in the table, BASES also tested three different product positioning statements for the concept: *Homemade* (positioned to match homemade taste and quality), *Pasta Dinner* (a hearty-enough dinner to satisfy meat-and-potato cravings), and *Superior* (a new line that is better than any pasta or sauce you have ever tried). The Superior positioning was slightly preferred over the other two on the attributes shown in Figure 9.7 (more likes and fewer dislikes), and was therefore selected for further consideration.

Next, the raw top-two-boxes results were converted to an A-T-A-R sales forecast. BASES calls on its database to convert statements of "definitely will buy" and "probably will buy" to actual purchase behavior. While this information is proprietary and varies across industries, we will apply a simple rule of thumb: We expect that 80 percent of the "definitely" and only 30 percent of the "probably" will actually buy. Our adjusted trial is therefore:

$$(0.8 \times \text{definitely}) + (0.3 \times \text{probably}) = (0.8 \times 24\%) + (0.3 \times 51\%) = 34.5\%$$

The next two components of the A-T-A-R model, awareness and availability, are assessed using managerial input. To keep the example simple, Nestlé is planning to spend $13 million on advertising, which is enough to achieve 48 percent awareness, and they are funding an intensive distribution strategy in which the product will be available to 70 percent of the population. We now have the first three parts of the A-T-A-R model:

$$(\text{awareness} \times \text{trial} \times \text{availability}) = 0.48 \times 34.5\% \times 0.70 = 11.6\%$$

The total number of target households was 77.4 million, so the number of trial households is 11.6% × 77.4 million = 9 million.

Finally, repeat rate is assessed at 39 percent based on similar products, with the average customer repeat purchasing 2.5 times, and with 1.4 units bought per purchase occasion. (This methodology is a little different from how repeat was calculated in earlier examples, but it makes sense for small, frequently purchased packaged goods such as this one.) Repeat therefore is calculated to be:

$$39\% \times 2.5 \times 1.4 = 136.5\%$$

Putting it all together, BASES predicts total sales to be:

$$9 \text{ million} \times 136.5\% = 12.3 \text{ million}$$

Nestlé also had the greatest amount of uncertainty in the 39 percent repeat rate, so BASES redid the calculations with a worst-case and best-case repeat rate. Even with a mediocre 27 percent repeat rate, the sales forecast still reaches 8.5 million units.

To support the launch of the follow-up product, Contadina refrigerated pizza and topping kits, a BASES II methodology was employed. This situation was a little different, because customers will be already familiar with two alternative product forms: frozen pizza and takeout pizza from the local shop. It was important, then, to determine if customers thought this new product was anything different or special relative to more familiar choices. First, top-two-boxes scores were obtained from a sample of about 600 respondents. The pizza-and-topping combo scored 76 percent, while a pizza-only concept scored only 58 percent, so the choice was made to move the pizza-and-topping concept forward. As noted above, the distinctive feature of BASES II is that customers actually try the product (in this case, in an in-home use test). At this point, the results gave some cause for concern. Respondents were asked how "new and different" the pizza-and-topping concept was compared to takeout or frozen pizza. Before use, the top-two-boxes score ("extremely new and different" plus "very new and different") reached 59 percent; this declined to 49 percent after use, suggesting some disappointment among the customers. After-use attribute testing identified a list of improvements as suggested by the respondents: Improve the overall taste and lower the price were the most important. With this information obtained from BASES II, Nestlé is in a position to decide whether to approve the product for launch, run more extensive testing (we will discuss market testing methods later in this book), or drop the concept altogether.[25]

---

[25]Interestingly, Nestlé decided to launch the pizza-and-toppings product without further market testing, but it did poorly. The name Contadina was sold to Del Monte Foods a few years later, and Nestlé is still in the refrigerated pasta and sauce business (under the Buitoni name), but not in the pizza business.

Conclusions

The advantages of concept testing and development prior to full screening are many. It can be done quickly and easily, gives the screeners invaluable information for the sorting out of less valuable concepts, proves market research technology exists, is reasonably confidential, helps us learn a lot about buyer thinking, and enables segments and positionings to be developed in tandem with the concept. Unfortunately, some developers (especially industrial designers) still refuse to do concept testing. Herman Miller, for example, was unable to market successfully a Hygiene System that incorporated a toilet, sink, and tub. It had not been concept tested, and after it failed, the designer claimed that industry people still did not understand it.

Nevertheless, concept testing is a bit treacherous—mistakes are easy and can be costly. It is not a tool for amateurs. There have been classic flops, most of which passed concept tests—dry soups, white whiskey, clear soda, and so on. The original chewable antacid tablet floundered because the concept test missed the idea that people then wanted water with antacids. One firm studied executions of a single new product idea by three copywriters and found that the most important determinant of high scores in the concept test was the skill of the copywriter.

People find reacting to entirely new concepts difficult without a learning period; the stimulus of a concept statement is very brief; many situation variables will change by the time the product is marketed; and certain attributes cannot be measured in a concept test—for example, rug texture, shower nozzle impact, and what color will be "in" next season. Perhaps most troublesome, the technique has just enough slippage in it that persistent product champions often argue successfully against its findings.

Summary

This was the first chapter covering the tools used to evaluate new product proposals. Because evaluation actually begins prior to ideation (that is, deciding where to seek ideas), we first looked at the product innovation charter. By focusing the creative activity in certain directions, the charter automatically excludes all other directions and thus, in effect, evaluates them negatively.

Once the strategic direction is clear, most firms undertake a market analysis of the opportunity described by it. The customer should be a major input to any product innovation program, and immediately after strategic decisions have been made is an excellent time to seek this input. Then, as the ideas begin to roll in, an initial response is made—highly judgmental, quick, and designed primarily to clean out the worthless ideas. Once an idea passes that test, more serious evaluation begins. The tool at this point is concept testing, or concept development, which now has a lengthy history of successful use. The chapter gave the overall procedure for concept testing, including its purposes, options in concept format, respondent selection, and the interviewing procedure. An immediate benefit of concept testing is that it gives management the information needed to make the judgments required by the scoring models used in the following step: the full screen of the concept, which is the subject of Chapter 10.

Applications

1. "You know, most of our new products people do a great deal of marketing research—concept testing, attitude surveys, and the like. But let me read something that one automobile designer thought about marketing research." (She then read from a yellowed clipping on her desk.)

   Market research is probably the greatest single deterrent to excellence in modern business. It's a crutch for managers with no vision and no conviction. On the surface, it sounds sensible enough: Find out exactly what the buyers want before you come to a design. But in practice, it's impossible. The public doesn't know what it wants without being shown the choices, and even then, preference is apt to veer off in the direction of Kmart. Market research gives you Malibus with Mercedes grilles, refrigerators in avocado hues, and Big Macs with everything. You do not, however, produce greatness with this technique.[26]

   "Perhaps you would comment on that statement."

2. "A cosmetics competitor is trying to speed up its new product work on lipsticks by a system that uses (1) brainstorming to create ideas (392 in a recent session); (2) evaluation of those ideas by the same group of people, down to only the best 50 ideas; and then (3) focus group sessions for concept testing those ideas down to the few that should be developed rapidly. Do you see anything wrong with this system?"

3. "I would be curious to test your personal judgment on some new ideas from one of our recent idea sessions. They were all accepted in later concept tests with consumers, and that concerns me. Are we safe to go ahead?

   a. A gasoline-powered pogo stick.

   b. A combination valet stand and electric pants presser.

   c. Transistorized golf balls and an electric finder.

   d. An arm wrestling device so you can arm wrestle with yourself.

   e. An electrically heated bath mat.

   f. Chocolate candy in an edible chocolate box."

Case: Nokia[27]

Nokia was founded in Finland in 1865, originally in the paper business, though it eventually became competitive in the rubber and cable businesses as well by acquisition, and by 1960 had established an electronics department too. By the 1980s, Kari Kairomo, the CEO, had recognized the emerging mobile communications market, and Nokia's technological capabilities were increased to include mobile phones as well as computer and television manufacturing. By 1992, under

---

[26]"The Best Car in the World," *Car and Driver,* November 1979, p. 92.

[27]Information from this case was obtained from public sources including Nokia Web pages www.nokia.com and research.nokia.com/research/index.html, and from "New Nokia Research Shows Customers Ready for M-Marketing via Mobile Handsets," *Wireless Internet,* February 2002.

new president and CEO Jorma Ollila, the strategic decision was made for Nokia to devote itself to mobile telecommunications, and also to expand geographically out of its traditional European home base. (As recently as 1991, a quarter of Nokia's sales still originated in Finland.) Nokia launched several mobile handsets over the next few years, and in fact, the first satellite call was made in 1994 using a Nokia satellite phone. By 1998, Nokia became the world's largest mobile phone manufacturer and was well established throughout North and South America as well as much of Asia. In 1999, Nokia launched the first wireless application protocol (WAP) handset, which facilitated Internet access. In the years since then, Nokia has continued to strengthen its worldwide competitive position in the mobile phone market.

In 2001, in conjunction with HPI Research Group, Nokia undertook a research study of its current customer base to determine the potential of a new concept: marketing to consumers via their mobile phones, or "m-marketing." The study encompassed about 3,300 respondents representing the core mobile phone market (the 16–45 age group) in eleven global markets: several Western European countries, Brazil, Japan, Singapore, and the United States. The respondents stated overwhelmingly (88 percent) that they would be receptive to text message coupons to be redeemed at nearby stores, and 31 percent noted that they would welcome such coupons. Four factors were identified as the most important in driving acceptance of m-marketing: choice (user can decide not to receive messages), control (user can easily bypass the messages), customization (user can filter received messages), and mutual benefit (user gets a reduction in service cost or some other similar benefit).

The study also looked into another concept: mobile visual entertainment (TV-like programs received on a mobile phone). About three-quarters of the respondents reported they would be fine with advertisements on such programs as long as they are short, and almost exactly half reported that they would not view such ads as an intrusion. Almost 90 percent agreed that advertising would be acceptable if they received a service cost reduction as a result.

Finally, the study surveyed the respondents on general desires and benefits sought in mobile phones. It revealed that the respondents showed interest in many different mobile phone features and functions, in particular text message, audio capability, video capability, and informational services. This suggests that more multifunctional phones would be welcomed by the core phone market, especially if the features are viewed as fun and stimulating. In particular, respondents tended to list messaging and photo capabilities, entertainment, and information functions as most important to them. The study also examined design implications for their cell phones and discovered that features such as circular key pads, touch-screen capability, and bright, interchangeable covers were popular with the teenage market.

How might Nokia put the results of this research study to use in developing its next-generation phones? Consider both the specific new product concepts listed above as well as the more overall considerations regarding desired features and functions.

Case: Dell Computers (B)[28]

Refer back to the Dell Computers (A) case at the end of Chapter 6. In addition to the competitive information made available there, Dell management also commissioned customer research. Customer preferences were gathered, and these were used to identify "ideal brands" and assess the number and size of customer benefit segments in the marketplace. Three segments were identified. Segment 1 (about 20 percent of the market) prefers highly flexible PCs; Segment 2 (about 50 percent of the market) likes high-performance machines; and Segment 3 (about 30 percent of the market) values a combination of the two attributes. The results of the study are summarized below.

	Attribute 1 (Performance)	Attribute 2 (Flexibility)	Size of Segment Relative to Market
Ideal Brands by Segment			
Segment 1	0.5	3	20%
Segment 2	2	1	50
Segment 3	1.5	1.5	30

Add these ideal points to the positioning map you drew for the case in Chapter 6. Which are Dell's most serious competitors in each segment? What are the competitive implications?

[28]This case was written by Prof. C. Anthony Di Benedetto and is based on public information, including www.dell.com. The "Executive" is a disguised product name. Market size and market share information is realistic for the leading competitors. Note that there are more than four key players in the computer industry but that some simplifying assumptions were made for the sake of presentation. Positioning information and company/industry financial information is not based on fact but is meant to illustrate concepts of product positioning, advertising decision making, and financial analyses.

CHAPTER TEN

The Full Screen

Setting

Remember the discussion of Lexmark International back in Chapter 1? Lexmark had instituted a new products process and reported increased ability to launch successful products on time and within budget, and the company had aligned its business and technical processes. Even so, management felt there was still room for improvement. In general, the most frequent problem was that too many projects were still getting through without adequate resources, and management was unable to prioritize the product projects effectively.[1] This problem is all too common: Managers often say that concept selection is one of their biggest challenges. All the product projects that have made it this far in the process have cleared all the hurdles and look promising. But there are not enough financial or human resources to go around, so what should be done? Too often, managers lack a good selection procedure and do one of two things: guess (and probably select the wrong project), or approve everything (and consequently underfund every project). Even for the top product developing firms, this can be a challenge. We tackle concept selection in this chapter by introducing you to the full screen. In this chapter, we cannot present what any particular firm should do. That's up to the new products manager. But we can present the range of alternatives and a middle ground that actually fits most firms. It can easily be modified. See Figure 10.1 for how screening relates to concept testing and the protocol step that follows from it.

Unfortunately for you, the step is not glamorous. It isn't discussed weekly in the business press, and, in fact, you may never have heard of a full screen step until you read about it in this book. But business has heard of it and has been using it for many years. Research on it continues, as we will see later, even in large firms like P&G known for their ability to generate successful new products.

Purposes of the Full Screen

Recall where we are in the product innovation process. After the original idea emerged, we put it into concept format and then gave it a brief initial exposure for reaction by key players. Concept testing then enabled us to add the thoughts of

[1] Ed Crowley, "Building a Gated Product Development Process at Lexmark International," *Visions,* 29(4), October 2005, pp. 22–23.

FIGURE 10.1

Flow of New
Product
Concepts
through
Screening and
Protocol

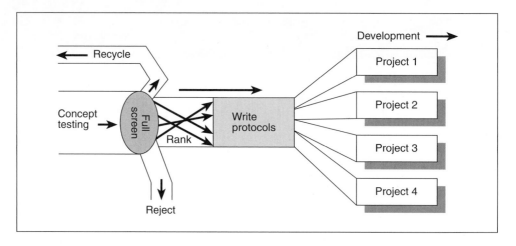

potential users to the set of market and other data collected since the time of the product innovation charter. Along the way, we have been compiling the inputs of key functional people in the firm—technical, marketing, financial, operational, and so on.

This work (which is situation dependent and may take a couple days up to several months) culminates in a step called the *full screen.* The term "full" here means that we now have as much information as we're going to get before undertaking technical work on the product. The full screen often involves the use of a **scoring model,** which is an arrangement of checklist factors with weights (importance) on them, though we will see some variations in this chapter.[2]

Why do the full screen? Actually, the full screen accomplishes three objectives. *First, it helps the firm decide whether it should go forward with the concept or quit.* Keep in mind that if a concept passes the full screen, the next phase in the new products process is development. The concept will become a new product development project and will require a serious increase in commitment of financial and human resources. The full screen helps us decide whether these resources (R&D personnel, systems design for services, engineering, etc.) should be devoted to the project and, if so, how vigorously. This decision rests on whether we *can* do the job and whether we *want* to do it. "Can do" means feasibility—is technology up to the task, do we have it, can we afford it? "Want to" means will we get out of the project the profits, market share, or whatever it is we are doing product innovation for? Sometimes these are called *feasibility of technical accomplishment* and *feasibility of commercial accomplishment,* and assessing these two types of feasibility (often through a scoring model) is central to most full screens.

Second, the full screen helps manage the process by sorting the concepts and identifying the best ones. The best of the concepts can be rank ordered or prioritized

---

[2]For a discussion and comparison of many of the most common full screen techniques, see K. L. Poh, B. W. Ang, and F. Bai, "A Comparative Analysis of R&D Project Evaluation Methods," *R&D Management,* 31(1), January 2001, pp. 63–75.

such that we have some options on standby when an ongoing project stalls or is canceled, while unacceptable, but possibly worthwhile, concepts get cycled back into concept development where more work may make them acceptable. Further, a record is kept of rejected concepts to prevent reinventing the wheel when a similar concept comes up again later. This latter may seem a trivial point, but to managers who screen hundreds or even thousands of new product concepts a year, it is not trivial. A good corporate memory helps settle arguments later. An old adage says that a winning new product finds scores of "parents" who proposed it whereas, a losing new product is always an orphan. In firms that like to reward creativity, it helps to know who suggested what, and when.

Third, the full screen encourages cross-functional communication. Scoring sessions are peppered with outbursts like: "Why in the world did you score that ratchet idea so low on such-and-such a factor?" The screening process is a learning process, particularly in making managers more sensitive to how other functions think. And it flushes out all basic disagreements about a project (including the ever-present politics) and sets them up for discussion. These disagreements put the spotlight on "potholes" or hurdles that the concept will face during development and show where new people may be needed. Many firms have difficulty with the full screen. They either select the wrong projects, or select too many projects. Inefficient screening means that financial resources and new product people are spread out over too many projects. New project approval should be made with human and financial resources and constraints in mind.[3]

Some firms bypass the full screen. Smaller firms not doing much new product work may prefer what really is an opinion poll where one or more people make a judgment on some informal checklist.[4] In some cases participants may have a printed list of evaluation points as memory joggers, taken from the more formal lists that follow. Some packaged goods firms whose development process is rather nontechnical (me-too products and simple variations on what is already on the market) also may skip the full screen. Technical feasibility and the firm's ability to market the product are already known, and the only issue is whether consumers will like the product if it were marketed. To compensate for a lack of a full screen, these firms may do a more complete concept test (Chapter 9) and what they call **premarket testing** sales forecasting models, which we will meet in Chapter 11. When there are major issues of technical feasibility (and more often than not, there are), even the packaged goods firms won't depend just on concept testing and will rely on a full screen employing a scoring model as seen below.

The Scoring Model

Scoring models are simple but powerful things. Let's look at them through the eyes of a student who has a decision to make.

[3]Robert G. Cooper, "Your NPD Portfolio May Be Harmful to Your Business Health," *Visions,* April 2005, pp. 22–26.
[4]Even some very capable firms feel they can't answer the issues in the more complete scoring models shown later. One unit of AT&T uses: Do customers care? Do we care? Can we do it? and Can we stay ahead if we do?

Introduction to Scoring Models

Assume a student is trying to decide what social activity to undertake this weekend. The student has several options, and more options may appear between now and then.

The student could list criteria on several decisions that are personally important, specifically:

1. It must be fun.
2. It must involve more than just two people.
3. It must be affordable.
4. It must be something I am capable of doing.

These four criteria (commonly called *factors,* but don't confuse these with the factors we discussed in factor analysis) are shown in Figure 10.2. Of course, 20 or 30 factors might be involved in this student's weekend social decisions, but let's stick with the four. These factors are not absolutes; they can all be scaled—some fun, lots of fun, and so on. Figure 10.2 shows a four-point scale for each factor.

Next, each scale point needs a number so we can rank the options. With that done, the student can proceed to evaluate each option (as indicated in Figure 10.2) and total the score for each. The final answer is to go boating—even though it isn't quite as much fun—primarily because it can involve lots of people, it is cheap, and the student is a capable rower.

But suppose the student protests at this point and says, "There's more to it than that. If I go hiking, I'll get more exercise; but if I go skiing, a certain person is apt to be there." Or the student may argue that affordability is more important than the other factors because without enough money, there is no need to score the other points. Or the student may say, "Having fun is really more important than skill, so let's double the points for fun." And then there are objections that "skiing really is not all that much fun, boating is more expensive than you think," and so on.

FIGURE 10.2   **Scoring Model for Student Activity Decision**

	Values			
Factors	**4 Points**	**3 Points**	**2 Points**	**1 Point**
Degree of fun	Much	Some	Little	None
Number of people	Over 5	4 to 5	2 to 3	Under 2
Affordability	Easily	Probably	Maybe	No
Student's capability	Very	Good	Some	Little
Student's scorings:	**Skiing**	**Boating**	**Hiking**	
Fun	4	3	4	
People	4	4	2	
Affordability	2	4	4	
Capability	1	4	3	
Totals	11	15	13	
Answer: Go boating.				

A scoring process is what we actually use in making decisions like this, whether we realize it or not. The student's objections contain the basic problems of new product scoring models, and we will see how the criticisms can be handled to fashion a system that works pretty well.

The Screening Procedure

It takes a while to develop a system; but once it is running, the fine-tuning does not require much effort.[5]

What Is Being Evaluated

In the case of the above student, we chose to base the model on four arbitrarily selected factors. Selecting factors in real life is not that easy, and how we pick them is no accident. *First, if we could, we would use only one factor.* There is one factor that covers both technical and commercial accomplishment, a financial term called *net present value of the discounted stream of earnings from the product concept,* considering all direct and indirect costs and benefits. That mouthful is simply the finance way of saying "the bottom line on an income statement for the product, where we have included all costs (technical, marketing, and others) and then discounted back the profits into what their value is today." That factor is shown on Level One in the abbreviated graphic of Figure 10.3. If it happens we can make a reasonably good estimate of that net present value, no other factors would be needed. But we almost never can; at this early spoint all financial estimates are quite shaky.

In that case, we use *surrogates* (or substitutes) for it. Level Two in Figure 10.3 shows the obvious two: the likelihood of technical accomplishment (whether we can create something that will do what customers want) and the likelihood of commercial accomplishment (whether we can sell it profitably). There is again nothing left to do. Those two convictions would predict financial success of Level One, and we are finished.

Unfortunately, experience shows we usually can't make these two estimates either. So we reach for more surrogates, this time at Level Three. To save space, Figure 10.3 shows only the three that produce commercial accomplishment; if we know our sales, our margins on those sales, and our marketing and administrative expenses, we have the commercial half of the answer.

However, again we fall short; we don't have a very good understanding of those figures either at this early point. Note, however, that the packaged goods firms developing marginally different new products, discussed above, *can* make these estimates and do so in their forecasting models. Most firms have to seek surrogates for the Level Three factors too. This leads us to Level Four, which is where the action is. Level Four factors have answers, or at least answers we can estimate

---

[5]Though quite easy when done in the mode of the scoring model example given later in this chapter, we should note that an immense body of theory lies behind all scoring decisions. For example, our scoring model is technically a linear compensatory model. That model, plus the conjunctive, disjunctive, and lexicographic models, is discussed (and compared in a new product screening exercise) in Kenneth G. Baker and Gerald S. Albaum, "Modeling New Product Screening Decisions," *Journal of Product Innovation Management*, 3(1), March 1986, pp. 32–39.

FIGURE 10.3
Source of
Scoring
Model Factors

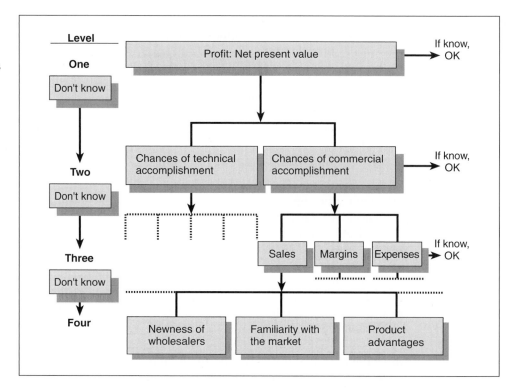

better than the factors at higher levels. Figure 10.3 lists only three of the many factors at this level.

The reasoning goes like this: If you tell me the new product will enter a market with which we already have great familiarity, chances are we will be able to communicate with buyers in that market. This raises the chances for good sales (up to Level Three), and greater sales make for more likely commercial fulfillment (up to Level Two), which, in turn, leads to profit (Level One, our objective). So the trick is to spot those Level Four factors that contribute to the technical and commercial operations in this firm on this particular product concept. Level Four factors comprise the scoring model shown in Figure 10.4. Some firms include profit, sales, and so on as factors even though their surrogates should be there already.

In general, a firm should start with the list of factors in Figure 10.4, scratch out any that clearly are not applicable, insert any obviously omitted, and then use it for a few times to see how the scores set with the people involved. Over time the list should be reduced as much as possible and always kept fluid. Nothing about this system should be set in stone; after all, it is just an *aid* to decision.[6]

[6]For further information, especially from a more corporate management view, see Thomas D. Kuczmarski, *Managing New Products* (Englewood Cliffs, NJ: Prentice-Hall, 2002). From the consumer products view, see Larry A. Constantineau, "The 20 Toughest Questions for New Product Proposals," *Journal of Product and Brand Management*, 2(1), 1993, pp. 51–54.

FIGURE 10.4   **Scoring Model for Full Screen of New Product Concepts**

Cate-gory	Factor	Scale 1	2	3	4	5	Score	Weight	Weighted score
Technical accomplishment	Technical task difficulty	Very difficult				Easy	4	4	16
	Research skills required	Have none required				Perfect fit	5	3	15
	Development skills required	Have none required				Perfect fit	2	5	10
	Technical equipment/ processes	Have none required				Have them	.	.	.
	Rate of technological change	High/erratic				Stable	.	.	.
	Design superiority assurance	None				Very high	.	.	.
	Security of design (patent)	None				Have patent			
	Technical service required	Have none required				Have it all			
	Manufacturing equipment/processes	Have none required				Have them now			
	Vendor cooperation available	None in sight				Current relationship			
	Likelihood of competitive cost	Well above competition				Over 20% less			
	Likelihood of quality product	Below current levels				Leadership			
	Likelihood of speed to market	Two years or more				Under six months			.
	Team people available	None right now				All key ones			
	Dollar investments required	Over 20 million				Under 1 million			
	Legal issues	Major ones				None in sight			
									Total 210
Commercial accomplishment	Market volatility	High/erratic				Very stable	2	3	6
	Probable market share	Fourth at best				Number one	5	5	25
	Probable product life	Less than a year				Over 10 years			
	Similarity to product life	No relationship				Very close	.	.	.
	Sales force requirements	Have no experience				Very familiar	.	.	.
	Promotion requirements	Have no experience				Very familiar	.	.	.
	Target customer	Perfect stranger				Close/current			
	Distributors	No relationship				Current/strong			
	Retailers/dealers	Trivial				Critical			
	Importance of task to user	No relationship				Current/strong			
	Degree of unmet need	None/satisfied				Totally unmet			
	Likelihood of filling need	Very low				Very high			
	Competition to be faced	Tough/aggressive				Weak			
	Field service requirements	No current capability				Ready now			
	Environmental effects	Only negative ones				Only positive ones			
	Global applications	No use outside national				Fits global			
	Market diffusions	No other uses				Many other areas			
	Customer integration	Very unlikely				Customer seeks it			
	Probable profit	Break even at best				ROI>40%			
									Total 240

Concept: _____

Date of screen: _____

Action: _____

Grand Total 450

FIGURE 10.5   **Industrial Research Institute Scoring Model**

Technical success factors:
- *Proprietary Position:* developing a strong, defendable patent in the technology to be researched.
- *Competencies/Skills:* Available technical resources have the competencies to undertake the research project.
- *Technical Complexity:* The impact of technical complexity on product success.
- *Access to and Effective Use of External Technology:* The availability of external technology and the firm's ability to use it successfully.
- *Manufacturing Capability:* Relates to whether the firm has internal or external capabilities to manufacture the product or incorporate the process into its operations.

Commercial success factors:

- *Customer/Market Need:* Is there a ready market for the product or the process, resulting from the project?
- *Market/Brand Recognition:* The likelihood that the product will be accepted in the marketplace, due to company strengths and/or image.
- *Channels to Market:* The ease with which the product will be introduced and distributed.
- *Customer Strength:* The probability that the product will succeed or fail based upon the strength of the customer in the business area of interest.
- *Raw Materials/Components Supply:* The effect of the availability of key components and materials.
- *Safety, Health, and Environmental Risks:* The probability that any of these effects will hinder project success.

Source: John Davis, Alan Fusfield, Eric Scriven, and Gary Tritle, "Determining a Project's Probability of Success," *Research-Technology Management,* May–June 2001, pp. 51–57. Reprinted with permission.

The WiLife Case, at the end of this chapter, will show how each situation is somewhat different. A new scoring model for new technical projects was recently developed by the Industrial Research Institute on how best to determine the success of an individual technical project. The model, developed with the help of this institute's member company managers, contains two parts: a set of technical success factors and a set of commercial success factors. Each project is rated on each of these factors on a 1 to 5 scale. Importance weights for each success factor are also established. Weighted sums of the technical success and commercial success factors are calculated; projects with the highest total scores are most likely to succeed. The Industrial Research Institute's model factors are as shown in Figure 10.5.

The Scoring

Given a scoring form such as that shown in Figure 10.4 or 10.5, the team members who will be doing the scoring first undergo a familiarization period during which they get acquainted with each proposal (market, concept, concept test results). Then each scorer starts with the first factor (in this case, the difficulty of the technical task) and rates each one by selecting the most appropriate point on the semantic differential scales given in the third column. These scorings are multiplied by the assigned importance weights, and the factor totals are extended. The scorings continue for the other factors, and the ratings are then totaled to get the overall rating for that concept by each individual.

Various methods are used to combine the individual team member's ratings, an average (mean) being the most common. Some firms use the Olympic method of dropping the highest and lowest ratings before averaging. Some firms have an open discussion after the averages are shown, so individuals can make a case for any view that is at odds with the group. Many firms have found that **groupware** (e.g., Lotus Notes) aids the process greatly.[7]

Unusual Factors

On some factors, a bad score constitutes a veto. For example, in the case of the student seeking to decide what entertainment to pursue this weekend, a money shortage may block anything costing more than $30. This problem should be faced in the beginning so no time is wasted drumming up options costing more than $30. Industry is the same, and a key role for the product innovation charter is to point out those exclusions. These are sometimes called **culling factors.**[8]

Another problem occurs when the factor being scored has all-or-nothing, yes-or-no answers; for example, "Will this concept require the establishment of a separate sales force?" This type of factor is handled by using the end points on the semantic differential scale, with no gradations. If possible, such factors should be scaled as, for example, "How much additional cost is involved in setting up sales coverage for this concept?" Columns might be None; Under $100,000; $100,000 to $300,000; and so on.

The Scorers or Judges

Selecting the members of a scoring team is like selecting the members of a new products team. The four major functions (marketing, technical, operations, and finance) are involved, as are new products managers and staff specialists from information technology, distribution, procurement, public relations, human resources, and so on, depending on the firm's procedure for developing new products.

Top business unit managers (presidents, general managers) should stay out of the act, except, of course, in small firms. Such people inhibit the frank discussions needed when assessing the firm's capabilities (for example, in marketing or manufacturing). Some CEOs are intuitively so good at this task they can't be excluded.[9]

Screening experience is certainly valuable. So is experience in the firm and in the person's specialty. Technical people generally feel more optimistic about probable technical success, and marketers are more pessimistic.

Problems with individuals are more specific. Research indicates that (1) some people are always optimistic, (2) some are sometimes optimistic and sometimes pessimistic, (3) some are "neutrals" who score to the middle of scales, (4) some are far more reliable and accurate than others, (5) some are easily swayed by the group, and (6) some are capable but erratic. Scoring teams need a manager to deal with such problems. Some firms actually weight each evaluator's scores by past accuracy (defined as conformity with the team's scores). Dow Brands uses a computerized groupware approach primarily because they like the scorings to be anonymous.

---

[7]For another matrix scoring model, see Bob Gill, Beebe Nelson, and Steve Spring, "Seven Steps to Strategic New Product Development," *The PDMA Handbook of New Product Development* (New York: John Wiley, 1996), pp. 19–34.

[8]See Rodger L. DeRose, "New Products—Sifting through the Haystack," *The Journal of Consumer Marketing,* Summer 1986, pp. 81–84. This article shows some direct connections between product strategy at Johnson Wax and the firm's new product screening; for example, its screening factors include "only safe products," "use existing capabilities," and "reflect the company's position and style."

[9]One leading packaged goods firm's CEO was such an expert at selecting among product manager job applicants that other evaluations were considered unnecessary.

Weighting

The most serious criticism of scoring models is their use of weights because the weightings are necessarily judgmental (an exception from new research will be discussed in a moment). Let's go back to the student seeking a weekend activity. To a money-cautious student, affordability deserves more weight than the other factors. But how much more? Should it be weighted at two and the other factors at one? Because of weighting's importance, some firms measure its effect using **sensitivity testing.** Scoring models are actually just mathematical models or equations, so an analyst can alter the scorings or the weightings to see what difference the alterations make in the final score. Spreadsheet programs handle this easily, and so does most groupware.

Profile Sheet

Figure 10.6 presents an alternative preferred by some firms for its graphic capability. The **profile sheet** graphically arranges the five-point scorings on the

FIGURE 10.6
The Profile of a New Product Proposal

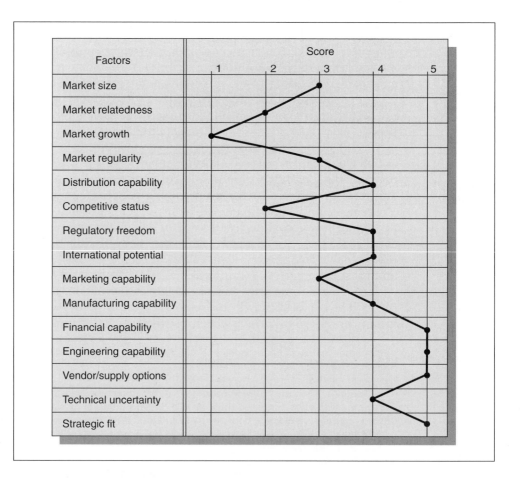

different factors. If a team of judges is used, the profile employs average scores. The approach does indeed draw attention to such patterns as the high scores given near the bottom of the profile (in Figure 10.6) compared to those near the top.

A Screening Model Based on Project NewProd

Project NewProd, a comprehensive study of new product success and failure, was undertaken by Robert Cooper in the late 1970s. Some 100 Canadian industrial firms cooperated in the original NewProd study, in which product managers identified a recent product success and a recent failure. Respondents provided information on dozens of descriptive variables that might have been related to the product's success or failure. From this study, the original New-Prod screening model, similar to the scoring models seen above, was derived and used to predict likelihood of product success and failure, and also to identify weak spots that ought to be rectified before approving the new product project.[10]

Since that time, the original NewProd model has been expanded and enlarged with the inclusion of data from many more firms and input from other new product managers. Most recently, Cooper and his coauthors have advocated a two-level screening model, which combines checklists with scoring models. The two levels of criteria are *must-meet* and *should-meet* criteria. Must-meet criteria include good strategic alignment between project and strategy, and acceptable risk-return ratio; should-meet criteria include strategic importance, product advantage to the customer, and market attractiveness. The full set of criteria are listed in Figure 10.7. As might be expected, must-meet criteria are designed to weed out the bad projects and function as high hurdles for the new product project. In fact, the authors suggest using a simple yes-no checklist for these, and a single "No" response might be enough to screen out the project. The should-meet criteria are those that characterize good business propositions. No one project would rate high on every one of these, so the authors suggest using a scoring model to combine all the criteria and rank the best new product projects by total score. What is notable in Figure 10.7 is that the must-meet and should-meet criteria both include a combination of both financial and strategic considerations. This is characteristic of the better product developing firms, which look beyond simple financial considerations when choosing new product projects to support.[11] We will return to this important topic in our discussion of financial analysis in Chapter 11.

[10]Robert G. Cooper, "Selecting Winning New Product Projects: Using the NewProd System," *Journal of Product Innovation Management*, 2(1), March 1985, pp. 34–44.
[11]Robert G. Cooper, *Winning at New Products,* 3rd ed. (Cambridge, MA: Perseus Publishing, 2001).

FIGURE 10.7   **Must-Meet and Should-Meet Criteria Based on the NewProd Studies**

Must-Meet Criteria: rated Yes/No

1. Strategic Alignment—does the product fit the business strategy?
2. Existence of Market Need—does it surpass the minimum required size?
3. Likelihood of Technical Feasibility—is it technically reasonable?
4. Product Advantage—does it provide the customer with unique benefits or good value?
5. Environmental Health and Safety Policies—does it meet the standards?
6. Return versus Risk—is the ratio acceptable?
7. Show Stoppers—any "killer" variables?

Should-Meet Criteria: rated on scales (like scoring models)

1. Strategic
    a. To what extent does the project align with business strategy?
    b. What is the strategic importance of the project to the business?

2. Product Advantage
    a. To what extent does the product offer unique benefits?
    b. To what extent does the product meet customer needs better than the competition?
    c. To what extent does the product provide excellent value for the money?

3. Market Attractiveness
    a. What is the market size?
    b. What is the market growth rate?
    c. What is the competitive situation? (the more intense and price based, the lower the score)

4. Synergies
    a. To what extent does the product leverage marketing, distribution, or selling strengths?
    b. To what extent does the product leverage technical know-how or expertise?
    c. To what extent does the product leverage manufacturing or operations expertise?

5. Technical Feasibility
    a. How big is the technical gap relative to other products? (the smaller the gap, the higher the score)
    b. How complex is the product technically? (the less complex, the higher the score)
    c. What is the technical uncertainty of the outcome? (the higher the certainty, the higher the score)

6. Risk versus Return
    a. What is the expected profitability (NPV)?
    b. What is the percent return (IRR or ROI percent)?
    c. What is the payback period—how fast is the initial investment recovered?
    d. What is the certainty of the profit or sales estimates (pure guess or highly predictable)?
    e. To what extent is the product low cost and fast to do?

Source: From Robert G. Cooper, *Winning at New Products*, 3rd ed., Perseus Books, 2001. Copyright © 2001 Robert G. cooper. Reprinted by permission of Basic Books, a member of the Perseus Books Group.

The Analytic Hierarchy Process

Another technique for product project screening and evaluation is the **Analytic Hierarchy Process (AHP)**.[12] AHP, developed in the 1970s by Thomas Saaty, is a

[12]For a full treatment of AHP, see Thomas L. Saaty, *The Analytic Hierarchy Process*. New York: McGraw-Hill, 1980.

general technique that systematically gathers expert judgment and uses it to make optimal decisions. It has been used in dozens of business and nonbusiness settings over the years and can be applied in full screening as a way to prioritize and select new product projects. When used as a full screen technique, AHP gathers managerial judgment and expertise to identify the key criteria in the screening decision, obtain scores for each project under consideration relative to these criteria, and rank the projects in order of desirability. Commercially available software such as Expert Choice makes AHP very easy to use.[13]

The product manager begins by building a hierarchical decision tree. The tree will show the manager's ultimate goal (in this case, choosing the best new product project) at the top. The next level below will include all the *primary criteria* the manager considers important in reaching the goal. There may be several levels of criteria (secondary, tertiary, etc.) under the primary criteria in the tree. Lastly, the choices (new product projects under consideration) are placed at the bottom of the tree.

Next, the manager provides comparison data for each element in the tree with respect to the next higher level. That is, the criteria are compared in terms of their importance in reaching the goal, and the choices are compared in terms of their ratings on each criterion. The AHP software takes over from this point. It converts the comparison data into a set of relative weights, which are then aggregated to obtain composite priorities of each element at each level. Ultimately, the available choices (new product projects) are rank ordered in terms of their preferability to the manager.

A sample, real-life application of AHP in a new automobile project screening setting is provided in Figure 10.8.[14] In this case, the product manager for one of the Big Three U.S. automakers screens projects with respect to four primary criteria: fit with core marketing competencies, fit with core technical competencies, total dollar risk profile of the project, and managerial uncertainty about the project's outcomes. (Again, much like in the NewProd-based model, both financial and strategic criteria are considered, though the specific criteria are somewhat different and more specific to the auto industry.) As shown in the figure, each of these primary criteria can be assessed in terms of several secondary criteria. For example, market fit considers the new product's expected fit with the existing product line, distribution channel, distribution logistics, market timing strategy, price, and sales force. Finally, there are four new automobile projects under consideration (P1 through P4); these are placed at the bottom of the decision tree.

After the decision tree is built, paired comparisons are obtained. Usually, this is done by asking the manager first to rate the relative importance of the primary criteria in pairwise fashion on a scale of 1 through 9 (for example, "how much

---

[13]Expert Choice is presented in Arvind Rangaswamy and Gary L. Lilien, "Software Tools for New Product Development," *Journal of Marketing Research* 34, February 1997, pp. 177–184. Expert Choice has a simple online AHP tutorial on its Web site, www.expertchoice.com, and also allows the user to download a small trial version of AHP from the Web site.
[14]Roger J. Calantone, C. Anthony Di Benedetto, and Jeffrey B. Schmidt, "Knowledge Acquisition in New Product Project Screening with the Analytic Hierarchy Process," *Journal of Product Innovation Management*, 16(1), January 1999, pp. 65–76.

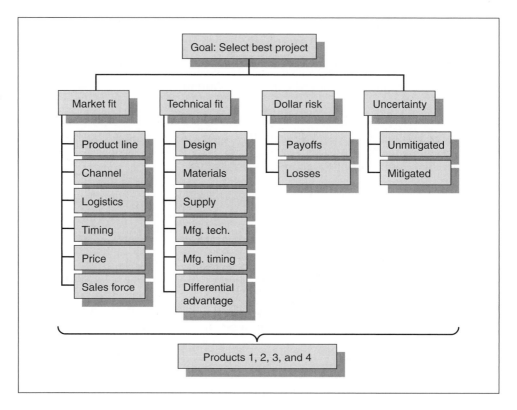

more/less important is fit with marketing competencies as compared to fit with technical competencies?"). Expert Choice allows several other ways for the paired comparisons to be entered by the respondent. Next, the relative importance of the secondary criteria are obtained (for example, "how much more/less important is fit with product line as compared to fit with distribution channel?"). Finally, comparisons of the new product projects with respect to each secondary criterion are made.

Using these data, the AHP software calculates overall global weights for each new product project. These weights can be interpreted as the relative contribution of each alternative to the overall goal. The AHP output, shown at the bottom of Figure 10.9, clearly shows P1 to be the preferred project, having the highest overall global weight (0.381). P2 is second best at 0.275, while P3 and P4 are also-rans.

While all the AHP results cannot be shown here, Figure 10.9 summarizes some of the key findings and provides some insights on how P1 came to be the top choice. The Level 1 weights indicate the relative importance of the primary criteria. This manager views dollar risk to be the most important criterion, followed by market fit, technical fit, and uncertainty. Similarly, the Level 2 weights indicate how important each of the secondary criteria are to this manager. For example, under market fit, timing and price are rated more important than sales force or product line fit. The last column shows the project that was ranked highest on each secondary criterion. P1 was ranked highest on most of the secondary criteria,

FIGURE 10.9
AHP Results and Overall Project Selection

	Level 1 Weights	Level 2 Weights	Highest Ranked Project
Dollar Risk	0.307		
Payoffs		0.153	P1
Losses		0.153	P1
Market Fit	0.285		
Timing		0.094	P1
Price		0.064	P2
Logistics		0.063	P1
Channel		0.036	P2
Product line		0.014	P1
Sales force		0.014	P2
Technical Fit	0.227		
Differential advantage		0.088	P1
Manufacturing timing		0.047	P2
Design		0.032	P2
Materials		0.027	P2
Manufacturing technology		0.023	P2
Supply		0.010	P1
Uncertainty	0.182		
Unmitigated		0.104	P1
Mitigated		0.078	P1

Ranking of Alternatives:

Project	Overall Weight	
P1	0.381	xxxxxxxxxxxxxxxxxxxxxxxxxxxxxxxxxxxxxxxxx
P2	0.275	xxxxxxxxxxxxxxxxxxxxxxxxxxxxxx
P3	0.175	xxxxxxxxxxxxxxxxxx
P4	0.170	xxxxxxxxxxxxxxxxx

and almost all of the really important ones (as judged by the Level 2 weights). P2 tended to do a little better on several of the technical fit criteria, but technical fit is less important to this manager than dollar risk or market fit. So it is not surprising that P1 comes out ranked first, with P2 in second place.

Special Aspects

A few other aspects round out our discussion of scoring models. One concerns the product champion (discussed fully in Chapter 14). Champions are sometimes needed to push past normal resistance to change and to see that the concept gets a fair hearing at all turns. They try to give the scorers all favorable information and may argue that standard forms don't fit their special situations.

Some developers are trying to use computer technology with **expert systems** (often called knowledge-based systems). Such systems are essentially scoring models, with the factors developed on the basis of expert experience.[15]

Last, experience shows that management sometimes misuses scoring models. One consumer products manufacturer threw out a scoring model system because it

1. Was rejecting products that would help round out the line.
2. Was rejecting products that would help forestall competitive entry into the market.
3. Was rejecting too many products, according to the sales department.

The first two problems arose from either faulty factor selection or faulty factor weighting and were easily solved. The third arose because the cutoff score was set too high. Scoring models require competent management.

Summary

If an idea progresses through early concept testing and development to the point where it is a full-blown concept ready for technical workup, it must then be screened. Screening is commonly done with scoring models, whereby the firm's ability to bring off the required development and marketing is estimated. If the concept scores well by whatever criteria the firm uses, it is sent into technical development.

Just prior to that, however, some firms try to spell out a protocol—an agreed set of benefits and other requirements that the technical development and marketing phases must deliver. And once the team feels the product parts of the protocol have been achieved, the concept is in prototype form. It can be taken to the field for further concept testing. The concept test is much more productive when the concept is in prototype form, though it may be more expensive because substantial technical expenditures have already been made. These matters of protocol and prototype testing will comprise Chapter 12.

Applications

1. "Our small electrical engines division recently threw out a screening system that was based on a fairly complete scoring model, as they called it. Seems the model kept rejecting too many of their product ideas, some of which looked like sure winners to them—and to me, incidentally. Under their new system, a top-management committee reviews these ideas personally, without all that paperwork, and it looks like things will be better. Do you have any reaction to that?"

[15]For a look at expert system performance, see Sundaresan Ram and Sudha Ram, "Validation of Expert Systems for Innovation Management: Issues, Methodology, and Empirical Assessment," *Journal of Product Innovation Management*, 13(1), January 1996, pp. 53–68.

2. "We experimented with a numerical scoring model some years back—it just didn't work. Brought in all the senior people, sales managers, product managers, you name it. We selected several dimensions of technical and commercial viability, not too different from the scoring model you presented. Rated everything on a scale of 1 to 5. Guess what? All the projects that were the pet projects of senior management came out as 5s. The ones they all could care less about came out as 1s. And all the ones we really lacked good information on came out as 3s. A lot of help that was! What went wrong?"

3. "If it happens that one of our divisions absolutely must use a scoring model, as you call it, I strongly prefer the one that we use at my company: Just get answers to four questions: Do customers care, Do we care, Can we do it, and Can we stay ahead if we do? What else could be more relevant? That list covers technical feasibility and commercial feasibility both, doesn't it?"

Case: WiLife, Inc. (A)[16]

Evan Tree had about two decades of experience working as a dealer-installer in the video surveillance industry, when he founded WiLife, Inc. in 2002. His partner in this venture, Andrew Hartsfield, had entrepreneurial experience, most recently in the beverage business. Evan had operated a local security dealership, Double Tree Security, for about ten years and had just sold the business to a nationwide concern. Evan's experience in video surveillance suggested that there was a gigantic hole in the marketplace. Video surveillance systems currently available on the market might cost as much as $4,000, even for a basic model. These were typically sold to business operators by big security companies such as Honeywell or ADT through dealer-operators like Double Tree. Not only was the price steep, but running wires and mounting cameras was complex work, and a central location would require a dedicated computer for monitoring. Big customers, or those such as jewelry stores or pharmacies with special surveillance requirements, would make the big investment. But the majority of small business owners found the price tag for video surveillance much too high. Evan and Andrew recognized that a small, inexpensive video surveillance system would fill a real market need for the small businessperson. The two partners began thinking of the market opportunity and the technical and commercial factors that would be most critical to success.

On the technical side, a place to start would be the weaknesses of the current systems. Systems available at the time used analog cameras. It would make sense to explore digital cameras for this application, especially as the costs would probably not be too high. Digital video clips could potentially be sent to a PC, or even to a mobile phone with video capability. It also makes sense to explore

[16]Information for this case was obtained from Jeanne Lee, "Simple Surveillance," cnnmoney .com, Feb. 1, 2006; Walter S. Mossberg and Katherine Boehret, "Setting Up Your Own Security Camera at Home," *The Mossberg Solution*, ptech.wsj.com, March 29, 2006; Edward C. Baig, "LukWerks Lets You Put Kids, Pets on Candid Camera," *USA Today*, www.usatoday.com, July 12, 2006; Paul Taylor, "Network Cameras on Watch for Intruders—and Family Pets," *Financial Times*, www.ft.com, January 18, 2007; and the WiLife Web site, www.wilife.com.

Ethernet networking to connect the cameras to the PC. This is a standard and readily available technology that would eliminate the need for new wiring, as it runs on the electrical power lines already in the building. One would then need to think about video image storage for review by business owners or the police (in the event of a break-in caught on tape, for example). Currently, images caught by analog cameras were videotaped, and the tapes were frequently reused after a certain number of weeks; this might be a reasonable starting point for storage requirements. Picture quality would have to be good, and it would be a nice feature to add digital time stamps for convenient playback and searching. Though WiLife thought first only of in-store surveillance, the concept might be developed for external cameras as well, though this might pose additional technical issues (making the cameras waterproof, for example, or using infrared technology so the camera can see in the dark).

There are obvious commercial factors to consider here as well, first and foremost being price. It is almost a certainty that more small businesspeople would buy video surveillance systems if the price were not so high. Still, there are non-price attributes to consider. As noted above, it should be technologically possible to send digital images system to the user's PC or phone; customers should like this because it eliminates the need for a dedicated PC. Plus, the system could be "smart," alerting the user to any unusual activity by sending an alarm message to the user's PC or phone. (If it is really smart, it should be able to distinguish a burglar breaking a window from a cat sitting on the windowsill.) Additionally, having the crew out to install video cameras is time-consuming and disruptive; ease of camera installation should be a consideration. Similarly, it should be painless to load the required software onto the PC.

You don't have the information to compose an entirely new scoring model for use on the new product concept discussed in this case, but you can put together the five most important factors under each part of the model in the chapter (technical factors and commercial factors). The case above gives you a few suggested technical and commercial factors to consider; try to add a few on your own to these. Give all of them weights. Then apply your model to the new product concept WiLife has recently been looking at (the new inexpensive digital video surveillance system). Beyond the task of *developing* a scoring model for WiLife, give some thought to the problems of *implementing* the scoring model system in this firm. Would any of the results of the scoring session potentially cause big problems for the firm? Why?

CHAPTER ELEVEN

Sales Forecasting and Financial Analysis

Setting

Now that we have finished the full screen, we know the product concept meets our technical capabilities (present or acquirable) and that it meets our manufacturing, financing, and marketing capabilities as well. Also, we know it offers no major legal problems, and so on. So we are ready to charge ahead.

Or are we? Most managers don't think so—they are very interested in the financial side of this proposition. In fact, they have been interested in money from the very start of a project—think back to the product innovation charter where we talked about the size of potential markets and objectives on market shares and profits. And they will still be interested in money when they look back and total up whether the whole project was worthwhile. In addition, more and more managers are learning that looking at the financial projections is not enough: To make the best possible choices from all projects being considered, one needs to keep in mind how well each project fits with the organization's strategic goals and competencies. Indeed, one of the biggest problems facing firms at this phase is that they commit to too many projects, spreading human and financial resources out too thin. That is, firms need to improve their project selection procedure—for many, that means considering strategic fit to a greater extent than previously.[1]

Now is a good time to take a closer look at the *managerial* side of analysis. How should we select and manage a new product project such that it achieves reasonable financial goals and is in keeping with the PIC? In this chapter we focus our attention on the financial analysis and in particular on the sales forecast, which is usually one of marketing's most critical contributions to the financial analysis. We then reconsider the product innovation charter to determine whether the project(s) under consideration are consistent with the firm's strategy for innovation. These activities make up part of the last box in Figure III.1: They are part of the project approval process. In the next chapter, we will develop a written protocol for the project—at that point, we are ready to move forward to the development phase.

---

[1] Robert G. Cooper, "From Experience: The Invisible Success Factors in Product Innovation," *Journal of Product Innovation Management,* 16(2), March 1999, pp. 115–133.

Sales Forecasting for New Products

We begin the financial analysis with the **sales forecast.** As noted above, this is typically the responsibility of the marketing person on the new product team. Once sales have been projected over the next several planning periods, we can assess costs, make profit projections, and calculate key financial benchmarks (commonly used ones include net present value [NPV], internal rate of return [IRR], payback period, etc.).[2] Other participants on the team (such as manufacturing engineers, R&D people, financial and accounting specialists, etc.) have a greater input in providing the costs and other data that will make up the financial analysis.

One of the hardest challenges in financial analysis is developing a reasonable sales forecast, especially for a very new product based on rapidly advancing technology. In 2000, forecasters were predicting that by 2007 there would be 36 million satellite radio subscribers; a year later this forecast was reduced to about 16 million. The actual number achieved by the end of 2006 was about 11 million, and revenues to Sirius and XM Satellite have been much lower than expected.[3] See Figure 11.1 for some other forecasts—good and bad—about today's society and products made by a panel of futurists a few decades ago. What the figure suggests, however, is that expert forecasters often do quite a good job predicting how advancing technologies will result in new products, even 30 years or more into the future, provided they keep a level head.

We must keep in mind several considerations when developing the sales forecast. First, a product's *potential* may be extremely high, but sales may not materialize due to insufficient marketing effort. Advertising may not adequately create awareness, or inadequate distribution may make the product unavailable to much of the market. The A-T-A-R model we discussed in Chapter 8 will help us adjust sales forecasts based on awareness and availability. Second, sales will grow through time if we successfully get customers to try the product and convert many of these customers into repeat purchasers, if they pass along favorable word of mouth to their friends, if greater demand encourages more dealers to stock the product, and so on. After this growth period, sales will eventually stabilize. Thus, we will be interested in developing projections of long-run sales or market shares. Third, we should recognize that our product's sales will depend on our competitors' strategies and programs as well as our own.

There are several general approaches that can be taken to forecast a new product's sales at this early phase in the new products process. We will review some frequently used ones here, focusing on approaches that directly incorporate customer input such as purchase intentions or trial and repeat rates. These generally are referred to as *assumptions-based* models, since they are built to a certain extent on judgment, and their accuracy depends on the validity of the judgments and assumptions.

[2]This book cannot go into the details of financial analysis, but it can give references to readers who wish to go deeper. Any general financial management book will give a step-by-step method for doing a net present value method of capital budgeting.
[3]See Sarah McBride, "Until Recently Full of Promise, Satellite Radio Runs into Static," *Wall Street Journal*, August 15, 2006, pp. A1, A9.

FIGURE 11.1 **What the Future Looked Like in 1967**

In 1967, noted authorities in science, computers, and politics made a series of long-term forecasts about the coming 30 years. Many of these turned out to be highly accurate:

- We would have artificial plastic and electronic replacements for human organs by 1982, and human organ transplants by 1987.
- Credit cards would virtually eliminate money by 1986.
- Lasers would be in common use by 1986.
- Many of us would be working at home by the 1980s, using remote computer terminals to link us to our offices.
- By 1970 man would have walked on the moon.
- By 1986 there would be explosive growth in expenditures on recreation and entertainment.

While about two-thirds of the forecasts were remarkably accurate, about a third were just plain wrong. Samples:

- Manned planetary landings by 1980, and a permanent moon base by 1987.
- Private cars banned from city centers by 1986.
- 3D television globally available soon.
- Primitive life created in the laboratory by 1986.

What can we learn from the correct, and from the incorrect, forecasts? Firstly, forecasts do not have to be absolutely perfect to be used for planning. Recall that old-time ship captains used maps that contained inaccuracies, but still got where they wanted to go. Secondly, incorrect forecasts seemed to fit into two categories: underlying factors driving the projections changed or the forecaster was overly optimistic in the speed of development. Space funding was substantially cut back after the 1969 moon landing, throwing off forecasts about future space exploration. 3D television may indeed be big a couple of decades from now—of course we were saying that about video phones back in the 1960s.

Sources: From Edward Cornish, "The Futurist Forecast 30 Years Later" *The Futurist*, January–February 1997, pp. 45–58. Originally published in *The Futurist*. Used with permission for the World Future Society, 7910 Woodmont Avenue, Suite 450, Bethesda, Maryland 20814 USA. Telephone: 01-656-8274; www.wfs.org.

Note that many other standard forecasting techniques such as those shown in Figure 11.2 can also be used in generating sales forecasts.[4]

Forecasting Sales Using Purchase Intentions

Think back to concept testing (Chapter 9). Among other things, we gathered purchase intentions from respondents. When presented with a concept, they were asked (typically using a five-point scale) to state their likelihood of purchasing that product if it were made available. As mentioned at that time, it is common to look at the top-two-boxes totals (the number of customers who stated they would either definitely or probably buy the product). This measure can be refined and calibrated through experience.

As an example, recall that in our example of a concept test for an aerosol hand cleanser (Figure 9.2), we found that 5 percent of the respondents would definitely

[4]For an excellent resource, see Kenneth B. Kahn, *New Product Forecasting: An Applied Approach* (Armonk, NY: M. E. Sharpe, 2006). Also see Kenneth B. Kahn, "Using Assumptions-Based Models to Forecast New Product Introduction," in A. Griffin and S. M. Somermeyer, *The PDMA Toolbook 3 for New Product Development* (New York: John Wiley, 2007).

FIGURE 11.2 Commonly Used Forecasting Techniques

Technique	Time Horizon*	Cost	Comments
Simple regression	Short	Low	Easy to learn
Multiple regression	Short-medium	Moderate	More difficult to learn and interpret
Econometric analysis	Short-medium	Moderate to high	Complex
Simple time series	Short	Very low	Easy to learn
Advanced time series (e.g., smoothing)	Short-medium	Low to high, depending on method	Can be difficult to learn but results are easy to interpret
Jury of executive opinion	Medium	Low	Interpret with caution
Scenario writing	Medium-long	Moderately high	Can be complex
Delphi probe	Long	Moderately high	Difficult to learn and interpret

*Generally, a short time horizon means under three months; medium time horizon means up to two years; and a long time horizon means over two years.

For more details on these and other forecasting techniques, please consult any good forecasting textbook.

Source: Adapted from Spyros Makridakis and Steven C. Wheelwright, "Forecasting: Framework and Overview," in *Forecasting*, S. Makridakis and S. C. Wheelwright (editors), *Studies in the Management of Sciences*, Vol. 12, Amsterdam: North-Holland, 1979. Reprinted with permission.

buy it, and 36 percent would probably buy it. Based on averages from data collected on similar products launched in the past, about 80 percent of those people who say they would "definitely" buy actually buy the product, and 33 percent of those who say they would "probably" buy actually buy. From this information, our first estimate of the percentage of potential purchasers would be $(0.05)(0.80) + (0.36)(0.33) = 16\%$. This estimate assumes 100 percent awareness and availability, and so it would have to be adjusted downward. If we expect that 60 percent of the market will be aware of the product *and* have it available to them at a nearby retail outlet, our predicted percentage of actual purchasers would be $(0.16)(0.6) = 9.6\%$. As a refinement to this method, we could also vary the concept and get separate purchase intentions for each variation. For example, we might have asked respondents to state their purchase intentions for an aerosol hand cleanser that disinfects as well as cleans, using the same five-point scale. As another example, consider satellite radio again.[5] In 2000, there were roughly 213 million vehicles in the United States. Let's assume 95 percent availability (due to heavy distribution at satellite outlets) and 40 percent awareness (attributed to heavy promotion by Sirius and XM Satellite). Market potential adjusted for awareness and availability is $(213\text{ million}) \times (0.40)\,(0.95) = 81$ million. Market research suggests that half of this market could afford satellite radio; the forecast now becomes 81 million $\times$ $0.5 = 40.5$ million. Of these, what percentage actually intends to subscribe to satellite radio? One way to estimate this is to estimate the percentage of customers who are among the first to try a new technology. If this percentage is estimated at 16 percent, then the forecast becomes 40.5 million $\times$ 16%, or a little over 6.4 million. Let's take this as first-year (i.e., 2001) subscriptions and project yearly effective growth

[5]The satellite radio example is adapted from Kenneth B. Kahn, "Using Assumptions-Based Models," op. cit.

rate at 10 percent. (Effective growth rate means that we are considering new subscriptions as well as defectors.) By the end of 2006, we would project a little over 10 million subscribers—below the actual number attained but much closer than the industry estimate of 36 million! Indeed, the two rivals (Sirius and XM Satellite) agreed to merge in early 2007.

Forecasting Sales Using the A-T-A-R Model

In Chapter 8 we worked through a simple example of the A-T-A-R model in action and briefly mentioned where some of the data could be obtained. This simple model can be used to construct a sales or profit forecast, and market researchers long ago pushed the early, simple models into far more powerful forecasting devices. These advanced research models are used largely on consumer packaged goods, where firms have lots of new product experience on which to develop model parameters and to calibrate the raw percentages they get from consumers.

The A-T-A-R model is the basis of many of the simulated test markets we will encounter in Chapter 18. This is one of the pseudo sale market testing methods used later in the new product process, typically when the physical product is available for the consumer to take home and try. Post-trial data are then collected from the consumer and used as input to the A-T-A-R model. At this early stage in the new products process, before product design and prototype manufacture, the A-T-A-R model can still be applied using data from other sources, and even assumptions. Trial and repeat rates that need to be achieved to reach sales or profit projections can be estimated early on and adjusted as the product goes through later stages and more information becomes available.

Here we are using a form of A-T-A-R that is commonly used in forecasting market shares. First-time product trial might be estimated using the purchase intention method described above. For frequently purchased consumer packaged goods, it is critical to get a good estimate of repeat purchase as well as trial, since long-run market share can be expressed as

$$MS = T \times R \times AW \times AV$$

where T = ultimate long-run trial rate (the percentage of all buyers who ultimately try the product at least once)

R = ultimate long-run repeat purchase rate (share of purchases of the product among those who tried the product)

AW = percent awareness

AV = percent availability

Repeat purchase rate, R, can be obtained by analogy to similar products for which such data are available. It can also be calculated using a switching model.[6]

---

[6]This switching model is an application of a Markov model (a form of model used to determine equilibrium states) in which the long-run repeat purchase rate is the equilibrium state. Details on the switching model are given in Glen Urban, "PERCEPTOR: A Model for Product Positioning," *Management Science,* 21(8), 1975, pp. 858–871.

We can define R_s as the proportion of customers who will switch to the new product when it becomes available, and R_r as the proportion of customers who repeat purchase the product. The switching model estimates long-run repeat purchase rate, R, as $R_s/(1 + R_s - R_r)$. If R_s and R_r are estimated as 0.7 and 0.6, respectively, repeat purchase is estimated as $0.7/(1 + 0.7 - 0.6) = 0.636$. If awareness and availability are 90 percent and 67 percent, respectively, and 16 percent of the market that is aware of the product and has it available to purchase tries it at least once, long-run market share is calculated as

$$MS = 0.16 \times 0.636 \times 0.90 \times 0.67 = 6.14\%$$

Furthermore, if the total number of purchases in this product category is known, this market share can be converted into long-run sales. If total number of purchases is 1,000,000 units, the firm's long-run sales are estimated to be 1,000,000 × 6.14% = 61,400 units. The process of calculating market share is illustrated in the bar chart in Figure 11.3. The y-axis represents the total market (100 percent). The figure shows that 90 percent of the market is aware of the product; 67 percent of the "aware" market (67% × 90% = 60.3%) also has the product available to them; 16 percent of the "aware" market that has the product available tries it at least once; and 63.6 percent of the latter become repeat purchasers.

As stated above, the accuracy of forecasts obtained using these methods depends on the validity of the measures. When building the forecasting models, one must also consider data availability, and also data precision. In the above example, we had assumed availability of 67 percent, but this might not be very precise; actual availability may be as low as 40 percent or as high as 80 percent. In such a case, it makes sense to do a **what-if analysis.** Substituting these values into the market share calculation, we see that the market share forecast falls into a range of 3.66 percent to 7.33 percent, representing the worst- and best-case scenarios.[7]

We shall return to A-T-A-R models of this type when we have a product prototype we are ready to test with customers, a little later in the new products process.

FIGURE 11.3
A-T-A-R
Model—
Results in Bar
Chart Format

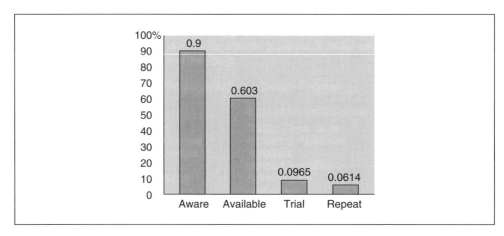

---

[7]See Kenneth B. Kahn, "Using Assumptions-Based Models," op. cit.

Techniques for Forecasting Product Diffusion

Diffusion of innovation refers to the process by which an innovation is spread within a market, over time and over categories of adopters. The adopter categories, which we will look at more closely in Chapter 16, are often called *innovators, early adopters, early and late majority,* and *laggards*. In theory, individuals in the earlier adopter categories influence the purchase behaviors of later ones through word of mouth and other influence processes. The rate of diffusion of a product can be difficult to assess, especially at this early stage in the new product process, since it is unknown how influential the earlier adopter categories will ultimately be. We have already seen, in the satellite radio example, how important it is to get an estimate of the number of innovators and early adopters (i.e., those users who will be among the first to try the product).

To get a handle on the growth potential of an innovative product, we can use an analogous existing product as a guideline. If we are assessing the market potential of a new kind of automobile tire (that could, say, run safely for 100 miles after being punctured), we could reasonably use common radial tires as an analogy. They are sold to the same populations (car manufacturers and service centers) and provide basically the same benefit. Thus, as a rough estimate, long-run market potential for our new tire is probably similar to the sales level achieved by radial tires. Managerial judgment regarding our new product might suggest that actual market potential be somewhat higher or lower than this initial estimate.

Quantitative innovation diffusion models can also be used in predicting future product category sales based on historical product sales levels. A diffusion model commonly used for durable goods is the **Bass model**,[8] which estimates the sales of the product class at some future time t, $s(t)$, as:

$$s(t) = pm + [q - p] Y(t) - (q/m) [Y(t)]^2$$

where p is initial trial probability,

q is a diffusion rate parameter,

m is the total number of potential buyers,

$Y(t)$ is the total number of purchases by time t

The Bass diffusion model is based on the diffusion curve of new products through a population. The initial diffusion rate (growth in total number of purchases) is based on adoption by innovators. Following these early purchases, the growth rate accelerates as word-of-mouth helps to promote the product and more of the market adopts the product. Eventually, however, we reach the point where there are not that many potential purchasers left that have not yet tried the product, and growth rate slows.

[8]The model was originally published by Frank Bass, "A New Product Growth Model of Consumer Durables," *Management Science*, 15(1), January 1969, pp. 215–227, and has since been extended in dozens of research articles. This stream of literature is reviewed in Vijay Mahajan, Eitan Muller, and Frank M. Bass, "New Product Diffusion Models in Marketing: A Review and Directions for Research," *Journal of Marketing*, 54(1), January 1990, pp. 1–26.

Managerial judgment, or standard procedures for market potential estimation, can be used to estimate m, the number of potential buyers. If the product category has been around for a while and several periods of data exist, one could use past sales to estimate the size of p and q. To set these values for a recent innovation, one might look at similar (analogous) products for which these values are known or rely on judgment or previous experience with this kind of model. Previous studies suggest that p is usually in the range of about 0.04, and q is typically close to 0.3, though these values will vary depending on the situation.[9]

A desirable feature of this growth model is that, once p and q are estimated, the time required to reach the sales peak (t^*) can be predicted, as can the peak level of sales at that time (s^*). These are given as:

$$t^* = (1/(p + q)) \ln (q/p)$$
$$s^* = (m)(p + q)^2/4q$$

Let's say you are working for a company that is assessing the viability of a new product category: a combination cappuccino maker–miniature convection oven. You believe the long-run potential for this product is in the area of 25,000,000 households. For similar small household appliances your company has sold in the past, innovation and imitation rates have tended to be in the area of 2 percent and 12 percent. Figure 11.4 presents a sales forecast derived for this new product category, based on applying the Bass model to these estimates. This preliminary forecast suggests that peak sales will occur about four years from now, and that total product category sales during that year will be a little over 4 million units. If these sales projections are combined with price, cost, and market share projections, the product's potential projected contribution to profit can be assessed. The Bay City

FIGURE 11.4
Bass Model Forecast of Product Diffusion

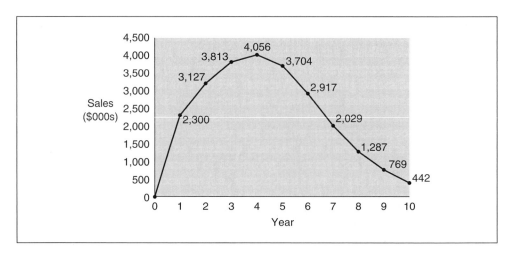

[9]Parameter estimation issues are discussed in Vijay Mahajan and Subhash Sharma, "Simple Algebraic Estimation Procedure for Innovation Diffusion Models of New Product Acceptance," *Technological Forecasting and Social Change*, 30, December 1986, pp. 331–346; and Fareena Sultan, John U. Farley, and Donald R. Lehmann, "A Meta-Analysis of Applications of Diffusion Models," *Journal of Marketing Research*, 27(1), February 1990, pp. 70–78.

Electronics case at the end of this chapter shows a set of sales projections for a new product (derived using Bass or some similar model) and takes you through these steps, finishing with an NPV analysis.

Bass showed that, despite its simplicity, his model did a good job at predicting the time and magnitude of the sales peak for many durable consumer goods, including clothes dryers, television, coffee makers, irons, and many others. Later researchers have used it to forecast the diffusion of many high-tech product categories such as satellite TV or music CDs.[10] Interestingly, it has also been used to predict the growth of Internet communities such as Facebook. The similarities to durable goods diffusion are striking: One is either a member of Facebook or is not; and some people will be the innovators and join right away. The more influential these innovators are in encouraging others to join, the faster the new community will grow.[11] Other extensions of the Bass model have shown how it can be applied to nondurable goods where repeat sales need to be considered.[12]

Observations on Forecasting Models

Model makers are rapidly accumulating experience and sharpening their models, which are now readily available to consumer packaged goods innovators, are quite inexpensive compared to test markets and rollouts, and allow diagnostic output as well as sensitivity testing.

Unfortunately, they also require massive amounts of data to work well, are built heavily on assumptions, and are so complex that many managers are wary of them. Having been developed initially in the 1950s and 1960s, they often incorporate assumptions no longer valid—for example, reliance on mass advertising and easy-to-get distribution. But they are now a mature industry, a large and profitable one.

It is interesting that the most successful firm by far uses the simplest methodology and requires the least data. In BASES II, Burke (a division of Nielsen) combines a concept test and a product use test, calibrates the trial and repeat percentages from their massive files of past studies, and uses a set of experience-honed heuristics (rules of thumb) to translate those percentages into market shares.

But product innovators outside of consumer packaged goods still most often use the simple version of the A-T-A-R model in Chapter 8, if they use any forecasting

---

[10]C. van den Bulte, "Technical Report: Want to Know How Diffusion Speed Varies Across Countries and Products? Try Using a Bass Model," *Visions,* 26(4), October 2002, pp. 12–15.

[11]D. R. Firth, C. Lawrence, and S. F. Clouse, "Predicting Internet-Based Online Community Size and Time to Peak Membership Using the Bass Model of New Product Growth," *Interdisciplinary Journal of Information, Knowledge, and Management,* 1, 2006, pp. 1–12. See discussion of this topic in C. Anthony Di Benedetto, "Diffusion of Innovation," in V. K. Narayanan and Gina C. O'Connor (eds.), *Encyclopedia of Technology & Innovation Management* (Chichester, UK: John Wiley, 2010), Chapter 16.

[12]See Vijay Mahajan, Eitan Muller, and Frank M. Bass, "New Product Diffusion Models in Marketing: A Review and Directions for Research," *Journal of Marketing,* 54(1), January 1990, pp. 1–26.

model at all. Research continues toward improving all of the sales forecasting models.[13]

Problems with Sales Forecasting

Doing the sales forecasts poses no problem as such. We have an immense arsenal of forecasting methodologies, as seen above in Figure 11.2. We know, based on the A-T-A-R model we encountered in Chapter 8, what makes for sales. This model does an excellent job and serves as the basis for some very advanced mathematical systems used by sophisticated new product marketers. And every firm has people who can make an income-statement-based net present value (NPV) or internal rate of return (IRR) calculation (using discounted cash flow methods),[14] as illustrated in the Bay City case at the end of the chapter. The real problems are getting the required information to do the financial analysis and not ignoring strategic issues when considering new product projects.

One can use A-T-A-R to assist in building the sales forecast for the financial analysis. A-T-A-R, however, requires a solid estimate of how many people/firms will become aware of our new item, how many of those will opt to try some of the item in one way or another, and so on. Each of these figures, however, is very difficult to estimate. For example:

- The folks at Google or Twitter did not *know* their Web sites would become that popular.
- Apple did not *know* so many of us, even dyed-in-the-wool Windows users, would buy iPods or iPhones.
- Amazon.com did not *know* we would buy millions of books over the Internet.
- Ganz did not *know* that its Webkinz stuffed animals would be all the rage in elementary schools.

Also, the financial model requires product cost, prices, the current value of money, probable taxes on the future income, the amount of further capital investments that will be required between now and when we close the books on the product, and much more.

These will never be certain, even after living out the product's life cycle. Sales will be known, but we might have had a better marketing strategy. Costs are always just estimates. We will never know the true extent to which a new item cannibalized sales from another product. If we had not marketed the new item, a competitor probably would have. The fact is, we rely on estimates. Management's

---

[13]For a discussion of the use of forecasting techniques used in new product development, see Kenneth B. Kahn, "An Exploratory Investigation of New Product Forecasting Practices," *Journal of Product Innovation Management*, 19(2), 2002, pp. 133–143; and Kenneth B. Kahn, *New Product Forecasting*, op. cit.

[14]While we use NPV analysis in this chapter, some analysts suggest internal rate of return (IRR) instead for financial evaluation of projects since the latter tends to select the largest projects, not necessarily the highest-return projects! See Carey C. Curtis and Lynn W. Ellis, "Satisfying Customers While Speeding R&D and Staying Profitable," *Research-Technology Management*, September–October 1998, pp. 23–27.

task is to make the estimates as solid as we can and then manage around the areas of uncertainty in such a way that we don't get hurt too badly.

On minor product improvements we do this quite well—a new Troy-Bilt lawn mower with a pepped-up engine is not a wild guessing game. On near line extensions, we also do well, but with more misses. Really new products, using technologies never so applied before, are pure guessing games. For over 30 years business schools used a Polaroid pricing case in which Edwin Land was trying to decide whether people would pay $15, or maybe $25, or (dream on) $50 for his first instant camera! They paid the top price in huge numbers, making Land a very rich "financial and technical genius."

Summary of the Problems

What makes forecasting so difficult? For one thing, target users don't always know what the new product will actually be, what it will do for them, what it will cost, and what its drawbacks will be, nor will they have had a chance to use it. And if they do know, they may want to keep some information from us or offer outright falsehoods. Complicating this problem is that market research on these potential users is often poorly done—for example, horror stories about focus groups abound.

At the same time, competitors don't sit still. In fact, they are trying very hard to ruin our data, just as we do to theirs. Resellers, regulators, and market advisers are in a constant flux.

Information about marketing support—what kind of service will be available in the firm, for example—may be lacking. No sales manager can make promises a year ahead about sales time and support. Internal attitudes can be biased, and politics are always present. Many new products managers will not be ready to show just how good the new item is for some time, so they try to delay official forecasting.

In their excitement to get to market, new products managers sometimes get themselves into trouble by rushing their products out, without stopping to field-test the new item. Steelcase management, responding to some disappointments, now demands that new office furniture systems be *thoroughly* tested in *end-user offices*.

Finally, most common forecasting methods are extrapolations and work well on established products. New products don't have a history. Even forecasting methods that seem free of history (use of leading indicators and causal models) use *relationships* established in the past.

Actions by Managers to Handle These Problems

Given that we badly need financial analyses and that good analyses are difficult to make, what is a manager to do?

Improve the New Product Process Currently in Use

Most of the horror stories given earlier from the trade press are embarrassing to their managers. In most of them a key step was skipped. In an effort to hurry, or to capitalize on the conviction of someone working in or around the project, a bad assumption was made. For example, New Coke was heavily taste-tested, but was not *market*-tested—that is, no one was actually asked to buy the product with that new name, and certainly no one was told in the test that if New Coke were launched, Classic Coke would be immediately dropped. So the emotional backlash over the loss of Classic Coke was totally missed. When it first launched the minivan in the early 1980s, Chrysler was wiser—it knew that consumers were negative toward the minivan because they couldn't see the value in it until they actually drove it for a while. So Chrysler made sure customers drove it and learned that, despite its size, it handled like a car (since it was, and still is, built on a car platform). Top new product professionals today know good new products process, but many others don't. They lack information and don't realize it. All the standard forms will not make up for omissions of key data pieces.

Use the Life Cycle Concept of Financial Analysis

Firms sometimes err by focusing their financial analysis at one particular point—perhaps a stage in a phased system. That point is often right where we are in this book, at full screen. Another popular time is later, near where some major financial commitment must be made—for example, building a plant or releasing an expensive marketing introductory program. Managers talk about a point of no return. It is indeed a phase, a hurdle, and new product managers may spend weeks getting ready for the meeting.

But both instances are exaggerated. Technical work can begin without committing the firm to a huge technical expenditure. Building a plant can often be avoided by contracting out early production or by building a large pilot system for trial marketing in a restricted rollout.

It is far better for managers to see their project as a living thing—a bottom line that is created gradually, over the life of the project, never being completely accurate, even well after the item is launched (see Figure 11.5). A product innovation charter is accepted only because the management believes the combined

FIGURE 11.5
Financial Analysis as a Living Thing: The Life Cycle of Assessment

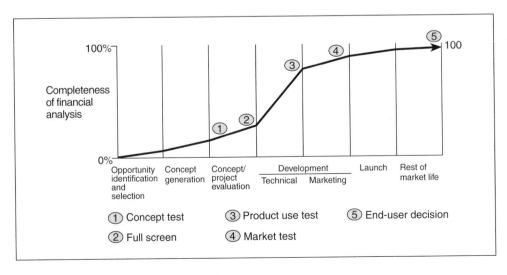

technologies and market opportunities fit well with each other and with the firm. A PIC describes a home field where we can't ever be sure of the final score, but where we should be able to win. A concept test result doesn't assure financial success either, but it can say we are one step further along—the intended user agrees there is a need for something like our concept and wants some to try out. An early field use test with a prototype also won't assure success, but it can say intended users like what they see. An advertising agency or a sales manager cannot guarantee success either, but they can assess whether the new item will be brought to the attention of potential end-users and that it will be tried. If it delivers, it will sell, and if manufacturing is able to do what it felt it could, there will be profit in the item. And so on. The best we can do at any point is to ask whether progress to date is consistent with a successful life cycle.

It is the same with financial analysis—where are we today, is what we know at this time consistent with profit goals, is there reason to change our past projections? Some financial analysts now prefer to set up with full financial sheets at the beginning and then compare progress against those spreadsheets. Many boxes are blank in the beginning, but will be filled in when we know them. But the profit figures at the bottom of the page are not current *forecasts*, just current *goals*. As long as current progress is consistent with those goals, we proceed. A successful cola taste-test is not a reliable indicator of consumers' ultimate trial. If we get to trial, the taste-test says the chances are we will get repeat business.

The life cycle concept of financial analysis enables us to avoid setting up systems where make-or-break decisions rest on one sales forecast or one cost forecast.

Reduce Dependence on Poor Forecasts

If it is difficult to make sales and profit forecasts, are there ways of avoiding having to make them? Yes, several, and many firms use them, though with precaution.

Forecast What You Know

This is actually an attitude toward forecasting. Why try to forecast what people in the marketplace will do, if there is no reasonable way we can do so? A blank in a spreadsheet can be filled in with a range of estimates to see where the failure point is. If that is very unlikely, then go ahead.

Approve Situations, Not Numbers

This is a variation on what was mentioned earlier. Analyze to find what the success factors are, and then look to see if the situation offers them. If so, go ahead, knowing that success should come about even though we don't know just how much. An extreme example of this occurred once when a marketing vice president was asked to predict what he would do if he could get a license to use the Coca-Cola trademark on a line of new products. His answer was, right now I don't know, but with that trademark it's only a matter of how much, not whether.

One way of betting on a situation has a parallel in horse racing; some betters bet on the jockey, not the horse (about whom they may be able to learn very little). Many firms "bet" on a top-notch scientist, sales force, trademark, or reputation.

Another situation variable is *leadership*. Some firms encourage the *champion system*. They expect champions to force their way past a restrictive financial system. This makes for a strange but very workable practice of evaluating teams and their leaders, rather than the ideas they come up with. These firms don't seek great new products; they seek concepts that they can *manage* into great new products. You may have heard about the movie producer who builds a staff of outstanding creative people and depends on them to work miracles with ordinary scripts. A competitor invests in top scripts instead. But both were avoiding the necessity of relying on complex forecasts and financial analyses.

People who love to fish do this all the time; they spend lots of money to find and reach top trout streams. One manager recently said, "If there is a good trout stream with lots of trout in it and a good angler with good equipment, we don't need an accountant to tell us how many fish we will catch. Whatever happens will be good." This strategy is not as folksy as it may sound. A firm must know what the success factors are in any situation. One of those two movie producers may be wrong. Notice how the manager included the trout stream, the angler, *and* the good equipment.

Recall from Chapter 8 the two potholes to success identified by Campbell Soup: the taste of the soup and the manufacturing cost. Their name and skills could overcome any other limitations. Precise forecasting wasn't necessary under this strategy, but being sure on taste and cost was.

Commit to a Strategy of Low-Cost Development and Marketing

There are times when a company can do the type of product innovation that some call temporary products. Develop a stream of new items that differ very little from those now on the market, insert them into the market without great fanfare, and watch which ones end users rebuy. Drop those that don't find favor. Japanese makers of electronics goods do this regularly, with Honda introducing several hundred new items in a year; there even are cities in Japan where firms introduce their food and since consumers know this, marketing costs can be kept low.

Go Ahead with Sound Forecasts But Prepare to Handle the Risks

This strategy especially appeals to managers who feel business is suffering from "paralysis by analysis." There are lots of ways to put risk back into product innovation while managing it well. One approach is to isolate or neutralize the in-house critics (a strong reason for setting up project matrixes and spinouts).

Another approach defers financial analysis until later in the development process. One firm realized it was consistently killing off good new product ideas by demanding precise financial analyses at the time of screening. It didn't have the data. Another strategy is to use market testing rollouts (see Chapter 18). If a financial analysis looks weak, but the idea seems sound, try it out on a limited scale to see where the solution might lie. This thinking may violate several popular management theories (e.g., empowered teams), but it may be necessary at times.

Managing risk is a major field in itself today, since we know business needs risk as a source of profits. Figure 11.6 shows the risk situation new product

FIGURE 11.6
Calculating
the New
Product's
Required Rate
of Return

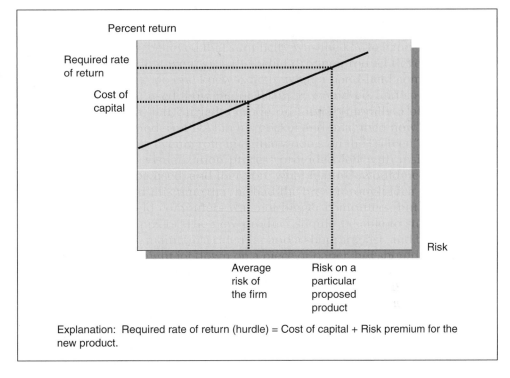

Explanation: Required rate of return (hurdle) = Cost of capital + Risk premium for the new product.

managers face in their evaluations—they know their product will bring more risk than the average risk of the firm, but how much? Conceptually, Figure 11.6 suggests that the riskier the new project is expected to be, the higher the **required rate of return** should be, but in practice it can be difficult to put real numbers into the diagram.

Product managers can borrow from options-pricing theory to make early decisions on product concepts. **Real-options analysis** may be used to estimate the net present value of a new product when it is still in the concept stage. It accounts for the fact that there still are unknowns at this early stage, and that the firm may need to abandon the project at some time in the future as more information is obtained, and uncertainty is reduced.[15] Consider the example detailed in Figure 11.7. A product concept under consideration would incur startup costs of $70,000. Demand is still uncertain; let's assume a 50-50 chance of generating a cash flow of either $40,000 or $10,000 per year for the next four years, depending on whether demand turns out to be high or low. In the case of low demand, the firm has the option of abandoning the project at the end of the first year and selling the equipment for an estimated $38,000. Assume a discount rate of 12 percent.

[15]For a good discussion of real-options analysis in financial evaluation of product concepts, see Edward Nelling, "Options and the Analysis of Technology Projects," in V. K. Narayanan and Gina C. O'Connor (eds.), *Encyclopedia of Technology & Innovation Management* (Chichester, UK: John Wiley, 2010), Chapter 8.

FIGURE 11.7
**Real-Options
Analysis of
a Product
Concept**

Data:
  Startup costs in Year 0: $70,000.
  The cash flows for Years 1 through 4 are estimated to be $40,000 in a high-demand scenario,
    or $10,000 in a low-demand scenario.
  The probabilities of a high- or low-demand scenario are both 50 percent.
  The product concept could be abandoned after Year 1, and the equipment could be sold
    for $38,000.
  Discount rate = 12%.
Procedure:
  Begin with by assessing cash flow in Year 1 for each demand scenario.

Demand	Year 1	Year 2	Year 3	Year 4	Total
High	40,000	$40,000/(1.12)$ = 35,714	$40,000/(1.12)^2$ = 31,888	$40,000/(1.12)^3$ = 28,471	$136,073
Low	10,000	$10,000/(1.12)$ = 8,929	$10,000/(1.12)^2$ = 7,972	$10,000/(1.12)^3$ = 7,118	$34,018

Next, assess cash flow for Year 1 if the option to abandon the project is taken and the equipment
is sold:

Demand	Year 1	Take Option to Abandon and Sell Equipment	Total
Low	10,000	38,000	$48,000

Since $48,000 > $34,018, management will choose to abandon the project after Year 1.
Next, go back to the present (Year 0) and assess NPV for each demand scenario, with the
knowledge that management will choose to abandon the project after Year 1 if demand is low.

Demand	Year 0	Year 1	Year 2	Year 3	Year 4	Total
High	−70,000	$40,000/(1.12)$ = 35,714	$40,000/(1.12)^2$ = 31,888	$40,000/(1.12)^3$ = 28,471	$40,000/(1.12)^4$ = 25,421	$51,494
Low	−70,000	$48,000/(1.12)$ = 42,857				−$27,143

Since each scenario is equally likely to occur, the expected value of the investment is:
$(0.5)($51,494) + (0.5)(−27,143) = $12,176$, and since this expected value is greater than zero, the
firm should make the investment.

Source: Edward Nelling, "Options and the Analysis of Technology Projects," in V. K. Narayanan and Gina C. O'Connor (eds.), *Encyclopedia of Technology & Innovation Management*, Chichester, UK: John Wiley, 2010, Chapter 8.

As shown in Figure 11.7, the way to begin is to calculate net present values as of
the end of Year 1, which is when the option would be exercised. The figure shows
that, as of the end of Year 1, the NPV is over $136,000 if demand is high, but is only
about $34,000 if demand is low. If the firm exercises the option and abandons the
project, the NPV increases to $48,000, so the firm will indeed choose to abandon
the project one year from now if demand turns out to be low.

With this information, we can now go back and calculate the expected value of the concept to the firm. The last part of Figure 11.7 shows that there is a 50 percent chance that demand will be high, and the product will generate a NPV of over $51,000. There is also a 50 percent chance that the demand will be low, in which case the project will be abandoned and the current NPV would be a loss of about $27,000. The expected value of the product concept's NPV is therefore a little over $12,000. Since this is positive, the firm should go ahead with the investment. The possibility that the project loses money is offset by the firm's ability to recover some of the investment should the project be abandoned.

Use Different Methods of Financial Analysis on New Products, Depending on the Situation

Most product innovation (in terms of sheer numbers of items) is singles, not home runs—product improvements and close line extensions. This innovation is managed deep within the ongoing operation, no empowered teams, no huge technical breakthroughs. The item is often demanded by a key customer or key channel, and the decision to develop it is not based on item profitability at all. The risks are relatively small; sometimes the development is in a partnership with a customer who will provide profitable volume.

But home runs are something else entirely. They involve big risks and potentially big gains. They need much attention and cannot be handled easily with methods such as those in the previous section. Here, the best approach is to have *two* systems of financial analysis, one for singles and one for home runs. Alternatively, some firms have no standard system at all, but develop a *financial analysis for each project*, keying the information to those issues where the risks really lie and unknowns prevail.

Improve Current Financial Forecasting Methods

For example, marketing people sometimes make use of mathematical sales forecasting models (such as A-T-A-R, or something similar). Although many of these models were developed for use on consumer packaged goods, efforts continue to make them work better on durable goods.[16] Some firms analyze their own past efforts as well. More progress will come when firms systematically study their most recent 50 (or 25, or whatever) new products to summarize what financial methods were used and how well they forecast the actual outcomes. This is what we now call success/failure analysis, and it leads to best practices. It is rather common in other phases of new product work—for example, recall the NewProd screening model of Cooper in Chapter 10. There have also been some improvements in accounting methods. Lastly, some new products managers make a general plea that all financial analysis should be advisory—not fixed hurdles and mandates but flags that warn of potential problems. Of course, hurdle rates can be *managed* in the sense of being situational (see Figure 11.8).

---

[16]See Glen L. Urban, John S. Hulland, and Bruce D. Weinberg, "Premarket Forecasting for New Consumer Durable Goods; Modeling Categorization, Elimination, and Consideration Phenomena," *Journal of Marketing,* April 1993, pp. 47–63.

FIGURE 11.8   **Hurdle Rates on Returns and Other Measures**

Product	Strategic Role or Purpose	Sales	Hurdle Rates	
		Sales	**Return on Investment**	**Market Share Increase**
A	Combat competitive entry	$3,000,000	10%	0 Points
B	Establish foothold in new market	$2,000,000	17%	15 Points
C	Capitalize on existing markets	$1,000,000	12%	1 Point

Explanation: This array shows that hurdles should reflect a product's purpose, or assignment. For example, combating a competitive entry will require more sales than would establishing a toehold in a new market. Also, we might accept a very low share increase for an item that simply capitalized on our existing market position.

Return to the PIC

So far in this chapter, we have focused on financial analysis for a new product project. Before leaving this topic, we should note that many of the very successful product developing firms have realized that financial analysis is not enough. One must also reconsider the PIC and the strategic criteria it implies: For example, does the new product project technology create a new market opportunity or reshape an existing one?[17] Firms are increasingly using a combination of financial analysis and PIC considerations when making the tough decisions on which new product projects to commit to. That is, projects need to be considered on how well they fit the firm's strategy for innovation.

As noted above, many firms report that too many new product projects get approved, and the human and financial resources end up getting spread too thin. This can happen for several reasons. Too many projects clear simple financial hurdle rates (such as minimum NPV), and all get approved; resource constraints are not included in the NPV calculations so tradeoffs are not made; or low-quality work at the fuzzy front end reduces the quality of information available to managers making Go/No Go decisions. Furthermore, the wrong mix of projects may be undertaken: Management approves several small, quick-hit projects while passing up the opportunity to develop a significant new product platform or technology.[18] These problems may stem from the firm's reliance on only financial projections when selecting projects. These projections may be unreliable (especially at this early stage in product development) and obviously do not provide any information about how well the project fits the firm's product innovation charter.[19]

[17]Edward U. Bond, III and Mark B. Houston, "Barriers to Matching New Technologies and Market Opportunities in Established Firms," *Journal of Product Innovation Management*, 20(2), 2003, pp. 120–135.
[18]See Robert G. Cooper, Scott J. Edgett, and Elko J. Kleinschmidt, "New Products, New Solutions: Making Portfolio Management More Effective," *Research-Technology Management*, March–April 2000, pp. 18–33.
[19]Randall L. Englund and Robert J. Graham, "From Experience: Linking Projects to Strategy," *Journal of Product Innovation Management*, 16(1), January 1999, pp. 52–64.

FIGURE 11.9
Hoechst-
U.S. Scoring
Model

Key Factors	Rating Scale (from 1–10)			
	1 ...	4 ...	7 ...	10
Probability of Technical Success	<20% probability			>90% probability
Probability of Commercial Success	<25% probability			>90% probability
Reward	Small			Payback < 3 years
Business-Strategy Fit	R&D independent of business strategy			R&D strongly supports business strategy
Strategic Leverage	"One-of-a-kind"/ dead end			Many proprietary opportunities

Source: Adapted from Robert G. Cooper, Scott J. Edgett, and Elko J. Kleinschmidt, *Portfolio Management for New Products*, McMaster University, Hamilton, Ontario, Canada, 1977, pp. 24–28. Reprinted with permission.

In Chapter 3, the strategic portfolio model for portfolio management was presented. It is typical of a **top-down** strategic approach—that is, the firm or SBU lays out its strategy first, then allocates funds across different kinds of projects. This approach can clearly be used in project selection. For example, if the firm is already involved in plenty of quick-hit projects, strategic portfolio considerations would indicate that new funding would be better routed to a long-term, major technology development.

Management can also take a **bottom-up** approach to strategy development by building strategic criteria into their project selection tools. The top-performing firms, in fact, often use a combination of top-down and bottom-up approaches and consider strategic as well as financial criteria when selecting projects, while the worst performers tend to rely only on financial criteria.[20]

Robert Cooper and his colleagues use Hoechst-U.S.'s scoring model as an example of how to balance strategic and financial concerns (see Figure 11.9). Of the five factors shown in the figure, two are clearly full-screen feasibility factors similar to those in Figure 10.5 (Probability of Technical and Commercial Success), one is a financial criterion (Reward), and two are strategic factors related to the firm's PIC (Business-Strategy Fit and Strategic Leverage). Similarly, Specialty Minerals, a spinoff of Pfizer, uses a seven-point scoring model that shows a similar combination of financial and strategic considerations:

- Management interest
- Customer interest
- Sustainability of competitive advantage
- Technical feasibility
- Business case strength
- Fit with core competencies
- Profitability and impact

[20]See Robert G. Cooper, "Portfolio Management: Results of New Product Portfolio Management Best Practices Study," in L. W. Murray (ed.), *Maximizing the Return on Product Development*, Proceedings of the 1997 PDMA Research Conference, Monterey, CA, pp. 331–358.

Dimension	Sample Questions
Strategic Fit	Does the concept fit with corporate vision?
	Does the concept fit with our sales force?
Customer Fit	Does the concept allow the customer to better meet consumer needs?
	Does the concept have a good value as perceived by the customer?
Consumer Fit	Does the concept satisfy an unmet or latent consumer need?
	Will consumer loyalty be increased?
Market Attractiveness	Is the concept unique relative to the competition?
	Could our firm be a Number 1 or Number 2 competitor?
Technical Feasibility	Is the concept feasible?
	Is the concept protectable?
Financial Returns	Will the project break even soon?
	Will the project achieve required earnings in the desired time?

Source: From Erika B. Seamon, "Achieving Growth through an Innovative Culture," in P. Belliveau, A. Griffin, and S. M. Somermeyer, *The PDMA Toolbook 2 for New Product Development,* John Wiley & Sons, Inc., 2004, Ch. 1. Reprinted with permission of John Wiley & Sons, Inc.

As another example, the screening criteria used by a real manufacturing company (whose identity was not revealed) included:

- Net Present Value
- Internal Rate of Return
- Strategic Importance of Project (how the project aligns with business strategy)
- Probability of Technical Success

Again, one criterion (the third) is clearly a measure of fit with PIC (albeit using slightly different terms), while the others are related to technical feasibility or financial expectations.[21] Research into this subject continues, but so far the results are suggesting that consideration of strategic, as well as, financial criteria is important when assessing new product projects.

Finally, Figure 11.10 presents the advice of Erika Seamon of Kuczmarski and Associates, a well-respected consultant group. It is clear that this consultancy is recommending that the firm consider both strategic and financial criteria when deciding which concepts to move into prototype development.

Summary

This chapter has dealt with the matter of how to make judgments on the financial merits of new products. It has also explored in depth the issue of sales forecasting, since this is one area where the new product team usually relies heavily on the

[21]The Hoechst, Pfizer, and manufacturing firm examples are from Robert G. Cooper, Scott J. Edgett, and Elko J. Kleinschmidt, *Portfolio Management for New Products* (Hamilton, Ontario: McMaster University, 1997), pp. 22–29.

expertise brought in by the marketing representative. There are good basic methods for doing financial analysis (net present value calculations using discounted cash flow) and for doing sales forecasting. Most firms use these daily. However, new products managers know they often do not have the data these sophisticated methods require. So they may also need to use "risk-reducers"—actions that give them nonquantitative guides to probable success.

The method of making financial analyses is given in the Bay City case, which comes after the Applications section. The case offers data for a new electronics product and gives opportunity as well to look at some nondata issues involved in financial analysis.

At this point in the new product development process, we are ready to begin Phase IV (development).

Applications

1. "You're still a student, but when you tell me about all the problems new product managers have putting together financial worksheets, you sound like the people we have around here. They complain that all finance numbers are unreliable, estimates, guesses, etc. What they really want is no financial appraisal at all—just leave them alone and they'll eventually bring back the bacon—big slabs of it. That's simply not true—our financial evaluations have a weak figure or two, sure, but how else can we keep reasonable managerial control over the use of sometimes very great corporate resources?"

2. "One thing I know for certain—I don't want any sales managers or technical research people making new product forecasts. I've never seen such lousy forecasting as we get from these people. Sales managers either love a new item so much they think it will outsell everyone, or they think it is a dud and under forecast just as badly. Absolutely no objectivity in them. And the technical people, well, they become so enamored with their inventions that they lose all objectivity too. What I like is forecasting done by independent people—project managers or new products managers in separate departments. Have you run into any good ways of keeping sales managers and technical researchers out of forecasting? You agree that they should be excluded, don't you?"

3. "Actually, I agree with one thing you said a while ago, and that related to the desirability of making financial analyses on a threshold basis. I realize how many unknowns there are in the new products business. As a president, I realize too that most of the financial projections I read are just air. If a new products group can convince me that they can sell *at least* X volume, and at that volume their costs will be Y, *or lower*, then I am inclined to go along with them. But, deep in my heart, I don't like it—those thresholds are just as much subject to manipulation as are the more structured NPV projections. You agree?"

Case: Bay City Electronics[22]

Financial analysis of new products at Bay City Electronics had always been rather informal. Bill Roberts, who founded the firm in 1970, knew residential electronics because he had worked for almost seven years for another firm specializing in home security systems. But he had never been trained in financial analysis. In fact, all he knew was what the bank had asked for every time he went to discuss his line of credit. Bay City had about 45 full-time employees (plus a seasonal factory workforce) and did in the neighborhood of $18 million in sales. His products all related to home security and were sold by his sales manager, who worked with a group of manufacturers' reps, who in turn called on wholesalers, hardware and department store chains, and other large retailers. He did some consumer advertising, but not much.

Bill was inventive, however, and had built the business primarily by coming up with new techniques. His latest device was a remote-controlled electronic closure for any door in the home. The closure was effected by a special ringing of the telephone: For example, if a user wanted to leave a back door open until 9:00 p.m., it was simple to call the house at 9:00 and wait for 10 rings, after which the electronic device would switch the door to a locked position. A similar call would reopen the door.

The bank liked the idea but wanted Bill to do a better job of financial analysis, so the loan officer asked him to use the forms shown in the Bay City Appendix as Figure 11.11 and Figure 11.12. After some effort, Bill was able to fill out the key data form, Figure 11.11, and his work is reproduced here. To date, Bay City had spent $85,000 in expense money for supplies and labor developing the closure and had invested $15,000 in a machine (asset). If the company decided to go ahead, it would have to invest $50,000 more in a new facility, continue R&D to validate and improve the product, and—if things went according to expectations—invest another $45,000 in year 3 to expand production capability.

He also had to fill out the financial worksheet, Figure 11.12; for this he used a friend of the family who had studied financial analysis in college. The friend had relied on a summary of how to do this, and this summary is attached. He also warned Bill that there were lots of judgment calls in that calculation, "so don't get into an argument with the people at the bank about details."

While waiting for his appointment at the bank, Bill spent some time just thinking about his situation. Did the numbers look good? Where were the shaky parts that the banker might give him trouble on? Most of all, he was curious about whether a friend of his at the LazyBoy chair firm in Monroe had to do the same thing, and would 3M require the same type of form from his daughter, who now worked for them? Frankly, he didn't feel he personally had learned much about his situation from the exercise and was already wondering whether there weren't better ways for him to go about reassuring the bank that their loan was a good proposition.

---

[22]This is a realistic, but hypothetical, situation.

FIGURE 11.11   **Key Data Form for Financial Analysis, Part A**

Financial Analysis Proposal: *Bay City Electronics Closure**
Date of this analysis: _____ Previous analysis: _____

1. Economic conditions, if relevant:
   Corporate scenario OK

2. The market (category):
   Stable—5% growth

3. Product life *5* years

4. List price: *$90*
   Distributor discounts: *$36*
   Net to factory: *$54*

   Other discounts:
   Promotion: *$1*
   Quantity: *$1*
   Average dollars per unit sold: *$52*

5. Production costs:
   Explanation of any unique costing procedures being used:
   None. Experience curve effect.

   Applicable rate for indirect manufacturing costs: _____
   20% of direct costs

6. Future expenditures, other capital investments, or extraordinary expenditures:
   Build production facilities: $50,000
   Ongoing R&D: $15,000; $10,000; $15,000; $10,000 for first four years after intro
   Special UL test during the 2nd year will cost $5,000
   Expand facilities in 3rd year for $45,000

7. Working capital: *35* % of sales
   10% inventory; recover 80% in period 5
   15% receivables; all recovered in period 5
   10% cash, all recovered

8. Applicable overheads:
   Corp.: *10* % of sales
   Division: *_* % of sales

9. Net loss on cannibalized sales, if any, expressed as a percent of the new product's sales: *10* %

10. Future costs/revenues of project abandonment, if that were done instead of marketing: *Abort now would net $3,000 from sale of machine.*

11. Tax credits, if any, on new assets or expenditures: *1% of taxes due to state and federal, based on positive environmental effect.*

12. Applicable depreciation rate(s) on depreciable assets: *25% on orig. plant and machines; 33 1/3% on expansion facilities*

13. Federal and state income tax rate applicable: *34* %
    Comments:

14. Applicable cost of capital: *16* %
    ± Premiums or penalties: *high-risk project 8* %
    _____
    Any change in cost of capital anticipated over life of product? *No*

*This key data form is filled in with demonstration data for the Bay City Electronics case.

FIGURE 11.11 (CONCLUDED)   **Key Data Form for Financial Analysis, Part B**

15. Basic overall risk curve applicable to the NPV: Standard OK   ✓

16. Key elements to be given sensitivity testing (e.g., sales, price cuts): *(see below)*	17. Sunk costs: Expenses to date: *Ignore* Capital invested to date: *$15,000*

18. Elements of new product strategy that are especially relevant on this proposal: (e.g., diversification mandate or cash risk):
Strategy calls for us to strengthen company in diversified markets, which this product will do.

19. Basic sales and cost:

Year	Unit sales	Direct production cost per unit	Marketing expenses
1	4,000	$16	$100,000
2	10,000	12	80,000
3	18,000	11	50,000
4	24,000	9	60,000
5	5,000	14	10,000

20. Hurdle rates:
Must have 40% gross margin after production costs.

21. Any mandatory contingencies: *None*

22. Other special assumptions or guidelines:
(1) The total $110,000 of facilities and machines will salvage for $10,000 when production is finished.
(2) The firm has other income to absorb any tax loss on this project.
(3) Ignore investment tax credit.

———————————

Sensitivity testing (Calculate the effect on NPV of the following):
(1) We may have to cut the price to $34 net at start of third year.
(2) Our direct manufacturing cost estimate may be overly optimistic. What if we never get the cost below the original $16?
(3) Competition may force much higher marketing costs—what if starting in year 2 the level we have to spend at is just twice what we forecasted above?
(4) How about a worst-case outcome, in which all of the above three contingencies are tested at one time?

FIGURE 11.12 Financial Worksheet, Bay City Electronics

Product Proposal: Electronic Closure   Date:

			Years of the Market			
	0	1	2	3	4	5
Unit sales	0	4,000	10,000	18,000	24,000	5,000
Revenue per unit	0	52	52	52	52	52
Dollar sales	0	208,000	520,000	936,000	1,248,000	266,000
Production costs:						
Direct	0	64,000	120,000	198,000	216,000	70,000
Indirect	0	12,800	24,000	39,6000	43,200	14,000
Total	0	76,800	144,000	237,600	259,200	84,000
Gross profit	0	131,200	376,000	648,400	988,000	176,000
Direct marketing costs	0	100,000	80,000	50,000	60,000	10,000
Profit contribution	0	31,200	296,000	648,400	928,800	166,000
Overheads (excluding R&D):						
Division	0	0	0	0	0	0
Corporate	0	20,800	52,000	93,600	124,800	26,000
Total	0	20,800	52,000	93,600	124,800	26,000
Other expenses:						
Depreciation	16,250	16,250	16,250	31,250	15,000	15,000
Cannibalization	0	20,800	52,000	93,600	124,800	26,000
R&D to be incurred	0	15,000	10,000	15,000	10,000	0
Extraordinary expense	0	0	5,000	0	0	0
Project abandonment	3,000	0	0	0	0	0
Total	19,250	52,050	83,250	139,850	149,800	41,000
Overheads and expenses	19,250	72,850	135,250	233,450	274,600	67,000
Income before taxes	(19,250)	(41,650)	160,750	414,950	654,200	99,000
Tax effect:						
Taxes on income	(6,545)	(14,161)	54,655	141,083	222,428	33,660
Tax credits	(65)	(142)	547	1,411	2,224	337
Total effect	(6,480)	(14,019)	54,108	139,672	220,204	33,323
Cash flow:						
Income after taxes	(12,770)	(27,631)	106,642	275,278	433,996	65,677
Depreciation	16,250	16,250	16,250	31,250	15,000	15,000
Production facilities	50,000	0	0	45,000	0	0
Working capital: Cash	0	20,800	31,200	41,600	31,200	(124,800)
Working capital: Inventories	0	20,800	31,200	41,600	31,200	(99,840)
Working capital: Acc. Rec.	0	31,200	46,800	62,400	46,800	(187,200)
Net cash flows	(46,520)	(84,181)	13,692	115,928	339,796	492,517
Discounted flows	(46,520)	(67,888)	8,904	60,803	143,725	168,001
Net present value	$267,025					
Internal rate of return	73.7					
Payback	Nov., Year 3					

Test 1: NPV = $88,885
Test 2: NPV = $149,453
Test 3: NPV = $196,013
All 3: NPV = ($99,699)

Worst case is very undesirable, even here where indirect effects, sunk costs, and salvage were omitted.

BAY CITY APPENDIX: FINANCIAL ANALYSIS FOR NEW PRODUCTS

New products financial analysis requires two separate activities: (1) gathering the full set of data and other "givens" in the situation, and (2) using them in calculations to derive whatever final figure is sought. These two tasks are shown in Figures 11.11 (the key data form) and 11.12 (the financial worksheet).

COMPILING THE KEY DATA

Economic Conditions. Most firms have ongoing economic forecasts, but sometimes a team wishes to differ. If so, the difference should be noted here.

The Market or Category. The "market" for the new product is defined carefully, and the growth rate assumption is noted. Also, the current total market unit and dollar volumes are recorded.

Product Life. The number of years used in the economic analysis of new products is usually set by company policy, but any particular project may be an exception.

Pricing. Start with the end-user list price, work back through the various trade discounts to get a factory net, then deduct any planned special discounts and allowances. The average dollars per unit sold is the price used in worksheet calculations.

Production Costs. Is anything unusual being done on this project? Actual anticipated cost goes directly onto the financial worksheet. Cite factory burden percentage rate.[23]

Future Special Expenditures. These typically include factory facilities, licensing rights, the one-time introductory marketing cost, up-front payments to suppliers, further R&D on improvements and line extensions, and plant expansions as volume grows. These are all *investment outflows*.

Working Capital. This estimates cash, inventories, and receivables needed to support the sales volumes. How are they to be recovered?

Applicable Overheads. Some firms assign only "direct" overheads—those caused by the new product (such as an expanded sales force or a new quality function). Other firms believe overheads tend to grow as functions of volume and should be included.

Net Loss on Cannibalized Sales. These are dollar sales lost as the new product steals sales from current products. This is to be deducted from revenue. Some experts believe if we don't do this a competitor will, so they omit it.

---

[23]Factory overheads are often assigned using an Activity Based Costing (ABC) system. If adopted, new items have a greater chance of realistic allocations. See Bernard C. Reimann, "Challenging Conventional Wisdom: Corporate Strategies That Work," *Planning Review*, November/December 1991, pp. 36–39.

Future Costs/Revenues of Project Abandonment. Along the way, the project may have accumulated facilities, people, patent rights, inventories, and so on. If abandoned now, disposal of these will produce revenue, money that is actually a *cost of abandoning the project.* But disposing of radioactive chemicals may be expensive, thus a *revenue* of going ahead.

Tax Credits. Federal or state incentives for activity in the public interest.

Applicable Depreciation Rate. Policy question, set by management.

Federal and State Income Tax Rate. Company figure, provided.

Required Rate of Return. This one tells us the cash flow discount rate to be used and can be complex and political. Theoretically, the figure to use is the *weighted average cost of capital,* including the three sources of capital—debt, preferred stock, and retained earnings. Often it is simply the *firm's current borrowing rate.*[24] It may be the *rate of earnings from current operations.* New product managers want it low, conservative financial people may want it high. The actual rate to be used is often an arbitrary decision. Whatever the rate, the next step is to decide how the riskiness of this project compares with the rest of the firm's activities. Look at Figure 11.6, which shows that a relationship between risk and rate of return exists for every business, as discussed in the chapter. Given the current average cost of capital and the level and slope of the line, the manager can mark off the risk of the particular new product, go up to the risk/return line, and then read off the required rate of return. Except in unusual circumstances, that required level will represent a premium over the current cost of capital. The premium is entered in section 14 of the key data form.

Risk Curve. Figure 11.7 shows the typical **risk curve** of possible profit outcomes from a given new product project, as discussed in the chapter. In the B pattern, for example, chances are the project will have a lower payout, but a very high payout is also possible. Imitative competition is expected; but, if it doesn't come, the profit will be high. This risk pattern information is good to keep in mind when making the financial analysis, though few firms undertake the probability-adjusted risk analysis it permits.

Sensitivity Testing. After an analysis has been completed using original data, the analyst goes back and recalculates the profit using other figures for especially sensitive factors.

Elements of Strategy. When evaluating new product proposals, it is important to remember the strategy that prompted them. Less-profitable products may well be warranted under certain strategies.

Basic Sales and Cost Forecasts. This section gives the primary data inputs—the number of units to be sold, the direct production cost per unit, and the total marketing expenditures.

---

[24]A variation on this is to use the current market risk-free cost of capital (interest rate on Treasuries, for example). We then add a premium reflecting the general level of risk in the industry at hand.

Hurdle Rates. A company sometimes has hurdle rates on variables other than rate of return.

Mandatory Contingencies. A firm may want one or more contingencies worked into the analysis every time, not left optional.

Other Special Assumptions or Guidelines. This is the typical miscellaneous section, totally situational.

Beyond the Key Data Form: Sunk Costs. Sunk costs should not enter into this analysis. Sunk money is just that—sunk. It stays sunk whether we go ahead at this time or abandon the project.

Salvage. NPV forms sometimes call for the dollars obtained at the end of the product's life from sale of salvaged equipment. The amounts are usually small and are best omitted.

Portfolio. If the new item is playing a special role as part of an overall portfolio of projects, the value of that role should be mentioned. The new project may be high risk but still worthwhile to balance a large number of low-risk projects—or the reverse.

CHAPTER TWELVE

Product Protocol

Setting

When a new products group finishes the full screen and the financial analysis co-incident with it, they have reached what many feel is the most critical single step in the new product's life—more critical than the market introduction and more critical than the building of manufacturing capacity. This is the point where very important things *all around the firm* begin to happen.

Granted, some managements still use a relay race system, where one department does its work, passes the product concept to the next department, which does its work, then . . . and so on. The leading product innovators do not—they use some type of **concurrent system**, one in which all of the players begin working, doing as much as they can at any time as the project rolls along. When technical work begins, process engineers are not sitting around waiting for the final prototype to be tossed to them. When process engineers are laying out the manufacturing system, procurement people are not waiting for final word about when certain components are going to be built. And while all of this technical/operations work is continuing, marketing people are not sitting around waiting for a hand-off that will trigger their thoughts about advertising and customer technical service.

No, they all begin work at the same time, and in fact many have been watching the concept testing and screening to see how positive the early word is. If a concept looks like a winner, even if financial screening won't take place for a couple months, these down-the-line people are already starting to do what they will *eventually* have to do. Some workers actually may be a year ahead of need, especially if there is some built-in delay in what they do.

For example, while process engineers are waiting for product specs so they can begin their work, packaging people have been thinking about the concept. Many products require packaging—durable, value-producing packaging, or impressive, shelf-talking promotion packaging. Packages, in turn, require product names. So purchasing cannot order new packages until brands are settled, and brands cannot be settled until product content is known and marketing strategy is settled. Marketing strategy involves price decisions, which must await costs, which must await final manufacturing systems and component costs, which is where this paragraph started.

The Product Protocol

What do we do? We do it all, side by side, doing what we can, when we can, making minor commitments at some risk, holding on costly commitments. All of these efforts are risky and will never work well without *something that keeps the team together*, something that allows them to make reasonable speculations.

That something currently has no standard form, no accepted name, and no established practice. But most firms are doing part of the task, a few all of it, waiting for the activity to gel. In this book we will call the activity *protocol preparation*, and the output is a **product protocol.** Other names that it goes by are *product requirements*, *product definition*, and *deliverables*. All terms mean the same thing—what is the final package of output from the development system—what benefits or performance will the product deliver to the customer, and what changes will the marketing program bring in the marketplace.

A protocol is, by definition, a signed agreement between negotiating parties. In a product protocol, the negotiating parties are the functions—marketing, technical, operations, and others. Signed agreement is a bit formal, perhaps, but the financial analysis that triggered this phase depended on certain assumptions—product qualities and costs, certain support facilities, certain patents, and certain marketplace accomplishments. If they are not delivered, all bets with management are off. Since most projects today involve some form of multifunctional team, the whole group is responsible for writing a protocol. Although new products do indeed require tradeoffs, they are negotiated in a very positive use of the term. Even if the multifunctional team works well together, technical limitations may emerge that may make quick agreement difficult. A humorous view of the kind of challenges that can crop up at this phase is presented in Figure 12.1.

One technique used by Toyota to get cooperation across functional areas, to speed up integration, and to focus the team is the "Oobeya Room," described in

FIGURE 12.1
A Marketing-R&D Conversation

> MKTG: We're going to be needing a solar-powered version of our standard garage door opener, soon.
> R&D: How reliable should it be? Should it be controllable from inside the house? Should we use new electronics technology? Should it be separate from the collector system already installed?
> MKTG: Well, you're the technical people, make some recommendations.
> R&D: In other words, you don't know what you want.
> MKTG: Cripes, do we have to tell you everything? What do you do for a living? How should we know where the collectors should be located?
> R&D: If we go electronic, you'll say it's too expensive. If we go electric, you'll say we're living in the 30s. Wherever we put the collectors you will say we are wrong. If we guess, you second-guess.
> MKTG: OK. Put the collectors on the garage roof.
> R&D: That probably can't be done.

FIGURE 12.2
The Oobeya
Room

One tool used by Toyota to speed up its product development is the Oobeya Room. "Oobeya" (from the word for "room" in Japanese, pronounced oh-beya) is, indeed, a big room, set up to accommodate the entire team for one new product project (usually containing people from marketing and sales, engineering, logistics, planning, design, and production). In the center of the Oobeya room is the prototype (a model, mock-up, or drawing) that encourages communication among team members, and helps the team visualize the product and identify potential problems early. All around the room are boards that guide discussion of the product project. These would include:

An objective board (containing Toyota's version of a PIC: background, objectives, technical specifications, and project organization)

A metrics board (showing current project status and allowing for team members to determine where they are at, or behind, target)

An action board (showing the activities of all members on the team that are required to reach the objective and indicating which activities are already completed)

A decomposition board (indicating which sub-projects need the most attention)

An issue board (showing the most critical problems that have arisen, used to stimulate discussion between team leader and team members and to assign accountability)

An important part of the Oobeya Room concept is that the roles of all the participants. The team leader is responsible for setting targets, assessing team member plans, negotiating with the team or with company management when the goals are not realistic, and to keep meetings under control. Team members' responsibilities include providing solutions that help the team attain desired goals, providing status reports (on target versus behind target), suggest how to overcome obstacles, understanding the activities of other team members, and resolving key issues. Generally, at each meeting, team members are expected to make a short presentation about their areas. The more experience they have, the easier it is for team members to keep their reports under three minutes. Total meeting time, including review of main and issue boards, usually is under one hour.

The Oobeya Room concept seems rather simple, but it is in fact a powerful tool. The payoff comes from the fact that the process requires the team members to integrate their behaviors, and to work in a very efficient and structured manner. That way, more information is generated and less time is needed. Problem detection and resolution speeds up and the value of each individual meeting is increased. No one can "loaf," read reports, or send e-mails, since there are strict time constraints. To get the work done well and on time requires a real commitment to collaboration and interaction.

Source: Toshi Horikiri, Don Kieffer, Takashi Tanaka, and Craig Flynn, "A Toyota Secret Revealed: The Oobeya Room—How Toyota Uses This Concept to Speed Up Product Development," *Visions*, 33(2), July 2009, pp. 9–13.

detail in Figure 12.2. The Oobeya Room is conceptually very close to the idea of the product protocol: It very effectively overcomes the challenges shown in Figure 12.1 by giving the team members little choice but to work together.

Protocol preparation is the subject of this chapter. In prior chapters of this book you had a chance to see the new product process from an overall perspective—how it goes from strategy through to market success, how the strategy gives the process focus, how concepts are created and gathered, how concepts are then tested and evaluated, and how the evaluation process comes to a temporary conclusion with the full screen and financial analysis.

FIGURE 12.3
The
Integrating
and Focusing
Role of
Protocol

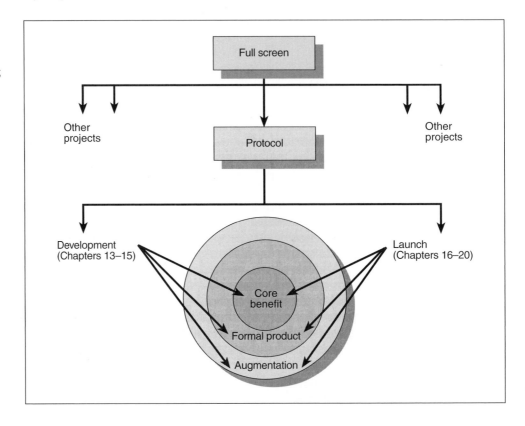

Figure 12.3 shows what happens now. In the middle of the figure lies a bull's-eye-like circle representing the **augmented product concept.** This shows that at the core of a product is end-user benefit, the real purpose for which the product was created.

Purposes of the Protocol

This can vary from market segment to market segment, and from time to time. What the customer actually buys, however, consists of one or more core benefits, a formal product presentation (physical form or service sequence), *and* an augmentation of things from presale technical service to a money-back guarantee. The point here is that customers and end users buy fully augmented products, and their core benefit may partly come from the augmentations. New products managers cannot focus only on the formal product. All three of the concentric rings of the bull's-eye must be designed and executed, and two functional groups play a role in all of them, as shown by the arrows leading into the augmented circles. Figure 12.3 also shows that the technical departments (with help from manufacturing, quality, procurement, and others) work pretty much as a unit, and marketing (with help from its allies in sales, market research, promotion, channel management, and others) does the same on the right side of the diagram. Both groups keep in close touch with each other.

The issue is: *What do these two groups need to do their work?* The answer differs by firm and industry and situation, but whatever, it should be consolidated into a protocol statement. The protocol is, in fact, one step in the evolution of a concept, as you saw in Figure 2.3 of Chapter 2. It is more than the simple statement approved in the screening, and less than what will exist when the first prototype appears. But it is what we need now, what all departments need to begin their work.

This idea of how others use the protocol is what gave it the name *product deliverables*. In fact, *the first general purpose of the protocol is to specify what each department will deliver to the final product that the customer buys*. For a new type of golf footwear, a deliverable from technical might be "Can be used in all types of weather and on all turf conditions." A deliverable from marketing might be personal trial use by at least 80 percent of the golf professionals in Europe, the United States, Australia, and South Africa. A deliverable from information technology might be "800 number service with less than five minutes' waiting time, covering the needs of 80 percent of callers from the United States this year and from the other markets by end of second year."

Not all deliverables are known at this time, of course, but the critical ones should be. Otherwise, we are not ready for release into a system of parallel (or concurrent) development. If, on that golf footwear, we don't know the importance of bad weather and turf conditions, the golf pro's influence on affluent golfers (what we are producing we can see will have to be expensive), the criticalness of trial (key benefits will be hidden), and the certainty of technical questions on a complex product like this, then we haven't done our homework. The fact is, protocol (like many things in use today) states requirements that force us to do what we should be doing anyway, such as good market research!

In Chapter 3, on the product innovation charter, you read that the PIC is rather like a soft harness on a team of horses, clearly directing and integrating the team. A second general purpose of the protocol statement is the same for the participants in new product development. *It communicates essentials to all of the players, helps lead them into integrated actions, helps direct outcomes that are consistent with the full screen and financials, and gives all players their targets to shoot for.* Some new products people think the mere call for the document leads to early customer contacts that should always be made, but often aren't.

A third purpose of the protocol relates to time through the process, or *cycle time*. As seen in Chapter 2, many firms place high priority on accelerated time to market, and better product definition can help cut development time. Consider how much development time would be wasted, and how many costly steps would have to be redone, if a new portable CD/MP3 player were fully planned, designed, and in prototype production when someone noticed it was too heavy for normal use! It would have been better to specify the desired and maximum weight before undertaking development. Seemingly small decisions like this at product definition, if done wrong, can result in extremely costly fixups late in the process.

Fourth, if done right, the protocol gives requirements in words that can usually be measured. It thus permits a development process to be *managed*. It tells what is to be done, when and why, the how (if that is required by some power beyond our control), the who, and perhaps most important, the whether. That is, we know at any time whether the requirements have been met; this will automatically caution that we are not ready to market an item if there is still an open requirement, unless specifically waived. Many of the techniques we have learned in preceding chapters (perceptual gap analysis, preference mapping, conjoint analysis) will provide us with information that can be used as inputs to various "requirements" of the protocol.

As the saying goes, if you don't know where you're going, any road will get you there. Without protocol and its call for measurements, you've no idea where (or when) you will end up.

Protocol's Specific Contents

You have just read what is in a protocol, in general terms. The details can vary greatly, and will for some time until our practice on this new step tells just how to do it. But we do know that there is a scale of demand or commitment. Not everything that we call for *must* be delivered. Some firms use the terms *Musts* and *Wants*—that is, some requirements we must have, and some are simply what we *would like* to have if feasible and practical within technology, cost, and time frames. But each firm has its own language for these things. Some have put the musts in a protocol and the wants or "hoped-fors" in an attachment (or literally, in one case, on the *backs* of pages!).[1] The following sections list items often found in protocols, and an abbreviated version of a simple protocol is given in Figure 12.4.

Target Market

Most firms *manage* most of their new product projects using techniques we have been presenting: PICs, concept testing, screening models, protocols, and so on. Other projects are *wildcatting*—betting on a technology that hasn't yet been shown to work, betting on a new application where some end-user will partner with us to see what works, or just betting on a scientist with a good track record for coming up with saleable new products. None of these is appropriate for a protocol; we just don't have the knowledge to write one, and its only effect would be to bother the developers, who, actually, will ignore it completely.

In most cases, however, we know the target market very well—first in finding their problems to solve, later in asking if our new product concept meets their need and seems reasonable to them, and still later in screening factors (e.g., do we have a sales force that can reach them or will we have to build a new one?). Perceptual and preference mapping techniques we discussed in earlier chapters can be very helpful in developing this part of the protocol, as benefit segments will have been identified and their specific needs will be understood.

The target market needs to be spelled out here, quite specifically. Some firms like to have a primary target market, selected perhaps due to size, growth rate, urgency of need, buying power, perceived ease of making competitive inroads,

---

[1]Puritan-Bennett uses one category of protocol benefits called "excitement needs," those that, if filled, would happily surprise the end user. John R. Hauser, "How Puritan-Bennett Used the House of Quality," *Sloan Management Review*, Spring 1993, pp. 61–70.

FIGURE 12.4 Simplified Protocol for a Home Trash Disposal/Recycling System

1. **Target market:**
   Ultimate: Top 30% of income group, in cities of over 100,000, with upscale lifestyle.
   Intermediate: Stakeholders in building industry for homes over $300,000, especially developers, architects, builders, bankers, and regulators.
2. **Product positioning:**
   A convenient, mess-free method for recycling items in the home.
3. **Product attributes (benefits if possible):**
   - The system must automate trash disposal in a home environment with recycling (separating trash, compacting, placing bags outside, and rebagging the empty bins and notifying user when the bag supply is running out) at a factory cost not to exceed $800.
   - The system must be clean, ventilated, and odor-free. The user will want an easy-to-clean appliance. Rodents, pets, and angry neighbors could become a problem if odors exist.
   - Installation must be simple. Distributors and other installation personnel must have favorable experience in installations.
   - The system must be safe enough for operation by children of school age.
   - The entire working unit must not be larger in cubic feet than twice a 22 cubic foot refrigerator.
4. **Competitive comparison:**
   None: First of a kind.
5. **Augmentation dimensions:**
   Financing arrangeable with us, if necessary. Generous warranty. Competent installation service, and fast/competent post-installation service. Education about recycling and about the product will be difficult and essential.
6. **Timing:**
   Being right overrides getting to market fast. But the window will not be open more than two years.
7. **Marketing requirements:**
   - Marketing announcement must be made at national builders shows and environment/ecology shows.
   - A new channel structure will be needed for the intermediate target market, but it will eventually be collapsed into our regular channel.
   - We will need a small, select sales force for this introduction.
   - To capitalize on announcement value, we need 50 installations during the first four months.
8. **Financial requirements:**
   - Development and intro period losses will not exceed $20,000,000. Break-even is expected by end of second full year on the market.
   - Ultimately, this project must achieve a five-year net present value of zero, based on 35% cost of capital.
9. **Production requirements:**
   - Once we announce, there must be no interruption of supply.
   - Quality standards simply must be met, without exception.
10. **Regulatory requirements:**
    Regulations are from many sources and vary by states and localities. There are various substakeholders here; we need to know them well. A surprise, significant holdup (after launch) cannot be allowed on this development.
11. **Corporate strategy requirements:**
    Corporate strategy is driving this project, and has personal leadership at the corporate general management level. We seek diversification of markets, enhanced reputation for innovativeness, and sustainable margins higher than those in our major markets today.
12. **Potholes:**
    This project has massive pothole potentials, because of its newness. The most worrisome ones are (1) regulatory approval of health issues, (2) accomplishing the $800 cost constraint, and (3) getting fast market approvals for early installations.

and so on. Typically, one or more secondary target markets will also be selected to move to after successful introduction, and at least one fall-back target market if the primary gets blown out of the water by technical failure, regulation, competition, or whatever during development.

Positioning

This is a real challenge for many firms. **Product positioning** is the concept that came out of the advertising world in the early 1970s. Essentially, it says, "Product X is better for your use than other products because . . . ." It announces the item as new and gives the end user a real reason for trying it. In the process, it shows the end user what problem it attacks and what about it makes it better than whatever they are using now. This concept will be developed more completely when we get to Chapter 16, but for now it is usually enough to state the target market and complete that sentence above. Fortunately, this should be easy because joint space mapping and other concept testing activities will have provided key information on desirable positioning options for our product. In effect, the concept test assures us stakeholders will be interested in trying an item and a positioning claim.

Technical people are often not told what the positioning of a new item will be. It's almost as though we say, develop a new item and do it in a way the customer will like. That's not management; that's abdication. Even in large packaged goods firms today, with their excellent staffs, products a bit off the beaten track often get neglected; many of these firms' R&D staffs have had to build market research departments to do concept testing on items they are originating. Misunderstandings on positioning have probably been the cause of more technical/marketing fights than anything else.

Product Attributes

As discussed earlier, product attributes define the product. They are of three types—features, functions, and benefits. Benefits include uses. Protocols can list any of these, and do. "The new bulk laxative will dissolve completely in a four-ounce glass of water in 10 seconds" (Merrill-Dow). This is function—how the item will work, not what it is (feature) or what the benefit is of fast dissolving. Note that by being asked for speed, technical people were allowed to select any chemical they wished (and did—it is now second only to Metamucil in this market).

Benefits

Benefits are the most desirable form for a protocol to use—better than functions or features. Information obtained from conjoint (trade-off) analysis and other concept testing techniques can be extremely useful in determining what combinations of features, functions, and specifications ought to be built into the product. An advantage of specifying the protocol in terms of benefits is that it places no (or very few) constraints on the R&D staff: They are given free rein to figure out how best to design the product so that it provides the desired benefit. For example, consider Built NY, which is a small design firm. A friend of the firm's owners suggested an idea for a new product: a convenient carrier for two wine bottles, which could be brought to a BYOB restaurant. The designers quickly developed a list of customer benefits for the ideal two-bottle wine carrier: protective (so the bottles wouldn't break), insulating (to maintain temperature), ergonomic (easy to carry), lightweight, reusable, inexpensive, maybe also flexible (easy to store when not in use). The challenge then was to select the material that could best deliver all these benefits. They hit upon neoprene, a synthetic material most commonly used for wetsuits. It offered all of the customer benefits, and also turned out to be easy to cut into shape and to dye into designer colors. The "Two-Bottle Tote" won awards for product design and also inspired a range of similar products, such as beer carriers and baby-bottle carriers.[2]

Functions

Function attributes sometimes cause confusion. Marketers tend to use them a lot, and they are often called performance specs, or performance parameters, or design parameters. One everyone knows is: "The car must accelerate from 0 to 60 miles per hour in 8 seconds." This requirement does not tell us what features will yield that performance. What it *does* is answer the question of how the customer achieves the benefits of exciting (or safe) start-ups.

Some people feel a performance parameter (a function) may come to be expressed as a design parameter. For example, on the matter of the car pickup above, the statement might be "Use the new German 11-Z4 engine." Such a new engine would be a technology but clearly might be a *solution* to a need, not a *description* of it; there are probably many other ways rapid pickup could be achieved. Car platforms are heavily laced with such statements.

Protocols for services are especially likely to be in performance terms since the production of a service is a performance, not a good. But protocols are also much less necessary on services because of the smaller investment in technical development. These producers can, in many cases, get to prototype very quickly, so that prototype concept testing or even product use testing can easily gain confirmation of customer need fulfillment.

Features

Features are also a problem. Technical people often come up with features first, based on technologies they have. Some scientist at a firm such as PPG might figure out a way to make a boat deck out of finely ground glass left over from some production operation. The thought is pursued for several months only to be knocked out by a shipbuilder's need for reduced weight. A full protocol statement might have avoided that waste of time. In another case, a scientist did in fact figure out a solution to a certain worm infestation in children, only to be told that this infestation occurs only on scattered Pacific islands and could never constitute a viable market for a pharmaceutical firm. For this reason, firms often ask scientists to keep others informed and to seek input about markets being worked on.

The bigger problem with features is that they deprive the firm's most creative and inventive people of the freedom to use their skills. A large computer firm 30 years ago was known for having a strong technical research staff. They

---

[2]The firm's Web site is www.builtny.com.

originated some useful technology. But the firm never achieved much success in reacting to changing needs in the marketplace. Some insiders said it was the result of a system that had a central engineering staff take each situation and spell out the features and characteristics their research staff were to produce. One such spec sheet ran for 13 pages, and the scientist getting it said he felt like a beginning law clerk. He left the firm as soon as he could.

An extreme version of a protocol was reported by a pharmaceutical firm in which a new products manager sent a comprehensive advertising layout to his technical counterpart in R&D with an attached note, "Please prepare an item that will back up this ad." The first reaction was negative, until technical realized they were given carte blanche to do whatever they wanted, so long as the result met the listed claims.

Occasionally, a firm knows from long-time market contact what features are associated with what functions (performance) and benefits. They occasionally will put through a work request that calls for "A new pump with electronic valves that give faster reaction to down-line stoppages and thus prevent blowouts." If the valves are standards, this protocol statement gives feature, function, and benefit.

Detailed Specifications

On occasions, customers make such decisions and call for products with specific features. This is dangerous. If the customers are qualified and have reason to know better than we do what features will do for them, we are wise to listen. In Chapter 4 we talked about getting finished product concepts from lead users (sometimes even a finished prototype).

Another case where features may be needed is where a firm is benchmarking competitive products. One strategy is to have the Best of the Best. Take the best features in the market, all products combined, and assemble them in your new product. This sounds great, but it means our product design is being led by competitors, not end users.[3]

Still other situations where features will appear in protocols are (1) where regulations stipulate a particular feature (e.g., prescription containers), (2) where end users own major items of equipment that impose limitations (e.g., under-dash space limitations for disk players), (3) where established practice in a customer industry is too strong for one supplier to change (e.g., for many years software makers had no choice but to put MS-DOS as a feature requirement), and regrettably (4) where upper managements have personal preferences.

In general, as a conclusion to this section on attributes, it is still the best policy to write protocols in benefits, using performance if that helps explain and doesn't inhibit too much.

Competitive Comparisons and Augmentation Dimensions

Benchmarking has been mentioned, but there are many other competitive standards that can be put into a protocol—matching some important policy, the

---

[3]This is explained by Milton D. Rosenau Jr., in "Avoiding Marketing's Best-of-the-Best Specification Trap," *Journal of Product Innovation Management,* 9(4), December 1992, pp. 300–302.

degree of differentiation we have to meet, and many aspects of the marketing plan (e.g., size of sales force, price, distribution availability, and more). Information on competitive comparison can be derived from perceptual maps, and the gaps appearing on the perceptual map can provide guidance on selecting an appropriate competitive position.

Just as the product itself was described in attributes above, the augmentation ring of the product can also be cited. Sometimes the product itself may be "me-too," but still is a legitimate competitive offering as it may offer the customer a new level of service, a better warranty, or better distributor support. Recall that there are three rings in the fully augmented product—ring one (core benefit) is covered in the positioning statement, ring two (the formal product) is covered in the attribute requirements, and ring three (augmentations) is covered here.

Other Components of the Product Protocol

There are several other components of the protocol that we will handle here very briefly. These are probably best illustrated through example, such as in Figure 12.3.

> *Timing:* Most new products today must come out faster, but not all do. Some involve major technical breakthroughs that cannot be put on the clock. The distinction needs to be clear to all. And if there is a date to meet, it should be right here.
>
> *Financials:* Typically, the protocol will include price level, discounts, sales volume, sales dollars, market share, profits, net present value, and many of the other financial data introduced in the previous chapter.
>
> *Production:* This one is much like marketing requirements, some focusing on what the function will prepare to do and what that will accomplish—thus, plants to be built, volumes, and quality to be achieved.
>
> *Regulatory Requirements:* These are highly varied, but managements today understand the need to have advanced understanding on them.
>
> *Corporate Strategy Requirements:* Key ideas (such as core competencies) will have already been captured in the product innovation charter. Also, at this time, the assurance of upper management support is important.
>
> *Potholes:* As we have seen before, there are potholes in product innovation, just as they are on that stretch of highway as you drive at night—and they are capable of bringing a new product down. Management that doesn't take a good look ahead deserves to hit one. We don't usually drive into *known* potholes, so listing them here helps.

Protocol and the Voice of the Customer

What Is the Voice of the Customer?

Back in Chapter 2, you were introduced to the concept of the voice of the customer (VOC). We return to it here, as it plays such an important role of the development of the product protocol.

VOC has been defined as a "complete set of customer wants and needs, expressed in the customer's own language, organized the way the customer thinks about, uses, and interacts with the product . . . , and prioritized by the customer in terms of both importance and performance—in other words, current satisfaction with existing alternatives."[4] Think for a moment about what is included in this definition. "Customer's own language" means exactly that—no scientific jargon. Printer users don't generally think in terms of edge resolution or number of pixels; rather, they think in terms of how well the letters come out or how nice the pictures look. Just because the terms don't sound scientific doesn't mean the opinions are unimportant! Also, the customers must organize and prioritize their needs in their own way, as they see fit; this is likely to be different from the way the firm sees it. Recall the Mexican cement company that was surprised to learn it could gain significant market share just by focusing on its customers' stated need for better on-time delivery? Or what about the pharmaceutical company that discovers its new drug product is highly prescribed by doctors, not because of its efficacy or lack of side effects, but because they like the fact that patients only have to take it once a day, while competitive drugs need to be taken three times a day?

Later in this chapter, we will learn how to translate the voice of the customer into a form that will be perhaps more helpful to the product engineers and R&D personnel who will actually design the product. First, however, we need to understand how best to bring the VOC to the new product team.

Hearing the Voice of the Customer[5]

Recall from Chapter 5 that we have several ways to access the voice of the customer: through direct interviewing, for example, or by conducting focus groups. The advantages and drawbacks of focus groups were reviewed in Chapter 5. As an alternative to focus groups, some firms go with individual interviews. Interviewing customers individually can provide very rich and detailed information, but might be time-consuming and costly. The real question here is, how many interviews should be conducted before one is relatively confident the VOC has been captured? Some groundbreaking research on interviewing by Abbie Griffin and John Hauser suggests a reasonable ground rule: about 30 individual interviews, each lasting about three-quarters of an hour, produce close to 100 percent of all customer needs; 20 interviews produce about 90 percent of the needs.[6]

The interviewer should be prepared with the right questions. Interestingly, one of the worst ways to elicit the VOC is to ask "What are your needs?" or "What are your requirements?" Customers are all too willing to provide a wish list of

---

[4]Gerald M. Katz, "The Voice of the Customer," in P. Belliveau, A. Griffin, and S. M. Somermeyer, *The PDMA Toolbook 2 for New Product Development* (New York: John Wiley, 2002), Ch. 7.
[5]Much of this section derives from Gerald M. Katz, op. cit.
[6]Abbie Griffin and John Hauser, "The Voice of the Customer," *Marketing Science*, 12(1), Winter 1993, pp. 1–27.

"must-haves," almost certainly taken from existing, available solutions. That is, car drivers might say "add more cup holders," or clock radio buyers might say "make the snooze alarm last longer," but rarely would anything really surprising emerge. From this faulty VOC, the best a firm could produce would be yet another "me-too" product! The better way to ask the question is to focus on experiences or desired outcomes, for example, by asking "What are the most difficult tasks you are trying to accomplish with the product?" "What do you like, and what do you dislike?" or "What is the best, and the worst, experience you have ever had with this product?"

Consider staying overnight at a hotel. If you were asked to state your needs, what would you say? Probably a clean room, a nice bed, shower, TV, maybe an Internet connection. But if asked what your worst experience was, what would it be? Couldn't find the plug for your razor? Bumped yourself on the shower head? Towels weren't clean? The interviewer will get many more ideas for product or service improvements this way.

It is also not enough to get the generalities, such as "I need my cell phone to be flexible," or "I need my Internet access provider to be consistent." The obvious follow-ups here are "What do you mean by flexible?" and "What do you mean by consistent?" This ensures that the VOC is clearly heard and not misinterpreted. A good rule of thumb is to keep asking why: "Why did you say that?" "Why do you feel like that?" "Why would it be better that way?" and so on. The goal, remember, is not to get technical solutions to the problems. That comes later. Rather, the customer's wants, needs, likes, dislikes, and so on must be articulated as well as possible at this point.

Good practice at this point suggests that all the interviews are taped (with permission granted ahead of time by the respondents), and transcripts are made. To boil down the dozens or even hundreds of transcript pages into a basic set of customer needs, it might be useful to write down the key phrases obtained from each interview (sticky notes are good for this), then sort and rearrange them into sets of needs. These are typically still too numerous, so they may need to be further grouped into bundles of needs. Experts in this procedure like to aim for about 15 to 25 bundles or groupings of customer needs.

Consider the Morton Salt company. What could product innovation possibly mean to them? Isn't salt just salt? Of course not. Morton sells over a dozen different types of salt, including kosher salt, garlic salt, seasoned salt, popcorn salt, and pickling salt. (This is in addition to salt sold for industrial use and de-icing salt.) A recent product launch was Hot Salt with added hot spice to be used in Mexican cooking, pasta sauce, and the like. Interviewed customers might say they love the idea. But to really get the voice of the customer, one would have needed much more specific information. How spicy? How different from regular chili powder? A sharp cayenne flavor, or a smoky chipotle? Translating a great idea into a product customers will actually buy and like is tricky; and without this level of detail from customers, the food engineers are left to just guess.

Protocol and Quality Function Deployment (QFD)

QFD and the House of Quality

To understand the role of the product protocol in the new products process, think of this process as shown in Figure 12.5. This figure emphasizes the role of the customer, as it shows that we begin with the voice of the customer, and end up with a product that satisfies the customer's needs. Through market research, sales calls, and other forms of customer contact, we are able to identify what the customer desires. The next step is a tricky one, but absolutely essential. We need to convert those customer desires into some kind of blueprint, perhaps an engineering schematic or a detailed service plan, that offers the customer those desired benefits in a format that is useful for the product development team. Once we get to this point, we can take it back to the customer and conduct the appropriate tests to fine-tune the product. It is indeed the product protocol, the subject of this chapter, that helps the firm get "around the bend" of Figure 12.5, because when carefully planned, the protocol allows the firm to translate customer desires into the appropriate product form.

This next section describes a technique, originating in Japan but now commonly used worldwide, that allows the VOC to become a driver of all later steps in the new products process.

Quality function deployment (QFD) was invented in the Japanese automobile industry years ago as a tool of project control in an industry with incredibly complicated projects. It can lead to reduced design time and costs, and more efficient communication between project team members from functional

FIGURE 12.5
The Role of Protocol in the New Products Process

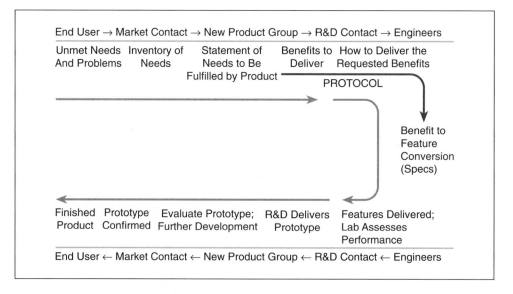

areas.[7] In fact, QFD has been credited with a major contribution to the U.S. auto-mobile industry's comeback against Japanese competition. We present it here, as it is one way in which many firms have fostered the kind of cross-functional in-teraction mandated by the product protocol. QFD has also been successfully used earlier in the new products process, very early in the fuzzy front end in concept generation, because it can help the new products team think of novel new concepts that will satisfy customer needs.[8]

In theory, QFD is designed to ensure that customer needs are focused on, all through the new product project: product engineering, parts deployment, process planning, and production. In practice, the first step of QFD has received the most attention and has been useful to the largest number of firms, and that is the so-called **house of quality (HOQ).** The value of the HOQ to firms is in the way it summarizes multiple product aspects simultaneously and in relationship to each other. Figure 12.6 shows a sample HOQ for the development of a new computer printer.

The HOQ requires inputs from marketing and technical personnel and encour-ages communication and cooperation across these functional areas. Down the left-hand side of the figure appear the *customer attributes* (CAs), variously called needs, whats, or requirements. This is a critical marketing input into the HOQ. Compat-ibility, print quality, ease of use, and productivity were identified in this case as the most important CAs for a printer. CAs are identified through market research: focus groups, interviews, and the like. This section of the HOQ corresponds to the part of protocol relating to what the end user will get from the product. It is usually filled with benefits, though occasionally (as above), features or functions (functional benefits) are so mandatory that they are put there. The CAs in this ex-ample seem to be primary attributes; in a more complex application there may be secondary or even tertiary attributes under each. For example, ease of use might include "easy to learn how to operate," "easy to connect," "easy to replace the paper," and so on. CAs are also frequently weighted in terms of importance.

At the far right of the HOQ are the ratings of the proposed new product and its main competitors on each of the CAs, where 0 = "poor" and 5 = "excellent." This section can be interpreted much like a snake plot of customer perceptions, as we have previously seen in Chapter 6, and identifies the strong points and areas for improvement of our new product.

The upper section of the HOQ shows *engineering characteristics* (ECs): edge sharpness, resolution, and so on. ECs are often technologies, but can also be stated

[7]John R. Hauser and Don Clausing, "The House of Quality," *Harvard Business Review,* 66(3), 1988, pp. 63–73; Abbie Griffin and John R. Hauser, "Patterns of Communication among Marketing, Engineering and Manufacturing: A Comparison between Two Product Teams," *Management Science,* 38(3), March 1992, pp. 360–373; and Abbie Griffin, "Evaluating QFD's Use in U.S. Firms as a Process for Developing Products," *Journal of Product Innovation Management,* 9(3), September 1992, pp. 171–187. For more information on QFD, try the Web site for the QFD Institute, www.qfdi.org.
[8]Gerald M. Katz, "Practitioner Note: A Response to Pullman, *et al.*'s (2002) Comparison of Quality Function Deployment versus Conjoint Analysis," *Journal of Product Innovation Management,* 21(1), 2004, pp. 61–63.

FIGURE 12.6
QFD and
Its House of
Quality

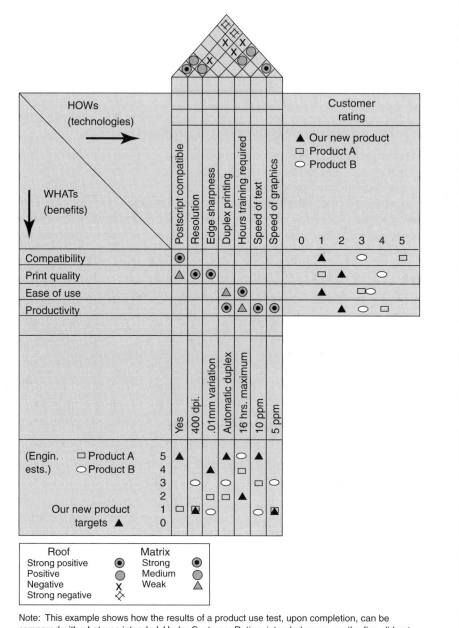

Note: This example shows how the results of a product use test, upon completion, can be compared with what was intended. Under Customer Rating, intended users say the firm did not achieve its objectives.

in terms of performance or design parameters. This is where the customer's needs are translated into technical specifications. The project team goes through the central grid of the HOQ, identifying those ECs that will affect one or more CAs either positively or negatively. In this case, "hours of training required" is positively related to both ease of use (strongly) and productivity (less strongly); "Speed of text" is strongly related to productivity. Obviously, this step requires real cooperation between marketing and technical personnel. Objective measures are then set for each EC (usually by engineers), and the team can now begin setting target values for the ECs based on customer need and competitive offerings. For example, speed of text can be objectively measured in pages per minute (ppm); and in this case, 10 ppm was set as the objective.

In the automobile example earlier of fast pickup speed, one CA might be "teenage pride among peers." Related ECs might be a new engine (a technology), the 0–60 time (a performance parameter), or a weight switch putting more load at the point of drive-wheel contact (a design parameter). Practice varies such that we can't give instruction here, but there are other sources.[9]

Finally, the top part of the house (the peaked "roof") shows the tradeoffs between ECs that the technical personnel must consider. Each diamond in the roof represents the interaction between a pair of ECs, and the technical staff must identify each significant interaction. The "strong negative" crosshatch (pound sign) at the crossing of "resolution" and "speed of graphics," for example, indicates that if the printer's resolution quality is boosted, it is likely to slow down speed of graphics printing. Some of these interactions are positive: A single design change may boost both speed of text printing and of graphics printing.[10]

As noted above, the HOQ is really only the first part of the full QFD procedure. Figure 12.7 shows what comes next. The HOQ, which translates CAs into ECs, is linked to a parts deployment house, which takes the ECs as inputs and converts them into parts characteristics. Subsequent houses specify the key process operations and production requirements. Nevertheless, experienced QFD practitioners will often find that 80 percent of the value of QFD can be obtained in the first HOQ matrix; consequently, few QFD projects go all the way through the process.[11]

In a very simple illustrative example, suppose we had decided on the concept of extra-hot, thick, green salsa on the basis of our conjoint analysis in Chapter 7.

---

[9]See Hauser and Clausing, "The House of Quality," for a general introduction. For applications, see John R. Hauser, "Puritan-Bennett, The Renaissance Spirometry System: Listening to the Voice of the Customer," *Sloan Management Review* 34, 1993, pp. 61–70; and Milton D. Rosenau and John J. Moran, *Managing the Development of New Products* (New York: Van Nostrand Reinhold, 1993), pp. 225–237.

[10]In a real-life application (iron ore products), increasing a metal's hardness reduces its malleability (how easily it can be formed into shapes). See Magnus Tottie and Thomas Lager, "QFD: Linking the Customer to the Product Development Process as a Part of the TQM Concept," *Research-Technology Management,* July 1995, pp. 257–267.

[11]Gerald M. Katz, "Quality Function Deployment and the House of Quality," in A. Griffin and S. M. Sommermeyer, *The PDMA Toolbook 3 for New Product Development* (New York: John Wiley, 2007), Ch. 7.

FIGURE 12.7
Later Stages
of QFD

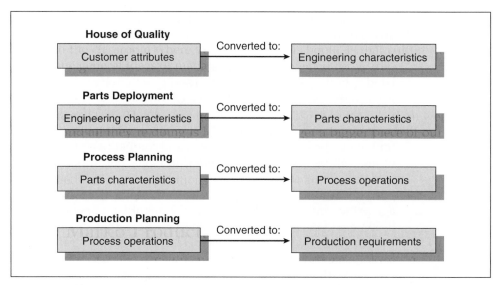

House of Quality

Customer attributes   → Converted to: → Engineering characteristics

Parts Deployment

Engineering characteristics   → Converted to: → Parts characteristics

Process Planning

Parts characteristics   → Converted to: → Process operations

Production Planning

Process operations   → Converted to: → Production requirements

The CA of extra-hot might be translated to an EC such as hotness on a 10-point scale (a kind of simplified Scoville pepper scale) where habaneros, the hottest peppers, are rated 10. We might aim at no more than 7 or 8 on this scale (as only the most daring would want salsa to be hotter!). Thickness could be translated into a viscosity measure, and we might aim at a score of between 4 and 6 on a 10-point thickness scale (where 7 and higher would be too thick, and 3 and lower would not be thick enough). The ECs in turn suggest which parts—or, in this case, ingredients—to use: which types of hot chile peppers, how much tomato and garlic, and so on. Process requirements might specify what kind of food processing (chopping, boiling, etc.) will be involved. Related production requirements would be the settings of the food processing equipment that give the desired consistency and appearance. Using the puree setting on the chopper might make the salsa too runny.

Outcomes of QFD

There are several benefits of applying QFD. For one thing, everything—from product engineering to designing the production process—is driven by customer needs (or, more specifically, by the stated customer attributes). The likelihood that the product about to be developed is one of those better mousetraps that doesn't have a market is minimized. Furthermore, to get the benefits out of QFD, the various functional areas really do have to work together. This is especially an issue in the development of some industrial products. While consumer-good firms may routinely collect the market data used in the HOQ, industrial product developers often question why they need to do customer needs assessment (or even talk to the folks in marketing)—after all, they say they know the market! QFD has been useful in such firms in promoting dialogue between disparate groups and in encouraging product developers with technical backgrounds to see the advantages of assessing customer needs. In sum, QFD encourages cross-functional dialogue and interaction throughout the technical development process—which is precisely the kind of agreement called for by the product protocol.

When QFD was first used extensively in the United States, mixed but generally favorable results were reported. Over 80 percent of teams using QFD reported a long-term strategic benefit and an improvement in cross-functional teaming.[12] A more recent survey of QFD use in the United States and Japan finds firms in both countries having success with QFD, but in somewhat different ways. U.S. firms tend to concentrate on the HOQ matrix and collect new primary data from their customers (for example, through focus groups). Japanese firms use more of the downstream matrices and rely more on existing product data (such as complaint information and warranty data). Interestingly, U.S. firms report greater benefits in cross-functional integration and decision making through QFD than do Japanese firms, possibly because the U.S. firms had the most to learn about listening to customer needs![13]

QFD has had only mixed results in some applications. It's expressive, in both cost and employee time, due to the extensive data collection at the VOC phase. It probably is best suited to major projects such as new platform development or major process reengineering.[14]

Use of QFD by firms tends to be related to better financial performance and greater customer satisfaction. Many firms, however, use it occasionally rather than consistently, and especially for exploratory products (that is, one that will be dropped unless a customer will support it). Besides, the data requirements can be overwhelming. The term *matrix hell* has been used to describe its application, and highly trained technical personnel may not be able to resolve conflicts that arise. In some cases, the customer firm may not know what it wants, so specifying the "whats" can be difficult. Nevertheless, QFD has been experiencing a resurgence lately, probably because it is viewed as one of the most thorough and objective ways to translate customer needs to engineering specifications.[15] Its proponents say it is the best way to uncover customer wants and boost cross-functionality, while its detractors call it overly lengthy and boring, leading some participants to wonder why they are doing it.[16] In general, the better the team, the more efficient

[12]Abbie Griffin, "Evaluating Development Processes, QFD as an Example," *Marketing Science Institute,* Report No. 91–121, August 1991.
[13]John J. Cristiano, Jeffrey K. Liker, and Chelsea C. White III, "Customer-Driven Product Development through Quality Function Deployment in the U.S. and Japan," *Journal of Product Innovation Management,* 17(4), July 2000, pp. 286–308.
[14]Gerald M. Katz, "Quality Function Deployment and the House of Quality," in A. Griffin and S. M. Somermeyer, *The PDMA Toolbook 3 for New Product Development* (New York: John Wiley, 2007), Ch. 7.
[15]Gerald M. Katz, "Is QFD Making a Comeback?" *Visions,* 27(2), April 2003.
[16]Gerald M. Katz, "Quality Function Deployment and the House of Quality," op. cit.

FIGURE 12.8
Criteria for
Good Team
Selection

Make sure the team is cross-functional. This means design, manufacturing, R&D, marketing, finance, technical support, and anyone else that might have a stake in the success of the product.

Appoint an administrator and an advocate for the Voice of the Customer. One person should be well-informed on all customer details, and able to explain exactly what customers mean when they express their needs.

Team members should have ultimate responsibility to act on the results. If key line managers are on the team, it eliminates the need to convince them of the correctness of the analysis and the need to act.

Other criteria: Team members should have knowledge of current practice and also a historical perspective; team members should be respected by their peers; include some top-level executives; include people from a range of levels within the firm; don't shy away from those who will try some "creative abrasion" to stretch team thinking (but keep the disrupters off the team).

Source: From Gerald M. Katz, "Quality Function Development and the House of Quality," in A. Griffin and S. M. Somermeyer, *The PDMA Toolbook 3 for New Product Development,* John Wiley & Sons, Inc., 2007, Chapter 7. Reprinted with permission of John Wiley & Sons, Inc.

the QFD; Figure 12.8 provides some guidelines in team selection. The efficiency of QFD can also be improved by doing one or more of the following:

- Concentrate on only some of the engineering characteristics: either the apparently most critical ones or some others where improvements might be easy to accomplish.
- Organize the engineering characteristics into groups and designate responsibility for these to specific functional areas (i.e., manufacturing, product design, even marketing).
- Do a cost-benefit analysis on each engineering characteristic to identify which ones provide the greatest benefit relative to associated cost of improvement on that characteristic.[17]

Some Warnings about the Difficulty of the Protocol Process

The protocol process is very complicated. For one thing, it is fraught with politics. The departments are all in natural competition for power and budget. Key individuals are as different as night and day, being scientist, marketer, accountant, and factory manager. The situation itself is fluid and changing, seemingly never nailed down. Management senses the importance of the various projects and puts heavy pressure on them. A big winner on the product frontier can make a career, exonerate a general manager's other disappointments, award very large bonuses; and of course, a major failure can make a mess of everything close to it.

[17]For good practical discussions of QFD, see Gerald M. Katz, "Is QFD Making a Comeback?" *Visions,* October 2001; Gerald M. Katz, "After QFD: Now What?" *Visions,* 25(2), April 2001, pp. 22–24; and Carey C. Curtis and Lynn W. Ellis, "Satisfying Customers while Speeding R&D and Staying Profitable," *Research-Technology Management,* September–October 1998, pp. 23–27. For a perspective on how to overcome QFD difficulties, see Rick W. Purcell, "Should the IV House Be a Duplex?" *Visions,* 27(2), April 2003.

FIGURE 12.9
Protocol
Accomplish-
ment

Requirement	Company Call	Customer Call
1. Reduce setup time	OK	OK
2. Lower initial cost	OK	Not needed
3. Easier replacement during manufacturing process	OK	OK
4. Safety in customer's plan	Doubtful	Later
5. Easier federal approval on finished item	?	Not needed
6. Lower cost disposal of trim	Vendor	Later
Date:		

Explanation: A form such as this, listing all protocol requirements, can serve as a good exercise for the team: How are we going to measure each of the requirements? Must we go outside? When do we do all this? Is a judgment call enough or do we need data?

This means that people have their own agenda for incorporating into a protocol (or not incorporating into it). Most want the other people nailed down to specific accomplishment requirements with dollar signs and dates clearly attached, but with no such promises from themselves.

Given that a protocol is needed early on, just prior to broadscale work being started, many people are not yet on the scene. They have more pressing, near-term problems, so they delay the process or weaken it by their absence.

But, beyond the politics and pressures, we also see a hardening of the requirements in a protocol. People think they were all wise when developing the document and presume the contents are all set in concrete. But it shouldn't be seen that way. It is an *aid to management,* not a *substitute for thinking.* All protocols have to change, some of them many times. But the burden of proof is on those who want to change a requirement.

Ironically, in some situations the protocol is ignored, so a smart new products team manager will prepare something like the protocol accomplishment form shown in Figure 12.9. It is needed, especially, for product requirements (such as customer benefits), and there should be agreement in advance about who is going to make the call on each. Some can be made by the team, but others must be made by the person the product is being made for.

Along the way, bureaucracy sneaks in. One leading computer firm recently made a presentation on product requirements that must have contained at least 25 acronyms; that presentation sounded as if it was right out of government.

Last, most of these problems go away if preparation of a protocol is assigned to a multifunctional new products team. Technical doesn't write one, and neither does marketing. Most assuredly, top management does not write one.

Summary

This chapter has dealt with a powerful concept—protocol. As an agreement among the functions about the required output or deliverables from a specific new product program, it sets the standards for it. The purpose is to communicate the required outputs as product benefits and other dimensions, integrate the team onto the same frequency, make clear the timing importance, and make it easier to manage the process against specific targets.

You saw a simplified version of a typical protocol. At this time we are ready to blow the whistle and charge into the development activity. As seen in the new products process of Chapter 1, action will now take place in marketing and technical in parallel, so we are going to need excellent communication among marketing, R&D, production, design, and other functional areas to get us through the next phase.

Applications

1. "Let's cut right to the quick on this one. I understand the theory of having benefits rather than features, but to me it is just that, theory. I knew one of the top people at that computer company your book talked about—the one where a corporate new product engineering group spelled out the specifications of each new product before technical work was funded. I heard the same criticism your author did, so I called this woman and asked her about it. She said the facts were right, but the implication was wrong—corporate staff did indeed spell out most of the features, but only to get the project moving. She said if they just gave their research people the benefits or needs of the customer, those dreamers would never reach a prototype. Every item would be a Taj Mahal. You know, I think she had a point. What do you think?"

2. "I really don't think you understand what parallel or concurrent new product development is all about. You said you had studied in your course that all of the functions get involved. No, concurrent development means just that—*technical development phases*—design engineering, etc. They are all doing work very much alike, they work with each other, they can feel how things are going and when they can take a chance and make a premature commitment. Marketing people can't do that. Even production people (process engineering) have trouble on this score."

3. "I heard a funny one two weeks ago that might interest you. Seems one of our R&D people went to a new products management seminar and heard about a thing called the protocol. They told him it was the device whereby the overall manager of new products communicated to R&D exactly what was wanted from the technical group. R&D even had to 'sign on the dotted line,' swearing that they thought it could be done. He was really steamed—said no one could tell R&D what they should come up with, not in advance, anyway. And R&D is responsible only to top management, not new products managers, so they don't have to promise anything. He said he considered that concept the most stifling single action imaginable. How would you answer that scientist, or would you?"

Case: WiLife, Inc. (B)[18]

Think back to the WiLife case (A) at the end of Chapter 10. The clock has rolled forward a few months, the full screen has now been conducted, and the inexpensive digital video surveillance product concept has passed easily. Evan and Andrew are

[18]See WiLife Inc. (A) for list of references.

very excited about the prospects so far. They have even come up with a name for the new product: LukWerks, pronounced "look works."

Here is what is known so far on the technical side. The digital technology is definitely there, and it works. It is possible to make a video camera that can be used for motion detection; in fact, it is possible to put the software required for motion detection, digitization, and data compression right into the camera itself. The data can be transported to any regular PC via Ethernet, thus eliminating the need for a dedicated computer for surveillance purposes as well as the need to drill holes in the walls and feed new wires through them. The user can download LukWerks software on his or her regular computer, and video images would be stored there.

The camera described above could be built relatively easily and could safely be used indoors. A few additional kinks would have to be ironed out to make an outdoor version (as noted before, protection against the elements and infrared capability for nighttime use become concerns for the external camera). These are not insurmountable, but would require additional technology and possibly some additional development time.

Finally, there is the issue of price. At the current time, Evan and Andrew think the product they have in mind, if commercialized, could be brought to market at a retail price of about $300 for one camera plus software. They are exploring the idea of selling add-on cameras for the user who wants multiple cameras, at perhaps about $250 each.

First, think about whether the protocol idea would fit the situation of LukWerks. Then, write five lines of benefits that customers would probably stress if they were interviewed. Decide how you would actually measure whether the benefits were being achieved when LukWerks was used.

Second, refer to the list of contents in a protocol and see if there are any other points that could be added to the benefits you just wrote. There won't be many in a simple situation like this, but there will probably be some. Look especially at the marketing requirements.

Finally, though you are (probably) not in the digital camera video surveillance business, there is enough technical information given in this case for you to try a very basic house of quality. Take each of the customer benefits and try to convert it into an engineering characteristic. As a simple example: The customer wants ease of installation. One possible engineering characteristic would be to eliminate any need for special skill or tools to install the camera. If it could be placed on a table or hung on a wall like a picture, it would require no skill beyond that needed to hang a picture.

FIGURE IV.1
Development

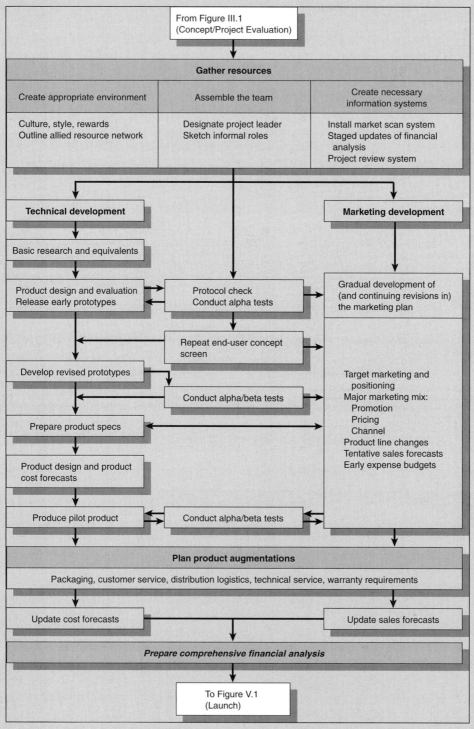

PART FOUR

Development

Somewhere during the preceding process of creation and early evaluation, a decision was made to develop the concept being considered. The decision may have come quickly (a key customer wanted the item and was ready to help develop it) or slowly, after concept testing and extensive review of capital and operational expenditures required. A product protocol was written, and an early financial plan released funds for the development.

The question now is fulfillment of that protocol. There may be extensive technical search (e.g., for a new pharmaceutical) or (as on service products) none. The key problem may be in industrial design or in the very technical characteristics of a 686 or 786 chip. Fulfillment may consist of nothing more than confirming a recipe that was used to produce new cookies for the concept testing. Or, as in the case of Frito-Lay's O'Gradys, two years of technical development may be necessary.

This is a point of high creativity, and there is usually a strong art form, even when dealing in scientific areas. Progress at this point has the attention of managers in all functions. No longer is the technical work isolated between protocol and prototype, as when everyone waited for the classic slot in the R&D door to open and disgorge the finished prototype.

Development today includes creation of everything needed to *market* the product, including funding, distribution, promotion, and technical service. Look at Figure IV.1. The technical work (including design, engineering, and manufacturing) is displayed down the left side of the stream. Testing, marketing, and legal, among others, are displayed on the right. Both continue through the launch.

Several things about that figure may surprise you.

- First, note that what we commonly think is the technical creation task is just one box on a page with 15 boxes in the technical (left-hand) stream. That one box, in practice, is broken down into literally thousands of other boxes. Many firms use a project control system called a Program Evaluation Review Technique (PERT) chart, or network diagram, originally developed for the first nuclear submarine, the Polaris, in the late 1950s. A network diagram uses boxes ("nodes") and connecting lines to indicate the flows of tasks in a project and how they all interrelate. In the automobile industry, a network diagram for just one assembly (e.g., the dashboard) is so complicated that it cannot even be printed out on paper.

- Note, too, the large box at the top of the diagram. Getting ready to do technical development sometimes takes months—finding the people, acquiring the rights to certain materials, creating a particular culture, training the team, and, so important today, creating the information system to support the complex of activities.

- Typically there is not just one prototype. Sometimes there will be dozens or even hundreds, depending on how lucky the team is. Granted, a new Frisbee with an edge shaped to grab a dog's teeth may be real progress for competitors in that sport, but hardly an afternoon's work for the designer. Edison was said to have tried hundreds of materials for the filament in the first electric light bulb.

- Developers must stop frequently to have their work checked—note terms like *evaluation*, *check*, *screen*, *test*, and *clearance*. Generally this is good, because to advance a design with a flaw is wasteful, yet to stop at every possible turn grinds things to a halt, including morale.

- The technical side is a *rolling evolution*. Even when an early prototype looks good, it must evolve into a tested prototype, then into a process, then into a pilot product, then into a production scale-up product, then into a marketed product. This follows the same route as the life cycle of a concept that was diagrammed and explained in Chapter 2 on process. We don't really *develop* a thing so much as we *evolve* one. There are fewer "eureka moments" than people think. It's hard work, step by step.

- Note, too, how items on the right-hand stream associate with items on the left-hand. Thus, producing a prototype may start design on a package; producing a scale-up product stimulates start on a technical customer service activity; producing a marketable product means a distribution network must be in place.

But rather than try to discuss both streams simultaneously, we cover marketing's role in the technical work here in Part IV and marketing's role in the other stream in Part V. Actually, we have been working on the marketing stream from Chapter 3 on—for example, target market is usually known at PIC time and new product positioning statements are used in concept testing.

Thus Chapter 13 talks about the players involved, the essence of design, and productivity in the development process. Chapter 14 covers the creation and management of today's cross-functional teams, and Chapter 15 tells how the team finds whether the latest prototype is indeed, ready to launch—a subject we will take up, in Part V of the book.

Before we get too far, let's be sure we know just what marketing's role is in the work that takes place on the technical side. There are nine important dimensions.

1. To make absolutely clear to everyone what the protocol calls for. What is the end point? How can technical groups know when they are finished?

2. To make sure that this protocol task is technically feasible and doable within the time and dollars imposed by the development budget. That is, do all technical people agree?

3. To provide an open window for industrial and systems designers to all influential forces in the marketplace. Marketing should not be a gatekeeper, but rather an enthusiastic tour guide. It is truly in their best interests, and in the firm's as well, that all development effort (technical and marketing) be based on market knowledge.

4. To provide a continuous interim of opportunity to pretest various versions of the new product. This means to cooperate in early in-house testing and in later customer use testing.

5. To be available to technical people at all reasonable times. Some marketing people seem to forget that technical work is going on. A common joke in the labs is the scientist who left for lunch with the request to an aide: "If my product manager calls, get their name."

6. To stay informed about technical progress via team meetings, lab visits, social contacts, and so forth. This is not spying. It is seeking an opportunity to pass along some market information technical people didn't know about. Well-led teams today soften this problem, but marketers have to learn how to be good team members.

7. To involve technical people in the decision making on the marketing side of the development stream—especially any changes in the givens at the start of development, target market for example. Again, teams help, but just as marketers can get distracted, so can technical people. We have to show them why we need their input on matters they may not feel are as important as the technical ones they are busy on.

8. To stay continuously alert to the project's progress and to be creative in finding ways to help. For example, in Chapter 14 you will see the benefits of cross-functional teams, one of which is to speed up a new product's development. Saving a day in marketing may be as good as saving a day in technical.

9. To flag the various ways that work in nonmarketing departments impacts marketing plans directly. This action, often called *internal marketing*, involves technical departments (for example, technical information for sales

brochures), manufacturing (for example, cost reductions and stand-by production capability), packaging (for example, promotion claims made on front panel), and human resources (for example, selection of new personnel needed in the launch effort).

It is the purpose of the material in Part IV to help you perform those roles, but be aware—the technical side of the development stream is immensely more complicated than most outsiders realize. Don't take the roles lightly.

CHAPTER THIRTEEN

Design

Setting

Part IV of this book explores all aspects of the development phase, which encompasses product design, product architecture and prototype development, and product use testing, as well as organizational and team management issues. Here in Chapter 13, we examine just what this development phase means to different companies, and we introduce design and its use as a strategic resource. We also examine the role of the product designer and the interface between design and other functions involved in the new products process.

As consumers, we have all been frustrated by poorly designed products and wonder how they ever got to market:

- Too-bulky or underpowered vacuum cleaners.
- Cereal boxes with protective packaging that rips when first opened and thus no longer protects.
- Oddly shaped spatulas that are useless for flipping pancakes.
- Unclear labeling on a self-serve pump.
- A combination CD-tape player, with the tape controls located near the CD drive and the CD controls near the tape drive.

Yet we recognize and appreciate outstanding designs—a new car, revolutionary office furniture, or even a universal screwdriver that really works—and reward the product manufacturers. The design and appearance of the Apple iPod certainly adds to its appeal; likewise James Dyson's vacuum cleaner. In a day and age of "don't sweat the small things," it may be those very small things that determine brand preferences and that the manufacturers should focus on![1]

What Is Design?

There is no doubt that top management also sees the importance of design and can use it as a tool in boosting competitiveness. In half of the companies surveyed in a

---

[1]Laurence P. Feldman, "But Have You Tried the Product?" *Visions*, October 1999. The examples are from this article, as well as Laurence P. Feldman, "Is Your Product 'Utility Challenged'?" *Visions*, April 2000, and from the Bad Designs Web site, www.baddesigns.com. This site features dozens of poorly or oddly designed products and includes ideas on how the design could have been easily improved.

recent study, the CEO had primary responsibility for design decisions![2] Excellence in design also benefits the bottom line. Firms that are judged to be higher in design effectiveness outperform other firms in return on sales and assets, net incomes, and cash flow, as well as higher stock market returns.[3]

But what is design? One writer defines it as "the synthesis of technology and human needs into manufacturable products."[4] In practice, however, *design* as a term has many uses. To the car companies, it can mean the styling department. To a container company it means their customer's packaging people. To a manufacturing department it most likely means the engineers who set final product specifications. According to product design expert Roberto Verganti, "Design introduces a bold new way of competing. Design-driven innovations do not come from the market; they create new markets. They don't push new technologies, they push new meanings. Customers had not asked for these new meanings, but once they experienced them, it was love at first sight."[5]

In any case, design should not be considered an afterthought where industrial designers are asked to pretty up a product that is about ready to be manufactured. The following section explores how firms in several industries have successfully used design to achieve key new product objectives.

The Role of Design in the New Products Process[6]

Interestingly, design's potential role in the new products process is sometimes underestimated. This may be because of a lack of understanding or appreciation of designers, design management, and the design function on the part of managers from other functional areas. Designers undergo rigorous training to learn how to design products that function well mechanically, that are durable, that are easy and safe to use, that can be made from easily available materials, and that look appealing. Clearly, many of these requirements will be in conflict, and it is up to the skillful designer to achieve all of them simultaneously.

---

[2]Peter Dickson, Wendy Schneier, Peter Lawrence, and Renee Hytry, "Managing Design in Small High-Growth Companies," *Journal of Product Innovation Management*, 12(5), pp. 406–414.

[3]Julie H. Hertenstein, Marjorie B. Platt, and Robert W. Veryzer, "The Impact of Industrial Design Effectiveness on Corporate Financial Performance," *Journal of Product Innovation Management*, 22(1), January 2005, pp. 3–21.

[4]See Michael Evamy, "Call Yourself a Designer?" *Design*, March 1994, pp. 14–16. This article was part of a series in this publication, all on the matter of design definition. Useful also is Karl T. Ulrich and Steven D. Eppinger, *Product Design and Development* (New York: McGraw-Hill, 1995).

[5]Roberto Verganti, *Design-Driven Innovation: Changing the Rules of Competition by Radically Innovating What Things Mean* (Cambridge, MA: Harvard Business School Press, 2009).

[6]Much of this section is drawn from Jeneanne Marshall, "Design as a Strategic Resource: A Business Perspective," Design Leadership Program, Corporate Design Foundation, 1991; and Eric M. Olson, Rachel Cooper, and Stanley F. Slater, "Design Strategy and Competitive Advantage," *Business Horizons*, 41(2), March–April 1998, pp. 55–61. For a good view of "hot topics" among design practitioners, read the periodic newsletter *@Issue*. Current and back issues are available online on the Web site for the Corporate Design Foundation, www.cdf.org.

FIGURE 13.1
Contributions
of Design
to the New
Products
Process

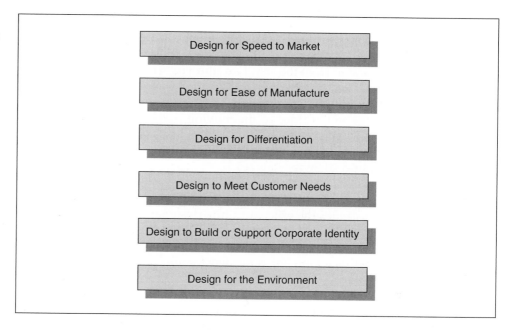

Design for Speed to Market

Design for Ease of Manufacture

Design for Differentiation

Design to Meet Customer Needs

Design to Build or Support Corporate Identity

Design for the Environment

Contributions of Design to New Product Goals

As proof of the importance of design, consider several ways in which design excellence can help firms achieve a broad spectrum of new product goals, as shown in Figure 13.1.

Design for Speed to Market

Ingersoll-Rand developed its Cyclone Grinder (an air-grinder power tool) in record time, thanks to an efficient cross-functional team and excellence in design. The team (composed of marketing, manufacturing, and engineering personnel) worked closely with Group Four Design to identify customer needs. Users of traditional grinders often complained that they were difficult to hold, and that their hands would freeze (the unit became cold during use). The new grinder was ergonomically shaped (better shaped for the human body meaning, in this case, easier to hold), lighter, and made of a new composite material that was both more durable and more comfortable to hold (since it conducted less thermal energy and thus did not get cold). Furthermore, the one-piece housing design was a cost improvement over the previous version, which required assembly of seven different components.

Design for Ease of Manufacture

A classic example here concerns IBM's development of its Proprinter dot-matrix printer in the mid-1980s. At the time, the Japanese owned the worldwide market for low-end printers. It was felt, however, that the competition was vulnerable: Their printers were not well designed, and in particular had hundreds of parts including dozens of rivets and fasteners. IBM set a performance target of

200 near-letter-quality characters per second (not the current standard, but the expected standard four years into the future) and had a motto of "no fasteners": Everything had to snap together easily. Furthermore, the development time had to be compressed from the standard four years to two-and-a-half years. All of the above was achieved: The original Proprinter had only 61 parts and could be assembled in three minutes. Similarly, Swatch watches are designed for ease of manufacture, having about a third of the moving parts of a traditional Swiss watch, a plastic casing without a removable back, a plastic strap incorporated into the casing, and many other design features. Swatch watches retail at a small fraction of the price of traditional Swiss watches.

Design for Differentiation

Haworth Inc., the office furniture designer, employs an Ideation Group, responsible for exploring and assessing customer acceptance of speculative products (high-risk products without a clear-cut market). Haworth believes that "nonstandard" product development is needed for speculative products. Few of the prototypes developed by Ideation may make it to the marketplace, and those that do (like the Crossings furniture line) may end up looking quite different. Good ideas from the Ideation Group can make their way into existing lines or other future products, and more importantly, Haworth has successfully differentiated its product offerings as being more original in design. Incidentally, excellence in design seems to be important in the office furniture industry: Steelcase Inc. is a majority owner of IDEO, the design firm we have met more than once in earlier chapters.[7]

Design to Meet Customer Needs

Deep understanding of customer needs is required in order for the firm to translate a high-potential technology into a product that provides meaningful benefits to the customer. Collaboration with end users (seen in Chapter 4) and capturing the voice of the customer (Chapter 12) are important ways to get this depth of understanding, now sometimes referred to as **user-oriented design**.[8]

The voice of the customer was extensively used in the design of the Infiniti QX4 sport utility vehicle. In fact, marketing director Steve Kight said at the time that "the QX4 was designed expressly for [our customers]." Interviews and surveys of Infiniti drivers in Westchester County, New York, revealed their preferences in an SUV: handles like a car, easy to get into, priced below $40,000. Infiniti drivers and nondrivers within the target market (35–64 years old, over $125,000 household income, willing to purchase a luxury car) were presented with five different designs. The best of these was molded into clay and fiberglass models with the additional input of dealers. Finally, the SUV was supported with a strong promotional

[7]Janis R. Evink and Henry H. Beam, "Just What Is an Ideation Group?" *Business Horizons,* January–February 1999, pp. 7–77; Bruce Nussbaum, "The Power of Design," www.businessweek.com, May 17, 2004.
[8]Robert W. Veryzer and Brigitte Borja de Mozota, "The Impact of User-Oriented Design on New Product Development: An Examination of Fundamental Relationships," *Journal of Product Innovation Management,* 22(2), March 2005, pp. 128–143.

campaign, advertising heavily in magazines such as *Smart Money*. As a result, sales far exceeded expectations.[9]

Crown Equipment Corporation, a manufacturer of forklift trucks, developed its RC (Rider Counterbalance) lift truck and launched it in 2008. An age-old problem expressed by forklift truck drivers is their inability to see clearly in front, especially if they have pallets raised on the forks. In some cases, a second person would be required to guide the driver, whose sight line was obstructed by the load carried at the front of the truck. Using an ingenious counterbalance system, the RC's forks are located to the side so as to remove the driver's obstruction. Additionally, the RC had extra design elements that addressed other common user complaints and appealed to the driver: a much larger than average operator compartment, a desk-top area allowing the driver to keep papers and tools nearby, a newly designed shock absorption system that smoothed the ride, and a stylish and ergonomic appearance. The RC significantly grew Crown Equipment's market share and also won several design awards.[10]

Universal design is the term sometimes used to mean the design of products to be usable by anyone regardless of age or ability. Principles of universal design can be used to develop products for new markets based on unmet customer needs. The designer considers the abilities of real people in real-world settings when applying universal design principles. For example, some people are visually impaired, while others have temporary vision problems due to eye fatigue, recovery from surgery, or even poor lighting. Phones with extra-large buttons address permanent or temporary vision problems and can be used by anyone. Closed-captioned television, automatic garage-door openers, and automatically opening doors to grocery stores also exemplify universal design. Figure 13.2 illustrates the principles of universal design.

Design to Build or Support Corporate Identity

Many firms have established *visual equity* across the products they sell: a recognizable look or feel that they use consistently. Product design can thus help build or support public perception of the firm and, ultimately, its corporate identity. Apple computers and other devices have always been designed to look user-friendly. Rolex watches all have a classic, high-prestige appearance, and Braun appliances have lines and colors that convey simplicity and quality.[11] Nokia phones share common design elements that make them unique, yet at the same time familiar. The company calls these commonalities "Nokia DNA." Radically designed new BMW models, such as the Z4, still share familiar design attributes with classic BMWs of years ago, such as the distinctive grille.[12]

---

[9]Constance Gustke, "Built to Last," *Sales and Marketing Management,* August 1997, pp. 78–83.

[10]Bruce Nussbaum, "The Best Global Design of 2008," *Business Week,* July 17, 2008; also see the firm's Web page, www.crown.com.

[11]Karl T. Ulrich and Steven D. Eppinger, *Product Design and Development,* 2nd ed. (Burr Ridge, IL: Irwin/McGraw-Hill, 2000), p. 219.

[12]Anonymous, "Online Extra: A Chat with Nokia's Alastair Curtis," www.businessweek.com, July 17, 2006.

FIGURE 13.2   Principles of Universal Design

Principle	Examples
Equitable Use: The design is useful to people with varied abilities.	Pay phones in public places with adjustable volume levels Powered doors to grocery stores are convenient to disabled shoppers and also people pushing carts, strollers, etc.
Flexibility in Use: The design accommodates a variety of preferences and abilities.	Phones with large buttons Scissors or knives that work left- or right-handed
Simple and Intuitive to Use: The design is easy for anyone to understand and use.	Color-coded labels on cough medicine Ikea furniture building instructions use illustrations and minimal text to avoid language barriers Newer DVD and DVR players are easier and more intuitive to program with on-screen commands
Perceptible Information: The design communicates the required information effectively to the user.	Plugs and jacks connecting DVD players and other electronic gadgets to televisions are color-coded Honeywell thermostats show numerical settings and also use audible click-stops when the dial is turned
Tolerance for Error: The design minimizes adverse consequences of inappropriate use.	Irons or coffeemakers that shut off if not used for five minutes Lawnmower handle that requires the user to squeeze a lever against the handle to keep the lawnmower running
Low Physical Effort: The design can be used efficiently by anyone with minimal fatigue.	Rollers and handles on luggage Angled computer keyboard easier for operator to use
Size and Space for Approach and Use: Regardless of the user's size or mobility, the product is easy to reach, manipulate, and use.	Whirlpool side-by-side refrigerator-freezers with full-length handles Copco chopping knife's handle is designed to be comfortably held in hands of any size Wide car door opening makes it easier for someone with a walker or wheelchair to get in or out

Source: From James L. Mueller and Molly Follette Story, "Universal Design: Principles for Driving Growth into New Markets," in P. Belliveau, A. Griffin, and S. Sodermeyer (Eds.), *The PDMA Toolbook for New Product Development,* John Wiley & Sons, Inc., 2002, pp. 297–326. Reprinted with permission of John Wiley & Sons, Inc.

Design for the Environment

Design for disassembly is the technique by which products can be taken apart after use for separate recycling of metal, glass, and plastic parts. Among other carmakers, BMW has designed disassembly and recycling into its cars. Used plastic parts are sorted, recycled, and made into new parts. Other components are either recycled or rebuilt, while unusable parts are incinerated to create energy.[13]

In fact, *green design* is now a driving force within many firms. The carmaker Subaru provides an example. Thomas Easterday, senior vice president, Subaru

---

[13]Jacquelyn A. Ottman, *Green Marketing: Challenges and Opportunities for the New Marketing Age* (Lincolnwood, IL: NTC Business Books, 1993), p. 119.

FIGURE 13.3
Range of
Leading
Design
Applications

Purpose of Design	Item Being Designed
Aesthetics	Goods
Ergonomics	Services
Function	Architecture
Manufacturability	Graphic arts
Servicing	Offices
Disassembly	Packages

Comment: Design is a big term, covering many areas of human activity, especially new products. The new products field contributes to two classes of items and to all six classes of purpose. Some people hold that even the other four classes of items are really products to the organizations producing them.

of Indiana, says that Subaru has "embraced the concepts of reduce, reuse, and recycle." He claims that Subaru has achieved zero landfill status and has attained a recycling rate of 99.8 percent (the remainder is hazardous waste that must be incinerated due to EPA regulations). Subaru works with suppliers so that they use recyclable packaging and with local companies responsible for collecting and recycling materials; the carmaker also finds markets for recycled materials. More recycling leads to less waste, and cost savings, at Subaru.[14] Apple also makes several green claims for the iPad on its Web site, noting that the display is mercury-free, there is no PVC plastic used, and the aluminum-and-glass enclosure is recyclable.[15]

Figure 13.3 shows a variety of design dimensions, using only the two criteria of Purpose of Design and Item Being Designed. Design is not just a field in which artists draw pictures of new microwaves. It blends form and function, quality and style, art and engineering. In short, a good design is aesthetically pleasing, easy to make correctly, reliable, easy to use, economical to operate and service, and in line with recycling standards. **Ergonomics** are also an important consideration; this can be defined as studying human characteristics in order to develop appropriate designs.[16] Many of the poorly designed products mentioned at the start of this chapter might have been improved with better attention to ergonomics. An excellent design can play a big role in determining how well a new product will meet the needs of customers, as well as retailers and other stakeholders, and therefore is an important determinant of success.

Consider one innovatively designed product: the Cross Action toothbrush by Gillette's Oral-B division. Researchers videotaped people using toothbrushes to determine actual brushing patterns, then built a robot arm to simulate brushing action. High-speed video cameras and computer imaging were used to test several

[14]Mary G. Wojtas, "32nd PDMA International Conference Delivers Expert Insights, Knowledge, and Tools to Enhance Innovaton Success," *Visions*, Vol. 32, No. 4, December 2008, pp. 22–25.
[15]The specifications are at www.apple.com/ipad/specs.
[16]Karl H. E. Kroemer, "Ergonomics: Definition of Ergonomics," National Safety Commission Web site (www.nsc.org).

different prototypes and to arrive at the bristle configuration that was most effective in cleaning teeth.[17]

The role of the design in a product's ultimate acceptance by customers is easily understood. Consider a new car design. If the new style is not that different from existing cars, customers might find it uninteresting or overly conservative. On the other hand, if the new design looks as if it came from Mars, most customers are likely to find it too revolutionary or even ugly. Given that as much as $2 billion may be invested in a new car design, it seems reasonable for the car companies to spend as much as $1 million on getting just the right balance of style and shape. Focus groups may be used to get initial reactions, then full-size models (or car shapes on a computer screen) may be shown to hundreds of potential buyers. Despite careful research, however, misleading results may be obtained: Customers often don't really know what they want as far as style is concerned.[18]

Product Architecture[19]

Product architecture has been described as the process by which a customer need is developed into a product design. This is a critical step in moving toward a product design, as solid architecture improves ultimate product performance, reduces the cost of changing the product once it is in production, and can speed the product to market.

To understand architecture development, consider that a product contains *components* (a portable CD player-recorder has a chassis, motors, disk drive, speakers, and so on) that can be combined into *chunks* (the base, the disk handling system, the recording system, and the sound production system). A product is also composed of *functional elements* (for a CD player, these might include reading disks, recording sound, producing sound, and adjusting sound quality). The product's architecture is how the functional elements are assigned to the chunks and how the chunks are interrelated.

A Process for Product Architecture

A stepwise process for product architecture development can be applied to make sure the product's design will be in keeping with customer needs and, ultimately, the product innovation charter.[20] The process is illustrated in simplified form in Figure 13.4. Careless product architecture results in products such as the CD-tape player mentioned earlier in this chapter. Although each component works perfectly

[17]Mark Maremont, "New Toothbrush Is Big-Ticket Item," *The Wall Street Journal*, October 27, 1998, p. B-1.
[18]Tom Moulson and George Sproles, "Styling Strategy," *Business Horizons*, September–October 2000, pp. 45–52.
[19]Much of this section derives from David Cutherell, "Product Architecture," in M. D. Rosenau, A. Griffin, G. Castellion, and N. Anscheutz (eds.), *The PDMA Handbook of New Product Development* (New York: John Wiley, 1996), pp. 217–235.
[20]The stepwise process described here is based on that of Karl T. Ulrich and Steven D. Eppinger, *Product Design and Development*, 2nd ed. (Homewood, IL: Irwin/McGraw-Hill, 2000), Chapter 9.

FIGURE 13.4
Product
Architecture
Illustration

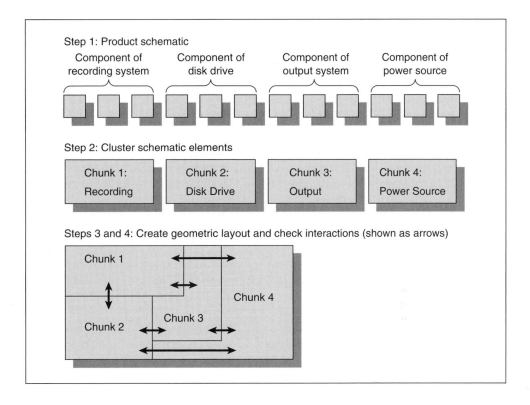

well, the way the pieces are put together makes little sense from the user's perspective, and minor rearrangement might have resulted in an easier-to-use product.

1. *Create the Product Schematic.* The schematic shows the components and functional elements of the product and how they are interconnected. Several alternative schematics may be developed and explored at this point. For the CD player-recorder, one might develop a version designed to plug into a standard stereo system, a stand-alone version with miniature speakers, or another to be used only with headphones. It would contain components connected with the disk drive itself, input (recording) functions, output (playback or speaker) functions, and power supply, among other things.

2. *Cluster the Schematic Elements.* Here, the chunks (or modules) are defined. In the figure, input, disk, output, and power chunks are identified. Interaction among the chunks should be simple so changes can be easily effected, and one should take advantage of manufacturing capabilities wherever possible. If rapid changes are expected in some part of the product, that part should most certainly be made into a chunk. For example, if new disk drive technology is expected to permit 10 times as much content to be recorded and stored on a quarter-sized disk, one should be able to replace the current drive with this new one if desired.

3. *Create Geometric Layout.* Here, using simulations, computer-aided design, or other techniques, the product is arranged in several configurations to

determine the "best" solutions. For example, should the disk load in the front or the side of the CD player? Where should the speakers (if there are any) be located? One possible geometric layout is shown in Figure 13.4.

4. *Check Interactions between Chunks.* Understand what happens at the interfaces between chunks. In the CD player, sound flows as a digital signal to the disk during recording, and also as a digital signal from the disk during playback.

Product Architecture and Product Platforms

Clearly, careful product architecture development is critical to a firm seeking to establish a product platform. As noted in Chapter 3, car manufacturers (with few exceptions) think in terms of designing platforms, not individual products. A successful platform (such as Chrysler's "cab forward" design) can result in a successful car (the Chrysler Concorde), and also lead to several other models in the future (the Eagle Vision and Dodge Intrepid).

If the architecture permits the designers to replace chunks or modules easily, several new products can be designed as technology improves, market tastes change, and manufacturing skill increases. This is how Sony can develop those 200 or so versions of the Walkman on just four basic platforms!

In the Chrysler example, the Vision and Intrepid models are referred to as *derivative products:* These are products based on the same platform as an existing product, but modified incrementally in terms of technology or customer need fulfillment. Depending on how many features are added, the derivative product may cost about the same to manufacture (such as new designs of Swatch watches), or may cost more but offer greater value to the user. Features may also be stripped out to achieve a lower-cost derivative product. Additional cost savings can be incurred by using standardized components across many products. Whatever the case, the key is to be able to make changes to the modules while still operating on the same platform.

Industrial Design and the Industrial Designer[21]

Industrial designers are, above all, creative types: Their job is to take a problem and somehow visualize a solution to it. They are concerned about how things work as well as how things look. Their university training will have included work in aesthetic design, mechanical engineering, materials and processes, and art or drawing. It is this unique set of skills and abilities that determines the special role the product designer plays in the new products process.

Consider this real-life example. An industrial designer was brought in by a leading manufacturer of liquid correction fluid (white fluid brushed over mistakes made when using a typewriter). A user problem was identified: The brushes got dried-out or misshapen, and thus became difficult to use. Some obvious solutions

---

[21]Much of this section derives from Walter Herbst, "How Industrial Design Fits into Product Development," in M. D. Rosenau, A. Griffin, G. Castellion, and N. Ancsheutz (eds.), *The PDMA Handbook of New Product Development* (New York: John Wiley, 1996), pp. 237–251.

might be: Make the bottleneck bigger, or improve the brush applicator. But better product design work results in more creative solutions. To accomplish this, designers can use techniques similar to the general creativity techniques seen in Chapter 5, such as brainstorming. Working together with the marketing and engineering personnel from the product team, the designer can sketch hundreds of thumbnail ideations for review. For the correction fluid, these ideations included sketches of pens holding the white fluid, variations of the pen's tip (including different angles, a spring-loaded version, and so on), different kinds of caps for the pen's tip—even several versions of a dispenser much like a tape dispenser. Instead of using sketches, the ideations can also be computer-generated using software such as Photoshop. The product team assesses each ideation based on appearance and manufacturability and chooses the best ones that are then more fully rendered by the designer.

No one ideation is likely to be the final design concept to be brought to prototype development. The best parts of each ideation are combined into a single design in a step called *design consolidation*. As much detail as possible is fleshed out at this time—including decorative graphics and brand name and logo (if known)—since this is typically one of the last evaluation points before a huge amount of financial and human resources are dedicated to the product. Generally, computer-generated renderings are preferred at this point. Other members of the new product team will provide information to determine if the product is manufacturable and marketable.

Using these procedures, two new correction fluid products were designed and launched. The first put the liquid into a ballpoint-pen-type dispenser which, when squeezed, emitted a smooth flow of correction fluid right on the mistake. The second, which required two years of additional development, was a tape-dispenser that put a strip of dry white tape over the mistake (thus allowing the user to make the correction right away without waiting for liquid to dry).

There are several factors that can be considered by industrial designers when deciding on the appropriateness of a design. These may include quality of user interface, emotional appeal, maintenance and repair, appropriate use of resources, and product differentiation (see Figure 13.5).[22] Emotional appeal could include, for example, the sound made by a cell phone when the lid is closed. A solid "thud" is more appealing than a cheap "click." Nokia knows this and Nokia engineers worked hard on the springs and ball bearings just to get the sound right.[23]

Industrial designers must also consider tradeoffs among these factors. Bright colors on a phone answering machine may add to its emotional appeal but diminish perceived quality. Furthermore, many of these more aesthetic factors differ among individuals, making the designer's job more difficult.[24]

---

[22]This set of assessment questions comes from Karl T. Ulrich and Steven D. Eppinger, *Product Design and Development,* 2nd ed. (Homewood, IL: Irwin/McGraw-Hill, 2000), pp. 227–230.
[23]Anonymous, "Online Extra: A Chat with Nokia's Alastair Curtis," www.businessweek.com, July 17, 2006.
[24]Mariëlle E. H. Creusen and Jan P. L. Schoormans, "The Different Roles of Product Appearance in Consumer Choice," *Journal of Product Innovation Management,* 22(1), January 2005, pp. 63–81.

FIGURE 13.5
Assessment
Factors for
an Industrial
Design: A Car
Example

> ### Quality of the user interface
> Will the user understand the product and its intended use? Is it safe for use? In a car dashboard design, for example, is it clear that the knobs and switches for lights, wipers, and horn are easy to locate and operate?

> ### Emotional appeal
> Is it an attractive, exciting design? Would the prospective owner be proud to own the product? Does the car make a satisfying "growl" when revved up?

> ### Maintenance and repair
> Is the procedure for maintenance obvious and easy? Can all the fluids be easily changed, and is it easy to tell which fluid goes where?

> ### Appropriate use of resources
> Does the product include unnecessary features, or does it lack key features? Were the best materials chosen, with regard to cost and quality? Were environmental and ecological factors considered when choosing, for example, types of body paint for the car?

> ### Product differentiation
> Does the design distinguish the product? Is it memorable? Does it fit with corporate identity? When prospective luxury car owners take a look in the showroom, will they say this new model really stands out?

Source: From Karl T. Ulrich and Steven D. Eppinger, *Product Design and Development*, 2nd ed., McGraw-Hill, 2000, pp. 227–230. Reprinted with permission of The McGraw-Hill Companies.

Prototype Development[25]

For most people, the word **prototype** conjures up the image of a fully functioning, full-size product essentially ready to be examined by potential customers. Industrial designers define the term more broadly. A **comprehensive prototype** would be one of these essentially complete prototypes. They also make use of what are called **focused prototypes,** which examine a limited number of performance attributes or features. Recall the development of the electric bicycle and the Iomega Zip Drive from Chapter 2. In these cases, we encountered several focused prototypes. The bicycle makers built a nonfunctioning bicycle out of foam or wood to determine customers' reactions to the product's form, and a crude working prototype to experiment with and determine how the product might work. Recall that dozens of nonworking prototypes of the Zip Drive, including some with a flip-up top, were built before arriving at a prototype that customers liked.[26]

[25]Much of this section derives from Ulrich and Eppinger, op. cit., Chapter 12.
[26]The Zip Drive story is told in Gary S. Lynn and Richard R. Reilly, *Blockbusters: The Five Keys to Developing Great New Products* (New York: Harper Collins, 2002).

Which type, or types, of prototypes should be built? The answer is, of course, it depends: Primarily, it depends on the intended use of the prototype. Focused prototypes are used in probe-and-learn ("lickety-stick") product development in the development of new-to-the-world products, such as the Zip Drive. Focused prototypes are also used in cases where the product is not so new to the world to learn about how the product works and how well it will satisfy customer needs. BMW designers, for example, built clay models of new car designs for the 3 Series and sent them to southern France to see what they would look like in the sunlight at a distance, and to determine if there were line or form defects. It is much cheaper to make required changes now, rather than later in the development process.[27]

A more comprehensive physical prototype is necessary to determine how well all the components fit together—as an additional benefit, the various members of the new product team are essentially required to cooperate to build the comprehensive prototype. Finally, more advanced prototypes can be used as milestones—the performance of the prototype can be tracked periodically to see if it has advanced to desired levels.

Once a comprehensive prototype exists, of course, it can be taken to potential users to be tested in a real usage situation, and improved and refined. This is known as product-use testing and will be taken up in Chapter 15.

Managing the Interfaces in the Design Process

New product managers have to keep in mind that product design should not be the responsibility of only the designers! Historically, in the era of powerful functional chimneys and slow, linear, stage-based development, industrial designers dominated the action in most firms making tangible products. Today, they have to share this traditional role with several other functions, an example being when NCR Corporation hired packaging engineers and cognitive engineers (psychologically trained) to help design products that complement the way people think and act.

The net result was recently expressed: " . . . large multinational companies have begun to 'unchain' product designers capable of bridging and building upon the expertise of both marketing and engineering. Working at last as equal members of multidisciplinary teams, under the new kings and queens of the product development process—'project,' 'product,' or 'program' managers. . . ."[28]

Ironically, by joining the team and seeming to lose power, design stands on the verge of winning its ultimate position of influence. But, it is the new product manager's task to bring this about.

There are several participants in the product design task, some in a more direct role than others, as shown in Figure 13.6. One model of how these people participate is shown in this figure. The representation there is somewhat linear, but with substantial overlapping or parallel effort.

[27]C. Bangle, "The Ultimate Creativity Machine: How BMW Turns Art into Profit," *Harvard Business Review*, 2001, pp. 47–55.
[28]Christopher Lorenz, "Harnessing Design as a Strategic Resource," *Long Range Planning*, October 1994, pp. 73–83. The author goes on to make it very clear that he considers the industrial designer as the greatest among equals.

FIGURE 13.6
Model of
the Product
Design
Process

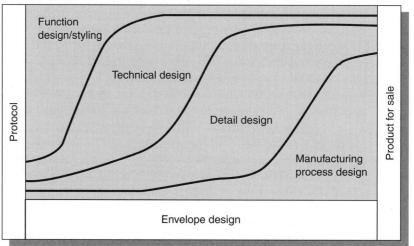

Development time scale

The members of a core team all participate in all four stages, but leadership in the first stage is often given to industrial designers, the middle two to engineering design, and the last to process design or manufacturing design. Terms in use vary widely. In chemical and pharmaceutical industries the design and engineering functions are replaced by research and development. And in some firms the term *product engineering* replaces engineering design; they want to contrast product engineer and process engineer.

For services, the same steps apply, but instead of a "thing" we are developing a service sequence and technical capability. Think of an investment service developed in a financial institution, or a cable TV system, or office design service.

Simultaneous with development (on goods *and* services) is the development of the augmented aspects of the product—pre- and postsale service, warranty, image, and so on. This activity, most often led by marketing people, is called *envelope design*, running across the bottom of the figure.

Participants in the Design Process

Direct Participants	**Supportive Participants**
Research & Development	Design Consultants
Industrial Designers and Stylists	Marketing Personnel
Engineering Designers/Product Designers	Resellers
Manufacturing Engineers and System Designers	Vendors/Suppliers
Manufacturing Operations	Governments
	Customers
	Company Attorneys
	Technical Service

It is easy to see how this model of operations gives people problems, particularly the designers. *Industrial designers,* trained to develop aesthetics (styling), structural integrity, and function (how the product works), directly overlap with the *design engineers,* who are technical people who convert styling into product dimensions or specifications. Technical people are not devoid of ideas on styling, and stylists are not devoid of thoughts on how the mechanics can work. This is especially true on common products (like shoes or dinnerware) where all parties have experience.

The other dimension of complexity is added by some of the supportive participants in the preceding list. Suppliers usually know their materials better than their customers do. That's why Black & Decker picked its supplier for the Snake Lite before its design was finished. Large firms like Philips have the funds to establish large central styling centers where styling skills exceed those of the typical plant stylist. Customers almost always have overriding ideas to contribute. Consequently, the styling function is a synthesis of many views beyond those of the direct participants. If we add all of the other company people listed as supportive, we get back to the list of functions usually represented on the teams discussed in Chapter 14.

The result of all this can be chaos, and in general the problems are thought to be at the heart of why some countries' producers are so often beaten by new products from Japan and Germany. In Japan, for example, product design means more than how a product looks and feels to the user; it often means engineering applications. To one observer, design in Japan "means the total-enterprise process of determining customer needs and converting them to concepts, detailed designs, process plans, factory design, and delivered products, together with their supporting services."[29] This merges a holistic view of end-user needs and a holistic structure to meet those needs. Design is seen as a vertical means of fulfillment, and individual skills are not central.

In the United States and Europe, participants end up playing musical chairs from one project to the next as roles change. Increasingly, the industrial designer gets fully integrated into a company team, as was the case in Chrysler's development of the LH line. Some design purists and traditionalists will likely resist this movement, however. Design and marketing operate in drastically different cultures, and cultural gaps are hard to erase.[30]

In some cases, designers are taking on an expanded role as a liaison from end user to top management. Greater integration with end users can lead to better information about what design changes are desired. Designers can also serve as a conduit of information from industry, for example, making recommendations to the product development team on new materials to use.[31]

Both the design engineer and the stylist have been accused of continually trying to make a product just a little better and refusing to release it for production. There

---

[29]Daniel E. Whitney, "Integrated Design and Manufacturing in Japan," *Prism,* Second Quarter, 1993, pp. 75–95.
[30]Matthew K. Haggerty and Brian L. Vogel, *Innovation,* Winter 1992, pp. 8–13.
[31]See Michael Evamy, op. cit.; and Jeneanne Marshall Rae, "Setting the Tone for Design Excellence," *Innovation,* Fall 1994, pp. 7–9.

used to be a statement around the auto industry that engineering never released anything; the new car managers had to go in and take it away. Too much design retooling can result in products that have too many engineering characteristics or gimmicks and are late onto the market. The quadraphonic sound system and the Xerox 8200 copier are products that failed to live up to expectations, partly because of their complexity. 1980s-era PCs could also fit in this category—Apple's initial success was based on its ease of use.[32]

The hard feelings sometimes run deep and lead to cross-functional animosity. The Japanese showed the world how to handle this when they began freezing the specifications at an early date in the technical cycle, forcing later ideas to be put into the schedule for the next model.

Improving the Interfaces in the Design Process

Most of the problems surrounding design have to do with concurrency, or over-lapping the steps in development. It is clear from the discussion of Chapter 12 that up-front product definition (product protocol and firm prototype) is important. Several techniques are currently being used to make sure that design is integrated correctly with other functions during the development phase and that the products being designed can be manufactured in a cost-efficient way.

Important among these is **colocation** (putting the various individuals or functional areas in close proximity). The development phase can be a communications snake pit. When the different groups are not in regular contact and cooperating, there is a tendency for information to be lost (or hidden). This causes wasted work and slows the whole operation down. Further, the problems intensify in large firms with their research centers hundreds of miles from the offices of marketers and the production lines of manufacturing people. Many firms have tried colocation to shorten communication lines and increase team cohesion. Motorola, for example, colocated its development team when developing the Bandit pager, completing the project in 18 months (less than half the normal development time), and Ford sped up time to market with the 1996 Taurus/Sable using colocation. Many other firms such as Honda, AT&T, and John Deere have used colocation successfully.[33]

Colocation helps integrate departments and improve information flow, and also allows the team members to identify and resolve product development problems quicker. It must, however, be carefully planned and handled. It is probably not a good idea to break up a center of technological excellence in order to colocate its members. Too-distant colocation (i.e., employees have to get in their cars and drive to another building rather than walk down the hall) might lead to team members

---

[32]Paul A. Herbig and Hugh Kramer, "The Effect of Information Overload on the Innovation Choice Process," *Journal of Consumer Marketing*, 11(2), 1994, pp. 45–54.

[33]Anthony Lee Pratt and James Patrick Gilbert, "Colocating New Product Development Teams: Why, When, Where, and How?" *Business Horizons*, November–December 1997, pp. 59–64; and Kenneth B. Kahn and Edward F. McDonough III, "An Empirical Study of the Relationships among Co-Location, Integration, Performance, and Satisfaction," *Journal of Product Innovation Management*, 14(3), May 1997, pp. 161–178.

letting their problems pile up rather than resolving them immediately. There may be an unintentional home court advantage (if the meetings are at the marketing facility, marketing team members may be perceived to be more powerful). And team members must be willing to tear down the functional walls and change their attitudes about working with individuals from other functions—otherwise, colocation facilitates social exchange, but doesn't really achieve cross-functional integration.[34]

In many firms, the effects of colocation are achieved without actual physical proximity of team members, using the resources of communications technology such as Lotus Notes provides. This is sometimes known as **digital colocation.** Interestingly, research suggests that digital colocation and face-to-face colocation complement each other in terms of facilitating knowledge dissemination.[35]

As a final note, there is a recent increase in the use of **global teams** (that is, teams comprising individuals from at least two different countries). Improved information technologies such as videoconferencing, teleconferencing, e-mail, and company databases combine with phone calls and regular mail to make global teams an increasingly feasible option. Global teams are increasingly popular in new product development, and we will take up their management in the next chapter.[36]

Other techniques are sometimes used. Some firms have sought a solution by bringing in a **produceability engineer:** an independent third party who understands both design and production and who can work in the design studios to see that production requirements are met by design decisions. Being third-party, turf battles are partially avoided. But it is not a satisfactory solution—adding another person rarely is.[37] As seen in Chapter 12, quality function deployment has also helped in getting cooperation across new product team members and in maintaining focus on customer needs and benefits. The customer's needs (counterpart of protocol) comprise an inherent part of the system and cannot be overlooked.

In addition, partnering upstream with vendors is a possibility. Of course, there are security risks, patent uncertainties, cooperation that cannot be mandated in an emergency, and the like. But most companies tell us they are doing it by using technology searches, demands that suppliers value engineer their product, and inclusion of supplier people on the new product teams. Chrysler, as an example, has cut its supplier base, establishing longer-term relationships with its suppliers, and insisted on high supplier quality in order to increase global competitiveness.[38]

---

[34]See Pratt and Gilbert, op. cit., and Farshad Rafii, "How Important Is Physical Colocation on Product Development Success?" *Business Horizons,* January–February 1995, pp. 78–84.

[35]Michael Song, Hans Berends, Hans van der Bij, and Mathieu Weggeman, "The Effect of IT and Colocation on Knowledge Dissemination," *Journal of Product Innovation Management,* 24(1), January 2007, pp. 52–68.

[36]Edward F. McDonough III, Kenneth B. Kahn, and Gloria Barczak, "Effectively Managing Global New Product Development Teams," *Proceedings,* 1998 Research Conference, Product Development and Management Association, pp. 176–188.

[37]See Gerda Smets and Kees Overbeeke, "Industrial Design Engineering and the Theory of Direct Perception," *Design Studies,* April 1994, pp. 175–184, for ideas on how users deal with the expressiveness of products, and the impact of that on industrial design activities.

[38]Jeffrey H. Dyer, "How Chrysler Created an American Keiretsu," *Harvard Business Review,* July–August 1996, pp. 42–60.

It is in any vendor's best interest to be offering something an end user genuinely needs, so both parties gain from integrated activities.[39]

Computer-Aided Design and Design for Manufacturability

Another development is helping to bring people together and at the same time show the importance of all players. **CAD** (computer-aided design), **CAM** (computer-aided manufacturing), **CAE** (computer-aided engineering), **DFM** (design for manufacturability), and other variations refer to computer-based technologies that allow for very efficient product design and development.

These technologies offer lots of advantages—people have to work together to understand and use them, they force the integration of all needs into one analytical set, they are fast, and they do more than the human can do alone even if there were ample time. They also help improve the images of team players who may lack status. For example, manufacturing used to have to take a back seat to design and marketing. It was uncommon in many firms for the factory people even to be invited to meetings; they were expected to take what came from design and make it, somehow. In most firms that time is gone, and should be in all firms.

Product designers often use **design for manufacturability (DFM)** techniques to find ways to minimize manufacturing costs. On average, up to 80 percent of a product's cost is determined by the time it is designed. The idea behind DFM techniques is that an apparently trivial detail in the design phase might have huge manufacturing cost consequences later on, so manufacturing implications need to be considered early in product design. Another term sometimes heard is **front-loading**: identifying and solving design problems in earlier phases of the new products process.

Probably the most important DFM process is **design for assembly (DFA)**, which is concerned with checking ease of assembly and manufacture and encouraging product simplification.[40] As was the case with the Proprinter example given above, DFA leads to fewer components, resulting in lower materials costs as well as savings in assembly time. There are several DFA programs, but the first one came from Boothroyd & Dewhurst, a Rhode Island software firm. By programming in the manufacturing conditions, and information about the particular assembly operation (for example, cars on an assembly line), the DFA program can react to any design proposal with information about its time and cost result. It also points out the major design elements contributing to slow time or high cost, so the designer can work directly on them. Unfortunately, the designer does not have comparable software that would be called DFM (design for marketing). Unless the protocol is very clear and accepted, or unless marketing or customer people are present during the design process, developers may be acting favorably to factory time/cost but unfavorably to customer value and usefulness.

[39]The good and the bad of this partnership are shown in Fred R. Beckley, "Some Companies Let Suppliers Work on Site and Even Place Orders," *The Wall Street Journal,* January 13, 1995, p. A1.
[40]Keith Goffin, "Evaluating Customer Support during New Product Development: An Exploratory Study," *Journal of Product Innovation Management,* 15(1), January 1998, pp. 42–56.

Three-dimensional CAD mock-ups have been successfully used to front-load design problem identification. Designers of aircraft or automobiles, for example, are working within space limitations. A traditional two-dimensional engineer's drawing might not be able to identify that the designed air conditioning duct would not fit well in a new aircraft's structure. The car dashboard designers might not realize that their desired position for the radio/CD player would protrude too far into the engine area. This sort of ill-fit can be identified and fixed readily using CAD. Iomega used CAM in designing the Zip Drive: Prototypes were built right from the three-dimensional computer-generated images.[41] Similarly, Boeing used CAM in its design of the 777. They simulated climbing into the newly designed aircraft for maintenance using a computer-generated virtual human—and found that one of the navigation lights would have been hard for a real serviceperson to reach. There was no need to build an expensive prototype to find this flaw, and the fixup was easily made.[42]

A similar benefit was obtained by Chrysler in the development of the 1998 Concorde and Intrepid models. Car engineers speak of *decking*—assembling the car's powertrain into the upper body (think of making a sandwich where all the parts have to fit together perfectly). Using CAD mockups, Chrysler identified (and solved) numerous fit problems digitally before any physical decking actually took place. In fact, the decking process was completed in 15 minutes since all potential problems had already been caught.[43]

Another application of CAD concerns car crashworthiness. BMW virtually "crashed" dozens of car designs using a crash simulator and was able to improve crashworthiness by about 30 percent as a result. Only two physical prototypes were actually built, crashed, and analyzed. The cost of building and physically crashing dozens of design iterations would have been prohibitive, not to mention time consuming.[44] In sum, digital preassembly (such as in the Chrysler example) and simulation analyses are among the biggest benefits of 3-D CAD to product development since they help to overcome costly and time-consuming stumbling blocks in the new products process.[45]

Other examples of current progress are (1) stereolithography and (2) mechanical computer-aided engineering (MCAE). Stereolithography is a technology that permits *free-form fabrication,* that is, the creation of a solid object directly from a three-dimensional computer model. This process is sometimes called **rapid prototyping**. In just one to three days, a container of liquid can be converted into a hard plastic prototype based on the 3D computer-designed model. The process sends

[41]Lynn and Reilly, *Blockbusters,* op. cit.
[42]Marco Iansiti and Alan MacCormack, "Developing Products on Internet Time," *Harvard Business Review,* September–October 1997, pp. 108–117.
[43]Stefan Thomke and Takahiro Fujimoto, "The Effect of 'Front-Loading' Problem-Solving on Product Development Performance," *Journal of Product Innovation Management,* 17(2), March 2000, pp. 110–127.
[44]Stefan Thomke, "Simulation, Learning, and R&D Performance: Evidence from Automotive Development," *Research Policy* 27, 1998, pp. 55–74.
[45]Yasunori Baba and Kentaro Nobeoka, "Towards Knowledge-Based Product Development: The 3D–CAD Model of Knowledge Creation," *Research Policy* 26, 1997, pp. 643–659.

hardening beams of electrons into the container causing the liquid to solidify in tiny bits at a time, yielding very precise models. At one time, a single model of this precise detail would have taken a modeler weeks to construct. MCAE permits engineers to test before they build, with all criteria being considered. It's a type of simulation that plays what-if games with a design.[46]

Continuous Improvement in Design

How can one go about improving product design even further? A familiar concept in new product development—the voice of the customer—might be revisited. Too often, the basic product is designed, then a product-user interface is slapped on without much thought to what the customer wants. Worse yet, it may be difficult to give the customer what he or she really wants without making major changes to the basic product. By starting with the customer's needs, a better basic product would be designed in the first place. This process is sometimes called *interaction design*. For example, if a given ATM user always requests service in English and always asks for a receipt, couldn't that behavior be tracked so that after a while the machine no longer asks him? Simple enough concept, but one that would require a substantial change to the basic product in order to give the customer what he wants.[47]

Summary

This chapter has dealt with the design process, the people and the activities. We have looked specifically at design process elements such as design architecture and prototype development, and explored some of the computer-aided techniques so important to design in so many firms. Design is many-faceted, however, so it will differ greatly from one industry to another. Marketing people have found it important to be flexible here, helping to shape a role for design that fits each situation and corporate policy. But in most firms, design joins manufacturing and other functions to form a working, multifunctional group (usually a team), and in Chapter 14 we will look at its structure and management.

Applications

1. "One of our divisions makes an electric scooter. Classic case of where a designer, looking for new modes of ultralight transportation, came across the scooter and electrified it. Boy, people said he was crazy. Kids begged their parents not to ride one (shame), and a cop said, 'It's not a moped. It's not a motorcycle. It's not

---

[46]See Otis Port, "A Smarter Way to Manufacture," *BusinessWeek*, April 30, 1990, pp. 110–117; and R. Van Dierdonck, "The Manufacturing/Design Interface," *R&D Management*, no. 3, 1990, pp. 203–209.

[47]The concept of "interaction design" and the ATM example are from Alan Cooper, *The Inmates Are Running the Asylum: Why High-Tech Products Drive Us Crazy and How to Restore the Sanity* (Indianapolis, IN: SAMS, 1999).

anything, and I don't ride anything when I'm not sure what it is.'[48] Best example I know of why designers have to be free to do their thing, without having market researchers be responsible for picking up on market trends."

2. "Most of our divisions believe in customer integration—involving the user in the new product process. I am a fanatic on it. But some people want us to carry this right into the technical design phase. This would be dangerous. A lot of what we do must be secret—we can't patent most of our ideas, and timing is everything. That's why we put so much emphasis on speed of development. But I still get pushed to do more. Help me. Tell me all the things we might do to get integrated customers but at the same time minimize the risks of losing our secrets."

3. "About this matter of design, I am stumped. I agree design is critical today, and I always support it. But you've got to admit that industrial designers sometimes get into arguments with the engineers who are trying to make products as functional as possible. For example, I once saw a beautifully styled computer mouse that had lost its ergonomic value. As a general executive matter, how do you suggest we evaluate these tradeoffs? How can we find where to stop styling and let the engineers rule?"

Case: The Mini[49]

In 1990, the U.S. car buying market was surprised and pleased with the latest new car: Mazda's new Miata. The Miata was designed to look and "feel" much like a 1960s-era British roadster, yet due to careful attention to costs, it was brought to market at a retail price of about $15,000, making it a realistic purchase even for a young, first-time new car buyer. In the years since then, many other carmakers have tried their luck with retro-designed cars. Volkswagen, of course, succeeded with the New Beetle. Prior to its launch, critics were sure that the New Beetle would find only a limited niche, among 1950s and 1960s Beetle enthusiasts. The car market had changed too much in the intervening years, and there were just too many better small cars out there (Japanese as well as American) to choose from. But Volkswagen designed the New Beetle on a Golf platform, retaining enough of the familiar Beetle shape while making it thoroughly competitive with other small cars of the 1990s in terms of performance, comfort, and price. Chrysler's PT Cruiser resembled a 1930s-style car, while Ford brought back its 1950s-era Thunderbird for a short period. The Nissan 350Z was an update of the popular Datsun 240Z of the 1970s.

BMW's chairperson, Helmut Panke, is known to have a clear mission for BMW: to continue to sell established models in established markets, while at the same time penetrating new markets with new models. In the mid-90s, BMW successfully launched the Z3 Roadster while maintaining its existing range of high-end

[48]Joseph Pereira, "Guffaws Aside, New Scooter Makers Zip Ahead," *The Wall Street Journal,* August 20, 1998, p. B1.
[49]This case was prepared from several public sources, including the BMW 2002 Annual Report, several articles in *Automotive News,* and articles appearing on the Web sites www.autofan .com and www.miniusa.com.

sedans; this certainly was evidence of the corporate mission at work. With its acquisition of the British carmaker Rover Group Ltd., BMW obtained the rights to the name and design of the Mini (or Mini Cooper), one of the best-known British cars. It clearly fit into BMW's mission to try to revive the Mini and bring it to the world market. And with the recent popularity of the New Beetle in the United States, it seemed evident that the American market might be very receptive to the Mini, especially if reasonably priced.

Still, any car launch carries risks. In the mid-90s, Mercedes teamed with Swatch to develop what is now known as the Smart Car in Europe. This sub-subcompact has caught on in many European countries in a big way, as it is ideally suited to city driving and parking. But would the Mercedes-Benz image be tarnished by association with such an inexpensive car? Similarly, BMW had to decide how much it wanted to stress its name in the marketing of the Mini. Clearly, BMW engineering would have to be viewed as a positive by prospective buyers. But BMW would not want backlash from current BMW owners who had paid in the $50,000 range for a new car and who believed they benefited from the prestige of the BMW nameplate. The decision was made not to stress BMW in the promotion of the Mini, but to let the latter's superior engineering and design speak for itself.

The Mini was launched in 2002 and was phenomenally successful. The retail price was highly affordable, in the $15,000 to $20,000 range, and the car delivered an economical 37 miles per gallon. Prospective buyers could consult popular car magazines to get ideas for customizing their Mini, then visit the Web site, www .miniusa.com, and design their own Mini online. Clubs such as the Independent North American Community of Mini Owners and Enthusiasts sprang up. BMW has been giving Volkswagen a run for its money in the U.S. small, fun car market.

In your opinion, what were the most important design considerations for BMW when redesigning the Mini for the U.S. car market? What would be the most important benefits to design into this car for the targeted market segment(s)? What would be the key points of discussion between design and other functional areas within BMW in order to deliver a car with the desired benefits? More broadly, when a car such as the Beetle or Thunderbird is redesigned or given a facelift for the modern car buyer, what are the design pitfalls and concerns, and specifically, what kind of market research should be conducted to ensure that the pitfalls are avoided?

Case: Palm Pilot[50]

This case is about the development of two products: the original Palm Pilot, launched in March 1996, and the Palm V, released only a couple of years later. Although we focus on the design of these two products, it is important to recognize how design was driven by both customer needs and the available technology, and also to consider just how important an element design was to Palm's overall corporate strategy.

[50]This case is based on Anonymous, "Beyond Techno Gadget," *@Issue*, Corporate Design Foundation (no date given), and Bill Moggridge, *Designing Interactions* (Cambridge, MA: MIT Press, 2007).

The story begins in the months leading up to the launch of the original Palm Pilot (the first personal digital assistant, or PDA) by Palm Computing. The inventor, Jeff Hawkins, believed that simplicity was the key to hand-held computers ("Do one thing; do it well" was the belief driving product development). Of course, in those days, no one knew exactly what a hand-held computer would do, how it would be used, how big or heavy it would be, and so on. In trying to visualize his idea, Jeff carried a crude prototype (literally a block of wood about the size of a modern PDA) in his pocket and imagined how he might use it through the day. He even wrote imaginary notes on the "screen" during business meetings! This visualization process provided Jeff with insights on how the product would be used, and therefore what features would need to be built into it. It was around this time that he had the breakthrough idea that the competition for hand-held computers was not bigger computers, but rather paper notebooks and organizers. The new product should be able to store addresses and phone numbers, maintain a calendar and a shopping list, and basically anything else someone might jot down on a piece of paper, but should do it quickly and conveniently. Based on his experiences, Jeff developed four design criteria for what was to become the Palm Pilot: It should be small enough that one could conveniently carry it in a shirt pocket; it should be aggressively low priced (he targeted $299 retail), it should offer synchronization (a core application), and it should be comparable to paper notebooks and organizers in terms of speed.

Soon after the Palm Pilot was launched, work began on product enhancements. During this time, Microsoft and others were beginning to launch competitive PDAs, and Palm would need to develop a competitive strategy to help them maintain market share. As always, Jeff's simplicity motto was adhered to. While competitive products offered as much as four times the memory, Jeff felt that was the wrong way to compete. As he said at the time, "Who cares . . . I don't need eight megabytes; I can't even fill up two. Let's show the world that this isn't about speeds and feeds; it's about simplicity."

The company soon realized that its early customer base comprised mostly of men who enjoyed electronic gadgets, and it was felt that the new generation of products should appeal to women as well. Jeff became more convinced that the right direction was to make the Palm Pilot look and feel more like an accessory than a computer.

In order to achieve the desired results, Jeff contacted IDEO (the creative firm seen in the P&G Carpet Flick case earlier in this text) for design ideas in late 1996. Dennis Boyle, manager of IDEO's Palo Alto studio and senior project leader, was chosen as the leader for what was to be known as the Palm V project. For product design inspiration, Dennis rounded up several brand-new electronics products recently launched, including a Sony Mini-Disk player, a Canon Elph camera, a Motorola StarTac cell phone, and a Panasonic minitape recorder. Compared to the boxy original Palm Pilot, these new products looked ultra-modern, sleek, and attractive. As Jeff said, "there was something [about the StarTac phone] that had visceral impact. It's so small and beautiful. It really grabs you." Jeff was impressed and requested that IDEO work on a new design that offered the same emotional qualities.

IDEO's first plans for the Palm V (still known internally by the code name "Razor") focused on thickness and weight. The new Palm should be about half the thickness of the original Palm Pilot and weigh about one-third less. To modify these plans, the IDEO team went to colleagues, friends, and typical PalmPilot users and distributed them to over 200 of their own staff. Informal feedback and e-mail followup found that most users were basically happy with the Palm Pilot, but found that it tended to break if dropped, thought the case was too rigid and the battery door hard to operate, and disliked the stylus storage compartment. Some even designed their own stylus holders.

Dennis was particularly interested in getting comments from female users, and he used two female design engineers, Amy Han and Trae Niest, to be his project leaders. They in turn solicited opinions from 15 female coworkers. These findings were also revealing. Female users found the design boxy and gray, not graceful at all. Interestingly, they also challenged both distribution and promotion programs used for the Palm Pilot. One wondered why PDAs had to be sold at electronics stores (which she called a "guy kind of place . . . why not places where women shop, like Nordstrom?"). Palm Pilot ads also tended to feature male actors. Dennis realized that the Palm V would have to appeal to both men and women in terms of design.

These design initiatives created technical challenges. First, the stylus and other accessories ought to be easily stored on the PDA, and appearance in general had to be spruced up. IDEO employed rapid prototyping, going through dozens of different crude versions, soliciting comments from customers, and making improvements. Dennis believed in "never going to a client meeting without a prototype" and became known for doing exactly that in the weekly consultations with Palm. Every week, a new feature was revealed: a new on-off button design, a new idea for an LCD panel, or a new type of stylus. Dennis liked being able to get feedback from Palm on a continual basis in this way. For example, the stylus storage problem was solved by going through different crude versions (pockets, hinges, etc.) before settling on a dual-rail system solution.

Two other technical challenges were more troublesome. First, the new thin design ruled out AAA batteries, which were the power source of the original Palm Pilot, and rechargeable lithium ion batteries were still something new in 1996–1997. Although resistant at first, battery makers agreed to develop a lithium ion battery that would work properly in a PDA. Second, the plastic case needed to be replaced, as it added to both weight and breakability. IDEO was inspired by looking at Japanese cameras and binoculars to try thin anodized aluminum instead. While it had the light and unbreakable properties IDEO desired, the aluminum case posed an aesthetic problem: It was held together with screws, which was considered unacceptable. Through trial and error, IDEO found an acceptable workaround that had never been tried before for PDAs or similar products: An adhesive turned out to work fine, and the need for screws disappeared.

The Palm V was readied for launch in 1998. By this time there had been organizational upheavals. Palm was bought by U.S. Robotics, which then was bought by 3Com. (3Com later spun off Palm, in 2000.) At the same time, Jeff left 3Com and started Handspring, a PDA that licensed the Palm operating system. None of this affected the launch of the Palm V, which went ahead as planned in 1998. Total development time was a little under three years.

The Palm V was an undisputable success. Although the cheaper Palm III was still on the market, customer response to the Palm V was enthusiastic. Buyers raved about the exact design points identified by Jeff and Dennis: the "cool" design and aluminum case, the rechargeable battery, and its incredibly thin and light form. Ads stressed its role as an accessory, not a new gadget—something rarely seen in previous PDA advertising. Female as well as male models were used in print ads, with the tagline "Simply Palm" effectively communicating Jeff's motto.

As Dennis Boyle said, "Technology is integrating into designed products that we use, wear, and ride in . . . it has become like the wristwatch, which has a very sophisticated mechanism inside but has evolved to a stage where people take that for granted. People buy the watch that looks beautiful and is a pleasure to use. Now they are coming to expect that of computer devices too."

What was the role of design in the success of the initial Palm Pilot, and how did design contribute to the continued success of the Palm V? Describe how design was driven by both customer needs and technology, and how indeed this product is an example of the dual drive strategy (see discussion of the product innovation charter earlier in the text). Design is clearly a key element of Palm's corporate strategy. Can you think of other firms (besides Apple!) where design plays such a major role in a firm's competitive advantage?

Case: Gillette Mach3[51]

For decades, the Gillette Co. has followed a simple strategy for success: Replace excellent blade technology with an even better one. Over the years, Gillette has brought us the Blue Blade, the Platinum Plus, the Trac II, the Atra, the Sensor, then the SensorExcel. In April 1998, Gillette announced the next generation of razor: a three-bladed pivoting cartridge system called the Mach3.

The idea of a three-bladed system was being investigated by Gillette engineers as early as 1970, without much success: They irritated the skin, yet didn't produce a closer shave. During the 1970s and 1980s, they launched the twin-bladed Atra and the Sensor, which had its blades mounted on tiny springs, meanwhile continuing the design work on the three-bladed system.

By the early 1990s, the design problems that had stalled the three-bladed system had been overcome. A prototype three-bladed razor (code-named the Manx) was developed and shown to outperform the Sensor in internal tests.

A key element of the Manx's design was the positioning of the three blades: Each blade was a little closer to the face than the previous one. This patented design reduced the irritation caused by the third blade. In addition, the pivot point

[51]This case is based on Mark Maremont, "How Gillette Brought Its Mach3 to Market," *The Wall Street Journal*, April 15, 1998, p. B-1.

was moved to the bottom of the cartridge (those familiar with Sensor know that its pivot point is in the middle of the cartridge). The new pivot point made shaving feel a little like using a paintbrush, added to the cartridge's stability, and ensured that the bottom edge of the cartridge always touched the face first (ensuring that hairs were lifted properly). Other design features were also built into the Manx. To the white lubricating strip found on the Sensor, a blue indicator was added that gradually faded, indicating when the blade needed to be changed. And engineers were working on better blades, perfecting a way to make them thinner and harder, thanks to new metal technology borrowed from the manufacture of semiconductors. Furthermore, consumer studies found an interesting problem incurred by Sensor users that suggested a potential product improvement: 18 percent of men put the cartridge on the razor upside down! A new snap-in mechanism was developed that would only work in the right direction.

Unfortunately, the new design was going to be costly to manufacture. There was internal resistance within the ranks of Gillette, with some managers believing that the company should go with a less-revolutionary, three-bladed SensorExcel rather than a costly and risky introduction of a totally new product. Alfred N. Zeien, Gillette's CEO and an engineer by training, favored the new design, believing that the best chance for a sure winner was to go with the most technologically advanced design. Michael T. Cowhig, director of manufacturing for the North Atlantic group, felt that the new metal technology, excellent for making computer chips, would not be ready to make blades, especially in the numbers Gillette expected to sell annually. He said, "I knew we could make one blade; I didn't know if we could make 3.6 billion." His assessment was that the Mach3 blade would cost about 50 percent more to manufacture than SensorExcel, the premium Gillette blade at the time.

Nevertheless, the new design (now called by the code name 225) was locked in during the month of April 1995. The next three years were spent in designing and producing the equipment needed to manufacture the new cartridges—most of the machinery had to be specially designed for the task. Meanwhile, product use tests with consumers were showing that the Mach3 was outperforming the SensorExcel 2 to 1 and doing even better against competitive brands. The consumer tests were also suggesting that users were fairly insensitive to price—the Mach3 tested well even at a 45 percent price premium over SensorExcel.

Gillette geared up for an April 1998 launch. All told, the Mach3 development took six years and $750 million, about four times what the Sensor cost. Further, $300 million was allocated for marketing in the first year ($100 million in the United States and $200 million elsewhere), so the up-front costs broke the billion-dollar barrier. The rollout began in the United States, Canada, and Israel in July 1998, then Western Europe and part of Eastern Europe in September. The plan was to have the Mach3 available in about 100 countries by the end of 1999. By comparison, the Sensor (largely regarded as a global marketing success) needed five years to reach that level of distribution. To accommodate the rollout, production ramp-up was targeted to 1.2 billion cartridges per year by the end of 1998. The price point was set high (about 35 percent above the SensorExcel's price of $1 per blade); sticker shock was reduced by putting less blades in each pack. At the time, at least one industry expert, Pankaj Ghemawat of Harvard, was saying that even SensorExcel's price was "outrageous," though Zeien and other top Gillette executives believed that the Mach3 was so good, it would sell itself.

Based on what you see in this case, what strategic role did design play at Gillette? What are the risks involved in the decision to go with the really new Mach3 design, versus making incremental design improvements to the older SensorExcel technology? Play the role of both Mr. Zeien and Mr. Cowhig. And what about that aggressive marketing and rollout plan? Would you recommend they take it slower? What are the pros and cons?

CHAPTER FOURTEEN

Development Team Management

Setting

In Chapter 14, we focus our attention on the **cross-functional team,** a form of management that is now a given in less routine new products processes. According to a study by the American Productivity Quality Center, about three-quarters of respondents reported that cross-functional teams were used by their firms in product development, and about the same percentage said that there was an identified team leader who pushed the product through from beginning to end.[1] Yet teams differ in their composition, whom they report to, how effectively the team members work together, and how productive they are. Increasingly, the team may comprise individuals who may live thousands of miles apart. Organizing and managing product teams are real challenges. Yet, as seen in earlier chapters, a well-functioning product team is critical to bringing in and using the voice of the customer, developing new product protocols, accelerating time to market while staying under budget, and in so many other ways. In this chapter, we take up the issue of product team organization and management.

What Is a Team?

Describing, building, and managing teams is treacherous because there are so many different kinds of teams. Drucker focused on the dilemma when he talked about sports teams:[2]

- *Baseball teams:* They are like assembly line teams. Their work fits together, and all the players are needed, but they generally work as individuals, in their own ways. The double-play combo is a clear exception. Work is generally in a series.

[1]Robert G. Cooper, Scott J. Edgett, and Elko J. Kleinschmidt, *Improving New Product Development Performance and Practices* (Houston, TX: American Productivity and Quality Center, 2002).
[2]Peter F. Drucker, "There's More Than One Kind of Team," *The Wall Street Journal,* February 11, 1992, p. A16.

- *Football teams:* These have fixed positions, but they play as a team. Japanese car teams are of this type. Work is parallel, not series. But one player does not come to the aid of another.
- *Tennis-doubles teams:* The players work with and support each other. The result is important only as the team scores a point or wins a match. Partners are dedicated. Volleyball teams are another example, as is the jazz combo.

Baseball and football managers are quite strong, but there are no tennis-doubles managers. Some training people feel that volleyball is the best analogy for today's teams: There are more players; they develop skills at all positions; and the unique role for the manager is comparable to that of the new products team manager.

The new products team is so far from the traditional and comfortable hierarchical world that great learning is required; there is a shortage of people who currently know how to play the game; and performance appraisal is tough, because only the team's overall performance matters. It offers the greatest risk to upper level managements. Since the team members all have different backgrounds and play different roles, there is no one to "score" them against.

Structuring the Team

The new products organization can be structured in many ways. One useful listing of **organizational structure options** is shown in Figure 14.1. The options shown in this figure can be thought of as a continuum: The further across the figure, the greater is the commitment of company personnel to the new product project.[3] The term that is sometimes used is **projectization**: the further to the right, the greater the projectization. You may also come across the terms *lightweight* and *heavyweight* teams, where heavyweight is synonymous with high projectization.[4] In Figure 14.1, then, the more to the right, the more heavyweight the team is.

The farthest left option, **functional,** means the work is done by the various departments with very little project focus. There usually is a new products committee or a product planning committee. The work is usually low risk and probably involves the present line of products—improvements, new sizes, and so on. The ongoing departmental people know the market and the business; they can get together and make the necessary decisions easily and effectively. There may be advantages associated with a lightweight team. The team leader can usually ensure relatively easily that members are informed about key issues, and communication

[3]New product organizational options have been expressed in scores of ways. But only one listing came from empirical research on the form and on the success or failure of actual new product projects. It was originally stated in David H. Gobeli and Eric W. Larson, "Matrix Management: More Than a Fad," *Engineering Management International*, 1986, pp. 71–76. The only change is that what the authors called *project team* is here called *venture* to reflect recent preferences. The same authors also later published a much larger empirical study on the same subject: Erik W. Larson and David H. Gobeli, "Organizing for Product Development Projects," *Journal of Product Innovation Management*, 5(3), September 1988, pp. 180–90.
[4]Gloria Barczak, "Innovation Teams," in V. K. Narayanan and Gina C. O'Connor (eds.), *Encyclopedia of Technology & Innovation Management* (Chichester, UK: John Wiley, 2010), Chapter 32.

FIGURE 14.1
Options in
New Products
Organization

	Options				
Functional	**Functional matrix**	**Balanced matrix**	**Project matrix**	**Venture**
With or without committee					Inside Outside
0%_____ 20%_____40%_____60%_____80%_____100%					
Degree of projectization*					

*Defined as the extent to which participants in the process see themselves as independent from the project or committed to it. Thus, members of a new products committee are almost totally oriented (loyal) to their functions or departments; spinout (outside) venture members are almost totally committed to the project.

is comparatively easy. A possible drawback is that functional area managers are strong and can dominate the project leader, weakening his or her effectiveness.[5]

To overcome these problems and give the product team and its leader more power, we have the other four options as shown in Figure 14.2. Three of them are variations of **matrix structures**. If the people in a matrix structure get together to make some decisions, they may be 50/50, or the power may lean toward the head of the functional department, or it may lean toward the project manager. The higher the projectization, the more the power leans toward the project manager as seen in Figure 14.1. Greater projectization might involve, for example, R&D personnel talking with customers along with marketing specialists. Taking off their functional "hats," team members develop new perspectives as well as a greater understanding of one another's roles in successful innovation.[6]

FIGURE 14.2   Considerations When Selecting an Organizational Option

High projectization encourages cross-functional integration.

If state-of-the-art functional expertise is critical to project success (e.g., in a scientific specialty such as fluid dynamics), a functional organization might be better, as it encourages the development of high-level technical expertise.

If individuals will be part of the project for only a short time, it might make more efficient use of their time if they were organized functionally. For example, industrial designers may be involved in any given project for only a short time, so different projects can simply draw on their expertise when needed.

If speed to market is critical, higher projectization is preferred as project teams are usually able to coordinate their activities and resolve conflicts more quickly and with less bureaucracy. PC makers, for example, often use project teams, as they are under severe time pressure.

Source: From Karl T. Ulrich and Steven D. Eppinger, *Product Design and Development*, 2nd ed., McGraw-Hill, 2000, pp. 28–29. Reprinted with permission of The McGraw-Hill Companies.

[5]S. Wheelwright and K. Clark, *Revolutionizing Product Development* (New York: The Free Press, 1992). See also discussion in Barczak, op. cit.
[6]Erika B. Seamon, "Achieving Growth through an Innovative Culture," in P. Belliveau, A. Griffin and S. M. Sommermeyer, *The PDMA Toolbook 2 for New Product Development* (New York: John Wiley, 2004), Chapter 1.

We have names for different kinds of matrix structures, as shown in Figure 14.1. The **functional matrix** option is the most lightweight of these. Here, a team exists, with people from the various departments (such as manufacturing, R&D, marketing, and finance), but the project is still close to the current business. Team members think like functional specialists, and their bosses back in the departments win most of the face-offs. In the **balanced matrix** option, both functional and project views are critical—neither ongoing business nor the new product should be the driver. The most heavyweight of the three is the **project matrix** option, which recognizes the occasional need for stronger project push. Here projectization is high. Team people are project people first and functional people second.

The **venture** option extends projectization to its ultimate and is most useful for new-to-the-world or new-to-the-firm products. Team members are pulled out of their departments and put to work full time on the project. A *think-tank* environment, designed to identify new ideas or solutions to new product-related problems, is one type of venture. The venture may be kept in the regular organization, or it may be spun outside the current division or company—a **spinout venture.** Lockheed's *Skunkworks*, a group of researchers pulled out of their familiar departments and routine activities to concentrate on specific innovation targets, is a good illustration of a rather extreme spinout venture.[7] German carmaker BMW, having acquired the Rolls-Royce luxury car name, sent designers from California and Munich to their design center, "The Bank" (literally an old bank building), in London to learn the Rolls-Royce culture and jointly develop what would become the 2003 Rolls-Royce Phantom. Similarly, the BMW Z4 sport coupe, launched in 2004, was also designed by a dedicated team of automotive engineers over the course of about ten months.[8] Both of these examples illustrate highly projectized teams.

While conventional wisdom suggests that ventures should be particularly suited for new-to-the-world products, there still remains the matter of how to manage the team, which is essentially working outside the organization. Many firms found these difficult to establish and/or to manage, decided venture teams weren't for them, and have moved back toward a more lightweight approach. For their part, matrix structures are notoriously difficult to manage, often becoming unreasonably complicated and incurring high overheads. There are inevitably role-conflict issues in any matrix organization: Should team members put first priority on the project or on the function they represent? In extremely complex cases, a matrix structure can actually be detrimental to innovation. Operational difficulties ascribed to a rigorous organizational structure have been blamed for Hewlett-Packard's lack of innovative performance over several years.[9] These firms find that encouraging cooperation among team members is perhaps more important

---

[7]Marianne Jelinek, "Organizing for Innovation," in V. K. Narayanan and Gina C. O'Connor (eds.), *Encyclopedia of Technology & Innovation Management* (Chichester, UK: John Wiley, 2010), Chapter 29.

[8]Gail Edmondson, "BMW's Dream Factory," www.businessweek.com, October 16, 2006.

[9]See Jelinek, op. cit.

than the details of the organizational structure of the team; one cannot just throw people together and call them a team.[10]

Other organizational issues arise as well. Should the radical innovation be "incubated" within the venture team, only to be integrated within the firm if it gains some acceptance in the marketplace? Recent research on twelve large firms and their ongoing innovative efforts suggests that the best procedure is to manage the relationship between the venture's management and that of the present firm, including all issues of leadership and transition of management. Three competencies tied to radical innovation were identified:

- Discovery. Creating, recognizing, and articulating radical innovation opportunities.
- Incubation. Transitioning the radical opportunity into a business proposal.
- Acceleration. Ramping up the business so that it is comparable to other businesses within the parent organization.[11]

Another Look at Projectization

Despite the difficulties in implementation, firms do need to consider projectization as a way to get the team members working together effectively. Any time two or more people from different departments or functions of a firm gather to work on a project, conflicts arise. When a sales manager, for example, goes to a new products *committee* meeting, there is little doubt about priorities because committee members are engineers or marketers first and committee members second. The sales manager is "functionalized," not projectized. Committee members want the company to make a profit; they are not disloyal. But they have independent opinions about how any particular new product may contribute to profit. The sales manager may see a new package size as meeting customer demands and adding sales; the engineer may believe production costs will go up more than the sales volume; accounting objects to another line item that may just split customers' current purchases and add to cost; R&D says work on the new package size will pull a key person off a far more important project needed next year.

These are not idle concerns. They are the reality of new product life, and they are legitimate. Increasing projectization can help to handle them. If a project is important and faces lots of opposition of the types just mentioned, then we increase the projectization. If the opposition is very high, a venture team organization may be called for. On the other hand, if the product development will entail only minor variations to a standard product or platform, it is possible that lower projectization will be the preferred option.

[10]Barbara Dyer, Ashok K. Gupta, and David Wilemon, "What First-to-Market Companies Do Differently," *Research-Technology Management*, March–April 1999, pp. 15–21.
[11]Gina Colarelli O'Connor and Richard DeMartino, "Organizing for Radical Innovation: An Exploratory Study of the Structural Aspects of RI Management Systems in Large, Established Firms," *Journal of Product Innovation Management*, 23(6), 2006, pp. 475–497.

Different firms manage these issues in different ways. Toyota, for example, has been successful with integrated product innovation while retaining a functionally based organization. It accomplishes this in several ways:

- Written communication between employees of different functional areas is stressed. Emphasis is placed on concise (one- or two-page) reports to minimize paperwork overload.
- There is close supervision between supervisors and new hires within each functional area, resembling a student-mentor relationship.
- "Chief engineers" are the lead designers on a new car project. Their role is to design the overall "approach" and to manage the large team of engineers that will actually "fill in the details."
- In-house training of engineers is stressed. Engineers are rotated widely throughout the company to avoid setting up "functional chimneys."
- Relatively simple, standardized work processes are used to keep everyone on track.
- A set of design standards is maintained to promote predictability in the new product process.[12]

We determine how much team power is needed by study of the situation. Some other factors that influence the correct projectization level are the need to encourage cross-functional integration, the level of functional expertise required, the likely duration of an individual's stay on the team, and the criticality of speed to market. Figure 14.2 expands on all of these important factors.

Building a Team

Most managers and almost all researchers have concluded that new products teams must be created to fit their situations. There is no right method or paradigm, just as there is no right method of concept testing or spelling out a product innovation charter. Neither are there right people; most team members and team leaders tell of their own personal growth during such assignments. Sales managers and scientists alike must become something else, something appropriate to a group task.

Establishing a Culture of Collaboration

Few people disagree with the importance of culture in business. There is even the saying that "Every firm should have a culture, even a bad one." For product improvements and near line extensions, the new products people must take the culture of the ongoing organization. At Heinz, for example, the Big Red brand team (tomato ketchup, etc.) will dominate its new products work. But as the task becomes tougher, firms will need to foster a culture of **collaboration** that will help

[12]Durward K. Sobek II, Jeffrey K. Liker, and Allen C. Ward, "Another Look at How Toyota Integrates Product Development," *Harvard Business Review*, July–August 1998, pp. 36–49.

them harness creativity, share information among departments, encourage growth of intellectual capital, and get more efficient in new product development.[13]

Collaboration is an intense and complex form of integration among functional areas (marketing, R&D, manufacturing, etc.). Each functional area has an equal stake in the new product's success, a lack of hidden agendas, and a focus on the team's common objectives. Ideally, collaboration results in *synergy*: The new product outcome is greater than the sum of the capabilities of the individual participants. Although cross-functional teams can greatly increase functional integration, more is needed to ensure proper levels of collaboration. Specifically, the participants have to be open to change, willing to cooperate, and trusting of one another. Top management's commitment to new products and its responsiveness to the needs and expectations of team members also contribute to increased collaboration.[14]

It is said that styles of management create cultures. But cultures come slowly; management change can come suddenly. Culture may be overemphasized; it only *permits* action and accomplishment. It does not itself produce any output from the new products system. Still, the team working with no clear culture (or with the wrong culture) in place is at risk. The next sections explore how a collaborative culture can be fostered by attending to issues of team building and management.

The Team Assignment and Ownership

A clear understanding by everyone involved as to what the team is for, its mission, and its strategy is critical. One manufacturer of reasonably technical medical care products wanted only the moderate risks of *innovative imitation*, so R&D was made responsive to the directions of marketing. New projects originated only in marketing, key product attributes were determined before R&D began, and a marketing manager ran each project. Another firm in an allied industry wanted to implement an *aggressive technical innovation* strategy, but two qualified R&D directors came and went before management realized the short-term focus of a dominant marketing department was totally misleading the teams. Funny things happen when new product teams lack strategy, because they pick up whatever strategy they think is correct, and technical people may feel that team success is measured by technical performance. The customer has a different opinion.

Also critical is "buy-in" on the part of everyone on the team—this is sometimes called taking **ownership** in the project. With ownership comes enthusiasm, commitment, energy and pride. Ownership is *not* entrepreneurship—white knights do not ride around a firm waving a sword and conjuring up new products. *Groups of skilled specialists* create new products, not individual leaders. Some firms use the term **product champion** to describe those who have taken ownership, but want all members of the team to join in the ownership.

[13]For a perspective on the importance of sharing information across functional areas, see Michael Song, Jinhong Zie, and C. Anthony Di Benedetto, "Message and Source Factors, Market Uncertainty, and Extrafunctional Information Processing: Hypotheses and Empirical Evidence," *IEEE Transactions on Engineering Management* 48(2), 2001, pp. 223–238.
[14]Edward U. Bond III, Beth A. Walker, Michael D. Hutt, and Peter H. Reingen, "Reputational Effectiveness in Cross-Functional Working Relationships," *Journal of Product Innovation Management*, 21(1), January 2004, pp. 44–60.

It takes three things to have ownership: training, empowerment, and motivation. *Training* helps assure that no one will take ownership without the skills and knowledge required by the task. **Empowerment** means that a person has been cut loose. It is far more than delegation (which usually has strings attached—budgets, policy, procedures, etc.). It is essentially a statement from senior management that they are ready and willing to trust the person's judgment. *Motivated* means the person has been encouraged to want to succeed, and we will talk about that in more detail later.

Functional people will sometimes not want to take ownership. Power yes, but not ownership. And they often can't, because the conditions above haven't been met. A Citicorp manager once said the bank had to move innovation of retail products to a corporate new products group because the line departments just weren't doing the job. They refused to take ownership (including the responsibility for failure).

Team empowerment must be carefully managed. For example, a team may be empowered to make key decisions, but at some later time management may need to step in and help out the team if it has run into difficulty—or may simply revise decisions already made by the team. Alternatively, the team itself may seek help from above. In other cases, a team may outstep its authority. Any of these situations can cause problems and potentially hurt the future use of teams within the firm. Management should resist the urge to intervene and make efforts to support team decisions. It also helps if the team's objectives and boundaries are clearly spelled out at the start—otherwise the team will either create its own (which may or may not be appropriate from the firm's viewpoint) or drift.[15]

Selecting the Leader

Given the overall strategy and the decision on just how much team the firm needs for the job at hand, it is time to select a leader. Sometimes this is automatic—for example, when the firm uses a product manager system and the new product concerns an addition to a particular person's product line or when, as in the case of 3M, the project originates from a particular person's technology.

Leaders must be *general managers*. They must be able to spot the need for change and convince others of this need. They also need to get potential team members to accept the idea of being on a team, ensure their commitment, encourage information sharing, increase interaction, and generally feel comfortable working with people from other functional areas.[16] They lead without direct authority and so must win personal support. Team leaders must have strong self-confidence (based on knowledge and experience, not just ego), have empathy (be able to look at things from another person's point of view), have a good self-awareness of how others see them, and be experts in personal communication. But the irony is that even all this is probably not enough. It has been said that a new products project really needs two leaders: a creative, inspiring type for early on, and a tough disciplinarian for the later phases. Rare is the person who can be both.

[15]Donald Gerwin, "Team Empowerment in New Product Development," *Business Horizons,* July–August 1999, pp. 29–36.
[16]Avan R. Jassawalla and Hemant C. Sashittal, "Strategies of Effective New Product Leaders," *California Management Review,* 42(2), Winter 2000, pp. 34–51.

Sometimes people wonder whether the leader should be chosen first or selected by the team members themselves. The latter is an attractive idea and is used occasionally. But senior management usually prefers to pick the leader and then let that leader identify the team players. This increases the likelihood of good team chemistry and commitment, but also assures that a capable leader is leading. Senior management can also help increase the leader's chance of success by providing appropriate resources and empowering the leader to make key decisions. In addition, the team leader should view his or her position as a full-time commitment![17] Many companies recognize the difficulties in locating talented leaders and highly prize those that they do find. Toyota and Honda, for example, have them stay on as managers of their cars after launch, and then assign them to the start of another new car project (rather than to the track to top executive positions).

Selecting the Team Members

When selecting the members of a new product team, it is important to remember that each one of them is on the team as the representative of a group of others "back home" in their department. The R&D team member can't do all the technical work and may do none, but does stimulate, direct, and encourage others in R&D to do it. This is usually in the face of competition from other R&D representatives on other teams, who are also trying to win time for *their* projects. The same goes for team members from the other functions. Chrysler wants team members to be change agents. Bausch & Lomb (B&L) wants members to have real functional influence and a broad-business view. B&L believes so strongly in teams that a conference speaker from the firm brought along (and introduced) five core members of his team.

So we seek people who are knowledgeable in their respective areas, have the respect of their departments, and want to be on the team. If they have to be talked into the job, they will probably not do it well.

Most people in a business are of three types regarding their interrelationships outside their departments. Teams need the *Integrators*, who love to relate to people from other departments or other firms. They naturally give, and get, respect. *Receptors* respect others and welcome information from them but do not desire personal relationships. They are good contacts but not particularly good team members. *Isolates* prefer to be left alone. They are deep specialists in their field and really want nothing to do with people from other functions. They are rarely able to play a role in new product team operations.

How many members should a team have? First, let's distinguish the core team, ad hoc team, and extended team. The *core team* includes those people who are involved in *managing* functional clusters. Thus, one marketing person may represent, speak for, and guide 10 to 12 others in the sales and marketing areas. The core team members are active throughout and are supported by *ad hoc team* members. Ad hoc members are those from important departments (e.g., packaging, legal, logistics) whose importance is brief in time and thus not needed on the core team.

Extended team members may come from another division of the firm, corporate staff, or another firm. Though extended team members can come from just about

---

[17]Jassawalla and Sashittal, op. cit.

anywhere, firms are increasingly seeing the value of including key suppliers on the team. Sharing of information on product and technical plans between manufacturing firms and their suppliers can reduce problems associated with technological uncertainty and help both participants reach their long-term goals.[18] The firm's purchasing department may be a core or ad hoc team member and serve as the liaison with the supplier firm. Additionally, greater coordination with external partner firms may also facilitate internal cooperation between functional areas.[19]

To illustrate the benefits of supplier interaction, Dell Computers has close ties with the external suppliers of its processors, peripherals, and software, and as a result can quickly and easily customize products in response to customer needs. DAF, a small European truck manufacturer, depends on the knowledge provided by its injection systems supplier, Bosch. These firms, in fact, view themselves as partners, despite the size difference between them. Bosch supplies injection systems to DAF, which in turn supplies quick, reliable information to Bosch. The partnership allows Bosch to better anticipate the needs of its other customers.[20]

Roles and Participants

People working on new products are sometimes not just functional representatives; they may assume other roles, some well known and necessary. Figure 14.3 shows the full set of roles, many of which are informal. Although these roles are not always present (for example, an *inventor* may not be needed), they usually are. Sometimes, who is playing which role isn't clear, and people may actually compete for the role they want.

The most well-known role is that of *product champion* (also called *process champion* or just champion). Projects get hung up at times by movements outside the team in the supporting infrastructure. People lose interest; political conflicts arise; volume and cost projections turn sour; technical breakthroughs aren't achieved. The champion within the corporation plays a role similar to that of the entrepreneur starting up a new business. His or her role is to push past the **roadblocks**; bypass corporate hierarchy and persuade other people in the firm (including from several functional areas) to support the innovation.[21] Champions can't win every time, but their task is to see that no project dies without a fight. Champions also

[18]Kenneth J. Petersen, Robert B. Handfield, and Gary L. Ragatz, "A Model of Supplier Integration into New Product Development," *Journal of Product Innovation Management,* 20(4), 2003, pp. 284–299; and C. Anthony Di Benedetto, Roger J. Calantone, Erik VanAllen, and Mitzi M. Montoya-Weiss, "Purchasing Joins the NPD Team," *Research-Technology Management,* 46(4), July–August 2003, pp. 45–51.

[19]Bas Hillebrand and Wim G. Biemans, "Links Between Internal and External Cooperation in Product Development: An Exploratory Development Study," *Journal of Product Innovation Management,* 21(2), March 2004, pp. 110–122.

[20]For the Dell example: G. Tomas M. Hult and K. Scott Swan, "Special Issue on New Product Development and Supply Chain Management: From the Special Issue Guest Editors," *Journal of Product Innovation Management,* 20(5), 2003, pp. 333–336; for the DAF example, Finn Wynstra, Mathieu Weggeman, and Arjan van Weele, "Exploring Purchasing Integration in Product Development," *Industrial Marketing Management,* 32(1), 2003, pp. 69–83.

[21]Stephen K. Markham and Lynda Aiman-Smith, "Product Champions: Truths, Myths, and Management," *Research-Technology Management,* 44(3), May–June 2001, pp. 44–50; and StephenK. Markham, "Moving Technologies from Lab to Market," *Research-Technology Management,* 45(6), November–December 2002, pp. 31–42.

FIGURE 14.3   Roles and Participants in the New Products Management Process

Participant*	Activity	Participant*	Activity
1. Project manager	Leader Integrator Translator Mediator Judge Arbitrator Coordinator	4. Strategist	Longer range Managerial Entire program
2. Product champion	Supporter Spokesperson Pusher Won't concede	5. Inventor	Creative scientist Basement inventor Idea source
3. Sponsor	Senior manager Supporter Endorses Assures hearing Mentor Increases output	6. Rationalist	Objectivity Reality Reason Financial
		7. Facilitator	Boosts productivity

*The participant's role may be either formal or informal.

play a key role in bringing information to the new product team through both their contacts within the organization and their external network.[22]

In most cases, the *project manager* plays the champion role. Other times the champion is self-appointed, often a technical person associated with the discovery that started the project. Today, many firms see the *core team* as the champion since all should have strong concept commitment. Some firms are beginning to think that the champion idea has outlived its usefulness since political obstacles should be addressed by the firm, not by an individual fighting what in many cases takes on a David/Goliath character. Some research finds, however, that champions do make a positive contribution to the performance of the overall new products process.[23]

There is still a lot more to learn about the role of champions. A recent study looked at what is commonly believed about champions and found many misconceptions as well as some beliefs that are essentially correct (see Figure 14.4). For example, it seems that product champions are likely to be found in both large and small firms, and in both technology-driven and marketing-driven firms. Champions are most

[22]Jane M. Howell and Christine M. Shea, "Individual Differences, Environmental Scanning, Innovation Framing, and Champion Behavior: Key Predictors of Project Performance," *Journal of Product Innovation Management,* 18(1), January 2001, pp. 15–27.

[23]Howell and Shea, op. cit.; see also Gloria Barczak, "New Product Strategy, Structure, Process, and Performance in the Telecommunications Industry," *Journal of Product Innovation Management,*12(3), June 1995, pp. 224–234; and Albert L. Page, "Assessing New Product Development Practices and Performance: Establishing Crucial Norms," *Journal of Product Innovation Management,* 10(4), September 1993, pp. 273–290.

FIGURE 14.4 **Myths about Product Champions**

Myth: Champions are associated with market successes. Champions are likely to support failures as well as successes. Champion behavior is not necessarily related to greater market success.

Myth: Champions are excited about the idea. Marketers champion product innovations, production people champion process innovations. The motivating factor may be self-interest, not idealistic excitement.

Myth: Champions get involved only with radical changes. Not necessarily: Champions get involved with radical as well as incremental products.

Myth: Champions only arise from high (or low) levels in the firm. The most famous stories often involve lower-level individuals (such as Mr. Fry, the scientist at 3M who championed Post-It Notes) or senior executives (Mr. Morita, the CEO of Sony, was the Walkman champion). In truth, champions can derive from all levels within the firm.

Myth: Champions are mostly from marketing. Actually, champions can emerge from marketing, R&D, general management, production and operations, and elsewhere.

The same research study did confirm some common beliefs about champions, however:

Champions get resources and keep projects alive.
They are passionate, persuasive, and risk-taking.
Champions work in firms with formal new products processes as well as firms without such processes.
Championing requires sensitivity to company politics.
Champions are likely to back projects that align with the firm's innovation strategy.

Source: From Stephen K. Markham and Lynda Aiman-Smith, "Product Champions: Truths, Myths and Management," *Research-Technology Management*, May–June 2001, pp. 44–50. Reprinted with permission of Industrial Research Institute.

effective if they have a positive personal relationship with the people within the firm they are trying to win over and use cooperative rather than confrontational tactics to win over these people. They also are found supporting incremental as well as radically new products. Obviously, this is a ripe area for more study.[24]

The second most important role in Figure 14.3 is that of **sponsor.** This person does not drive anything but is higher up in the firm, is supportive, and lends encouragement and endorsement to the champion. Teams are wise to develop sponsors, whom some call godfathers or mentors.

To interest a sponsor in a new product project, one must clearly define the project and its objectives, show how the project will affect the sponsor and his or her organization, and state the expected effects on revenues, costs, and profits. One should also consider the level within the firm from which to seek a sponsor: If the project will likely cut across functional boundaries in the organization, it is advisable to seek sponsorship from among the ranks of senior management. Also, don't forget to keep the sponsor interested and enthusiastic: Involve him or her in team meetings and provide progress reports.[25]

[24]Stephen K. Markham, "A Longitudinal Examination of How Champions Influence Others to Support Their Projects," *Journal of Product Innovation Management*, 15(6), November 1998, pp. 490–504; and Stephen K. Markham and Abbie Griffin, "The Breakfast of Champions: Associations between Champions and Product Development Environments, Practices, and Performance," *Journal of Product Innovation Management*, 15(5), September 1998, pp. 436–454.
[25]Gary Tighe, "From Experience: Securing Sponsors and Funding for New Product Development Projects—The Human Side of Enterprise," *Journal of Product Innovation Management*, 15(1), January 1998, pp. 75–81.

The other roles in Figure 14.3 are indicated by the activities listed for them.

Network Building

So far our people focus has been on the team leader and the team members. But sometimes there is no team. As seen in Chapter 1, many new products are simply improvements or close line extensions, and often these are developed in the functional mode, within the ongoing organization, and without a special team. In addition, the extended team includes people well outside the core and ad hoc team. In all of these cases, the participants who actually do the new product work comprise a network.

A **network** consists of nodes, links, and operating relationships. *Nodes* are people important to the project in some way. *Links* are how they are reached and what important ties they have to others in the network. *Operating relationships* are how these people are contacted and motivated to cooperate in the project.

Who are the nodes? This is the toughest part. Any given project may enlist the support of hundreds (or even thousands) of people. Only judgment can decide how many of them should be put into a formal network and managed.

Networks drawn up on paper or computer are not meant to substitute for intensive, walk-around management styles. And they are fluid—changing from time to time in the life of the project, and from project to project as the importance of various functions ebb and flow. For example, the purchasing department was for a long time omitted from networks or placed way out on the edge. But today's focus on speed, quality, cost, and value has moved purchasing to a front row seat.

Network makers admit it's a lot easier to draw nodes and linkage lines than it is to work them. But there is no choice, and networks are an aid, even if quite informal or just mental pictures. Perhaps their greatest danger is that they can easily become bureaucracies. One manager, when asked during a training program, refused to draw up the network for a project he was then managing. He said he didn't want to see it all on one sheet and risk being overpowered by its complexity. And he didn't want his boss to see it and thus get a better idea of the massive indirect costs involved in the activity.

Training the Teams

An appointed team is not yet ready to operate. There must be **top management support** (discussed later) and, hopefully, a good image around the firm. Other managers sometimes come to doubt or fear a team, and they can isolate or ostracize it.

But the real need at this time is training. It would be nice to say we have a large cadre of experienced new product team members and leaders. We do not. Generally, firms start a team off with an intensive two- or three-day training session for the team members. At many firms, this pretraining is so critical that teams may spend a month on it. But training sessions cannot bring team members up to the needed skill levels unless there is considerable skill to begin with.

Managing the Team

Managing a team of the type being developed for more important projects in the new products field is extremely difficult. A couple of recent studies found that most firms reported having well-defined new products processes but were often less successful in implementation. Firms with the most success in new products tended to have several common principles guiding implementation, including clarity of roles and responsibilities, a sense of commitment and ownership, cooperation, strong team leadership, and flexibility. Figure 14.5 provides more

FIGURE 14.5
Guiding Principles in New Product Process Implementation

Clarity of Goals and Objectives. Spell out what needs to be done, by whom, and when, at all phases of the new products process. Provide materials, training, and clearly specified metrics for measurement of new product impact. Make sure there is a shared vision, common focus and direction, and excellent communication across all team members.

Ownership. Commitment (a desire to do whatever is needed to make the project succeed) is important, but so is ownership, which goes beyond commitment. Ownership means that team members feel they can make a difference and want to do so. Their very identity is tied up in the project's outcome. Provide the kinds of rewards and recognition that encourage all team members to share the new products process and to put forth that extra effort. Build mutual confidence across team members.

Leadership at both senior and team levels. Senior management must visibly support new products and lead by example. Responsibility ultimately resides at the top, though decision making can be assigned appropriately to different managerial levels. At the team level, leadership can take the form of support, facilitation, and encouragement.

Integration with business processes. This means all upstream activities affected by the new products process. Their inputs and outputs need to be linked to new product development; a centralized business process organization may facilitate this.

Flexibility. Adjust the new products process as the environment and objectives change. The goal is to remain a world-class product developing organization; this requires the firm to allow each project or each team the required amount of flexibility in, for example, the number of projects currently underway or the length of time devoted to each stage.

Source: Based on Jeffrey M. Davidson, Allen Clamen and Robin A. Karol, "Learning from the Best New Product Developers," *Research-Technology Management,* July–August 1999, pp. 12–18; and Edward F. McDonough III, "Investigation of Factors Contributing to the Success of Cross-Functional Teams," *Journal of Product Innovation Management* 17, no. 3, May 2000, pp. 221–235.

detail.[26] A term that is now emerging to describe high-performance teams is **charged behavior**: In addition to commitment and cooperation, team members derive enjoyment from working together. Encouragement to take risks, quality focus, interdepartmental linkages, exposure to customer input, and the nature of competition, among other factors, are positively related to charged behavior.[27]

A few special thoughts on management and implementation follow.[28]

Cross-Functional Interface Management

As we have seen, product innovation involves people from many different functional areas and backgrounds: sales and marketing, R&D, design, engineering, manufacturing, operations, and so on. Part of the challenge of new products is managing the **interfaces** across the functional areas, as the key functions *must* cooperate often and effectively to improve product development performance.[29] Most new products people can identify with stereotypical complaints such as "Those marketers can't get through the day without a two-hour lunch at the most expensive restaurant in town." And this one: "Ever try to get a scientist to say clearly yes or no?" Or, "Why don't manufacturing people ever admit they goofed up?" These are wildly unfair generalizations. In fact, cross-functional problems are often much less combative than they are sometimes depicted, and people on these interfaces often get along very well.[30] But they do differ on their general time frame, for one thing, and on their measure of success for another. And frictions between functional areas can exist, threatening the project. All participants, including top management, must recognize these frictions and deal with them to minimize any possible negative effects.

Most interface management is straightforward, and experienced managers often know just what to do. Much research has focused on managing the friction

---

[26]Jeffrey M. Davidson, Allen Clamen, and Robin A. Karol, "Learning from the Best New Product Developers," *Research-Technology Management,* 42(4), July–August 1999, pp. 12–18; Edward F. McDonough III, "Investigation of Factors Contributing to the Success of Cross-Functional Teams," *Journal of Product Innovation Management*, 17(3), May 2000, pp. 221–235.

[27]Rajesh Sethi and Carolyn Y. Nicholson, "Structural and Contextual Correlates of Charged Behavior in Product Development Teams," *Journal of Product Innovation Management*, 18(3), May 2001, pp. 154–168.

[28]For a discussion of the performance appraisal, pay, promotion, organizational culture, team leader, member selection, empowerment, and related topics, see Patricia J. Holahan and Stephen K. Markham, "Factors Affecting Multifunctional Team Effectiveness," in M. Rosenau, A. Griffin, G. Castellion, and N. Anscheutz, *The PDMA Handbook of New Product Development* (New York: John Wiley, 1996).

[29]See Kenneth B. Kahn, "Market Orientation, Interdepartmental Integration, and Product Development Performance," *Journal of Product Innovation Management*, 18(5), September 2001, pp. 314–323.

[30]For evidence that there is general agreement across functional areas, see Roger J. Calantone, C. Anthony Di Benedetto, and Ted Haggblom, "Principles of New Product Management: Exploring the Beliefs of Product Practitioners," *Journal of Product Innovation Management*, 12(3), June 1995, pp. 235–247; and X. Michael Song, Mitzi M. Montoya-Weiss, and Jeffrey B. Schmidt, "Antecedents and Consequences of Cross-Functional Cooperation: A Comparison of R&D, Manufacturing, and Marketing Perspectives," *Journal of Product Innovation Management*, 14(1), January 1997, pp. 35–47.

between functional areas. The highlights of the research findings can be summed in three statements:

- Top managers get the interfaces they deserve because they can eliminate most of the problems any time they choose to do so.
- Interface management primarily takes time, not skills. One new product manager said he solved his team's problems by giving at least 40 percent of his time to seeing that all key players spent a lot of time with each other, on and off the job.
- Participants who continue to be a problem should be taken out of new product team situations; they get some perverse satisfaction out of reactions to their behavior.

At the most innovative firms, one sees real relationships across functions, and not just structured work assignments. 3M, for example, encourages early, informal communication among marketing, technical, and manufacturing staff (3M employees refer to this as the three-legged stool). Team members bounce ideas off one another and provide resources and information informally to each other. Design of employees' working environment can be used to stimulate cross-functional integration. Many new facilities (such as Hoffman-LaRoche's New Jersey research and marketing facility and Glaxo-Wellcome's lab in the United Kingdom) are designed with coffee bars on every floor to encourage cross-functional shop talk, and workstations can be designed such that they are easy to move (thus facilitating the process of reorganizing into teams). Sony and other Japanese companies rotate their managers through marketing, product development, manufacturing, and finance, thus developing well-rounded managers.[31]

Keep in mind, however, that even with these new approaches to teams, conflicts can still arise. In fact, a little conflict is a good thing. Healthy disagreements between functional areas can lead to more critical analysis and, ultimately, bring vitality to new product development. How conflict is managed, however, is of critical importance. Integrative conflict management styles such as confrontation (collaborative problem solving to reach a mutually agreeable solution) and give-and-take (reaching an acceptable compromise solution) are better at fostering a positive environment for innovation than dysfunctional styles such as withdrawal (avoiding the issue), smoothing (seeking a superficial solution), or forcing a solution (see Figure 14.6).[32] Also, no one functional area should dominate the process.

---

[31]See Eric M. Olson, Rachel Cooper, and Stanley F. Slater, "Design Strategy and Competitive Advantage," *Business Horizons,* 41(2), March–April 1998, pp. 55–61; S. W. F. (Onno) Omta and Jo M. L. van Engelen, "Preparing for the 21st Century," *Research-Technology Management,* 41(1), January–February 1998, pp. 31–35; and Karen Anne Zien and Sheldon A. Buckler, "From Experience: Dreams to Market: Crafting a Culture of Innovation," *Journal of Product Innovation Management,* 14(4), July 1997, pp. 274–287.

[32]David H. Gobeli, Harold F. Koenig, and Iris Bechinger, "Managing Conflict in Software Development Teams: A Multi-Level Analysis," *Journal of Product Innovation Management,* 15(5), September 1998, pp. 423–435; and Barbara Dyer and X. Michael Song, "Innovation Strategy and Sanctioned Conflict: A New Edge in Innovation?" *Journal of Product Innovation Management,* 15(6), November 1998, pp. 505–519.

FIGURE 14.6 **Five Conflict Management Styles**

Conflict Management Style	Definition	Example
Confrontation	Collaboratively solve the problem to reach a solution the parties are committed to.	Debate the issue, conduct customer interviews, generate possible solutions, find the one most supported by customers.
Give and Take	Reach a compromise solution that the parties find acceptable.	Negotiate a set of features to build into the product to keep the project moving ahead.
Withdrawal	Avoid the issue or the disagreeable party.	Team members with unpopular positions don't think it's worth the trouble and back out of the decision.
Smoothing	Minimize the differences and find a superficial solution.	Accommodate to the team members that are strongly committed to certain product features, for the sake of group harmony.
Forcing	Impose a solution.	Project manager steps in and makes the decisions.

Source: Adapted from David H. Gobeli, Harold F. Koenig, and Iris Bechinger, "Managing Conflict in Software Development Teams: A Multi-Level Analysis," *Journal of Product Innovation Management* 14, no. 5, September 1998, pp. 423–435.

If marketing, or manufacturing, or R&D is viewed as the *de facto* leader, good cross-functional collaboration and better new product performance are unlikely to be facilitated. Equal status seems to work best.[33]

Overcoming Barriers to Market Orientation

We still see signs of compartmentalized thinking in many new product developing firms; that is, functional areas tend to focus on their own goals. Information either does not flow across departments efficiently, or it is interpreted differently by different departments. This problem should be surmountable by establishing empowered cross-functional teams (discussed in this chapter) and implementing a house of quality procedure for translating customer input to product specifications (as seen in Chapter 12). A related problem that still surfaces is inertia: Market information is not used if it does not conform to specifications. As we have seen in this chapter, it is critical for management to create an environment of mutual trust among employees of all functional areas; higher levels of trust mean that managers will be more open to suggestions that might cause change in "the way things are done." Clearly, while we have seen great improvements in recent years on these issues, the problems remain, and more improvement still needs to be made.[34]

[33]Kenneth B. Kahn, "Department Status: An Exploratory Investigation of Direct and Indirect Effects on Product Development Performance," *Journal of Product Innovation Management,* 22(6), November 2005, pp. 515–526

[34]Marjorie E. Adams, George S. Day, and Deborah Dougherty, "Enhancing New Product Development Performance: An Organizational Learning Perspective," *Journal of Product Innovation Management,*15(5), September 1998, pp. 403–423.

Ongoing Management of the Team

A pressing problem on new product teams is keeping the group enthusiastic. As work goes on, as creative needs are not met, as efforts fail, and as people get tensed up, it is imperative to give what one manager calls pep talks. Burnout is a genuine and not uncommon problem, and the innovation-derailing patterns of behavior that new products face are almost unbelievable. Some team leaders set up defenses against the well-intentioned suggestions they know will come up—a product variation, a technology that just appeared, or a new advertising approach. Such suggestions are terribly distracting if not kept away from the team.

Another aspect of the team management problem may appear trivial—the ability to run *effective meetings*. New product people seem to be in meetings continuously. Some product innovators have caught on to this need and are now studying their own team meetings for ways to speed them up and improve the decisions.

Changes in team membership over the duration of the project can also cause problems. Losing key people from the team might cause important information to get lost. There is also a *job security* issue. In many firms, climbing the corporate ladder within one's functional area (from junior to senior marketer or researcher, for example) is seen as a more secure road to promotion than is team membership. A clear career path for scientists seems to be especially important. One study showed that, among the most innovative firms, there was a "dual ladder" system: Scientists could be promoted into management or choose to stay in the laboratory without financial penalty. At the more poorly performing firms, the common feeling is that "you have to get out of research to get ahead in this company."[35]

Team Compensation and Motivation

A delicate issue in team management is the matter of compensation. Team leaders and team members are usually paid a straight salary or salary plus bonus. Bonuses are equally split among company performance, individual performance, and project accomplishment. It is rare to have compensation ride on the new product's performance.[36] The reasons for this are strong: Employees should be treated equally (fairly), team members do not have the financial risks of an entrepreneur, and it is easier to transfer managers into and out of teams if compensation plans are equal. Still, all agree that finding good people willing to risk career-bypass by serving on a new products team and motivating them to give the necessary high level of effort and stress is a legitimate problem.[37] Firms that use equity awards, such as stock shares and product profit-sharing, tend to be smaller ones in Silicon Valley (that is, those that survived the Internet bubble of 2000).

[35]S. W. F. (Onno) Omta and Jo M. L. van Engelen, op. cit.
[36]See Albert Page, op. cit., p. 278.
[37]Hollister B. Sykes, "Incentive Compensation for Corporate Venture Personnel," *Journal of Business Venturing*, 7, 1992, pp. 253–265.

Many firms use a combination of monetary and nonmonetary rewards (such as prizes, formal recognition, or even permission to work on pet projects on company time) to motivate their teams. According to the CPAS study, the most commonly used rewards are project completion celebrations, the opportunity to work on a bigger and more meaningful project, getting written up in a special newsletter, plaques and pins, and award dinners.[38]

Using only monetary rewards can lead to problems. Some may feel that the satisfaction of being on a successful team is reward enough, and the money isn't necessary. Others may complain that all team members get rewarded (even the lazy ones!)—a problem that is compounded if the same dollar figure is awarded to everyone on the team. Some may be resentful if their multimillion-dollar idea was rewarded with only a $1,000 bonus![39]

It has been suggested that firms align their reward structures to characteristics of the project. If the project is relatively long or less complex, rewards tied to the project's profit outcome tend to enhance performance; for risky projects, it is preferable to reward the team's processes during product development (procedures, behaviors, completion of phases in the new products process, etc). Outcome-based rewards in this latter case may be viewed as too risky or difficult and may be rejected by the project team. Firms can also consider rewarding the team at frequent milestones (much like mountain climbers celebrate getting to the first base, then celebrate again at the summit), as this can help boost team spirit and positively affect organizational culture.[40]

TRW's Cleveland automotive group has instituted Project ELITE (Earnings Leadership in Tomorrow's Environment) to motivate and compensate its teams. In this endeavor, specific goals are set for each team project and also for each individual, and 10 to 25 percent of pay is tied to the accomplishment of these individual and team goals. DuPont uses a "360-degree" review process in which team members are evaluated by peers, subordinates, and supervisors. Motorola is one of many firms that rewards team behavior rather than team results. Motorola recognizes that teams often need to take risks to make progress, and rewarding only results might make them risk-averse. It also makes sense to have one person in charge of the nonmonetary recognition programs, modifying them occasionally to make sure they are always worthwhile rewards.[41]

[38]Gloria Barczak, Abbie Griffin, and Kenneth B. Kahn, "Perspective: Trends and Drivers of Success in NPD Practices: Results of the 2003 PDMA Best Practices Study," *Journal of Product Innovation Management,* 26(1), January 2009, pp. 3–23.

[39]Perry Pascarella, "Compensating Teams," *Across the Board,* February 1997, pp. 16–22. See also Shikhar Sarin and Vijay Mahajan, "The Effect of Reward Structure on the Performance of Cross-Functional Product Development Teams," *Journal of Marketing,* 65(2), April 2001, pp. 35–53.

[40]Shikhar Sarin and Vijay Mahajan, "The Effect of Reward Structures on the Performance of Cross-Functional Product Development Teams," *Journal of Marketing,* 65(2), April 2001, pp. 35–53; and Erika B. Seamon, "Achieving Growth through an Innovative Culture," in P. Belliveau, A. Griffin, and S. M. Somermeyer, *The PDMA Toolbook 2 for New Product Development* (New York: John Wiley, 2004).

[41]These examples and suggestions are from Pascarella, op. cit., and J. Gregory Kunkel, "Rewarding Product Development Success," *Research-Technology Management,* 40(5), September–October 1997, pp. 29–31. See also Tom Kiely, op. cit.

Closing the Team Down

Strong differences of opinion arise regarding when a new product team should be closed down and the product turned over to the regular organization. Some firms *close out early,* well before the item is marketed; they bring in operating people bit by bit.[42] A second practice lets the team prepare for the marketing (for example, write the plan or train the people) but, at the last minute, the *regular people launch it.* When this is done, the key team people are usually kept close to the action to help solve problems. A third, and rarer, practice lets the team actually *market the item* and either become the nucleus of its standing management as a new division or turn it over to the regular organization after it has been successfully established. Honda keeps team leaders as ongoing managers of its new products for two or three major design upgrades (six–nine years), and then reassigns them to a new development program.

No matter when the ongoing staff takes over, they should be brought into the action in a way that lets them link into the new product organization. As one manager put it, "Treat this as a whirling gear being meshed with an idle gear; send a few people into the ongoing organization early, to get the idle gear up to a speed where it can accept the rest of the new operation."

Virtual Teams[43]

Many firms now take advantage of available technology to assemble virtual teams that meet and share information "electronically" in place of traditional or colocated teams. Virtual teams are a way for firms to take advantage of local expertise and incorporate it into their global new products processes, and also to develop products that could be sold globally. By definition, a **virtual team** is one whose members are linked electronically (e.g., via the Internet) to each other and also to partners such as customers, contractors, and the like. The obvious benefit of virtual teams is the ability to communicate despite geographic dispersion. In addition, virtual teams can meet in *synchronous* mode (everyone is on the computer or the phone and communicating at the same time), or in *asynchronous* mode (participants enter the site individually and can come and go as they please). Synchronous methods of communication include video or audioconferencing, instant messaging, live application sharing; e-mail and shared document repositories are examples of asynchronous methods. Both are commonly used; however, asynchronous meetings avoid time zone problems and working around holidays. Virtual product teams

---

[42]Charles Heckscher, "The Failure of Participatory Management," op. cit. Heckscher notes that permanent or "semi-permanent" teams tend to build walls around themselves, and recommends that teams get abandoned as soon as possible.

[43]Much of this section is drawn from Hans J. Thamhain, "Managing Product Development Project Teams," in Kenneth B. Kahn, George Castellion and Abbie Griffin (eds.), *The PDMA Handbook of New Product Development* (New York: John Wiley & Sons, 2005), pp. 127–143; and Mitzi M. Montoya, Anne P. Massey, Yu-Ting Caisy Hung, and C. Brad Crisp, "Can You Hear Me Now? Communication in Virtual Product Development Teams," *Journal of Product Innovation Management*, 26(2), March 2009, pp. 139–155.

have certainly become popular in recent years: According to the Gartner Group, demand for team collaboration software exceeded $1 billion in 2008.

Virtual team participants will note that these teams pose their own sets of challenges. Team members must be familiar and comfortable with the technology. Performance measurement and managerial control may be more difficult, and dealing with power conflicts may be more challenging than in a face-to-face format. Further, the whole idea of virtual teams may not fit too well with the values or cultures within many firms, or may not be universally adopted by all team members. Firms with a very hierarchical chain of command, or poor teamwork skills in general, tend to have difficulties with implementing virtual teams. Because of problems like this, firms often complement virtual teams with at least some traditional team meetings. In fact, research in both the United States and the Netherlands finds that traditional and virtual communication channels complement and strengthen each other, and that firms should explore both colocation and information technology that supports virtual teams, depending on the nature of the knowledge that needs to be shared among members.[44] Nevertheless, experienced virtual team participants admit that the latest communication technologies have put virtual teams on a par with traditional team structures, as long as commitment and trust are maintained.[45]

Although virtual teams can be used whenever there are geographic distances between team members, they really become important in the case of global teams. Given the available technology, team leaders will see virtual teams as a wonderful opportunity to bring in firm expertise residing in research facilities located throughout the world. But the challenge posed by global virtual teams is greater, as they must overcome cultural as well as communication barriers. More on global teams in the next section.

Managing Globally Dispersed Teams

More firms than ever are taking a global perspective to new product development and building teams composed of individuals based in different countries. A summary of some results from a recent series of interviews with senior executives appears in Figure 14.7. In a recent survey, more than half of the responding firms reported using globally dispersed teams (GDTs) for at least some of their new product efforts, and that the use of GDTs is expected to continue increasing.[46]

---

[44]Michael Song, Hans Berends, Hans van der Bij, and Mathieu Weggeman, "The Effect of IT and Co-location on Knowledge Dissemination," *Journal of Product Innovation Management*, 24(1), January 2007, pp. 52–68.

[45]See Robert Jones, Robert Oyung, and Lisa Pace, *Working Virtually: Challenges of Virtual Teams* (Hershey, PA: Cybertech Publishing, 2005).

[46]Edward F. McDonough III, Kenneth B. Kahn, and Gloria Barczak, "An Investigation of the Use of Global, Virtual, and Colocated New Product Development Teams," *Journal of Product Innovation Management*, 18(2), March 2001, pp. 110–120. For a good reference on coordinating global R&D efforts, see Yves Doz, Jose Santos, and Peter Williamson, *From Global to Metanational: How Companies Win in the Knowledge Economy* (Boston, MA: Harvard Business School Press, 2001).

FIGURE 14.7
Some Insights on Global Innovation from Senior Executives

On Idea Generation:

It is important to leverage knowledge from around the world.

New ideas can come from customers, employees, competitors, distributors, suppliers, and so on.

On Product Development:

U.S. firms tend to work toward "home run" type breakthroughs, while Japanese firms concentrate more on continuous, incremental improvement. This can even hold true at the launch stage, where the prototype may be initially launched; if it does badly, it is viewed as a learning experience rather than as a failed launch.

Development costs may be shared, as new technology development may be prohibitively high. Technology licensing or trading may be the result.

Standardization is increasingly used to better manage a global company, not necessarily in response to similar customer needs.

For some products categories, such as image-based or children's products, standardization may be easier.

On Commercialization:

Many firms recognize the costs and risks of being an early entrant, and actually prefer to be a later entrant in certain markets. A clear hierarchy, for example, may exist among Japanese firms, some being leaders, others being followers.

Strong local support is an important factor deciding where products will be introduced. For durables, customer needs may be rather standardized across countries so a global launch may be attempted to recover development costs quickly. A few special cases notwithstanding, most consumer nondurable launches are still initially local launches. Success in the U.S. market often confers "signal value" for entry into other markets, but a U.S. failure can be costly. Europe, by contrast, might be attacked one country at a time.

It is often better to introduce innovations in a foreign market with the help of a local partner. This reduces costs, capitalizes on the local partner's capabilities in manufacturing and distribution, and helps overcome cultural barriers.

Source: From Peter N. Golder, "Insights from Senior Executives about Innovation in International Markets," *Journal of Product Innovation Management* 17, no. 5, September 2000, pp. 326–340. Reprinted with permission of John Wiley & Sons, Inc.

It is easy to see why GDTs have increased in prominence. Increasing product complexity and accelerated product life cycles put pressure on new product teams to gather expertise wherever it resides. If Braun, for example, were to develop a new battery-powered shaver suitable for use in the shower, it would need to gain expertise in materials and components, mechanics, and shaving emulsion that normally would be out of its purview. Additionally, changes to the battery or other components may also be required. Since we now have the capacity to coordinate team activities using computer-driven communication technology, it would be possible for Braun to tap into expertise on these issues even if it resides on other continents![47]

These teams pose special challenges to managers, over and above the difficulties involved in managing domestic teams! Global business meetings are often carried out in English, and while all team members may speak English, their levels of ability may vary considerably. Then there is the issue of cultural differences. Potentially, having a multicultural, heterogeneous team should lead to greater creativity and better problem solving, but communications breakdowns are likely to be more common, and it is up to top management and team leadership to get the desired cross-cultural synergy.[48] The meetings are usually conducted electronically, as the members are physically distant from one another. More communications problems can occur since in-person meetings may occur only rarely. Nevertheless, despite these challenges, some research has found that globally dispersed teams may be better than colocated teams in terms of effectiveness and efficiency, so long as they are good at teamwork issues such as good communication, good cohesion, strong effort, and mutual support.[49]

GDTs also have a more difficult task in completing design reviews, as regular meetings in a central location obviously are nearly impossible. GDTs use e-mail and phone to discuss design changes, but these tools are limited in that team members cannot work easily with three-dimensional models. Many firms operating globally have turned to Visual Issues Management software that allows all participants to visualize the designs in three dimensions, do mark-ups, flag problems, and track changes. Designers, engineers, and other experts can be brought into the new products process at the very earliest phases and easily identify potential problems before they become costly to fix. Overall, engineering and reengineering costs are reduced and speed to market is increased using such tools.[50]

There are many examples of virtual GDTs that have successfully overcome these communications difficulties. Boeing used Web-based new product systems to integrate its rocket engine designers and its partner firms scattered across several geographic locations, resulting in enormous reductions in design time, development

[47]The shaving example is from Roger Leenders, Jan Kratzer, and Jo van Engelen, "Building Creative Virtual New Product Development Teams," in P. Belliveau, A. Griffin, and S. M. Somermeyer (eds.), *The PDMA Toolbook 2 for New Product Development* (New York: John Wiley, 2004), Chapter 5.
[48]X. Michael Song and Mark E. Parry, "Teamwork Barriers in Japanese High-Technology Firms: The Sociocultural Differences between R&D and Marketing Managers," *Journal of Product Innovation Management,* 14(5), September 1997, pp. 356–367; B. M. Wren, W. E. Souder, and D. Berkowitz, "Market Orientation and New Product Development in Global Industrial Firms," *Industrial Marketing Management,* 29(6), November 2000, pp. 601–611; Preston G. Smith and Emily L. Blanck, "From Experience: Leading Dispersed Teams," *Journal of Product Innovation Management,* 19(4), July 2002, pp. 294–304; and K. Sivakumar and Cheryl Nakata, "Designing New Global Product Teams: Optimizing the Effects of National Culture on New Product Development," *International Marketing Review,* 20(4), 2003, pp. 397–445.
[49]M. Hoegl, H. Ernst, and L. Proserpio, "How Teamwork Matters More as Team Member Dispersion Increases," *Journal of Product Innovation Management,* 24(2), pp. 156–165.
[50]Steve Bashada, "Visual Issues Management: Improving Product Development," *Time Compression,* September–October 2009, pp. 24–25.

costs, and the number of component parts. As another example, Xerox uses the Web to integrate the efforts of its product designers in Rochester, New York, its engineers in Shanghai, and its manufacturing plants in Hong Kong.[51] Certainly, multinational firms that encourage globally dispersed research and development activities accumulate and use knowledge more effectively, resulting in greater innovative capability. In sum, the most important drivers of successful international new product teams are having an innovative, global culture, committing sufficient resources to R&D, and obtaining the support of top management.[52]

Ford Motor Company attributes much of its recent success to increased efficiencies stemming from its Global Product Development System and Global Vehicle programs. As far back as the development of the Contour/Mondeo, Ford was using a GDT that communicated using the Web and videoconferencing. As with car companies worldwide, Ford makes use of global platforms to support multiple brands (see discussion of platforms in Chapter 3). But, according to Derrick M. Kuzak, group vice president for Global Product Development, the global platform approach is even more all-encompassing. He says, "Think about a product development that allows you to be faster in time to market, depending on the complexity of the vehicle, by 25 to 40 percent. . . . Think about one group doing the engineering on a system for every vehicle globally."[53] Where in the past, each new products project would have its own, say, exhaust engineer, one group would handle the exhaust system for all cars sold globally on the same platform. This uniformity contributes to what Ford calls "Vehicle DNA." Since steering wheel design and engineering is done by one team and applied across all cars, steering wheels on all Fords will have a distinctive, familiar grip or "feel," regardless of where they were made or sold. This familiarity runs through all components of the car, even down to the same "sound signature" emanating from a Ford I-4 engine. Ford claims to have slashed new car engineering costs by 60 percent between 2005 and 2008 thanks to their global product development efforts, while launching successful new products (the Ford Fusion) and breathing new life into older models (the F-150 truck).

Digital Equipment Corporation had great success with its GDT (which it named the "Columbus Team"), composed of members from five U.S. locations as well as Switzerland, France, and Japan. It had to put several measures into effect to overcome GDT-related hurdles, however. A major problem was team motivation: The typical team member felt more allegiance to his or her own local network and not

[51]Rajesh Sethi, Somendra Pant, and Anju Sethi, "Web-Based Product Development Systems Integration and New Product Outcomes: A Conceptual Framework," *Journal of Product Innovation Management,* 20(1), January 2003, pp. 37–56; and Muammar Ozer, "Using the Internet in New Product Development," *Research-Technology Management,* 46(1), January–February 2003, pp. 10–17.

[52]See Ajax Persaud, "Enhancing Synergistic Innovative Capability in Multinational Corporations: An Empirical Investigation," *Journal of Product Innovation Management,* 22(5), September 2005, pp. 412–429; and Ulrike de Brentani and Elko J. Kleinschmidt, "Corporate Culture and Commitment: Impact on Performance of International New Product Development Programs," *Journal of Product Innovation Management,* 21(5), September 2004, pp. 309–333.

[53]The Ford example and quote are from Gary S. Vasilash, "Developing More Faster at Ford," *Time Compression,* September–October 2009, pp. 34–35.

to the Columbus Team, and getting agreement on team goals proved difficult. To overcome this problem, Digital allowed team members some say as to the tasks they should perform, so that they would contribute to the team project while at the same time "look good" to others in their local network. To overcome communications barriers, Digital found that team members liked audioconferencing at the start of the project (since casual comments could be made). Computer conferencing and e-mail worked better in later phases when team members were working more at their own pace, and it became increasingly important to retain transcripts of conversations.[54]

Kodak's Entertainment Imaging Division created two global teams to develop and launch new products in its line of premixed chemicals used in movie film processing. The development team included R&D scientists from France, technical personnel and film system developers from both the United States and Europe, the U.S.-based worldwide product marketing managers and planners, manufacturing engineers, and packaging engineers from both sides of the Atlantic. And a launch team was assembled comprising members from Europe, the United States and Canada, Asia, Australia, and Latin America, and also the product marketing manager and other engineers and developers. Needless to say, finding a time to hold phone meetings that worked for all team members was difficult. The teams also faced the above-mentioned language problem: All members spoke English but their levels of understanding varied widely. Kodak discovered that having the occasional face-to-face meeting was valuable in overcoming communication problems.[55]

Many firms such as Philips, AT&T, and IBM have programs in place that actively support team diversity. Philips uses job rotation in which employees ("expatriates") are sent to foreign locations, often to serve in a different functional area within the company, for an average of five to seven years. The drug company Schering shuttles its technical people between its Berlin and Richmond, Virginia, research centers. Other firms use "visiting researchers," foreign technical specialists who visit R&D headquarters to pick up firm knowledge. Recognizing that hair care varies across countries, the Japanese chemical company Kao uses reciprocal visiting researchers—from Japan to Germany and from Germany to Japan—to develop hair care products. Predevelopment takes place in Tokyo, while development activities are centered in Darmstadt, Germany.[56]

For many firms, GDTs are here to stay since they offer a practical and cost-efficient alternative to relocating employees and research facilities to a central location. GDT members in foreign markets can also provide local expertise for developing new products for their particular markets. So far, GDTs have, in general,

---

[54]Edward F. McDonough III, "Meeting the Challenge of Global Team Management," *Research-Technology Management*, 43(4), July–August 2000, pp. 12–17.

[55]Marian Herz, "Case History: Eastman Kodak: Using Global Teams to Overcome the Challenges of Multinational Product Distribution," *Visions*, 26(4), September–October 2002.

[56]Oliver Gassmann, "Multicultural Teams: Increasing Creativity and Innovation by Diversity," *Creativity and Innovation Management*, 10(2), June 2001, pp. 88–95. A good step-by-step resource for managing dispersed teams is Parviz F. Rad and Ginger Levin, *Achieving Project Management Success Using Virtual Teams* (Ft. Lauderdale, FL: Ross Publishing, 2003).

not performed as well as domestic teams. This may be partially due to the fact that GDTs are such a new concept for many firms. There is also some new evidence suggesting that GDTs have their own drawbacks: For example, it may be more difficult to discuss or interpret very complex problems using e-mail or a company intranet than by meeting in person. Some researchers are finding that "in-between" teams that offer flexibility in physical proximity and mode of communication are more creative than either in-person teams or totally virtual teams. With greater experience in global team management, however, GDT performance will likely increase.[57]

Summary

This chapter covered issues surrounding the subject of the team: what a team is, the various organization options, setting up a team and managing it through to completion—selecting the leader, selecting the team members, training them, and so forth.

As a closing thought, there are two new types of new product teams emerging on the scene. One is a higher-level, multifunctional group (often heads of the key functions) whose task is to *manage the project teams*. As teams proliferate, they need a reporting home of some type. The other emerging team is a group of experienced new products people whose task is to *assist project teams in developing appropriate processes to follow*. The latter may just be a person with the title *New Products Process Manager*. Process is critical, and a firm needs some place to house the **organization learning** constantly taking place.

Applications

1. "Actually, I'm not convinced that any particular organization formats are better than others. I've run into too many exceptions. For example, that great portable tape player, Walkman by Sony, was conceived and pushed through by Akio Morita, Sony's chairman of the board. He got the idea from seeing a past chairman wearing a headset in the office, and he personally directed the project through its technical phases, even over the opposition of his people in manufacturing and sales. Even gave himself the title of project manager. I'll bet that approach doesn't fit any of your academic formats. And I'll bet you wouldn't discourage it."

2. "You mentioned culture! Now there's a human relations cult if I ever heard one. Human resource and organization design people are great, and out of their work has come some of the most valuable new business methods of the past 15 years. But culture isn't one of them. It's vague, never defined, full of soft terms like *happy, egalitarian,* and *forthright*. Life just doesn't work this way. Don't misunderstand me; managers must respect their people, and we can't let strong opinions get in the way of our increasing productivity. But good people want

---

[57]See Leenders, Kratzer, and van Engelen, op. cit., and McDonough, Kahn, and Barczak, op. cit.

honest motivations, not games or manipulations. Yeah, I said manipulation, because that's what the culture thing is. Tell me, what kind of a culture do you like best in the classroom where you are using this book? Is that culture consistent with the general ideas of management we have had for years?"

3. "Several of our divisions say they get tremendous help from their vendors when it comes to new product development. But, to tell you the truth, I think they're just lazy. They've got good talent in those divisions, or darn well should have, and all they're doing is letting vendors get a bigger piece of our innovation profits. Most vendors don't pull their share in these funny partnerships. Besides, the initiative should be theirs, not ours; they stand to gain more from so-called integrated operations and alliances than we do."

Case: Marko Products

As a major and very profitable division of a large conglomerate for the past seven years, Marko Products was one of those acquisitions that worked out well. They specialized in medical supply products (items bought by physicians for use in their offices, not medical products for the patient).

Marko's president, Bill Wong, was an aggressive executive who tried to keep his firm poised for maximum market impact. He had installed the product manager system three years ago and was pleased that it seemed to be working well. The product managers were in the marketing department, and although they did not have the almost unlimited informal authority of their packaged goods counterparts, they were respected around the firm.

Marko had two manufacturing divisions: one for consumer supplies (e.g., bandages, rubber gloves) located in a different state, and another for equipment (examining tables, cabinets, ophthalmoscopes, etc.) located at headquarters. All R&D was physically centralized, but the VP for that function had divided her staff into six parts, each dedicated to a particular technology such as rubber, laminated materials, electronics, and more.

One sales force sold the entire line, but in the more populated regions the firm used separate salespeople for supplies and for equipment.

Top-management staff included a long-range planning group, an international marketing division organized by areas of the world, a governmental/public relations department, finance, human resources, and legal. Packaging and quality control were part of the manufacturing staff.

Marko Products' management chased tough goals in profit and market dominance. They planned to hold the number one or two spots in each major market or else would pull back promotional and R&D support.

They recently held a two-day planning retreat, which produced new product innovation charters for each of their businesses. It had been a productive session but not without controversy because most of the managers thought Marko should concentrate on what they did best: manufacture top-quality examining room furniture. They argued that furniture earned most of the profits and that supply was a commodity business Marko entered only because it came with the cabinetry business of Mainline Medical (a firm Marko acquired six years ago). Bill Wong was pleased that he had persuaded them to become more aggressive and to set their sights on bigger and better things.

Following are two of the charters:

Medical Office Equipment, Nonscientific: Marko will actively develop any and all new products in what might be called the "furniture" category, for use in doctors' and hospitals' examining and consultation rooms. The items will typically (and desirably) utilize our skills in "metal bending" and our knowledge of examining room procedures. The goals of this activity are (1) to add $70 million profit contribution over the next four years, and (2) to assure that we dominate (actual or close) in each major market we enter.

To do all this we will rely primarily upon our marketing department for input on market needs, supported by input from knowledgeable technical staff who maintain market contacts. Each new product will be unique in at least one critical dimension, and we hope it will make a contribution to examining room procedure. We intend to continue our reputation as the leading light in this industry, and all new items will be of the highest quality ("absolutely no schlock," as Wong put it). Our major contribution will be in designing products that can be manufactured to the traditionally high standards of our operations group.

Disposables: In recent years the medical community has turned to disposables to solve many of their operating problems, and Marko wants to take advantage of this trend. Our two small lines of disposable gloves and disposable aprons will be the springboard for this activity. The key to dominance here is predicting what new methodologies the medical personnel will agree to convert to disposability next. We want to develop products that extend disposability and are thus unique. Finding these product concepts will be difficult and will require a combination of office procedure knowledge, attitude study, and technical capability.

Profit goals are not clear for this operation, but we do want the program to get us into at least 10 new lines over the next five years, to dominate at least eight of those lines (plus gloves and aprons), and to be the firm contacted by persons in medicine who see an opportunity for disposability. Minimum ROAs will be developed as the projects come along.

Some new disposable products will be reasonably nondifferentiated add-ons to capitalize on our position in a given market.

Wong now wondered which of the five organizational structures in Figure 14.1 would be appropriate for each of the two PIC groups.

Also, Wong knew that putting a structure into place was not enough—the people in any structure had to work effectively as a group. So please take whatever organization option you choose for the nonscientific medical office equipment and then go through the following topics, commenting on how each topic would relate specifically to the equipment group management: (1) culture, (2) team ownership, (3) selecting the leader, (4) need for product champions, (5) compensating the team.

Case: Ford Mondeo[58]

In the mid-1980s, Ford and other carmakers were noticing that car requirements in different parts of the world were converging. For example, North American drivers accustomed to larger cars were demanding smaller ones, while many Europeans were looking for somewhat bigger and more comfortable cars with more powerful engines. This trend suggested to Ford the possibility of developing a new car for the global market, using the skills and specializations of its U.S. and European R&D centers. Ford set out to replace its Sierra model in Europe and its Tempo model in the United States with a single car commercialized in both markets.

Ford began with a benchmarking study to determine levels of customer satisfaction with existing models, followed by extensive surveys to identify the most pressing needs for performance improvement. Subsequently, the "global car" project went into development, with Ford Europe taking project leadership (as the car was more similar to European than to American Ford models). Ford selected its assembly plant in Gand, Belgium, as the coordination site for the project.

From the beginning, the project operated on a global scale. There were several global working groups addressing specific technical issues, a Program Control Group consisting of the leaders of the working groups, and a Product Committee chaired by Ford Europe's president. A Coordination Group was established to keep the activities of all other groups coordinated. Suppliers too were global: 47 were European and another 20 were North American–based.

Different groups worked on different phases of the new product process. During product design, a group in Dearborn, Michigan, handled the six-cylinder engine and transmission; one in Merkenich, Germany, worked on the four-cylinder engine and aesthetics; and one in Dunton, United Kingdom, specialized in interiors. At the same time, 35 Americans were working in European technical labs.

Similarly, during prototype development, groups were assigned specialized responsibilities. The Bridgend, Wales, plant developed prototypes of smaller four-cylinder engines; Chihuahua, Mexico, handled larger four-cylinder engines; Cleveland, Ohio, concentrated on six-cylinder engines; and Dagenham, United Kingdom, worked on diesel engines. CAD-CAM was used extensively and shared between prototype and design engineers. Teleconferencing and other telecommunication systems were used to coordinate all efforts.

Engineering was done in Gand; it was felt necessary to colocate engineers from the various design and prototyping units to a central location for this step. Some members of the Gand team were then transferred to Kansas City for U.S.-based engineering preproduction.

[58]This case is derived from Vittorio Chiesa, "Global R&D Project Management and Organization: A Taxonomy," *Journal of Product Innovation Management,* 17(5), September 2000, pp. 341–359.

The Mondeo (known in the United States as the Contour) was introduced at the Geneva car exhibition of 1993 and launched in the United States a little over a year later. It was also sold in Japan through a Ford-Mazda joint venture.

How did Ford do managing the efforts of the various global teams? What would be the strengths and, importantly, the weaknesses of the procedure used in the development of the Mondeo? What would you recommend for Ford to have done differently, if anything? Could they have used GDTs as described in this chapter to any greater extent? If so, how?

CHAPTER FIFTEEN

Product Use Testing

Setting

The first output of technical development is a prototype, which is checked against the protocol statement that guided its development and perhaps sent it to the marketplace for a confirmatory prototype concept test. The methodology for that is essentially the same as the original concept test except now, we have a more tangible expression of the idea. Usually the end user is not satisfied that the prototype would work, so more development work is done. The cycle continues until the firm has a good approximation of what will be the eventual product—a prototype that stakeholders like.

At this time, most firms like to make up a quantity of prototypes, whether on the bench (i.e., a single working unit of a new remote control, made by designers) or in some small-scale pilot production setup. And for the first time they can give the end user a product concept that is in a *form for extended use*—no more guessing about whether it *would* or *might* satisfy the needs, based on internal laboratory, or bench, testing. Our task is to devise a method for testing the end users' experience with the new item, and we call the activity **product use testing (PUT)**, or *field testing*, or *user testing*. Sometimes it is called **market acceptance testing**, though this term may also mean *market* testing, as in Chapter 18. Product use testing is the topic of this chapter.

We begin the chapter with a statement on the role of marketing through Phase IV, development. Though the actual designing of the prototypes may be out of the marketer's hands, marketing makes important contributions throughout this phase, and its contributions accelerate rapidly as we near the end of Phase IV and approach Phase V, launch. With this in mind, we then explore the process of product use testing in detail.

The importance of product use testing is clear, as it shows up in several of the key concepts driving the whole new product process—the *unique superior product*, the *repeat buying percentage* in the A-T-A-R paradigm, and the *requirements in the protocol*. A product that does not meet end-user needs fails on one of the three key causes of failure.

One other reminder: This chapter applies equally to services and to goods. On the www.baddesigns.com Website are many examples of poor signage marking roads, highways, parking lots, and the like. It is almost a certainty that these poor signs had not been tested for clarity.

The Role of Marketing During Development

Marketing Is Involved from the Beginning of the Process

The role of the marketing personnel changes and accelerates as the product nears the end of the development phase and moves closer to launch. Years ago, when firms were still predominantly practicing the "selling concept" (i.e., "we sell what we make"), the role of marketing was simple: to sell the products that the firm makes. Marketing didn't really need to get involved in product development until technical personnel had basically done their job. With all this discussion of teams and speed to market, it is clear most firms aren't following this concept any more—or can't, if they want to stay competitive. Marketing people are now involved from the very beginning of the new products process. Throughout the process, they advise the new products team about how the product development underway fits in with the firm's marketing capabilities (such as sales and sales training, service availability, distribution strengths, etc.) and the market's needs. By early involvement, they can help the product succeed, as they represent the issues and concerns having to do with the marketing of the product.

It is too easy to say that marketing's role is to gather information from the marketplace. Too often, that means that marketing plays a gatekeeper role, funneling information from the marketplace to the new product team that it thinks is important and possibly missing out on other, more critical information in doing so. The whole team needs to focus on the marketplace, not just marketing. All team members, be they technical personnel, design engineers, or marketing, can gather information. Indeed, the whole idea behind lead user analysis (see Chapter 4) is that key customers are part of the team itself and provide information directly. A really market-oriented firm thinks of marketing's task not as information *gathering*, but as information *coordination*—deciding what information the various sources have (customers, lead users, distributors, etc.), and what information the members of the new products team need.

A good illustration is provided by DuPont's development in the 1960s of an unusual ethylene polymer named Surlyn.[1] It was originally a totally technology-driven product with apparently interesting properties: It was strong, resilient, clear, and bouncy. It was envisioned, among other things, as a coating for golf balls—and, after much initial resistance from the golf ball manufacturers, was eventually adopted as the replacement for rubber-based ballata golf ball covers. Marketing eventually found out that there was a bigger market out there that was very interested in Surlyn—but not for the attributes originally thought to be most important. Surlyn, as it turned out, has exceptional oil and grease resistance properties that made it an excellent sealer for the meat packing industry. Further applications were found over the years: as an adhesive for juice boxes and an extrusion coating for paper. As more market information was gathered, the scientists were able to modify the process and develop related polymers for other applications,

[1]Parry M. Norling and Robert J. Statz, "How Discontinuous Innovation Really Happens," *Research-Technology Management,* 41(3), May–June 1998, pp. 41–44.

such as bowling pins and ski boots. Clearly, the original technology-push innovation had done an about-face, and market needs were now driving further technical development.

Manufacturing's role has similarly evolved over the years. They also are involved in the new products process from the beginning, advising the team on the manufacturability of the product under consideration. Like marketing, manufacturing understands the need to be involved early and resents being left out of the early phases of the process. The Hewlett-Packard DeskJet printer, for example, represented a new direction for HP: new products, markets, and customers, and a new product development process. Manufacturing got involved in the process at the very beginning; in fact, manufacturing engineers were moved to the R&D site and used as a resource by the design engineers throughout. The process went so well, designers lobbied to get even more manufacturing engineers! As a result of this project, manufacturing engineers increased in status within HP.[2]

Marketing Ramp-Up, or the "I Think We've Got It" Phase

While they make contributions to the process throughout, the roles of both marketing and manufacturing change as the process moves along. Often, an important turning point occurs when the early prototypes are made and are passing performance tests. A new pharmaceutical to combat hypertension, for example, may be showing promising results in early animal testing. We might call this point the "I think we've got it" phase, and it is here that the team's whole attitude toward the project changes. Up to this point, the technical people on the team played the predominant role, with marketing and manufacturing acting more in an advisory capacity. Now, however, marketing's role increases, as marketing people have to "rev up" their operations. They have to begin planning field sales and service availability for the product, investigating packaging and branding options, bringing in the advertising agency representatives, and so on. In short, the "I think we've got it" phase is where marketing's work for launch begins.[3]

It's also where manufacturing's responsibilities pick up. In new product development, we often hear of "manufacturing ramp-up"—the point at which manufacturing personnel plan the full-scale production of the product (which up till now has just been manufactured in small quantities, sufficient for prototype evaluation). Just like manufacturing ramps up from prototypes to full production, marketing can be said to ramp up for product launch—and marketing ramp-up begins here.

[2]Dorothy Leonard-Barton, H. Kent Bowen, Kim B. Clark, Charles A. Holloway, and Steven C. Wheelwright, "How to Integrate Work and Deepen Expertise," *Harvard Business Review*, September–October 1994, pp. 121–130.

[3]See discussion of the relative workloads of the marketing and technical personnel as the product moves from development to launch in Behnam Tabrizi and Rick Walleigh, "Defining Next-Generation Products: An Inside Look," *Harvard Business Review*, November–December 1997, pp. 116–124.

Why Do Product Use Testing?

Once the prototype is ready, marketing begins an important part of the ramp-up process: assessing the physical prototype among real customers. Note: As we saw previously in Chapter 3, a prototype could be in a crude, early form, or could be a finished or nearly finished product. **Use testing** means testing the prototype under normal operating conditions. Consumers put a tire on a car and drive it; technicians put notebook computers in the hands of warehouse personnel; a bank installs a new check cashing service at three branch points, and so on. Makers of a building-block set for children will put kids in a focus group room and watch how they play with the set (Do they like it? Do they follow the instructions or use their imagination? Do they get tired of it quickly?), while at the same time the parents are surveyed regarding price points (Would you pay $70 for a set with 100 pieces, or $50 for a set with 75 pieces?). We previously saw product use testing as part of the testing seen in the Tastykake Sensables case of Chapter 2. The product will probably not be perfect at this time, for more reasons than poor design. An example of *manufacturing* difficulties came from Weyerhaeuser. Their new UltraSofts disposable diapers worked well, very well, and sold at a discount price. But the pilot plant was a poor predictor of full-scale production. There were production line fires and other breakdowns, and suppliers refused to sign long-term contracts on the key diaper liner.[4] Testing should continue until the team is satisfied that the new product does indeed solve the problem or fill the need that was expressed in the original protocol.

Is Product Use Testing Really Necessary?

Here is a composite statement of what we commonly hear at product use testing time:

"We've been working on this thing for months (or years), and we've spent a ton of money on it. Experts were called as needed. Market research showed that end users would want a product like this. Why dally around any longer? Top management is leaning on us for the revenues we promised, and we continue to hear that a key competitor is working on something similar. Look, we're now in an up mode; stopping to test suggests to management that we don't have faith in what we've been doing. Besides, customers can't just take the new item and try it fairly; they have to learn how to use it, then work it into their system, listen to our ads (or reps) advising them what to do and how good the results are. Worst of all, a competitor can get his hands on our creation and beat us to the market! No, it's just not worth the time and money to do extended use testing."

Now, sometimes that statement is a fact, not an argument. For example, the first fax machine probably could not be use tested by end users—there was no network of others with whom to communicate. Same for the picture telephone. Same for the first color TV when there were no programs being broadcast in color. How

---

[4]Alecia Swasy, "Diaper's Failure Shows How Poor Plans, Unexpected Woes Can Kill New Products," *The Wall Street Journal,* October 9, 1990, p. B1.

could the Internet have been use-tested? Hopefully it won't be as bad a situation as that in a well-known cartoon, where one lab scientist holds up a flask and says to another scientist, "It may well bring about immortality, but it will take forever to test it."

Are These Arguments Correct?

These arguments are persuasive, especially when put forth by the person on the top floor who has funded the work to date. But, except for very rare cases such as with the fax machine, they are incorrect. What we have is an unknown, with lots yet to be learned. The user whose problem started the project still hasn't told us that our product *solves* that problem.

Even more, the risks and costs of use testing are usually small compared to the loss of the earnings flow from a successful product (see Figure 15.1). About the

FIGURE 15.1
Variable Gains and Losses from Program of Product Use Testing

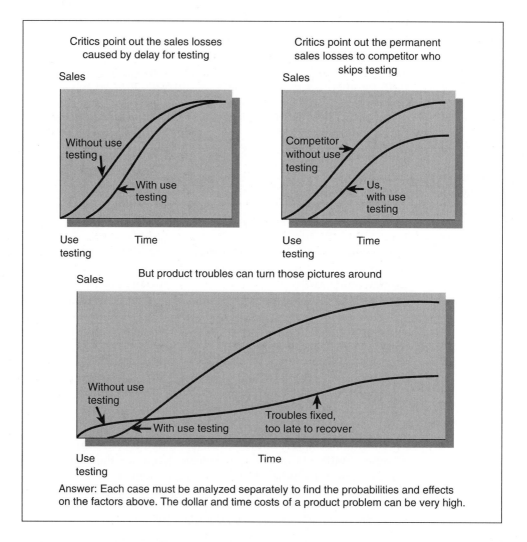

Answer: Each case must be analyzed separately to find the probabilities and effects on the factors above. The dollar and time costs of a product problem can be very high.

only argument that really carries weight is the competitive one, and then only when our new product can be copied and marketed, fast. Many food products are like this, as are other items where there is no technical accomplishment involved. If use testing clearly makes us second (or even third) into the market, most firms will opt for immediate marketing—without use testing. And, of course, they expect to fail often. Food products suffer an 80–90 percent failure rate, based on the minor improvements they offer, the small retail availability such products can get, and the fickleness of consumers who apparently cannot predict their behavior in a concept test.

But, even in consumer packaged-goods industries, there should be more serious consideration of the counter arguments *for* use testing. They include the following:

Assessing Competitive Reaction

A firm developing new items is well advised to build its innovation on a technology base where it has some insulation from competitive copying (see the strategy discussions in Chapter 3). Second, competitors today are finding that copying someone else has small gains—others will copy *them,* price competition will take the profits away, the imitator usually copies the innovator's mistakes too, and the competitors we must worry about most are themselves involved in technology-based developments that cannot be thrown over on short notice.

The Complexity of Customer Needs

In almost every industry, there is no one, simple, end-user need. Any new item foists onto the end user a learning curve. There are tradeoffs, and there is "baggage"—things that came with the new item that often surprise even the developer. For example, consider the case of GTE Airfone, the technology that permits phone calls to go from ground to seated individuals on airborne planes. What seemed like a natural is going very slowly—turns out that many fliers don't want to be disturbed during their rare quiet times. And nearby passengers don't think much of the idea either. End use is indeed complex, and there is no way it can be simulated in laboratories, where use is isolated from user mistakes, competitive trashing of the concept, and objections by those in the user firm or family whose work or life is disrupted by the change. In addition, for new-to-the-world products, several product use tests may be needed for a company to get it right—what is important is that the company learns from its errors. Recall from Chapter 2 the convoluted process followed by GE in the development of their CT full-body scanner.[5]

Customers' Communication of Their Needs

End users also often have trouble communicating their wants and their satisfactions, short of having the finished item. Two firms (Mars and Hershey) marketed food items with new synthetic fats (from NutraSweet and P&G, respectively). Both cases faltered on a surprise difficulty: Just what do consumers really want in a

---

[5]Gary S. Lynn, Mario Mazzuca, Joseph G. Morone, and Albert S. Paulson, "Learning Is the Critical Success Factor in Developing Truly New Products," *Research-Technology Management,* 41(3), May–June 1998, pp. 45–51.

dessert or a candy bar? Is sweetness an index of enjoyment? Does the term *fat substitute* destroy expectations of pleasant taste? And so on. One firm went national and the other into an expensive test market before these obstacles became clear.[6]

Assurance of Delivery of a Quality Product

Recall the idea of the augmented product—where there is a core benefit, then a formal product, and then the many augmentations of service, warranty, image, financing, and so on. The new products process tends to focus on the core benefit and the formal product, and even that may have implementation problems. But firms often just *assume* they will be able to deliver the outer ring of augmented product quality—the sales force will be able to explain the new item well; early product breakdowns will not chase other potential buyers away; the finance division will approve generous financing arrangements; the advertising effectively answers competitors' claims; and warehouse personnel won't make a simple mistake and destroy half the product. These things happen, and often. As just one example, Black & Decker once pulled thousands of flashlights off store shelves and stopped shipment on a new line of smoke detectors that carried the Ultralife battery after Kodak discovered an unexpected buildup of material that affected its shelf life. The discovery was made during marketing, not during use testing.

To bypass product use testing is a gamble that should be considered only when there is just cause. The burden of proof is on whoever argues for skipping it. Intel seemed to have a very good reason to cut short its testing of its highly publicized Pentium chip, and perhaps they did—the problems that appeared occurred only rarely (one needed ninth decimal calculation for one glitch to appear). But if Polaroid had thoroughly use-tested its new children's camera, it would have discovered that children love pressing all the buttons—including the one that opens the camera and ruins the film! Who would have guessed that making something too *easy* to open would have been a problem?[7]

Knowledge Gained from Product Use Testing

As can be seen from the above examples, there is ample opportunity for the firm to learn from product use testing and to use the knowledge gained to make the product more suitable to the desired market. Figure 15.2 shows the key pieces of knowledge that use tests provide.

Pre-Use Sense Reactions

Almost every product gives the user a chance to react to immediate sensations of color, speed, durability, mechanical suitability, and so on. Initial reactions are important, especially on service products. For example, managers at Saturn feel the most important single reaction of a potential new car buyer is the impression

---

[6]For Mars: Gabriella Stern, "Attempt to Cut Candy Calories Sours for P&G," *The Wall Street Journal,* August 25, 1993, p. A1. For Hershey: Anonymous, "Simple Pleasures," *Across the Board,* May 1994, p. 39.
[7]This example is from www.baddesigns.com.

FIGURE 15.2
Set of New Knowledge from Product Use Tests

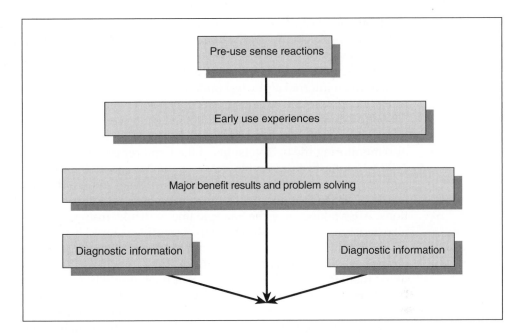

upon first entering a dealership. In the marketing of the first Saturn managers designed dealerships for a good impression and measured to see they got it.

Early Use Experiences

This is "does it work" knowledge. Key specifics are such things as ease of use, surface variables, can they manage it, are there still bugs, and is there any evidence of what the item will eventually do.

Alpha and Beta Tests

This latter point is a special problem. Computer hardware and software firms, for example, are under great competitive pressure and prefer to run **beta tests**. These are short-term use tests, at selected external customer sites, sometimes preceded by internal **alpha tests** with employees. These are designed to tell the manufacturers one thing: Does this product work, free of bugs? In fact, some have their people competing to see who can find the most bugs in a new item—better now than later.[8] Beta tests are not designed to tell them about meeting customer needs and solving problems—such testing takes longer than the few weeks usually allowed on computer products.

The term *beta testing*, originally used in the computer industry, is now frequently heard in all sorts of other settings, but computer firms still seem to be the leaders at beta testing. Netscape launched Navigator Release 2.0 in January 1996 and had an early alpha version of Release 3.0 up on its internal Web site by February. After getting early feedback from hundreds of employees, a second alpha was made

[8]Douglas W. Clark, "Bugs Are Good: A Problem-Oriented Approach to the Management of Design Engineering," *Research-Technology Management,* 43(3), May–June 1990, pp. 23–27.

available two weeks later. A third version, this time a beta version available to the public, was released by early March. This procedure continued through several more beta versions until Release 3.0 was launched in August. Throughout this period, Microsoft was developing its competitive Explorer product. It began in March 1996 with an internal alpha test (among its 18,000 employees) with only 30 percent functionality, enough to get early feedback and begin design improvements. External beta testing followed: The first beta version was released in April 1996, and by June, Microsoft had a beta version that was 90 percent functional. Netscape was also monitoring the beta versions of the Explorer product over this time.[9]

Most alpha tests resemble those of the Microsoft Explorer—a quick test of a very early version of the product with employees, where the product often is not nearly ready to release to customers, even as a beta version. But there are exceptions. After taking over the Snapple line of drinks from Quaker, Triarc eliminated all extensive customer testing. Triarc executives would just order new flavors and try them out themselves—that is, new products were launched after passing the alpha test! Management figured that, if the product ultimately didn't sell, the worst that would happen would be that they would have to discount some excess inventory. While this seems a risky way to launch new consumer products, Triarc successfully launched the Snapple Elements line (three new drinks named Rain, Sun, and Fire) in exactly this way. (Do you think a big firm like Quaker would have readily taken such a risk?)[10]

Beta tests are conducted under such time pressures that managers must be sure not to ignore danger signals. What might become a classic was NCR's development of its Warehouse Manager computer package. In hurrying this product to market, the firm committed several mistakes:

- Concluded the beta tests before there was time for key bugs to show up. The program actually sabotaged customers' accounting and cost systems.
- Neglected to test thoroughly a part of their package that they licensed from another firm—Taylor Management.
- Continued selling and installing the $180,000 program after hearing of horrendous problems with it. Several big installations were made even after NCR ordered a halt to further sales.
- Promised "single-source solution" to technical problems when in fact they depended on Taylor to handle problems on their part of the package.
- Took the stance with individual customers that the product worked well, so the problems must be caused by the customer.

Note that inadequate use testing can lead to far more problems than product adjustments. NCR's court hassles multiplied the cost of adequate product testing

[9]Marco Iansiti and Alan MacCormack, "Developing Products on Internet Time," *Harvard Business Review*, September–October 1997, pp. 108–117; Alan MacCormack, "Product-Development Practices That Work: How Internet Companies Build Software," *Sloan Management Review*, 42(2), Winter 2001, pp. 75–85.
[10]John Deighton, "How Snapple Got Its Juice Back," *Harvard Business Review*, January–February 2002, pp. 47–53.

FIGURE 15.3 Common Pitfalls of Beta Testing

- Beta test site firm has no internal capacity to test the performance of the product at the required level and lacks the funding to hire an outside firm to do the test.
- Developer puts in a wishy-washy performance requirement like "user-friendly," which is meaningless unless a measurable specification is defined.
- Testing is done too late in the new product process, which almost ensures that development time will be extended and production delays will occur. Doing testing in increments throughout the process is a way to avoid this pitfall.
- Developers attempt to bypass beta testing, relying only on alpha testing of their own products. By definition they are too close to the product to critically test it and find problems.
- Developers ignore early negative results, hoping that the product will improve by itself during the new product process. All beta test results, whether positive or negative, need to be honestly evaluated.

Source: From Robert Stoy, "Assembled Product Development," in M. D. Rosenau, A. Griffin, G. Castellion and N. Anscheutz, eds., *The PDMA Handbook of New Product Development*, John Wiley & Sons, Inc., 1996, pp. 271–86. Reprinted with permission of John Wiley & Sons, Inc.

many times.[11] There are other concerns regarding beta test implementation. If done too late in the new products process, design may already be essentially fixed—or, if design changes are required, they may delay the launch. But if a beta version of a new computer program is released before major bugs are worked out, the lukewarm results may get picked up in the popular computer press, damaging the product's reputation. (This was one reason why Microsoft chose to release only two or three beta versions of Explorer, rather than the six or seven versions of Navigator 3.0 released by Netscape.) Further, the firm testing the new product may need to obtain information from the beta test site customer (such as economic value), which might strain the supplier-customer relationship. Figure 15.3 summarizes the more common pitfalls of beta testing.[12]

Gamma Testing

Beta testing may not meet all of the developer's needs. In a beta test, users may not have had time to judge whether the new product met their needs or was cost-effective for them. Apple Computer's PowerBook notebook had faulty disk drives that were not discovered until after marketing, even though they did field testing. As a result, a third term is becoming popular, **gamma testing** (gamma being the third Greek letter after alpha and beta). It designates the ideal product use test, where the item is put through its paces and thoroughly evaluated by the end user. To pass this test, the new item must solve whatever problem the customer had, no matter how long it takes. Gamma testing is so critical on new medicines and

[11]Mile Geyelin, "How an NCR System for Inventory Turned into a Virtual Saboteur," *The Wall Street Journal,* August 8, 1994, p. A1.
[12]Beta testing is a large and complex subject. One very helpful study is Robert J. Dolan and John M. Matthews, "Maximizing the Utility of Consumer Product Testing: Beta Test Design and Management," *Journal of Product Innovation Management,* 10(4), September 1993, pp. 318–330. For a full discussion of the benefits and risks of beta testing, see Robert Dolan, *Managing the New Product Development Process* (Reading, MA: Addison-Wesley, 1993), pp. 221–232.

medical equipment that the United States demands it; such testing can take up to 10 years.

Even though gamma testing is the ideal test (and is urged here), firms anxious to save time and money or to leapfrog competitors nevertheless opt to go with beta testing. Some virtually have to—carmakers, for example. The very successful Saturn was beta-tested by market users who drove them on a prepared track, dealers who drove them at the Arizona proving grounds, and automotive magazine writers and test drivers. But there was no testing over a time needed to really judge whether the new car actually met family needs.

Diagnostic Information

New products managers are looking for how items are used and what mistakes are made. Use tests often suggest ways to improve performance or to reduce cost. General Foods carried to the very last test the issue of the relative proportions of instant coffee and roasted grains for Mello Roast; it needed the best tradeoff between the lower cost of the grains and the effect on flavor. New product developers also seek specific pieces of information needed to back up their claims. Marketers want confirmation of target markets and product positionings. Product integrity is also on trial during a use test since only the users' perceptions tell us whether the parts tie together into a meaningful whole and whether product fits application. Lastly, developers are watching for any other red flag, a signal that users had some problems understanding the new item, or were slow to accept the results they got, and so on.

Apple and other software manufacturers may use *case-based research* as a very comprehensive form of product use testing that runs parallel to the software's development process, from early concept to finished product. The first stage is *investigation:* The developer interviews users to learn their expectations and how they will likely use the product. In the *development* stage, users are encouraged to try early prototypes of the new software and explore its menus and features. As an interesting twist, they speak out loud during product use, describing any problems they encounter. This stage is followed by a preliminary beta test with end users in a real work environment. Product use problems are identified at this stage, and solutions to all of these will be provided in the software instruction manual. This is all followed by a standard beta test.[13]

Decisions in Product Use Testing

Any product use test, whether one of several or alone, whether industrial or consumer, whether for Egypt or Alabama, should be crafted carefully, and several key decisions must be made. First and foremost, managers should decide what it is they *need to learn* from the product use test. Though what we need to learn is totally situation specific, the objectives should still be clear and should include the

[13]Matthew Holloway, "A Better Way to Test Interface Design," *Innovation*, Summer 1994, pp. 25–27.

requirements spelled out in the protocol. (See Chapter 12.) Some managers like to do what is often called a *potential problem analysis* at this point. The remainder of this section examines other key questions faced in product use testing.

Who Should Be in the User Group?

Some use testing is done with *lab personnel* at the plants where the products are first produced. Alexander Graham Bell became the first telephone user when he called his assistant.

Experts are the second testing group (e.g., the cooking staff in a test kitchen). Car companies have styling professionals; wine companies have tasters. Experts will give more careful consideration than will typical users and probably will express more accurate reactions. They will not be interested in the same things that interest customers, however.

The third test group option, *employees,* is widely utilized though often criticized. Company loyalties and pressures and employees' lifestyles and customs may distort opinions and attitudes. Obvious problems of possible bias can be overcome to some extent by concealing product identities and by carefully training and motivating the employee panel.

Stakeholders are the next choice, and the set includes customers and noncustomers, users and nonusers, resellers, end-user advisers (such as architects), users of competitive products, repair organizations, and technical support specialists whose reactions to new products have been sought.

SmarterKids.com Inc. sells educational toys on the Web. They select prospective new toys and games that seem to have educational merit and subject them to product use testing using a jury of elementary school kids. Employees will spread toys out on a table, set the kids loose, and watch what they do (and do not) play with. A new Monopoly-like game set in remote Alaska had a "Go to Lunch" square in place of "Go to Jail." While the second graders seemed to love the game, one was disappointed she could not make her classmates serve time![14]

Market researchers doing the use testing are very careful to pick the right number of stakeholders. Sample size may vary from 3 to 6 on experts, 30 or more for employees, and from 20 to several thousand for end users. A joint operation between Whittle Communications and Philips Electronics bet $70 million on a use test for a medical news service via TV; it involved 6,000 physicians.[15] As we have seen earlier, Netscape's Navigator and Microsoft's Explorer were tested at thousands of internal and external sites.

As usual, sample size is primarily a function of what is being tested. Any sample should be representative of the entire population for which the product is targeted and the results should be accurate (have *validity*) and reproducible (have *reliability*). A hair products firm marketed a new hair tonic for men after use testing, and it flopped primarily because it was tested in humid areas of the country. In drier areas, the product evaporated too quickly to do the user any good.

---

[14]Stephen D. Solomon, "The Next Next Thing," *Inc.*, June 2000, pp. 84–95.
[15]Patrick M. Reilly, "Whittle, Philips Plan Interactive M.D. TV," *The Wall Street Journal*, June 26, 1992, p. B1.

How Should We Reach the User Group?

There are several options here. First we must decide on mode of contact: *Mail* and *personal* are the most common. The mail method is more limited than personal contact in type of product and depth of questioning, but it is more flexible, faster, and cheaper. Burlington Industries used the telephone to ask people to serve on special one-time mail panels that evaluated new fabrics. Business-to-business firms often insist on personal contact, since they need a closeness far beyond that on most consumer products.

Second, there is a choice between *individual* contact and *group* contact. Most firms prefer individual contact, especially at this critical point in the development cycle, but it may be cheaper to deal with groups.

Third, the individual mode of contact brings up the question of *location*. Should the test be conducted at the *point of use* (home, office, or factory), or should it be conducted at a *central location* (test kitchen, shopping center, theater, or van)? The point-of-use location is more realistic and permits more variables to operate. But it offers poor experimental control and permits easy misuse. In contrast, the central location offers very complete facilities (such as kitchens, two-way mirrors, eating areas, pseudo stores), good experimental control, speed, and lower cost. The central location approach is winning out, but industrial firms will almost certainly stay with on-site studies. Sometimes one can be creative—TV networks sometimes test new pilot programs in Las Vegas, not at all representative, but oddly, a place where a wide range of people have time and desire to look at pilots between runs at the slot machines and blackjack tables. Other possible central locations for product use testing include marketing research firm facilities, trade shows, and even factory tours, such as at Ben & Jerry's Vermont headquarters.

Should We Disclose Our Identity?

A key issue, **identity disclosure**, concerns how much the user should be told about the brand or maker identity of the product. Some testers prefer open disclosure, while others (the majority) prefer to keep it secret. It may be that the brand cannot be hidden—as with many cars, some shoes, and many business products. Persons have perceptions about various firms and brands. Knowing a new item's brand introduces halo-image effects, maybe distorting user reactions. It helps to think about what is being tested. Developers may need a competitive comparison (only **blind tests** can determine this). Or they may want to know if users *perceive* the new item to be better (honest perception requires brands). A good compromise is to do both, first a blind test, followed by a branded test. This covers most of the issues. Service products can rarely be tested blind.

How Much Explanation Should We Provide?

Some people conduct use tests with virtually *no comment* other than the obvious "Try this." But such tests run the risk of missing some of the specific testing needs. A second degree of explanation, called *commercial,* includes just the information the customer will get when actually buying the product later. The third level is *full explanation*. It may be necessary to include a great deal of information just to ensure the product gets used properly. Rolm gave Nissan's employees 90 days of training in the use test for its CallPath system. Some people do one round of testing with full explanation, followed by a brief round at the commercial level.

How Much Control over Product Use Should There Be?

Most new medicines can be tested legally only under the control of physicians. This *total control* is essential when accurate data are required and when patient safety is a concern. Many industrial products also require total control to avoid dangerous misuse.

But most testers want users to experiment, to be free to make some mistakes, and to engage in behavior representative of what will happen later when the product is marketed. For example, a new blend of coffee may be tested under conditions of perfect water, perfect measuring, and perfect perking, but it should also be tested in the kitchen the way the average person will do it—right or wrong.[16] By providing this kind of freedom, the company can see how the product is likely to be misused. If Heublein had extensively product-use-tested its 1970s-era Wine & Dine meals (pasta, sauce mix, and a bottle of salted cooking wine in a box), they would have identified a problem that hit them in the marketplace instead: Many customers just drank the salted wine, gagged, and vowed never to buy the product again![17]

So two modes of looser control—*supervised* and *unsupervised*—have developed. If a conveyor belt manufacturer wants to test a new type of belting material, company technical and sales personnel (maybe even their vendor's people) will be at the user's plant when the material is installed (supervised mode). After early runs indicate there are no mistakes, the belting people go back home, and the material is left to run in an unsupervised mode for the full testing period (though developer personnel are never "very far away").

Services are almost always under some supervision because they cannot be "taken home" to use. Often, restaurants test new menus in a few locations (supervised mode) and then roll them out if everything works well.

How Should the Test Be Conducted?

The product may be tested in many combinations, but four ways are standard (see Figure 15.4):

- In a **monadic** test where the respondent tests a single product for a period of time. Services usually must be monadic, though there are exceptions.
- In a **sequential monadic** test where there are back-to-back monadic tests with the same respondent. It is sometimes called a *staggered paired comparison*.

[16]It has been said that one of the best ways to mislead product planners is to establish exacting controls in product use tests that won't be duplicated in the real world. See Robert J. Lavidge, "Nine Tested Ways to Mislead Product Planners," *Journal of Product Innovation Management*, 1(2), 1984, pp. 101–105.

[17]Robert M. McMath and Thom Forbes, *What Were They Thinking?* (New York: Times Business, 1996).

FIGURE 15.4 Types of Product Use Tests, as Applied to a New Toothbrush

Type	Products	Instructions
Monadic	The new product alone.	Try this new toothbrush, and tell me how you like it.
Sequential monadic	Back-to-back monadic tests.	Same as on monadic
Paired comparison*	The new product and another toothbrush (1)—the market leader or (2) one known to be the best or (3) the leader in the segment selected for the new product or (4) the one currently used by the testee.	Try these, and tell me how you like them, which you prefer, etc.
Triangular comparison*	The new product and two of the others. A variation is to use two variants of the new product and one of the others.	Same as on paired comparison.

*These multiple-product techniques can employ either of two product use approaches:
Side-by-side: Please brush your teeth with this toothbrush, and then brush again with the other one. Then give me your reactions.
Staggered (often called a sequential monadic): Please use this toothbrush for a week, and then switch to the other for a week. Then give me your reactions.

- In a **paired comparison** where use of the test product is interspersed with that of a competitive product.
- In a **triangular comparison**, similar to paired comparison but with two competitive products versus one test product (or two test products versus one competitor).

More sophisticated experimental designs exist, but they are only used in special situations.[18] The monadic test is the simplest; it represents normal usage of products. It is probably also the most *valid* of these tests (that is, it most closely represents normal product usage). But it is less *sensitive* in results (that is, changes in price or other attributes affect customer preferences markedly). The usual *side-by-side* or simultaneous form of paired comparison is the most unrealistic test, but it is by far the most sensitive. A *sequential monadic* is probably the ideal combination, though it takes longer. In the staggered format, a user may try out a toothbrush for one week, then change to another for the second week, then go back to the first one.

Even monadic tests usually involve a silent competitor—the product being used before the new one appeared. When an established category (such as photocopiers) is involved, then it is almost a must to test a new product against the category leader. But in the absence of an established category, as was the case with the first fax machine, what does the developer do? The first cell phone should have been tested against traditional landline phones, for example. If there is no direct predecessor, product developers usually just run a monadic test and then ask the user to compare the new product with whatever procedure was being followed before.

[18]For added information on such matters as experimental designs, sequencing of stimuli, and sample design, see Howard R. Moscowitz, *Product Testing and Sensory Evaluation of Foods* (Westport, CT: Food and Nutrition Press, 1983).

Over What Time Period Should the Test Be Conducted?

Some use tests require a *single* product experience (this may be all that is needed for a taste test); some require use over *short periods* of up to a week; and some require use over *extended periods* of up to six months. The longer period is needed if substantial learning is required (a shift in a paradigm), if initial bias must be overcome, or if the product entails an acquired taste. A longer period is also needed if the product faces a full range of variations in use (for example, a new PDA may find application by final consumers, small business owners, multinationals, and hospitals or other institutions). Again, researchers opt more often to use several modes. The initial, quick test predicts the early reactions of those people we call innovators. Failure here, even if perceptions are unjustified, often dooms a good product. On the other hand, favorable initial impressions must be sustained well past the novelty stage. Many products have flared briefly before sputtering to an early death.

Tests over a month long are rare on consumer products and difficult to defend to management. But if a new piece of business equipment will be positioned on its cost-cutting advantage, the use test had better run long enough for the user to see a significant cost reduction. Incidentally, those long tests of paint panels in the fields along highways are lab tests, not use tests. There is no testing of user carelessness in application, thick versus thin paint coatings, and the many other variations one gets in a true home use test. Apple gets closer when they test PowerBooks with common indignities such as spilled soda and simulated bouncing in a car trunk. But again, this is not true use testing, where customers are far more inventive of destructive ways.

What Should Be the Source of the Product Being Tested?

Generally speaking, three different sources of the product are employed in a use test—*batch*, *pilot plant*, and *final production*. If the firm will employ just one type of use testing, then the final production material is far and away the best. Batch product should be used alone only if the production process is prohibitively expensive.

As with many other phases of product development, the decision on source of product is a tradeoff between the cost and value of information. Being penny-wise at this point has proven over and over to be pound-foolish.

Often overlooked is the product left in the hands of users at the end of the test. In most cases, the product should be collected and examined for clues about user problems and actions during the test. If a patent application will follow soon, it is very important to pick up *all* of the product; otherwise, developers risk losing the originality requirement of the patenting process.

What Should Be the Form of the Product Being Tested?

One view favors testing the *best single product* the organization has developed, as identified by concept tests or market analyses. The opposing view favors building *variants* into the test situation—colors, speeds, sizes, and so on. The latter approach is more educational but also much more costly. Services are almost always tested in multiple variations, given that it is usually easy to make the changes.

The decision rests on several factors, the first being how likely the lead variant is to fail. No one wants to elaborately test one form of the product and then have that form fail.

Further, what effect will added variants have on users' understanding of the test? The more they test, the more they understand, and the more they can tell us. For example, a maker of aseptic packaging for fruit juices realized the juice and the package were both new to consumers, so the firm tested orange juice in the new package first and subsequently tested the new apple and cranberry juices. (Incidentally, the firm shipped the orange juice to its European factory for packaging so that it would spend the same time in the box as did the apple and cranberry juices.)[19]

How Should We Record Respondents' Reactions?

Essentially, three options are available, as demonstrated by Figure 15.5. First, a five- or seven-point verbal rating scale is generally used to record basic *like/dislike* data. Second, the respondent is usually asked to compare the new product with another product, say, the leader or the one currently being used, or both; this is a *preference score.* This can be obtained several ways; for example, a respondent may be asked to allocate 11 points between the new and comparison products. A 10–1 allocation would show strong preferences while a 6–5 allocation would reveal that the respondent is almost indifferent between the two. Third, for diagnostic reasons, testers usually want *descriptive information* about the product that covers any and all important attributes. Examples include taste, color, disposability, and speed. A semantic differential scale is the most common here. This is where we gather all of the other information called for in the objectives.

The researchers of a new sausage product presumed from early concept testing that the ideal sausage would have low levels of greasiness and saltiness, and several test products were developed accordingly. Needless to say, use testing proved just the opposite—the two top sausages in the test ranked first and second in saltiness, and they were among the greasiest. Some of the least greasy test products had some of the lowest overall scores. We have come to expect the unexpected and plan for it.

Marketing research has spawned a large group of exotic research methodologies found to be useful occasionally in new product testing. For example, brain wave measurements help disclose users' inner thoughts, especially if they have a strong emotional reaction to the product being tested. Voice pitch analysis (that is, testing for stress in the respondent's voice patterns much like in lie-detector tests) has been used to overcome product testers' efforts to be "helpful" and avoid hurting the tester's feelings.

---

[19]Regardless what the form is, the test product should be representative of the product that will actually be launched—not of significantly higher or lower quality (yes, this happens!). This is another of Lavidge's ways to mislead product planners. See Robert Lavidge, op. cit.

FIGURE 15.5
Data Formats
for Product
Use Tests

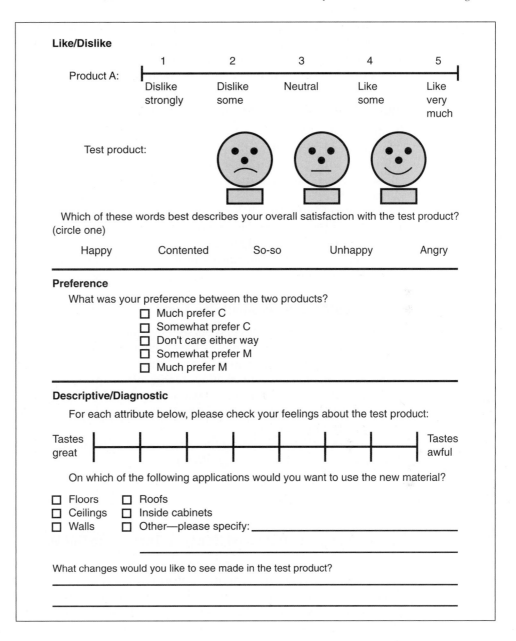

One additional piece of information is very important at this point—intent to purchase. Recall that near the end of the concept test, we asked respondents how likely they thought they would be to try the product if it became available on the market (the top-two-boxes question). We have now asked them how well they liked the product and whether it was preferred to their currently used product. So again, we ask the buying intention question, this time as a measure of use test results, still not a predictor of actual trial rates.

In many *business* product use tests the market research flavor of this section is missing. They want all relevant information and get it by close personal investigations and observations. Users may find applications the developers didn't even think of. There are few formal questionnaires in evidence.[20]

How Should We Interpret the Figures We Get?

Testers have long realized that they want *comparative* figures, not just *absolutes*. That is, if 65 percent of the users liked a product, how does that percentage compare with previous tests of somewhat similar items? If previous winners all scored over 70 percent on the "like" question, then our 65 percent isn't very impressive.

The 70 percent figure is a *norm*. Where we get norms and how we use them is often a serious question. The major source is obvious—the library of past experiences, thoroughly studied and averaged. The files of marketing research supplier firms are also helpful, but norms pulled from the air at committee meetings are virtually worthless.

Who Should Do the Product Use Test?

The first choice here is between personnel *within* the company and personnel *outside* the company. The firm may or may not have the necessary personnel skilled in information technology analytical capability.

Second, the *functions* (marketing, technical) historically have jockeyed for control. But today, the development team is responsible—the same team that handled the prototype concept testing. If vendor personnel are members of such teams, then they too participate.

Some special ideas holding the attention of veteran new products people run through all product use testing situations.

Special Problems

Don't Change the Data Just Because They Came Out Wrong

One firm discovered a user problem in a use test, but the president said, "They're just going to have to live with it." Unfortunately, the use test did not ask whether users were *willing* to live with it. They weren't, and the product failed. In some tests technical and marketing people warn of user problems only to be told that they are being negative—a real-life case of "kill the messenger."

Be Alert to Strange Conditions

One industrial firm noticed that several electrical measuring instruments showed signs of tampering after a field test. On examination, they found users were making

---

[20]A review of some practice along these lines is Aimee L. Stern, "Testing Goes Industrial," *Sales and Marketing Management,* March 1991, pp. 30–38.

a particular change to aid the product's function; after a few telephone calls, they had an improved product design ready to go out for more testing.

What If We Have to Go Ahead without Good Use Testing?

Try to work some use testing into the early marketing of the product (e.g., in the rollout method discussed in Chapter 18) and try to have some alternatives ready to switch to as a hedge against negative outcomes.

There are also surrogate tests available if time or money limitations prevent a full product use test. Quick results are possible, for example, through *constructive evaluation* (the respondent uses the item, describing activities and explaining problems encountered) or *retrospective testing* (the user reviews videos of conventional product use testing previously done).

Summary

Chapter 15 has dealt with the issues of whether a product solves customer problems, how it compares to other products in this regard, and what else can be learned about it at this point. Getting this type of information would seem critical, but strong pressures are exerted to skip product use testing. We talked about the arguments for skipping and showed why they should be followed only when they are overpowering.

That paved the way for discussion of the 13 dimensions of product use tests, ranging from "What we want to learn from the test" to "Who should conduct it?" Each dimension has several options and selecting from among them usually follows an analysis of the situation.

At the end of the testing, the product may have to be routed back into technical work to resolve problems, or it may be dropped. Otherwise, we now proceed to commercialization and the preparation of finished product, which, of course, is just a later version of the concept going into the greatest use test of all: marketing. Marketing is the topic of Chapters 16 and 17.

Applications

1. "I think some research suppliers oversell a bit—they want us to do too much market research. For example, one of the biggest published data on a 'blind' versus 'identified' product test. Here are the results:

Branded	Preferences	Unbranded	Preferences
Prefer A	55.5%	Prefer A	45.6%
Prefer B	44.5%	Prefer B	54.4%
Prefer A	68.0%	Prefer A	60.7%
Prefer C	32.0%	Prefer C	39.3%
		Prefer B	64.4%
		Prefer C	35.6%

I'm told the differences were highly significant statistically. The research firm concluded that there was no choice *between* blind and identified but that both should be used in just about every case where there was any reason to even suspect an effect of branding. Do you agree?"

2. "Colgate's marketing people apparently had some trouble a while back with a new detergent laced with a dye that turned laundry blue during introductory marketing. Another product of theirs, a dishwasher detergent packaged in waxy cartons like those used for orange juice, was rejected by test market parents who were afraid their children might think the cartons contained juice. Seems to me those errors were inexcusable. Shouldn't they have been discovered earlier, in product use testing? How would you have made sure of that?"

3. "Our pharmaceutical division, of course, develops new pharmaceutical products for use by doctors and hospitals. The technical research department does all the testing (they have different names for the various tests). The last phase is clinical testing, where the drugs are given to humans in a manner that will substantiate claims to the Food and Drug Administration. The clinical tests are conducted by MDs in the clinical research section, which is in our R&D department along with all the other technical people. Now it seems to me those clinical tests are designed to satisfy more people than just the FDA—physicians, pharmacists, nurses, and so on. But MDs in clinical testing are not too high on marketing research–type thinking, so it dawned on me that I should see that at least one thoroughly trained marketing research person was assigned to clinical research—to help me make sure the clinicals have maximum impact later in marketing. Do you agree?"

Case: Product Use Testing for New Consumer Nondurables[21]

In the competitive consumer nondurables market, new products seem to be launched all the time. Failure rates tend to be on the high side, mostly because the manufacturers often try out several products, see what "sticks," and prune out the rest. Nevertheless, with careful product use testing, one can identify potential problems with the product and seek to correct them before a costly launch mistake is made.

Here are several new products that have been launched recently by some of the bigger name packaged goods manufacturers. Few could really be called "new-to-the-world" products, though all of them posed at least some risk to the manufacturer.

[21]This case is based on products appearing on the NewProductWorks Web site, www .newproductworks.com. When you access this site, try the Hits and Misses link. This link is periodically updated and gives expert "hit-or-miss" predictions on recently launched new consumer products. NewProductWorks, a division of Arbor Strategy Group, houses the New Product Showcase, which includes countless new product failures through the years.

- *Kellogg's Special K Plus:* A Special K cereal brand extension with added calcium. The product is sold in a milk-carton-shaped box (a gable top) to reinforce the calcium idea. The package contains about the same amount of cereal as a standard cereal box and is easily reclosed using a plastic seal to keep the product fresh. About $15 million is planned for the product launch.

- *Coca-Cola Surge:* Coca-Cola's response to Mountain Dew, Pepsi's popular drink aimed at active Generation Xers. Surge has a citrus flavor and is designed to compete for the extreme-sports segment against Mountain Dew and Gatorade, as well as other established soft drinks and sports drinks. A Norwegian launch (under the name "Urge") has already proven successful, and about $50 million is slated for product commercialization.

- *Uncle Ben's Rice with Calcium:* Another familiar brand to which calcium was added, Uncle Ben's Rice with Calcium was supported by the American Dietetic Association. Extensive television and print advertising featuring Eloise the "spokes-cow" was planned.

- *Avert Virucidal Tissues:* Developed and marketed by Kimberly-Clark, this was essentially Kleenex treated with vitamin C derivatives that killed cold and flu germs if you used it when you sneezed or blew your nose.

- *Wheaties Dunk-A-Ball Cereal:* From the makers of Wheaties, General Mills. This was a sweetened corn-and-wheat cereal for kids, shaped like basketballs. Advertising noted that kids could "play with it before eating" and that it would be "available for a limited time only."

Given that these products were all launched into highly competitive markets, time was of the essence in rolling them out. For the moment, however, the issue of product use testing is at hand. What do you think would be the biggest concerns, or unknowns, about each of these products that might be unearthed using product use testing? Using the list of product use testing decisions given in this chapter, make recommendations as to how some (or all) of these could have been product use tested prior to launch.

FIGURE V.1

Launch

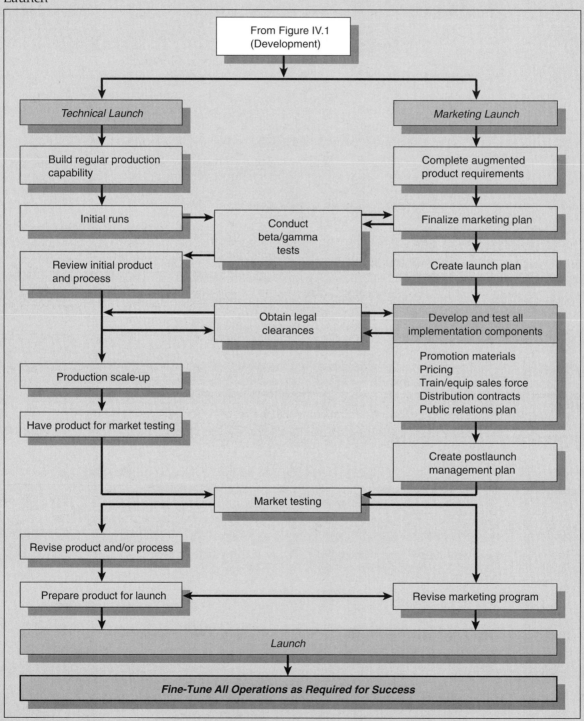

PART FIVE

Launch

We saw in Part IV that both marketing and technical activity take place throughout the development process. The intensity of activity on the marketing side may be relatively low, especially early in development, and there may be long periods of almost total inactivity as technical work gets hung up somewhere. But, as we have seen in Chapter 15, a point is reached in the development process where the balance of activity shifts more toward marketing. We depicted the parallel marketing and technical activity during the development phase in Figure IV.1. Similarly, these "twin streams" of activity carry on through the launch phase, as is shown in Figure V.1.

Somewhere in the process, management becomes convinced that the new product should be marketed. This starts what we will call the launch phase, sometimes called *commercialization*. All of the functions (engineering, production, marketing, and so on) are working before and after the launch decision. The change is often triggered by a commitment to produce the new item and to risk the high costs of building a plant.

At the end of development and throughout launch, marketing activity picks up intensity. But remember, that marketing actually begins near the start of the project. The product innovation charter calls for a market focus—usually a particular use or user. That will eventually become our target market. After concept generation, concept testing uses a concept statement that soon will turn into our product positioning statement. But marketing activities after that cool for a while, until technical can come up with a prototype that seems to show it meets the protocol statement of requirements (see Chapter 11). Of course, this brief description does not match most service products—on them, there is far less technical development work, and the whole process telescopes dramatically. And, as Figure V.1 shows, there is a lot happening on the technical side of the launch, including making the initial production runs, scaling up to full production, getting sufficient product prepared for market testing, and making last-minute revisions to product and process.

The next three chapters deal with the activities during launch. Launch planning decisions use all of the previous activity and a great deal of new thinking and testing to build eventually toward launch capability. As will be shown in upcoming chapters, launch planning can be thought of in several phases. In strategic launch planning, the strategic decisions of marketing (such as targeting and positioning) are made; in tactical launch planning, tactics are developed to implement the strategic plan. In a later phase, the strategic and tactical decisions are tested in the marketplace. All of these phases comprise Chapters 16 through 18. One could also add the phase of launch management, or managing the new product to success. Chapter 19 examines launch management because its planning is done at the same time and it concerns the postannouncement period.

In the final launch plan, the new products team must accept some givens. That is, the firm has an established operation—one or more sales forces, a financial situation, and so on. Teams can skirt some of these limitations, but not all of them. So the first several launch plan "decisions" are not really decisions in the voluntary sense; they are called **strategic givens.** Next, the team will make a set of **strategic decisions** on matters where there are options, such as positioning, branding, packaging, and the like. These are difficult, often critical, and usually hard to change. Some may even be included among the strategic givens. Finally, many **tactical decisions** must be made, though in this book we will only be able to include the most important of these. As you will see, these align rather closely with traditional marketing program decisions such as promotion, pricing, and distribution. Chapter 16 deals with the strategic givens and the strategic decisions, and Chapter 17 looks at the tactics. Be warned, of course, terms in the new products field are "flexible," and one person's tactic is another person's strategy and still another person's given.

Closing out Part V is a chapter on public policy issues. These are with us throughout the process, but they come to the fore at time of launch and thereafter. One caution is appropriate: Chapters 16 and 17 cover an activity that many people do not understand. They *think* they do, and some of them are actually in marketing departments. Our problem is not that people draw a blank—blanks are easy to fill in. Instead, we suffer from the existence of many myths—conditions *people think exist but do not.* Figure V.2 lists 11 of these myths. We encourage you to keep these in mind and perhaps refer to them from time to time. As you read the next two chapters, see if you can find what makes each one of them a myth. Check your answers with those at the end of Chapter 17.

FIGURE V.2   **Some Common Myths about Marketing Planning for New Products**

Here are some statements that we often hear around people who have not done much new product marketing. All are myths, as explained at different places in Chapter 16 and 17. See if you can figure out the reasons on your own, and then check your answers with those at the end of Chapter 17.

1. *Marketing people make the decisions that constitute a marketing plan.*
2. *The technical work is essentially complete when the new item hits the shipping dock. Marketing people take over.*
3. *It's important that marketing people be required to use strategy-tactics paradigms. Clear thinking helps rein in their excess exuberance and excitement.*
4. *The marketer's task is to persuade the end-user to use our new product.*
5. *The more sales potential there is in a market segment, the better that segment is as a target candidate.*
6. *The PIC guides the development stage and the marketing plan guides the launch stage.*
7. *The pioneer wins control of a new market.*
8. *A new product's goals are of two general types: sales (dollars or shares) and profits (dollars or ROIs).*
9. *People generally are pretty smart buyers—they will not be influenced by meaningless package designs.*
10. *A launch is no game—when we say go, that's it, sink or swim, and it had better be swim.*
11. *As with Broadway shows, opening night is the culmination of everything we have been working for.*

CHAPTER SIXTEEN

Strategic Launch Planning

Setting

At this point in the new products process, the team is ready to build the actual marketing plan. The task should be easy if the new item is an improvement to items already in the line. In such cases there is actually little to decide, as little is changed. If the product is "really new" (to the world or to the firm), the challenge facing the firm is more substantial, as it may need to rely on new communication or distribution strategies in order to sell unfamiliar products, often to unfamiliar markets.[1] Firms often do not place enough emphasis on up-front strategic planning for product commercialization (such as defining strategic purpose or competitive positioning), especially in the case of new-to-the-world products.[2] Weak strategic planning then shows up when the product reaches the market, and tactical errors (such as insufficient resource allocation) can compound the problem.

No matter how new-to-the-world the product is, the firm should think of product commercialization in two sets of decisions. **Strategic launch decisions** include both *strategic platform* decisions that set overall tones and directions, and *strategic action* decisions that define to whom we are going to sell and how. **Tactical launch decisions** are marketing mix decisions such as communication and promotion, distribution, and pricing that are typically made after the strategic launch decisions and define how the strategic decisions will be implemented. For example, one platform decision that often gets overlooked is the level of aggressiveness. If it is decided to be very aggressive (a platform decision), the target market (an action decision) must be rather broad, and the introductory advertising plan (a tactical decision) will probably call for mass media and a strong attention-getting campaign.

[1]Yikuan Lee and Gina Colarelli O'Connor, "The Impact of Communication Strategy on Launching New Products: The Moderating Role of Product Innovativeness," *Journal of Product Innovation Management*, 20(1), 2003, pp. 4–21.

[2]Michael Song and Mitzi M. Montoya-Weiss, "Critical Development Activities for Really New versus Incremental Products," *Journal of Product Innovation Management*, 15(2), March 1998, pp. 124–135.

Aside from those mentioned above, strategic launch decisions include the desired innovativeness of the product, the time to market, the competitive stance or positioning, the driver of new product development (market, technology, or both), and many others. Many of these decisions will have been made earlier in the new products process, at PIC or product protocol specification, and may be very difficult or expensive to change at this point, hence the term **strategic givens.** They are frequently difficult or costly to change once made. They do, however, determine the strategic context for the marketing plan and thus influence the tactical decisions made later. The tactical decisions are more easily modified. The strategic launch decisions are covered here in Chapter 16; the tactical launch decisions come in Chapter 17.

Product commercialization often turns out to be the most expensive and risky part of the new products process due to the financial commitments to both production and marketing made once the go-ahead is given. It is also often the most poorly managed.[3] As seen in the Chapter 13 case, the Mach3 incurred total production and marketing costs in the range of $1 billion. Despite the financial risks, proficiency in carrying out the launch process is critical to success. Researchers that study launch tend to find that most of the factors contributing to new product success are controllable—that is, rather than taking a "hope for the best" attitude, managers can achieve better success rates by improving product launch practice.[4]

To improve practice at the launch phase, it is important to have heavy marketing input, primarily because marketing will guide the implementation of the plan. The launch plan itself may be called a business plan, but more commonly it is the marketing plan or marketing program. In today's business, the marketing plan is recognized as a plan for the full business activity of launch; that's why full function teams are essential. But this is not the place to discuss plans. Instead, Appendix C contains an outline of a marketing plan and a discussion of some aspects of it.

The Strategic Givens

We begin by assessing the strategic givens, seen first in the introduction to Part V. These are "decisions" that are already made for us, so to speak; they "come with the territory" when a project is undertaken. Often we tend to forget them and their importance. They cover the full range of the organization's operations and are often "set in concrete" without our knowing it. They comprise that awful "resistance to change" that new products people frequently lament. In fact, they are such a problem that top managements often set up

[3]Roger Calantone and Mitzi M. Montoya-Weiss, "Product Launch and Follow-On," in William E. Souder and J. D. Sherman (eds.), *Managing New Technology Development* (New York: McGraw-Hill, 1994), pp. 217–248.
[4]Mitzi M. Montoya-Weiss and Roger Calantone, "Determinants of New Product Performance: A Review and Meta-Analysis," *Journal of Product Innovation Management,* 11(5), November 1994, pp. 397–417.

skunkworks, in order to try to be immune from whatever restrictions are common within the firm.

Some of the most common examples of problems we have with these givens can be indicated by an example. Sybron Corporation had a division in the dental furniture business; the division desperately needed new cash flow, and they had a new, unique, superior chair ready to go. But the corporation had a mandatory 50 percent gross margin requirement that the division product planners were sure would be waived when management saw the new chair. It wasn't, even when the gross margin came in at 47 percent. The division collapsed.

If these restrictions are really important and recognized in advance, they are put into the PIC guidelines. But some items here called givens are far more subtle, perhaps being held for reasons that new products people don't even know about. Many are pure and simple habit, convenient and comfortable routines. The point is: They need to be identified and studied. The launch team needs to be aware of such restrictions and to consider whether it wants to challenge them.

Revisiting the Strategic Goals

Early in the new products process, when the product innovation charter (PIC) was being developed, a basic set of strategic goals was outlined, and these goals have led the new products team up to this point. That original set may still be complete. Usually, though, much has been learned in the new products process, competitive conditions may have changed, and customer or management needs may have changed. Therefore, at this early point in the launch planning process, the goals should be revisited and updated.

Unfortunately, business firms use a complex set of measures as goals, and there is no one universally accepted set.[5] The most used set of measures for individual products is as follows (from lists numbering in the hundreds):

Customer Acceptance Measures	Product Level Performance
Customer acceptance (use)	Product cost
Customer satisfaction	Time to launch
Revenue (dollar sales)	Product performance
Market share	Quality guidelines
Unit volume	
Financial Performance	**Other**
Cash-to-cash (time to break even)	Nonfinancial measures peculiar to the new product being launched
Margins	Example: competitive effect, image change, morale change
Profitability (IRR, ROI)	

[5] Abbie Griffin and Albert L. Page, "An Interim Report on Measuring Product Development Success and Failure," *Journal of Product Innovation Management*, 10(4), September 1993, pp. 291–308.

The **cash-to-cash** metric listed above, sometimes called the **time-to-break-even metric**, is simply the time between the initial cash investment and the time of payment for the finished product, and it is becoming increasingly popular.[6] Using the cash-to-cash metric, the firm must also keep in mind that they need to be efficient and effective in getting the product to market—not just fast. The cash-to-cash metric is improved by using suppliers that efficiently achieve order fulfillment, practice effective inventory management, and successfully collect accounts receivable. Perhaps for this reason, cash-to-cash first caught on with supply chain managers, though new product teams have recognized its usefulness. As one example, Toyota uses lean manufacturing techniques in its Japanese manufacturing plants and has applied these same techniques in its U.S. plants. These techniques focus on just-in-time delivery of parts from suppliers, reducing inventory levels at parts distribution centers, increasing supplier on-time delivery, and improving inventory turnover. As a result, Toyota continuously improves its cash-to-cash metric, both in its domestic and U.S. production.[7]

Regardless of how measures are expressed, there should be absolutely no doubt in the minds of any launch planners about what the launch is to produce or achieve.

Strategic Platform Decisions

Each launch planning team will want to make up its own list of platform decisions because they vary much from industry to industry, goods to services, industrial to packaged goods. One place to start, however, is by considering just how new the product is to the world and to the firm (recall our discussion of "what is a new product" back in Chapter 1).

Type of Demand Sought

Different levels of product newness require different kinds of impact the launch activities must have on demand:

- For a new-to-the-world product: The firm must develop an entry strategy with the emphasis on stimulating **primary demand** for the product category. The launch plan must stimulate adoption of the new product category and lead to diffusion through the marketplace. Ford recently released MyKey, a system for parents to monitor and control teen driving via a computer chip in the key (it can limit speed, limit the volume of the sound system, and give off a signal if the driver is not wearing a seat belt). To stimulate adoption by

---

[6]For resources on the cash-to-cash metric, see R. Bowman, "From Cash to Cash: The Ultimate Supply-Chain Measurement Tool," *Supply Chain Brain,* June 2001; M. Farris and P. Hutchinson, "Cash to Cash: The New Supply Chain Metric," *International Journal of Physical Distribution and Logistics Management,* 32(4), 2002, pp. 288–298.

[7]For more information on Toyota's cash-to-cash initiatives, see T. Feare, "Optimizing a Supply Chain," *Modern Materials Handling,* 55(13), 2000, p. 61; and J. Liker and Y. Wu, "Japanese Automakers, U.S. Suppliers and Supply-Chain Superiority," *Sloan Management Review,* Fall 2000, pp. 81–94.

prospective parents, Ford tied MyKey into its overall safe-driving initiative for teens, including a "Driving Skills for Life" program in which teens can participate.[8]

- For a product improvement or upgrade to existing product (such as the newest release of Windows or the newest Ford compact car): The launch is expected to achieve **customer migration** (that is, existing customers should be encouraged to migrate to the new product), with switch-in from competitors' customers where possible. We could say that the goal here is to stimulate **replacement demand**.

- For a new entry or line addition in an established market (such as a new soft drink by Pepsi or a new cereal by Kellogg): The emphasis is on stimulation of **selective demand** (drawing market share away from competition). The launch plan must stimulate trial purchase, which is a precursor to adoption. Pepsi's objective is to get loyal Coca-Cola drinkers to break their habit at least once to try the newcomer brand.[9]

In addition to type of demand sought, several other strategic platform decisions may need to be made.

Permanence

On *permanence,* there are three options. The first is the usual one—we are *in to stay,* and no thought is given to getting out. The second is *in to stay if we meet our goals.* This cautions against alliances that would make escape difficult; it is especially useful when a firm is using the new product to enter another sphere of activity. Such a market development project can be tentative—probe an area, try hard to make it a winner, but pull out if competitive capability is inadequate.

The third option is *temporary.* This may sound strange—spending months or years developing a new item only to limit its life to a few months or a couple years. But some new brands are planned to be only temporarily on the market. Think of how many new toys and games, frozen yogurt flavors, diet products, and exercise programs seem to appear every year. Customers like variety and are more willing than ever to try something new, especially if it seems fashionable, youthful, or modern.[10] Baskin-Robbins, for example, has a basic range of ice cream flavors but runs others in and out to give variety. A food company may have a short-term product designed as a tie-in to a popular movie or TV program (for example, recent Kellogg's products have included Disney *Phineas and Ferb* Fruit Flavored Snacks and Disney Pixar *Finding Nemo* Fruit Flavored Snacks). Occasionally, a temporary product will catch on and become permanent. Many tactical decisions change if the plan is temporary—using contract manufacturing

---

[8]Sharon Silke Carty, "Ford's MyKey to Safety for Teen Drivers Controls Speed, Stereo," *USA Today*, September 1, 2009.

[9]Joseph P. Guiltinan, "Launch Strategy, Launch Tactics, and Demand Outcomes," *Journal of Product Innovation Management,* 16(6), November 1999, pp. 509–529.

[10]Dan Herman, "Introducing Short-Term Brands: A New Branding Tool for a New Consumer Reality," *Journal of Brand Management*, 7(5), May 2000, pp. 330–340.

rather than building a new plant and borrowing a sales force from agents or other manufacturers.

Aggressiveness

Aggressiveness refers to an attitude as much as to dollars. An *aggressive entry* seeks lots of attention early on, so most of the promotional dollars are spent early, and most of the resources go to getting early trial. In contrast, some firms will slink into the market with a *cautious entry*. They are uncertain about something important—maybe product performance, maybe competitive reaction, maybe sales force capability to deal with a new type of market. This is not a negative posture, just one where being aggressive has a risk the firm wants to avoid. For example, some firms like to enter a new market cautiously so as not to alarm the leaders in that market.

Third, the aggressiveness can be *balanced*. This simply means the firm is not trying to be pugnacious or slinking. The average of all new product introductions in a given industry would be balanced, but this does not mean normal; for some firms, aggressive is normal.

Sometimes this is a good place to raise the issue of marketing costs as *an investment*. Much of the marketing budget for a new product will pay off over many years; it is not an expense in the sense of an annual advertising budget. If the spending strategy is too stingy, try getting it thought of as an investment.

Competitive Advantage

Another decision that tends to come up early concerns the basic offer we make to the marketplace: Will our product lower end-user costs by virtue of its *price,* or will our product offer new benefits by virtue of its *differentiation?* Today we often hear that a firm is committed to the triad of quality, cost, and speed. Its managers fully expect to have new products that offer benefits by virtue of differentiation *and* that can be sold at a price below leading competition. So there is a middle choice on this option too: *both.*

Product Line Replacement

Most new products relate to existing products in the company's **product line**; they do not enter markets new to the firm. Naturally, the issue arises: How should we manage the replacement of the existing by the new? The firm has several clearly different strategic options, as shown in Figure 16.1.[11]

The technologically strongest firms cannibalize their own products (and production processes) with newer, higher-performance versions (Gillette has done this for years, most recently with the Fusion razor). Probably any one industry will have no more than a few innovators that can build their new product strategy

[11]John Saunders and David Jobber, "Product Replacement: Strategies for Simultaneous Product Deletion and Launch," *Journal of Product Innovation Management*, 11(5), November 1994, pp. 433–450.

FIGURE 16.1 Product Line Replacement Strategies

Butt-on product replacement	The existing product is simply dropped when the replacement is announced. Example: Ford's marketing of Focus and dropping of Escort.
Low-season switch	Same as butt-on, but arranging the switch at a low point between seasons. Tour companies use this switch when they develop their new catalogs.
High-season switch	Same as butt-on, but arranging the new item at the top of a season. Example: Polaroid used this strategy often, putting new replacement items out during the holiday buying season.
Roll-in, roll-out	Another version of butt-on, but arranged by a sequence of market segments. Mercedes introduced its C series country by country.
Downgrading	Keeping the earlier product alongside the new, but with decreased support. Example: Older computer chips are marketed alongside newer ones but with less channel support.
Splitting channels	Putting the new item in a different channel or diverting the existing product into another channel. Example: Old electronic products often end up in discounter channels.

Needless to say, there are variations on these. Casio has so many calculators that it is continuously renewing older ones, shifting the emphasis as it goes along. The important point is: Have *some* strategy decision and a plan. And have it early enough in launch planning that the total market offer (including augmentation such as service, warranty, and brand image) can be built to suit the strategy.

Source: From John Saunders and David Jobber, "Product Replacement: Strategies for Simultaneous Product Deletion and Launch, "*Journal of Product Innovation Management* 11, no. 5, November 1994, pp. 433–450. Reprinted with permission of John Wiley & Sons, Inc.

around cannibalism. Other firms, the imitators, succeed by following the leader firms and making incremental improvements to their products. In other words, imitators move up the performance curve (with, say, improved typewriters) while the innovators create whole new curves with higher performance limits (such as computer printers and word processing software).[12]

The decision on when to launch the next generation of product is a tricky one, but is likely to depend on at least three important forces: the competitive environment, customer expectations, and profit margins. Intel is a good example of a firm that considers each of these when planning a launch. When the competitive environment for chip manufacture heated up in the mid-1980s, Intel realized it was time to become its own producer (rather than relying on secondary chip suppliers). By 1990, it was focusing on increased chip performance and shorter development cycles and was able to maintain its competitive lead. Intel also carefully studied expectations of home computer users and concentrated on improving computing power in its Pentium chip. As it turned out, the home computer market drove demand for the Pentium chip in the mid-1990s. Finally, given the steep discounting of chips over the last several years, Intel has carefully chosen its prices on succeeding generations of chips. It reduces price low enough to keep competitors out while not so low as to dry up the margins needed to develop the next generation of chip.[13]

[12]Michael C. Neff and William L. Shanklin, "Creative Destruction as a Market Strategy," *Research-Technology Management*, May–June 1997, pp. 33–40.
[13]Neff and Shanklin, op. cit.

Competitive Relationship

Occasionally a product innovation charter will have a statement something like this: "The product(s) that will come from this program will not be aimed at XYZ Company, nor threaten a piece of business that is important to that firm." Colgate once had such a statement relative to P&G, but abandoned it years ago. Other firms do just the opposite, shooting their new item directly *at* a specific competitor.

The practices lead to a three-option set: *Make no reference to specific competitors, aim directly at a specific competitor,* and *avoid a specific competitor.* Unintentionally trying to do two or three of those mires the tactical managers in a frustrating set of conflicts.

Scope of Market Entry

This issue relates to a firm's desire to do market testing. Some introduce their new items into part of a market, watch what happens, and then roll them out to the entire market as they overcome any problems. The difference in these approaches will be discussed more in Chapter 18.

Even in a **rollout**, there is still the option of trying to *roll out very rapidly* (barely holding up long enough to find crisis problems) or to *roll out deliberately, as performance warrants.* And, of course, it appears most firms *go to the total market at the beginning.*

Image

The issue here is: Will the new product need *an entirely new image, a major change in an existing image, a tweaking of an existing image,* or *no change whatsoever in an image?* For example, the butt-on strategy of market replacement can destroy the prior brand if necessary to properly position the new. But the side-by-side strategy needs a continuing positive image in the item being upgraded. Images can be quite resilient and long-lasting, so changing them should not be undertaken lightly. Yet an image can also be distorted by an almost trivial mistake in an ad or a label, and establishing a new image can be expensive.

In the above analyses leading to *givens, guideline decisions,* and *strategic platform decisions,* one could conclude that we must be about finished. Most of the thinking in those sets is unpleasant because we are deliberately focusing effort or attention on single options from sets.

On the other hand, once these higher-order decisions are made, the rest are easier. So we now turn our attention to what you may think of as the *real* marketing planning decisions: target market, product positioning statement, and creating unique value for the chosen target.

The Target Market Decision

Competition today forces the overwhelming majority of companies to market new items to specific target groups. Markets are so complex that one product cannot come close to meeting all needs and desires.

Alternative Ways to Segment a Market

There may be thousands of ways that new product marketers use to target a specific market segment. Yet each of these can be classified into one of several categories.

End-Use

Athletic shoes are specific for various types of athletic activity. Plastics are sold for hundreds of different applications. CD buyers have different time frames in mind. To test your own end-use orientation, try listing the many different items of clothing you have in your possession. Women, start with designer blouse, dress blouse, and so on. Men, start with T-shirt, golf shirt, dress shirt, and so on. Notice how often the type of garment is defined by the activity it is worn for. Clothing manufacturers design for use, though not only for use.

Geographic and Demographic

Convertibles are not marketed aggressively in Norway, and Golden's fried pork skins are made for the southern United States. Bran cereals are often targeted to the mature segment, Grey Poupon to the upscale, and Right Guard to males (originally). Fitness equipment manufacturers such as Precor have been designing simpler-to-use gear with large-display consoles as the senior market's interest in fitness increases.[14]

Behavioral and Psychographic

Markets can be segmented according to psychographic variables: values, activities, and lifestyles. Lotus Notes was developed for people who needed to communicate in groups across great distances, and Kevlar bulletproof jackets are for people exposed to guns. Products are targeted to lifestyles—tax shelters, clothing, cars, and so on. SRI Consulting follows trends in these variables, as well as in key demographics, using its well-known VALS (Values, Activities, and Lifestyles) questionnaire.[15]

Benefit Segmentation

As we saw in Chapter 9, benefit segments are of great interest in new product development. Through surveys of customers and potential customers, we can identify segments based on benefits sought and develop products to satisfy the needs of one or more of these segments. Recall that in the joint space mapping example of Chapter 9 we identified three benefit segments in our maps of the swimsuit market (see Figure 16.2). Of course, benefit segment information in combination with brand perceptions can be very helpful in developing a positioning strategy, a topic to which we return later in this chapter.

The PIC usually makes quite clear what market group the new project will focus on, and the target market may be clear from the *original concept generation*. For instance, a sales rep notifies management that offices with southern exposure

---

[14]Terence B. Foley, "Muscle Machines: Makers of Fitness Gear Are Tailoring Their Products to an Older Market," *The Wall Street Journal*, September 4, 1998, p. R-15.
[15]Try the online version of the VALS questionnaire at www.sric-bi.com.

FIGURE 16.2
Joint Space Map Showing Ideal Points (from Figure 9.4)

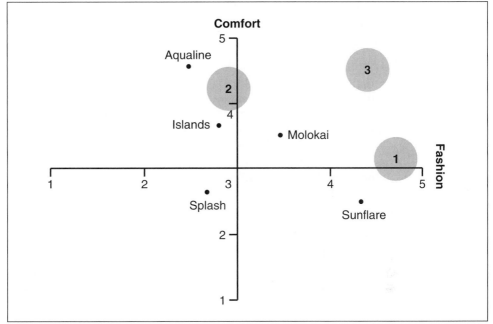

Numbers along the axes represent factor scores.

are having problems with the new personal computer screens, and a new monitor evolves.

Second, the firm's *method of operation* may constrain the choice. If a firm's sales force calls on hospital accounting departments, its new line of tabular records will probably be so targeted.

Third, a focus may come from *concept testing or product use testing*. An early target market may reject a concept in an early trade-off analysis or when they actually try out a prototype. Thus many firms use **parallel development**, keeping two or three target alternatives in development.

Micromarketing and Mass Customization

A current twist in target market selection is the trend toward smallness. Retail scanners and sales information systems yield the databases that display very small targets (neighborhoods or industrial subsets) with unique purchase patterns. These clusters have been labeled **micromarkets**. David Olson, new product researcher at the Leo Burnett advertising agency, uses scanner data to cluster food buyers into six groups:

Loyalists, who buy one brand at all times, like it, and don't use deals.

Rotators, who have a 2- or 3-product set, move around in that set, and don't use deals.

Deal-selectives, rotators whose movement is determined by presence of deals.

Price-driven, who buy all major brands, always on deals.

Store brand buyers, who do as their name implies.

Light users, who buy too little for a pattern to show. Light users comprise the biggest group in most categories.

Direct marketers and online marketers use tighter segments than mass media marketers, stemming from their databases. *Database marketing* has grown exponentially in recent years and allows firms to target their customers in new ways. Amazon looks at a customer's online purchase (for example, a popular book), scans its database for products that tend to be bought by other people who ordered that same book, and makes suggestions for multiple purchases. The more one purchases from Amazon, the richer the database, and the better the recommendations become. Similarly, Blockbuster recommends movies to rent based on past rentals. As one of countless other examples, Fingerhut (a catalog company) has a database of over 30 million households, with about 1,400 pieces of information per household (demographics, hobbies, interests, birthdays). They use their database marketing skills to support online shopping and also to tailor their direct mail offers depending on what customers are likely to buy. Mars, the candy manufacturer, is also a leader in pet food and has a database of practically every household in Germany that owns a cat, gathered from veterinarians and customer questionnaires. Mars periodically sends out samples or coupons, as well as cat birthday cards, much to the delight of the cat owners.[16]

The ultimate smallness, and the ultimate building customer value, is **mass customization** (tailoring a good or service to the unique specifications of individual customers). Great advances in information technology and changes in work processes make mass customization feasible for many products; the challenge is for managers to decide how best to proceed. Firms can practice mass customization in a variety of ways, as seen in Figure 16.3. One such firm is Lands' End. By going to www.landsend.com, customers can create a product online by choosing the combination of features and components that satisfy them directly, then immediately place the order. On its site, www.niketown.com, Nike allows running shoe buyers to go online and customize the style and color of their desired shoe, and even the message appearing on the sides (though, presumably, "Buy Adidas" would not be permitted). An extension of this customization is **virtual product testing**. Customers build the desired product, get an assessment of the resulting price, and then state their likelihood of making a purchase. Researchers can track the way customers make the tradeoffs between product features and price, and thus better understand what features are and are not important in the purchase decision.[17]

A large Japanese bicycle manufacturer, NBIC, pursues both mass customization and mass production simultaneously. The larger mass production plant uses robotics and automated assembly and is designed for high efficiency. The smaller plant is set up to produce bicycles in direct response to customer online orders.

---

[16]See Philip Kotler, *Marketing Management*, 11th ed. (Upper Saddle River, NJ: Prentice-Hall, 2003), pp. 53–55.

[17]Bill MacElroy, "Computer Configuration Figures to Change MR," *Marketing News*, April 4, 2002, p. 23.

FIGURE 16.3 Types of Mass Customization

- *Collaborative customizers* work with the customer in arriving at the optimal product. Japanese eyewear retailer Paris Miki inputs customer frame style preferences with facial features into a design system that makes frame and lens recommendations, which are further refined by customer and optician working together.
- *Adaptive customizers* let the customers do the customizing themselves according to their performance needs. Lutron Electronics markets a lighting system that allows customers to adjust lighting in several rooms simultaneously to obtain a desired ambience.
- *Cosmetic customizers* sell the same basic product to different segments, but adapt the product's presentation (such as its promotion or packaging) depending on segment needs. For example, Wal-Mart likes larger sizes of Planter's Nuts than does 7-Eleven. Planter's now offers a wide range of package sizes and adjusts its production order-by-order according to the wishes of the retailers.
- *Transparent customizers* do not inform their customers that they are customizing the product for them. ChemStation formulates industrial soap specifically to its customers' needs but packages everything it sells in the same kind of tanks. In this case, the customer cares about whether the product works and is delivered on time, not necessarily whether it is customized.

Obviously, any of these strategies has pitfalls that need to be avoided. It would be cost-inefficient for Planter's, for example, to offer too wide a range of package sizes.

Source: Reprinted by permission of *Harvard Business Review.* Exhibit from "The Four Faces of Mass Customization," by James H. Gilmore and B. Joseph Pine II, January–February 1997. Copyright © 1997 by the Harvard Business School Publishing Corporation; All rights reserved.

The online system allows customers to choose from literally millions of variations, and the bicycle is produced and shipped within about two weeks, at a slight price premium. What makes the two-plant system work is that product trends and changing preferences among online customers are tracked, and this customer information is forwarded to the mass-production plant. The online customers essentially act as lead users! Among other reported benefits, the craftsmen from the mass customization plant rotate to the other plant to train their mass-production colleagues, and robots designed for painting in the mass-customization plant eventually found their way into the mass-production factory.[18]

As we approach the marketing date, intense pressure builds up in the organization to add just a few more buyer types, a few more store types, a few more uses or applications because, "The product is good for them too, isn't it?" We call this the *broaden the market* fallacy. The new item cannot be good for lots of different groups unless it is so general it doesn't have any zing for any of them. And targeting to diverse groups can cause dissonance in the promotion. Does a fourth grader want a peanut butter sandwich like the one shown being eaten by a senior citizen? Further, changing the target can be a disaster if promotional and trade-show materials and dates are all prepared; packaging, pricing, and branding are fixed; and the concept and product use tests were conducted only with the original target group.

Lastly, keep in mind that whatever we do, the end users may disagree. A few years ago, sports utility vehicles (SUVs) were adopted by boomers for regular use. They were tired of minivans, and it didn't matter what the car companies *told* us

[18]Suresh Kotha, "Mass-Customization: A Strategy for Knowledge Creation and Organizational Learning," *International Journal of Technology Management*, 11(7/8), 1996, pp. 846–858.

these vehicles were for (or that the government said they were trucks). Some firms capitalize on this end-user penchant by just launching the product and following up to see who the buyers are, then focusing their promotions accordingly. This is strictly a wildcat operation—no charter, no concept testing, no use testing.

Targeting May Also Use Diffusion of Innovation

New products are innovations, and we call the spreading of their usage the *diffusion of innovation*. The original adoption and diffusion of the microwave oven was very slow, but it has been quite rapid for the cellular phone. For a cancer cure, it would be almost instantaneous.

When we used the Bass diffusion model in sales forecasting (Chapter 11), our forecasts rested on two key values: the rates of innovation and imitation. Taken together, these values define the speed of an innovation's adoption. Let's look closer now at the factors that affect this speed of the **product adoption process**: the characteristics of the innovative product and the extent to which early users encourage others to follow.

Product Characteristics

According to the classic diffusion theory of Everett Rogers, there are five factors that measure how soon a new product will diffuse into the marketplace.[19]

1. The *relative advantage* of the new product. How superior is the innovation to the product or other problem-solving methods it was designed to compete against? Google spread rapidly through the Internet community as the preferred search Web site, as it was seen to offer better search capability than other available alternatives.

2. *Compatibility.* Does it fit with current product usage and end-user activity? A *continuous* innovation requires little change or learning by customers, as compatibility with prior experiences and values is high; the more *discontinuous the* innovation, the more learning is required. Microwave ovens were slow to be adopted initially, due to the perceived differences in cooking compared to conventional methods.

3. *Complexity.* Will frustration or confusion arise in understanding the innovation's basic idea? Many people gave up on the Apple Newton, perceiving that it was too hard to make its handwriting recognition feature work; several years later, they adopted Apple's iPod rapidly for many reasons, one of which was certainly its ease of use.

4. *Divisibility* (also called *trialability*). How easily can trial portions of the product be purchased and used? Foods and beverages are quite divisible, but new homes and word processing systems are much less so. A satellite TV service provider faces a bigger divisibility problem, for example, than does Kellogg's with its newest cereal.

---

[19]The classic source on this subject is Everett M. Rogers, *Diffusion of Innovations* (New York: The Free Press, 1962). The illustrative examples (Google, etc.) are from C. Anthony Di Benedetto, "Diffusion of Innovation," in V. K. Narayanan and Gina C. O'Connor (eds.), *Encyclopedia of Technology & Innovation Management* (Chichester, UK: John Wiley, 2010), Chapter 16.

5. *Communicability* (also called *observability*). How easy is it for the user to see the benefits of using the product? The benefits of a new cologne with a nice scent are immediately noticed by the user; the benefits of using a new decay-preventing toothpaste are, by contrast, more difficult for the user to discern.

An innovation can be scored on these five factors, using primarily personal judgment plus the findings from market testing during earlier phases of the development. Launch plans can then be laid accordingly.

Next is the degree to which early users actively or passively encourage others to adopt a new product; if they do, its spread will be rapid. So interest has focused on the **innovators** (the first 5 to 10 percent of those who adopt the product) and on the **early adopters** (the next 10 to 15 percent of adopters). The theory of innovation diffusion states that, if we could just market our new product to those innovators and early adopters, we could then sit back and let them spread the word to the others. Other categories of adopters include the **early majority** (perhaps the next 30 percent), the **late majority** (perhaps another 30 percent), and the **laggards** (the remaining 20 percent).[20]

The obvious question is, "Who will be the innovators and early adopters?" Can we identify them in advance so as to focus our early marketing on them? Not always, but several traits (shown in Figure 16.4) have often emerged from the studies, and they apply to business firms as well as to individuals.

Early users do come typically from the innovator group, but it is difficult to predict which ones. In the industrial setting, early *business* adopters are often (not always) the largest firms in the industry, those who stand to make the greatest profit from the innovation, and those who have presidents who are younger and better educated.[21]

A more recent diffusion model, Geoffrey Moore's **crossing the chasm** model, provides an extension to the Rogers model. Briefly, Moore suggests thinking of the innovators and early adopters as the *visionaries* and later categories as the *pragmatists*. These two new groups of adopters will differ in their expectations of the new product, and the pragmatists may not use the visionaries as their opinion leaders. That is, in Rogers's model, a neat transition from one category to the next is predicted to occur; Moore says that this is not necessarily so, as what the two groups are looking for in the new product can be very different. For example, visionaries may snap up the latest cell phone or music player, almost regardless of price, because it's the newest thing, they like the performance features, or they simply think it's cool. Pragmatists may be unimpressed by the newness factor and might care less about the new device's "coolness"; they may just be looking for something that works pretty well and is not so expensive. They may care more

[20]Note that these are percentages of those who end up *adopting* the item. They are not percentages of the target market. Late majorities and laggards would seem to be slow, but if a product fails they may simply be the last of those daring to try the item! The last group of users who wait 90 days to try a cancer cure are quite a different group from the last of the microwave oven adopters who waited for five years.
[21]Ralph L. Day and Paul A. Herbig, "How the Diffusion of Industrial Innovations Is Different from New Retail Products," *Industrial Marketing Management*, August 1990, pp. 261–266.

FIGURE 16.4
Traits of
Innovators
and Early
Adopters

Venturesomeness—the willingness and desire to be daring in trying the new and different; "sticks his neck out"; "deviates from the group social norms."

Social integration—frequent and extensive contact with others in one's area whether work, neighborhood, or social life; a strong industrial counterpart.

Cosmopolitanism—point of view extending beyond the immediate neighborhood or community; interest in world affairs, travel, reading.

Social mobility—upward movement on the social scale; successful young executive or professional types.

Privilegedness—usually defined as being better off financially than others in the group. Thus the privileged person has less to lose if the innovation fails and costs money. This trait tends to reflect *attitude* toward money as much as possession of money.

Source: Reprinted from *International Journal of Research in Marketing*, Vol. 10, June 1993, "Innovativeness in Industrial Organizations: A Two-Stage Model of Adoption," by Stephane Gauvin and Rajiv K. Sinha, pp. 165–183. Copyright © 1993, with permission from Elsevier.

about the reviews in the mainstream publications (probably not where the visionaries get their information). This is the chasm that Moore is referring to: A firm that offers a value proposition that attracts all the visionaries may never "jump over the chasm" and successfully sell into the (much larger) pragmatist market. Moore's model suggests that the firm should consider developing a value proposition that will work for pragmatists and develop a launch strategy designed to reach pragmatists.[22]

However it comes about, the target market decision essentially measures (1) how much *potential* is in each target market option, (2) how well our new product *meets the needs* of people in each of those markets, and (3) how prepared we are to compete in each—that is, our *capacity to compete* there.

Product Positioning

A **product positioning statement** is created by completing this sentence: Buyers in the target market should buy our product rather than others being offered and used because: _____. Positioning originated as a concept in advertising but is now seen as an ingredient of *total* strategy, not just an advertising ploy. Product, brand, price, promotion, and distribution must all be consistent with the product positioning statement.

[22]The main reference is Geoffrey Moore, *Crossing the Chasm* (New York: Harper Business Essentials, 1991); for a comparison of the Rogers and Moore models, see Di Benedetto, op. cit.

New products managers have a big advantage on positioning—*the end user's memory slate is clean;* potential buyers have no previous positioning in mind for a new item. Now is the best chance ever to effect a particular positioning for their item.

Positioning alternatives fall into two broad categories. The first is to position to an **attribute** (a feature, a function, or a benefit). Attributes are the traditional positioning devices and are most popular. Thus, a dog food may be positioned by a **feature** as "the one with as much protein as 10 pounds of sirloin." **Function** is more difficult and rarely used, but an example is the shampoo that "coats your hair with a thin layer of protein." (You are not told how this is done or what the benefit is.) The **benefits** used in positioning can be *direct* (such as "saves you money") or *follow-on* (such as "improves your sex life," an indirect result of the cleaner teeth or cleaner breath given by this toothpaste). Miller's tag line for years has been a simple statement of one direct benefit and one follow-on: "Tastes great, less filling."

Feature-function-benefit work as a triad, and they are sometimes used that way. For example, a new Drano product was headlined with just three words: THICKER, STRONGER, FASTER. These in fact are: feature, function, benefit. But trying to use all three can be confusing, and target buyers won't spend much time on clarification.

The second alternative in positioning is to use **surrogates** (or metaphors). For example, "Use our dietary product *because it was created by a leading health expert.*" This says the product differs because of its designer. Specific reasons *why* the product is better are not given; the listener or viewer has to provide those. If the surrogate is good, the listener will bring favorable attributes to the product. See Figure 16.5 for the various surrogate positioning alternatives, their definitions, and examples of each.

The perceptual mapping techniques we first encountered during concept generation and evaluation, in Chapters 6 and 9, can be profitably put to use in positioning strategy development. Consider the joint space map of Figure 16.2 again. It indicates not only the positions of the ideal brands of each benefit segment, but also the perceptions of the existing brands. We can use this map to hunt for worthwhile market gaps. We can, for example, select a position for our new brand such that it is near an ideal brand that is not served very well by existing brands. Segment 2 may be relatively large, but if there is heavy brand loyalty to the Aqualine and Islands brands, it may be difficult to get many sales there, and Segment 3 may be a better option. As a simple example, the Taylor Wine Company once identified a small group of heavy wine users and asked them what brands of wine they preferred. Surprisingly, none of the wines the heavy users bought was being positioned on its great taste. Taylor did so position a wine of theirs and succeeded immediately.

If there is no longer an open feature-function-benefit positioning that users want, developers can try to *build* preference for some unique attribute their product has, or they can turn to surrogates. This is where the art begins. Studying the list of alternatives in Figure 16.5 should reveal some good possibilities. These can then be copy tested with the target market to see if they communicate ideas we want the buyers to have. For example, when the Skil Corporation, makers of a successful circular handsaw, developed a line of benchtop tools such as a table

FIGURE 16.5 **Surrogate Positioning—Alternatives and Examples**

Listed below are the types of surrogates currently being used. No doubt there are many others awaiting discovery. For each, the definition is given, followed by one or more examples. The surrogates are listed in order of popularity in use. The claim in each case would be that "Our product is better than, or different than, the others because. . . ."

Nonpareil: . . . because the product has no equal; it is the best (Jaguar cars and Perrier water are sold this way).

Parentage: . . . because of where it comes from, who makes it, who sells it, who performs it, and so on. The three ways of parenting positioning are *brand* (Le Temps Chanel timepieces), *company* ("Everything we know about peanut butter is now available in jars" for Reese's peanut butter, "No one potpourries like Glade" for the new Peachpourri, and new "Adventures in Wonderland" TV show that has no features in its advertising but clearly comes from Disney), and *person* (the RL 2000 chair, designed by Ralph Lauren, the newest book by Dan Brown).

Manufacture: . . . because of how the product was made. This includes *process* (Budweiser beer is beechwood-aged), *ingredients* (Fruit of the Loom panties of pure cotton), and *design* (Audi's engineering).

Target: . . . because the product was made especially for people or firms like you. Four ways are *end-use* (Vector tire designed especially for use on wet roads), *demographic* (several airlines have service specially designed for the business traveler), *psychographic* (Michelob Light for "the people who want it all"), and *behavioral* (Hagar's Gallery line for men who work out a lot, "fit for the fit").

Rank: . . . because it is the best-selling product (Hertz and Blue Cross/Blue Shield); not very useful on a new item unless also positioned under parent brand.

Endorsement: . . . because people you respect say it is good. May be *expert* (the many doctors who prescribed DuoFilm wart remover when it was prescription-only) or a person to be *emulated* (NEC cellular phone keys were designed for Mickey Spillane).

Experience: . . . because its long or frequent use attests to its desirable attributes. Modes are *other market* (Nuprin's extensive use in the prescription market), *bandwagon* (Stuart Hall's Executive line of business accessories are "the tools business professionals rely on"), and *time* (Bell's Yellow Pages). The latter two of these are also of limited use on new products.

Competitor: . . . because it is just (or almost) like another product that you know and like (U.S. Postal Service Express Mail, just like the leading competitor except cheaper).

Predecessor: . . . because it is comparable (in some way) to an earlier product you liked (Hershey's Solitaires addition to the Golden line).

saw, the announcement said: "Besides evaluating its features, one should also consider its *ancestry*." And, "Over *six decades ago* Skil introduced the world's first circular saw. . . . Today we are continuing the Skilsaw *tradition* . . . lives up to its *namesake* . . . member of our new *family* . . . long-standing *reputation* for quality." This is surrogate positioning.

Creating Unique Value for the Chosen Target

Once a market segment has been targeted and a positioning statement created for it, we have a chance to cycle back to the product itself and see if we can enhance its value to the chosen market. After all, the role of a new product is usually to build gross margin dollars, dollars that come primarily from the values it has over its price.

FIGURE 16.6
Purchase Configuration—
What the
Buyer
Actually Buys

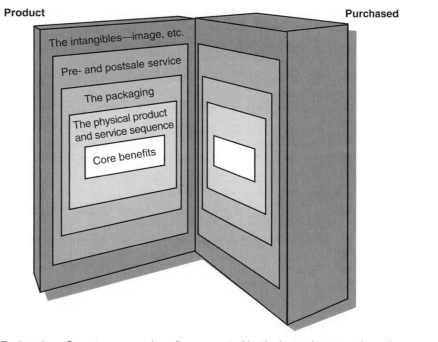

Product   Purchased

The intangibles—image, etc.

Pre- and postsale service

The packaging

The physical product
and service sequence

Core benefits

Explanation: One or more core benefits are wanted by the buyer; but to get them, the buyer must also take delivery on the physical product or service sequence, its packaging, its attendant service, and all intangibles that go with the brand and firm making/selling it. These other purchase "layers" may enhance the total value or detract from it, but they each offer opportunity for differentiation or for the core benefit to be destroyed or overpowered if not handled correctly by the new products manager.

Figure 16.6 shows how the buyer actually receives a bundle of things a product consists of. Here we view it as a package, bought and taken home, but the augmentation idea is the same as the bull's-eye shown in Figure 12.3. The core benefit of the product may receive the greatest attention during the development phase. But from the buyer's point of view, the bundle that he or she receives and takes home can comprise much more. During later phases of the new products process, we try to add extra benefits to the core product through branding, packaging, warranty, presale service, and so on—such that we increase the value of the augmented product to the customer.

Most firms now try to freeze specs late in development and schedule others for soon after launch to sustain value in the product. As the first product is coming down the pike, the first couple of line extensions should be in development. Then, after launch, when competitors are casting around for ways to come out with catch-up versions, we market them first.[23]

[23]C. Merle Crawford, "How Product Innovators Can Foreclose the Options of Adaptive Followers," *Journal of Consumer Marketing*, Fall 1988, pp. 17–24.

In the remainder of this section, we will focus our attention on two of the ways in which we can increase unique value to the targeted customer—**branding** and **packaging**.

Branding and Brand Management

Trademarks and Registration[24]

Every new product must be identified, and the accurate term for what identifies products is **trademark**. Under U.S. federal law, a trademark is usually a word or a symbol. That symbol may be a sequence of letters and/or numbers (such as the Z3 Roadster) a logo (for example, Apple Inc.'s multicolored apple), or a design (for example, the stylized lettering in GE, or the golden arches of McDonald's). A *word string* such as "just do it" can be a trademark, as can a *sound signature* such as the 3-note NBC chimes or the "Intel Inside" sound.[25] The law doesn't care how unusual the trademark is and just requires it to identify and differentiate the item using it. The law also requires that the firm uses, or intends to use, the trademark—this requirement is called *bona fide intent.*[26]

Most businesspeople and their customers use the term *brand* instead of *trademark*. This book uses *brand* when talking about marketing strategy and *trademark* when talking about the legal aspects. Technically speaking, services have *service marks,* not trademarks, and businesses have **trade names,** not trademarks.

Another definition is very important: **registration**. Historically, and still today in most countries, the *first user* of a trademark had exclusive rights. But in the United States you can ask that your trademark be registered. If you can get it registered, you can keep that trademark forever, even if another firm later displays proof of prior use.

The Patent and Trademark Office has certain conditions it considers when allowing a trademark to be registered. One obvious condition is that the trademark should not be immoral or misleading. The trademark should also not be too descriptive of a product type; for example, a judge once ruled that Light was too descriptive a name to be used as a cigarette brand, since the name would have identified any low-tar cigarette, not just the one firm's brand. Another condition is that the trademark should not be confusingly similar to trademarks belonging to other products. Quality Inns once tried to name a cheaper line of hotels McSleep—until McDonald's lawyers objected. The argument is that the "Mc" *formative* would lead people to believe that the hotel chain was part of McDonald's and could pose problems to McDonald's at the time the latter was building a chain of truckstop operations called McStop. Quality changed the name of the hotels to Sleep Inns.

---

[24]There are many sources for information on this topic, but the best thing a new product manager can do is make contact with the employer's in-house (or local area) trademark attorney. Most such departments have brochures for employees to study, but experts we should not try to be!

[25]Rob Osler, "On the Mark," *Marketing Management,* January–February 2007, pp. 31–36.

[26]Rob Osler, op. cit.

FIGURE 16.7 **Categories of Brand Names and Trademark Protection**

Famous Names. Certain well-known trademarks (such as Coca-Cola and Disney) are protected by the Federal Trademark Dilution Act, which prevents other companies from using similar names, even on unrelated items. A prominent 1998 case involved the famous Victoria's Secret store, and an adult-oriented store, Victor's Secret (later Victor's Little Secret). Interestingly, the U.S. Supreme Court ruled in favor of the latter, arguing that Victoria's Secret's capacity to identify its goods were not lessened by the presence of the competitor.

Fanciful Names. Also known as neologisms, these are made-up names either comprised of real words or parts of words (Bluetooth, Ameriprise) or totally unique (Kodak, Exxon). These are distinctive and easy to protect via trademark laws, but the firm must create a meaning for a word that, by definition, doesn't have one.

Arbitrary Names. These are real words that appear to have been chosen as brand names without concern for the nature of the product or industry (Apple computers, Virgin airlines, and Web sites like Monster.com or Amazon.com). These enjoy trademark protection much like fanciful names.

Suggestive Names. These are defined as those that require some imagination to link them to the nature of the product (Coinstar coin machines, Quadra Tred tires). Suggestive names can communicate a product benefit to customers, but might be harder to protect via trademark laws. As an example, boatmaker AMF owned the Slickcraft trademark for recreational boats, but courts ruled that competitor Nescher could use the name Sleekcraft for its racing boats (since the product categories were ruled to be different enough).

Descriptive Names. (Lean Cuisine, HotJobs) are harder to protect since they are, by definition, not inherently descriptive. These names go onto a different trademark list at first (the Supplemental Register), but if the owners can create sufficient awareness after a five-year period, they can obtain a higher level of legal protection. This is what happened in the case of Rollerblades.

Generic Names. These names have become synonymous with the product category, and the original trademark holder loses the exclusive rights (see text for examples).

Source: Reprinted with permission from *Marketing Management,* published by the American Marketing Association, Rob Osler, "On the Mark," January–February 2007, pp. 31–36.

Apple Corps (the Beatles' recording company) once sued Apple Computers (now Apple Inc.) when the latter entered the music business through iTunes. In that case, however, it was ruled that the two uses were not *confusingly similar* and both companies were permitted to keep the Apple trademark.[27]

Different types of brand names offer different amounts of protection under trademark laws. See Figure 16.7 for a description.

What happens if, shortly after launch, other manufacturers begin encroaching on our mark? We move aggressively to stop them. Aladdin began putting on its labels "Aladdin thermos bottle." Do you know what thermos bottles are? If you do, as most people do, then the term no longer just describes one maker's brand of vacuum bottles. Aladdin was sued by the firm that owned the thermos mark, and won; the original owner did not protect it. *Thermos* became a generic. Any company can use it. Over the years, so did aspirin, cellophane, brassiere, dry ice, shredded wheat, trampoline, yo-yo, linoleum, corn flakes, kerosene, high octane, raisin bran, lanolin, nylon, mimeograph, and scores more. Billions of dollars in value lost. But today, makers of in-line skates know that Rollerblades is aggressively protected,

[27]May Wong, "Apple, Cisco, Ready for an iPhone Trace?" businessweek.com, February 1, 2007.

as is Mattel's Frisbee. Some Xerox Corp. advertising reminds customers that the word "Xerox" is a trademark and therefore a proper adjective. It should always be followed by a descriptive noun (as in "Xerox copier"), and never used as a verb (as in "xerox this for me").[28] Incidentally, don't forget to seek protection for the new brand in all countries where it might be marketed.

Companies can also seek **trade dress** protection. Trade dress refers to a wide range of product identifiers: In addition to brand name, it can include packaging (the familiar Coca-Cola bottle shape), product color (Brillo is the pink soap pad, SOS is blue), or décor (the distinctive look inside a certain fast-food chain, for example). The extent of protection a company has is not always clear-cut, but if a firm has data that show customers identify a given trade dress with a particular brand, protection is often allowed by the courts using the concept of *secondary meaning*. That is, the color, décor, or packaging takes on a secondary meaning, which is the name of the brand. Private brands often use trade dress to establish themselves as competitors of well-known brands—the drugstore brand of aspirin may be in a package that resembles the Bayer Aspirin package. Typically, courts deny the private brand absolute rights to copy the well-known brand's trade dress.[29]

What Is a Good Brand Name?

Getting a good brand is not easy, because most good combinations of letters have already been taken. But, if Billy Fuddpucker's and Orville Redenbacher can be successful brand names, then there is hope for all. Experts have given us several rules-of-thumb to follow and pitfalls to avoid (Figure 16.8).

Beyond these general principles, there is no end to the specific advice given by branding experts. The branding decision is often very important; it can be botched or brilliant. Consider some of the poorer brand name choices:

- A new high-tech product was named "Killer" as management thought it would "kill the competition." Needless to say, it did not.[30]
- A real misfire was La Choy's Fresh and Lite line of low-fat frozen Chinese entrées—critics thought it might be a feminine hygiene product, or perhaps a beer or soft drink.[31]

By contrast, the Motorola RAZR phone, Apple's iPod, and the Swiffer mop from Procter & Gamble are such popular brands that they have become associated with entire product lines.[32]

---

[28]Maxine S. Lans, "On Your Mark: Get Set or It May Go," *Marketing News*, September 26, 1994, p. 12.
[29]Paul F. Kilmer, "Trade Dress Protection 1995: A U.S. Perspective," *Journal of Brand Management*, October 1995, pp. 95–103.
[30]Lee Schaeffer and Jim Twerdahl, "Giving Your Product the Right Name," in A. Griffin and S. M. Somermeyer, *The PDMA Toolbook 3 for New Product Development* (New York: John Wiley, 2007), Chapter 8.
[31]"Flops," *BusinessWeek*, August 16, 1993, p. 76.
[32]Lee Schaeffer and Jim Twerdahl, op. cit.

FIGURE 16.8

Issues and Guidelines in Brand Name Selection

Question	Guideline
What is the brand's role or purpose?	If the brand is to aid in positioning, choose a brand name with meaning (DieHard, Holiday Inn). If purely for identification, a *neologism* (made-up word) such as Kodak or Exxon will work.
Will this product be a bridgehead to a line of products?	If so, choose carefully so as not to be a limitation in the future (Western Hotels changed name to Western International, then finally to Westin).
Do you expect a long-term position in the market?	If not, a dramatic, novelty name might be useful (such as Screaming Yellow Zonkers).
Is the name irritating or insulting to any market segment?	P&G intended to name a new detergent Dreck until it was noted that Yiddish or German definitions included garbage or body waste, and the name was changed to Dreft.

Others: Easy to understand; no hidden meanings; translates well; simple and memorable; fits corporate mission; and complements other products in the marketplace.

Brand Name Pitfalls to Avoid

Not anticipating future uses of the name. A cute name can become irrelevant; a bad name may be chosen because there was time pressure to make a decision; a regional name becomes a hindrance as the firm goes national or international. Consider US Airways, originally known as Allegheny Airlines, a name that suggests it should serve the Pittsburgh area only. An acceptable name in English or some Spanish dialects may be offensive in other Spanish dialects (the Toyota Fiera was unsuitable in Puerto Rico where the name means "ugly old woman"). Even differences between American, British, and Canadian English need to be considered. A new U.S.-made product with the brand name "EZ" (pronounced "easy") would just not sell as well in either Great Britain or Canada where most readers would pronounce the name "e-zed."

Not allocating enough time for the process. This corresponds with the idea of marketing activities being conducted throughout the product process. The brand name should not be a last-minute rush job, especially if the brand is going to be marketed across multiple countries. Consider that Procter & Gamble went to the trouble of assigning two different French brand names for Mr. Clean due to slightly different usage patterns: M. Propre in French Europe, and M. Net in Quebec.

Choosing the wrong comfort level. A provocative and controversial brand name such as Yahoo! may be a great strategy, certainly better than a comfortable yet uninspiring name.

Having too many individuals involved in the brand naming decision process. It works better if a team is assigned that understands brand naming and its consequences, than to let democracy or consensus rule.

Other pitfalls: Not identifying who the key decision makers are; getting "stuck" on a brand name early in the process and, knowingly or not, it is adopted without any objective feedback; not checking negative meanings in foreign markets, and, of course, not hiring the best patent attorney.

Sources: Some of these points are adapted from Lee Schaeffer and Jim Twerdahl, "Giving Your Product the Right Name," in A. Griffin and S. M. Somermeyer, *The PDMA Toolbook 3 for New Product Development*, Wiley, 2007, Chapter 8.

Some of the newest work in brand name selection considers the semantic meanings of the *phonemes,* or the raw sounds of the letters. Some letters are associated with pleasant or unpleasant feelings, others may suggest size or speed. Using this viewpoint, the BlackBerry PDA has a great name: the "b"s evoke reliability, and the short "e" speed. "StrawBerry" just wouldn't have been as good. Viagra (the erectile dysfunction drug) has a good name too: "Vi-" suggests vitality, "-agra" suggests aggression. It also rhymes with "Niagara," as in powerful Niagara Falls, which happens to be a favorite honeymoon spot. What a great name![33]

As a final word, be sure the budget is sufficient for adequately creating customer awareness and understanding. If you don't have the funds to put meaning into a meaningless combination of letters, avoid that type of brand.

Given an overall marketing strategy and the role that brand will play, it is useful to have some discussions with intended users (to learn how they talk about things in this area of use)—and also with phonetic experts, who know a great deal about such things as word structures. Then brainstorm or use computers to generate large numbers of possible combinations. Computer software (such as NamePro, developed by The Namestormers, and IdeaFisher by IdeaFisher Inc.) is available to assist in brand name selection and development.[34]

Conduct interviews with users to screen the list down. Ask what the brands on your list mean—including in global markets (see Figure 16.9 for classic misfires). There is much support available for branding decisions at this point. A check at www.register.com should identify any similar brand names that might cause negative connotations or even a legal challenge. One can also turn to the Patent and Trademark Office site (www.uspto.gov) and search under Trademarks, as well as any trademark databases in targeted foreign countries. The site www.trademark.com can also help access trademark databases. A quick check of possible offensive or unintended meanings in foreign languages can be easily made using one of the familiar translation Web sites, like www.freetranslation.com. Needless to say, make sure to have a good trademark attorney on your side.[35]

Managing Brand Equity

There is more to brand management, of course, than brand name selection. The best brand names—Coca-Cola, Levi's, Campbell, AT&T, and so on—are important assets that provide value to both the firm and its customers, as they communicate quality, build positive brand images, and encourage customer loyalty. This value is known as **brand equity**, and the firms that benefit the most from brand

---

[33]Sharon Begley, "New ABCs of Branding," *The Wall Street Journal*, August 26, 2002, pp. B1, B4.
[34]Check out these firms' Web sites: www.namestormers.com and www.ideafisher.com. The Namestormers site has links to a NamePro software demonstration as well as to a naming guide providing useful guidance on good brand name selection (including domain name selection for your firm's Web site).
[35]Useful guides in brand name development are Chiranjeev Kohli and Douglas W. LaBahn, "Creating Effective Brand Names: A Study of the Naming Process," *Journal of Advertising Research*, January–February 1997, pp. 67–75, and Lee Schaeffer and Jim Twerdahl, op. cit.

FIGURE 16.9 Bad Brand Names

Sometimes it seems that foreign companies choose brand names that would seriously limit their sales potential in English-speaking markets.

Crapsy Fruit	French cereal
Fduhy Sesane	China Airlines snack food
Mukk	Italian yogurt
Pschitt	French lemonade
Atum Bom	Portuguese tuna
Happy End	German toilet paper
Pocari Sweat	Japanese sport drink
Zit	German lemonade
Creap	Japanese coffee creamer
I'm Dripper	Japanese instant coffee
Polio	Czech laundry detergent
Sit & Smile	Thai toilet paper
Barf	Iranian laundry detergent
Cream Pain	Japanese snack cake
Porky Pork	Japanese pork snack

Of course it works in both directions. Two famous examples are the Rolls Royce Silver Mist ("Mist" means "manure" in German), and Colgate Cue toothpaste ("Cue" is the name of a French porno magazine). Clairol also experienced problems launching its Mist Stick curling iron in Germany. The lesson is that we need to be careful when introducing brands into foreign markets.

More recently, Mon Cuisine frozen entrées were launched in the U.S., the French name undoubtedly selected to add an upscale image. Only problem was the manufacturer made a basic grammatical error (it should have used "Ma Cuisine").

Sources: Anonymous, "But Will It Sell in Tulsa?" *Newsweek*, March 17, 1997, p. 8; Ross and Kathryn Petras, *The 776 Even Stupider Things Ever Said* (New York: Harper-Perennial, 1994); www.engrish.com; and others.

equity have invested in protecting this equity to maintain the value of their brand names.[36]

A brand with high equity encourages loyalty among customers, making advertising and other forms of promotion more efficient. High equity also means high brand awareness, which makes it easier for the firm to create other associations (for example, McDonald's is associated with children, clean restaurants, Ronald McDonald, etc.). Brand equity can also be associated with higher perceived quality and thus can support a premium positioning for a brand. Due to its high familiarity and positive associations, a high-equity brand can more easily be used as a bridgehead for launching **brand extensions**. In short, brand equity can provide sustainable competitive advantage—and recent work suggests that all of these brand equity advantages hold for business-to-business products as well as consumer goods.[37] One authority on branding, Kevin Lane Keller,

[36]The authoritative books on brand equity are David A. Aaker, *Managing Brand Equity* (New York: Free Press, 1991); and David A. Aaker and Erich Joachimsthaler, *Brand Leadership* (New York: Free Press, 2000).
[37]Paul Mitchell, Jacqui King, and John Reast, "Brand Values Related to Industrial Products," *Industrial Marketing Management*, 30(5), July 2001, pp. 415–425.

FIGURE 16.10 A Brand Report Card

Many different factors work together to make a strong brand. Brand managers often focus on only one or two of these factors. Here is a list of several characteristics shared by the world's strongest brands that can be used to assess the strengths of a brand and to identify points of improvement.

Characteristic	Examples
Delivers benefits desired by customers.	Starbucks offers "coffee house experience," not just coffee beans, and monitors bean selection and roasting to preserve quality.
Stays relevant.	Gillette continuously invests in major product improvements (Fusion), while using a consistent slogan: "The best a man can get."
Prices are based on value.	P&G reduced operating costs and passed on savings as "everyday low pricing," thus growing margins.
Well-positioned relative to competitors.	Lexus competes on excellent customer service, Mercedes on product superiority. Visa stresses being "everywhere you want to be."
Is consistent.	Michelob tried several different positionings and campaigns between 1970 and 1995, while watching sales slip.
The brand portfolio makes sense.	The Gap has Gap, Banana Republic, and Old Navy stores for different market segments; BMW has the 3-, 5-, and 7-series.
Marketing activities are coordinated.	Coca-Cola uses ads, promotions, catalogs, sponsorships, and interactive media.
What the brand means to customers is well understood.	Bic couldn't sell perfume in lighter-shaped bottles; Gillette uses different brand names such as Oral-B for toothbrushes to avoid this problem.
Is supported over the long run.	Coors cut back promotional support in favor of Coors Light and Zima, and lost about 50% of its sales over a four-year period.
Sources of brand equity are monitored.	Disney studies revealed that its characters were becoming "overexposed" and sometimes used inappropriately. It cut back on licensing and other promotional activity as a result.

Source: Reprinted by permission of *Harvard Business Review.* Exhibit from "The Brand Report Card," by Kevin Lane Keller, February 2000. Copyright © 2000 by the Harvard Business School Publishing Corporation; All rights reserved.

suggested a brand report card—a list of characteristics shared by the strongest brands worldwide that can be used to assess a brand's strengths and weaknesses (see Figure 16.10).[38]

Brand extensions can be either vertical or horizontal depending on whether the new brand is in the same product category as the parent one. Procter & Gamble

[38]One firm that specializes in brand identity and corporate identity development is Landor Associates, www.landor.com. Their site contains a portfolio of dozens of applications, including Kellogg's, FedEx, Kodak, Seven-Up, and many others.

extended Crest toothpaste vertically into Crest Tartar Protection, Crest Sensitivity Protection, and Crest Multicare toothpastes, and also horizontally into Crest toothbrushes and Crest Glide floss, among others. Regardless of the direction, a brand extension can boost acceptance of the new product, but problems with the new product can result in dilution of the parent brand's equity.[39]

Brand extensions must be managed carefully as an unsuccessful extension, or too many extensions, can lead to brand equity erosion. Some companies have tried extending a well-known brand name into an inappropriate product category, with disastrous results. The Frito-Lay brand has been successfully extended to many snack foods, but Frito-Lay Lemonade didn't sell. Neither did Ben-Gay aspirin (what would that taste like?), Smucker's ketchup, nor Fruit of the Loom Laundry Detergent.[40] We have already seen how firms seeking to extend their brands globally should check for unanticipated humorous or objectionable meanings. Perhaps more subtle is the fact that humor often doesn't cross national or linguistic barriers. As a rule of thumb, humorous names tend to work best only in cases where the product will have only a limited, local market (which presumably will see the humor).[41]

Although there is no one right way to extend a brand name, there are some guidelines to follow to avoid mistakes. For instance, emphasizing the product's name or benefits might create a safe distance from the brand being extended. When the Audi 500 automobile was allegedly experiencing problems with sudden acceleration, Audi 400 sales were hurt, but not Audi Quattro sales. Another consideration is whether the brand being extended has a functional or a prestige image. Gillette could probably launch a downscale extension of the Fusion razor easily, while Mercedes risks tarnishing its reputation if it launches a low-end Mercedes car. Often, a **flagship brand** (a dominant brand in a product category, such as Hallmark Cards or Planter's Peanuts) is extended in this way, as its brand equity is already quite high. But flagship brands should be extended carefully, and then probably only to brands of similar or better quality to avoid risking brand name dilution and consumer confidence. There may also be international considerations. The Bayer name is best known in North America for over-the-counter pharmaceuticals, yet in Europe it is well known also as a producer of agricultural products and chemicals. Bayer pesticide might do well in Germany, but probably not in the United States. Of course, concept testing a potential extension can identify any possible negative associations.[42] On the positive side, a strong parent brand, successful previous brand extensions, strong marketing support, good acceptance at the retailer level, good fit between parent brand and

---

[39]Kuang-Jung Chen and Chu-Mei Lu, "Positive Brand Extension Trial and Choice of Parent Brand," *Journal of Product and Brand Management*, 13(1), 2004, pp. 25–36.

[40]Robert M. McMath and Thom Forbes, *What Were They Thinking?* (New York: Times Business, 1996).

[41]Lee Schaeffer and Jim Twerdahl, op. cit.

[42]Dennis A. Pitts and Lea Prevel Katsanis, "Understanding Brand Equity for Successful Brand Extensions," *Journal of Consumer Marketing*, 12(4), 1995, pp. 51–64; see also Sieu Meng Long, Swee Hoon Ang, and Janet Liau, "Dominance and Dilution: The Effects of Extending Master Brands," *Journal of Consumer Marketing*, 14(5), 1997, pp. 280–288.

extension, and low perceived risk of the extension are all associated with more successful brand extensions.[43]

Brand Equity and Branding Strategies[44]

There is a variety of different branding strategies available, each with pros and cons, and there is no one-size-fits-all solution. In all cases, however, the firm must consider how the branding strategy will protect and possibly build brand equity.

Think of a spectrum of branding strategies. On one end of the spectrum are businesses that put their corporate name on every product they make. This is sometimes called an **umbrella brand** strategy. At Kellogg's, for example, every cereal carries the word "Kellogg's" as part of the brand name: Kellogg's Corn Flakes, Kellogg's Rice Krispies, and so on. The Kellogg's name is synonymous with excellence and quality in cereal, and the appearance of the company name on a new cereal (or a new snack, as seen in the Kellogg's case in Chapter 3) extends this brand equity to the new product. In similar fashion, Kraft Foods has dozens of decades-old products that include the name Kraft in the brand (Kraft Salad Dressing, Kraft Singles), or at least display the Kraft logo prominently on the package (Philadelphia Cream Cheese, Velveeta). The firm will also use corporate brands other than Kraft to roll out new product. A new nut product will carry the Planters name, a new pizza will be Di Giorno, and a new coffee is likely to be Maxwell House. Other examples are Virgin Airlines (which entered many other businesses including publishing, soft drinks, and cell phones, all under the Virgin name), and Hard Rock Café (which extended into Hard Rock Café Resorts in Asian markets).[45]

On the other end of the spectrum are firms that seem to go out of their way not to mention the company name in the brand. None of the many detergents and cleaning products marketed by Procter & Gamble includes P&G in the brand name; the names are simply Tide, Bold, Mr. Clean, and so on. This **individual brand** strategy is consistent with P&G's historically strong brand management. The Clorox Company uses the Clorox brand on all of its bleach products. Its environmentally friendly Green Works brand also displays the Clorox brand on the packaging, to communicate that the all-natural line is as effective as conventional cleaners. (More on Green Works in the case appearing in Chapter 20.) But other products acquired by the Clorox Company over the years have never undergone a name change. The Clorox Company owns Hidden Valley Ranch salad dressing, KC Masterpiece barbecue sauce, Glad Bags, and Burt's Bees. These are high-equity brands in their own product categories, and there is nothing to be gained by using

[43]Franziska Volckner and Henrik Sattler, "Drivers of Brand Extension Success," *Journal of Marketing,* 70(2), 2006, pp. 18–34; see also Eva Martinez and Jose M. Pina, "The Negative Impact of Brand Extensions on Parent Brand Image," *Journal of Product and Brand Management,* 12(7), 2003, pp. 432-448.

[44]For dozens of examples, check out www.kelloggs.com, www.kraftfoods.com, www.thecloroxcompany.com, www.pg.com, or www.conagrafoods.com.

[45]Muammer Ozer, "A Survey of New Product Evaluation Models," *Journal of Product Innovation Management,* 16(1), January 1999, pp. 77–94.

Clorox as an umbrella brand here. Interestingly, the Clorox Company does not even extend the Clorox brand to other cleaners it produces, such as 409, SOS, or Tilex (though its Handi Wipes disposable cloth towels do carry the Clorox logo on one corner of the package).

There are often possibilities for improving one's branding strategy so as to take advantage of synergies or co-branding opportunities. As a case in point, ConAgra Foods produces dozens of brands familiar throughout North America: Hunt's tomato products, Orville Redenbacher popcorn, Reddi-Wip whipped cream, Healthy Choice frozen entrees, Peter Pan peanut butter, just to name a few. None of these brands carries the ConAgra corporate name; the equity resides in the strong brands, similar to P&G or Clorox. Unlike Clorox, ConAgra's line is entirely within one category: consumer packaged food products. Consumer research showed that the ConAgra name was not well known among consumers. Executives felt that a new corporate identity would reinforce the individual brands, reinforce ConAgra's position as a top food manufacturer, and make the company more competitive. But what should they do? Adding "ConAgra" to familiar brand names like Hunt's or Peter Pan probably doesn't help them that much. ConAgra decided instead on a new slogan to be attached to every brand and advertisement ("Food You Love"), together with a new logo (a contemporary-looking smiling plate with a spoon), both unveiled in 2009. ConAgra's plan was to move on the branding spectrum closer to Kraft in terms of having a unified corporate identity, while still taking advantage of its strong individual brands.

Global Branding and Positioning: Standardize or Adapt?

One consideration in global brand management is the extent to which brand names will be standardized around the world (that is, the same name is used worldwide). Gillette blades, Coca-Cola, and Kellogg's cereals are known to customers by those names everywhere they are sold. These firms use essentially the same positioning in every market as well; Gillette positions its blades as "the best a man can get" virtually everywhere.

For many other firms, achieving a standardized global presence is not an option, and quite possibly not even desirable. These firms will choose instead an adaptation strategy for its position and/or its brand names. Honda, for example, uses a high-quality position in the United States, but a speed/youth positioning in Japan. Canon launched the AE-1 in the United States under the slogan "so advanced, it's simple," while in Japan the same camera was positioned as a high-tech product for experienced camera users.

A firm may also choose different names for the same product in different markets. While Tide is P&G's leading brand in North America, Ariel is their best-known name throughout Europe and Japan; similarly, Liquid Tide is Liquid Ariel in Europe. A major North American competitor of Kellogg's, General Mills, entered the European market in a joint venture with Nestlé called Cereal Partners Worldwide (General Mills provided the cereal making expertise while Nestlé contributed experience in European distribution, sales, and advertising). Familiar North American General Mills brands such as Cheerios (as well as Europe-only brands such as Chocapic) are sold in Europe under the Nestlé name.

An interesting case is Unilever, the Anglo-Dutch conglomerate, which uses a blend of standardization and adaptation in brand name selection. Several Unilever products are sold under the same names worldwide: these include Lipton, Bertolli, Knorr, Dove, Vaseline, and many others. Cif household cleanser, originally sold in France, is known under that name there and in several other markets such as Italy, Switzerland, Turkey, and Greece, but is also known as Viss in Germany and Vim in Canada. Perhaps the most extreme case of brand name adaptation is the fabric softener known in North America as Snuggle. In Italy, the brand name is Coccolino; in France, Cajoline; in Germany and Austria, Kuschelweich; and in the Netherlands, Robijn. In all cases, the familiar teddy bear character is prominent on the package. Even though the actual product is standardized throughout the world, Unilever provides it with a local-sounding brand name in every market. (In multilingual Switzerland, the name is Comfort: simple, and easy to understand in any language.) Similarly, Unilever has acquired several ice cream manufacturers around the world, including Good Humor in the United States, Langnese in Germany, Algida in Italy, and Kibon in Brazil. In each case, the familiar brand name was retained; a red heart-shaped logo is used as an identifying mark in all markets and, collectively, these are known as Heartbrand within Unilever.[46]

Global Brand Leadership[47]

The preceding section suggests that the goal is not necessarily to pursue a single global brand, but rather to create a strong presence in every market through **global brand leadership**. This requires an overall global brand strategy that coordinates the brand strategies used in the individual countries, and a commitment to allocate sufficient resources to brand building.

There are many ways to work toward global brand leadership. In order to achieve consistent brand management across countries, firms can develop brand manuals, set up workshops, or distribute newsletters or videos to all brand managers to serve as a guide on what the brand stands for. This goes beyond simple product attributes, as these may be copied by competitors. Intangibles (such as a quality reputation) and symbols (such as the Ronald McDonald clown) should be considered as well. Mobil has set up a knowledge bank on marketing topics accessible via company intranet, while Frito-Lay runs a "market university" three times a year. Activities such as these encourage communication and sharing of successful practice among managers throughout the company. Employee empowerment is also important. P&G's Taiwanese brand team for Pantene Pro-V came up with a novel positioning: "Hair so healthy it shines." The ad campaign built around this slogan was so successful in Taiwan, it was picked up by P&G and used in 70 other countries.

---

[46]Reference: www. unilever.com.
[47]Much of this section is adapted from David A. Aaker and Erich Joachimsthaler, "The Lure of Global Branding," *Harvard Business Review*, November–December 1999, pp. 137–144.

Packaging

To many firms, packaging is less important, either because the goods require little packaging or because the shelf persuasiveness of packaging is not a priority. In these firms, packaging is for the most part assigned to packaging design departments. Of course, most services require no packaging. But in many other firms, packaging is of great importance, especially when the new item will be distributed through self-service environments, when the product category is already established so the new item will have to force its way in, and when many strongly entrenched competitors sit next to one another on store shelves. In such firms, packaging decisions are often made at the highest levels. In fact, more money is spent on packaging food and beverage products than on advertising them.

The Role of Packaging

Packaging can refer to *primary packaging* (the material that first envelops the product and holds it, such as a pill bottle), *secondary packaging* (the box that holds the pill bottle), or *tertiary packaging* (bulk packaging that holds secondary packages for shipment). All forms of packaging serve several roles: *containment* (hold for transporting), *protection* (from the elements and the careless), *safety* (from causing injury), *display* (to attract attention), and *information* and *persuasion*. All are important to a new products manager, sometimes enough so that there are legal problems; packaging design is a part of logo and trademark, where rights can be valuable.

But there are other roles. For example, assisting the user in some way—with instructions (pharmaceuticals or food) and with a use function (beer cans and deodorant dispensers). Other times packages are designed to permit reusability, meet ecological demands on biodegradability, carry warnings, and meet other legal requirements. They may also aid in disposability.

The Packaging Decision

Packaging is part of the new product manager's network. The packaging decision centers on a person most often called the director of packaging. It is, however, a complex decision. Packaging decisions can involve participants from engineering, distribution, safety, legal, cost accounting, purchasing, R&D, and other departments, in addition to marketing and sales, not to mention outside interests such as vendors, distributors, shippers, advertising agencies, and the government. The packaging decision may take months; it is a key target in most accelerated development programs.

Each company tends to develop a somewhat unique approach to packaging, but there are common steps. First, a packaging person is put on a new products team. Field trips are mandatory, as is access to the various market studies that have been made. A unique packaging approach for Pfeiffer's salad dressing was found when a packaging staffer visited supermarkets and noted that salad dressings were displayed by type rather than by brand; most competitive bottles were shaped like whisk brooms with flat iron heads.

The process for package development resembles that for the product itself. Tests include dummy packages, in-store displays, color tests, visual tests, psychographic tests, physical tests, distribution tests, warehouse legibility, and even some in-store selling tests. One of the strategies sometimes used in package design is family packaging, that is, using a key design, or some other packaging element, to integrate the packaging of several individual items. A package for a new Häagen-Dazs or Ben & Jerry's ice cream flavor, for example, is immediately recognizable. Coca-Cola and Pepsi are red and blue, respectively. In each case, the packages clearly belong to one set, but there are usually some individualizations, such as brand name.

Packaging can be a very powerful competitive tool. In recent years, wine and spirits have made up a larger share of the alcoholic drink market at the expense of beer. One of the ways Anheuser-Busch and competing brewers have tried to counteract this trend is through innovative packaging. See-through beer labels (technically, pressure-sensitive adhesives made from acrylate ester) that stick on the side of the bottle and look painted on are one of the newest packaging innovations. Soon after their introduction, growth in see-through labeled bottles was at over 10 percent in the United States and near 40 percent in Europe and Asia. The labels are not only attractive, but can be easily designed to add special messages, such as around playoff football or Olympics time, and also allow the brewer to use the whole package—from the bottle cap to the base—for graphics and copy. Among other packaging innovations are shrink-wrap labeling, and aluminum bottles for Budweiser, Bud Light, and several other Anheuser-Busch brands (including shamrock green aluminum bottles for St. Patrick's Day), and Halloween-themed aluminum bottles printed with ultraviolet ink that glow under black lights.[48]

Summary

In Chapter 16, we have extended our look at the launch planning process by going into the platform decisions and the driving decisions. Both sets have a strong effect on the strategies chosen. The chapter also looked at three of the biggest areas of decision—target market or segment, positioning of the new item for that segment, and creating unique value for that segment. We can now turn to those many things that make up the tactics portion of the marketing plan. But there is far too little space for an in-depth study in the many areas of operational marketing. We will look at those issues that give new products managers the most difficulty.

Applications

1. "My daughter is a newly appointed assistant professor at a school in North Carolina, and she recently was joking about how similar the development of courses is to the development of new products. In fact, she said courses have to be planned for and their marketing has to be just right, even to using positioning as a concept. I wonder if you could take a new college course, say, one on the application of new computer and telecommunication technologies to the

---

[48] "Beer Has an 'Image Crisis'; Wine and Spirits Gain," *USA Today*, January 11, 2005; Anonymous, "Labels Brewing Up Acrylate Esters Demand," *Chemical News & Intelligence*, February 27, 2006; and www.anheuser-busch.com.

operation of a retail store, and show me how you could position that course, using each of the various methods for positioning a new product."

2. "We're in the furniture business, and I'll bet you have used some of our stuff if you spent any time in your college dorms. But, I'll tell you something, there's not much profit in that business—too many competitors, too much standardization in products. You know, buying on bids from purchasing department product spec sheets. I was aware of what you said a while ago about core benefits and creating product value *around* that core, like in service, image, warranty, and so on. But I'm not sure we could use that approach. Given that, physically, our desks and beds have to meet specs, how might we create value around that to help us defend slightly higher prices?"

3. "Packaging must be terribly important today on lots of products. We spend a fortune on it. I read recently about a detergent packaging gimmick—an 'over-cap.' It goes onto a bottle, over the regular cap. It can be torn away and sent in for a refund. Less likely to be cheated on than a coupon. Now that's creative. Are you creative? Could you come up with some ideas like that? We think there is a big packaging opportunity to differentiate our nonalcoholic beer. New products people on that line would sure appreciate some packaging ideas they have never heard of. Good ones, that is, not just a bunch of foolishness."

Case: Wii[49]

Soon after the launch of its GameCube gaming system, Nintendo immediately began development on what was to become its next-generation product. Known initially by the code name "Revolution," this new product was designed to be competitive with the two leading competitors, Microsoft's Xbox 360 and Sony's PlayStation 3, yet at the same time target a wider demographic of customers. A prototype was revealed at the Tokyo Game Show in September 2005 by no less than Satoru Iwata, Nintendo's president. It was launched in December 2006. The world knows it as the Wii, pronounced "we." (Note: According to the company, the name is simply Wii, not Nintendo Wii.)

According to Nintendo's vision of the market, the next generation of product should not necessarily have been a more powerful GameCube. (Both the current Sony and Microsoft products were considered quite fast and powerful products with excellent graphics.) Rather, player interaction was stressed in product and game design. Unusually small for a gaming system, the Wii features a wireless controller (the Wii Remote), which detects motion and rotation and also works as a pointing device. Another feature is WiiConnect24, by which the Wii can receive messages over the Internet. These innovative features have led reviewers to praise

---

[49]Information for this case is from: the Wikipedia entry on Wii (wikipedia.com); Al Ries, "Nintendo Will Win Game Wars by Thinking 'Different,' Not 'Better,'" adage.com, February 19, 2007; Alexander Sliwinski, "Nintendo Wii Marketing to Exceed $200 Million," joystiq.com, November 12, 2006; Erik Sofge, "Nintendon't: The Case Against the Wii," slate.com, November 20, 2006; Cliff Edwards, "Nintendo Wii: One Ferocious Underdog," businessweek.com, November 22, 2006; and James Brightman, "Exercise + Entertainment = Wii Is Good for Your Health," businessweek.com, February 15, 2007. The quote from Mr. Iwata is from the Wii Web site, wii.nintendo.com.

Nintendo for "thinking differently," not "thinking better." The Wii Remote allows the player to control screen action just by tilting his or her hand; the effect has been called "virtual reality in your living room." In a car race game, the user mimes driving a car; in a combat game, the user "wields" a sword. Sports games let the player mime swinging a baseball bat, tennis racket, or golf club. Players say they feel they are doing more than controlling the game; they "feel like they are a part of it." The aerobic benefits (to both young and old) of playing these video games have led to the creation of a new term: "exertainment." So, despite being quite underpowered next to the competitors and featuring comparatively poorer graphics, the Wii has been winning the market wars and also getting mostly favorable reviews. The *New York Times* said that Wii "radiates fun" and "is eclipsing Sony," while the *Wall Street Journal*'s Walter Mossberg wrote that the "modest Wii" was "more exciting, fun and satisfying." Not all reviews were so glowing, however. One reviewer for *Slate* wasn't impressed with the accuracy of the remote.

The wider targeted demographic is critical for Wii's success. Mr. Iwata was quoted as saying that the goal is not to fight Sony, but "to get new people playing games." Over $200 million was spent on TV and Internet ads during late 2006 and through 2007, urging viewers to "experience a new way to play." The ads stressed family-friendliness and showed all sorts of individuals, from grandparents and parents to urban types and ranchers, enjoying playing Wii games. Needless to say, the bulk of the promotional effort was to change the perception that Nintendo is for teenagers and children only. The units are priced at about $250, and the games are priced at about $10 less than similar Microsoft or Sony games. The units are also compatible with GameCube games.

Address Nintendo's vision and new products process for the Wii gaming system. According to Mr. Iwata, the Wii "could not have been accomplished if we had tried to make a new game console in the conventional manner." What does this mean? Then address the positioning attempted by Nintendo in this highly competitive market. Which positioning strategy or strategies discussed in the chapter seem to have been used, how successful has Nintendo been in achieving this desired position, and what are the major drawbacks? Finally, comment on the brand name, using the criteria discussed in the branding section of the chapter. In answering this question, you should know that the original code name, "Revolution," was actually favored by many people within Nintendo, and the final selection of Wii was somewhat controversial at the time.

Case: Iridium[50]

Iridium is a mobile communications network that allows any kind of phone transmission (voice, data, fax, and paging) via a system of satellites. Iridium attracted several large investors, including Motorola, Kyocera, and Lockheed Martin, all of

[50]This case was based on several published sources, including Peter Elstrom, "Iridium Is Looking a Little Star-Crossed," *BusinessWeek*, April 14, 1997; Bill Menezes, "Handsets Too Expensive?" *Wireless Week*, May 4, 1998; Laurel Wentz, "Creating Brands: Three Companies Compete to Market New Satellite Phones Worldwide," *Advertising Age International*, January 11, 1999; Monica Alleven, "The Ball and Chain: Should Motorola Shed Iridium?" *Wireless Week*, June 21, 1999; and Rikki Lee, "Opinion: Iridium, the Flawed Dream," *Wireless Week*, June 21, 1999.

whom had ownership shares of 7 to 20 percent. The Iridium system was composed of 66 satellites as well as a range of ground stations, which allowed the user to reach any destination in the world. The first Iridium satellites were launched in May 1997, and by June 1998 all satellites were launched. By mid-November 1998, both phone and paging service were available. The total cost to build the Iridium system was about $5 billion.

Despite the substantial financial backing, Iridium never caught on. By mid-1999, there were just over 10,200 subscribers, far below breakeven (Iridium management were hoping to have over 300,000 subscribers by the end of 1999), and Iridium found itself in a precarious financial position. Corporate clients were reluctant to subscribe until Iridium's financing was in order, though lenders were hesitant to extend credit until more subscribers were attracted. After several tense months, Iridium finally declared bankruptcy early in 2000, and the fate of the Iridium satellites was undecided.

What happened? Several things, actually. Notably, the initial purchase price for a handset was $3,000, and user charges ranged from $1.10 to $7.00. These were substantially higher than similar costs for cellular phones and service available in 1998 and 1999 (basic cellular phones were available for well under $100). Iridium had certain advantages over cellular, at least on paper (all-digital technology, as compared to a digital-analog mix in cellular phones; compatibility with multiple local services; can use solar power; signal cannot be obstructed by tall buildings, mountains, etc.). But these advantages apparently were not enough to convince enough customers to buy a handset that cost more than 20 times the price of a cheap cell phone.

Iridium faced a series of technical problems related to the complex new technology. For one thing, all parties knew that launching the system would take at least 10 years, though unavoidable delays in development and deployment of the system were encountered. There were quality control problems with the handsets that resulted in a lengthy debugging period. Additionally, the phones could not be used indoors without an adapter, and these proved to be troublesome, leading to more delays. Some gateway providers were not ready to offer full service at launch, causing delays in key regions such as Japan and Russia. Furthermore, many users were dissatisfied with the sound (described by some as tinny) and disliked having to recharge the phone two or three times a day. And despite expectations to the contrary, outdoor service was not reliable: Buildings or tall trees proved to be obstacles to transmission after all.

Despite early enthusiasm from initial investors like Motorola and Lockheed Martin, Iridium was soon facing vexing financial problems. Lenders had set a deadline of June 30, 1999, for Iridium to line up 27,000 subscribers, and to reach this goal, Iridium planned a new marketing strategy aimed at a new target market: Instead of aiming at high-ticket international business travelers and explorers, Iridium targeted federal government users and similar markets. Despite some limited success reaching federal employees, many investors were wishing for Motorola to cut its losses on Iridium. Lockheed Martin and other members of Iridium's operating consortium also had a major influence on Iridium's fate. Put bluntly, Iridium's financial troubles could be described as a vicious circle: Potential subscribers were waiting to see if Iridium could get stable financing, while lenders were waiting to see if Iridium could attract more subscribers before committing any more credit! By the end of June 1999, there were just over 10,000 subscribers (far short of the goal), and Iridium was desperately trying to stave off bankruptcy proceedings.

What could Iridium management have done strategically in the critical 1998–1999 opportunity window? The attempted price cuts (to about $1.59 per minute) appeared to be too little and too late. Could deeper price cuts or other incentives have made a difference? Was it truly already too late? Or was the mistake made years earlier, when the investors decided to commit funds to this project?

Case: Dell Computers (C)[51]

Refer back to the Dell Computers cases (A) and (B) at the end of Chapters 6 and 9. Suppose now that Dell competitive intelligence indicates that Hewlett-Packard is planning a strategic repositioning within six months. Assume that all prices remain about the same among these competitors. Using its best judgment, Dell management believes that HP is most likely to reposition positively on the performance attribute, to about 2 or even 2.5.

How serious is this competitive attack? What, if anything, should Dell do now to minimize the threat posed by HP? Or is it better for Dell to wait until the HP repositioning occurs and then react?

[51]This case was written by Prof. C. Anthony Di Benedetto and is based on public information, including www.dell.com. The "Executive" is a disguised product name. Market size and market share information is realistic for the leading competitors. Note that there are more than four key players in the computer industry but that some simplifying assumptions were made for the sake of presentation. Positioning information and company/industry financial information is not based on fact but is meant to illustrate concepts of product positioning, advertising decision making, and financial analyses.

CHAPTER SEVENTEEN

Implementation of the Strategic Plan

Setting

Chapter 16 set up the strategic platform decisions and the strategic actions decisions. It then went into the building blocks of marketing by talking about the target market and the product positioning statement. That led to actions for building value into the product for the chosen target and positioning and into the matter of brand—part of the product and part of the promotion. Now, we can move into the tactics area—how management actually sets up to communicate all of these things to the end user. The strategic implementation often calls for considerable creativity, and gets it.

The Launch Cycle

First, let's correct an impression many people have about the launch of a new product. They see the launch as a matter of announcing to the world the good news about our great new product. If it could be that simple!

What actually takes place is a **launch cycle.** The launch cycle is an expansion of the familiar introductory stage of the **product life cycle (PLC)** into substages; see Figure 17.1. It picks up the preparations during the prelaunch period, the announcement, the beachhead phase, and then the early growth stage that links the launch cycle back to the PLC.

Prelaunch and Preannouncement

The **prelaunch** stage is when we are building our capability to compete. This means the training of sales and other promotional people, building service capability, putting out *preannouncements* if they are in order, and arranging for stocking of the product at the reseller level.

The new products novice almost invariably focuses on announcement as the culmination of the entire new products process, which it clearly is not. In fact, only on very rare dramatic occasions is there one day when the announcement takes place. The car companies once keyed their announcements (with appropriate

FIGURE 17.1

The Launch
Cycle

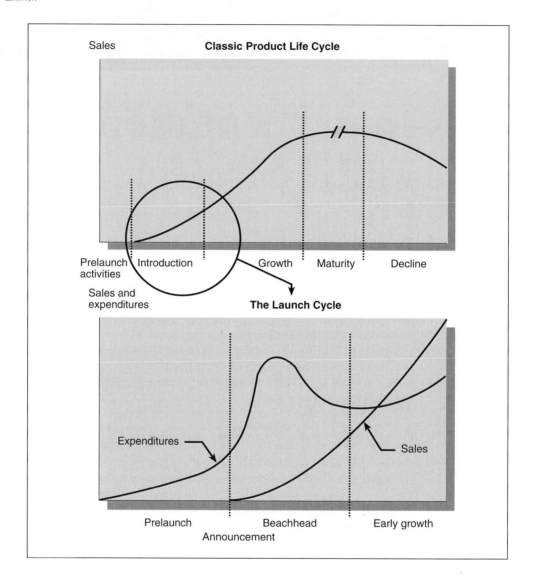

Classic Product Life Cycle

Sales

Prelaunch activities

Introduction Growth Maturity Decline

Sales and expenditures

The Launch Cycle

Expenditures

Sales

Prelaunch Beachhead Early growth

Announcement

on-camera unveilings) to a date in the fall. But such drama does not play well today. In the first place, it is almost impossible to keep a secret, especially as the firm's formal announcement day approaches.

Instead, we see a planned sequence of announcements, often geared to keeping competitors guessing and to keeping competitors' customers from stocking up just prior to our being available. One sequence of periods goes like this: (1) nondisclosures; (2) product testing—beta testers sign confidentiality forms; (3) anticipation—position releases telling about the problem being solved; (4) influentials—press kits for editors, industry researchers, and some customers; (5) broadcast PR—full press releases, product for reviews; (6) promo pieces—the start of advertising. Stages 3 and 4 are used for preannouncements, usually subtle *signaling*, sometimes orchestrated through planned leaks by selected individuals and sometimes just allowed to happen.

Preannouncement can be used to hype interest in the upcoming product, to keep current customers from switching to a competitor, and to encourage prospective buyers to wait for the new product (rather than becoming part of the competitor's installed base of customers). Of course, in many markets, there is almost no attempt to keep secrets. The whole world knew Microsoft Corporation was announcing their new Windows 95 on August 24, 1995. It had been in beta tests with over 2,000 firms, some for more than a year. Its full details were known to every computer editor in the world. This practice has occasionally received criticism, however, especially if the new product's launch is uncertain or likely to be delayed. Microsoft has sometimes been criticized for not delivering software on the date promised in the preannouncement.[1] More recently, Microsoft Windows 7 was preannounced well before its launch, as was the Apple iPad.

Signaling can be done using several marketing tools. An obvious one is price. Others are advertising, trade shows, comments by salespeople, a speech by a CEO at a security analysts' luncheon in New York City, London, or Tokyo, tips from vendors of packaging or production machinery, stocking calls made on distributors or retailers, appointment of new sales representatives with certain industry experience, and on and on. Some are so subtle they are missed. But in general, they can be very effective, so much so that they constitute a field of unfair advertising law.[2]

The preannouncement decision is often tied to whether there are *network externalities*. *Indirect network externalities* exist if product sales are dependent on sales of complementary products (the more Xbox games there are, the more Xboxes Microsoft can sell). *Direct network externalities* exist if product sales are dependent on the number of people that have adopted it (the more people that have e-mail and fax, the more useful these products are; by contrast, videophones never caught on with consumers). For high-tech products with indirect network externalities, there may be two preannouncements, first to program developers, then to consumers. Indeed, Microsoft preannounced the Xbox at a game developer conference, releasing software tools enabling developers to begin designing games for use with the Xbox. When the Xbox was launched to consumers, plenty of games were already available.[3]

Preannouncement can also be used to block a competitive entry. When it became known that Ford was introducing the new Windstar minivan, Chrysler put into operation an aggressive price promotion. This brought them many buyers who otherwise might have awaited Windstar, but it also tweaked interest in Chrysler's own new minivan scheduled for the following year.[4] It is somewhat dangerous to

---

[1]See discussion in T. S. Robertson, J. Eliashberg, and T. Rymon, "New Product Announcement Signals and Incumbent Reactions," *Journal of Marketing* 59(3), July 1995, pp. 1–15.
[2]Oliver P. Heil and Arlen W. Langvardt, "The Interface between Competitive Market Signaling and Antitrust Law," *Journal of Marketing*, 58(3), July 1994, pp. 81–96.
[3]E. Le Nagard-Assayag and D. Manceau, "Modeling the Impact of Product Preannouncements in the Context of Indirect Network Externalities," *International Journal of Research in Marketing*, 18(3), September 2001, pp. 203–220.
[4]Jerry Flint, "A Van for All Seasons," *Forbes*, December 20, 1993, pp. 43–44.

cut the price of an item being replaced, because this can result in current buyers all deciding to await the new product; this makes it tough to clear out trade stocks of the old item. The president of Compaq once remarked at an international conference that there really is no "announcement" any more: New items are just developed and moved into the market, usually on a limited market area basis. (This will be called a *market rollout* in Chapter 18.)

Occasionally a firm can use preannouncement signaling to keep the finance markets happy, but there is a danger of not being able to fulfill the signal. In the software field this has resulted in what is called *vaporware*—signaled but not delivered until much later, if ever. One preannouncement gone awry was made by Pacific Scientific Corporation, makers of the Solium dimmable fluorescent light bulb. In 1994, the company hired a PR firm to announce the pending launch and the signing of a contract with a big-name industry partner to handle marketing. Annual revenues were projected in the $100 million range. Meanwhile, there were delays in product development and technology bugs were beginning to emerge. Stockholders began suing the company. By first quarter 1997, Pacific Scientific took a $12 million loss disposing of the Solium technology and watched its stock value plummet.[5]

One study showed that firms with smaller shares are more likely to preannounce; large firms will avoid preannouncing if they fear government criticism of monopoly; there will be less preannouncing in industries that are very competitive; and there will be more preannouncing where switching costs are high.[6] More recent research has suggested that software firms use vaporware intentionally to gain competitive advantage, and that this seems to hold true for large as well as small firms.[7]

Announcement, Beachhead, and Early Growth

The second stage of the launch cycle—**beachhead**—gets its name from a military landing on enemy soil, a good metaphor for many launches. Other expressions are priming the pump, getting a fire started, getting the ball rolling, getting off the ground. In each situation, a standstill is followed by movement in a manner similar to that of a kite pulled into the wind, a descending bobsled, or a military invasion force expanding from a small strip of shoreline. In a product launch setting, beachhead refers to the heavy expenditures necessary to overcome sales inertia—Figure 17.1 illustrates this with a steeply rising expenditures curve up to the point where sales are increasing at an increasing rate.

Announcement kicks off the beachhead phase, and the conditions at the time are hardly conducive to good management. Communication systems fail, unexpected problems arise, supplies become scarce, and general confusion may reign.

[5]Stacy Kravetz, "Light Bulb Couldn't Match the Glow of Its Own Press," *The Wall Street Journal*, May 28, 1997, p. B1.
[6]Jehoshua Eliashberg and Thomas S. Robertson, "New Product Preannouncing Behavior: A Market Signaling Study," *Journal of Marketing Research*, 25(3), August 1988, pp. 282–292.
[7]Barry L. Bayus, Sanjay Jain, and Ambar G. Rao, "Truth or Consequences: An Analysis of Vaporware and New Product Announcements," *Journal of Marketing Research*, 38(1), February 2001, pp. 3–13.

As the months go by, a subtle change in emphasis occurs as initial announcement gives way to "reason why" and then to the rationale of trial and the reinforcement of successful experience.

The key decision in the beachhead phase is to end it—inertia has been over-come, the product has started to move. This decision triggers a series of actions. Improvements and flankers will now be brought along as scheduled; new budgets will be approved and released; temporary marketing arrangements will be made permanent (such as a temporary sales force, an advertising agency, or a direct-mail arrangement). One new products manager said he knew this decision had been made when the firm's president stopped calling him every couple of days for the latest news.

Decisions made at launch and throughout the product life cycle need to be made in accordance with the strategic decisions made earlier. The most recent work on new product launches, interestingly, finds three common patterns for launch strat-egies and tactics.

- *The innovative new product.* For some products, the strategic objective is to get a foothold in the market early in the product life cycle. Common tactics accompanying this kind of launch are a broad product assortment, a new brand name and distribution channels, and a higher price.

- *The offensive improvement.* The strategic objective here is different: to erect bar-riers to entry. Managers find it more beneficial to use existing distribution channels, high consumer promotion and advertising, and a broad product assortment.

- *The defensive addition.* For other products, the strategic objective is to increase penetration in existing markets; appropriate tactics include smaller assort-ments, penetration pricing, and promotions to the customer and the sales force.[8]

Launch Tactics

Launch tactics planning includes selecting distribution channels, setting price and the marketing communications mix, training salespeople, and so on. For many firms, the launch phase is the single most costly and risky part of the new products process, and proficient implementation of launch tactics is related to improved new product performance.[9] We begin by reviewing the prevailing marketing mix. Consider Figure 17.2, which shows the major product launch decisions and actions pertaining to each component of the marketing mix. The product manufacturer (or service provider) can allocate its limited funds across the components of the

[8]E. J. Hultink, Abbie Griffin, Henry S. J. Robben, and Susan Hart, "In Search of Generic Launch Strategies for New Products," *International Journal of Research in Marketing*, 15(3), July 1998, pp. 269–286.
[9]Fred Langerak, Erik Jan Hultink, and Henry S. J. Robben, "The Impact of Market Orientation, Product Advantage, and Launch Proficiency on New Product Performance and Organizational Performance," *Journal of Product Innovation Management*, 21(2), March 2004, pp. 79–94.

FIGURE 17.2   Tactical Launch Decisions and Actions, Showing Influences on Demand

Launch Tactic	Effective for
Promotion	
Advertising	Cases where awareness will stimulate trial
Coupons	Reinforcing awareness
Publicity	New and controversial technologies with high perceived usage risk
Sampling	Cases where product advantages best learned through usage
Beta Test Sites	Stimulating "sampling" and as a reference for other potential buyers
Sales and Distribution	
Shows/Demonstrations	Clarifying relative product advantages or where uncertainty exists
Technical Support	Cases of incompatibility in usage process
Distribution Structure	Cases where relative advantage strong (direct channels)
Intensity of Coverage	Cases where warranty/maintenance service needs to be offered easily
Distribution Incentives	Cases where availability needs to be stimulated
Pricing	
Introductory Pricing	High relative advantage and compatibility (skimming policy); early adoption needs to be stimulated (penetration policy)
Price Administration	Cases where economic risk needs to be reduced (i.e., through rebates or money-back guarantees)
Product	
Breadth of Assortment	Introducing new product categories with high relative advantage
Timing	
Product Deletion	High margin but strong relative advantage (fast deletion); high switching costs (slow deletion)
Preannouncing	Building hype for new products; useful if relative advantage is high

Source: Adapted from Joseph P. Guiltinan, "Launch Strategy, Launch Tactics, and Demand Outcomes," *Journal of Product Innovation Management* 16, no. 6, November 1999, p. 519.

marketing mix given in Figure 17.2—from spending to improve the product or add line extensions to it (to make the item more attractive to buyers) to having a retailer put on a big in-store promotion around the new item.

Developers have been following a mix from the very beginning—where decisions were made on R&D budgets. Pharmaceutical firms put the bulk of their money into technical research, White Consolidated (white goods) puts it into manufacturing process development, and Avon and Mary Kay into personal selling.

The Communications Plan

Communications is the term most widely used to cover all of the information and attitude effort we put into changing how the end user sees our situation. It involves everything from technical products data to strong persuasion. The communications *requirements* are the specifics that must be communicated in our plan. They have been with us almost since the beginning of this project—for example, when we focused on skiers because we were sure our new plastics technology could deal more effectively with the need for skis to both slide and hold. A communications requirement would be to remind skiers about their problems with sticking skis, tell them we have a solution, what it is, how they can get it, and so on. This comes from the PIC, from concept testing, and especially from the product protocol statement (where marketing requirements were listed alongside technical requirements). It can be quite short or long, but is a powerful tool in all that follows. It should be based on a solid understanding of the end user's attitudes and behavior.

The communications task is performed with a **communications mix.** There can be as many as four mixes: one for communications to the reseller by us, a second for communications to the end user by the reseller, a third for communications to the end user by us, and a fourth for the total communication effort by our team to the end user. Service firms and direct-selling manufacturers appreciate a simplification of this task because there is usually no reseller. Direct-selling manufacturers also benefit this way. The job here is to make the best choices—a mix from each set, imaginatively implemented. New products people, in particular, have wide freedom—a clean sheet of paper. There are some restrictions (from the "givens" in ongoing company operation), but still there is always room for creativity. For example, some firms take advantage of Internet newsgroups to boost communication among user groups and also to do follow-up customer support, though generally such impersonal communication should be coupled with human communication, if possible, to stay in touch with customers effectively.[10]

The Copy Strategy Statement

Given the requirements that communications tools are to deliver, let's look at a device designed to communicate these requirements to those who, for example, create advertising. Its name varies a lot in practice, but **copy strategy statement** is a common one. It can be used to convey to every advertising and promotion creative person the following items (among many others):

The market segment being targeted;

The product positioning statement;

The communications mix and the pieces covered by this statement;

The major copy points to be communicated.

The major points are usually product attributes, including features, functions, and benefits as well as uses, but they can be almost anything important to that end user making a favorable decision. For example:

The provider of this insurance policy is the largest in the world.

Black Pearls perfume was designed by Elizabeth Taylor personally.

This cellular phone has no geographical limitation.

Dockers are available at Penney's.

Future neurosurgeons benefit from the hand-and-eye skills of computer games like this one.

---

[10]Muammer Ozer, "Using the Internet in New Product Development," *Research-Technology Management,* 46(1), January–February 2003, pp. 10–17.

There is no limit. But there must be focus on any one list. Communication capabilities today are under great pressure—humans are exposed to millions of messages and thousands of firms. It's fine to list lots of points in a selling piece or an ad, but only a few of them should be on the requirements list. Only a few *must* be accomplished at this time. And the copy strategy statement should be written by the team, not by the person who will create the pieces for it.

Personal Selling

The salesperson is the workhorse of most new product introductions. Even on packaged goods **personal selling** is clearly essential, in this case, the important role of the detail salesperson in getting good retail availability and shelf position in key retail stores. The new products manager probably has to work harder than ever meeting the needs of these new professional sales operations. But, being professional, they know what will sell and are anxious to have new products if they are based on meeting customer needs. Because we are competing with other marketing managers for the limited pool of selling time with customers, getting sales support means internal marketing.

One issue that is sometimes difficult to decide is, how early should we involve salespeople? An industrial firm developing new metal-grinding machinery will have downstream customer coupling, and by the time the project is ready for marketing, the sales department has been involved for a long time. Advertising people have not been. For consumer packaged goods, advertising people (including advertising agency personnel) are involved early on, but the sales department usually is not. For services, the new product developer is apt to *be* in the sales department.

Some managers want to keep salespeople away from product development ("no need for them to know," "we must continue selling today's products today"). Some firms find the answer in having sales *managers* involved. A common tactic is to have small groups of district or regional sales managers rotating on advisory teams.

A much more difficult question comes up when the new product needs a new sales force—that is, one reaching markets the current one doesn't cover. Hopefully less-disruptive adjustments can be made. Sometimes it is possible to add *some* of the uncovered customers or hire a small group of specialists to hit the major pockets of new customers.

A new product is an intrusion for the sales force. It takes time. It disrupts schedules. It involves change and risk. Salespeople often want new items to sell, but there are still negatives. Salespeople are not usually given reduced territories when asked to sell a new product. So it is important to (1) *investigate* in advance any possible reasons why salespeople might object to the new product, (2) give them all the *training and materials* they need to be effective, and (3) make sure the product is *available* in their territories when they start seeking orders.

The key is to do our job such that they can do their job. That means, have a product that customers will understand and want to try, and train the sales force to understand and communicate these things.

Over the last several years, under the prodding of very large buyers, business firms are reluctantly turning to a new mode of customer contact. Rather than have product-line-based sales forces, they are going to customer-based sales forces. Each rep sells a longer line, but brings to the customer a team of company people who can address customer problems. The new approach makes customers happy (Walmart had to force the system upon its suppliers but is now P&G's biggest single customer). A customer-based sales organization requires less of the hard-sell pushing that product-based sales forces can provide.[11]

Alliances

Technical departments have, in recent years, come to realize that they needn't have every possible technical capability required on a new product project. Instead, they form **strategic alliances** with universities, government units, private research centers, and even competitors to access what they need. Marketing people have been doing this for many years, and still do. In fact, the trade channel itself is a strategic alliance. Independent firms sign a franchise agreement wherein each side promises to do certain things, the result of which is to accomplish a task. Manufacturers don't *have* to use retailers—Avon dropped theirs many years ago.

Advertising is another area for alliances—long-standing agreements are signed with advertising agencies. Service organizations are often brought into a franchise situation. Ditto for warehousing companies, for competitors (to gain sales forces that can reach markets where it is more profitable to use an established organization than to do the whole thing ourselves), and exhibit firms (for trade shows).

It has been said that today, one can form an alliance with someone, somewhere, for every task that needs to be done.

A-T-A-R Requirements

In Chapter 8, you met the A-T-A-R model. It displayed the four key steps that an end user must move through if there is to be satisfied adoption of a new product—Awareness, Trial, Availability, and Repeat use. It is the task of the marketing organization to accomplish these in a sufficiently large set of users to achieve the financial and other goals. They make a good framework for deciding just what marketing activities will be undertaken.

Awareness

Awareness is the necessary first step toward adoption (though there are rare cases where a product can be consumed in ignorance or in a hurry, with awareness following that trial). Awareness means different things on different products and is sought aggressively by almost all new product marketers.

---

[11]For more on this trend in sales force thinking, see Benson P. Shapiro, Adrian Slywotzky, and Stephen X. Doyle, "The High Impact Salesforce: The Investment You Can't Afford Not to Make," Harvard Business School Press, Publication No. 9-999-002, 1998.

Measuring Awareness

Let's look at three quite different situations. First is a new candy bar. To a lover of candy bars, the mere mention of a new bar is enough to trigger interest and probably trial purchase. Second is a new word processing software package being considered by a leading author of novels. Mere mention is not enough; there must be considerable information because of the inconvenience of trial and the cost of the package. Third is a new method of cleaning up black water in municipal water-treatment systems, and the target is civil engineers specializing in recommending municipal water treatment systems. There is so much at stake in their first trial recommendation that they may compile information over several years before making it.

All three people "heard of" their new items on a single day and in a single message. They may even have heard the positioning and understood it. But one is minutes away from trial and the others months or years away.

Given that we want trial to follow awareness, what constitutes awareness differs greatly. There is no accepted definition, though consumer packaged goods usage tends to become standardized. For example, "Have you heard of a new candy bar made from burned raisins and ground barley?" Some element of the positioning must be present.

Methods for Getting Awareness

People working in every industry have a good understanding of how to get awareness of a new product in their industry. The ideal probably is a mix: an announcement ad or sales call, then favorable mention by a friend, then seeing the item in use, then a reminder of some type, then getting some professional endorsement in a news account or column, then a reminder of some sort, and then an opportunity to buy it (which stimulates consideration of all the information previously gathered).

Providing all these stimuli is apt to be expensive; the less the product has going for it, the more we have to spend on it. And there is never enough money to "do the job right."

Fortunately, the marketplace can help us on awareness and trial if we are following the process of this book. That's because we made sure there was a problem and then worked until we had a good *solution*. If the activity (bowling, eating, machining, surgery, whatever) is important to the customer, so much the better. An interested, dissatisfied customer, for whom we have good news, needs little more than announcement to get awareness. It helps even more if the situation is newsworthy (sports, politics, financial markets, health, etc.) and if the product is one that customers see in use frequently (car, TV set, clothing, and the like).

Stocking and Availability

Services are usually sold directly, and so are many goods. But most goods use resellers, such as distributors and retail dealers. They help us push the product down the channel, but only rarely does a new product offer them really new business without any major troubles. For example, Abbott's of New England nearly went broke trying to get its new chowder products into supermarkets. So, it persuaded some of the stores' deli counters to offer single portions of hot chowder. The products were soon in 20 percent of U.S. supermarkets.

Most resellers do a large volume of business in a rather standardized way with a small margin. Many have constraints on what they can and cannot do—franchise agreements, long-time personal relationships with sales representatives, channel leadership roles, and selling and service systems of their own. They are not at all anxious to make changes in their systems.

Therefore, their thinking should be represented in the product development process. If a distributor is large and powerful, it is a candidate for including very early in the new products process—when product attributes are still being worked on, when packaging is being designed, and so on. Otherwise, it is usually sufficient to have the resellers' views represented by experienced salespeople—sales managers and what are sometimes called *trade relations directors*.

We start with a statement of what the reseller's role will be. This role normally includes, for stocking distributors, (1) prestocking activities such as training and installation of equipment, (2) stocking of the new item, (3) preparation for promotion, including training salespeople and service people, and (4) actually doing the promotion, whether just listing the item in a catalog, adding the item to selling schedules, or working with individual buyers to determine their needs and convert interest into sales.

Somewhere along the line we have to know that resellers *can* do what we want and need, and that they *will* do it. Assuming they "can do," the "will do" is a matter of motivation, and for this we arrange a program of encouragement, based on items from the list in Figure 17.3. Without any question, proof that the new item will sell is the best motivation.[12] But channel firms can be tough if they feel mistreated. Elizabeth Arden Division of Unilever had to cancel a planned introduction of a new Elizabeth Taylor fragrance called Black Pearls because the firm slashed monies for department store salespeople. The stores refused to stock it, forcing Arden to plan distribution through mass merchandisers, but the whole deal was ultimately canceled, even though Black Pearls advertising had started running. The division looked to lose millions of dollars, and its president resigned by mutual consent. Moral: Don't deal carelessly with a necessary team player.

In several nonfood product categories, the practice of *stocklifting* is spreading. As an example, Midwest Quality Gloves purchased from Lowe's Home Improvement Warehouse 225,000 pairs of garden gloves made by its competitor, Wells Lamont, thus clearing the shelves to fill them with its own product. The competitor's product is then sold off to industrial customers as commodity goods or sold to firms that dispose of stocklifted goods by reselling them to close-out stores or foreign distributors.[13]

---

[12]A 3M division tells how they choose the best channel for a new industrial product in V. Katsuri Rangan, Melvyn A. J. Menezes, and E. P. Maier, "Channel Selection for New Industrial Products: A Framework, Method, and Application," *Journal of Marketing*, 56(3), July 1992, pp. 69–82.

[13]Yumiko Ono, "Where Are the Gloves? They Were Stocklifted by a Rival Producer," *The Wall Street Journal*, May 15, 1998, p. A1.

FIGURE 17.3   Alternative Tools and Devices for Motivating Distributors

A. Increase the distributor's unit volume.
1. Have an outstanding product.
2. Use pull techniques—advertising, trade and consumer shows, public relations, missionary selling.
3. Give the distributor a type of monopoly—exclusivity or selectivity.
4. Run "where available" ads.
5. Offer merchandising assistance—dollars, training, displays, points of purchase, co-op advertising, in-store demonstrations, store "events," and repair and service clinics.

B. Increase the distributor's unit margin.
1. Raise the basic percentage margin.
2. Offer special discounts—e.g., for promotion or service.
3. Offer allowances and special payments.
4. Offer to prepay allowances to save interest.

C. Reduce the distributor's costs of doing business.
1. Provide managerial training.
2. Provide dollars for training.
3. Improve the returned-goods policy.
4. Improve the service policy.
5. Drop-ship delivery to distributor's customers.
6. Preprice the merchandise.
7. Tray pack the merchandise or otherwise aid in repackaging it.

D. Change the distributor's attitude toward the line.
1. By encouragement—management negotiation, sales calls, direct mail, advertising.
2. By discouragement—threats to cut back some of the above benefits or legal action.
3. Rap sessions—talk groups, focus groups, councils.
4. Better product instruction sessions—better visuals, better instructions.

One trade channel where the players seem to have run out of creativity is that of food products. Large retailers now often "sell" their scarce space, charging manufacturers sizeable *slotting allowances*—so much per store for minimum shelf positions. Large firms can buy their way in, but smaller firms are pretty much shut out. Again, however, a really new item for which there is consumer demand will face a softer resistance.

Trial

Getting awareness is often difficult, but usually possible. The same goes for availability and some reseller promotion. Trial is another matter. This is the stumbling point for most products that fail; and it is the cause of winning products not winning a great deal more.

Trial of a new product is *limited usage,* hopefully under normal usage conditions, that will permit the customer to verify claims and learn the advantages and disadvantages of the good or service. Trial is on a scale from a taste test of a new cheese in a supermarket to a three-year experiment by a major company on a new telecommunications system. A firm can spend a fortune on free samples to generate trial, as Pepsi did with its launch of Pepsi One. An estimated 5.5 million cans were given away to Pizza Hut customers who ordered a pizza to go, and countless more were handed out to Walmart shoppers by the greeters at the front door.[14] There must be learning, relative to the adoption decision; thus the cheese taste may be a full trial if taste by the tester is the only issue. But if the rest of the family has a say, or if the package may or may not keep the cheese fresh, or if the product tends to turn gray while sitting on a table or in a sandwich, then the taste test was not a trial.

Trial may be *personal, vicarious,* or *virtual.* With elevators, plant location services, and burial services, satisfactory personal trial conditions are difficult, though visiting the site of a previous buyer simulates trial. So buyers gather the trial experience of others in a vicarious experience. Virtual trial can be achieved by various electronic setups, even a pseudovirtual experience via video.

A key requirement is that a trial must have some "cost" associated with it. The more important the trial, the more the cost, or there is not enough motivation for the necessary learning to take place. The cheese taste test, just mentioned, had very little cost (a few seconds of time, possible embarrassment in the store if the taste is awful), so the customer would consider little more than the taste and perhaps color, aroma, and texture.

That is usually not enough for the next step in the process—the acceptance of the item, its adoption into a usage system, or its repeat purchase. The cheese taster probably would want to buy a small package and take it home for the *real* trial.

Barriers to Trial

Barriers to trial cause customers to delay or even permanently postpone trial. In Chapter 16, you saw several new product characteristics that influence trial rates: relative advantage, compatibility with current product usage, complexity, divisibility, and communicability. Of these, the first two, relative advantage and compatibility, probably have the greatest influence on trial and adoption. Furthermore, they can be influenced directly by launch strategies and tactics: that is, if high perceived relative advantage and/or compatibility can be achieved at the time of launch, desired levels of trial (and, ultimately, demand) will be attained.

A framework for choosing launch tactics given levels of relative advantage and compatibility is given in Figure 17.4. In each cell of this figure, the selected launch tactics are designed to leverage opportunities (such as a high level of compatibility) or to offset a constraint (e.g., distinguish a new product from other similar ones).

Low Relative Advantage and Low Compatibility

Start with the upper left cell in Figure 17.4. Novelty products (such as Coors' Zima clear malt beverage) and some service products (such as the debit card) will fit this category: low incremental advantage and relatively incompatible with buyers' experiences. The launch plan must therefore be designed to reduce any economic or other risks associated with the product's purchase. Intensive distribution reduces search costs, while penetration price minimizes buyers' financial risk. Since the

---

[14]Nikhil Deogun, "Pepsi Takes Aim at Coke with New One-Calorie Drink," *The Wall Street Journal*, October 28, 1998, p. B4.

FIGURE 17.4   **Appropriate Launch Tactics Given Relative Advantage and Compatibility**

	A. Low Relative Advantage	**B. High Relative Advantage**
1. Low Compatibility	Penetration price Slow deletion Risk-based promotion (leasing, money-back guarantees, equipment allowances) Intensive distribution	Preannounce Broad product assortments Information-based promotion (shows, demonstrations, Web sites, publicity/education) Selective distribution
2. High Compatibility	Secrecy before entry Narrow product assortments Awareness promotion (coupons, etc.) Intensive distribution	Skim price Fast deletion Usage-based promotion (samples, beta tests) to clarify benefits received Selective distribution

Source: Adapted from Joseph P. Guiltinan, "Launch Strategy, Launch Tactics, and Demand Outcomes," *Journal of Product Innovation Management* 16, no. 6, November 1999, p. 520–521.

new product may not offer great advantage over products currently on the market, customer migration will be slow, and one should not delete the older product from the market quickly (and potentially annoy current customers). Promotion should also aid in risk reduction by offering money-back guarantees, warranties, or tie-ins to existing products.

High Relative Advantage and High Compatibility   Now go diagonally down to the lower right cell in Figure 17.4. Here one finds products that are clearly superior on attributes that buyers consider important (such as a cell phone with more features and smaller size or a computer with faster operations). These are the diametric opposite of the products in the upper left cell, and recommended launch tactics consequently are the mirror images of the ones recommended above. Sampling or beta testing allows the potential user to see the product's advantages for themselves. Skimming pricing and selective distribution are recommended if the early adopters are likely to exert high search efforts in order to get the desired attributes. Because of the product's inherent benefits, customer migration will occur swiftly and deletion of the older products can be fast.

High Relative Advantage and Low Compatibility   In the upper right cell of Figure 17.4, one finds the new-to-the-world products that, due to their very newness, are likely to be somewhat incompatible in terms of values or use (think microwave oven or electric car). Launch tactics must center around directing extensive product information to prospective customers both to emphasize relative advantages and to reduce perceived incompatibility. Preannouncements may be necessary to warn prospects to prepare for the impending changes in their usage systems. Additionally, a broad assortment may be useful, especially if this helps to customize the product to different high-potential segments.

Low Relative Advantage and High Compatibility These are the direct opposite of the products in the upper right cell of Figure 17.4: familiar products yet low relative advantage. In this cell, generating brand awareness and capitalizing on brand equity will be the most important factors in getting trial. As seen in Chapter 16, care must be taken in brand extension as a new brand with little relative performance advantage (but a cheaper price) might erode brand equity. Coors apparently was thinking of this when they launched the lower-priced Keystone brand under its own name. Intensive distribution makes sense here; additionally, distributors will be more amenable to carrying and selling a narrower assortment.

How to Overcome Those Barriers

Fortunately, development of the marketing program begins well ahead of launch because that's when most of the barrier problems should be addressed. And most of them come to developers' attention during concept testing and product use testing, as well as from experience in the industry. And most of the barriers respond to more than one solution.

Note how many of the launch tactics concern price—penetration pricing or skimming, for example. Other price tactics can include free goods, couponing, a signing bonus, deferred payment, refunding cost of competitor's stocks, price, discounts, rebates, free service, free replacement offer, cooperative advertising, direct cash payment for trying, and so on. Why is this? In most cases, the buyer is deferring trial because of anticipating loss of something—loss of time, money, or prestige, for example. The most obvious answer is to pay the buyer for such loss.

This emphasis on price has led sellers to adopt complex discount schedules (it's easier later to drop a discount than to raise the list price). Using discounts also fits with the most popular of the new product price strategies:

Premium—a very high price, intended to stay that way, with clear product differentiation.

Skim—a price clearly above the market, but appropriate to a differentiated product, nonthreatening to competition, and with room for some price manipulations.

Meet the market—though there may be no *one* market price, this strategy says pick a price that takes price out of the play as much as possible. It is a waste for a clearly superior product unless the marketer has no market acceptance.

Penetration—the price that is clearly low and designed to buy one's way into the market. Will be met perhaps, but in the meantime share is gained. Dangers: little room to discount, tough to raise later after share is achieved, and if met immediately, just wastes the opportunity and at a lower price.

Skim seems to achieve the benefit both ways—brings some of the product's value to our bottom line and gives marketers freedom to meet special opportunities, yet doesn't price ourselves out of the market. Of course, if the differentiation is worth a great deal, a true obsoleting of the earlier item, then premium pricing is defensible.

Repeat Purchase

If our target market buyers do a serious trial on our new item, and if we had previously been assured from the product use test that people would like it, repeat buying is virtually assured. There are competitive actions to repel and counter. There is the continuing problem of complacency especially in markets where our item's benefits are not crucial to anything. There is the careless new product manager who fails to keep a ready supply available for the buyer who wants to repeat.

And, as always, we need to be sure customers are satisfied with their total relationships with our firm, well beyond the product itself.

Usually we have actions in the marketing program to encourage further usage (e.g., long-term discounts, new uses for the item, ready availability of additional product as well as of continued service). And we will see in Chapter 19 how a measure of repeat purchase is a key part of the postlaunch control program, in which we prepare to deal with at least some of the problems that may come up. If there is any evidence of product failure (which may be expected to happen if the product use test had to be skipped), it will be investigated promptly and corrections negotiated through the technical members of the team.

Summary

Chapter 17 was the second of a two-chapter set on the subject of marketing planning. It dealt with what some call the tactical portion of the planning task. So we looked at the launch cycle, the communication program, and the requirements for success: Awareness, Trial, Availability, and Repeat purchase (A-T-A-R). Each is very difficult to attain, given the ongoing nature of life and business out there in the market and the actions of other players such as competitors. Since a marketing launch entails hundreds or even thousands of actions, we focused on those that seem most critical and most difficult in practice.

Once the full marketing launch plan has been worked out, many firms like to devise some way to hold a dress rehearsal—just to see if there are any glitches. After all, millions of dollars may be spent in the next few months. So, in Chapter 18, we will look at what is called market testing. It is the third of a testing triad—with concept testing (Chapter 9) and product use testing (Chapter 15).

Applications

1. "You frighten me when you mention alliances in the marketing launch. Hardly a week goes by but what some scientist says we simply must join an alliance. Don't scientists ever work alone any more? Anyway, even though we need alliances on the technical side, that's no reason for them on the marketing side. I don't think I recall hearing about alliances over there—you mention ad agencies? And resellers? No, those are just contracts for service, and in almost every case those are pseudo contracts—they can be broken if it's important. Why does your text call them alliances?"

2. "Some of the folks in the software division have come up with an idea for a new service. They found out that computer people around the world have trouble learning about new software—not about its existence, but how good it really is. What we're going to sell is reports of all comments—good and bad—that appear in the press about all new software. The customer can access this information online, with reports classified by type and brand of software, and in six languages. They think software users outside the mainstream of personal business contacts will like it. But, and this is a problem they worry about, since the whole field of software is so full of announcements and news, how can they break through the noise to make prospects aware of the new service where they can *make a decision to try it?* (They have a trial package: five days, 20 inquiries, for a small fee.)"

3. "Sampling is another tool we like—you know, like that trial package I just mentioned. Samples are really effective in getting trial among the people who are somewhat inclined toward a new product in the first place. But several of our divisions can't use samples per se because of the nature of their products. Could you tell me what might be a substitute for samples in the marketing of a new type of each of the following?

   a. Heavy industrial elevators.
   b. Coffins.
   c. Milling machines.
   d. Diamond rings.
   e. Replacement tires."

CASE: Hulu[15]

The enormous success of YouTube (now owned by parent company Google) was a wake-up call to the major TV networks and movie studios. Since its inception in 2005, YouTube has allowed user-provided content, which of course meant there was the possibility that someone would post copyrighted material. With the sheer number of uploaded videos and daily visitors, YouTube has relied on self-policing to control copyright infringement (a video is removed if viewers or companies complain). This continues to be a serious issue for YouTube, even though the company does have an official policy prohibiting the posting of copyrighted material. Entire episodes or short clips from TV shows such as *The Simpsons* or *Family Guy* have been uploaded illegally, as well as entire music videos. In one case, an entire episode of the popular show *24* was uploaded even before it was played on network television!

[15]This case was compiled from D. Chmielewski and A. Pham, "At Hulu, 'Free' May Soon Turn to 'Fee,'" *Los Angeles Times*, January 21, 2010; several pages at hulu.com, including its "Launch Statement"; C. Salter, "Can Hulu Save Traditional TV?" Fastcompany.com, Dec. 1, 2009; Eric Schonfeld, "Hulu Could Still Launch on the iPad," techcrunch.com, Feb. 10, 2010; Tushar Mital, "Hulu: Know the Co," knowtheco.com, March 13, 2010; and other public sources.

Early in its existence, YouTube had posted a short video called "Lazy Sunday" originally shown on the NBC program *Saturday Night Live*. In February 2006, NBC Universal asked YouTube to remove "Lazy Sunday," videoclips from the 2006 Olympics, and other copyrighted material. To minimize illegal uploading of TV programs, YouTube instituted a 10-minute maximum length on practically all clips, a rule circumvented by cutting a desired program into a number of approximately nine-minute segments. But by this time, the publicity from NBC's action was making YouTube more popular than ever. By June 2006, NBC announced it would partner with YouTube and make promotional clips for upcoming shows like *The Office* available for viewing. In July, CBS struck a similar agreement with YouTube. CBS President of News and Sports Sean McManus said at the time that "the more exposure we get from clips like that, the better it is for CBS News . . . in retrospect we probably should have embraced the exposure, . . . [rather than] saying 'let's pull it down.'" By August, major music labels such as Warner and EMI were working out deals to have music videos available in return for a portion of YouTube's advertising income. In October, Universal Music Group and Sony BMG followed suit.

The first major legal challenge to YouTube arrived in March 2007, when Viacom sought over $1 billion in damages for "massive intentional copyright infringement." Viacom is the parent of MTV, Nickelodeon, and Comedy Central, among others, and therefore owns countless shows and clips appealing to the teenage and child markets. It claimed that about 160,000 of its clips were published on YouTube without permission. For its part, Google was confident that its YouTube policy was respectful of copyright law. At about the same time, major media companies such as NBC and News Corp. were wary of letting Google gain such a dominant position in Internet video. The challenge for NBC and other networks was to provide some way to offer a YouTube-like product but at the same time retain control of their valuable, protected content. As Jeff Zucker, NBC Universal's CEO, said at the time, "if we didn't do this, we knew someone else would." The product in question turned out to be Hulu.

In 2007, Hulu was founded by NBC Universal, Fox Entertainment Group, and ABC Inc., though it operates independently from all of these. It was made available in beta form in late 2007 and was officially launched to the public in March 2008. The beta test was judged a success, as millions of viewers visited and watched at least one TV program or movie. On its website, hulu.com, Hulu offered a simple search interface familiar to online viewers who were already enjoying programming on YouTube or on Web sites such as abc.com. Hulu CEO Jason Kilar said that Hulu "[crosses] a milestone in its mission to help people find and enjoy the world's premium content, when, where, and how they want it."

Hulu achieved almost immediate success. The business magazine *Fast Company* rated it one of the best innovative companies of 2009, noting that it "is a model of what's possible when rivals work together and embrace disruptive technology." Indeed, the top networks not only worked together, but achieved a first-to-market position, which seems to have worked, at least initially.

The success of Hulu certainly rests on its wide range of available videos. While online viewers were already enjoying movies and TV programs, there was not one

Web site that brought all of these together. Where one might previously have had to visit NBC, ABC, and Fox Web sites to search for favorite TV shows or sports programs, or one of the movie providers for an online movie, Hulu provides a kind of one-stop shop for videos of all kinds. For consumers lacking TiVo or DVR, Hulu is the go-to place for watching older episodes of many popular programs. In addition, due to its partnerships with broadcasters, the streaming video technology provided by Hulu was state-of-the-art, providing high-quality video to the viewer. There are also easy video sharing options.

From the networks' point of view, Hulu is an improvement over YouTube, since it does not accept user-provided content; thus they retain the desired level of control over the content. Hulu generates money through ad revenue. Ads average about two minutes per show (compared to about eight minutes per show on regular TV), and viewers get to pick which ad they want to watch, thereby increasing the percentage of effective exposures. To gauge customer satisfaction and generate ideas for improvement, Hulu CEO Jason Kilar personally monitors Twitter and assesses what bloggers are writing about Hulu.

Hulu started as a free service, much like YouTube, and ads were the only source of revenue. After a couple of years of operation and constant increases in popularity and viewership, Hulu management was considering a fee-for-service model. The new fee-based model was in concept testing with customers for months, as Hulu executives tried to determine what customers would be willing to watch online for a fee. The fee-based model would not be unprecedented, of course; major sites such as newyorktimes.com and others have used a fee-for-service model, at least for the highest-volume users.

Assess the launch strategy used by Hulu. To what extent was being a first mover critical to its success? What about the relatively less-common practice of severe competitors (in this case, the three top networks) working jointly in the foundation of this company? What are the risks to Hulu of being first to market? Also, since they were already successful with the original free-service model and profitable through advertising revenue, is it wise for them to move to a fee-for-service model?

Case: Dodge Nitro[16]

Although the sport utility vehicle (SUV) market has been declining in recent years, this car category has continued to be profitable for carmakers competing in the North American marketplace. Dodge, a division of Chrysler, has competed in the SUV market with one product: the full-size Dodge Durango. By contrast, in 2006, Ford and Chevrolet were carrying four and five SUVs, respectively, and Toyota

[16]Information for this case is from the Dodge Nitro Web site (www.dodge.com/nitro); "Marketing Campaign for the All-New 2007 Dodge Nitro Is Set to Reignite on November 5 Across Multiple Media Platforms," press release from Chrysler, www.prnewswire.com, November 3, 2006; Jim Mateja, "Will Dodge Dealers Regret Getting What They Wished For?" *Chicago Tribune*, December 21, 2006; Ann M. Job, "Dodge Nitro SUV Explodes onto Scene," *Newhouse News Service*, January 18, 2007; Mark Vaughn, "She's Gonna Blow!: 2007 Dodge Nitro Fuels Brand Expansion," *AutoWeek*, October 9, 2006, p. 8; Joe Lorio, "Liberty's Child: Dodge Nitro Concept," Automobilemag.com, May 5, 2006.

had five in its line and was about to add a sixth. Much of the action in recent years has been in the smaller or "mid-size" SUV segment with another Chrysler product, the Jeep Liberty, being one of the big competitors. Dodge wanted to add a mid-size SUV to its lineup. There are two major hurdles facing Dodge: First, it must figure out how best to leverage its carmaking skills to design a competitive mid-size SUV; then, it must carefully plan the launch strategy and tactics so that sales of the new vehicle, to be named the Dodge Nitro, will reach new target markets and not just cannibalize sales of the Durango or the Jeep Liberty.

The design problem would seem easy to overcome. Platform sharing is, of course, quite common in the car industry. Car platform development is notoriously expensive, and carmakers like using a single platform to support several models over the course of a few years in order to spread out the cost of the platform over a large number of vehicles. At Chrysler alone are several examples of cars that share platforms: The Dodge Durango shares a platform with the Chrysler Aspen, while the Dodge Grand Caravan and Chrysler Town and Country also are twins. The Dodge Charger, Dodge Magnum, and Chrysler 300 are triplets, as are the Jeep Patriot, Jeep Compass, and Dodge Caliber. It would be logical to use the Jeep Liberty platform as a basis for the Dodge Nitro. According to Chrysler policy, however, Jeep platforms are not shared with non-Jeeps. But company policy also said that Mercedes components would not be used in Chrysler or Dodge products and vice versa, and under new company leadership, these policy rules have begun to be broken. For example, the Chrysler Crossfire featured a Mercedes engine, and the Chrysler 300 and Dodge Magnum used Mercedes components as well. The decision was made to break company policy: The new Nitro would be built on the Liberty platform.

Every effort was made to distinguish the Nitro from its close relative, the Liberty. The design was noticeably different, as the Nitro was given a bold, athletic look, including options such as 20-inch chrome-finished wheels and a four-inch longer body. Both 210 horsepower and optional 260 horsepower engines are available. A Load 'n Go cargo floor, located in the trunk, slides in and out making loading and unloading heavy cargo much easier. The Nitro dashboard comes with an optional entertainment and navigation system with a 20-gigabyte hard drive. Needless to say, the Nitro and Liberty, when parked side by side, look very different from the front, the Nitro having the Dodge "cross-hair" grille while the Liberty has the familiar Jeep seven vertical "slots." Among mid-size SUVs, often described as having bland styling, the Dodge Nitro is viewed as being much more masculine in appearance. In fact, in the Nitro marketing literature, the Liberty was surprisingly not even mentioned as one of the direct competitors: The Nitro was designed to go head to head against competitive mid-size SUVs such as Ford Escape, Nissan Xterra, and Chevrolet Equinox.

The focus on masculine styling is no coincidence. The entry-level SUV market is dominated by female buyers (about 55 percent in 2006). Dodge marketing director Tom Loveless notes that the masculine styling of the Nitro is designed to appeal to the male segment while at the same time being attractive to women. The more masculine positioning for Nitro seems to fit well with the established position of Dodge and its "Grab Life by the Horns" promotion for the Dodge Ram.

The launch tactics for the Nitro must be consistent with this positioning strategy. First, Dodge realized the importance of the Internet as an information source. No expense was spared in designing the Web site, www.dodge.com/nitro, where prospective buyers could virtually walk around the Nitro and, if inclined to buy, even easily go through the credit process linking them to Chrysler Financial. TV advertising included a spot on the the 2006 World Series in October, followed by a more intense campaign beginning in November with advertising on NFL football, NHL hockey, and NASCAR car racing coverage, as well as popular prime-time shows such as *Law and Order* and *My Name Is Earl* and late-night talk shows. DirecTV is also well represented: Dodge is a major sponsor of *NFL Sunday Ticket* and is advertised on several other programs. Print ads were run in dozens of magazines, including those aimed at the general market (*Men's Fitness, Rolling Stone, Sports Illustrated*) and at multicultural markets (*Jet, Fox Sports en Español, India Today, Korean Journal*). The Nitro was integrated into the Xbox NHL 2K7 game and offered as first prize in an online video competition held in late 2006.

In addition to the above, movie theater ads, radio, direct mail, and other promotions were also planned. Several humorous 15- or 30-second TV spots aimed at the African American and Hispanic markets were developed. Media typically used for the "Grab Life by the Horns" campaign (such as men's magazines) as well as media aimed more at women were used. The latter included TV programming such as *Desperate Housewives*, magazines such as *Martha Stewart Blueprint*, and Web sites such as hgtv.com. Nevertheless, the prime target remained men, and in particular, men passionate about sports, fitness, and social networking.

Comment on the strategic and tactical elements of the Nitro launch. How did Dodge do, in your assessment? If you were a Dodge dealer, would you be thrilled about adding this new SUV to your lineup, or would you be fearful that the new vehicle would just draw sales away from Jeep Liberty? Explain your assessment of the tactical components of this launch using the terminology of this chapter.

Case: Celsius and Enviga[17]

Now here is something you don't hear about too often: a drink with negative calories. How does it work? By stimulating metabolism in the body, such that the small number of calories consumed in drinking the product is more than offset by the number of calories burned off in the hours after consumption. Coca-Cola certainly saw the market opportunity: Soft-drink and fruit-juice sales were flat in the years leading up to 2005, while both nutrient drinks and green teas were experiencing enormous growth. The potential for a green-tea based energy drink was initially conceived by Beverage Partners Worldwide, a joint venture of Coca-Cola and Nestlé. Scientists at Nestlé had studied certain green tea extracts

---

[17]This case was based on information in Anonymous, "2007 Beverage Innovation Awards," www.beverage-innovation.com; Anonymous, "Celsius, Inc. Executive Takes the Temperature of the Functional Beverage Market," *Nutrition Business Journal*, March 2005; Burt Helm, "A Slick Pitch for 'Negative Calories,'" businessweek.com, January 15, 2007; and the product Web sites, www.celsius.com and www.enviga.com.

and found that they increased the body's metabolism, leading to calorie burning. While Coca-Cola may have been among the first to begin development of a green-tea energy drink, it was actually a much smaller firm, Celsius, Inc., that hit the market first with its Celsius product. The Coca-Cola product, Enviga, followed soon thereafter.

Celsius and Enviga represent a new beverage category: thermogenic calorie-burning beverages ("thermogenic" refers to the increase in body temperature resulting from stimulation of the metabolic rate). Both products are tea-based, carbonated, and come in a variety of flavors. Enviga is available in green tea, berry, and peach flavors, while Celsius comes in lemon-lime, ginger ale, cola, orange, and wild berry. Both are promoted as soft-drink replacements, offering all the benefits of energy drinks together with a soft-drink taste, yet none of the sugar, preservatives, high-fructose corn syrup, or other "bad" ingredients typically found in soft drinks. Price per 12-ounce can is approximately $1.45.

The back of the Enviga can states that the average 18- to 35-year-old person drinking three 12-ounce cans per day will consume about 15 calories, but will also burn about 60 to 100 calories more per day due to the increased metabolism.

These new products have received much media attention. *DataMonitor* named calorie-burning beverages as the "Number One Food and Beverage Trend for 2007," and *Beverage Industry* magazine named Celsius as the "Best New Product of 2005." Celsius was featured prominently on the *NBC Today Show.* In addition, Celsius is regulated by the FDA for food safety and manufacturing quality.

With the backing of Coca-Cola, Enviga has the larger advertising budget of the two drinks. A *BusinessWeek* article noted that Enviga ads and promotional literature do not specifically say that Enviga promotes weight loss, though Americans who love soft drinks but want to lose weight could barely miss the Enviga message. The FTC (Federal Trade Commission) monitors product packaging claims, and any packaging statement that oversells the health claims would come under FTC jurisdiction. In the words of *BusinessWeek* writer Burt Helm, "both the ingredient dosages and carefully worded health claims should land just below the radar of regulators who would take action if they spot bogus health claims. . . . though one watchdog group has threatened to sue over false advertising, [Coca-Cola and Nestlé] say the claims for the drink are justified."

Skeptics wonder about the claims made by the makers of Celsius and Enviga. Burning off about 100 calories per day won't make too much difference in terms of either weight loss or overall health, they say. In addition, what is really new about these drinks? Couldn't someone consume any other sugar-free drink containing caffeine and get the same effect? The Enviga people counter this skepticism by stating that the green tea extract, EGCG, increases the effect of the caffeine in Enviga (about 100 milligrams per can, similar to the amount of caffeine in a cup of coffee). To prove the point, Coca-Cola scientist Rhona S. Applebaum shows the results of an internal Enviga study, in which test subjects who drank Enviga over a three-day period burned more calories than when they drank a placebo over the same length of time. Similar controlled studies by Celsius revealed that consumption of the product increases metabolism by about 12 percent and boosts both calorie-burning and energy for a three-hour period.

Consider the A-T-A-R model. What problems would Enviga and Celsius have in terms of awareness, trial, availability, and repeat? Which of the four components of this model is likely to cause the greatest difficulty, given the case information and what you know about the beverage industry? Importantly, would Celsius (made by the smaller company) face different problems from Enviga (which has Coca-Cola's backing)? What are your recommendations to the management of these two brands for overcoming problems of awareness, trial, availability, and repeat purchase?

ANSWERS TO THE ISSUES IN FIGURE V.2

1. *Teams* make these decisions, not one functional group.
2. Marketing people have been in all along. And there should be no "taking over" because technical people should stay.
3. These paradigms *aid thinking.* Exuberance and excitement we have, but they don't replace thinking.
4. Not *marketing's*—the *entire firm's.* Every part of the firm has contributed to what we offer the end user. Hopefully, the end user has a problem and will welcome the product.
5. A good target market has several dimensions, not just sales potential. A large piece of a favorable segment may be much more profitable.
6. The PIC guides *all* phases—it is a strategic plan for the entire operation through to whatever its goals call for.
7. Data don't support this. Quite often, a follower comes up with the winning design.
8. Goals may be expressed in customer satisfaction terms too, but there are usually other goals unique to the situation—e.g., build a bridge to new market dominance.
9. Perhaps if really meaningless, but they should be meaning*ful,* helpful in telling the product story.
10. The launch is *managed*—if we start to sink, let's hope there is a large dipper handy. (See Chapter 19.)
11. Opening night is the first salvo in a drive to achieve the project goals—success. A successful opening night brings little profit, but a long run brings a big one.

CHAPTER EIGHTEEN

Market Testing

Setting

At this time, glance back at Figure V.1 in the introduction to Part V. It shows the basic new products process and where we are at this time. We have a physical product or the complete specifications for a new service. Early concept testing showed a need, and the use test indicated the emerging product met that need without serious drawbacks. And we have a marketing plan.

Now what do we do? Market the item quickly before competition finds out what we are up to? Or find a way to check out what we have done to see if it really looks as if we will be successful, before spending a lot of money on the launch? The option open to us is called **market testing.** This chapter gives the overall picture for market testing and introduces several methods commonly used: pseudo sale, controlled sale, and full sale.

We also discuss trends in market testing: As firms make a greater commitment to accelerated time to market, we are seeing a movement toward quicker, less costly market testing methods that provide the required information as efficiently as possible. For example, **test marketing** (sell the product in two or more representative cities) is in fact now a relatively minor market testing technique. It's still done on some occasions, but it's lost much ground to newer, faster, and cheaper methods. (Don't confuse the terms *test marketing* and *market testing*!) Scanner-based methods are, of course, a big part of the trend in obtaining quick, reliable marketplace information. Many firms have replaced the traditional test market with a product rollout (initially limited-distribution sale, gradually expanded to the full market).

Recall that we have been stressing speed to market and the role of the new product team in accelerating time to market, starting in Chapter 1 and throughout this book. It is only fitting that we are seeing many new types of market testing grow in popularity relative to test marketing, given their advantages of cost, speed, and accuracy.

The Market Testing Decision

The full set of market testing technique options will come later. First, we need to get a feeling for the decision to test or not to test.

FIGURE 18.1
Decision
Matrix on
When to
Market Test

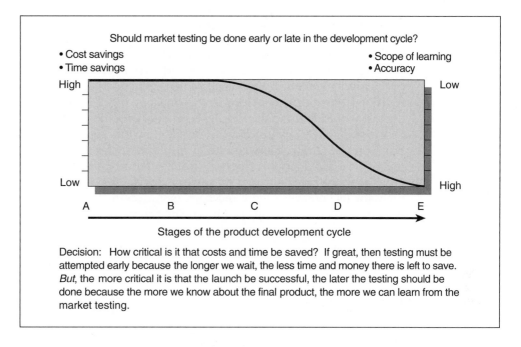

Should market testing be done early or late in the development cycle?

• Cost savings
• Time savings

• Scope of learning
• Accuracy

High — Low

Low — High

A B C D E

Stages of the product development cycle

Decision: How critical is it that costs and time be saved? If great, then testing must be attempted early because the longer we wait, the less time and money there is left to save. *But*, the more critical it is that the launch be successful, the later the testing should be done because the more we know about the final product, the more we can learn from the market testing.

When Is the Decision Made?

The decision of whether and how to test can be made at many different times (see Figure 18.1). On the one hand the longer we wait, the more we will know about our product and its marketing program; that makes testing more useful and more reliable. But the longer we wait to do the test, the higher the costs, the later the entry, the more damage competitors can do, and so on. The solution is to begin the testing as soon as a technique can be found that will tell us *what we need to know*. Some consumer products market testing actually begins before the product is even firmed up—it works with a concept statement! Other market testing, such as that with an appliance manufacturer or carmaker, cannot be done until we have everything in place ready to go.

Is This an Easy Decision to Make?

Any time we make a new product, we cannot really be sure about *anything*. With a few rare exceptions, *everything* we think we know about the new product and its marketing is not a fact—it is an opinion, a guess, a judgment, a hope, an order from above. The full scenario of the new item's marketing will be played out on a playing field where all too many people still have to react to something. Even they cannot be sure of their reaction, especially when we aren't completely sure what our offer will be and we sure cannot anticipate what competition will tell buyers about it.

It takes a strong manager to say at this point, "I know we have spent a fortune, and we are running late, but I am not convinced we have made the right decisions.

I want to take a couple of months (or more) to be sure." What kind of confidence does that inspire in the typical top management?

Keep in mind that asking for a market test is not a confession of failure on the team's part. This is also true in other fields. Trial performances of a new Broadway play may be staged in Detroit, Boston, or the Midwest to make minor or major revisions. In product development, as in stage productions, the decision *not* to do the test would seem to require the burden of proof.

It is true that many products underwent no market testing and were successful. But there are far too many counterexamples that show what can happen when the market test is skipped or does not test the entire marketing plan. Carter-Wallace, the makers of Nair hair removal cream, developed a version of their product for men, for use on arms, legs, and back (some swimmers, cyclists, or other athletes would be interested in this product). They chose the name "Nair for Men." Would you advocate going to the market without at least testing the name? To the target audience, does "Nair" mean "the most established name in hair removal cream," or "something my sister would use?"[1]

Recall the Iridium case at the end of Chapter 16. Potential users might have said they were crazy about the satellite phone, but that answer is unreliable without testing the price dimension. Think about some of the new product failures introduced in the case at the end of Chapter 15: Avert virucidal tissues, Uncle Ben's Rice with Calcium, and so forth—or about whatever favorite new product failure comes to mind. We may never know to what extent these products were market tested. But it is a safe bet to say that these manufacturers wish they had done a better job in the market test!

Market Tests Must Have Teeth

Figure 18.2 shows how market testing relates to other testing—the three major tests covering the three major causes for new product failure—concept testing for "lack of need," product use testing for "product does not meet need," and market testing for "marketed poorly." Many times a firm is in a hurry at all three of those times, so it first skips the concept test, then it skips the field use testing, and then, if it also skips market testing, it will be flying blind. Once in a while, the firm gets it right, and nothing is lost by skipping the market test. Campbell executives were reportedly so excited about the concept of Spaghetti-Os that they bypassed test markets and went right to launch, and never looked back. This is very risky, of course, and not what we recommend here; most firms would do at least some kind of market test of the type we will see in this chapter. But the market test must have teeth, meaning that managers are willing to take action based on the results. In some cases, negative market test results are ignored, because the product team does not want to kill the CEO's pet project!

Regardless of the kind of market test used, planners go to the trouble of market testing to gain two important insights. First, this is the opportunity to obtain *solid forecasts of dollar and unit sales*—not the general market figures or ranges of possible

---

[1] When in market testing, Nair for Men was featured on the "Hits or Misses" page of the www .newproductworks.com Web site, and scored reasonably well on the online survey.

FIGURE 18.2
How Market
Testing
Relates to the
Other Testing
Steps

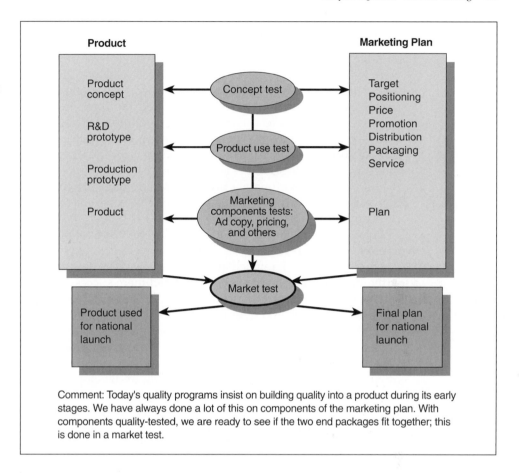

Comment: Today's quality programs insist on building quality into a product during its early stages. We have always done a lot of this on components of the marketing plan. With components quality-tested, we are ready to see if the two end packages fit together; this is done in a market test.

shares that guided earlier planning decisions. Second, the planners need *diagnostic information* to help them revise and refine anything about the launch that seems to require it—product, packaging, communication effort, or anything else. To gather solid quantitative forecasts and the diagnostic information, and then for whatever reason not use it, is asking for trouble.

Hoping to ride the wave of "new-age," clear products, Coors Brewing Company developed a clear malt liquor it named Zima. The test marketing was conducted in late 1992 in three markets: Nashville, Sacramento, and Syracuse. Six months later it was in about three dozen markets; within a year it was distributed nationally. An extensive advertising campaign stressed what Zima was not—neither a beer nor a wine cooler. A couple of potential potholes were identified in the early roll-out results: Repeat sales were not at expected levels (suggesting a possible taste problem), and sales were higher among females (who drink less than males and thus comprise less of the heavy half). The potholes were ignored, however, as the advertising spending was taken up a notch to as much as $38 million in 1994. Industry observers said that one of the main problems was the fact that the advertising message left consumers confused: Do you drink it like beer or pour it over ice? Distributors were reporting that many customers were mixing it with fruit juice, yet Coors resisted adding fruit flavors to avoid Zima being perceived as just another wine cooler. In short, the early warning signs were there, but apparently were ignored.[2]

Campbell Soup was working on a microwaveable soup-and-sandwich concept named Souper Combo. The concept passed the screening phase, went into development, and was test marketed in preparation for national launch. Based on the test market results, two forecasts were prepared: Marketing research projected sales of about $45 million, while the product team's forecast was in the $68 million range. Marketing research essentially forecasted poor repeat sales, accounting for the difference. Unfortunately, no one in senior management doubted the high-end forecast, the product was launched nationally, never made the projected sales figures, and was pulled after nine months.

Polaroid had a similar experience with the Captiva instant camera. Although market research revealed that consumers would be unwilling to pay more than $60 for this camera, it retailed at twice this price. The new product team had apparently forgotten a principle that had earned them success with previous products; sell the camera at cost, and make profits on film sales.[3]

These examples and countless others illustrate that market tests must have teeth. Remember in Chapter 8 when we noted that in early phases we could have relatively low hurdles so as not to terminate a promising concept before it was fully worked out? We needed to establish more difficult hurdles at the time of concept evaluation, because committing to development of a new concept is costly and time-consuming, and it incurs opportunity costs since other promising concepts are not developed. At this very late phase in the process, the same principle applies. For a product that passes the market test, the next phase is launch, and as the examples show, the amounts at stake escalate sharply at this point!

The Factors for Deciding Whether to Market Test

Each new product project has a unique situation, but here are the most common important factors considered in the market test decision.

Any Special Twists on the Launch

Did the original charter dictate a tight time schedule? There may be special considerations such as the need for new volume to help sell off an operation or the need to assist a new CEO to get off to a quick start. Does the charter limit the funds for the project such that it *must* be rolled out, growing to each new phase as profits come in from earlier phases? Is this launch part of a far bigger launch program, for example, where the firm is trying to gain new industry experience in one world market to permit a critical expansion into another world market?

---

[2]The Zima story is summarized in Richard Melcher, "Why Zima Faded So Fast," *BusinessWeek*, March 10, 1997, pp. 110–114.

[3]The Campbell and Polaroid examples are from Calvin L. Hodock, "Honest Innovation," *Marketing Management*, March-April 2009, pp. 18–21.

What Information Is Needed

We look first to see if this is one of those situations where huge sums of money have been spent and careers staked, yet no one knows what will really happen out there when the item becomes available. Conditions permitting, there is a strong argument for thorough market testing. This is partly to avoid a huge loss from market rejection, but also to protect against being surprised by too *much* volume. Nabisco launched Ritz Bitz directly to the national market and immediately found demand outstripping their bakeries' output capacity. Later launches have been supported by the rollout market testing process discussed later in this chapter.

One experienced P&G market researcher said he considers skipping the market test if the following conditions exist:

1. Capital investments are small and forecasts are conservative.
2. The use tests went well and consumer interest is high.
3. The company knows the business well and has been successful there.
4. Advertising is ready and successfully tested; sales promotion plan does not depend on perfect execution.[4]

Interestingly, one way P&G market tests new products is to list them, together with their retail price, on their Web site. They judge likely interest in a new product by how many customers click on the site and order the product! P&G's Crest Whitestrips, a home tooth-whitening kit, sold at a relatively high $44 and were initially offered only on whitestrips.com. E-mails to potential consumers were used to encourage visiting the Web site, in addition to TV and magazine ads. The response to the online campaign was very promising: About 12 percent of visitors to the site bought the kit, accounting for about 144,000 kits sold in the first eight months. With these results, it was relatively easy for P&G to overcome retailers' skepticism about the high price per kit and to convince them to stock the product.[5]

Another type of information need is more *operational*. It is for learning, learning *how* to do something that the launch requires. A launch involves all functions, each with its own needs. The manufacturing and production department needs to plan around solid volume estimates and must also at this point identify any difficulties in ramping up from smaller batch sizes to full-scale production. The service department (whether internal or contracted out) needs to know what the likely service demands will be so that it can be sufficiently prepared. The firm needs to know about any special needs or requirements from outside vendors or resellers. In addition, will product acceptance by customers be as expected, or will customer adoption require a significant, unforeseen change in purchasing habits? And what is the likely effect of product cannibalization? To what extent will the new product's sales volume come at the expense of other products already on the market?

[4]Robert E. Davis, "The Role of Market Research in the Development of New Consumer Products," *Journal of Product Innovation Management*, 10(4), September 1993, pp. 309–317.
[5]John Gaffney, "How Do You Feel about a $44 Tooth-Bleaching Kit?" *Business 2.0*, October 2001, p. 46.

The above conditions argue *for* information, but today's managers anticipate this problem by building in customer involvement. Firms that involve customers from the very beginning (as we have seen back in Chapter 4, even having customers as members of their new product teams) get early answers to lots of questions. Some firms approach this level of involvement by having customers pay for the material used in product use testing. Additionally, **total quality management** programs familiar in many firms force some of the learning needed for items earlier in this list.

Costs

Market test costs include: (1) direct costs of the test—fees to market research firms, and (2) costs of the launch itself—for production, selling, and so on, and (3) lost revenue that a national launch would have brought. Sometimes the costs of launch are so great that firms don't even consider market testing. For example, in the automobile industry their big cost is getting the finished product; once they have cars, there is little inclination to market them in a limited geographical area, or so they have felt. Many Japanese firms, however, will roll out new cars through the West Coast first as a market test.

Nature of the Marketplace

If competitors can take retaliatory action that will hurt us, chances are the testing will be quick, if at all. Most new products have some protection, just by being first in the customers' minds, but few have the ability to keep a market for themselves.

Another marketplace characteristic is that customers may literally demand the new item. New pharmaceuticals, for example, are rarely market tested upon getting Food & Drug Administration permission for marketing. One can only imagine the public outrage if a confirmed remedy for AIDS was put into a six-month test market in Phoenix and Des Moines.

The marketplace may not be good for market testing, especially in the case of global launches. Many markets outside North America and Europe are still very weak on scanner technology and other capabilities for testing.[6]

Methods of Market Testing

Marketers have developed a seemingly endless array of market testing methods for new products. One firm uses a very large company cafeteria. Another uses small foreign divisions. Still another uses the facilities of a chain of radio stations owned by a subsidiary. But the methods tend to fall into one of the following three general categories. Figure 18.3 shows where each of the methods is most useful.

---

[6]A check of ACNielsen's or IRI's Web sites, www.acnielsen.com and www.infores.com, respectively, will show which countries they do scanner-based market testing in: North America and Western Europe are well covered. Nielsen, for example, provides consumer purchase decisions in over 60 countries.

FIGURE 18.3
Methods
of Market
Testing and
Where Used

	Product Categories Where Useful				
	Industrial		Consumer		
	Goods	Services	Packaged	Durables	Services
Pseudo sale					
Speculative sale	▓			▓	▓
Simulated test marketing			▓		
Controlled sale					
Informal selling	▓			▓	▓
Direct marketing	▓				▓
Minimarketing					
Full sale					
Test marketing	▓				
Rollout					
By application	▓				
By influence	▓				▓
By geography					
By trade channel	▓		▓		

Pseudo Sale

This approach asks potential buyers to do something (such as say they would buy *if* the product were actually available, or pick the item off the shelf of a *make-believe store*). The action is distinct and identifiable, and much of the marketing strategy is utilized in the presentation; but the key factor here is little pain for the buyer—no spending, no major risk. It is, as the name says, a **pseudo sale.** It can be done early on.

Controlled Sale

Here the buyer must make a purchase. The sale may be quite formal or informal, but it is conducted under *controlled conditions.* The method is still research because the product has not been released for regular sale. Some key variable (often distribution) is not opened up but is contrived. **Controlled sale** is more vigorous than the pseudo sale, however, and much more revealing.

Full Sale

In a **full sale,** the firm has decided to fully market the product (this is not the case in the above methods). But it wants to do so on a limited basis first, to see if everything is working right. Barring some catastrophe, the product will go to full national launch.

Pseudo Sale Methods

Product innovators use two approaches to get potential users to make some expression of commitment resembling a sale without actually laying out money. The **speculative sale** method asks them if they would buy it, and the **simulated test market (STM)** method creates a false buying situation and observes what they do.

Speculative Sale

This is a technique used primarily by firms in business-to-business markets and consumer durables. It sounds very similar to the technique used in concept and product use tests, differing as follows:

> In the *concept test* we give the new item's positioning claim and perhaps something about its form or manufacture. Then we ask, "How likely would you be to buy a product like this, if we made it?"
>
> In *product use testing*, we give customers some of the product, have them use it in some normal way, and then ask the same question, "How likely would you be to buy a product like this, if we made it?"
>
> In the *pseudo sale method called "speculative"* we go to the customer, give them the full pitch on the product in a version close to ultimate marketing, answer questions, negotiate prices, and lead up to the closing question, "If we make this product available as I have described it, would you buy it?"

This testing is typically done by regular salespeople using selling materials that are developed and ready to go. They make pseudo sales calls—presenting the new product as though it were available for purchase. The difference this time is that the product is real, as are the price, delivery schedules, selling presentation, and so on. The target customer is real, and the positioning is clear. The buyer has little to do except make a decision. That decision may be just to ask for some samples to try, but that's okay. Trial is industry's way of making the first purchase and is really what we are trying to measure at this time.

Although the tool is typically used for business products, it can be used for certain consumer products. Rubbermaid is an example. Rubbermaid sells its products essentially by a push strategy, with some image advertising to consumers, but product presentation is confined to store counters. This setting can be duplicated easily, so Rubbermaid uses the speculative method in a setting that looks much like a focus group concept test (except using finished product with information on usage, pricing, and so on). The consumer faces a situation much like that in a store and can easily speculate on whether a purchase would be made.

Situations where the speculative method fits include:

1. Where industrial firms have very close downstream relationships with key buyers.
2. Where new product work is technical, entrenched within a firm's expertise, and only little reaction is needed from the marketplace.
3. Where the adventure has very little risk, and thus a costlier method is not defendable.
4. Where the item is new (say, a new material or a completely new product type) and key diagnostics are needed. For example, what set of alternatives does the potential buyer see, or what possible applications come to mind first?

There is no advertising in a speculative sale market test, and the ways of using it are many. For example, some people reject the idea of making a presentation to a buyer and then admitting there is actually no product available to buy. In such cases, they simply tell buyers, "We are getting ready to market a new product, and I want to know if you might be interested."

Simulated Test Market

Packaged goods firms do a great deal of product development, yet the speculative sale method, above, wouldn't work for them. They too wanted a method that was cheaper, more confidential, and faster than the controlled sale and full sale methods that follow. They found it in the A-T-A-R model discussed in Chapter 9. The method was a spinout from concept testing and comes very early in the development process. For being early, it is sometimes called *premarket testing*—testing that is done prior to getting ready to market—but *simulated test marketing* is the more common term today. Most usage is well ahead of the time other market testing can be used.[7] The name *simulated test market* came to be used because mathematical formulas are used to simulate the marketplace and at the time we were still calling all market testing "test markets."

The central idea is to get estimates of *trial purchasing* and *repeat purchasing*. *Awareness* comes from the advertising agency's component testing, and the firm's managers supply the other factors of *market units, availability, prices,* and *costs* that are required to turn A-T-A-R into a sales forecast. An example of a typical simulated test market procedure is given in Figure 18.4, though keep in mind that practice varies considerably from one market research supplier to another.

These pretests usually involve 300 to 600 people, require 8 to 14 weeks, and cost from $50,000 to $300,000, depending on the number of sales waves. Among the prominent suppliers of STMs is BASES, a division of ACNielsen. BASES combines

---

[7]Don't confuse these STM models with other models, such as TRACKER, that are used for interpreting early results in test marketing cities. Marketing scientists have models to cover almost every step in the new product development and marketing process, but here we can cover only the usage leaders.

FIGURE 18.4 A Sample Simulated Test Market Conducted as a Mall Intercept

1. Respondents are approached as they walk through the mall and invited to participate in a marketing study. (At least one major supplier does this step by telephone.) Respondents are qualified by observation before interviewing (estimates of age, sex, income, family status, and so on) and by questioning (such as product category usage) during a brief interview in the mall corridor. Employees of competitors will be eliminated at this step. Selected respondents are invited to step into a nearby research facility, which usually is one of the empty mall store areas.

2. In the facility, the respondents may be given a self-administered questionnaire asking for their attitudes and practices in one or more product categories. Then comes either individual or small-group exposure to broad-casting or print advertising stimuli. TV ads may or may not be couched in a television presentation (for example, a TV pilot program that is itself being tested). Print ads may be in what appears to be a magazine or on separate tear sheets. Several ads are presented so the respondent isn't sure what is being tested. One of the ads is for the new product being market tested. It gives the full story, including claims and price. (Note: Practice can vary, depending on the client and the company doing the testing.)

3. The respondent is then taken into another room, usually what appears to be a very small convenience store with shelves of products. The test manager gives the respondent cash or play money, not usually enough to make a purchase but enough to make such a purchase less painful. A respondent so inclined can walk right out without making a purchase, even with actual cash. The respondent shops and, hopefully, purchases the new product advertised in the first room—this yields the variable *Trial*. (One leading company does not use a mock-up store, but simply asks respondents standard buying intention questions as we used in Chapter 16 on product use testing, then gives the trial product to those who express buying interest.)

4. Most of the participants are then free to go. Perhaps 10 percent are taken into another room where a focus group is held. Another 10 percent may be asked to fill out another self-administered questionnaire covering post-exposure attitudes, planned product usage, and the like. Those that purchased the product are contacted later, nonbuyers are questioned as to why they did not buy the product, and participants may be given trial packages of the product as a thank-you for doing the study.

5. Some time later (time varies with the product category involved), the respondent is contacted by telephone. The call may be identified with the mall experience or it may be camouflaged. Information is sought about such things as product usage, reactions, and future intentions. Many diagnostics are obtained at this time, such as who in the family used the product, how it was used, and products it was used with.

At the end of the call, the respondent may be offered a chance to buy more of the product. This is the first step in a *sales wave*. Product is delivered to the respondent's home by mail or another delivery system, and the call is later repeated, new information gathered, and another sale opportunity offered. The sales wave provides information on another critical variable—*repeat*.

consumer response data (similar to that shown in Figure 18.4) with the firm's marketing plans to assess new product sales potential, allowing the manufacturer to tailor the allocation of marketing resources to improve the product's success potential. Another major supplier is Information Resources Incorporated, or IRI. Among other services, IRI provides a new product benchmarking service that scans an extensive database of new products to determine critical trial and repeat levels that can spell success or failure for the new product being tested.[8]

[8]Check out both of these sources' Web sites, www.acnielsen.com and www.infores.com (the latter is IRI's site). Other notable providers include the NPD Group at www.npd.com, Simmons Market Research Bureau at www.smrb.com, and TNS at www.tns-global.com.

STM services are offered in various forms and are continuously being improved. Recently, for example, BASES began stopping people as they *entered supermarkets,* gave them the pitch, asked them questions, gave them a coupon, and then followed up with the store later to see how many actually bought the item that was then available in the store.[9]

Output

Consumers give their opinions on the product, they buy or ask for some, they react to it, and so on. But the key purpose is to estimate how well the product will sell so the various services offer trial rate, repeat rate, market share estimates, and volume estimates. The latter come when they combine trial-and-repeat rates with the client's assumptions on awareness, retail availability, competitive actions, and the like.

A key aspect of the method is its mathematical simulation. If the client doesn't like the sales forecast from a study, variations are easily tested. For example, the model can be "asked" what amount of trial would be necessary to get to the desired market share. In turn, the cost of getting that trial (for example, by doubling the number of coupons currently planned for the introductory period or by lowering the price for a while) can be evaluated.

There are two variations on the above procedure, and the difference comes in how the data are analyzed. The current leading provider of the service (BASES Group, first introduced in Chapter 9) takes a fairly simple approach, relying on heuristics (rules of thumb derived from trial-and-error experience with previous, comparable situations). They gather the raw trial-and-repeat data from the test and calibrate them using their vast data set of thousands of comparable product introductions from the past to come out with adjusted trial and repeat measures. They then put these adjusted data through their version of the A-T-A-R model to project sales and market share.

Other leading suppliers use mathematical models, not heuristics, to derive their forecasts. This approach demands that more information be supplied by the client, but it is more useful in running simulations. One of the more prominent models is ASSESSOR, which is distinguished by its ability to make two forecasts (one using an A-T-A-R model and one using a preference model) and comparing the two to come up with market share predictions.[10] Consumer goods producers such as SC Johnson often test new products using the ASSESSOR simulated test market procedure.[11]

---

[9]An excellent (though dated) evaluation of these STM models can be found in Allan D. Shocker and William G. Hall, "Pretest Market Models: A Critical Evaluation," *Journal of Product Innovation Management*, 3(3), September 1986, pp. 86–107.

[10]The ASSESSOR model is described in A. J. Silk and G. L. Urban, "Pre-Test-Market Evaluation of New Packaged Goods: A Model and Measurement Methodology," *Journal of Marketing Research*, 15(2), May 1978, pp. 171–191; also see G. L. Urban and G. M. Katz, "Pre-Test-Market Models: Validation and Managerial Implications," *Journal of Marketing Research*, 20(3), August 1983, pp. 221–234.

[11]Gary L. Lilien, Arvind Rangaswamy, and Timothy Matanovich, "The Age of Marketing Engineering," *Marketing Management*, Spring 1998, pp. 48–50.

ASSESSOR's A-T-A-R model projects market share for a new product based on estimates of awareness, trial-and-repeat purchases. Customer data are gathered using a procedure much like that outlined in Figure 18.4. Based on the marketing mix variables of advertising (affecting awareness), distribution (affecting availability), and sales promotion (affecting number of samples received), estimates of long-run or steady-state trial-and-repeat are obtained. Multiplying steady-state trial-and-repeat rates gives the projected long-run market share. ASSESSOR allows the product manager to do "what-if" analysis, that is, to evaluate the effects of changes in marketing mix variables on market share and profit.

New Advances in STMs

We had discussed information acceleration (IA), a virtual concept testing technique, back in Chapter 9. Virtual testing techniques have been combined with traditional simulated test market procedures as well. One such development is called the *visionary shopper* (VS). Here, the respondent is brought into a virtual retail store environment and encouraged to shop around, "take products off the shelf" (by touching the image on the screen) and read the label, and make purchases. Recent work suggests that VS can be built into a shopping model as part of an STM, and advanced development of this technique is underway in the United Kingdom.[12]

Criticism

The STM technique has its critics. All major packaged goods firms use one or more of the methods, but we don't know how often or with what confidence. Mathematical complexity is a problem, and some managers may therefore be suspicious of the techniques. Second, everything in the system is slightly false: The mall intercept creates false conditions at the start, then the stimuli are unrealistically administered, the store is obviously fake, and much attention is focused on the behavior of the consumers being tested. Third, the calculations require a set of givens from the client before the formulas can be run (on the percent of stores that will stock the item, for example, or on the advertising budget, on how good the advertising will be, and on competitive reaction). Most of these numbers are assumptions and/or may be biased.[13] Further, the method may be less applicable for products that are totally new to the market or that are sold predominantly by personal selling or point-of-purchase promotion.

The firms supplying the service simply ask, "What other method comes close at such an early date?" Besides, their sales forecasts are often accurate, although it is

[12]For a discussion of the use of virtual stores in sales forecasting, see Raymond R. Burke, "Virtual Shopping: Breakthrough in Marketing Research," *Harvard Business Review,* March–April 1996, pp. 120–131. This technique is also presented in Phillip J. Rosenberger III and Leslie de Chernatony, "Virtual Reality Techniques in NPD Research," *Journal of the Market Research Society*, October 1995, pp. 345–355.
[13]For a good list of pros and cons of STMs, see Muammer Ozer, "A Survey of New Product Evaluation Models," *Journal of Product Innovation Management,* 16(1), January 1999, pp. 77–94.

felt that perhaps as many as half of all such tested products that go on into some later form of market testing are unsuccessful there.[14] So, usage and controversy continue.

Controlled Sale Methods

Pseudo sale methods are laboratory experiments that can provide very useful information in early market tests. Marketers also require market testing methods that involve real purchasing under some real competitive environment, but which can control one or more dimensions of the situation. Marketers have also wished for a market testing method that assumes distribution, or gets it automatically, without having to spend time and money to get it. This wishing has resulted in the **controlled sale** market testing methods.

Informal Selling

Much industrial selling is based on clearly identifiable product features. Product developers want potential buyers to see the product and hear the story, to make a trial purchase (or accept the offer of free trial supply), and to actually use the product. Repeat sales should follow unless product use testing was poorly done. Personal selling is the primary promotional tool, and there is little need to assess advertising.

So the obvious approach is to train a few salespeople, give them the product and the selling materials, and have them begin making calls. This informal selling method can even be handled at trade shows, either at the regular booths or in special facilities nearby. An example came from a 3M division that was in a crash program to market a new optical fiber splice; for market testing the item, the team manager found a trade show running just three months prior to launch date, where almost every potential buyer of the item would be present. As a footnote on this successful test, the night before the show opened it was necessary for the team to find why some fibers were slipping out of the splices; for this, they used a toy microscope purchased at a nearby mall.[15] New product marketers have to be quick on their feet.

The presentations in the informal selling method are for real, and cash sales take place. Often, enough time remains between the order and the expected date of shipment that production can be arranged after sufficient orders are obtained.

Informal selling differs from the speculative sale method discussed earlier. There, we asked people if they *would* buy; here we ask them *to* buy. And, just as Rubbermaid was mentioned as a consumer products firm using speculative selling, we find consumer firms using informal selling. All products sold primarily by salespeople directly to end users can use it (most controlled sale methods avoid the retailer/distributor stocking problem). So can services of most types.

[14]Bruce D. Weinberg, *Roles for Research and Models in Improving New Product Development.* Cambridge, MA: Marketing Science Institute, 1990, p. 8.
[15]Steve Blount, "It's Just a Matter of Time," *Sales & Marketing Management,* March 1992, pp. 32–43.

Direct Marketing

Another simple method of controlled sale is by **direct marketing.** Though usage of the term *direct marketing* varies, here it includes the sale of a (primarily) consumer product by the maker directly to the consuming unit by means of the mail, telephone, TV, fax, or computer network. As examples, LLBean and Lands' End are large direct marketers. They can easily test a new service of some type, or a new product or product line, simply by listing it in *some* of their catalogs and counting the orders. The advantages are several: secrecy, quick feedback, low cost, database support, and ease of testing multiple variations (by using multiple catalogs).

Minimarkets

Whereas the informal selling and direct marketing methods essentially avoid distributors and retailers/dealers, a third method involves outlets on a very limited basis. The new products manager first selects one or several outlets where sale of the new product would be desirable. In no way a representative sample, these are more likely to be bigger outlets where cooperation can be obtained. Instead of using whole cities (as in test marketing), we use each store as a minicity or **minimarket,** thus the name.

Black & Decker, for example, could contact Walmart or Home Depot and make arrangements to display and sell a new version of its Snake Lite. It could not use local TV or newspaper advertising because the item is available in only one or two outlets, but the stores could list the item in *their* advertising, there could be shelf display and product demonstrations, and sales clerks could offer typical service. Some methods (such as offering a rebate or a mail-in premium) could get the names of purchasers for follow-up contact by market research people.

The minimarket situation is more realistic, actual buying situations are created, great flexibility is allowed in changing price and other variables, somewhat more confidentiality is possible than with test marketing, and it is cheaper. Of course, it is still somewhat contrived in that the ability to get distribution is not tested—minimarket testing is a still controlled sale. Store personnel may overattend the product, that is, pay too much attention to it and give it assistance the item will not get when fully marketed. And, of course, sales cannot be projected to any national figure.

Several market research firms offer this service to manufacturers, using stores with which they have previously set up relationships and also using their fleet of vans to rapidly get the product out to more than just a few stores. At least one of the firms has special new product racks in supermarkets, where the new items are displayed. Note that this method is not very scientific; it is used to catch the first flavor of actual sale and/or to work on special problems the developers are having (such as brand confusion, price, package instructions, product misuse, or different positionings). It tells us the trial and gives some feeling about repeat.

One variation on minimarkets, **controlled-distribution scanner markets (CDSMs),** is based on scanner technology and has received much attention in the consumer packaged goods field. Information Resources Inc. (IRI) and ACNielsen offer CDSM service to packaged-goods manufacturers. IRI's BehaviorScan CDSM uses eight cities of around 100,000 people, for example, Marion, Indiana and Visalia, California. In each city, it contacts all of the retail outlets for grocery store products and asks them to install scanner systems if they don't already have them, at IRI's expense. In return the retailers agree to share the scanner data with IRI and to cooperate in a few other activities. Next, IRI sets up two panels of 1,000 families in each city. Participants agree to (1) have electronic technology installed on cable-based television sets, (2) report their exposure to print media, (3) make all of their purchases of grocery store products in the BehaviorScan stores, and (4) use a special card (much like a credit card) identifying their family. The families get various incentives (such as lottery participation) to get their initial and sustained cooperation. The key parts of this system are (1) cable TV interrupt privileges, (2) a full record of what other media (such as magazines) go into each household, (3) family-by-family purchasing, and (4) a complete record of 95 percent of all store sales of tested items from the check-out scanners. Immediate stocking and distribution in almost every store is assured by the research firm (this too is a controlled sale method). IRI knows almost every stimulus that hits each individual family, and it knows almost every change that takes place in each family's purchase habits.

For example, assume Kraft wants to market test a new version of cheddar cheese called Cajun. It contracts with IRI to buy the cheese category in one or more of the eight cities. It then places Cajun in a city and starts local promotion. Another of the cities can be used temporarily as a control. Kraft gets the right to put its commercials (via cable interrupt) into whichever of the homes (for example, younger families) it chooses. Kraft knows whether the families watched TV at the times of the commercials, whether they bought any of the Cajun, whether they bought it again, and so on. The two panels in each city allow Kraft to use two different positionings in its TV advertising, one positioning for each of the panels. The variations and controls stretch the imagination. Kraft can find out how many of the upscale homes that watched the initial commercial bought some of the product within the next two days and what they bought on their prior purchase, what they paid, what else they bought at the time, and the like.

ACNielsen offers a similar CDSM, its Consumer Panel Service. Nielsen's panel includes well over 120,000 households nationwide. It differs from BehaviorScan in a couple of major ways. Instead of the special card used by IRI families, Nielsen families have a scannerlike wand with which they record their purchases at home; this information is transmitted daily to Nielsen. This means that the Nielsen panel can track purchases from all retailers, not just participating stores, but has the drawback that panel members must actively scan all their purchases at home. Nielsen is also equipped to send test TV ads over the air, rather than only to cable households.[16]

Scanner Market Testing

There are many variations on minimarket testing, all designed to meet special situations and needs. One of them, **scanner market testing,** also came out of IRI's BehaviorScan system.

---

[16]For more information, check out the IRI and Nielsen Web sites: www.infores.com and www.acnielsen.com.

Once BehaviorScan was established, clients began asking the firm for more scanner data (fast and detailed in contrast to traditional market audit data that were slow and with less detail). They wanted to keep the BehaviorScan laboratories, but they also wanted data on large areas, preferably the entire country. So IRI developed what became known as InfoScan, a system of auditing sales out of outlets selling grocery store products. These audits were done in stores with scanner systems, and the data were reported for major metropolitan markets—first a few, and now over a hundred. In fact, the coverage is so complete that the InfoScan total market service is bought now as a national system, or it can be bought for single markets.

IRI has such good contacts with the stores it uses that, for a price, they can assure stocking of a new product. Without this assurance, the sell-in is left to whatever the firm can do. So InfoScan data can be used in a *minimarket test*—say, buying market stocking in Indianapolis and Denver and measuring sales of the new item there. Most minimarket test methods (see above) are in a small subset of stores and thus do not allow advertising in the areas' leading media—all local media are available in an InfoScan market. Or InfoScan data can be used in a *test market* where they introduce the new item by *natural sell-in*, regular calls on retailers and wholesalers in, say, Nashville and Albuquerque. If they want to, they can buy store data for two other cities, say, Rochester and Kansas City, where they do *not* sell the new product, for comparison with the two where it is being sold. The city pairs are not as carefully selected and matched as they are in traditional test marketing. Or, third, InfoScan data can be used where a firm starts selling a new product in major markets of the west, moves it out to nearby markets in the mountain states, and so on across the country. In a moment, we will see that this is a *rollout* market test.

InfoScan thus is a *method of market test design and data gathering*. By itself, it is not a method of market testing, but supports most of them. To help in this, IRI has also developed household panels in all of their markets so clients can follow individual family purchases, taking on some aspects of their own BehaviorScan laboratory system. Some consumer firms' managers call InfoScan a *live* test market, to distinguish it from the simulated test marketing models, and others call it an *in-market* test to distinguish it from the smaller city laboratories of the BehaviorScan electronic testing service.[17] Since the manufacturer can obtain so much information from one provider (purchases, household demographics and media behavior, and response to promotions and prices), InfoScan and its competitors are known as **single-source systems**. The excitement of single-source systems is the flexibility to do many different things in many different markets, with coordinated services, in rich detail, and (best of all) in days, not months.

Again, ACNielsen is a direct competitor with a similar offering, SCANTRACK Services, which gathers data weekly from over 4,800 food and food/drug stores in 50 major markets. Data are also available from drug stores, mass merchandisers,

---

[17]IRI goes much further in designing variations on the basic service. For example, besides the controlled *market* testing just described, they also offer controlled *store* testing where activities in one chain are studied.

and convenience stores, and for product categories in which nonscanner sales are more common, such as tobacco or candy, the scanner data are augmented with store audit data. Nielsen also provides Nielsen Food Index (NFI) reports. Managers can then obtain SCANTRACK and NFI reports online from Nielsen. Retailers also use their own scanner data to test alternative price points and shelf placements.

To meet the ever-increasing demands of consumer-packaged-goods marketers, both Nielsen and IRI offer expert system services that cut through the enormous amount of scanner data to provide useful reports to managers. IRI offers Sales Partner, which cuts through retail scanner data to identify key selling arguments and write reports that manufacturer sales reps can use when calling on retailers. Another IRI product, CoverStory, writes a brief market research report (including visuals and graphs) for product managers highlighting notable trends and events regarding their products. Nielsen offers Sales Advisor, which develops summaries of sales data and effective presentations of marketing information, again for the manufacturer's sales force to use on sales calls.[18]

Full Sale Methods

In full sale market testing *all* variables are *go*, including competition and the trade. They test the realities of national introduction. First will come test marketing and then the fastest growing method of all, rollout.

Test Marketing

Test marketing refers to that type of market testing in which a representative piece of the total market (usually, one or more metropolitan markets in and around cities) is chosen for a dress rehearsal. When we hear that a new product is being tested in Evansville, Boise, or Dubuque, it is probably in the form of a test market. What typically happens is that a firm first picks, say, two cities in which to sell the new product and two cities very similar to the first where the product is not sold. All four are watched closely, stocking of the new product is audited, sales are audited—either by the InfoScan system or some other method of collecting store purchase data and store inventories from which sales can be calculated. What they had, plus what they bought, less what they have left over on the auditor's next call, equals what they must have sold (ignoring what walked out).

The *purpose* of most test marketing today has changed. Whereas the early purpose was to predict profits and thus help decide *whether* to go national, firms today use it more to fine-tune their plans and learn *how best* to do so. Test marketing is too expensive to be used as a final exam.

This is a critical distinction, as shown by the market testing traditionally used for Broadway plays and musicals. Some of them *have* to play Detroit or Boston to prove their worth, but these are small, shoestring operations destined for an off-Broadway location. Big-time shows spend the real money getting *to* Detroit,

---

[18]Check the two firms' Web sites for the most up-to-date information.

where they fine-tune the operation, confirm volume and cost forecasts, and so on. A major production that fails in Detroit is a rarity.

An illustrative example of how a firm fine-tuned a marketing plan is given by Searle in their development of NutraSweet (aspartame) artificial sweetener. When NutraSweet was first developed, Searle originally thought the natural target market would be artificial sweetener users who disliked saccharin's aftertaste. In regional test markets, they found that the real target market was quite different and actually much larger and more lucrative: dissatisfied sugar users. It turned out that many saccharin users actually preferred saccharin's taste.[19] Similarly, when P&G was preparing to launch Febreze fabric refresher designed to lift odors from fabrics (a new product category), an extensive two-year test market was conducted in Phoenix, Tucson, Salt Lake City, and Boise. While Febreze was originally targeted to a niche market (smokers looking to remove cigarette odor from clothes), the test market showed that the potential market was much wider: Families with young children or pets were found to be heavy users.[20]

Countries, too, are sometimes used as test markets when firms are seeking international expansion or looking to minimize launch risks. P&G or Colgate-Palmolive may market a new soap or shampoo in Brazil to test the likely acceptance of the product in Latin America, or in Ireland to test European acceptance. Both Pepsi-Cola and Miller launched new drinks in Canada as a kind of test market for eventual U.S. launch.[21]

Pros and Cons

In contrast to other test methods, test marketing is intended to offer typical market conditions, thereby allowing the best sales forecast and the best evaluation of alternative marketing strategies. It reduces the risk of a total or major flop.

The test market offers the most abundant *supply of information* (such as sales, usage, prices, reseller reactions and support, publicity, and competitive reactions) and many less important but occasionally valuable by-products. For example, a smaller firm can use successful test market results to help *convince national distributors* to chance stocking the item.

The test market also permits *verifying production.* Nabisco had trouble with Legendary Pastries when a seemingly harmless ingredient in the canned topping mix caused the product to explode on kitchen shelves. Nabisco saved great sums of money by opting for a test market. Other firms have been surprised by the effects of *humidity* or *temperature, abuse* by distribution personnel, *ingenious undesirable uses* of the product, and *general misunderstanding* by company or distributive personnel.

---

[19]Gary S. Lynn, Mario Mazzuca, Joseph G. Morone, and Albert S. Paulson, "Learning Is the Critical Success Factor in Developing Truly New Products," *Research-Technology Management*, May–June 1998, pp. 45–51.
[20]Anonymous, "Odor Removal Spray Introduced," *Supermarket News*, July 13, 1998, p. 44; and Jack Neff, "P&G Shifts Ad Focus for Rollout of Febreze," *Advertising Age*, April 6, 1998, p. 16.
[21]Masaaki Kotabe and Kristiaan Helsen, *Global Marketing Management, Update 2000* (New York: John Wiley & Sons, 1998), pp. 324–325.

FIGURE 18.5   A Risk of Test Marketing: Showing Your Hand to the Competitor

- Kellogg tracked the sale of General Foods' Toast-Ems while they were in test market. Noting they were becoming popular, they went national quickly with Pop-Tarts before the General Foods' test market was over.
- After having invented freeze-dried coffee, General Foods was test-marketing its own Maxim brand when Nestlé bypassed them with Taster's Choice, which went on to be the leading brand.
- While Procter & Gamble were busy test-marketing their soft chocolate chip cookies, both Nabisco and Keebler rolled out similar cookies nationwide.
- The same thing happened with P&G's Brigade toilet-bowl cleaner. It was in test marketing for three years, during which time both Vanish and Ty-D-Bol became established in the market.
- While Campbell was test-marketing Prego spaghetti sauce, Ragú increased advertising and promotion (to skew the results of the Prego test), and also developed and rolled out new Ragú Homestyle sauce.
- General Foods' test market results for a new frozen baby food were very encouraging, until it was learned that most of the purchases were being made by competitors Gerber, Libby, and Heinz.

Sources: J. P. Guiltinan and G. W. Paul, *Marketing Management: Strategies and Programs*, 4th ed. (New York: McGraw-Hill, 1991); G. L. Urban and S. H. Star, *Advanced Marketing Strategy* (Englewood Cliffs, NJ: Prentice-Hall, 1991); E. E. Scheuing, *New Product Management* (Columbus, OH: Bell & Howell, 1989); Robert M. McMath and Thom Forbes, *What Were They Thinking?* (New York: Times Business, 1998); G. A. Churchill, *Basic Marketing Research* (Fort Worth, TX, Dryden, 1998); and others.

Of course, the method is *expensive:* Direct costs easily run $500,000 or more per city; many indirect costs (for preparing product, special training, and so on) must be considered as well. In the Pepsi-Kona case at the end of this chapter, the Philadelphia test market alone certainly exceeded this amount in cost when one considers production and bottling, distribution, production of a professional television commercial and other advertising and promotion costs, media buying, and so on.

These costs are often acceptable if the data are accurate, thus allowing the test markets to be projected to a national sales figure. But *test market results are not really projectable.* We cannot control all *environmental factors;* company people tend to *overwork* a test program; dealers may *overattend or underattend;* and the constant temptation exists to *sweeten the trade package* unrealistically in fear that inadequate distribution will kill the entire test.

In addition, there is the question of *time.* A good test may take a year or more, which gives competition a full view of the test firm's strategy, time to prepare a reaction, and even the chance to leapfrog directly to national marketing on a similar item (see examples in Figure 18.5). At one time, P&G would test market most new products extensively. Now, it goes directly from a successful STM to national launch with many products, though in some cases where higher risks or uncertainties were present (such as Febreze, as noted earlier), a full-scale test market of as long as three years may still be employed. Similarly, Starbucks conducted traditional test markets in selected cities when launching Via, its instant coffee product, before rolling out into the North American market, then worldwide. Though seemingly a simple product launch, management correctly recognized the risks, which justified the extensive testing. For example, Starbucks needed to determine if Via would be perceived as a high-quality product worthy of the Starbucks name, whether the features most desired by Starbucks drinkers (rich, flavorful coffee) would be deliverable in instant form, whether Starbucks drinkers would be skeptical of any instant coffee, whether the individual packet format would be accepted or desired, and so on. Moreover, a major failure with Via might have tainted the overall Starbucks brand equity.[22]

Also, *competitors can mess up a test market city* with a flood of coupons and other devices to falsely decrease the test product's sales. A product manager in the cereal industry once said that his firm used to drop valuable coupons for its own product when it noticed a competitor was conducting a test market. When asked why his company didn't try anything more involved or exciting, he simply replied, "It works!" As another tactic, competitive salespeople might even be tempted to make bulk new product purchases, falsely increasing the test product's sales reports.[23]

The Test Parameters

A large body of test market literature is available, and most of the leading market research consulting firms stand ready to design tests appropriate to any situation, so no depth of detail is needed here. The most common questions are "Where should we test?" and "How long should the test run?"

Picking Test Markets   Each experienced test marketer has an ideal structure of cities or areas. Ad agencies keep lists. Picking two or three to use is not simple, but usually the demographics and level of competition should be representative, the distribution channel should not be too difficult to get in, and there are no regional peculiarities in product consumption. One interesting consideration is media coverage: To avoid wasted exposures, the selected market usually has print and broadcast media that cover just that market, not a huge surrounding area.

Duration of Test   There is no one answer to the question of how long a test market should last, as made clear by one marketing vice president who said he needed 24–36 months for a new plant care item, but only 6–9 months for a candy snack. See Figure 18.6 for some data on purchase cycles; the wide variations are just one factor in the duration decision.

The Rollout

Test marketing is not dead, but marketers now prefer a market testing method called **rollout.** It gives the dress rehearsal value of a test market but avoids many of its problems. It is sometimes called *tiered marketing* or *limited marketing.* Indeed, many firms will say they do not do market test, but frequently use rollouts.

Assume a major insurance company develops a new policy giving better protection, at lower rates, for people who exercise regularly. Management decides to

---

[22]Julie Jargon, "Starbucks Takes New Road with Instant Coffee: Company Launches Marketing Campaign and Taste Challenge to Tout Its Portable, Less Expensive Product Via," *The Wall Street Journal,* September 29, 2009, p. A29.
[23]This technique is still being used, this time in the book industry, where some authors have made purchases in those stores whose sales are being audited for inclusion in national bestseller lists. Most firms have urged salespeople to recruit neighbors to make purchases and spur stocking by stores.

FIGURE 18.6 Purchase Cycles on Selected Product Categories

	Average Purchase Frequency (weeks)	Average Four-Week Penetration (percent)		Average Purchase Frequency (weeks)	Average Four-Week Penetration (percent)
Air fresheners	6	12.3%	Fruit drinks	4	27.8%
Baking supplies:			Presweetened		
Brown sugar	17	13.6	powdered		
Cake mixes	10	29.6	drinks	8	13.2
Chewable			Laundry care:		
vitamins	26	0.8	Heavy-duty		
Cleaners:			detergents	5	50.4
All-purpose			Soil and stain		
cleaners	35	3.4	removers	25	4.7
Window			Liquid bleach	6	18.3
cleaners	27	7.1	Margarine	3	71.7
Rug cleaners	52	2.4	Milk additives	9	11.8
Bathroom			Mouthwash	13	9.7
cleaners	25	4.2	Pet food:		
Coffee	3	53.1	Cat (total)	2	14.1
Frozen foods:			Dog (dry)	4	23.2
Frozen entrees	6	19.5	Dog (total)	2	41.8
Frozen pizza	8	21.1	Raisins	18	8.3
Furniture polish	27	7.0	Salad dressings	6	32.9
Hair care:			Salad toppings	8	1.2
Hair color	12	4.7	Snacks	3	17.7
Shampoo	8	23.4	Steak sauce	23	5.4
Juices/drinks:			Toothpaste	9	33.1
Fruit juices	3	33.6			

Note: The first column is the average time between purchases of the category cited, by the households in the ADTEL panel. The second column is the percentage of panel households that make at least one purchase in a four-week period. Both figures contribute to the decision on test market duration. Source: ADTEL, Inc.

market test the new service by first putting it out for sale in California, an area presumably prime for such a policy. Its independent agents do their job, the policy sells well, so the company offers it to the rest of its West Coast agents. Again, it sells well, and the *geographical* extension continues. One 3M division markets items in Argentina before rolling them out to the countries in Europe. Colgate follows a lead country strategy and recently marketed Palmolive Optims shampoo in the Philippines, Australia, Mexico, and Hong Kong before rolling into Europe, Asia, and other world markets.[24]

[24]U.S. multinationals have been urged to use Russia as a geographical rollout area. It offers a large market with much less world-class competition, allowing the test company to gain experience and volume. Russian leaders have adopted policies on reexporting, etc., to aid such tests. James L. Hecht, "Let Russia Be Your Product Testing Lab," *The Wall Street Journal*, August 24, 1992, p. A8.

FIGURE 18.7
The
Patterns of
Information
Gained at
Various Stages
of a Rollout

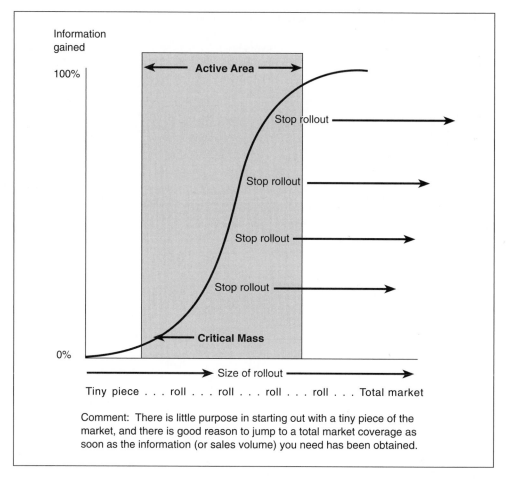

Comment: There is little purpose in starting out with a tiny piece of the market, and there is good reason to jump to a total market coverage as soon as the information (or sales volume) you need has been obtained.

The starting areas are *not representative areas* but, rather, areas where the company thinks it has the right people, and perhaps the right markets, to get the thing going. Some firms want the area to be difficult, not easy. For example, Miles Laboratories was marketing diabetes self-testing glucometers and realized that two of its sales divisions would have to cooperate; the Diagnostic salespeople knew the technology, and the Consumer Healthcare salespeople knew the retail druggists. They picked New York City, saying, "Because of the complexity of the market, if we could be successful in New York City, we could roll it out to other parts of the country with reasonable assurance of success."[25]

Second, there was no doubt about what the company was doing in the roll-out: *It was launching the new product.* See Figure 18.7 for the decision on when to roll out and how far to increase the rollout before switching to a full national launch.

[25]Leslie Brennan, "Meeting the Test," *Sales and Marketing Management*, March 1990, p. 60.

Kodak attempted a nationwide launch for its Advanced Photo System (APS), also known as Advantix, which in retrospect maybe should have been a rollout. The plan was to launch in early 1996, backed with a $100 million advertising campaign, catalogues, and other promotional items. The problem here was that demand far exceeded expectations. The trade press had given the APS system lukewarm reviews, possibly because product developers at Kodak did not give them complete information about the system's benefits. As a result, sales projections and production plans were tempered. The heavy advertising resulted in the unexpectedly high demand, and Kodak had to scramble to ramp production up to the new higher levels. Chains such as Walmart and Phar-Mor had APS cameras and film in only some of their stores, if any, as late as August (when the peak summer picture-taking season was winding down). By this time, advertising support and in-store promotions had slowed considerably. Industry insiders felt that if Kodak insisted on a nationwide launch, they probably ought to have waited until at least June, if not the fall. A rollout might have helped Kodak calibrate the level of sales in a small market and adjust full-scale production and advertising support upwards as the product went national.[26]

Let's take another example. Assume an industrial adhesives firm develops a new adhesive that works on many *applications,* including fastening bricks to steel plates, fastening insulation siding to the two-by-four studs in a house, and fastening shingles onto plywood roofing sheets. It has been field-tested in all three applications and has been tested in informal selling to roofing firms in one use (shingles), where it received a good response. Should the firm offer it for all three applications at once? Arguments against this include (1) the adhesive has not been market tested in the first two applications, (2) such action would strain resources, (3) multiple uses might confuse customers, all of whom are in the construction field and will hear of all three selling efforts, and (4) the new products manager wants to have some successful experience to talk about when entering the brick and siding fields because they are highly competitive. The answer here is to roll out by *business segments.* Market the new adhesive in the shingles business first, gain experience, build up some cash flow, and establish credibility. Then gradually begin selling it to the siding firms and make whatever changes are indicated. Still later, roll it on into the brick field.

Another kind of rollout would be the same adhesives firm if there were only one major application and the product (1) was only marginally better and (2) required lots of training for the distributors' reps. The adhesives firm could choose to begin selling the adhesive through one of its best (and friendliest) distributors, a firm willing to go along on the new item. When that went well, it could gradually roll it out to other distributors with whom it had increasingly less *influence,* using prior successes to persuade them.

A final example can be found in the magazine publishing field, where new magazines are often offered first through the newsstand *channel* and then, if they sell well, they are offered in direct-mail promotion for mail subscribers. Toy companies

[26]Wendy Bounds, "Camera System Is Developed but Not Delivered," *The Wall Street Journal,* August 7, 1996, pp. B1, B6.

use this kind of channel rollout as well. A new line of dolls or miniature cars might be rolled out just at Walmart or Toys "R" Us since both of these represent an enormous percentage of toy sales in the U.S. market. If the product sells well there, and the retailers experience no difficulties in inventorying or restocking the toy, they move to smaller chains and independent toysellers.

Other Forms That Rollout Takes

Those examples catch the leading forms taken by rollouts—geography, application, influence, and trade channel. Here are some other rollout situations:

- Sega wanted to get a jump on Nintendo and Sony for shelf space ahead of fall and holiday sales. So it used selected stores of Toys "R" Us, Babbage, Software City, and Electronic Boutique to sell some new items in April.[27]
- P&G's competitive response to Kimberly-Clark's move of their Pull-Up diapers into Europe was to introduce Pampers Trainers into Ireland and the Netherlands. They also rolled the new Trainers into Canada, but refused to state when (or if) the rollout would continue throughout Europe or from Canada into the United States.
- Prodigy was first rolled into San Diego and Discover card into Atlanta, both examples of using a rollout when the nature of the service was still being worked out.
- Tom's of Maine toothpaste uses rollouts to enter markets one at a time without the costs of advertising and slotting allowances. They use radio with a localized personal approach.
- Lastly, we will long remember one of the most ballyhooed introductions of all time—that of Windows 95 in August 1995. But Microsoft had been running beta-site tests for over two years, adding new applications and users every month, to a total of over 2,000. This was a rollout, and August 1995 was not a single, total-market introduction.

Contrasts with Test Marketing

A rollout has many advantages. The biggest are that it gives management most of the knowledge learned from a test market, it has an escape clause without losing the full budget if things bomb, and yet we are well on our way to national availability as early rollout results start coming in. This is important in the competitive battle because test marketing gives the competition time to launch their products while we are still in test market or getting geared up to go national.

Does this sound like the best of all worlds? What's the catch? In many situations, there isn't any catch, and the technique is justifiably growing rapidly. Other firms may find rollouts to be just as big a risk as full launch. Here is why:

1. Their biggest investment may be in a new production facility and to roll out requires the full plant at the start.

[27]Jim Carlton, "Sega Leaps Ahead by Shipping New Player Early," *The Wall Street Journal,* May 11, 1995, p. B1.

2. They may be in an industry where competitors can move very fast (for example, because no patent or new facilities are required), so a slow marketing gives them as much chance to leap-frog as would test marketing.

3. Available distributors are powerful, and none are friends willing to trust them.

4. They need the free national publicity that only a full national launch can get them; rollouts tend not to be newsworthy.

Wrap-Up on Market Testing Methodologies

Each of the 10 methods in the three categories of Figure 18.3 can be used alone, and many firms use the one they think is best in terms of cost and what they can learn. But some firms want a system of two or more techniques.

Such firms usually begin with a pseudo sale method—the speculative format if they are industrial or in a business where personal selling is the major marketing thrust, or a form of STM if they are in consumer packaged goods. Pseudo sale is cheap and quick. Learning is limited, but it is a good leg up on the problem. It often doesn't hold up the process.

The firm then turns to one of the controlled sale methods, especially informal selling for industrial firms or minimarkets for consumer firms. If the second test will be the last, firms tend to slide directly into a full-sale method. Thus, an industrial firm might use a speculative sale followed by an applications rollout. A packaged goods firm might start with an STM followed by a geographical rollout, or an STM followed by a minimarket and then full launch. Advances in information technology ensure that firms will have quicker and better data available at the individual household and business firm level far out into the future.

Summary

This chapter has presented market testing: the evaluation of the product together with its marketing plan. The techniques of market testing vary from the simplistic (and quite unreliable) one of making a sales presentation about the new product to potential buyers and then asking them if they would buy it if available, to a rollout.

The appropriate market testing methodology for any particular new product cannot be stipulated here. Some new product innovation is of such low risk that no market testing can be defended. The toughest issue of all is probably that of technology-based firms that develop what they feel the customer needs and *will* want; but customers don't *know* they want these new items until they have had a long chance to see them and think about them. Examples are many, ranging from the bathtub to the microwave oven. As a result, technical innovators sometimes distrust any kind of intermediate testing.

At the time of entering any market test (including rollout) and at the time of national launch, many firms have adopted some of the thinking of space launches: using a launch control system to prepare them for unexpected, but possible, traumatic events. This is the topic of Chapter 19.

Applications

1. "Several of our divisions have lately been using this so-called minimarket testing method. We had some shaving products use BehaviorScan, and a new upscale bandage line used a somewhat similar service from ACNielsen. But I am increasingly concerned about the panel members in those test cities. My concern is not that the people become accustomed to the testing or that they overreact to stimuli. These are valid concerns, but there's not much I can do about them. I am concerned, however, that our people do not *know the effect* of these things on the data we get. How would the results of our tests be affected if people like the testing too much? Or if they tend to become professional test participants and begin thinking like judges?"

2. "You know, we recently had a soft drink product (an exotic berry seltzer line) go through one of those simulated test markets, and it was a disaster. The new products people forgot completely about the possibility that the customers who bought the product in the shopping center pseudo stores might not actually get around to trying it. But it happened. Based on in-store purchases, everything was okay, but a good percentage of the purchasers changed their minds later; and, if they used the product at all, it was a limited trial by just one person. Solution, of course: A sales wave test added to the end of the store test. But that increases the cost considerably. Could you tell me when we should use the added sales wave and when we shouldn't?"

3. "I really was confused by something a corporate market researcher said in a seminar we held last week. It concerned our industrial tubing division, which sells extruded aluminum tubing of various smaller sizes for encasing wiring in commercial buildings. She was recommending that they market test their new items by going out to the customers and making what she called fakes—pretending to sell something they wouldn't have yet. This was so silly. Surely you don't agree with her, do you? Besides, it sounds dishonest to deceive potential buyers that way."

Case: PepsiCo—Pepsi-Kona and Pepsi One[28]

Pepsi-Cola's famed "Cola Wars" advertising, aggressively pitting Pepsi against arch-rival Coca Cola, seems symbolic of the competitive style of the beverage, snack, and fast-food corporation. In a competitive industry like soft drinks, new products that satisfy rapidly changing consumer demands are critical to sales growth and success. PepsiCo has had remarkable success with new product introductions such as Diet Pepsi (first launched in 1964) and has successfully repositioned Mountain

[28]This case was developed from several published sources, including the Pepsi Web site (www .pepsico.com); "The Best and Worst of the New Food Products of 1996," *Orange County Register*, January 2, 1997, p. 8; Bruce Horovitz, "Pepsi's One for All: One-Calorie Product May Spell Sweet Success," *USA Today*, October 6, 1998, p. B-1; Nikhil Deogun, "Pepsi Takes Aim at Coke with New One-Calorie Drink: Beveragemaker Plans Heavy-Duty Marketing Attack with Its Number-One Cola," *The Wall Street Journal*, October 5, 1998, p. B4.

Dew to the twentysomething market. Not all new product launches have been successful, however. Crystal Pepsi was launched in the midst of the "clear products" craze of the early 1990s. Its appearance and taste did not match customer expectations, and as a result it experienced very low repeat purchase rates and was soon withdrawn.

In the mid-1990s, highly caffeinated soft drink products (such as Coca Cola's Surge and Jolt Cola) were booming in popularity among the youth market, as were Starbucks and other coffee chains. Competitors such as Arizona Iced Tea were adding ginseng, another energy booster, to some of their products. Pepsi already had a working relationship with Starbucks, having produced and marketed Frappuccino as a joint venture. Based on these environmental trends, Pepsi decided the time was right for a coffee-flavored cola, to be known as Pepsi-Kona.

Technical development of Pepsi-Kona went successfully, thanks to PepsiCo's core competencies in soft drink development and its knowledge of the coffee business gained through its relationship with Starbucks. A coffee-brown label, prominently displaying the Pepsi logo and the Kona name in script, was prepared, and the decision was made to package the product in 20-ounce bottles and 12-ounce cans.

In May 1996, Pepsi-Kona was put into test market in Philadelphia. A full-scale promotional assault was readied. Several weeks before the launch, Philadelphia television stations began airing 15-second teaser spots with the themes "Spank Your Senses" and "Grab Life by the Konas." Once Pepsi-Kona was launched, it was on sale virtually everywhere, from the supermarket, to the 7-11, to street vendors (who had Pepsi-Kona posters prominently displayed on their trucks). A very entertaining full-length TV commercial was aired in which singer Tom Jones stood on a table in a crowded cafeteria and belted out "It's Not Unusual" while sipping Pepsi-Kona. Consumers kept their eyes peeled for the "Kona Hummer," a large vehicle from which samples of Pepsi-Kona were distributed.

The Philadelphia test market went poorly. While brewed coffee continued to be popular, the ready-to-drink coffee market (i.e., soft drinks containing coffee) was leveling off and actually declined during the mid-1990s. Some observers commented that the Kona Hummer and the TV spots were rarely seen. Furthermore, many consumers stated that they just didn't like the flavor combination of Pepsi-Cola and coffee. Pepsi-Kona was withdrawn from Philadelphia and never went into national distribution.

The clock rolls forward to October 1998, when Pepsi-Cola announced it was launching its newest product, Pepsi One. Pepsi One contains Sunett (otherwise known as Ace-K), a sweetener that had just been approved by the FDA, and thus contains only one calorie per serving. Interestingly, Pepsi One was not promoted specifically as a diet drink, nor was Diet Pepsi withdrawn from the market. Males in the 20–39-year-old age group were the primary target market. The advertising campaign for Pepsi One avoided mentioning "diet" (an unpopular word among that target group) and stressed that "Only One Has It All." Actor Cuba Gooding Jr. (who had just starred in *Jerry Maguire,* a movie about athletes and sports agents that was popular with the young male market) was chosen as the spokesperson. Sports tie-ins and other complimentary promotional activities (such as handing out Pepsi One at Walmart stores) were also undertaken. An important facet of Pepsi One's introduction was that there was no time for test marketing: In fact, Sunett (Ace-K) was approved by the FDA in June 1998, and Pepsi announced its intentions to develop Pepsi One on the same day.

What could be learned from the Pepsi-Kona failure that could help PepsiCo successfully launch Pepsi One? Specifically, consider the following issues. What might have been the PIC for Pepsi-Kona? What do you suppose happened in early concept testing? Why, after careful product development, did Pepsi-Kona do so poorly in the test market? Now, Pepsi One needs to be launched with virtually no test market. Given the prior experiences with Pepsi-Kona, should Pepsi One managers be worried? How might they lessen the risks of Pepsi One's launch?

Case: Square D Remote Lamp Dimmer[29]

In the late 1980s, the Consumer Products Division of the Square D Company had completed technical development of a new product designed for the home: a remote dimmer to use on table lamps. It used a fairly new technology for its time, but of course would now be well out of date. The product would soon join other consumer division products (particularly door chimes, weatherproof wiring devices, circuit breakers, and smoke detectors) for sale to the retail market.

The idea for the product had come originally from Ron Rogers, national sales manager of the division, and was based on his previous experience with motor speed controls and his having read a report on dimmer technology. The development had taken 14 months and cost less than $20,000. The product used a radio frequency that did not interfere with radios, TVs, or other household items. Its signal could go through house walls, with a 30-foot range. The remote unit had an on/off control as well as brightness-level control over lamp wattage. At the time of launch the unit would work only on upright lamps, but eventually they thought they could make the dimmer technology work for wall lamps and even ceiling lighting.

Ron decided that the U.S. market (the product's major potential at this time) consisted of 75 million households with an average of eight table lamps in each. That would indicate a potential sales volume of 75 to 600 million units. There was no direct competitor to the new dimmer, although wall-switch dimmers had been available for many years. It was not known whether there would be any patent protection, but the likelihood was not strong.

The product was primarily designed for use by a person returning home after dark. After entering the garage, a click on the Square-D Dimmer would turn on one or more lamps inside the house or apartment, so that the person never had to enter a totally dark area. It would also appeal to handicapped persons, who would use it from bed and going from room to room. As a third use, parents could use it to turn off or on a lamp in a child's room without disturbing sleep. And there were many more possible uses, such as one to turn on a lamp in the basement or on an outdoor porch if a strange sound occurred.

[29]This case was compiled from information provided by the firm.

The unit would come with four possible channels, A to D. Thus, the user might buy one unit with the A channel to turn on a lamp in the kitchen or entry hallway, and a B channel unit for use inside the house to turn on lamps in some other room.

The lamp dimmer retail package consisted of two pieces heat-sealed inside a display hanger. The first piece was a small space-capsule-shaped control that screwed into the lamp; the bulb was then screwed into the unit so that the control piece was between the bulb and the lamp socket. The second product piece was the remote control, which was much like a small TV remote control unit. The product was priced to retail for $33.50, with better than average trade margins because retailers would be doing most of the promotion.

Square D was a large and prosperous firm in the industrial equipment arena, although the Consumer Products Division was much younger. The lamp dimmer product had not been use-tested in the home, although some engineers and company managers had used it in their homes. The principal market study to date was a survey of manufacturers' reps, who endorsed the concept. This division sold through a national force of reps who called on such retail organizations as hardware stores, mass merchandisers, and department stores. Most marketing strategy was push-oriented with a minimum of consumer advertising. They thought retailers would be willing to stock the item and to put up in-store displays that encouraged potential buyers to pick up a unit and use it on a small lamp incorporated into the displays. They also hoped some retailers would give it some space in their weekly advertising if they allocated them an additional $2 promotional discount per unit bought. Granted, the technology was not exciting, and there were many more advanced electrical adjustment products on the market. But none of them did what this product would do, and none of them could offer something similar at the low price.

The issue for you is, how would you have recommended to Mr. Rogers that the product be market tested? Or would you have recommended no market testing? Please state your recommendation with supporting logic.

CHAPTER NINETEEN

Launch Management

Setting

Once the new product is ready to market, the long trek through the development process may appear to be ended. The people involved in the program are happy, satisfied, and anxious for a well-earned rest.

But the group was charged with launching a *winning* product. Just as managerial control over the *development process* was needed (checking actual progress against the plan and making adjustments where it appeared there would be trouble meeting the schedule), control over the *marketing of the new product* is needed. Launch management lasts until the new product has finished its assault on given objectives, which may take as long as six months to a year for industrial goods and commercial services or as little as a few weeks for some consumer packaged goods.

What We Mean by Launch Management

Comparing a NASA space capsule to a youngster's slingshot will explain the subject of this chapter. After firing at a crow in the upper branches of a tree, the youngster quickly panics and runs if the rock sails well over the crow and heads directly for the kitchen window in the neighbor's house. That's when the youngster would rather be in the NASA control headquarters in Houston, Texas, because NASA scientists launch *guided* space capsules, not *unguided* slingshot rocks. NASA would have anticipated that an in-flight directional problem *might* occur and thus would simply make an in-flight correction allowing the space capsule to continue its *controlled* flight. Not having in-flight corrective powers, the youngster simply runs.

This analogy isn't as farfetched as it may sound. It literally offers the new products manager a choice—NASA or a run for cover. Good tracking systems make successful launching of new products more likely. The manager who has to run for cover simply wasn't a manager.[1]

Unfortunately, only a minority of firms systematically use new product launch management. Historically, the day of launch was thought to seal the fate of a new

[1]People marketing new products are not the only ones using NASA-type systems today. Manufacturing quality control managers have the same difficulties in anticipating problems that might endanger product quality, watching to see if these problems are coming up, and being ready to do something if they do.

product. Prior to launch, management could pour overtime dollars into a project that was behind schedule, but there was no counterpart of overtime on the launch side.

That view is being rejected. If troubles are anticipated properly, and if contingency plans are thought out at least informally, then there is indeed time and opportunity to correct marketing troubles early—perhaps early enough to achieve original goals.

Apparently, most managers today are at least receptive to the concept of a guided launch; a few use such a system, some are experimenting with parts of systems, and the rest are watching what the others are doing.

The Launch Management System

A launch management system contains the following steps.

1. *Spot potential problems.* The first step in getting ready to play NASA on a new product launch is to identify all potential weak spots or potential troubles. These problems occur either in the firm's actions (such as poor advertising or poor manufacturing) or in the outside environment (such as competitive retaliation). As one manager said, "I look for things that will really hurt us if they happen, or don't happen."

2. *Select those to control.* Each potential problem is analyzed to determine its expected impact. Expected impact means we multiply the damage the event would cause by the likelihood of the event happening. The impact is used to rank the problems and to select those that will be "controlled" and those that won't.

3. *Develop contingency plans for the control problems.* Contingency plans are what, if anything, will be done if the difficulties actually occur. The degree of completeness in this planning varies, but the best contingency plans are ready for *immediate* action. For example, "We will up commission on the new item from 7 percent to 10 percent, by fax to all sales reps" is a contingency plan. It's ready to be put to work immediately. "We will undertake the development of a new sales compensation plan" is no contingency plan.

4. *Design the tracking system.* As with NASA, the *tracking system* must send back usable data fast. We must have some experience so we can evaluate the data (Is our slow-down in technical service typical on big electronic devices like ours, or do we have a problem building?). There should be *trigger points* (for example, trial by 15 percent of our customers called on, by the end of the first month). These points (if not met) trigger the contingency plan. Without them, we just end up arguing. Remember, money to execute a contingency plan has to come from somewhere (someone else's budget), and thus every plan faces opposition from people who want to delay implementing it.

If a problem cannot be tracked, no matter how important its impact may be, then we don't have it under control. For example, a competitor's decision to cut price by 35 percent is an act; it cannot be tracked like dealer stocking percentages can be. But we *can* have a contingency plan ready if it happens. This situation is not

FIGURE 19.1
Graphic
Application
of the General
Tracking
Concept (with
Remedial
Action)

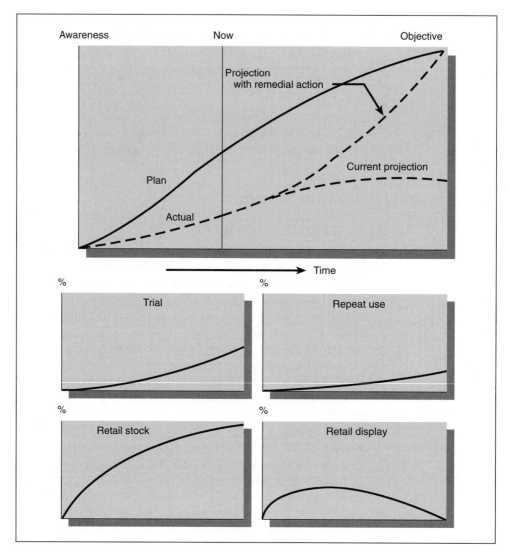

ideal because managerial control tries to anticipate a problem before it gets here; then we implement the remedial action in time to soften the negative effects. (See Figure 19.1.)

On the following pages, we will look in depth at each of these four steps in planning and executing a launch management system.

Step One: Spot Potential Problems

Four techniques are used to develop the list of potential problems. First is the *situation analysis* made for the marketing planning step. For example, government lawyers may recently have criticized an ingredient used in the product. Or buyers may have indicated a high level of satisfaction with present products on the market, suggesting trouble in getting them to try our new one. The *problems* section in the marketing plan will have summarized most of the potential troubles from the situation analysis.

A second technique is to *role-play what competitors will do* after they have heard of the new product. Vigorous devil's advocate sessions can turn up scary options that competitors may exercise—they usually have more options than we think of at first glance.

Third, we *look back over all the data* accumulated in the new product's file. Start with the original concept test reports, then the screening forms, the early lab testing, the rest of the use tests (especially the longer-term ones with potential customers), and records of all internal discussions. These sources contain lots of potential troubles, some of which we had to ignore in our efforts to move the item along.

For example, a food product had done well in all studies to date, except when the project leader ran a simulated test market (see Chapter 18). The sales forecast from the research firm came out very low. Study of the data indicated that consumers interviewed by the research firm had given a trial forecast of 5 percent, whereas the agency and the developer had been anticipating a trial of 15 percent. The difference was highly significant because success depended on which estimate was right. The developers believed *they* were right, so they stopped the STM tests and introduced the product. But they made trial the top-priority item on the problem list. Shortly after introduction, surveys showed that 15 percent was the better estimate, and the contingency plan was happily discarded. But they were ready if action had been warranted.[2]

Fourth, it is helpful to start with a satisfied customer or industrial user and work back from that satisfaction to determine the *hierarchy of effects* necessary to produce it. On consumer packaged goods, this hierarchy is the same one used earlier in the A-T-A-R model. Figure 19.2 shows that model when applied to the marketing of three ethical pharmaceutical and nutritional specialty items. Note that each product had a different problem and required different remedial action (contingency plan). All three items were marketed by one firm in one year.

But the hierarchy of effects will vary in other situations. Thus, for example, the satisfaction point for an industrial drill may be "known, provable, substantially lower output cost." But reaching that point requires the customer to measure actual costs. It also requires the customer to have data on what the drills cost previously. These are like rungs on a ladder—the customer cannot get to the top (satisfaction) without having stepped on the rungs of "know previous costs" and "know actual costs of the new drill." Both are potential problems, given that most firms do not have such sophisticated cost systems.

Later in this chapter (in Figure 19.7) you will see a sample launch management plan for a new industrial multimeter. There the five key potential problems were salespeople will fail to call as requested, salespeople will fail to understand the product, potential customers do not order a trial instrument, buyers do not place quantity orders after the trial, and a competitor markets a similar item. All were potential "killers," and one of them did strike.

[2]From the files of David W. Olson, vice president of New Product Research at Chicago advertising agency Leo Burnett.

FIGURE 19.2
A-T-A-R
Launch
Control
Patterns
(Actual)
for Three
Pharma-
ceutical/
Nutritional
Products

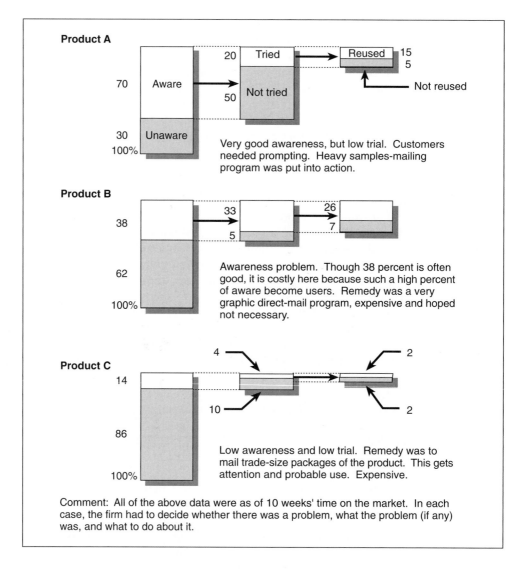

Product A

70 Aware

30 Unaware
100%

20 Tried

50 Not tried

Reused ⌐15
        ⌐ 5

Not reused

Very good awareness, but low trial. Customers needed prompting. Heavy samples-mailing program was put into action.

Product B

38

62

100%

33

5

26

7

Awareness problem. Though 38 percent is often good, it is costly here because such a high percent of aware become users. Remedy was a very graphic direct-mail program, expensive and hoped not necessary.

Product C

14

86

100%

4

10

2

2

Low awareness and low trial. Remedy was to mail trade-size packages of the product. This gets attention and probable use. Expensive.

Comment: All of the above data were as of 10 weeks' time on the market. In each case, the firm had to decide whether there was a problem, what the problem (if any) was, and what to do about it.

For another contrast, let's look at a new service. Peapod is an online grocery shopping service, used via computer from the home. Introduced into the Chicago area in 1990, Peapod was concerned about the common claim that consumers would not pay extra for the convenience of shopping online. In their case, conventional wisdom was wrong, and in fact, consumers were willing to pay a $29.95 start-up fee, $4.95 monthly service fee, plus $6.95 and 5 percent of their grocery total per order! But the firm was ready.[3]

Another example concerned a consumer durable product—this time a combination of the sturdy mountain bike and the thin-framed nimbler racing bike.

[3]Susan Chandler, "The Grocery Cart in Your PC," *BusinessWeek*, September 11, 1995, pp. 63–64.

But Huffy, the maker, failed to anticipate one potential problem that became a $5 million mistake. Huffy chose to distribute the new bike through their regular channels (mass merchandisers and chain specialty shops like Toys "R" Us). Unfortunately, the special hybrid bikes needed individual sales attention at the point of sale; such knowledgeable salespeople only work at bike specialty shops. A launch management system might have discovered this soon enough to permit necessary changes.[4]

Another example is the digital compact cassette machine (DCC) marketed by Philips Electronics. Their original launch of this product met with the following problems, all of which could have been anticipated and managed:

- *Advertising:* Missed on the matter of product understanding—example: the ads used the acronym DCC without defining it.
- *Resellers:* Sent it out to all dealers, but in the relaunch marketed only to those dealers who supported the concept and were willing to invest their money in the educational effort it required.
- *Price:* Early models didn't sell, so they cut the price to move them out of the stores before the replacements arrived. Not being sure how much of a cut this would require, they cut too much—shelves were bare before the new ones came in, and dealers started sending back their stock of tapes.
- *Consumer attitudes:* Consumers did not believe that digital tape could be as good as compact disks. True or not, this belief was a potential disaster, and it worked against them.[5]

All of this is not to say the companies were wrong—all new products are a gamble, and we never have enough time and money to do the job "right." But the problems represent what we are looking for when we do our launch management—knowing what bad event might happen, we can at least be on the lookout for it and hopefully have something in place ready to go if it does happen.

Oddly, one problem usually overlooked is the possibility of being too successful. It sounds like a nice kind of problem to have, but it can be expensive and should be anticipated if there is any particular reason to think it might happen.

Before leaving the matter of potential killer problems, don't forget that the firm has yet to prove it can do what it proposes to do—that is, produce and distribute a product that does what we claim it will. So launch management plans also contain problem items such as:

- Vendors fail to deliver the new parts in the volume promised.
- The new conveyor lines will be stretched to their limit. The stress limits provided by suppliers may be in error, and/or our manufacturing workforce may misuse the technology.
- Samples of the new product are critical in this introduction, yet we have not proven our ability to package the small units needed.

[4] "Flops," *BusinessWeek*, August 16, 1993, pp. 76–82.
[5] Kyle Pope, "Philips Tries, Tries Again with Its DCC," *The Wall Street Journal*, October 3, 1994, p. B1.

These too are potential problems. Any one of them can cause the new item to fail, so we must manage our way through them too. Incidentally, this reinforces a key issue in new products management today: The development does not end when the item arrives at the shipping dock. It ends when enough good-quality product has performed satisfactorily in the hands of the end user. The full team manages the launch management operation.

Last, note that one item has not been mentioned—actual sales. We do not "control" sales and do not have tracking lines and contingency plans for low sales. It might seem we should, and most launch management plans put together by novices include sales. But stop to think. If the sales line is falling short of the forecast, what contingency plan should be ordered into action? Unless you know what is *causing* poor sales, you don't know what solution to use.

Instead, we use the above efforts to list the main reasons why sales may be low and then track *those reasons*. If we have anticipated properly, tracked properly, and instituted remedies properly, then sales will follow. Otherwise, when sales lag, we have to stop, undertake research to find out what is happening, plan a remedial action, prepare for it, and then implement it. By then, it's far too late. Contingency planning is a hedge bet; it is a gamble, like insurance. Most contingency planning is a waste, and we hope it all will be.

Step Two: Select the Control Events

No one can managerially control the scores of potential problems that come from the analysis in step one. So the planner's judgment must cut the list down to a number the firm can handle. (See Figure 19.3 for a graphic representation of what

FIGURE 19.3
Decision Model for Building Launch Control Plan

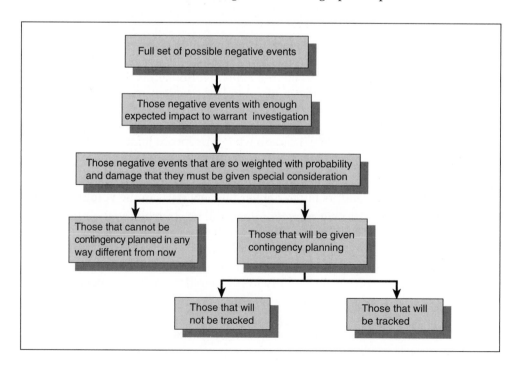

FIGURE 19.4
Expected
Effects Matrix
for Selection
of Control
Events

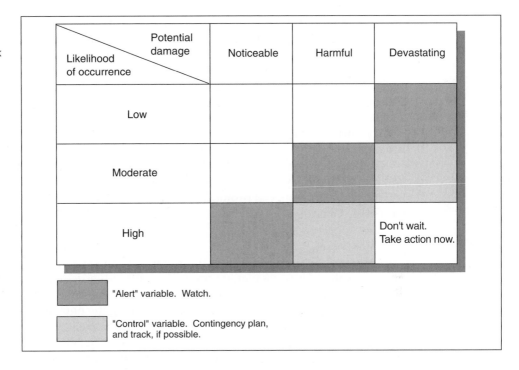

follows.) Some people say never more than six, but a new televised shaving product would surely warrant more contingency planning than the launch of a new line of jigsaw blades.

The judgment used to reduce the list of problems is usually based on the potential damage and the likelihood of occurrence. Figure 19.4 shows an **expected effects matrix,** indicating how the two factors combine to produce nine different categories of four types. Those with little harm and little probability can safely be ignored. Others farther down the diagram cannot be. At the bottom/right are problems that should be taken care of now; they shouldn't have gotten this far. In between are problems handled as suggested by the patterns on the boxes. How they are handled is very situational, depending on time pressure, money for contingencies, the firm's maturity in launch management, and the managers' personal preferences.

For example, most new products managers have been burned on previous launches and so have developed biases toward certain events. They may have been criticized so severely for forgetting something on a previous launch that they never forget it again. One new products manager recommended that the problems be sorted into two piles—potholes and sinkholes. Potholes are harmful, but sinkholes are disaster. Potholes rarely hurt us because we anticipate them; sinkholes are tough to anticipate.

Step Three: Develop Contingency Plans

Once we've reduced the problem list to a size the firm can handle, we have to ask: "If any of those events actually comes about, is there anything we can do?" For example, although competitive price cuts and competitive product imitation are on many lists, there is usually little the firm can do. The competitor is going to try to hold most of its share, and the developer is usually better off to ignore those actions and sell on the uniqueness of the new item.

For the other events, our planned reaction depends on the event. Let's take two different types: a company failure and a negative buyer action (consumer failure). The most common company failure is inadequate distribution, particularly at the retail or dealer level. Correcting the problem usually just depends on how high a price the company is willing to pay.

Retailers sell the one thing they have—shelf space exposure to store traffic. Shelf space goes to the highest bidder, so if a new product comes up short, the remedy is to raise the bid—special promotions, more pull advertising, a better margin, and so on (see Chapter 17).These were rejected options when the marketing program was put together, so contingency planners usually have lots of alternatives from which to choose.

A consumer failure is handled the same way. To get awareness, the marketers' program called for particular actions (sales calls, advertising, and so on). If it turns out that awareness is low, we usually do more of the same action—increase sales calls, or whatever. If people are not actually trying the new item, we have ways of encouraging trial (such as mailing samples or trade packages as in Figure 19.2 or giving out coupons).

Many product developers have marveled at how easy good contingency thinking is while preparing to launch, compared to doing it under the panic conditions of a beachhead disaster.

Step Four: Design the Tracking System

We now have a set of negative outcomes, for most of which we have standby contingency plans ready to go. The next step is developing a system that will tell us when to implement any of those contingency plans. The answer lies in the concept of tracking.

Tracking

The tracking concept in marketing has been around for a long time but probably got its greatest boost when Russia launched the Sputnik satellite. This launch led to the absorption of the rocketry lexicon into all leading languages. Though we had guided missiles for some time before that, they lacked the drama of a launch into outer space, especially with the spectacle of television.

The concept of tracking as applied to projectiles launched into space fits the new product launch well. There is a blast-off, a breakout of the projectile into an orbit or trajectory of its own, possible modification on that trajectory during flight, and so on. The launch controller is responsible for tracking the projectile against its planned trajectory and for making whatever corrections are necessary to ensure that it goes where it is supposed to go.

Applying this tracking concept to new products was as natural as could be. Earlier, Figure 19.1 showed the graphic application of the basic concept to a new product.

FIGURE 19.5   Advertising Weight versus Awareness Created for Selected Products

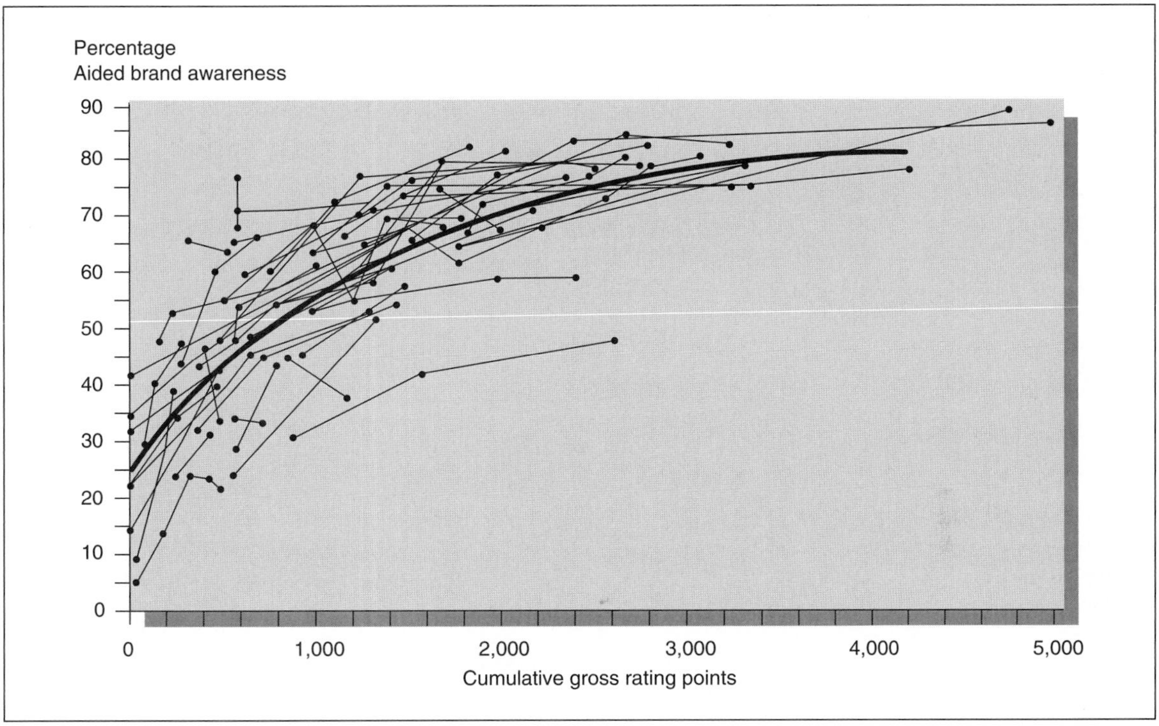

Source: David Olson, unpublished working paper, Leo Burnett Company.

Three essentials are involved: First is the ability to lay the *planned trajectory*. What is the expected path? What is reasonable, given the competitive situation, the product's features, and the planned marketing efforts? Although it is easy to conjecture about such matters, setting useful trajectory paths requires a base of research that many firms do not have when they launch a new product.

The new product research department at Leo Burnett Company, a large advertising agency, studied all of the new product launches that the agency had participated in and plotted the actual awareness tracks and trial tracks.[6] From these scatter diagrams, the director of research computed generalized paths that could be applied to future new product situations (see Figure 19.5). A firm that lacks experience can sometimes acquire the data it needs from such outside sources as advertising agencies, marketing research firms, trade media, or industry pools. Such ready-made options are important in these days of global marketing; fortunately, there is an increase of market research data and service organizations with international operations.

[6]David W. Olson, "Anticipating New Product Problems—A Planning Discipline," unpublished working paper. See also David W. Olson, "Postlaunch Evaluation for Consumer Goods," in M. Rosenau, A. Griffin, G. Castellion, and N. Anscheutz (eds.), *The PDMA Handbook of New Product Development* (New York: John Wiley, 1996), pp. 395–411.

FIGURE 19.6   Questions from a New Product Tracking Study

Category Usage Questions

In the past six months, how many times have you bought (product category)?
What brands of (product category) have you ever heard of?
Have you ever heard of (brand)? (Ask for four to six brands)
Have you ever bought (brand)? (Ask for four to six brands)
About how many times have you bought (brand) in the past six months?

Advertising Awareness Questions

Do you recall seeing any advertising for (brand)? (Ask all brands respondent is aware of.)
Describe the advertising for (brand).
Where did you see the advertising for (brand)?

Purchase Questions

Have you ever bought (brand)?

If "Yes":

How many times have you bought (brand)?
How likely are you to buy (brand) again?
What did you like/dislike about (brand)?
What do you think of the price of (brand)?

If "No":

Did you look for (brand) in the store?
Why didn't you try (brand)?
How likely are you to try (brand) in the future?

Each response is interpreted by Leo Burnett Company according to standard guidelines or norms. For example, the repurchase likelihood is measured on a five-point scale, and a modified "top-two-boxes" score is used: 100% of the "Definitely's" +50% of the "Probably's." For the price question, the norm is no more than 30% should say "fair" or "poor" value.
Source: Adapted from David W. Olson, "Postlaunch Evaluation for Consumer Goods," in M. Rosenau, A. Griffin, G. Castellion, and N. Anscheutz (Eds), *The PDMA Handbook of New Product Development*, John Wiley & Sons, Inc., 1996, pp. 395–411. Reprinted with permission of John Wiley & Sons, Inc.

Second, there must be an *inflow of actual data* indicating progress against the plan. This means quick and continuing marketing research geared to measure the variables being tracked. As an illustrative example, a short list of the kinds of questions used by Leo Burnett Company when tracking a new product is provided in Figure 19.6.

Third, we have to *project the probable outcome* against the plan. Unless the outcome can be forecasted, we have little basis for triggering remedial action until the outcome is at hand. The key is speed—learning fast that a problem is coming about, early enough to do something that prevents it or solves it.

Selecting the Actual Tracking Variables

Now we hit perhaps the toughest part of launch management. How will we actually measure whether one of our key problems is coming about?

If the problem is some specific step of action or mind, like awareness, then the answer is clear—find out how many people are aware of the new item. Trial is easy; repeat purchase is easy. What about trade support? Many new product marketers fear they will not get the push they need. But does trade support mean stocking the product? Displaying the product? Advertising the product locally? Giving presale service? Gearing up to give postsale service? The launch planner has to decide.

We need relevant, measurable, and predictable tracking variables. A variable is *relevant* if it identifies the problem, *measurable* if we can get a statistic showing it is or isn't, and *predictable* if we know the path that the statistic should follow across the page.

Look back to Figure 19.1. The top graph displays awareness: "Have you heard of . . . ?" It is a percentage of all people in the target market. The track line, labeled *plan*, shows what we *expect* to happen. The broken line shows what we find *is* happening and what we fear *will* happen if we do nothing. The tracking variable is relevant, measurable, predictable.

But let's look at dealer support. At the bottom of Figure 19.1 is a track of retail stocking, the percentage of target dealers who have stocked the item so far. This too is relevant, measurable, and predictable (based on our past experience). But what about shelf space? The height of the stocking, the number of facings, and the department in which it occurs are all aspects of shelf space. They differ in relevance; they are all tough to measure without actually calling on stores and looking at the shelves; and we are apt to lack the experience we need to predict them. Figure 19.1 also shows retail display, but such a track is mainly a guess.

In addition, watch out for situations where even a fairly obvious variable may be tricky to define. Take awareness (perhaps the most common variable tracked), for example. In Chapter 17 we talked about the marketing program to achieve awareness and how it can be the ability to recognize the brand name, or knowledge of the product's positioning, or ability to recall the brand. Awareness is a state that leads to trial, and that varies across product classes.

There is no way to settle this argument, so most firms just arbitrarily pick a reasonably good definition that they can measure and use it every time.

Many developers shun launch management because of problems in finding good tracking variables. If they can't easily measure the emergence of a problem early on, the whole idea of controlling the way to success makes a lot less sense.

Selecting the Trigger Points

Given that we have found useful variables for warning that a problem is coming about, the last step is deciding in advance how bad it has to be before turning the contingency plan loose. Say, for example, we have a low budget situation and are worried that customers may not hear of our new item—low awareness. If our objective for three months out is 40 percent of customers aware, and tracking shows we actually have only 35 percent, should we release the standby direct-mail program?

This is not an easy decision to make under beachhead conditions, for political reasons as well as for time constraints. Throwing the switch for direct mail admits that the original advertising has failed. This admission is not popular, and arguments will be made that the advertising is working as planned and the awareness will soon increase.

To avoid these no-win situations, agree in advance what level will be the trigger and put the triggering decision in the hands of a person with no vested interest.

With this, the tracking plan is complete. With diligent implementation, the launch will probably be "controlled to success."

Nontrackable Problems

What do we do when we have a problem that worries us but cannot be tracked because we can't find a variable for it, or because we don't have a track that the variable should follow, or because there is nothing we can do if the problem is found to be coming about? The answer is, very little.

Typically, management watches sales, and, if they are falling below the forecast, someone is asked to find out why. This means interviewing salespeople, customers, distributors, and so on. It's a difficult inquiry because things are changing so fast and because most participants have vested interests—they may not reveal the true problem even if they know it.

When the cause is found, a remedy is devised. If it's not a fast-moving market, time may be available to get the new product back into a good sales pattern. If it's too late, the new item is dumped or milked for a while. The loss may be very little if the costs of launch were low, as they often are for small firms, for line extensions, and for products that were never expected to amount to much.

Effective Metrics: Learning from Experience[7]

Deciding on the right metrics to use to evaluate a firm's new products process is clearly difficult. Yet effective metrics are needed for success with current projects, as well as for continued improvement. Much can be learned about metrics by examining the practices of some of the best-performing firms.

Boeing obviously uses cost, quality, and reliability metrics in the development of new airplanes. But Boeing VP Chris Chadwick says that *soft metrics* are also very useful. One used at Boeing is "help needed." Product team leaders are encouraged to ask for help when they run into a development problem; no requests for "help needed" is a signal that a project might be running into trouble. Boeing also uses forward-looking metrics to predict possible problems ahead of time. A metric such as weight maturity, for example, alerts Boeing to whether they are on track to meet eventual target weight constraints.

Another useful idea is to get external validation for metrics. ChevronTexaco has metrics for its capital programs, which it benchmarks using an external firm that specializes in this kind of analysis. This allows ChevronTexaco to assess its own cost and performance, not just with respect to internal goals, but also in comparison to competitive firms. ChevronTexaco also makes metrics meaningful for decision makers. Too often, managers don't pay attention to metrics, since their impact is never really communicated to them. At ChevronTexaco, managers are trained and certified in the use of metrics in decision making. In addition, Boeing,

[7]The examples in this section are taken from Mark J. Deck, "An Up-Close Look at Using Metrics Effectively Across the Life Cycle: Examples from Boeing, ChevronTexaco, Air Products, and Sprint," *Visions*, 24(1), January 2005, pp. 14–16.

ChevronTexaco, and many other firms tie individual incentives to performance on important metrics.

If there are too many or overly complex metrics, they will become a problem unto themselves. To avoid "paralysis by analysis," for example, Air Products (a gas and chemical company) uses only a handful of metrics at the highest level, such as financial return relative to objectives. At the middle level of management, a few additional metrics are added, such as product cost indexes and marketing efficiency; lower levels within the firm are concerned with more tactical metrics. Sprint, the communications services provider, does much the same thing. According to Assistant Vice President Mike Coffey, Sprint senior management uses a scorecard with eight or fewer metrics for each product they offer. Sprint also prioritizes metrics, recognizing that in their line of work, customer satisfaction and operational performance are the most important. Coffey says, "When customers are happy, that's a leading indicator of their intention to keep using the service."

An additional advantage of having fewer metrics is that metrics can be in conflict. Accelerated time to market is a good thing, but not if it means sacrificing quality. Air Products focuses on product reuse, which improves total cost of capital (one important metric), but lower cost of capital also has the effect of worsening an engineering efficiency metric, engineering cost divided by total capital. According to Naser Chowdhury, director of Global Product Management, this sort of metric conflict does occur, but needs to be avoided.

Finally, metrics need to be adjusted and fine-tuned through time, so that they are aligned with business goals—and firms need to learn from their metrics. At Boeing, a review known as Program Independent Assessment is designed to help identify new metrics and drop older ones, and also to assess how well current metrics are being used on each product project.

A Sample Launch Management Plan

Figure 19.7 shows a sample launch management plan. In it are samples of real-life problems, specific variables that were selected to track them, trigger points, and the standby contingency plans ready to go into effect. Note particularly that this was not a large firm, it had no market research department, and it was not then sophisticated in how to launch new products. Still, the plan covers the main bases, permits launch management to be in the hands of available managers, and provides effective action if any of the possible problems come about.

Larger firms with big budgets will have more sophisticated plans, but in principle they will be exactly the same—problem, tracking variable, trigger point, and remedial plan ready to go. Very small firms may have the energy to deal with only a couple of problems; the manager may use what we call *eyeball control* to move around the market and find if they are coming about, and then have in mind what will be done if they are.

But, whether in the mind, in the format of Figure 19.7, or in a sophisticated formal plan, the essentials are the same.

FIGURE 19.7   Sample Launch Management Plan

Setting: This launch control plan is for a small or medium-sized industrial firm that is marketing a unique electrical measuring instrument. The device must be sold to the general-purpose (i.e., factory) market, whereas past company products have been sold primarily to the scientific R&D market. The firm has about 60 salespeople, but its resources are not large. No syndicated (e.g., audit firm) services are available in this market.

Only a few parts of the marketing plan are presented here, but the control plan does contain the total set of control problems, a plan to measure those that could be measured, and what the firm planned to do if each problem actually occurred.

Potential Problem	Tracking	Contingency Plan
1. Salespeople fail to contact general-purpose market at prescribed rate.	Track weekly call reports. The plan calls for at least 10 general purpose calls per week per rep.	If activity falls below this level for three weeks running, a remedial program of one-day district sales meetings will be held.
2. Salespeople may fail to understand how the new feature of the product relates to product usage in the general-purpose market.	Tracking will be done by having sales manager call one rep each day. Entire sales force will be covered in two months.	Clarification will be given to individual reps on the spot, but if first 10 calls suggest a widespread problem, special teleconference calls will be arranged to repeat the story to the whole sales force.
3. Potential customers are not making trial purchases of the product.	Tracking by instituting a series of 10 follow-up telephone calls a week to prospects who have received sales presentations. There must be 25 percent agreement on product's main feature and trial orders from 30 percent of those prospects who agree on the feature.	Remedial plan provides for special follow-up telephone sales calls to all prospects by reps, offering a 50 percent discount on all first-time purchases.
4. Buyers make trial purchase but do not place quantity reorders.	Track another series of telephone survey calls, this time to those who placed an initial order. Sales forecast based on 50 percent of trial buyers reordering at least 10 more units within six months.	No remedial plan for now. If customer does not rebuy, there is some problem in product use. Since product is clearly better, we must know the nature of the misuse. Field calls on key accounts will be used to determine that problem, and appropriate action will follow.
5. Chief competitor may have the same new feature (for which we have no patent) ready to go and markets it.	This situation is essentially untrackable. Inquiry among our suppliers and media will help us learn quicker.	Remedial plan is to pull out all stops on promotion for 60 days. A make-or-break program. Full field selling on new item only, plus a 50 percent first-order discount and two special mailings. The other trackings listed above will be monitored even more closely.

Launch Management and Knowledge Creation[8]

Of course, we are learning throughout the new products process. During product development, we may discover activities or processes that we would like to duplicate in other product projects or standardize throughout the firm, or may identify technologies that could be reused elsewhere to minimize risks and costs and shorten development time. But in particular, much important knowledge can be created at the postlaunch phase by conducting an After Action Review (AAR), and AAR practitioners include some of the most successful innovating firms today, with Harley-Davidson, Sprint, and Ford among them.

An AAR is designed to capture the events leading up to the product launch and to try to understand the thinking behind the actions taken. The goal is to identify what went right (so it can be duplicated) and what went wrong (to identify weak areas in the firm's processes that need to be fixed). A good AAR includes statements of planned objectives and actual results, an attempt to rationalize the observed variances, a statement of what has been learned, and an outline for the next steps. An illustrative example is provided in Figure 19.8. AAR need not be terribly formal—in some cases, a couple of individuals meeting briefly after a customer

FIGURE 19.8   **A Sample After Action Review**

Objectives:

1. Send the customer sample by end December
2. Send the revised samples by end February
3. Reduce test time in half (from one minute to 30 seconds)

Results:

Objective 1 missed by a week, objectives 2 and 3 achieved

Reasons for Variances?

New product did not achieve performance requirements spelled out in the product spec.
Too much time (six weeks) was lost in redesign and remanufacturing as a result.
Not enough time was allocated for hardware or software changes.
But:
Team was able to reduce test time due to newly developed efficient testing.

Lessons Learned:
We probably relied too much on generic, off-the-shelf processes and packages, not all of which were appropriate in this setting.
Internally, we had been calling this product a "derivative" of existing products, but indeed the testing procedure was much more complex than for existing products, which should have been accounted for in the plan.

Source: From Ken Bruss, "Gaining Competitive Advantage by Leveraging Lessons Learned," in A. Griffin and S. M. Somermeyer, *The PDMA Toolbook 3 for New Product Development*, John Wiley & Sons, Inc., 2007, Ch. 15. Reprinted with permission of John Wiley & Sons, Inc.

[8]Much of this section is taken from Ken Bruss, "Gaining Competitive Advantage by Leveraging Lessons Learned," in A. Griffin and S. M. Somermeyer, *The PDMA Toolbook 3 for New Product Development* (New York: John Wiley, 2007), Chapter 15.

visit might suffice—but nevertheless it must be done. Some firms delay the AAR till a year after release, in order to assess how well the new product did, or whether it achieved its planned targets. Participants in the AAR should include the new product team leader and possibly just about anyone else who has some direct experience with the project: If this results in an unworkably large number of individuals, break them up into meaningful subgroups, run several AARs in parallel, then bring the subgroups together to discuss what had been learned. As is often the case in group discussion settings, having a good, trained facilitator can make all the difference.

Some products unintentionally live short lives. Occasionally, however, products are marketed that the managers know from the start will be on the market only a short time. Such products include fad products, temporary fillers of a hole in a product line, products keyed to a market participant's special needs, and *occasional* products. One producer of occasional products is Baskin-Robbins, which has a standing set of flavors always available and another stable of flavors that move into and out of the line.

Temporary products have much less need for launch management, mainly because there is nothing that can be done—everything is committed. Advertising and personal selling monies are needed to load up distributor/retailers (no out-of-stocks can be allowed because they represent permanently lost sales) and to build immediate sales. Sales promotion works only on awareness and trial. There are no follow-on products scheduled, production is contracted out if possible, inventories are moved out, and production runs are matched to the reorder rate. No long-term service facilities are built, prices are held steady (or at the most, reduced), and most effort after announcement is put into market intelligence needed to know when sales are leveling and heading down. By the time any launch problems are identified, the time to solve them is past.

Product Failure

Despite everyone's best efforts, products do sometimes fail or appear to be failing. When the product appears to be in decline, the firm first thinks of how additional money can best be spent, and strategy is reviewed. Of course, time permitting, the product can be changed or standby add-ons can be sent to market while longer-term changes are being made. If the market situation is particularly difficult and solutions lie only in longer-time product changes, it may be necessary to pull the product temporarily, or, at best, stop all promotion and hold the market in a freeze until the problem solution has been found. If things in the development area don't move along successfully fast, it is usually necessary to abandon the product; that is, to abandon the market opportunity. Most firms have many new product options and like to get their losers out of sight and out of mind. The politics are bad, people are scurrying to escape the sinking ship, critics are reminding everyone how they predicted this trouble, and so on. Of course, if new plants were built, if major promotional programs were undertaken, or in any other way major financial commitments were made, then there will be efforts to hold on—at least until there has been time to put through a relaunch.

FIGURE 19.9
A Stepwise
Product
Deletion
Process

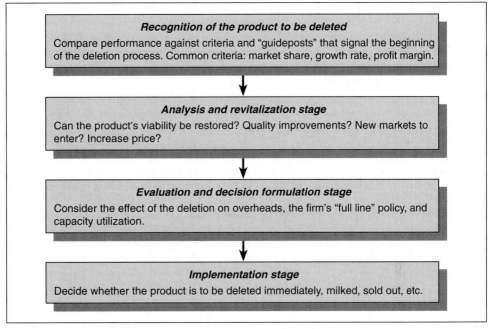

Source: From George J. Avlonitis, Susan J. Hart and Nikolaos X. Tzokas, "An Analysis of Product Deletion Scenarios," *Journal of Product Innovation Management* 17, no. 1, January 2000, pp. 41–56. Reprinted with permission of John Wiley & Sons, Inc.

The product deletion decision is obviously a complex one with a potentially strong ripple effect. One team of researchers has suggested a stepwise process for the product deletion decision (see Figure 19.9). In this process, the firm must first decide whether the product's performance merits consideration for deletion. It then explores ways by which the viability of the product might be restored through quality or price adjustments or perhaps targeting new markets. Before making the deletion decision, the firm must systematically evaluate the full effect of the deletion on overheads, expenses, and capacity utilization and also determine whether the deletion would leave a major hole in the firm's product line. Finally, if deletion is necessary or inevitable, its speed must be determined (i.e., get rid of the product immediately, milk it for several quarters or even years, sell it off, etc.).[9]

Some evidence exists that new-to-the-world product projects may be harder to shut down. In these cases, managers tend to be more optimistic about the chances of success, be more emotionally committed to the project, and be more likely to want to continue the project right through to launch. The Apple Newton personal digital assistant and RCA's SelectaVision videodisk system are both cases where the evaluation steps in the new products process identified strong signals indicating potential problems, but were ignored. In other cases, the evaluation is not done thoroughly, and clear Go/No Go decisions are not made. Some products that do get eliminated may even come back, possibly under another name. In our rush to

[9]George J. Avlonitis, Susan J. Hart, and Nikolaos X. Tzokas, "An Analysis of Product Deletion Scenarios," *Journal of Product Innovation Management*, 17(1), January 2000, pp. 41–56.

FIGURE 19.10 Consolidation Strategies at Work

About a hundred years ago, detachable, disposable paper collars were part of a waiter's uniform. As these fell out of style, there remained only one firm still making the collar. When this firm was acquired by another company, it sent out letters to its customers that the price of its paper collars would double. The new owner recognized that there was a small yet captive demand for this kind of collar.

A kitchen cabinet manufacturer bought a large wagon-wheel manufacturing plant, with the intention of turning it into a location for cabinet manufacture. It soon found that it had just taken over one of the last wagon-wheel plants in the U.S., and continued to sell wagon wheels profitably for some time thereafter.

Push lawnmowers declined in popularity as gasoline-powered mowers of all shapes and sizes, and riding mowers, took over the suburban lawn care market. One firm, American Lawnmower, had about a 95 percent share of the market for push mowers. In recent years, many homeowners have switched back to push mowers for their simplicity, environmental friendliness, and nostalgia, and sales have rebounded. In 1998 alone, American Lawnmower sold 250,000 units.

After transistors had completely replaced vacuum tubes in televisions, radios, and other devices, RCA and GE abandoned vacuum tube manufacture. One company located in Illinois realized that there would be demand for vacuum tubes in special applications, aggressively bought out small competitors, and achieved a profitable position in the market.

The advantage here is that there is little threat of new competition entering the market. (Would GE really want to reinvest in vacuum tubes at this point, or Ford in wagon wheels?)

Source: Examples are from Laurence P. Feldman, "From Paper Collars to Vacuum Tubes: Life at the End of the Product Life Cycle," *Visions,* October 1997, p. 10. Copyright © 1997 by Product Development and Management Association. Reproduced with permission of Product Development and Management Association via Copyright Clearance Center.

speed products to market quicker, we must not lose sight of the need to halt poor products sooner![10]

If a product or product line is discontinued, it may still hold revenue opportunities. It can be sold to another firm outright. Alternatively, the firm can sell the rights to the product or its brand name, its formulation or blueprints, its manufacturing process, its distribution channel, its technology or core subassemblies, or the whole business unit.[11] Another possibility is for the firm to consolidate its position—to become the "big fish" in an admittedly shrinking pond (see some examples in Figure 19.10). Actually, there is an advantage to this strategy: There is low threat of new competition entering the market. Any of these opportunities should be explored if feasible.

If **abandonment** is necessary, the manager's job is not finished. A lot of people need to be notified (including customers, governments, distributors, and trade groups). If persons or firms have become dependent on the product, it may be necessary to have a gradual stock-reduction program, a stockpiling of parts, and a period of repair service. The cost and required time duration of this after-the-fact support needs to be estimated.

[10]Jeffrey B. Schmidt and Roger J. Calantone, "Are Really New Product Development Projects Harder to Shut Down?" *Journal of Product Innovation Management,* 15(2), March 1998, pp. 111–123; and Jeffrey B. Schmidt and Roger J. Calantone, "Escalation of Commitment during New Product Development," *Journal of the Academy of Marketing Science,* 30(2), 2002, pp. 103–118.

[11]Patricia A. Katzfey, "Product Discontinuation," in M. Rosenau, A. Griffin, G. Castellion, and N. Anscheutz (eds.), *The PDMA Handbook of New Product Development* (New York: John Wiley, 1996), pp. 413–425.

Summary

This chapter brings us to the point where we introduce the product. We have the product, we have the marketing program for it, and we are prepared to control its way to success.

The requirements of launch management are a plan, measurement of progress in the market, analysis of events to determine if prearranged contingency actions should be put into play, and continuing study to ensure that any problem becomes known as soon as possible so action can be taken to avert or at least ameliorate it.

Launch management and tracking are especially tough because most of the activity is out in the marketplace, variables will change, and measurements are difficult and expensive (not like walking through the factory in the eyeball control method). But the methodology is available, and when the situation warrants this effort, a new products manager can certainly gain from it.

We can now turn our attention to a topic ever-present in new products work: Are there public policy issues involved in the new product's manufacture, distribution, use, or disposal? Are there ethical issues involved? What the developer thinks is, of course, not the point. What does the public think? What do government people think? This issue is the subject of Chapter 20.

Applications More questions from that interview with the company president.

1. "Thanks for telling me about that launch management idea you were studying. But, look, I'm a bit mixed up on one thing. You mentioned (1) critical events, (2) control events, and (3) tracking variables. You say you have to list all three things? Isn't one event likely to be on all three lists? For example, take awareness of the new product's key determinant attribute. Not getting it is a critical event, selecting it for control makes it a control event, and tracking it makes it a tracking variable. Right? Help!"

2. "I've had occasion several times over the past year to see a new product land in trouble—great expectations and terrible sales. And the saddest part is that so many people try so hard to deny the inevitable—the product has bombed, and the quicker one gets away from it the better. Otherwise, it's just sending good money after bad. In fact, I'm going to make a speech to that effect at our next general executive meeting, and you could do me a favor. Would you please develop a list of all possible reasons why someone might want to string a loser along? That would help me be sure I've answered all of the objections before I give the speech."

3. "If I remember right, the whole idea of launch management depends partially on having a track or plan that each variable should follow if everything is going okay. I believe you showed me some figures with those plan lines on them. But it seems to me those plan lines are just pure conjecture, at least in the case of really new products. For example, one time I was reading about Arco Solar Inc. (a division of Atlantic Richfield). It had a solar-powered plate that could be set on a car's dashboard and feed power to the car's battery. That power was

to make up for the natural self-discharge of a battery, the drain from electric clocks, and so on. Now, how in the world would they know what the normal path of awareness or trial would be? Are they unable to use launch management? Lots of our divisions are developing really new things like that."

Case: Levitra[12]

Erectile dysfunction (ED) is a condition that carries an obvious social stigma for many men. ED can occur for a variety of reasons: cardiovascular disease, medications such as diuretics and beta blockers, or other factors such as smoking or prostate surgery. Prior to 1998, men suffering from ED had few choices for treatment. Penile injections and suppositories had their own drawbacks and did not provide consistent results. Other men seeking to overcome ED turned to psychotherapy, surgery, or vacuum-related devices. The market was ripe for a safe, oral medication that would increase blood flow and thereby provide the desired effect. On top of this, many men with ED find it difficult even to speak with their doctors about the condition; a recent study suggested that 90 percent of patients have not consulted their physicians, and of those, only about half were receiving treatment. These numbers suggest that the total size of the market for Viagra might exceed 25 million men just in the United States, with this figure likely to double by the year 2025.

In 1998, with great promotional support, Pfizer launched Viagra, the first effective and safe oral treatment for ED. Viagra (sildenafil) showed impressive results in treating ED; according to a Johns Hopkins study at the time, Viagra was showing 65 percent effectiveness rates. It seemed impossible to avoid the launch of Viagra that year. Prominent politician Bob Dole was selected as the spokesperson for broadcast advertising, the theme of which was that it was acceptable for men to talk about ED with their physicians. To add to the promotional fanfare, a Viagra race car soon appeared in the NASCAR circuit. It was clear that the market was eagerly awaiting this product: By 2002, Viagra sales revenue was in the $1.7 billion range.

Other drug companies could hardly fail to take notice of this emerging market. It is true that Viagra was not a silver bullet. About 30 percent of users showed no positive results from taking Viagra, even in its highest dose (100 milligrams). Further, it requires about an hour after taking Viagra for results to occur, and the results last about four hours before wearing off. There were also a few minor side effects noted: headache, nasal congestion, and, interestingly, an altering of blue vision in some individuals. So perhaps research could identify a compound similar to Viagra but lacking these side effects or offering other benefits. But that would be only half of the solution: Even if such a compound is identified, how could it ever take on the popular, well-known Viagra brand in the marketplace?

In August 2003, GlaxoSmithKline and Bayer launched Levitra. This new compound is a direct competitor to Viagra and is in fact in the same class of pharmaceuticals. GlaxoSmithKline and Bayer conducted tests to demonstrate the superior performance

---

[12]This case is based on several public sources, including the Web sites www.webmd.com, www.bayer.com, www.gsk.com, and various news articles reported on www.reuters.com during 2003.

of Levitra. One study in particular showed that Levitra was effective in men who, most of the time, did not respond to Viagra treatment. Levitra also offered some dosing advantages: Results began to occur 16 minutes after taking and last about five hours: Both of these figures show improvement over Viagra's performance. In addition, Levitra does not impair blue vision.

Despite the performance and dosing advantages, GlaxoSmithKline and Bayer took no chances in the launch of this product. Former football star and coach Mike Ditka was recruited as the spokesperson. Like Dole, he would be recognized by his target audience as a strong, masculine role model and would help encourage more men to seek treatment for ED. GlaxoSmithKline and Bayer have become sponsors of the NFL. The Levitra tagline seems thoroughly appropriate: "Stay in the game— when you're in the zone it's all good." GlaxoSmithKline and Bayer relied on their existing global marketing and distribution networks to narrow the gap between the two drugs and to get worldwide distribution and acceptance of Levitra. Further, given the importance of cost to managed care providers, Levitra was launched at a lower price point: Thirty Levitra pills cost between $291 and $299 depending on the strength; comparable prices for Viagra ranged from $7 to $25 higher.

Within the first few months of its launch, Levitra captured about half of Viagra's market share, and, seeking protection, Pfizer is assessing whether Levitra constitutes a patent infringement on Viagra.

Clearly, GlaxoSmithKline and Bayer prioritized ED in its research efforts, given the phenomenal success (and market potential) of Viagra. The performance superiority of Levitra was evident, at least for some Viagra patients, and the price point made it the drug of choice in today's health care climate. One cannot argue about the choice of spokesperson or advertising message, nor about GlaxoSmithKline and Bayer's ability to launch a new product into the global marketplace effectively. What does the case tell you about first mover advantage? Is Levitra's sustainable advantage assured? If you're managing this brand for GlaxoSmithKline, what would you be most concerned about, and what could you do?

Case: SpinVox[13]

Christina Domecq and Daniel Daulton cofounded a new venture, SpinVox, in London in 2003. The vision of SpinVox was to develop and market a new message technology: voice-to-screen. The principle is easy to understand: A caller leaves a voice-mail message. The message is converted into text, then routed to one's e-mail inbox or to a cell phone as a text message. The system is powered by speech recognition software coupled with some specially developed and patented technology.

Given the rapid growth in messaging of all kinds, it was felt that the market was wide open for such a product. Plus, conventional voicemail retrieval poses its own set of problems. You might be unavailable or busy when a call comes in, but when

---

[13]This case was derived from Bruno Giussani, "Voicemail Breaks into Print," businessweek .com, January 8, 2007, and information from the SpinVox Web site, www.spinvox.com. In reality, SpinVox launched in the United States in late 2006, but the case is written as if this launch has not yet occurred.

you return the call the sender is now unavailable; phone tag is frustrating. Just as annoying are long, rambling messages (is this person *ever* going to leave his phone number?), or, conversely, detailed messages spoken so quickly that you must listen two or three times. In fact, Christine hit on the idea of voicemail text conversion out of frustration at the voicemail she received from her consulting clients.

SpinVox launched in Great Britain in 2005, and by the end of 2006, it was starting to do business in Spain and France. It was expected that it would have a presence in Germany by the end of 2007. There are currently 120,000 users Europewide (though mostly in Britain) and the system now can handle French, Spanish, and German calls as well as English. The company has grown from its two founders to about 150 employees. A typical customer pays five British pounds (about $10) per month and has about 20 voicemails per month transcribed.

Customers see plenty of advantages to SpinVox. Someone accustomed to SMS text messaging appreciates having the whole message text appear, rather than just a notification of a new voicemail. A person who could not take a phone call at a business meeting could surreptitiously glance at the screen of his or her cell phone to see if the call is important without disturbing anything. And users speak very highly about transcription accuracy. A few naysayers note that background noise or thick accents cause problems: Imagine if "I can't meet you at noon" is transcribed as "I can meet you at noon!"

SpinVox claims many advantages, in particular to business users: a 50 percent reduction in "slam-downs," a 17 percent increase in text traffic, and a 92 percent return message rate.

SpinVox sees the U.S. market as being their next logical expansion target. As was the case in their European expansion, it is company policy to have launch management plans. You have been called in to assist. Your job is to prepare a list of possible problems, narrowing them down to the ones the company president will have to do something about, and then planning how SpinVox should track them, and what they should do if any of these problems occurred.

Public Policy Issues

Setting

Along the way through the past 19 chapters, we have been dealing with the various problems of developing and launching a new product. But, to simplify things, we have deferred until now some major questions of public policy. They concern the relationship between the firm (people, product, whatever) and the citizenry. In every country on earth, there are ways in which the new product function is limited or directed, and usually for very good reason. So managers need to understand the rules, and they need to understand the edges of the law where issues are usually under movement or unclear.

Chapter 20 gives the life cycle of a public concern, discusses the attitudes of business regarding product innovation and public policy, and deals with the most critical of the concerns—product liability. It then goes into the other concerns, such as the environment, and some related managerial issues.

Bigger Picture: A Cycle of Concerns

The environment has been on the public consciousness more than ever before, and many companies have decided to seek solutions in their own ways. Walmart has looked into building low-energy stores, while General Electric is building ultra-high-efficiency products. Why so much attention all of a sudden? Certainly, media coverage of environmental concerns has been high, and the U.S. Environmental Protection Agency has established a comprehensive climate policy. These factors have led to greater awareness at the grassroots level. CEOs sometimes explain their sudden environmental concerns as a "personal awakening" to climate threats. But there is more to it: Big investors know that limits on carbon dioxide outputs may be coming, and sooner than expected, so they exert pressure on firms to find a solution. The environment is squarely in the mainstream, and if they hadn't been doing so already, firms have to develop policy on what to do next.[1]

---

[1]Michelle Conlin (ed.), "The Best Ideas." *BusinessWeek,* December 18, 2006, pp. 97–107; and the U.S. Environmental Protection Agency Web site, www.epa.gov/climatechange/policy/index.html.

FIGURE 20.1
Life Cycle
of a Public
Concern

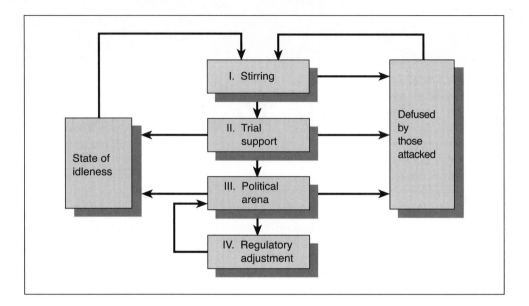

The fast-food companies have also been under public scrutiny. In 2003, McDonald's had been sued by parents of obese teenagers, who felt that their fast-food diet contributed to their girls' heart disease, diabetes, high cholesterol, and other conditions. (The suit was thrown out by a federal judge.) The company was also the target of the film *Supersize Me*, released in 2004. Many (not just within McDonald's) criticized the movie as a misrepresentation of facts (one member of the Competitive Enterprise Institute suggested the movie should be classified under "Comedy" at Blockbuster). Nevertheless, McDonald's committed to a "balanced lifestyles" program in 2004, which included public education as well as changes in the menu and in its advertising. As an example, famed personal trainer Bob Greene was recruited to visit major cities to talk about exercise and healthy eating. While things may be more under control in North America for McDonald's, their menu offerings still face harsh criticism in France, Britain, and elsewhere.[2] Similarly, the fast-food restaurants, as well as grocery chains, have had to make major decisions regarding the use of partially hydrogenated oils (trans fat) used in cooking and frying and which have been linked to heart disease.[3]

All public pressure situations go through a life cycle of the following phases (see Figure 20.1). See if you can identify each of these phases in the emergency of global warming public policy concerns or fast-food nutrition.

[2]Jonathan Wald, "McDonald's Obesity Suit Tossed." money.com, February 17, 2003; and the McDonald's listing on the SourceWatch Web site, www.sourcewatch.org. For an international perspective, see Peter Allen, "France Targets 'Le Snack' in Obesity Battle," telegraph.co.uk, March 2, 2007; and Catherine Elsworth, "Restaurants 'Promoting Extreme Eating' in U.S.," telegraph.co.uk, February 28, 2007.
[3]For one view on how complex the trans fat issue is, see Steven J. Milloy, "Trans Fat Hysteria Could Be Lawsuit Bonanza," foxnews.com, November 9, 2006.

Phase I: Stirring

Individuals begin to sound off long before enough people have been injured or irritated to cause a general reaction. Letters to company presidents, complaints in newspaper articles, letters to political representatives, and tentative expressions of concern by knowledgeable authorities are typical of phase I. Most people ignore these periods, but they are easy to identify, looking back. Consequently, the stirring phase may last a long time—decades, in fact.

The problem for new products managers is that they don't know what will happen. Flare up, or die away?

Phase II: Trial Support

As the stirrings over an issue increase, a champion may decide to take it on as a cause. Such champions used to be individuals and were often unknown, as Ralph Nader was when he tackled auto safety. Today, cause support tends to come from organizations whose leaders are attempting to marry the basic unrest in a situation with a desire for contribution and publicity. The key question to these organizations often is, "How widespread is the unpublicized unrest?" Or, "How dramatic can the headlines be made?" This may sound crass, but remember, there are scores of budding issues at any time, and an organization may lose its power if it squanders its scarce resources on issues that die out.

In phase II, a complex set of loosely affiliated parties may emerge over time. In July 1996, *USA Today* reported the danger of seating children under 13 directly in front of a car air bag. At the time, automakers, regulators, insurers, and consumer advocacy groups (who had pushed for air bags) all shared responsibility for the fact that parents were not warned of this danger. By 1998, however, parents who had lost children through such accidents were teaming with the consumer advocacy groups to take the automakers to court—something the advocacy groups have much experience in.[4]

In any event, phase II is a period when the would-be leader and the muted cause are on the stump, seeking a political base. If achieved, the action moves to phase III unless the industry being attacked can defuse the situation or the cause fails to capture broad support.

Phase III: The Political Arena

By the time an issue has acquired a political base among the voting public, the opportunity for defusing has usually passed. Now, companies must gird up for political battle in state and/or federal legislatures or in the various regulatory arenas. The issue is the content of new laws or regulations, and companies usually recognize the widespread consumer demands and are only trying to achieve the least costly and least restrictive mode of meeting them. Occasionally, companies fight vigorously against settlement. The cereal industry did, and won on several dimensions. However, the political base is usually all the cause leader needs to

---

[4]Jayne O'Donnell, "Child-Death Cases Say Automakers Failed to Act," *USA Today*, July 13, 1998, p. 3B.

force some modification in a practice, one severe enough to require legislation or a court ruling.

Phase IV: Regulatory Adjustment

New regulatory legislation is rarely precise, and this imprecision leads to a period of jockeying by the adversaries over its interpretation. The Consumer Product Safety Act, for example, directed the **Consumer Product Safety Commission** to order the seizure of any "imminently hazardous consumer products," four terms each impossible to define. Imprecision may well be a necessary or even wise approach in regulation. The phase often lasts for years, and sometimes general shifts in a country's political thinking cause various issues to move into or out of the idle state.

Business Attitudes toward Product Issues

Business firms deal with public policy issues on a much broader base than just new products. So they have reached a structure of beliefs on this matter of interface between business and society. Most of those beliefs support product innovation, and society agrees. Granted, there are some issues that we haven't yet figured out. For example, how do we pay the costs of product misuse where the consumer was unable to read and understand labels? What is the responsibility of a food company whose customers want great taste but whose government wants quality nutrition? In general, most of the headlines today are for problems that came up years ago, and our concerns are "at the margin"—that is, dealing in areas of temporary uncertainty and change.

For example, around the year 2000, people were honestly confused on whether sharing of music files on Napster and similar Web sites was legal, ethical, or somewhat justified. After court injunctions, well-publicized large fines to abusers, attempts by the music labels to set up fair, fee-based systems for legal downloading, and the emergence of the iPod, we have moved toward a solution.

The new product that causes unexpected concern on the public policy front is probably the result of careless management. Note, *unexpected*. A lot of our problems we expect and in most cases have methods to avoid them, or hedge bets, or prepare to deal with them. Of course, no manager can walk through the minefield of federal and regional legislators, regulators, trial lawyers, aggrieved customers, and leaders of popular causes without occasionally tripping up.

Current Problem Areas

New products managers face many specific problem areas as they attempt to deal with social and legal pressures—product liability is the most complex, and at the moment the most frustrating, partly because of the seriousness of the potential suits and the costs of error.

These issues are worldwide, though our discussion will mainly use American examples. Members of the European Union are still wrestling with the product liability question because of their 1985 commitment to strict liability. Although going slower than it was supposed to, the directive will apparently be implemented. Germany is a world leader in environment. China has only recently instituted a product liability law, while many other nations in the world have yet even to face this issue.

Product Liability

The scenario here is simple: You buy a product and are injured. The injury may have come when you carried the product home, when you opened it, when you stored it, when you used it, when you tried to repair it, or when you disposed of it. If you were injured and if you think the maker or the reseller of the product did (or didn't do) something that caused the injury, then you have a product liability claim. If guilty, the accused party is liable for the cost and the pain of the injury, plus punitive (punishing) damages as well.

Historically, **product liability** applied to goods, not services, and there have been many lost attempts to extend the law to cover services. Yet services are products (both in fact and as we use the terms in this book); they are sold and bought in good faith, injuries do occur, and some redress should be possible. For example, an engineering consulting firm gave an opinion that a building was in good shape; the buyer later found this untrue when an injury took place. Negligence on services can produce a product liability case.

How important is product liability? Most suits are settled out of court so we don't have good dollar data. Many billions of dollars are at stake (though suits are not as common as the press on asbestos, breast implants, and cars make it appear), and as a result, it can get complicated. As Figure 20.2 shows, the costs can be enormous for the company involved.

Typology of Injury Sources

Here is a list of the ways we get into trouble, and most of them are double trouble on *new* products.

1. Many products have *inherent risks*. For example, blood transfusion carries the risk of hepatitis infection, and dynamite will explode. Because the risk cannot be avoided, we get more understanding in the courts.
2. *Design defects* can cause the manufacture of an unsafe product in three different ways. First, the design may create a *dangerous condition,* say a steam vaporizer whose center of gravity is so high that the unit is likely to spill. Second, an essential *safety device* may be absent. For example, a hair dryer may lack an overheat cutoff switch. Third, the design may call for *inadequate materials,* which perform their function at first but may eventually deteriorate and become dangerous.
3. *Defects in manufacture* have perhaps always been a new products problem. Inadequate quality techniques may result in defective units even if the product is well designed. Poorly welded ladders are an example.

FIGURE 20.2   The Toyota Recalls of 2009–2010

In April of 2010, Toyota Motor Co. thought the news could not get worse . . . but it did. The company had just agreed to pay a large fine to the U.S. government – the largest fine ever imposed on an automaker – when it heard that there was a stability control problem with its luxury SUV models Lexus GX 460 and Land Cruiser Prado. This recall affected 9,400 vehicles in the U.S. alone and 34,000 vehicles worldwide. The consumer magazine *Consumer Reports* was reporting that these SUVs slid excessively during sharp turns.

Late in 2009, problems arose with the accelerator pedal in several models which allegedly sometimes stuck. In a later recall, the spare tire carrier on Sienna minivans was found to have a faulty cable, resulting in the tire falling off the vehicle. Including the luxury SUVs, about nine million Toyotas have been recalled since November 2009. The $16.4 million fine was due to government allegations that Toyota concealed information related to the sticking accelerator pedal. Government regulators believed that Toyota knew about the accelerator problem, or should have known about it, several months before. Toyota decided not to fight the fine to avoid a lengthy dispute and to focus instead on strengthening quality assurance. Under the terms of the fine, Toyota admitted no wrongdoing, but still faced several lawsuits filed by crash victims and their families. The amount at stake could be in the billions of dollars.

Regarding the SUV recall, a software update was offered to Lexus dealers by the end of April, to be installed in recalled GX 460s to fix the steering problem. The update would take no more than an hour at the dealership. At the time, the chief quality officer for North America, Steve St. Angelo, said that "Toyota's objective is to provide a high level of safety and quality, while meeting or surpassing governmental regulations . . . our engineers have conducted tests to confirm the [steering control] performance issue raised by *Consumer Reports*, and we are confident this . . . software update addresses the concern."

While the SUV recall affected a relatively small number of vehicles, it was felt to be another significant black mark against Toyota, for a couple of reasons: the company was already taking heat in the press for the earlier recalls and had just paid a huge fine, and the *Consumer Reports* recommendation of "do not buy" also gathered media attention because this rating is rarely given. Altogether, a lot of precious brand equity was lost relatively suddenly, and as of mid 2010 it was up to Toyota to take action to build it back up again, through a focus on quality assurance and also through improving its publicity efforts.

Source: Nick Bunkley, "Lexus to Recall S.U.V. in Another Black Mark to Reputation," *New York Times*, April 20, 2010, p. B3.

4. The manufacturer may produce an acceptable product but *fail to provide adequate instructions for use or warnings against particular uses.* If used improperly, the lawnmower is a potentially dangerous device. The instructions should tell the user how to use it *and* how not to use it. But courts are much more interested in how strong the warnings are against misuse, even of the unforeseeable kind. With the high risk of lawsuits, firms often go to what seem to be absurd lengths to ensure they have adequate warning labels (thus a lawnmower may sport a label reading, "do not pick up the mower to trim hedges"; see Figure 20.3). What constitutes adequate warning will never be known for sure, but here is what courts have used in recent years. The warning should be placed conspicuously on the product; it should be where the user most likely can be expected to see it; it should communicate the level of danger; it should instruct the user in how to avoid the potential hazard; sellers should not engage in marketing activities that vitiate an otherwise adequate warning; and it should not be accompanied by statements that the product is safe. The user should be told what may happen if the warning is ignored. Makers must also be prepared to prove that the user *got* the warning, not just that the maker *posted* it.

FIGURE 20.3
Which Are the
Real Product
Warning
Labels?

1. On a disposable razor: "Do not use this product during an earthquake."
2. On a rock garden: "Eating rocks may lead to broken teeth."
3. On a roll of Life Savers: "Not for use as a flotation device."
4. On a hair dryer: "Do not use while sleeping."
5. On a piano: "Harmful or fatal if swallowed."
6. On a cardboard windshield sun shade: "Warning: Do not drive with sun shield in place."
7. On shin guards: "Shin guards cannot protect any part of the body they do not cover."
8. On syrup of ipecac: "Caution: may induce vomiting."
9. On an iron: "Do not iron clothes while being worn."
10. On a plastic sled: "Not to be eaten or burned."
11. On work gloves: "For best results, do not leave at crime scene."
12. On a cell phone: "Don't try to dry your phone in a microwave oven."
13. On a carpenter's router: "This product not intended for use as a dentist's drill."
14. On a blender: "Not for use as an aquarium."
15. On a stroller: "Always remove child from stroller before folding."
16. On a washing machine: "Do not put any person in this washer."
17. On a fireplace log: "Caution: risk of fire."
18. On a laser printer cartridge: "Do not eat toner."
Solutions appear at the end of the Chapter 20 case.

Sources: '20/20' report, ABC Television, October 28, 1998, Michigan Lawsuit Abuse Watch Web site (www.mlaw.org), and other sources.

5. Finally, dangers sometimes appear *after use,* and the manufacturer's liability may continue into this period. For example, manufacturers of spray cans have to urge that the discards not be burned in fireplaces.

Note: We must approach the product liability matter cautiously because of the tendency of the press to distort problems. For example, it was widely publicized recently that an overweight physician with a heart condition had bought a Sears mower, suffered a heart attack while starting the mower, and was awarded $1.8 million. In fact, court records showed that the mower mechanism *was defective* and required an *abnormally large number of pulls*. The doctor, incidentally, *did not have a heart condition*. Casual readers of the press rarely have enough information to reach a good judgment, though they do form opinions.

The Four Legal Bases for Product Liability

The four main routes to liability for a product manufacturer are shown in Figure 20.4. All cases require a basis for the claim, and the manufacturer has to have done something—at the very minimum, make, sell, or lease the product to someone.[5]

Negligence

In the 1880s, under common law, injury claimants had to prove that (1) the manufacturer was *negligent* in operations, let the product become defective and thus injurious, and (2) there was direct sale from the manufacturer to the injured

[5]A good general source on the following issues is George D. Cameron, *Business Law: Legal Environment, Transactions, and Regulation* (Plano, Texas: Business Publications, 1989).

FIGURE 20.4   **Forms and Sources of Product Liability**

A manufacturer or reseller may be found guilty of product liability via these four routes:			
	Negligence	**Warranty**	**Strict Liability**	**Misrepresentation**
Source	Common law, 1800s; Once required privity, but dropped in 1960.	Uniform Commercial Code; Enhanced by Magnuson Moss Act.	Court decisions, 1960s.	Common law.
Conditions	Defective product by design or manufacture, and with failure to warn.	Defective product: Implied warranty of merchantability or of fitness for particular purpose. Express warranty; Untrue claim.	Defective product: No requirement for negligence or privity, and no disclaimer is allowed. Reasonably foreseeable.	Untrue claim or misrepresentation that led to injury. User relied on it. No need for defective product.
Defense	Not negligence; product not defective	Not implied by common usage; Not actually stated; Normal puffery.	Buyer knew, so assumed risk. Unforeseeable misuse. Product not defective.	Was truthful. Normal puffery. Buyer should have known better.

user *(privity).* Perhaps a wagon maker was careless and failed to attach a wheel securely to the axle. The wheel came off, the driver was injured, and **negligence** was easy to establish. The wagon maker failed to exercise ordinary care (the care that a reasonable person would use). The mistake could be made by salespeople, advertising, labeling, retailers, and wholesalers because one aspect of negligence is *failure to warn.*

In 1916 a court ruled that a defectively manufactured product was "inherently dangerous"; it didn't have to be sold direct. By 1966, every state had accepted this line of reasoning, and lack of privity as a defense against negligence was useless.

Warranty

It was still difficult to prove negligence. Thus warranty, a development of the first half of the 20th century, is relevant. **Warranty** is a promise, and if a promise can be proved and is not fulfilled, the seller can be charged with breach of warranty, whether negligent or not. A careful manufacturer of a new product may still be found guilty of causing injury.

Warranty is express or implied. An *express warranty* is any statement of fact made by the manufacturer about a product, whether made by salespeople, retailers, or others. The major issue with express warranty is the degree of puffing a court will allow. *Implied warranty* arises when a maker offers a product for a given use. An implied *warranty of fitness for a particular purpose* is part of the sales contract and means the product is of average quality and can be used for the purposes for which such products are customarily used. The buyer is justified to depend on the seller being right—an expert who knows how people customarily use the item.

But there was constant court bickering over who said what to whom and whether the distributor could have known as much as the maker. Our society is too complex for law that confuses more than clarifies, so we next saw the development of the strict liability concept.

Strict Liability

Under the concept of **strict liability**, the seller of an item has the responsibility for *not putting a defective product on the market*. If the product is defective, the manufacturer can be sued by any injured party even if that party was only a bystander. *There need be no negligence; there need be no direct sale; no statement by the seller will relieve the liability.*

However, the manufacturer may be able to use three key defenses. The first is *assumption of risk*. If the user of the product learns of the defect and continues to use it regardless of the danger, a suit may not be sustained. Second, the manufacturer has the defense of *unforeseeable misuse*, meaning the injury occurred because the user misused the product in a way that the seller could not reasonably have anticipated. Managers of new products may lack the expected experience, yet courts expect them to be completely marketwise. Third, the defense may be that the product, though causing injury, is not defective. For example, a man hit his eye on the pointed top of a small ventilation window on the side of his car. Though he leaned over and accidentally bumped the window, the jury held that this injury did not mean the window was defective. Presumably, the plaintiff should have been more careful.

Misrepresentation

Actually, a product itself doesn't have to be defective (as it does in the three other situations above) so long as an injury took place when the product was used on **misrepresentation** (intentional or not) by the seller. These cases are rare, but an example was the helmet manufacturer who made a helmet for motorcyclists and showed a motorcyclist wearing one in a picture on the carton. An experienced police officer bought one for use while riding on duty, but the helmet was not made to be used as a safety helmet. The court ruled there had been misrepresentation.

Other Legislation

Many industries have had unique problems leading to specialized legislation. The Food and Drug Administration, for example, was created in 1906. There are restrictions on alcoholic beverages, automobiles, scientific instruments, metals, and scores more. Attention frequently goes to the Consumer Product Safety Act and its Consumer Product Safety Commission (CPSC). Although the commission's direct impact has been much less than anticipated, the indirect impact has been substantial. It has the power to set standards for products, order the recall of products (see next section), issue public warnings about possible problem products, stop the marketing of new products, ban present or proposed products, and levy substantial civil and criminal penalties. Manufacturers have made many changes to avoid trouble with the law.

Planning for the Product Recall[6]

It seems that any firm may one day face a product recall. To ensure that the recall will be handled properly and successfully, there are steps that can be taken prior to, during, and after the recall.

Prior to the Recall

Designate a single individual as the recall program coordinator. He or she will be the spokesperson to the media and to regulatory bodies. Make sure this individual is well informed in dealing with the media and will not buckle under the intense media questioning that might occur. Also, make sure there are effective channels for communicating with consumers as well as intermediaries. Many firms use returned warranty cards to keep track of their customers, but often very few of these are actually returned, and in any event later owners are not tracked. Perhaps an incentive for sending in the card or a simpler way to register the product (such as a phone number printed right on the product) could be offered.

During the Recall

Assess the safety risk and take corrective action. When a single blood sugar level meter was found to be defective, LifeScan (a Johnson & Johnson subsidiary) recalled all 600,000 meters then on the market. Make sure final customers as well as intermediaries are informed of the risks. Mattel had no trouble recalling all of the defective Cabbage Patch Snacktime Kids (in which some children got their hair or fingers caught) from store shelves, but getting them back from consumers proved far more challenging. More recently, toys painted with lead paint posed the same problem. Also, recall notices mailed to consumers that resemble junk mail are likely to be thrown out. Finally, car companies strive to make the recall experience as pleasant as possible for customers.

After the Recall

Strive to restore the company's reputation and to monitor recall effectiveness. After the Perrier benzene scare of 1990, new bottles were marked "nouvelle production" to reassure customers they were safe. Some Schwan's ice cream was tainted with salmonella in the shippers' tanker trucks. In response, the company required that shippers devote their truck fleet only to Schwan's ice cream and not use their trucks to carry any other products, and tested all ice cream mix delivered to the plant for salmonella. After the pet food recall of 2007, Procter & Gamble placed full-page newspaper ads reassuring pet owners that their Iams and Eukanuba dry pet foods were safe and unaffected by the recall; safety information was also prominent on the brand Web sites. Finally, in the classic Tylenol tainting case in the early 1980s, Johnson & Johnson relaunched the product in gelcap and geltab form and in tamperproof bottles; sales were soon higher than they had been before the tainting incident.

[6]This section (including many of the examples) derives from Barry Berman, "Planning for the Inevitable Product Recall," *Business Horizons*, March–April 1999, pp. 69–77.

Attempts at Standardization and Clarification

Manufacturers have had special troubles dealing with the varying laws of 50 states and object to cases where a user changes safety equipment on a machine and then sues when injured, or when a machine was built before better technology was discovered, yet they are responsible by today's standards. Their biggest complaint concerns the discouragement of innovation. High-technology firms are reluctant to develop new products if there are major risks of trouble. Pharmaceutical companies call it "drug lag." New medical devices have almost ceased to come out. Evidence is piling up on this point.[7]

Many in government agree with these concerns, and attempts have been made to pass federal legislation to settle them. Opposition by consumer and trial lawyer groups have beaten these proposals back every year. There is some progress in particular product areas, such as general aviation, where some of the above issues have been taken care of selectively.

Environmental Needs

Public policy debate on new products is a huge topic, and in a book like this we can only scan the issues, point out why they are important, and cite some sources for readers who would like to investigate one or another of them. In this section we explore environmental concerns and needs.

A new product is said to hurt the environment (1) if its raw materials are scarce or hard to get to, (2) if its design or manufacture causes pollution or excess power usage, (3) if its use causes pollution, and (4) if any disposal problem cannot be handled by recycling. Firms seek to act in a socially responsible manner by including such "green" concerns into their product development efforts. Customers and stakeholders expect it, and increasingly, government measures are requiring it. Generally, *green product innovation* refers to either new product design or delivery that reduces negative impacts on the environment.

All too often, though, there is a gap between good intentions and execution.[8] Managers want to do the right thing environmentally, but are under pressure to make profits, especially when the economy is weak. Therefore, strong support for environmental concerns from top management is critical. The best success in green product development occurs when the firm aligns its business objectives with its environmental initiatives. If this occurs, product teams will feel supported in pursuing projects that have longer-term environmental benefits and not feel obliged to "pick the low-hanging fruit" (make only incremental

---

[7]Laura Jereski, "Block That Innovation," *Forbes*, January 18, 1993, p. 48. See also Paul A. Herbig and James E. Golden, "Innovation and Product Liability," *Industrial Marketing Management*, 1994, pp. 245–255, and W. Kip Viscusi and Michael J. Moore, "Product Liability, Research and Development, and Innovation," *Journal of Political Economy*, 1993, pp. 161–184.

[8]For a good discussion of these issues, see Jim Todhunter, "Going Green Without Seeing Red," *Visions*, 33(3), October 2009, pp. 6–7.

green improvements to their products). Firms that take a leadership position in green product development may discover that this becomes their sustainable competitive advantage. Government mandates on fuel emission, waste management, and other environmental issues are becoming more stringent; managers can effectively incorporate these mandates into their long-term business objectives.

A firm that effectively combines green business practices with achieving revenue objectives is Leggett & Platt, a manufacturer of box spring mattresses. This firm developed a new semi-folding box spring mattress, which provides added value to customers (anyone who has ever tried to move a box spring up several flights of stairs can immediately see the value!) and boosted their bottom line. At the same time, product delivery is greener: The folded mattress takes up about one-fourth the space of a conventional box spring, therefore four times as many mattresses can be loaded onto a truck, and a significant reduction in the carbon footprint is achieved.[9]

In addition to these concerns, there is still much we do not know—even about the environmental effects of our new products. Social costs and social benefits are not easily measured. Even environmental firms have found the swamp here—such as when Greenpeace badly overstated the damage done by destruction of oil drilling platforms in the North Sea. Interestingly, we are finding we don't even know what happens in landfills—new anthropological studies show that material in dumps reacts differently than we thought.

Improvements are many, involving action in all of the needed areas. Honeywell asks buyers of its home smoke alarms to return them to the factory for disposal. Some firms have begun market testing in Germany and Scandinavian countries to pass what is felt to be the world's toughest greenness test.[10] Toyota researchers were working on developing new, unique trees that can absorb car pollutants and may counteract global warming.[11] Cars pollute less, recycled paper is appearing in packaging, and so forth. Of course, there are occasional bloopers—P&G was congratulated for its ecology-friendly Ariel Ultra detergent in Europe, but was blindsided when critics found they had used animal testing in its development.

There are many times, even today, when the cost-benefit analyses come out wrong, but a strong need for environmental protection is here to stay. We are even learning better ways to do "green" marketing. Years ago, many firms noted that making "environmentally friendly" claims and catering to "green" concerns was becoming a hot marketing strategy—which resulted in exaggerated claims of environmental benefits on packaging and in advertising, and ultimately, increased

[9]This example is from Todhunter, op. cit.
[10]Though maybe not a precursor for the rest of the world, the situation in Germany is worthy of study. New laws implemented in the middle 1990s sharply changed the new products picture. For example, much product packaging (including foam packing and aspirin boxes) must either be returned by retailers to the manufacturers who used it, or returned by consumers to retailers who will shunt it to recyclers who will then bill manufacturers for the costs.
[11]See Emily Thornton, "Only God and Toyota Can Make a Tree," *BusinessWeek*, March 30, 1998, p. 58.

FIGURE 20.5
Public Policy Problems and the New Products Process

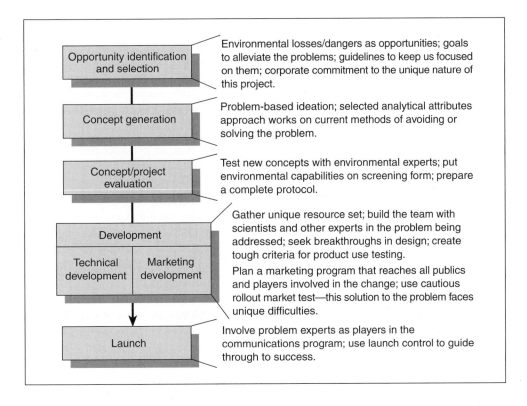

Opportunity identification and selection — Environmental losses/dangers as opportunities; goals to alleviate the problems; guidelines to keep us focused on them; corporate commitment to the unique nature of this project.

Concept generation — Problem-based ideation; selected analytical attributes approach works on current methods of avoiding or solving the problem.

Concept/project evaluation — Test new concepts with environmental experts; put environmental capabilities on screening form; prepare a complete protocol.

Development / Technical development / Marketing development — Gather unique resource set; build the team with scientists and other experts in the problem being addressed; seek breakthroughs in design; create tough criteria for product use testing.

Plan a marketing program that reaches all publics and players involved in the change; use cautious rollout market test—this solution to the problem faces unique difficulties.

Launch — Involve problem experts as players in the communications program; use launch control to guide through to success.

customer skepticism.[12] Thankfully, it is now no longer enough to slap a green label with pictures of ferns and waterfalls, or the words "environmentally friendly," on the product. It is now up to us to focus on environmental consequences of our products throughout the new products process: to understand customer needs, to design products to solve environmental problems creatively, and to learn the effects of our creations by testing.

Occasionally, a firm will go beyond this and even design its building to be more environmentally sound. The Hearst Tower in New York, for example, has floor-to-ceiling windows that let in natural light and reduce power consumption by as much as 25 percent. Other notable "green" buildings include Google headquarters in Mountain View, California, and the Bank of America Tower in New York.[13] See Figure 20.5 for how the overall new product system contributes to public policy problems just as it does to other problems.

[12]Joel J. Davis, "Federal and State Regulation of Environmental Marketing: A Manager's Guide," *SAM Advanced Management Journal*, Summer 1994, pp. 36–44; and Hector R. Lozada and Alma T. Mintu-Wimsatt, "Green-Based Innovation: Sustainable Development in Product Management," in *Environmental Marketing: Strategies, Practice, Theory, and Research*, Michael Jay Polonsky and Alma T. Mintu-Wimsatt (eds.) (Binghamton, New York: Haworth Press, 1995), pp. 179–198.
[13]Michelle Conlin, op. cit.

Product Piracy[14]

In some industries (video/audio products, computer software, pharmaceuticals, and brand-name clothing and fragrances), **product piracy** is a major problem, especially in foreign markets. Product piracy is actually a catchall term that includes several categories of illegal activities, which threaten the brand equity and intellectual property of firms in these and other industries:

1. *Counterfeiting.* This is the unauthorized production of goods that are protected by trademark, copyright, or patent. Counterfeit goods range from low price and quality to excellent quality; often a giveaway is that the product lacks the manufacturer's original warranty.

2. *Brand Piracy.* This is defined as the unauthorized use of copyrighted or patented goods or brands. Again, product quality can range from very low (the "$20 Rolex") to extremely high. Cartier and other watch and fragrance companies have initiated thousands of legal actions to attempt to stamp out brand piracy.

3. *Near Brand Usage.* Here, the pirate manufacturer uses slightly different brand names such as Channel fragrances, Panasanic camcorders, or Tonny Hilfiger clothes (all real examples!). Moral: Buyer beware, and check the package carefully.

4. *Intellectual Property Copying.* Some of the most highly publicized cases in recent years have involved the unauthorized copying of intellectual property, especially CDs and DVDs containing computer software or entertainment. One estimate figures that 75 million CDs are illegally copied in China alone. Other industries such as pharmaceuticals and car or plane parts are also affected.

In many foreign markets, especially developing economies such as China, the laws governing intellectual property protection and product piracy are very lax. In fact, in many lesser-developed countries (LDCs), intellectual property is seen as a public good, and easy access to it boosts economic development, ultimately closing the gap between the LDC and developed economies.[15] Figure 20.6 shows several ways that firms from developed economies can protect themselves from product piracy, or at least reduce its effects to some degree. In addition to seeking legal recourse or government protection, simply communicating with the market and educating them about the risks of buying pirated products can be an effective action to take.

Worthy Products

The makers of Folgers, Maxwell House, and Nescafe were under strong pressure from a consumer group in 1991 to stop buying coffee beans from El Salvador. P&G decided to offer a new blend of coffee, under the Maryland Club label, without

[14]Much of this section draws from Laurence Jacobs, A. Coksun Samli, and Tom Jedlik, "The Nightmare of International Product Piracy," *Industrial Marketing Management*, 30, 2001, pp. 499–509.
[15]Subhash C. Jain, "Problems in International Protection of Intellectual Property Rights," *Journal of International Marketing*, 4(1), 1996, pp. 9–32.

FIGURE 20.6 **Protection against Product Piracy**

1. Communication: Announce that your product has been pirated and that only the real thing offers top value and should be sought out. It was good enough to have been pirated, suggesting that it is of good quality! Especially works if there is a safety or health risk involved. Brazilian consumers were concerned about pirated contraceptives and anticancer drugs.
2. Legal recourse: A NAFTA agreement requires trading partners to enforce intellectual property rights. GATT allows a nation to restrain imports from countries where piracy is a problem. A firm can begin the process of getting legal protection by registering with the U.S. Customs Service.
3. Government: The U.S. Trade Representation lists the countries with the biggest piracy problem—currently China and Taiwan. A country can get a nation with a poor track record denied most-favored-nation status, but this is a severe penalty and rarely imposed. A problem is that there are not enough "policemen" to enforce all the international agreements.
4. Direct Contact: Get the counterfeit goods off the store shelves. Sometimes the counterfeiting is ignored, because of the costs of litigation and enforcement, risk of bad publicity, and the fact that top government officials may be in on the deal! Another possibility is for the injured company to try to buy the pirate firm.
5. Labeling: Put holograms or "DNA security markers" (that encode product manufacturing information) on the genuine goods' labels. Holograms can be copied but do increase the counterfeiter's costs. The security markers are generally too costly for most counterfeiters.
6. Strong Proactive Marketing: Cut prices, spend aggressively on advertising, encourage customers to buy the genuine article. Get distributors' support in cutting down on the counterfeit products. Keep changing the product or its packaging.
7. Piracy as Promotion: Wide availability of pirated Word software could have the effect of spreading the adoption of Word as the world's word processing standard. Microsoft could then add features available only to genuine product owners via valid registration numbers or could offer product support only to genuine owners.

Source: Reprinted from *Industrial Marketing Management*, Vol. 30, Laurence Jacobs, A. Coksun Samli and Tom Jedlik, "The Nightmare of International Product Piracy," pp. 499–509. Copyright © 2001, with permission from Elsevier.

such beans, though Folgers would continue to contain them. Other manufacturers have been asked to create special exercising equipment for handicapped individuals, better foods for people who need to diet, modified products for the elderly (e.g., with bigger printing on washer dials), and products keyed to the special interests of smaller ethnic groups. The Orphan Drug Act provides federal aid for the development and marketing of drugs that otherwise may not be commercially feasible because of the relatively small number of potential users. An example resulting from this law is Rituxan, a new drug for treating chronic lymphocytic leukemia.[16]

Morality

It used to be the satellite receiver makers who were criticized for bringing pornography into our living rooms. Today it is the Internet, and by the time you read this it may be some other mode of communication. Here, morality concerns whether society should be denied certain new products for its own good. We have new

[16]For more information on orphan drugs, visit the FDA's Web site devoted to the topic, www.fda.gov/orphan.

alcoholic beverages, new gambling devices, and new sex devices. Radar-detectors get better and better. Anheuser-Busch was forced to withdraw a product from the test market when the public complained that the level of alcohol in what was a "kid's drink" would "train" youngsters to like alcoholic beverages. R.J. Reynolds marketed Dakota cigarettes targeted to 18- to 24-year-old women with a high school education or less.

Product innovators know what is going on and carefully position their products as they wish. Society stops them when they are wrong. They rarely walk into a surprise, and no one expects a weakening on this point. But it is difficult to predict the outcome of any particular controversy, something product developers must try to do in advance.

Monopoly

The charge of monopoly is occasionally applied to new products. Some economists believe market dominance constitutes monopoly and outstanding new products can lead to (or protect already achieved) market dominance.

Apart from fringe exceptions, the free market forces have almost always prevailed. Bell and Howell once claimed that Kodak secretly developed some film products and introduced them before Bell and Howell had a chance to retool its own cameras and projectors to use the film. Bell and Howell lost, as did others. But recently, in the United States things have turned, and right now we cannot predict where they will go.

In 1994, a vigorous Justice Department challenged a patent licensing agreement of a type that had been approved for years. For example, in 1996, Steelcase (the office furniture maker) was ordered to pay competitor Haworth over $211 million for a patent infringement on prewired office panels. A Haworth spokesperson said that, while copying was frequent in that industry years ago, there has been an increase in the number of patents filed and firms have to be much more careful.[17]

Personal Ethics

Some criticisms are difficult to fit into the above categories. People who react to them more often call them matters of personal ethics, not economics or business management. They are issues where people pretty much reach individual decisions, rather than seek court decisions. Here is a set of them—not complete, but in sufficient variety to let you see the problems product innovators deal with. As with all personal ethics situations, they are not just in the marketplace—they are in the labs, factories, and offices too. As the cartoon character Pogo said, we have met the enemy and they are us.

---

[17]Rebecca Blumenstein, "Steelcase Must Pay Big Sum Over Patent," *The Wall Street Journal*, December 31, 1996, p. A10.

To get the full effect of this problem, try to find a person who will make an individual set of answers for comparison with your answers—both having been made privately first. Would you, or would you not, support continuing each of the following practices? How you would handle them if they came up in *your* new products organization? That is, what would you do *managerially*, not individually? Note that personal ethics situations exclude the clearly illegal—for example, scientists have been known to steal company secrets and sell them to competitors, but such cases are not issues in ethics.

1. Ideation or concept generation often leads us to explore the minds of customers to find something they want or will want when they hear about it. Your firm uses *intrusive techniques,* such as unannounced observation and psychological projective techniques. A customer recently said it is unethical to trick people into telling you what they want.

2. Your market research director uses focus groups for concept testing and lets company people *secretly sit behind the mirrors* as your customers react to the new concepts. They often joke about customers' product usage practices.

3. You introduce a temporary product that will be replaced when a better one in development is ready a year from now. You are told *not to let distributors or your sales force know* it is only temporary.

4. You work for a management training firm and are about to market a new seminar service for banks. Your firm, for a fee, will run seminars during which you will train bank personnel in investment counseling. But there is no product use test on the seminar, and *you don't know that the bank people will really learn how to counsel.*

5. You work for a detergents company and recently learned that over the years thousands of rodents have been force-fed each new product, including versions in development. The *force-feeding goes on until half of the rodents die* (the so-called LD50 test).

6. You are currently working on a patented item that schools will use for map displays. It is so good that virtually every K–12 school will buy several of them. You come across the cost figures and calculate that the *gross margin will run about 80 percent.* A co-worker comments that the price could be cut in half and the company margin would still be a healthy 60 percent.

7. You work for a database service that recently began collecting patient records from physicians and now offers a new service of *information for pharmaceutical firms.* The records sometimes contain names and often include age, sex, and so on of the patients. Information includes nature of illnesses and treatments.

8. The Food and Drug Administration has charged that your new Freshland spaghetti sauce is processed and sold nonrefrigerated; it therefore cannot be called "fresh" in its brand name. Your firm counters that it is fresher than the leading competitor, and besides, lots of products are advertised as being fresh when they technically aren't, by the arbitrary FDA definition.

9. A set of "educational" game cards, made by your firm and not really very educational, are known to be bought by less intelligent parents for their children. There are several far better sets of such cards on the market.

10. Your strategy is to stir up the waters—marketing a long line of similar products to confuse customers and keep them from being able to "buy intelligently."

11. You have a line of party products that seem to be in sync with many younger people, but are sexually oriented. You market them through mass outlets, not adult stores, and although some retailers won't stock the items, many will. Sales have been outstanding.

12. You work as a sales rep for a pharmaceutical company. Food and Drug Administration rules prohibit "off-label promotion," that is, marketing a drug for uses other than those approved by the FDA. Your company funds thousands of medical-education programs yearly at which doctors and other health professionals make presentations about the use of certain drugs, some of which are not yet approved by the FDA (but are written up in the medical journals as effective). They say they are doing nothing wrong, but you see this as a clear violation of off-label promotion rules. For you, the last straw is when you attend a sales meeting at which you are instructed to recruit medical speakers to talk about approved *and unapproved* uses of a new blood clot drug.[18]

The Underlying Residual Issues

A few really tough issues thread their way through the above confusions. They are such that we will never be free of problems working in the public policy area. One of them is, *What are reasonable goals for action here?* A risk-free existence is totally unreasonable. Zero-defect quality control is a goal in many firms. But, with the complexity in most of today's consumer products, nothing short of government decree would stop consumers from making errors—and then only because they would not be making any decisions at all. Besides, even if we could hope to reach a 99.99 percent level of risk reduction, that would still leave 27,500 people on the wrong side of the statistic in the United States alone. Worldwide, the number would certainly be much higher.

Another one is the *trade-off problem.* Even when a particular situation seems to have a clear-cut guiding principle, we often find a contrary principle of equal merit. Which of two worthy options should be accepted?

A third is, *Where should the costs fall?* In many of the controversies that affect new products, the argument is not so much *what should be done* as *who should pay for it.* Assuming (1) no production system can ever make products perfectly and (2) no consumer group will ever use products with perfect wisdom, there will always be injuries and waste. Who should pay? Governments are already under pressure for tax reduction. Insurance companies know the negative reactions to inflated rates. So the no-fault approach is becoming popular—or, as the manufacturer says, the

[18]This example is real. See Elyse Tanouye, "Staffers of Drug Maker Say It Pushed Product for Unapproved Uses," *The Wall Street Journal*, September 15, 1997, pp. A1, A7.

total-fault approach. The manufacturer assumes all responsibility and is expected to pass along the costs somehow.

What Are New Products Managers Doing about All This?

At the start of this chapter, it was stated that managements today generally have the public policy problem in hand. They have learned how to run the new products process to minimize the problems. The previous sections showed many ways in which actions are being taken. Here are a few more general ones.

Strategy and Policy

More top managers are personally involved today. They want safe and useful products because they sell better. For example, at a firm making V-style accordion gates for children, the CEO rejected a proposal, said the team could do better—they came out with something better *and* less expensive. Second, product innovation charters set the standards in guidelines and also point out opportunities where there is new product opportunity in regulations.

Control Systems

Managements today demand tough standards, rigorous auditing at all points, good record keeping, and training of new product employees. Disaster plans help. When Campbell's routine checking program disclosed a can containing botulin, the company immediately stopped shipments from the plant involved, canvassed 102,000 food outlets in a 16-state area, and inspected 65 million cans. A new manufacturing process was abandoned, two dozen spoiled cans were discarded, and the firm was back on top of the situation. Pfizer found a potentially flawed heart valve and had to contact 55,000 people with the implant. They had the records to do so.

Product Testing

Firms learn how customers will use products; and, if that use looks as if it will cause problems, then action is taken now, not after injuries mount. Then they add stress testing to catch misuse and overuse. They use common sense: Anybody could have seen that the all-terrain vehicles would be problems, and they were.

Marketing and Market Testing

They prepare adequate warnings. The Manville Corporation was defending against asbestos-death lawsuits as early as 1929. The firm's chief physician allegedly urged caution labels in 1953, but they didn't go on until 1964 and even then apparently did not indicate the gravity of the risk. Bankruptcy was ultimately necessary to survive. Firms today manage the marketing and distribution process with the same vigor they manage design and manufacturing. If a product is unsafe in lay people's hands and must go through professional channels, it is plainly labeled with an explanation of why. Market tests, combining product and promotion, are another way to spot miscommunications. Distributors may not understand promotions, discounts, instructions, or service. People who shouldn't buy an item may be doing so.

Customer Education and External Affairs

Managements now consider themselves in the education business, first with *company personnel* (through ombudsmen, consumer affairs officers, scientific advisory panels, etc.) and second with the *consumer* (through labels, warranties, how-to sheets, and more instructional advertising). In addition, most industries aggressively greet every legislative thrust on new products, and vigorous public affairs programs are standard fare. They work together more, and even include consumer units on their task forces.

Summary

This concludes our trip through a troublesome dimension of the new products process. The pressures are very real, and the difficulties are at times almost overwhelming. Some unresolved issues have no answers, and new variations in the general problem areas will continue to unfold.

New products managers, however, are finding they can manage under these circumstances if they do their homework well. Avoiding needless troubles requires that they understand the process, stay close to their legal departments, get management's support at critical times, and follow up marketing with more aggressive launch management than ever before used in American industry. All temptations are to do just the opposite because time can be the Achilles' heel of new products management, as we have seen more than once.

Although we have covered the major areas of product policy concerns in the new products field, you should know that there are far more problems and issues buried in the labs, plants, and offices of today's new products manager. Every industry has scores of them. As a final example, think of the problems scientists in the pharmaceutical industry have when they go to do field testing on an experimental drug known to be dangerous. With whom must they work, whose approvals are necessary, what controls should they have to use on the actions and record keeping of physicians and hospital personnel, and how far and hard should they search for side effects—to the third generation? Does it matter if the medicine being tested came from a rare frog on the endangered species list? Does it matter if the drug (assuming it is successful) will cost over $4,000 a month for 10 months of treatment, and have a lifetime dosage level of $1,000 a month?[19]

The point here is this: Thousands of people deal with these troublesome issues every day—they know the problems and they have worked out a balance between need to know and need to move ahead. They manage, risks and all.

[19]For an interesting summary of the problems, see George Anders, "Testing a New Drug Entails Daunting Costs and Clashing Interests," *The Wall Street Journal*, January 7, 1994, p. A1.

Applications

1. "The worst thing about product liability is what they call strict liability. Now, I know it's hard to prove negligence against a typical large corporation of today, but that's no reason to go to the other extreme and say a company is guilty when there is no evidence it did anything wrong. We market thousands of products involving thousands of people. Strange things are going to happen. Employees are not robots—they make human errors. You've probably already made a mistake or two today, yet if you were in a business, you could be sued, found guilty, and then hit with a punitive damages ruling like a common criminal. That's just not fair."

2. "We're currently about to market a new type of hair dryer. It's not a blower in the usual sense—there are no wires that get hot. Instead, we have combined two chemicals that tend to heat up if they are charged with an electrical current. The air is directed through the wire mesh container in which these chemicals are kept (they're solids, not liquids), and whenever there is electricity, there is heated air. If you feel you understand the moral and legal issues of product liability, would you please tell me what you think we should have done, and what we should do in the future, to conform with what the public generally expects of us and with what the law requires of us? We still have several months before we market the new dryer, but the product specifications are frozen and the item is currently about to be started through production."

3. "Two other firms I know about were less fortunate. Morton-Norwich Products introduced Encare, a vaginal suppository contraceptive, and American Home Products came out with a similar product called Semicid at about the same time. Both advertised that the products were safer than IUDs and that, unlike the 'pill,' they had no hormonal side effects. They called the items a safe, medically tested, positive method of birth control, which they are. But the Federal Trade Commission has ruled that the firms cannot claim a comparative advantage over other methods unless they also state that the new product is not as effective as the others. The FTC says the only novel aspect of the new products is the suppository form, and that has very little advantage to the consumer. Both firms now have to distribute a new pamphlet telling the advantages and disadvantages of all forms of birth control. All of this may be well and good—I don't know—but the aspect that bothers me is that the two firms were ruled responsible for telling consumers the *good* things about their competitors, not just the bad. Why do you suppose the FTC ruled the way it did, and is this a forecast of what we are all going to face? Since when am I responsible for helping potential customers choose a competitor's product?"

4. "When you first told me about those, what do you call them, public policy issues, I was thinking about our health industry group. It is rapidly developing a line of health maintenance organizations (HMOs) by acquisition, primarily, and several by invitation of leading hospitals. They will all be in the service business, and not-for-profit operations (they have other advantages for us), so it is pleasing to think that at least this part of our corporate family won't raise public policy issue problems. That's right, isn't it?"

Case: Clorox Green Works[20]

In the last fifteen or so years, concerned consumers have demanded "environmentally friendly" or "green" versions of their favorite products. Manufacturers soon learned that meeting this emerging demand posed particular challenges. For one thing, consumers are skeptical of green claims, possibly because some products with questionable credentials were marketed aggressively, and misleadingly, as environmentally friendly. Customer skepticism is likely to keep getting stronger. Consumers are becoming more educated about green issues and concerns, and the days of slapping a green flag on the label and calling your product environmentally friendly are over. Another issue is that many consumers have come to expect that the green version of items such as household cleaners may be twice as expensive as the conventional brand, and may also be less effective. Even labeling becomes an issue. What do you write on the label that properly conveys the intended message and doesn't unintentionally put off customers? Green? Natural? Good for the environment? Organic? Ecologically friendly? Small wonder that green products have not experienced expected levels of market penetration.

The Clorox Company set out to approach the green consumer market with a new line of household cleaning products. The Green Works line was launched in 2008 and was in fact the first family of natural cleaning products ever launched by a major consumer-goods manufacturer. The line, which includes an all-purpose cleaner, a toilet bowl cleaner, and the like, was an immediate success and had captured a large share of the natural cleaning products market only a few months after launch. What accounts for the success of this line? Industry experts suggest that Clorox did two things very well with this launch: (1) They identified a new, underserved market segment and learned everything they could about them, and (2) they designed and launched a product that met all of that segment's key needs, not just a couple of important ones.

For years, Clorox was interested in the issues of health and wellness, and had accumulated a large bank of consumer data. This came in handy as the Clorox product team was able to identify an emerging segment relatively early. While many consumers had a general objective of "doing something good for the environment," this particular segment had something more in mind: their health and well-being, and that of their family. They liked the performance of standard cleaning products but thought they contained too many potentially dangerous chemicals. Members of this market segment saw themselves playing a key role in their family: keeping the home safe. The product team named this segment the "Chemical-Avoiding Naturalist." Clorox market research found that this target consumer was very likely to be the primary shopper for the family, and 85 percent of the segment membership was female.

For women in this market segment, not just any "green" product would do. This consumer's belief (that she was first and foremost the protector of the family)

---

[20]This case draws largely from Sumi N. Cate, David Pilosof, Richard Tait, and Robin Karol, "The Story of Clorox Green Works™—In Designing a Winning Green Product Experience Clorox Cracks the Code," *Visions*, 33(1), March 2009, pp. 10–14.

would imply that she might not be fanatical about buying green products in any case; rather, this customer has a strong emotional commitment to the family. Nevertheless, a line of products with the cleaning power of conventional cleaners, but with no harsh chemicals, would be attractive to this customer.

Development of the new product line began with the positioning statement. Clorox first had to choose what terminology should figure in the value proposition that would best appeal to their targeted segment. Their demographic research found that terms like "green," "sustainable," or "carbon-neutral" would not be clear enough or could be interpreted multiple ways. "Organic" was considered, but its use is government-regulated and might be troublesome for Clorox. The product team settled on "natural," mostly because it worked with the target customer and also team members felt it played to Clorox's core competencies (it could be easily communicated and advertised, and it was a reasonable and reachable objective for the firm).

With a combination of personal interviews and in-home ethnographic "fly-on-the-wall" research, the product team gained an understanding of the Chemical-Avoiding Naturalist. This research suggested that this segment had several must-have expectations of the product, all of which would have to be met. It would have to support the emotional commitment of protecting her family and the environment (by drastically reducing the amount of harsh chemicals), but without compromising performance, convenience, or ease of use. It would need to be priced at an acceptable level and widely available, and the information about the product's benefits would need to be credible and trustworthy. The product team realized that focusing exclusively on one or two of these expectations would not be good enough. This consumer will not switch over to an all-natural product if performance was sacrificed or if the price premium was too high.

The ethnographic research found that customers knew that natural ingredients like vinegar could be used as cleaners, and some even made their own cleaners at home. Many expressed familiarity with plant-based cleaning ingredients and wondered why cleaners had to have harsh chemicals in them at all. These and related research findings led the Clorox team to develop its own definition of natural: 99 percent free of petrochemicals, derived from plants or minerals, biodegradable and nontoxic, and not chemically processed or tested on animals. (The ideal, 100 percent free of petrochemicals, was not considered feasible, because components such as fragrances, colors, and preservatives are not always available in natural form; 99 percent was close enough for Clorox to make a "virtually" all-natural claim.)

Care was taken such that the product line would have all of the must-have expectations. Conventional cleaning products sold in the $2.00 to $3.00 range, while many natural competitors sold for over $7.00 per bottle. The targeted retail price for the new line was set at $3.00 to $4.00 per bottle, which was felt to be acceptable to this segment. Since conventional products were sold almost everywhere (grocery stores, convenience stores, pharmacies, and so on), it was felt that intensive distribution was critical for the new line as well. The credibility angle was covered by having full disclosure on the label as well as providing extensive information on the product Web site. Clorox also received a rare endorsement from the Sierra Club and was recognized by the Environmental Protection Agency's "Design for the Environment" Formulator Program. The aesthetic appearance was also not forgotten: The product itself as well as its packaging would have to convey cleanliness and simplicity, as well as performance. For example, while a colorless and odorless product might have conveyed an all-natural image, customers might wonder if it would be any more effective than plain water! Finally, a clever brand name (Clorox Green Works) was chosen. "Green Works" effectively summarizes the dual benefits of the product line: environmentally conscious, but also power-ful ("it works"). The inclusion of "Clorox" in the name was not accidental, as the team wanted to leverage the Clorox effectiveness and trust brand equity. Finally, the word "natural" appears prominently on every label.

Of course, the products really had to deliver, but new advances in surfactant (cleaning agent) and solvent chemistry were making plant-based ingredients more effective. Clorox was able to rely on natural ingredients such as coconut oil (surfactant), natural polysaccharides (thickeners), and corn-based ethanol (solvent) to deliver acceptable levels of cleaning power that might not have been possible several years earlier. In fact, once launched, Green Works products per-formed as well or better than conventional products.

The product launch was a success. Clorox was able to get Green Works prod-ucts into all major retailers and encouraged them to display them prominently in their stores. The launch of a highly effective new green product also received a fair amount of publicity in the press at the time.

What can be learned from the development of Clorox Green Works? What accounted for the remarkable success of the line? (Think of at least three clear reasons.) What were the major difficulties or hurdles faced by the product team? How could a firm in a different product category, or a service provider, apply some of the best practices described in this case?

Case: Hybrid or Hydrogen Vehicles at General Motors?[21]

Rising fuel costs and a concern over the environment have led automakers to experiment with alternative-fuel cars. One of the most promising alternative-fuel technologies was the hybrid engine. Hybrid technology combines a gasoline-powered engine with a battery-powered electric motor. The battery is designed to recharge whenever the car brakes, or more conventionally by a generator supplied by the gasoline engine. The gasoline engine is designed to shut down completely at times, such as at stoplights, leaving the car to run only on the electric motor. As a result, a much smaller amount of gasoline is required for driving: Hybrid technol-ogy cars can obtain well over 500 miles per tank of gas.

The first attempts to market hybrid-technology vehicles in the U.S. market and worldwide were made by the Japanese carmakers. In 1999, the first hybrid vehicle

---

[21]This case was compiled from several published sources, including Gail Edmondson, "BMW's H-Bomb," *BusinessWeek Online*, businessweek.com, September 12, 2006.

was launched in the U.S. market, the Honda Insight. Seventeen Insights were sold that year. Soon thereafter, the Toyota Prius was launched, and by 2002 about 40,000 hybrid vehicles were sold. Industry projections suggest that by 2012, U.S. hybrid sales could increase to a million units, though other alternative-energy technologies might be commercially viable by then. U.S. carmakers soon launched their own upcoming hybrid launches. General Motors announced its plans for hybrid Chevrolet and GMC pickups, and both Ford and Chrysler revealed plans for hybrid sport-utility vehicles (SUVs) or trucks. Meanwhile, Toyota was planning to add hybrid technology as an option on both the Toyota Highlander and the Lexus RX330 SUV.

It was felt that the Insight suffered from some initial negative perceptions and misconceptions. The potential buyer had to trade off seating space, as the Insight was a two-seater. Some car buyers didn't like the silent idling of the electric motor at stoplights. Many also thought that the price premium over conventional gas engines was too high: J.D. Power and Associates research suggested that consumers would be reluctant to pay over $1,000 more than for a comparable gas engine car to get hybrid technology. By contrast, the Toyota Prius received early favorable publicity from an unexpected source: Several Hollywood actors (notably Leonardo Di Caprio and Cameron Diaz) were Prius drivers and spoke highly about their new cars (they did not receive incentives from Toyota to promote the Prius).

In late 2002, Honda introduced the Civic Hybrid as its latest entry in this market. It was based on the familiar and popular Civic body style and could carry five people, and a hybrid Civic had fuel efficiency reaching 650 miles per tank of gas. Many desirable features, such as air conditioning, cruise control, antilock brakes, and a top-quality stereo system, were standard in the Civic Hybrid. It carried a slightly higher sticker price than the gas-powered Civic and offered 20 percent less horsepower. At the time of the launch, Thad Melesh of J.D. Power spoke highly of the Civic Hybrid's market potential: "[Hybrid sales] growth . . . comes from buyers who want hybrid versions of regular vehicles, and not a 'quirky-type greenish vehicle.'"

The market environment seems to be improving steadily for hybrid vehicles. Due to the promotional efforts by the carmakers and the positive coverage resulting from the antipollution benefits of these cars, media attention has continued to escalate. Celebrities driving $20,000 hybrid cars (who could easily afford cars 10 times that price) add to the prestige and perhaps overcome some of the initial negative perceptions. Furthermore, the U.S. government has offered a one-time $2,000 federal tax deduction on hybrid cars as an incentive to purchase. Add to this the unrest in the oil-producing Middle Eastern countries and the desire of many Americans to minimize dependence on foreign oil, and it is clear why the market was primed for a steady growth period. In fact, Honda spent only about a half million dollars on the rollout of the Civic Hybrid; Honda executives see little reason to promote heavily given the strong sales growth with relatively small promotional expenditures.

Many observers in this industry see hybrid technology as only a stop-gap solution, and that ultimately the market is moving toward hydrogen or fuel cell cars. BMW has been a major investor in hydrogen cars, as it feels that only hydrogen engines can deliver the kind of performance expected by BMW drivers accustomed to sportiness. In fact, BMW rolled out a very limited number of hydrogen cars (7-series luxury sedans, to be exact), with the intention of leasing them to politicians and other opinion leaders. It's critical to hydrogen-car acceptance that BMW shows the feasibility of the technology, since as of 2007 there were only a handful of gas stations that sold hydrogen fuel. (These had been mostly built, in fact, to supply BMW's hydrogen car research and development.) The good news is that hydrogen cars can also run on regular unleaded gasoline, though investment in infrastructure is obviously required. Governor Arnold Schwarzenegger of California has spoken of supporting a "hydrogen highway" lined with hydrogen stations. Still, even BMW projects that by 2025, only about 2 percent of new cars sold in Germany will be hydrogen powered.

Apply any of the models discussed in Chapter 3 to assess the attractiveness of the electric car market for GM, which is about to launch the hybrid versions of the Chevy Silverado and GMC Sierra. Go past the obvious (for example, that hybrid technology is in the middle of market growth). What are the opportunities in the marketplace, and what are the threats? Then assess GM's business position in this market. If you agree that the hybrid technology market is attractive, what are GM's relative strengths and weaknesses in pursuing this market? In responding, keep in mind the public policy issues surrounding the development and launch of an alternative-fuel car. Should GM jump on the hybrid bandwagon now, or wait and continue development of the next (and presumably even better) generation of alternative-fuel automobile? Could GM gain from being a leader in hydrogen cell or other alternative-fuel technology? And are there any risks in having it both ways: launching a competitive hybrid Silverado and Sierra while at the same time pursuing alternative technologies?

Case: Product (RED)[22]

The Global Fund, founded in 2002, is a leading fundraiser and supporter of programs fighting AIDS, tuberculosis, and malaria in the developing world. As of late 2006 the Global Fund had raised well over $6 billion, and it makes up about 25 percent of total world funding for AIDS programs. The money is earmarked for treatment of current patients, as well as education and community programs to slow down the spread of the disease.

In 2006, a new global initiative, Product (RED), was started by two internationally known public figures, rock singer Bono and lawyer and philanthropist Bobby Shriver (nephew of John F. Kennedy). The idea behind Product (RED) was to get corporations to team up and help the Global Fund raise money that would be used for developing new treatments for developing nations (such as one that would prolong an AIDS patient's life by up to twenty years) and counseling.

[22]Information for this case was obtained from "How The Fund Works," a November 2006 publication of the Global Fund downloaded from www.theglobalfund.org; Jim Edwards, "Will Bono's Red Make Charity Cool?" *VNU Business Media*, 2006; as well as articles found on www.gap.com, www.americanexpress.com, and www.joinred.com.

Participating firms would create their own products in support of the initiative. They would, however, give up some brand equity, as all products would carry the Product (RED) logo as the brand. This boosts recognition of Product (RED) as a "super-brand" and essentially unites all participating firms behind the initiative. The target market for Product (RED) is the 19–32-year-old Generation X age group. Among the first firms taking part were The Gap, American Express, Motorola, and Converse.

Product (RED) developed an advertising book (basic message, logo, and so forth). Participating firms must follow the book's guidelines, which were designed to provide them with much flexibility in how they choose to promote their own Product (RED) lines. An accompanying Web site, www.joinred.com, was founded to allow targeted customers to support the initiative, download pictures, post blogs and videos, and link to participating firm Web sites. A sophisticated Web site of this type is essential to reaching the targeted Generation X group effectively. Product (RED) also had a presence on myspace.com, another favorite site of this age group, where information on new products or events could be found.

The Gap was one of the first participants in Product (RED), and Gap management believed that associating with this initiative would help their brand equity in a crowded marketplace while at the same time doing something good for society. Gap developed a new clothing line, promoted using taglines such as Inspi(RED), Uncenso(RED), Empowe(RED), and so on. Fifty percent of profits from this new line is aimed to the Product (RED) initiative. In addition, Gap set up manufacturing plants in South Africa, Madagascar, and other African countries, so that the workers would be the ones to directly benefit from the profits made by sales of the clothing line. For their part, American Express launched a (RED) card, first in the United Kingdom but with plans to go worldwide. One percent of purchases on the (RED) card are targeted to The Global Fund, while the cardholder gets benefits such as discounts on (RED) merchandise and (RED) events.

Other firms show many other diverse ways in which Product (RED) was manifested. Motorola developed (RED) versions of the RAZR flip phone, popular among the target audience due to its thin shape, Bluetooth-enabled technology, and MP3 compatibility. Motorola's Product (RED) Web site also allowed visitors to download screensavers or ringtones. Converse, the running shoe company famous for Chuck Taylor sneakers, launched Product (RED) Chucks and also initiated a promotion with celebrities and designers to create their own custom shoes. Apple launched a (RED) iPod Nano (red in color, obviously, to distinguish it from other iPods) together with a gift card so the buyer can begin adding songs. A certain percentage of the sales of products from all of these firms are to be donated to Product (RED).

What other firms potentially could also become part of Product (RED), and are there some firms that would actually not benefit that much from participation? Does a Product (RED) firm face any potential downside to participation in the project? Is Product (RED) a one-time-only initiative? If not, what other kinds of initiatives could get similar corporate interest? Also, comment generally about social marketing. What other social issues of today might stimulate similar corporate activity?

SOLUTIONS TO FIGURE 20.3

Almost all of the warning labels in the exhibit are real. The real ones are: 2 (rock garden), 4 (hair dryer), 6 (windshield sun shade), 7 (shin guards), 9 (iron), 10 (sled), 12 (cell phone), 13 (router), 15 (stroller), 16 (washing machine), 17 (fireplace log), 18 (printer cartridge). In fact several of these have won "worst of" awards. The best source for details on odd warning labels is the Michigan Lawsuit Abuse Watch Web site, www.mlaw.org.

Sources of Ideas Already Generated

New product ideas come from many places, some of which are peculiar to particular firms or industries. Here are the more broadly used sources.

Employees

Many types of employees can be sources of new product concepts. Salespeople are an obvious group, but so are technical groups, manufacturing, customer service, and packaging employees, and, in the case of general consumer products, any employee who uses the products. Manufacturing and engineering personnel are frequently part-time inventors who should be encouraged to submit their ideas. These people need to know that their ideas are wanted, and special mechanisms (and even cultures) must usually be constructed to gather those ideas.

Employee suggestion systems are not dependable ways to turn up ideas, and special idea contests have an equally disappointing record. Toyota ran an Idea Olympics for some time and in one year produced 1,300 employee-inventor entries. The firm did not comment on the quality of the ideas.

The most helpful suggestions come from employees whose work brings them in contact with customer problems. For example, a drill manufacturer's service department found that many drills were burning out because customers were using them as electric screwdrivers. Adding a clutch mechanism to the drill created a new product. Complaint-handling departments also become familiar with consumers' use of products. Salespeople know when a large order is lost because the firm's product is not quite what the customer wanted.

Dun & Bradstreet had a fine new products track record and reported that most of its new product ideas came from field personnel. Eligible D&B employees could receive $5,000 for suggesting an idea that went national. Some firms have used an "idea miner"—an employee whose job is to scout around among other employees, encouraging and collecting their ideas.

Customers

The greatest source of new product ideas is the customer or user of the firm's products or services, although their ideas are usually only for product improvement or nearby line extensions. Some people believe the majority of all new products in certain industries originate with users. Because some specialized user groups are personally involved with devices, new products people occasionally delegate new product concept development to them. Similarly, most auto parts and components manufacturers look to their giant OEM buyers for new product initiatives. On the other hand, one firm solicited 2,800 ideas from customers and was not able to use a single one.

The most popular ways to gather customer ideas are surveys, continuing panels, special focus groups, and the mail. Nowadays, these traditional methods are commonly supplemented by e-mail contact or online discussion with customers. Some firms get so many suggestions in the mail that they do not read them. Industrial firms usually take the initiative of using personal contacts by salespeople or technical staffs, especially lead users.

Resellers

Brokers, manufacturers' reps, industrial distributors, large jobbers, and large retail firms may be quite worthwhile sources. In fact, some mass merchandisers have their own new products departments and invite manufacturers to bid on specifications. Many industrial representatives are skilled enough to be special advisers to their clients, and selling agents in the toy industry not only advise but actually take on the new products function if the manufacturer wishes.

One chemical distributor suggested using a low-cost polyethylene bag to line steel drums to prevent corrosion; and a millwork producer learned about a new competitive entry from a dealer and then suggested how the new item could be improved. Both suggestions were successfully implemented. Kroger once told manufacturers that its customers want more easy-to-cook, single-portion frozen dinners, and another chain suggested a low-calorie enchilada.

Suppliers/Vendors

Most manufacturers of plastic housewares are small and thus look to the large plastics firms for advice. Virtually all producers of steel, aluminum, chemicals, metals, paper, and glass have technical customer service departments. One of their functions is to suggest new products made of the firm's basic material.

Competitors

New product idea generators are interested in competitors' activities, and competitors' new products may be an indirect source for a leapfrog or add-on new product; but competitors (as with government-mandated cross-licensing of ideas) are rarely sources of new product ideas except in industries where benchmarking has been accepted as a strategy. The first firms bringing a new product to a particular market segment (such as the smaller city banks) do use their innovative competitors as sources, but this is effective only when market segments are insulated. At Ford Motor Company, once the engineers get their hands on a new competitive product, it is systematically torn down into its 30,000 parts. All are cataloged and then mounted on panels so others can examine them.

The Invention Industry

Every industrialized country has an "industry" consisting of a nucleus of inventors surrounded by firms and organizations that help them capitalize on their inventions. Though tending to lose out to corporate research centers, individual inventors still submit almost a fourth of all patent applications. The auxiliary or supportive group includes:

Venture capital firms	Banks
Inventors' schools	Inventors' councils
Attorneys	Small Business Administration
Trademark and patent offices	Technology expositions
Consultants on new business	Patent shows
Patent brokers and others	Inventor newsletters
Inventor assistance firms	State entrepreneurial aid programs
Individual investors	University innovation centers

Currently, both the inventor and the potential manufacturer are frustrated by the communications, legal, and funding problems existing in this supportive network. Fortunately, this highly fragmented new "industry" is in the process of shaking down and should soon settle on several dominant organizational formats with which manufacturers can deal.

One example of this emerging format was InstanTechEx, a service provided by Dr. Dvorkovitz & Associates. Dvorkovitz sponsored an annual international technology exchange exposition where hundreds of firms and scores of governments displayed technological advancements that they wanted to sell. The show was a supermarket of technology and an emerging format for standardizing the new invention industry.

Other new organizations are merging the financial, legal, and managerial consulting assistance that inventors usually require, either as venture firms that actually take over and develop the idea or as facilitator firms that reach out to established manufacturers. In the meantime, some firms have what they call "inventors' farm systems" to get both quantity and variety of invention input. NordicTrack makes inventors their primary source of new products and cultivates that group with almost as much marketing effort as used on their customers.

Miscellaneous

Among the many other sources of outside new product ideas are the following:

1. **Consultants.** Most management consulting firms do new products work, and some specialize in it—for example, McKinsey, A. D. Little, Mercer, and PRTM. Some consulting firms are devoted exclusively to new products work and include idea generation as one of their services. Unfortunately, the stigma of being "outsiders" is strong in the new products field, as exemplified by the not-invented-here syndrome. Companies report very favorable experiences but also many horror stories. One alternative is to bring industry experts to discussion sessions with company personnel. General Mills has used a newspaper food editor, a trade journal editor, an advertising copywriter, a restaurateur, a division manager of a food chain, and four company junior executives.

2. **Advertising agencies.** This source of new product ideas is badly underrated. Most agencies have the creative talent and the product/market experience to generate new product concepts. Some agencies have full-blown new products departments, and some take their concepts all the way to market, including premarket tests and rollouts. Consumer product agencies do more new products work than industrial agencies do, although the West Coast agencies specializing in the computer industry render a wide range of services because their clients are often small.

3. **Marketing research firms.** Normally, marketing research firms get involved in the idea-generating process by assisting a client with need assessment. They rarely stumble across an opportunity that they pass along to a client. Some of the bigger marketing research firms also serve as management consultants.

4. **Retired product specialists.** Industrial new products people, particularly those with technical strength, often retire from their firms and become part-time consultants to other firms. One company actually tracks the retirements of all qualified specialists in its industry. Conflict-of-interest problems may arise, and divulging competitive secrets is ethically questionable, but most arrangements work around these problems easily.

5. **Industrial designers.** Industrial design firms sometime function as part of a team implementing a new product decision that has already been made. However, many industrial designers are extremely creative. Industrial design firms and individual industrial designers are increasingly capitalizing on their own new product strengths. Industrial design departments of universities are sometimes assigned by government and other service organizations to do original new products work.

6. **Other manufacturers.** Most firms have potentially worthwhile new product ideas that they do not want because these ideas conflict with the firm's strategy. These ideas are usually allowed to remain idle. General Electric once established a Business Opportunities Program in which it offered its "spare" technologies for sale. Sometimes, the offering was just an idea; but

other times, prototypes and even molds, dies, and finished goods inventories were offered, depending on how far GE had taken an idea before deciding not to develop it further. In later years, GE expanded this service by listing the technologies of others in its monthly editions of *Selected Business Ventures* and in annual compilations in its *New Product New Business Digest*.

7. **Universities.** Professors and students occasionally offer new product ideas, especially in schools of engineering, the sciences, and business. Dentists, physicians, and pharmacists are scientific groups that play a major role in new products work.

8. **Research laboratories.** Most of the world's leading countries now have at least one major research laboratory that will do new products work on contract from manufacturers and that occasionally comes up with interesting new product ideas. The Battelle Memorial Institute in Columbus, Ohio, received millions of dollars for its role in getting xerography off the ground. Other leading research laboratories are the Illinois Institute of Technology, the Stanford Research Institute, and Great Britain's National Engineering Laboratory.

9. **Governments.** The Patent Office of the U.S. government offers several services designed to help manufacturers find worthwhile new product ideas. The *Official Gazette* provides a weekly listing of (1) all new patents issued, (2) condensed descriptions of the patented items, and (3) which patents are for sale or license. Patent Office reports and services also make known what government patents and foreign patents are available.

   The military services have a want list of products that they would like to buy; the Department of Agriculture will help manufacturers with new products; and state governments have programs to aid industries.

   One by-product of today's regulation of business is increased assistance from regulators for solving such problems as unsafe products and unsafe working conditions. For example, the Occupational Safety and Health Act stimulated several companies to develop first-aid kits.

10. **Printed sources.** The hundreds of technical and scientific journals, trade journals, newsletters, and monographs are occasionally sources of ideas for new products. Most of the ideas indirectly result from accounts of new products activity. Some publications are more direct sources of new product ideas—for example, *Newsweek's* annual *New Products and Processes*, *New Technology* (London), and such compilations as *New Product News*. Though not new product ideas directly, there are now at least two online computer databases of actual new products marketed: Thomas New Industrial Products and Predicasts, New Product Announcements.

11. **International.** Minnetonka executives got the idea for pump toothpaste while browsing in a German supermarket. Powdered Tide was developed by scientists in Cincinnati, but Liquid Tide used a formula for surfactants from Japan and a mineral salts antagonist from Belgium. Unfortunately, few firms have systematic programs to find ideas from other countries. Some establish foreign offices to monitor various technologies, others ask their advertising

agencies' foreign offices to gather ideas, and still others subscribe to one or more reporting services.

12. **Internet.** At this time we can only guess what will happen, but some Web sites already are getting into new product ideas, and various bulletin boards post suggestions for product changes.

Managing These Idea Sources

These sources of ideas do not function without special effort. For example, salespeople must be trained how to find users with good ideas and how to coax the ideas from them. International markets must be covered on the spot by trained people. Studying the competition must be systematic to catch every change in competitors' products. Each special source is also a potential source for the competition, and the firm that uses these sources most appropriately will acquire the best ideas.

Other Techniques of Concept Generation

Chapters 4, 5, 6, and 7 presented the leading ideation techniques with the best track records and the greatest chance of producing valuable new product concepts. Perhaps hundreds of other techniques are available, some of which are proprietary (confidential to the consulting firm that originated each), and some of which are techniques given here but with different names.

Forty-five of the other techniques have been selected for brief review here. They are probably not necessary, but different individuals have found them useful. Perhaps you will too.

Techniques to Aid Problem Analysis

Composite Listing of Needs Fulfilled

By simply listing the many needs met by currently available products, there is a good chance some otherwise overlooked need will come to mind. This mechanical process is successful only if the listing is pushed to one's mental limits.

Market Segmentation Analysis

By using one segmentation dimension on top of another, an analyst can develop a hierarchy of smaller and smaller market segments. For example, bar soap segmentation could use sex, age, body part cleaned, ethnic groups, and geographic location. All possible combinations of these would yield thousands of groups—for example, elderly Jewish women washing their faces in New York City. Each combination is potentially a group whose needs are peculiar and currently unmet. (Psychographic and behavioral segments are especially useful today.)

Dreams

This approach analyzes the dreams of people who have the problem(s) under study. Dreams offer a greater range of insights, equitably involve other persons in the problem situation, and offer paranormal aspects of the dream itself. Various famous people, one of whom was Robert Louis Stevenson, have attributed part of their creativity to dreams.

Techniques to Aid Scenario Analysis

There are many techniques for finding meaningful seed trends (trends that could be extended). Some are discussed in Chapter 5, and here are nine more.

Trend People

Many believe certain people have a predictive sense and should be watched. *Women's Wear Daily* is one publication that uses this method, and the people it watches are well known to regular readers.

Trend Areas

Major changes in American life and practice traditionally begin on the West Coast and gradually make their way east. Although television and other mass media have reduced the time lag, some firms station personnel in California just to be closer to the changes going on there.

Hot Products

The automobile, television, the computer, and the Internet have had a dramatic effect on lifestyles. Others that may do so include fiber optics, biogenetic engineering, condominiums, and TiVo. One way to gather meaningful seed trends is to study such products and their effects. But watch out for false prophets, such as the CB radio of the 1970s.

Newspapers

Some persons like to read leading newspapers, particularly the *New York Times*, cover to cover and make note of every trend, activity, or idea around which significant scenario change might take place.

Hypothetical

A few persons believe one should just use any seed trend to create arbitrary scenarios. The more hypothetical the better, because the exercise is to stimulate creativity.

Technological Changeover

This approach predicts when one technology will substitute for another and seeks the implications of the substitution for all products and systems involving either the new or the old. Doing this involves time series analysis, graphic analysis, and forecasts by technical people.

Technical Innovation Follow-On

This procedure analyzes the implications for technical breakthroughs across a broad spectrum of technology, not just the immediate technology in which the breakthrough came. For example, a breakthrough in solar heating could be analyzed for effects in plumbing, clothing, furniture, or even entertainment.

Technological Monitoring

Some scientists keep journals of technological progress. Every meaningful event is carefully logged, and from time to time the journals are studied for meaningful trends. The technique helps guarantee the analysis of one event in the construct of other events.

Cross-Impact Analysis

First, list all possible changes that may occur over the next 20 years in a given area of activity (say, transportation). Then, apply these changes to other areas of activity, much as is done in technical innovation follow-on. The difference is that this method is not restricted to forecastable breakthroughs.

Techniques to Enhance Group Creativity

Phillips 66 Groups

To increase participation, Dr. J. Donald Phillips broke Osborn's 12-person groups into subgroups of 6 members each, sending the subgroups to break-off rooms for six minutes each, rearranging the subgroups, sending the new subgroups off for another six minutes, and so on. Rearrangement was Phillips's key to eliminating the problem of dominant or conflicting personalities. The Phillips 66 groups are sometimes called *buzz groups*, *free association groups*, and *discussion 66 groups*.

Brainstorming Circle

This approach forces the conversational sequence around a circle, and each person expands or modifies the idea expressed by the prior person in the circle. The brainstorming circle is more orderly and forces all persons to participate equally.

Reverse Brainstorming

This approach concentrates on a product's weaknesses or problems rather than on solutions or improvements. The discussion attempts to ferret out every criticism of, say, a vacuum cleaner. Later, attempts are made to eliminate the weaknesses or solve the problems.

Tear-Down

The rule of suspended judgment is reversed in this approach. Instead of avoiding criticism, tear-down requires it, and participants must find something wrong with the previous idea to get a talking turn.

And Also

In this approach, each speaking participant enlarges or extends the previous idea. No lateral moves are permitted unless the chain runs dry. The approach has been called *idea building and modification*.

Synectics

In its pure form, synectics does not differ much from brainstorming. Synectics provides more structure and direction by having the participants think along the lines of certain operational mechanisms—usually analogy and metaphors. The system has a forced sequence through these mechanisms and other steps—viewpoint, forced fit, and so on. However, in recent years the two individuals involved in creating this approach have led their respective creativity firms into the use of many ideation techniques. Analogy prevails as a critical feature, but the term *synectics* has come to mean two businesses running creativity seminars.

Gordon Method

Prior to developing synectics, W. J. J. Gordon used groups that were not told what the problem was. In this method, if a discussion is to develop new ideas for recording musical performances, the group is encouraged to discuss opera. Eventually the leader turns the discussion toward the problem but still without divulging it.

Delphi

Although occasionally touted for ideation, Delphi is really a method of organizing a forecasting survey. Panels of experts are compiled; they are sent a questionnaire calling for forecasts within a given area of activity (e.g., hospitals or data processing); the questionnaires are tabulated and summarized; the results are returned to the panel for their reaction and alteration; new summaries are prepared; the results are sent out again, and so on. The iterations continue until conformity is reached or until impasse is obvious. The method is essentially a cop-out because the individuals still must use some method to make their own forecasts. But in certain situations, it has been deemed effective, and it can be used quite easily in modified format. It is especially desirable where the industry itself is new and there are no historical data to aid forecasters.

Think Tanks

This too is more a matter of organizing people than a mechanism of stimulating creativity. Think tanks are centers of intensive scientific research. Xerox, for example, maintains a center in Palo Alto, California, at which, among other things, scientists are working on artificial intelligence. What they are studying today may be meaningful 5 to 20 years from now. The key to success here is the environment, which is thought to be stimulating to creativity. If the people in a think tank are charged with converting their outlandish ideation into useful products for marketing, the term *skunkworks* is often applied.

Techniques of the Analytical Attribute Approach

Benefit Analysis

All of the benefits that customers or users receive from the product under study are listed, in the hope of discovering an unrealized benefit or unexpectedly absent benefit.

Use Analysis

Listing the many ways buyers make use of a given product is also sometimes revealing. Some firms, 3M among others, have spent large sums of money asking consumers to tell them of new uses. Johnson Wax got into the car-polishing business when it found that its floor wax was being used on cars. One must contact users, however—not just list the uses already known to the company.

Function Analysis

In between feature and use is an activity called *function*. Thus, for shampoos, we know the chemicals and product features present, and we may know the full reasons for using shampoos. But it is also creative to list all possible ways that shampoos function—scraping, dissolving, depositing, evaporating, and so on. One could also list all the possible consumer uses of shampoo: cleaning, conditioning, making hair manageable, fighting split ends or grease, and so on.

Attribute Extension

Also called *parameter analysis*, this technique begins with any attribute that has changed recently and then extends that change. Thus, for example, bicycle seats have gotten smaller and smaller. Extending that idea, one might imagine a bicycle with no seat at all; what would such a bicycle look like, and what would it be used for?

Relative Brand Profile

Every brand name is flexible or elastic, meaning it can be stretched to cover different product types. People can understand a Minute Maid jelly or Minute Maid soup. But people also tell us that they cannot accept other "stretchings"—such as Minute Maid meats. Various market research techniques can be used to make these measurements, and any stretch that makes sense to the buyer is a potential new product. Incidentally, this thinking applies to goods and services, industrial as well as consumer.

Pseudo Product Test

By using what psychologists call a *projective technique*, one can ask consumers to evaluate what is presented to them as a proposed product but is actually an unidentified product currently on the market. They will typically find unique characteristics matching the needs they have. These attributes can then be the base for a new product.

System's Analysis

This is a technique for studying complete systems of activity rather than products. Standard Brands once studied food preparation systems that involved margarine. It noted that virtually every one included an instruction to "melt the butter or margarine, stir in flour," and so on. From that came a stick-form sauce base called Smooth & Easy.

Unique Properties

This technique is primarily valuable in technological fields. The analyst seeks unique properties of any product or material currently on the market. To aid in this, one usually begins by listing all common properties because the unique ones quickly pop out.

Hierarchical Design

Here an organization chart design is formed, with product usage at the top and material types fanning out below. One such design began with deodorants, followed at the second level by roll-on, stick, and aerosol. The brands were listed under roll-ons. Under each brand could be package size or target market segment. Another design had light construction at the top, followed by wood, steel, and concrete. Wood was broken into metal roof, tar or shingle roof, and so on. The technique is mainly a way of forcing one to see all aspects of a situation, which is the essence of the analytical attribute approach.

Weaknesses

All weaknesses of a product or product line (the company's own and those of the competition) are identified. This primarily defensive technique identifies line extensions and flanker products, and possibly even new-and-improved products. Every resolvable weakness offers a new product concept.

Achilles' Heel

Some analysts prefer to prune the list of weaknesses to one or two that are so serious, a competitor might capitalize on them.

Theoretical Limits Test

Both opportunities and threats can be visualized by pushing a known apparatus or device to its theoretical limits. The technique works especially well on a reasonably new technology that appears to have exhausted its usefulness.

Techniques to Enhance Lateral Search

One school of thought holds that all "nearby" creativity produces only insignificant line extensions and modifications. These people have only disdain for matrixes, analogy, and attribute analysis. They insist the mind must be pushed beyond where it wants to go, in a lateral search. Marketers too often think "vertically" when coming up with new ideas. Does introducing yet another soft drink flavor or shampoo name create any new customers or profitability? The authors Philip Kotler and Fernando Trias de Bes suggest applying Edward de Bono's "lateral thinking" concepts to product development to come up with truly creative new ideas. As an example, the authors propose the iPod. Typical vertical marketing extensions would include a smaller iPod, a more colorful one, or one that holds several more songs. Lateral-marketing thinking would explore ways in which the iPod could be *inverted* (to record rather than play music), *exaggerated* (improve sound quality to be superior to CDs), *reordered* (music goes from iPod to computer rather than vice versa), and so on.[1]

Here are some recommended techniques to stimulate lateral search.

Free Association

This approach begins when the ideator writes down one aspect of the product situation being studied—a product attribute, a use, or a user. The trick then is to let the mind roam wildly while jotting down every idea that comes out. The process is repeated for other aspects of the product situation. The associations are usually quite direct in the early stages when creativity is being stimulated; but with time, they become much less related and much more valuable as insights.

Stereotype Activity

Here one asks, "How would _____ do it?" The blank is filled in with a stereotype. Particular individuals can also be used, and the question can be reversed to ask what the stereotype would not do. Thus, a bicycle manufacturer might ask, "What type of bicycle would a senator ride? Loudspeaker on it? Pedal both ways?"

Cross-Field Compilation

As scientific disciplines have become increasingly blurred, a creative technique has been developed to bridge the between-field barriers. If a firm works primarily in the chemical area, its product developers may systematically scan developments in, say, physics or biology. Scientists in those fields may not know that some of their ideas have applications in chemistry.

Key-Word Monitoring

This approach involves monitoring newspapers and magazines and tallying the number of times key words appear. One firm used this approach to spot increasing use of the zodiac, and it promptly marketed a series of successful products featuring the zodiac symbols. Some take this approach with electronic databases and call it "database tracking." This method is closely allied to the Big Winner approach discussed later.

Use of the Ridiculous

Just to show that anything can be done, some ideators deliberately try to force themselves to use ridiculous approaches. In one session, participants were asked to write out the most preposterous methods of joining two wires together. One answer was, "Hold them with your teeth," and another was, "Use chewing gum." Those present were astounded to realize they had just reinvented alligator clips, and they promptly gave serious consideration to the chewing gum. It turns out that some ingredients in chewing gum may sometime be marketed for use in wiring!

[1]This section draws from Philip Kotler and Fernando Trias de Bes, *Lateral Marketing: New Techniques for Finding Breakthrough Ideas* (New York: Wiley, 2003).

Study of Other People's Failures

Any product that has failed offers a chance for the next trier to spot its problem. Robert McMath displays over 10,000 actual failed products in the New Products Showcase and Learning Center in Ithaca, New York (now part of New Product Works, which you saw in the Product Use Testing case in Chapter 15). The failures apparently stimulate creativity.

Lateral Thinking—Avoidance

Some people have stressed the use of avoidance techniques to keep an idea from dominating thinking as it has in the past.

Keep asking, "Is there another way of looking at this?"

Keep asking, "Why?"

Deliberately rotate attention to a phase or aspect of the problem other than the logical one.

Find an entry point into the problem other than the one habitually used.

List all possible alternatives to every aspect of the analysis.

Deliberately seek nonstandard concepts other than those inherent to the problem. Try "unconcepting" or "disconcepting," or try dropping a concept.

Fractionalize concepts and other aspects of the problem.

Bridge two or more concepts to form still other concepts.

Other people call the approach *disparate thinking, zigzag,* and *divergent thinking.* This method was claimed to have partially solved a long-standing problem of light bulb theft in the Boston subway—light bulbs were made to screw in counterclockwise.

Forced Relationships

The two-dimensional matrix and the morphological matrix are based on relevant product or market characteristics. Sometimes, however, interesting viewpoints are achieved by forcing relationships between normally unrelated (or even opposed) things. The forced relationships technique has spawned many preferences; the most quoted is the catalog method. In this method, a catalog, journal, or magazine is selected, and then a relationship is forced between everything in it and something else (perhaps a product or a consumer group). Some suggest using the table of contents in magazines or the Yellow Pages in telephone directories. Other names for the forced relationships approach are *pick-a-noun* and *random walk.*

Creative Stimuli

The idea subject is specified first—the problem, the product, and so on. Then the tangible goal is stipulated—the desired result or what the specified idea should accomplish. Last, a long list of words, names, and phrases is studied for ideas that accomplish the tangible goal. These are proven stimulants (why, we don't know). Some of them are:

Guest stars	Charity	Family	Photography
Alphabet	Education	Timeliness	Interview
Truth	His and hers	Videotape	Testimonials
Outer space	Style	World	Decorate
Chart	Nation	Birth	Showmanship
Gauge scale	Weather	Ethnic	Floor, wall
Zipper	Habit, fad	Push button	Participation
Fantasy	Transportation	Snob appeal	Music
Folklore	Symbolism	Romance	Direct mail
Subconscious	Calendar	Parody	Seasons
Hobbies	Rhinestones	Graphics	Strawberry
Holidays	Curiosity	Sketch	Telephone

For a complete set of the stimuli words and phrases, see Donald Cantin, *Turn Your Ideas into Money* (New York: Hawthorn Books, 1972). A newer version that combines stimulating terms with variations on a checklist is the product improvement checklist (PICL) by Arthur VanGundy. It is available from New Product Development Newsletter, P.O. Box 1309, Point Pleasant, NJ 08742.

Big Winner

Many successful firms, teams, or individuals in sports, politics, television, and so on are uniquely in tune with the thinking of society. Studying these big winners may lead to principles that can be generalized to new products. Currently, for example, something might be found by studying iPads, cellular picturephones, the World Wide Web, BlackBerries, hybrid cars, Steven Spielberg, and Arnold Schwarzenegger. One consulting firm compiled a list of the 20 all-time best-selling packaged goods; from this list, the firm generalized principles to transfer to clients' new products.

Competitive Analysis

Many firms claim that by studying the strategic plans and actions of competitors, they can detect new product approaches, especially defensive ones. For this purpose they watch competitive announcements, surveys, financial reports, trade show exhibits, detailed analyses of their products, and other such techniques. Life-cycle models help a firm estimate when competitors will take over any of its markets and thus stimulate new products to defensively cannibalize sales.

Technological Mapping

This is a form of relevance-tree forecasting in which the competitive capability of each competitor is predicted. It lays the groundwork for decisions to push or play down certain technologies in the home firm. Strategic analysis permits direct forecasting of probable future changes in competitors' technological commitments by studying mergers, acquisitions, sell-offs, patent applications, patent sales, and so on. A keen analyst can predict major market swings and thus suggest new product opportunities (or lack of opportunities) for the firm.

The Marketing Plan

Basic marketing management books have rather complete descriptions of the marketing planning process. This appendix will not duplicate that material, but will focus on the actual form of the marketing plan itself, that is, the plan, not so much the planning that is covered in Chapters 16 and 17.

No two firms use quite the same format of marketing plan, but Figure C.1 gives a marketing plan outline based on the best information we have. The plan generally follows these guidelines:[1]

Summarize the analysis done for this plan.

Give overall strategic thinking.

Give the tactical actions, including those for departments other than marketing.

Make sure everyone knows the financial situation and how the plan will be measured and evaluated.

The outline should communicate the plans to everyone involved, have built-in control mechanisms, and serve as a permanent record.

Contents

Certain sections of the marketing plan deserve additional comment. But remember: If the new product is a line extension, many of the early sections of the plan are unnecessary because the information is not new. You will recall that as part of the early evaluation process it is wise to thoroughly study (or restudy) the industry in which concepts are going to be generated. The list of information gathered for this is shown in Figure C.2.

Consumers/Users/Buyers

This section addresses the key element in the product's rationale. Data are given on the various buyer categories, the extent to which buying differs from using, the

---

[1] A still-excellent source of guidance is David S. Hopkins, *The Marketing Plan*, Report No. 801 (New York: The Conference Board, 1981).

FIGURE C.1 **Outline of Marketing Plan for a New Product, to Be Adapted to Fit Individual Firms**

I. Introduction. This section briefly describes the product, tells who prepared the plan, and its timing.
II. Situation analysis.
   A. Market description.
     1. Consumers, users, and other market participants.
     2. Buying processes pertinent to this plan.
     3. Direct and indirect competitors.
     4. Current competitive strategies.
     5. Market shares on sales, profits, and budgets.
     6. Available distribution structure, plus attitudes and practices.
     7. Key environmental or exogenous factors.
   B. Full description of new product, including all pertinent test data and comparisons with competition.
III. Summary of opportunities and problems.
   A. Key exploitable market opportunities.
   B. Key problems that should be addressed by this plan.
IV. Strategy.
   A. Overall guiding statement, including key actions and their quantitative and qualitative objectives.
   B. Market targets/segments, with positioning for each.
   C. Overall marketing efforts.
     1. General role for product, including planned changes.
     2. General role for advertising, including copy platforms.
     3. General role for personal selling.
     4. General role for such other tools as sampling and trade shows. Copy platforms for any creative units.
     5. General role for distributors (wholesale, retail).
     6. Price policy, including discounts and planned changes.
     7. Any special roles for nonmarketing departments.
V. Economic summary.
   A. Sales forecasts in dollars and units.
   B. Expense budgets by category of activity.
   C. Contribution to profit, with pro forma income statement.
   D. Risk statement: major problems, with cash flows.
   E. Future capital expenditures, with cash flows.
VI. Tactical plans. This section is situational to the firm. It includes each tool, what will be done with it, objectives, people responsible, schedule, creative units needed, etc.
VII. Control.
   A. Key control objectives for reporting purposes.
   B. Key internal or external contingencies to watch.
   C. Information generation schedule.
VIII. Summary of major support activities needed, including data processing, warehousing, technical service, R&D, finance, personnel, public relations.
IX. Chronological schedule of activities.

existence of influencers, and the specific process by which users acquire the merchandise. This includes buying motives, brands considered, information sought, product preferences, images, and unmet needs. It also covers how products are actually used and by whom.

FIGURE C.2   **Basic Market Description**

Market Size

Definition: By nature of product, by supplier, by user.
Sales: Dollars, units, by total and subgroups.
Trends: Growth total and rate by subgroups.
Key segments: Demographic, attitude, behavior.
Special aspects where appropriate: Cyclicality, seasonality, erratic fluctuations.
International variations and trends.

Distribution Structure Available

Retailers: Types, shares, demands, activities, current margins and profits, trends and forecasts, attitudes.
Wholesalers: Distributors, jobbers, agents, types used, function performed, policies, compensation, attitudes, trends, variances, by segments.
Bargaining power and channel control.
Degree of, and trends in, vertical integration. Variations by geographic area.
Use of multiple or dual channels.

Competition

Current brands.
Manufacturer source for each.
Sizes, forms, materials, etc. All variations, temporary and permanent. Quality levels.
Prices: Final discounts, special, changes.
Market shares: Dollars, units, by segments, using various definitions of *market*.
Changes: Trends of entries and exits, reaction times.
Profits being achieved: Sales, costs, Rols, paybacks, trends.
Promotional practices: Types, dollars, effectiveness.
Manufacturing and procuring practices.
Financial strengths.
Special vulnerabilities, instabilities.
Possible new entrants, current R&D activities, skills, track records.
Full description of derived demand aspects.
Industry life cycle analyzed by segments.

Special Aspects

Government and regulatory restrictions, especially trends and expectations.
Third-party influences: Scientists, institutions, research centers, associations, standards, pressure groups.
Effects of inflation, labor rates, union activity.
Upstream participants: Supplier manufacturers, importers, technology control.
General social attitudes and trends.
Industry productivity and efficiency in use of personnel and other resources.
Trends in industry costs: Materials, labor, transportation.

This section will help anyone who reads the plan to understand the decisions described later—for example, on targeting, positioning, and push-pull strategy. It also summarizes the general equilibrium of the market and highlights any instabilities that can be capitalized.

Competition

All plan readers must be told about the competitive situation because many of them are not in a position to have regular contact with it. Specific company and brand names should be listed, and a detailed comparative description given for each. All of our differences should be clear. If the product manager doesn't know the determinant attributes in this market or how the new product compares on those attributes with products already out there, the firm isn't ready to market the new item.

The competitors' overall business and marketing strategies are also needed, especially those which appear to be effective. This includes positioning, pricing, claims, and distribution.

Exogenous Factors and Change

Markets are not static, and everyone involved needs to be apprised of likely changes. No surprises should appear, and none will if the planner has been careful. Some often overlooked changes are government regulations, competitive product improvements, direct selling (skipping a distributive level), price breaks, new competition based on new technologies, and future changes in how this type of product is bought and/or used.

Product Description

In some cases, a product can be described in a few sentences; in others, readers of the plan almost need a seminar. Product complexity cannot be allowed to destroy understanding. The plan should guide other people in doing their parts in the overall marketing effort, so they need to know just how good this new product really is. The plan should summarize the key findings of concept testing and product use testing. It should include product strengths and weaknesses, perceptual problems, unusual uses of the product, physical characteristics, costs, and restrictions applied to any applications.

Objectives

A statement of what is expected from marketing this new product should be included near the start of the strategy section. But let's differentiate between objective and goal. A goal is a long-term direction of movement (sometimes not easily quantified) used for guidance, not internal control. For example, "It is our goal to become a leader in the snacks market." An objective is an intermediate point on the road toward attainment of a goal. For example, "It is our objective to capture a 15-percent share of the snacks market during our first year on the market." Objectives should be clearly and precisely stated in fairness to the new products manager. A narrative at this point in the plan will help clarify objectives.

Restraints

Every new product marketing effort has some built-in restraints that should be made clear. Here are some examples from previous marketing plans:

The new product will be marketed in accordance with the division's customary reliance on its industrial distribution system.

The sales force is currently questioning the ability of the new products department to come up with winners. Because the morale of the sales force is quite important to this division, actions will be taken to ensure the success of this particular product.

The strategy will not introduce potential problems of interpretation by the Federal Trade Commission, nor will it conflict with outstanding consent decrees.

Such restraints as these can have obvious effects on a marketing plan; if they are not stated, readers may not understand why certain actions are being taken.

Management of the Task

Putting together a marketing plan is a complex process, filled with grand strategic decisions interspersed with trivia. Experienced new product marketers never underestimate the contribution of the many nonmarketing departments in the firm, but novice new products people often do. For this reason, the new products team should be doing the marketing planning right along with the product development. As team members help construct the plan itself, they will have suggestions to make. Each function involved in the new product's marketing has ideas about what that function should do; they differ from what other people think that function should do. All are experienced people, and we have worked with them for some time. We would like to just ask each of them what they want to do and then put their requests into a package and call it a marketing plan. Some plans are actually developed that way.

Such plans don't work very well, however, unless we have a new product that essentially sells itself or unless the new item is a simple line extension, marketed totally as a new member in a line of products. The product line marketing plan captures the new item and tells what will be done.

In rare instances our new item doesn't have to be marketed at all, in the usual sense. For example, we may be making it in response to a military order, where the sale was made at the time our bid was accepted. Or we may be developing an item for a major producer of complex products (such as automobiles); in such a case, the producer essentially told us what to make, and all we have to do is deliver it and stand by to service it.

But these are exceptions; in most cases, the new item needs its own strategy, at least in concept. Otherwise, the various players will never come together to make up a team.

Let's distinguish between planning and a plan. Planning yields a strategy; the plan states the strategy, adds the tactical details, and directs the implementation. New products can use both, but the strategy is critical. Once the new products manager begins to concentrate on the plan, with its many budgets, dates, and other details, no strategy in the world can keep the players motivated, integrated, and effective.

Some new products managers orchestrate the team by dint of personal leadership. These people may miss dates and budgets but market a successful product. In some situations, a product marketed well over budget—but on time—makes more money than a product marketed within budget but three months late.

This line of thinking does not apply to established products, which need annual or quarterly marketing plans. They already have the infrastructure, the stature, the support base within the firm, and the experienced players that the new product lacks.

So as you go through the actual marketing planning process, keep in mind that we are looking at things that really make a difference. That's all that most new product managers have the time to seriously think about.

One other thought: Top-management approval is needed on marketing plans. "Whoever pays the fiddler calls the tune," so new products managers must deal with the frustrations caused by highly participative top managements.

The Strategic Components

Chapters 16 and 17 explain the components of marketing strategy for a new product and the general approach to how they are derived. This section of a marketing plan simply summarizes them and explains the background thinking on any issue known to be controversial in the firm. The target markets are explained first, followed by the product positioning statement (several of the items are being positioned differently for different target groups). After that the marketing plan becomes very situational, reflecting company practice and personal interests. Marketing mixes differ so in nature, complexity, and implementation that it does little good to outline a method for telling people about them.

It is typical that firms state their general mix strategy—what is the lead horse and how the other tools support that one. All people who will be implementing the plan should understand how the product, the price, the promotion, and the distribution partner up, and what their individual roles are. If they work well together, it is like any other team situation—good synergy can double the power.

Details and Implementation

What follows the general statement about strategic components is the full listing of what each tool will be doing, when, managed by whom, etc. Media schedules, sales staffing and calling schedules, all of the printed materials needed, sales meetings, and (in some cases) the hundreds of things that must be done to implement the launch. This section of marketing plans tends to give marketing planning a bad name. To many people, the plan document (actually a very large book in many cases) is the purpose of planning, yet huge planning documents quickly become file documents under the relentless pressures of change. Better to have a smaller overall plan and a set of tool documents prepared and implemented by the various departments in the firm.

Guidelines for Evaluating a New Products Program

This is a unique checklist. It is made for use by anyone evaluating the new products program of some organization—an internal review, a consultant, whatever. It presumes the organization uses all of the recommended methods, and it would be nice if the world worked this way. But product innovation managers face many problems—people, resources, competition, and so on. They make many compromises, so if you use these guidelines to evaluate a program, think of the gaps as suggestions or possible considerations. Most people who have tried the form find that they have to say no (or a very qualified yes) to a third or more of the items. The form is especially good at covering important activities that are especially difficult or of recent development.

The terminology used in this checklist matches that used throughout this text, but occasionally a second statement has been added for clarity.

If the form is being used within an organization, a good approach is for two or more people with experience in the firm's new products activity to go through the list separately, checking each item individually, as they know it. Then the scorings can be discussed in a joint session to bring out differences, which in turn can be discussed for clarification and possible remedial action.

Yes Maybe No
Some

_____ _____ _____   1. The senior managers of this firm or division (general manager plus top key functional heads) are committed to innovation in general. They want innovation in all phases of the operation, including that of product line.

_____ _____ _____   2. This management attitude toward innovation has been clearly and unequivocally communicated throughout the organization.

_____ _____ _____   3. Senior managements, both at corporate and at division, have gone through a planning exercise that established the overall goals for the product innovation function in each division.

_____ _____ _____   4. Outside directors know the future role for product innovation and support actions to achieve it.

———— ———— ———— 5. We have an innovation reward system. It includes insulation against punishment for failure, and there is evidence for all to see.

———— ———— ———— 6. The firm's or division's top executive has assessed the ability and inclination of each senior functional manager to generate innovation, particularly product innovation. This assessment has included input from persons reporting to those senior managers.

———— ———— ———— 7. General managers have learned the art of delegating full authority on new product projects while still sharing fully in the responsibility for them. (This managerial approach is unique to the product innovation function.)

———— ———— ———— 8. New product project responsibility is nonfunctional. That is, project leaders report in such a way that they are free of functional constraints and biases. Specifically, responsibility for new products is no longer housed in R&D.

———— ———— ———— 9. Senior management attempts to assess the productivity of the new products program. Standards of measurement have been established and communicated.

———— ———— ———— 10. If senior management is dissatisfied with the overall product innovation program, specific causes have been determined and remedial plans put into place. Continuing dissatisfaction is not acceptable.

———— ———— ———— 11. The firm's failure rate on marketed new products is somewhere between 10 percent and 20 percent. Less than that suggests no commitment to innovation, and more than that suggests an inadequately managed program.

———— ———— ———— 12. Senior management has studied the industry's new product situation and has shared ideas with other industry leaders. Work is under way to find industrywide solutions to obstacles hindering product innovation in this industry.

———— ———— ———— 13. Specific people in each division have been charged with opportunity identification—the creative assessment of technologies and markets available to the division.

———— ———— ———— 14. Senior management is aware of the fundamental conflict between process innovation and product innovation. Efforts are taken to keep either from dominating the other and to see that decisions at the interface are made at general-management levels.

———— ———— ———— 15. The firm has an overall process for developing new products, and its phases are known to participants.

———— ———— ———— 16. Product innovators on each project know their group's focus (arena of operation or turf).

———— ———— ———— 17. They also know the general goal and specific objectives of their project.

———— ———— ———— 18. Each project group is making use of both market drive and technology drive. That is, they are working to resolve one or more specific problems in a selected marketplace, and they are bringing to that solution one or more technologies at which the firm is very good.

———— ———— ———— 19. There are no hidden agendas on our new product projects.

———— ———— ———— 20. All people playing major roles in new product groups are rewarded in some way that reflects the group's accomplishment of assigned goals/objectives.

———— ———— ———— 21. For every new products project, it is clear who is the one person heading up that project and responsible for its success.

———— ———— ———— 22. Every project is assigned one of three projectization levels—functional matrix, balanced matrix, or project matrix. We try to avoid the purely functional approach, and we use a venture (spin-out) only when absolutely necessary. Players understand projectization.

———— ———— ———— 23. We recognize the values of design. To the extent appropriate, we actively integrate both industrial (esthetic/functional) designers and engineering (technical/functional) designers as key team players.

_____ _____ _____ 24. Our technical/marketing/manufacturing people are close together physically. Preferably, they are no farther than a five-minute walk apart.

_____ _____ _____ 25. We use the concept of the rugby scrum rather than that of the relay team's hand-off. All functions are represented at all phase points in the project, including project specification and postlaunch.

_____ _____ _____ 26. Managers of new products projects understand that they are really nontitled general managers and that they should manage their team of people as a general manager would. They also understand what a network is and how one should be built and managed.

_____ _____ _____ 27. We actively use upstream and downstream coupling by building in roles for suppliers and other vendors as well as direct involvement of potential customer personnel. These people are almost like members of the team.

_____ _____ _____ 28. We have an overall concept evaluation system in place and use it to carve out a special system for each project.

_____ _____ _____ 29. A basic market or technology study is made of each strategic arena before ideation begins, and that study is updated as needed during the project's life.

_____ _____ _____ 30. We believe in building the marketing plan right alongside the building of the product. It is a twin-streams, or coincident, operation.

_____ _____ _____ 31. We accept the idea that new products come into existence only after they have been successfully established in the marketplace. Even after they go to market, they are still only concepts (being modified as necessary) until we meet the objectives set for them.

_____ _____ _____ 32. We have proactive concept generation. That is, we don't just wait for new ideas to come in from the field, the lab, etc.

_____ _____ _____ 33. Our technical people are familiar with what customers think about products now on the market, what they use, and how.

_____ _____ _____ 34. To the extent possible, our new concepts begin their lives stemming directly from solutions to proven problems/needs of the intended customers.

_____ _____ _____ 35. We use a quantitative scoring model for screening concepts prior to any substantial development expenditures.

_____ _____ _____ 36. After screening, we make sure that technical people have a statement of the product requirements (product attributes in benefit format and any other deliverables). The marketing people also receive a statement of marketing requirements (what the marketing program is to accomplish—market penetration, speed, etc.). The product requirements speak to what the product should do for the customer. Both sets of requirements combine into a product protocol statement.

_____ _____ _____ 37. We do user-based product use testing on every item we develop, whether a good or a service. At least part of the testing is with typical potential users who are not our friends.

_____ _____ _____ 38. We believe product use testing should measure whether the product actually works as we had hoped, and also whether it solves the problem we started with and is satisfactory overall to the customer. That is, if we have been using beta testing, we want to do gamma testing too.

_____ _____ _____ 39. Our marketing program also is tested by exposure to the intended consumers of the new product. The testing method used is situational, but at the very least a rollout is employed.

_____ _____ _____ 40. Our marketing efforts recognize that getting trial use is the most critical (and difficult) of the several steps to sales success.

_____ _____ _____ 41. When marketing a new item, we have identified each potential problem that would be very damaging and that has a reasonable probability of coming about. We have agreed in advance what we would do about each, if it occurs.

_____ _____ _____ 42. We use postlaunch tracking systems for guiding the product to success. That is, we have set up measuring systems to track each critical problem and give us early warning. We have also agreed in advance about what will constitute evidence that each problem is actually coming about.

——— ——— ——— 43. Marketing strategy is built around the accomplishments of awareness, trial, availability, and repeat use (satisfaction). The plan clearly shows how each will be achieved.

——— ——— ——— 44. Marketing plans for new products are distributed in draft form to all persons who are key to the launch process, certainly to the basic functions of technical, production, and finance.

——— ——— ——— 45. Unless the new item is itself a line extension, we have at least the next two line extensions to it already on their way down the pike. Each follow-on item is intended to foreclose an option our adaptor competitors would find lucrative.

——— ——— ——— 46. All financial evaluations are much more than net present value calculations. In fact, we try to use a sales or profit threshold test rather than a specific dollar test.

——— ——— ——— 47. We try to anticipate ways in which customers will misuse a new product, we develop legally sufficient warnings for those misuses, and we keep records relevant to all aspects of product liability.

——— ——— ——— 48. Attention is given to any potential conflicts between the ethics of an operation and the ethics of the people working on it. Attempts are made to resolve these.

INDEX

Page numbers followed by n indicate material found in notes.